University of London Historical Studies

XXII

UNIVERSITY OF LONDON HISTORICAL STUDIES

THE DOUKAI

This volume is published with the help of a grant from the late Miss Isobel Thornley's Bequest to the University of London

The Doukai

*A Contribution to
Byzantine Prosopography*

by

DEMETRIOS I. POLEMIS

UNIVERSITY OF LONDON
THE ATHLONE PRESS
1968

Published by
THE ATHLONE PRESS
UNIVERSITY OF LONDON
at 2 Gower Street London WC1
Distributed by Constable & Co Ltd
12 *Orange Street London* WC2

Canada
Oxford University Press
Toronto

U.S.A.
Oxford University Press Inc
New York

485 13122 6

Printed in Great Britain by
ROBERT MACLEHOSE AND CO. LTD
THE UNIVERSITY PRESS
GLASGOW

TO MY FATHER

PREFACE

Investigation into the fortunes of medieval Greek families is a comparatively old branch of Byzantine studies and the extremely high standard achieved in this field by the great Ducange is everywhere recognised. His almost three-hundred years old *Familiae Augustae Byzantinae* still stands unsurpassed and in part continues to remain the standard work of reference, even though somewhat outdated for imperial Byzantine genealogy and prosopography. The swift development of Byzantine studies in the course of the last hundred years has indeed brought to light numerous previously unknown sources, thus substantially enriching the abundant material which still awaits scholars studying problems connected with both families and individuals in the Byzantine Empire, whether of noble origin or commoners.

It is true that the house of Doukas never attained the fame and the popularity of such dynastic families as the Komnenoi or the Palaiologoi, but all the same the Doukai rose to the top of the Byzantine aristocracy during the later part of the eleventh century. The aim of the present work is to assess the contribution of this family — or more exactly of the persons or groups of persons who bore the name — to the political and cultural history of Byzantium down to 1453. A first draft of Parts I, II and III of this study to 1204 was submitted as a doctoral thesis to the University of London (a brief summary of this was published in the *Bulletin of the Institute of Historical Research*, 37 [1964], 257-8).

It is a privilege to acknowledge here the encouragement and help which I have received while writing this book from Professor J. M. Hussey. I have benefitted greatly from her constant advice and experienced judgement and am most grateful for her assistance in revising the manuscript. I would also like to thank most sincerely Professor Robert Browning who read the work at various stages and offered valuable criticism. I am much indebted to Professor Paul Wittek for allowing me to consult the unpublished thesis on the Komnenoi by his late wife Dr S. Wittek-De Jongh. I should also like to thank my friend Dr N. M. Panagiotakis for various constructive suggestions.

A Research Fellowship at the Institute of Historical Research, University of London, during the session 1963-4 enabled me to extend my stay in Great Britain and greatly facilitated my work. The publication itself has been made possible by grants from the Marc Fitch Fund, the Isobel Thornley Bequest, and the Twenty-Seven Foundation, and I gratefully record my appreciation of this assistance.

Finally I would like to express my thanks to the Board of Management of the Athlone Press for accepting the book for publication and to their staff for invaluable help in many ways.

D. I. P.

CONTENTS

ABBREVIATIONS

(a) *Sources*

Akrop., Akrop., II	*Georgii Acropolitae Opera* (ed. A. Heisenberg), I–II. Leipzig, 1903.
Alexias, I–III	Anne Comnène, *Alexiade. Règne de l'Empereur Alexis I Comnène.* Texte établi et traduit par B. Leib. 3 vols. Paris, 1937–45.
Attal.	*Michaelis Attaliotae Historia.* Opus a W. Bruneto de Presle instituti Gallici socio inventum descriptum correctum rec. I. Bekkerus. Bonn, 1853.
Bryen.	*Nicephori Bryennii Commentarii*, rec. I. Bekker. Bonn, 1836.
Chon.	*Nicetae Choniatae Historia*, rec. I. Bekker. Bonn, 1835.
DAI, I–II	Constantine Porphyrogenitus, *De Administrando Imperio*. Vol. I, Greek text edited by Gy. Moravcsik, English translation by R. J. H. Jenkins. Budapest, 1947. Vol. II, Commentary edited by R. J. H. Jenkins. London, 1962.
Doukas	Ducas, *Istoria Turco-bizantina (1341–1462)* Ediţie critica de V. Grecu. Bucharest, 1958.
Ephraim	*Ephraemii monachi Imperatorum et Patriarcharum Recensus* interprete A. Maio. Bonn, 1840.
Eust.	Eustazio di Tessalonica, *La Espugnazione di Tessalonica.* Testo critico, introduzione, annotazioni di St. Kyriakidis, proemio di B. Lavagnini, versione italiana di V. Rotolo. Palermo, 1961.
Georg. Cont.	Theophanes Continuatus, Ioannes Cameniata, Symeon Magister, Georgius Monachus, rec. I. Bekker (Bonn, 1838), pp. 761–924.
Glykas	*Michaelis Glycae Annales*, rec. I. Bekkerus. Bonn, 1836.
Greg., I–III	*Nicephori Gregorae Byzantina Historia.* Vols. I–II edited by L. Schopen, Bonn, 1829–30. Vol. III edited by I. Bekker, Bonn, 1855.
Kallikles	L. Sternbach, 'Nicolai Calliclis Carmina,' *Rozprawy Akademii Umiejętności. Wydział Filologiczny.* Serya II, 21 (Cracow, 1904), 315–92.
Kant, I–III	*Ioannis Cantacuzeni Imperatoris Historiarum Libri IV*, cura J. Schopeni. 3 vols. Bonn, 1828–32.
Kedr., I–II	Georgius Cedrenus, *Ioannis Scylitzae ope* ab I. Bekkero suppletus et emendatus. 2 vols.

Kinn.   *Ioannis Cinnami Epitome Rerum ab Ioanne et Alexio Comnenis Gestarum*, rec. A. Meineke. Bonn, 1836.

Lampros, 'Μαρκιανός 524'   Sp. P. Lampros, "Ο Μαρκιανὸς κῶδιξ 524', *NE*, 9 (1911), 3–59 and 113–92.

Leon Gram.   *Leonis Grammatici Chronographia*, ex rec. I. Bekker. Bonn, 1842.

Man.   *Constantini Manassis Breviarium Historiae Metricum*, rec. I. Bekkerus. Bonn, 1837.

Pach., I–II   *Georgii Pachymeris de Michaele et Andronico Palaeologis Libri XIII*, rec. I. Bekkerus. 2 vols. Bonn, 1835.

Philes (Martini)   *Manuelis Philae carmina inedita*, ed. Ae. Martini. Naples, 1900.

Philes (Miller), I–II   *Manuelis Philae carmina*, ed. E. Miller. 2 vols. Paris, 1855–57

Psellos, I–II   Michel Psellos, *Chronographie ou Histoire d'un Siècle de Byzance (976–1077)*. Texte établi et traduit par E. Renauld. 2 vols. Paris, 1926–8.

Ps. Sym. Mag.   Theophanes Continuatus, Ioannes Cameniata, Symeon Magister, Georgius Monachus, rec. I. Bekker (Bonn, 1838), pp. 603–760.

Scripta Minora, I–II   *Michaelis Pselli Scripta Minora magnam partem inedita*, ed. E. Kurtz et F. Drexl. 2 vols. Milan, 1936–41.

Skout.   ''Ανωνύμου Σύνοψις Χρονική' in Sathas, *MB*, VII.

Skyl. Cont.   *Excerpta ex Breviario Historico Ioannis Scylitzae Curopalatae* in Kedr., II, pp. 639–744.

Sphrantzes   Georgius Phrantzes, Ioannes Cananus, Ioannes Anagnostes, rec. I. Bekker. Bonn, 1838.

Theoph.   *Theophanis Chronographia* rec. C. de Boor. Vol. I. Leipzig, 1883.

Theoph. Cont.   Theophanes Continuatus, Ioannes Cameniata, Symeon Magister, Georgius Monachus, rec. I. Bekker (Bonn, 1838), pp. 1–211.

Zon., III   *Ioannis Zonarae Epitomae Historiarum Libri XIII–XVIII*, ed. Th. Büttner-Wobst. Bonn, 1897.

(b) Collections of Sources, Periodicals and Other Works Frequently Cited

AB   *Analecta Bollandiana.*

Annuaire   *Annuaire de l'Institut de Philologie et d'Histoire Orientales et Slaves.*

B   *Byzantion.*

BCH   *Bulletin de Correspondance Hellénique.*

BNJ   *Byzantinisch–neugriechische Jahrbücher.*

Bompaire, *Actes de Xéropotamou*   J. Bompaire, *Actes de Xéropotamou*. Paris, 1964.

BS   *Byzantinoslavica.*

BZ   *Byzantinische Zeitschrift.*

Chalandon, *Les Comnène*, I–II   F. Chalandon, *Les Comnène: Etudes sur l'Empire byzantin au XIe et au XIIe Siècles*. Vol. I, *Essai sur le Règne d'Alexis I Comnène (1081–1118)*. Vol. II, *Jean II Comnène (1118–1143) et Manuel I Comnène (1143–1180)*. Paris, 1900–12.

De Jongh, *Généalogie des Comnène*   S. De Jongh, *La Généalogie des Comnène de Byzance*. Unpublished thesis, University of Brussels, 1937.

ΔIEEE   Δελτίον τῆς Ἱστορικῆς καὶ Ἐθνολογικῆς Ἑταιρείας τῆς Ἑλλάδος

Dmitrievskii, *Typika*   A. Dmitrievskii, *Opisanie Liturgicheskikh Rukopisei*. Vol. I, *Typika*. Kiev, 1895.

Dölger, *Regesten*, I–V   F. Dölger, *Regesten der Kaiserurkunden des oströmischen Reiches von 565–1453*. 5 parts. Berlin and Munich, 1924–65.

DOP   *Dumbarton Oaks Papers*

Ducange, *Familiae*   Ducange, *Familiae Augustae Byzantinae*. Paris, 1680.

EB   *Etudes Byzantines* (continued as *REB*).

EEBΣ   Ἐπετηρὶς Ἑταιρείας Βυζαντινῶν Σπουδῶν

EO   *Echos d'Orient*

Grumel, *Regestes*, I–III   V. Grumel, *Les Regestes des Actes du Patriarcat de Constantinople*. Vol. I, fasc. I–III. Paris, 1932–47.

Halkin, *BHG*, I–III   F. Halkin, *Bibliotheca Hagiographica Graeca*. 3 vols. Brussels, 1957³.

Hussey, *Church and Learning*   J. M. Hussey, *Church and Learning in the Byzantine Empire, 867–1185*. London, 1937.

JÖBG   *Jahrbuch der Österreichischen Byzantinischen Gesellschaft*.

Lampros, *Λεύκωμα*   Sp. P. Lampros, Λεύκωμα τῶν Βυζαντινῶν Αὐτοκρατόρων. Athens, 1930.

Laurent, *Bulles métriques*   V. Laurent, *Les Bulles métriques dans la Sigillographie byzantine*. Reprinted from Ἑλληνικά, 4 (1931), 191–228, 231–360; 5 (1932), 137–74, 389–420; 6 (1933), 81–102, 205–30; 7 (1934), 63–71, 277–300; 8 (1935), 49–64 and 319–43.

Laurent, *Collection Orghidan*   V. Laurent, *Documents de Sigillographie byzantine: La Collection C. Orghidan*. Paris, 1952.

Laurent, *Médaillier Vatican*   V. Laurent, *Les Sceaux byzantins du Médaillier Vatican*. Vatican, 1962.

MGH   *Monumenta Germaniae Historica*

MM, I–VI   F. Miklosich and J. Müller, *Acta et Diplomata Graeca Medii Aevi Sacra et Profana*. 6 vols. Vienna, 1860–90.

Moritz, *Zunamen*, I–II   H. Moritz, *Die Zunamen bei den byzantinischen Historikern und Chronisten*. 2 parts. Landshut, 1897–8.

NE   Νέος Ἑλληνομνήμων

OCP   *Orientalia Christiana Periodica*

Ostrogorsky, *History*   G. Ostrogorsky, *History of the Byzantine State*. Oxford, 1956.

Papadopoulos-Kerameus, *'Ανάλεκτα*, I–V	A. Papadopoulos-Kerameus, *'Ανάλεκτα 'Ιεροσολυμιτικῆς Σταχυολογίας*. 5 vols. St Petersburg, 1891–8.
Papadopoulos-Kerameus, *'Ιεροσολυμιτικὴ Βιβλιοθήκη*, I–V	A. Papadopoulos-Kerameus, *'Ιεροσολυμιτικὴ Βιβλιοθήκη ἤτοι κατάλογος τῶν ἐν ταῖς Βιβλιοθήκαις τοῦ ἁγιωτάτου ἀποστολικοῦ τε καὶ καθολικοῦ ὀρθοδόξου Πατριαρχικοῦ θρόνου τῶν 'Ιεροσολύμων καὶ πάσης Παλαιστίνης ἀποκειμένων ἑλληνικῶν κωδίκων*. 5 vols. St Petersburg, 1891–1915.
Papadopulos, *Genealogie der Palaiologen*	A. Papadopulos, *Versuch einer Genealogie der Palaiologen, 1261–1453*. Munich, 1938.
Petit, *Actes de Chilandar*	L. Petit, *Actes de Chilandar*. St Petersburg, 1911.
PG	J. P. Migne, *Patrologiae Cursus Completus. Series Graeco-Latina*.
PL	J. P. Migne, *Patrologiae Cursus Completus. Series Latina*.
REB	*Revue des Etudes Byzantines*
REG	*Revue des Etudes Grecques*
Regel et al., *Actes de Zographou*	W. Regel, E. Kurtz, and B. Korablev, *Actes de Zographou*. St Petersburg, 1907.
RH	*Revue Historique*
RIS	*Rerum Italicarum Scriptores*
RN	*Revue Numismatique*
Sathas, *MB*, I–VII	K. N. Sathas, *Μεσαιωνικὴ Βιβλιοθήκη ἢ Συλλογὴ 'Ανεκδότων Μνημείων τῆς 'Ελληνικῆς 'Ιστορίας*. 7 vols. Venice, 1872–94.
SB(N)	*Studi Bizantini (e Neoellenici)*
SBBAW	*Sitzungsberichte der Bayerischen Akademie der Wissenschaften. Philosophisch-historische Klasse*.
Stein, 'Untersuchungen'	E. Stein, 'Untersuchungen zur spätbyzantinischen Verfassungs- und Wirtschaftgeschichte', *Mitteilungen zur Osmanischen Geschichte*, 2 (1925), 1–62.
TT, I–II	G. L. F. Tafel and G. M. Thomas, *Urkunden zur älteren Handels- und Staatsgeschichte der Republik Venedig*. 3 vols. Vienna, 1856–7.
Vogel-Gardthausen, *Schreiber*	M. Vogel and V. Gardthausen, *Die griechischen Schreiber des Mittelalters und der Renaissance*. Leipzig, 1909.
VV	*Vizantiiskii Vremennik*
N	Denotes a man of unknown name.
Na	Denotes a woman of unknown name.

NOTE ON THE SPELLING OF GREEK NAMES

The names of all Greek persons referred to have been simply transliterated into Latin characters. In order to achieve uniformity this principle has been consistently followed throughout this work, even though it occasionally results in unfamiliar forms, such as Konstantinos, Ioannes, Anna Komnene and so on. It does also result in the surname 'Doux', which admittedly looks somewhat odd side by side with the title of *dux* from which it derives.

Geographical names, apart from a few minor exceptions, are always given in their traditional form.

PART I

INTRODUCTION

THE FAMILY

The designation of Doukas as a distinctive cognomen applicable to a particular family or person[1] appears for the first time in Byzantium in the middle of the ninth century, and from then on it is frequently met, despite some obscure decades, up to the last years of the empire and then through the period of the Turkish domination to present-day Greece where the name is not uncommon in various parts of the country. The numerous people who bore it belonged to different strata of Byzantine society: emperors and aristocrats, loyal soldiers and ambitious rebels, state officials and obscure gentry of the provinces, writers and monks.[2] Widespread as the surname was and however numerous its branches eventually become, in no circumstance can it be claimed that the Doukai represented a single family (like the Komnenoi or the Palaiologoi, for instance). And indeed simultaneously with the imperial house of Doukas in the eleventh century, a parallel shadowy group of persons of the same name can be shown to have existed in south Italy and Sicily.

The vast majority of the Doukai mentioned by the sources, especially those before 1204, indisputably belong to the Byzantine nobility, yet in actual fact it is the name itself which characterizes all persons so described, and it is therefore this name which will provide the terms of reference for the present work. The sources have preserved little on the general impact of the family (or rather of the groups of persons called Doukai), and thus the introductory part is necessarily based on relatively limited information. What the Byzantines themselves have to say about the families of the Doukai is far from adequate in forming a picture of what their place in general in contemporary society really was. Fortunately much more about the careers of certain individual members is known. Several of the Doukai are not only prominent figures but they themselves played a major part in shaping the history of Byzantium.

The main part of this study consists of prosopographical sketches of all known bearers of the name, including compound versions of it. As a general rule, only those are included who have been called Doukai by the sources at least once,[3] while children of Doukai who had assumed, or who were mentioned by, a

---

[1] For the different Greek terms employed by the Byzantine sources to denote a family name see Moritz, *Zunamen*, I, pp. 31–9.

[2] There is no satisfactory work devoted to the family. The account of Ducange, *Familiae*, pp. 160–6, covers the tenth and the eleventh centuries sufficiently but is totally inadequate for the twelfth since much of the rhetorical and poetical material now available was inaccessible to the learned author. For some brief and general observations on the Doukai see K. I. Amantos, Ἱστορία τοῦ Βυζαντινοῦ Κράτους, II (Athens, 1957²), p. 385.

[3] It should be noted however that this has not been applied in the earlier period, that is the tenth and the eleventh centuries where all traced descendants of the Doukai have been described

different name (such as the emperors Isaakios II and Alexios III Angeloi, sons of
Andronikos *39*), have been omitted as belonging to other families.

Conspicuous as the name has been in the history of Byzantium, it nevertheless
lacks continuity, thus preventing any attempt at a comprehensive genealogical
study. As already pointed out, it would be a mistake to consider the groups of
people designated by the cognomen of Doukas as forming one large family. In
particular, before 1204 three distinct groups of Doukai are found, and these are
not linked genealogically by any reliable evidence. The first person who can
definitely be regarded as a Doukas (or rather Doux) appears in *c*. 855 (see
N Doux, no. *1*, *infra*), but during the following half century the name apparently
entirely disappears. However, in the course of the first two decades of the tenth
century six other men of the house (nos. *2–7*) become active in military
affairs. Nearly all of them are known to have been related to one another, and
furthermore it is likely that they were all descended from the first Doux. Of the
known members of this group all but one (who was castrated) are mentioned as
having died at different times, and there appears to be no evidence that they
left heirs of their body. It is very likely that the male issue of this group became
extinct by about 917, and something similar to this is claimed by a late Byzantine
source.[1] It is only after an interval of some fifty years that another bearer of the
name is met. Towards the end of the tenth century a certain Andronikos Doux
and his two sons (nos. *8–10*) appear, but there is no direct indication that these
were connected either with their predecessors or with the imperial house of the
eleventh century.

It was in the eleventh century that a family emerged which was certainly the
most numerous and most distinguished branch of the Doukai proper. It gave an
imperial dynasty to Byzantium and also produced several high officials who
took a major share in the civil and military administration of the period.The
exact family connections of some of its members can be established, while
others remain isolated figures who, as their surname shows, must however have
been related to the imperial house itself, though sometimes only distantly. From
the mid-eleventh century onwards, down to the last days of the empire, and in
various parts of the Greek world, the name of Doukas is very frequently met.
Some of its bearers (like the Palaiologoi or the Doukai-Angeloi of Epirus) had a
legitimate right to it. Intermarriage between the Doukai and other representatives of the Byzantine nobility led to the adoption of the name by other persons,
or even families, strictly speaking not Doukai themselves but having some link
with the family, often through a female issue. Similarly various compounds
including the name of Doukas were coined and this became in fact very fashionable in the twelfth century. Such cases are very common both at that time and
later.

The modern usage of transmitting a father's surname to all his children,
though prevalent in the middle Byzantine period, was nevertheless not generally
accepted. Consequently there are numerous examples of persons designated
after the maiden names of their mothers or even their grandmothers,[2] a habit

[1] See below, p. 7, n. 4.

[2] It will suffice to cite two striking cases. The historians Nikephoros Bryennios and Anna
Komnene *107* had at least four children, three of whom are known by their full names. As far
as can be ascertained, none of them are ever mentioned with the appropriate cognomen of

which tends to confuse genealogical research. It therefore follows that some Doukai enumerated below may have sprung from houses other than that suggested by their name; on the other hand, some of the scions proper of the family may have assumed different names.

Origin

Certain Byzantine writers of the eleventh and the twelfth centuries, lavish as might be expected in their praises of the contemporary Doukai, regarded all bearers of that name as belonging to a single noble family, embracing the branch of the early tenth century and allegedly having its roots as far back as the first years of the Eastern Roman Empire. This traditional claim was asserted by Bryennios who categorically states that the first Doukas was in fact a cousin and close colleague of Constantine the Great who moved from Rome to Constantinople and adds that he was appointed there as the *dux* of the City. This unnamed *dux* became the founder and the common ancestor of all the later Doukai who naturally derived their surname from his rank.[1] Less explicit is the anonymous author of the dialogue *Timarion* who also relates the claim but in vaguer terms, only saying that the family originated in Italy whence it moved to, and settled in, Constantinople.[2] This is not a unique example of a wealthy family claiming ancestry from a noble Roman. Several other Byzantines might easily have made similar claims,[3] but no credence whatsoever can be given to such late inventions of palace scholars.

Bryennios; the eldest, Alexios, was called Komnenos, the other son Ioannes Doukas *78*, and there was also a daughter Eirene Doukaina *79*. In other words, the children chose to bear the names of their maternal grandparents which naturally appealed to them more than that of their own father Bryennios. Similarly, in the fourteenth century two of the sons of the learned *megas logothetes* Theodoros Metochites (died in 1332) carried the names of Angelos and Laskaris respectively. See Kant., I, pp. 209–10.

It should also be noted here that a married woman did not necessarily assume her husband's surname. Of those empresses before the thirteenth century whose full names are recorded the wife of Alexios I (1081–1118) was always called Eirene Doukaina and never Eirene Komnene. The wife of Alexios III (1195–1203) is known as Euphrosyne Doukaina or Kamatere and never as Euphrosyne Komnene or Angelina after her husband. The same can be said about the empresses of Nicaea. Only Theodora, the wife of Michael VIII, appropriately chose her husband's names (for references see the respective accounts of these two, *74* and *142*).

---

[1] Εἰ γάρ τις ἀνάρρουν ὥσπερ ἀναδραμεῖν βούλοιτο εὑρήσει τὸ τῶν Δουκῶν γένος ὥσπερ ἐκ πρώτης ἀναβλύσαν τῆς τοῦ μεγάλου Κωνσταντίνου φυλῆς, καθότι καὶ ὁ πρῶτος Δούκας ἐκεῖνος, εἰς ὢν τῶν μετὰ τοῦ μεγάλου Κωνσταντίνου τῆς πρεσβυτέρας 'Ρώμης ἀπαναστάντων καὶ πρὸς τὴν νεωτέραν μετοικησάντων, καθ' αἷμα τῷ μεγάλῳ Κωνσταντίνῳ καὶ γνησιώτατα προσῳκείωτο. ἐκείνου τε γὰρ ἐξάδελφος ἦν καὶ τὴν τοῦ δουκὸς Κωνσταντινουπόλεως ἀξίαν παρ' αὐτοῦ ἐγκεχείριστο. κἀντεῦθεν καὶ πάντες ἐξ αὐτοῦ κατωνομάσθησαν οἱ Δουκώνυμοι, Bryen., p. 13.

[2] 'Ηρωϊκόν ... τὸ γένος τοῦτο (sc. the Doukai), καὶ ὡς ἐξ 'Ιταλίας καὶ τῶν Αἰνειαδῶν μεταβὰν πρὸς τὴν Κωνσταντίνου πολλοῖς ὑποψιθυρίζεται; see A. Ellissen, *Analekten der mittel- und neugriechischen Literatur* (Leipzig, 1860), p. 50. Cf. R. Guilland, 'La collation et la perte ou la déchéance des titres nobiliaires à Byzance', *REB*, 4 (1946), 47.

[3] The most frequently quoted example is that of Basileios I, the founder of the Macedonian dynasty, who although of humble origin was eventually thought to have descended from the Arsacids. See Theoph. Cont., pp. 215 and 216; Ps. Sym. Mag., p. 687; Kedr., II, p. 183; cf. A. Vogt, *Basile I, Empereur de Byzance, et la civilisation byzantine à la fin du IXe siècle* (Paris, 1908), p. 21. Anna Komnene speaks of an Armenian noble Aspietes who apparently also claimed

The cognomen of Doux-Doukas[1] appears for the first time in *c*. 855 and no doubt derived from the military rank of *dux*, presumably held by the founder of the house that flourished in that century. Indeed similar family names emanating from corresponding army titles were quite usual in Byzantium.[2] The rank of *dux* was not particularly widespread at that time and was applicable to those army commanders who were in charge of rather remote military districts falling outside the jurisdiction proper of the theme *strategoi*.[3] The first Doux mentioned might have been the son of such an unknown *dux*, since the sources specify him as ὁ τοῦ Δουκός, and he might well have been the first person to be designated in this manner and to assume the military rank as a surname. To be sure, a couple of earlier references are sometimes associated with supposed members of the Doux family,[4] but this seems extremely doubtful. There is no justification

ancestry from the same noble house of Parthia (*Alexias*, III, p. 58). Similarly the emperor Nikephoros III Botaneiates boasted of being a scion of the famous Phokas family, which in turn was supposed to be genealogically linked with the Roman Fabii, allegedly transplanted by Constantine the Great to Georgia (Attal., pp. 217–20 and 229). The family of Gregorios Antiochos went back to the Seleucid King Antiochos Soter (reigned 281–61 B.C.) for its ancestor. See J. Darrouzès, 'Notice sur Gregoire Antiochos (1160 à 1196)', *REB*, 20 (1962), 76. This notion was not confined to the Greeks alone. Chon., pp. 45–6 (cf. Skout. 205), records that Muhammed, a Danishmend lord of Caesarea contemporary of Ioannes II Komnenos, also took pride in considering himself as being a descendant of the admired Arsacids. The fifteenth-century Kritoboulos went even further. He complimented his patron Muhammed II the Conqueror by asserting that the Ottoman sultans were direct descendants of the Persian Achaemenids. See Critobul din Imbros, *Din Domnia lui Mahomed al II–lea anii 1451–1467* (ed. V. Grecu; Bucharest, 1963), pp. 39–41. On these Byzantine tendencies cf. the remarks of R. Jenkins, *Byzantium and Byzantinism* (Cincinnati, 1963), p. 8. For a parallel practice in Italy during the Renaissance see J. Burckhardt, *The Civilization of the Renaissance in Italy* (London, Phaidon Press, n.d.), p. 111.

---

[1] Δοὺξ is the archaic form in use during the tenth century. Later the demotic version of Δούκας found almost general acceptance (the imperial family seems to have adopted it officially) though there is very occasional usage of the form Δοὺξ at a much later date.

[2] Thus the family name of *Strategos* is attested in 1342 (Kant., II, p. 279) and in 1369 (MM, I, p. 506). That of *Stratiotes* in the thirteenth century in Cos (MM, VI, p. 184), and the form *Kalostratiotes* is also found in 1340 (MM, I, pp. 194 and 195). Some other examples: *Drungarios* (1372, MM, I, p. 595), *Drungaropoulos* (11th/12th-century seal, Laurent, *Bulles métriques*, p. 217, no. 633), *Domestikos* (1019 and 14th century, S. Eustratiades, Ἱστορικὰ μνημεῖα τοῦ ῎Αθω,' Ἑλληνικά, 2 [1929], 362 and 382), *Domestikopoulos* (12th-century seal, Laurent, *Collection Orghidan*, pp. 217–18, no. 427; Laurent, *Bulles métriques*, p. 204, no. 582), *Komitopoulos* (1342, Kant., II, pp. 282–3; 1363, N. A. Bees, 'Σερβικὰ καὶ βυζαντιακὰ γράμματα Μετεώρου', Βυζαντίς, 2 (1911/12), 15), and *Tourmarchopoulos* (12th-century seal, Laurent, *Collection Orghidan*, p. 238, no. 475). Equally common are other Byzantine family names which derive from the offices of civil administration.

[3] For the rank of *dux* see J. B. Bury, *A History of the Eastern Roman Empire from the Fall of Irene to the Accession of Basil I (A.D. 802–867)* (London, 1912), p. 223; Stein, 'Untersuchungen', pp. 21–4; St. P. Kyriakides, Βυζαντιναὶ μελέται II–v (Thessalonica, 1937), pp. 278–81; Ostrogorsky, *History*, p. 326, no. 1; H. Glykatzi-Ahrweiler, 'Recherches sur l'administration de l'empire byzantin aux IXe–Xe siècles', *BCH*, 84 (1960), 53; V. Laurent, 'La chronologie des gouverneurs d'Antioche sous la seconde domination byzantine', *Mélanges de l'Université Saint Joseph*, 38 (1962), 225; R. Guilland, 'Etudes sur l'histoire administrative de l'empire byzantin. Les termes désignant le commandant en chef des armées byzantines', *EEBΣ*, 29 (1959), 56–7; T. Wasilewski, 'Les titres de duc, de catépan et de pronoétès dans l'Empire byzantin du IXe, jusqu'au XIIe siècle,' *Actes du XIIe Congrès International d'Etudes Byzantines* (Belgrade 1964), II, pp. 233–9.

[4] Theoph., p. 455, mentions a certain Nikephoros *dux* (Νικηφόρον τὸν δοῦκα) who took part in the revolt of the governor of Sicily Elpidios against the empress Eirene and after its suppression fled to the Arabs of North Africa (782). The word *dux* in this context is taken by the editor

for supposing that the cognomen was already in use as early as the eighth century.

The first Doux was then a man of entirely unspecified family connections except that he might have belonged to a house active in military circles. The opinion has been expressed that the Doukes descended from the Amorian dynasty through a female issue, but again no reliable evidence in support of this can be found.[1] In the early tenth century the Doukes are to some extent associated with Paphlagonia, and it is probable that the family sprang from that region.[2]

It has been suggested that the Doukes were of Armenian background. It is an established fact that the Armenian element was influential, especially in the army, during the ninth and the tenth centuries, and the view has therefore been expressed that the Doukes, like other leading contemporary houses (such as the Kourkouas, Kourtikes, and Mosele), were of Armenian origin.[3] But this cannot be substantiated since there appears to be no evidence at all showing that the Doukes as a whole, or even a single member or group of them, could

---

(*ibid.*, II, p. 598) as implying '*potius cognomen Nicephori*'. This is also the opinion of C. Sathas and E. Legrand, *Les Exploits de Digénis Akritas, Epopée byzantine du dixième siècle* (Paris, 1875), p. lxvii, and of R. Guilland, 'Etudes sur l'histoire administrative de Byzance: Le domestique des scholes'. *REB*, 8 (1950), 27, no. 5, who regard Nikephoros as being the first known member of the Doux family. On the other hand, J. B. Bury, *A History of the Later Roman Empire from Arcadius to Irene (A.D. 395 to A.D. 800)* (London, 1889), II, p. 482, considers him simply as being the *dux* of Calabria. This interpretation appears more convincing. In 793 Theoph., p. 469, mentions a certain Andronikos σπαθάριος καὶ τουρμάρχης 'Αρμενιακῶν whom R. J. H. Jenkins, 'The "Flight" of Samonas', *Speculum*, 23 (1948), 223, considers, presumably on account of the name Andronikos, to be a member of the Doux family. This cannot be accepted.

---

[1] A. Vogt, 'La jeunesse de Léon VI le Sage', *RH*, 174 (1934), 420–21, n. 2, attempts to explain (in my view on insufficient grounds) the alleged legitimacy of the Doukes over the first Macedonians by an imaginary descent from the emperor Theophilos. It appears extremely unlikely that an imperial descent in the ninth and the tenth centuries would have encouraged such high hopes. Had such a claim been put forward, it would undoubtedly have found an echo in contemporary historiography, which was in fact biased in favour of the Doukes and the other army aristocrats. The fact that some versions of the epic of Digenes form genealogical connections between the families of Doukas and Mouselom (=Mosele) (for references see J. Mavrogordato, *Digenes Akrites* [Oxford, 1956], pp. 254–5) and that Alexios Mosele married a daughter of Theophilos (Theoph. Cont., p. 107) cannot be taken in support of Vogt's assumption. The genealogy of the epic appears to be totally fictitious and should not be regarded as an historical source. For the question of the Doukai in the epic of Digenes see below.

[2] Theoph. Cont., p. 385, and the other chronicles drawing from Symeon Logothetes (cf. Stephanos 5) state that after the death of Konstantinos *3* his wife was sent back to her home in Paphlagonia (εἰς τὸν ἐν Παφλαγονίᾳ οἶκον αὐτῆς ἐξαπέστειλαν). We are however told that this woman was a daughter of the general Gregoras Iberitzes who was actually living in Constantinople, and his house there is mentioned (Theoph. Cont., p. 382). The former reference is therefore applicable only to the house of Konstantinos *3*. Since it is improbable that he ever held a position in the militarily unimportant Paphlagonia, a fact that would perhaps indicate a residence there, it is likely that the mentioned house represented a paternal heritage.

[3] This was voiced by N. Adontz, 'Les fonds historiques de l'épopée byzantine Digénis Akritas', *BZ*, 29 (1929/30), 205–7, who, however, did not cite any historical evidence to support it. R. J. H. Jenkins, 'The "Flight" of Samonas', p. 223, is also inclined to subscribe to this view and as possible fresh evidence he cites Theoph., p. 469, who speaks about an Andronikos wrongly thought to be a member of the Doux family (cf. p. 4, n. 4, above). On the basis of the fact that the partisans of Konstantinos *3* in 913 included several persons of Armenian origin, P. Charanis, 'The Armenians in the Byzantine Empire', *BS*, 22 (1961), 227, asks whether the Doukes were not actually of the same ethnic descent.

have been of any origin other than Greek. Though this cannot be conclusively proved, the cumulative effect of the evidence strongly supports this view. For instance, the surname of the family is Greek, or more correctly, hellenized Latin. Most families of Armenian origin bear Armenian names. Then there is a conspicuous absence of Armenian first names among the Doukes. That of Bardas *10*, which is the exception, may presumably be explained by a marriage of that group of Doukes (Lydoi) with another family which transmitted this name. Otherwise the first names of the family's members are all Greek, with Andronikos, Konstantinos, and Michael predominating. Further the Doukes originated in Paphlagonia where the Armenian impact was not at its strongest.

Lastly, if the Doukes had been of Armenian origin, this would surely have found an echo in the tale of their ancestry. The Armenian, or at least the eastern, background of Basileios I is betrayed in the claim that he descended from the Arsacids; likewise, the Phokades who may have originated in Armenia took pride in supposing that they had as ancestors the Roman Fabii but only through the intermediary of Georgia.[1] This tale of an oriental descent is however absent in the eleventh-century tradition on the origin of the Doukai.

The groups of the Doukai

Before 1204 there were three distinct families of Doukai, those of the early tenth century who are always referred to by the archaic form of Doux, the small group which flourished under Basileios II and are occasionally called Lydoi, and finally the imperial family the members of which are active during the period 1050–1150. Much more numerous than these three groups taken together are the various Byzantines, originally of other families, who acquired the name of Doukas, often in compound form with other surnames (e.g. Doukas-Angelos-Komnenos-Palaiologos). The many cases in which the name of Doukas entirely overshadowed the patronymic proper should also be mentioned in this category. The great majority of such families belong of course to the nobility, or at least to the well-to-do classes, but very occasionally the sources also mention Doukai in humbler walks of life.

No matter how strong the Byzantine concept of the unity of the family, even a superficial comparison shows that there was indeed not much in common between the tenth-century Doukes and the imperial family of the later period. The attested activities of the former hardly fill a decade, and the house owed its unusual fame to the deeds performed by Andronikos *2* and Konstantinos *3*. Some modern scholars have advanced the view that these men belonged to the all-powerful landed aristocracy of the eastern provinces which could not reconcile themselves to the rather humble social background of Leon VI. In a sense this view suggests that their revolts (i.e. that of Andronikos *2* from the fortress of Kaballa and the attempted coup of 913) are significant because they inaugurated those frequent tenth-century challenges to imperial authority which culminated in the far more serious revolts of Skleros and Phokas during the first years of Basileios II.[2] There is however no evidence that the Doukes possessed

[1] Cf. above, p. 3, n. 3.

[2] See for instance Jenkins, 'The "Flight" of Samonas', *passim*; R. H. Dolley, 'The Lord High Admiral Eustathios Argyros and the Betrayal of Taormina to the African Arabs in 902', *SBN*, 7 (1953), 340–53.

extensive estates, although it cannot be denied that they were at least wealthy.[1] Their prestige and genuine popularity among the masses does not point to a background of the kind traditionally associated with the misery of the Asia Minor peasantry. It is evident from the events in which they were implicated, from their popularity with the chroniclers and populace, and from the curious incident of *c.* 932 when an impostor gained wide local support only because he was clever enough to adopt the name of the dead Konstantinos *3*, that the fame of the Doukes rested not upon wealth and privilege but sprang from their daring military exploits on the eastern frontier. They were then pre-eminently brave and successful soldiers who could expect to command widespread support both from among their own ranks and from among the populace who knew and admired them. They lived and flourished in a milieu which nourished the legend around their name which is found in the epic of Digenes Akritas. It is probable that their spasmodic revolts against the lawful government were devoid of any serious foundation, and there appears to be no deep-rooted cause for these outbreaks. The incidents of 906–7 and 913 can best be understood as the action of ambitious and popular generals who had overreached themselves. The backing they received, sentimental rather than real, was far from adequate to cope with the situation that emerged. Herein lies the tragedy of the house, and to a certain extent explains the special consideration with which the Doukes were treated in Byzantine literature.

The relationship of these Doukes with the imperial house of the Macedonian dynasty presents no particular problem. No doubt the family's popularity had exceeded the permissible limit and even went so far as to link the name of Konstantinos *3* with the crown in the face of the evident discomfiture of Leon VI.[2] Otherwise they acted like other military commanders of similar background and mentality. Their professional experience was highly valued, but their loyalty was often questionable. Given a chance, they were capable of risking everything with the gravest consequences for the state and for themselves. But in the early tenth century, the family found in the chief minister Samonas a most dangerous opponent.[3] The blow sustained by the house in 913, following the annihilation of Konstantinos *3*, put an almost permanent end to its activities. Most of its members were either killed[4] or rendered harmless. If any Doukes

---

[1] In noting the withdrawal of Andronikos *2* to Kaballa, Theoph. Cont., p. 372, observes that he was accompanied by his own relatives and slaves (ἅμα συγγενέσι καὶ δούλοις αὐτοῦ), a remark which is not further elaborated. It is of course possible that those δοῦλοι were settled in some unknown lands of Andronikos *2*, but it can be equally reasonable to assume that during these times of relative abundance of war prisoners (cf. A. Hadjinicolaou-Marava, *Recherches sur la vie des Esclaves dans le Monde byzantin* [Athens, 1950], p. 40) it would not have been unusual to find a considerable number of them in the service of every successful army general.

[2] See below on Konstantinos *3*, p. 22, n. 8.

[3] Theoph. Cont., pp. 371–2; cf. Kedr., II, p. 266.

[4] According to Zon., III, pp. 675–6, during the abortive revolt of Konstantinos *3* in 913 all male members of the Doux family perished, and Konstantinos *12* allegedly descended from a female issue of it (ἀλλὰ τοῦ γένους ἐκείνων [sc. the Doukai] πάλαι πανοικὶ ἐξολοθρευθέντος, ὅτε Κωνσταντῖνος τυραννίδι ἐπικεχείρηκεν, ὡς ἔμπροσθεν εἴρηται, τοῦ πορφυρογεννήτου Κωνσταντίνου τοῦ παιδὸς τοῦ ἄνακτος Λέοντος, τοῦ φιλοσόφου φημί, βασιλεύοντος, καὶ ὑπὸ ἐπιτρόπους τελοῦντος ἔτι διὰ τὴν νηπιότητα, καὶ μηδενὸς ἄρρενος περιλειφθέντος, ἐκ θηλείας τινός, ὡς λόγος, οἱ τούτου [sc. the emperor Konstantinos *12*] κατήγοντο πρόγονοι, ὅθεν οὐδὲ Δούκας λελόγιστο καθαρός, ἀλλ' ἐπίμικτος καὶ κεκιβδηλευμένην ἔχων τὴν πρὸς τοὺς Δούκας συγγένειαν). Cf. H. Grégoire, Ὁ Διγενὴς Ἀκρίτας.

existed in the period afterwards (such as Nikolaos *7*), they were not particularly outstanding and certainly not comparable to their predecessors.

Very little can be said about the small branch of the Doukes which flourished in the later part of the tenth century and who were also referred to as 'Lydoi',[1] (nos. *8–10*). It is impossible to surmise their relationship to the earlier Doukes, though the name Andronikos found in both groups might possibly point to a genealogical link. These Doukes-Lydoi also belonged to the military aristocracy, but the sources do not pay much attention to them. They supported and took part in the revolt of Bardas Skleros, and there is also further evidence of their insubordination to the imperial authority. However, they were eventually pardoned, and at least one of them subsequently had a military career.

The Doukai of the eleventh century, thanks to the providential elevation of Konstantinos *12* in 1059, assumed a predominance which was strongly felt until the accession of Alexios I Komnenos, and for some time afterwards certain of them continued to hold responsible positions, especially in the army. The family flourished as far as numbers went but unfortunately it lacked the more constructive gifts which characterized its successors on the throne. In spite of their extensive power, their unusually vast wealth, and their close relations with the Komnenoi, after the end of the eleventh century the Doukai entered a period of obscurity. Although their name continued to be used and to be popular, the male lines of Konstantinos *12* and Ioannes *13* most probably became extinct by the middle of the twelfth century. The Doukai who subsequently appear do not owe their surname to a male ancestor but rather to a family which had meantime acquired it through marriage.

This family of the eleventh-century Doukai seems to have originated in Paphlagonia.[2] With regard to its ancestry and background little has been

---

'Η Βυζαντινὴ ἐποποιία στὴν ἱστορία καὶ στὴν ποίηση (New York, 1942), pp. 25–6; idem, 'La carrière du premier Nicéphore Phocas', Προσφορὰ εἰς Στίλπωνα Π. Κυριακίδην (Thessalonica, 1953), p. 232. The statement of Zonaras reflects a much later tradition, obviously hostile to the imperial family of Doukas, and although what he says cannot be refuted, the appearance of Nikolaos 7 some five years after the event does at least indicate that the Byzantine historian's account is somewhat exaggerated.

---

[1] The cognomen Λυδός, used by the sources as a designation for Andronikos Doux *8*, undoubtedly has a regional origin and was already in use (not as a surname) in the fifth century (cf. the name of the historian Ioannes Λυδός, the Lydian). A totally unknown historian of the same name is mentioned in the introduction of Skylitzes, see Kedr., I, p. 4. As a family name it is not widely met. A Theodoros Lydos who lived in c. 1190 (Skout., p. 399; Ephraim, p. 247, v 6039) is certainly Theodoros Mankaphas of Philadelphia. Another Ioannes Lydos (or perhaps Lydenos) is known from a tenth-century seal, see Laurent, *Collection Orghidan*, p. 210, no. 411. Some derivatives of the name can also be mentioned. In the ninth century a *protospatharios*, Theophilos Lydiates, was married to a lady of the Melissenos family (*Vita S. Nicolai Studitae*, PG, 105, col. 916 D), and in 1213 a priest, Georgios Lydiates, signed a document as a witness (MM, VI, p. 163). There is also another seal from the eighth century belonging to 'Theodoros Lydenos son of Theodoros', see Laurent, *Médaillier Vatican*, pp. 197–8, no. 185.

[2] In a letter of Psellos to Ioannes *13* he alluded, in a rhetorical manner, to the fact that the latter came indeed from Paphlagonia (Πυνθάνομαι δ'οὖν, οὐχὶ πατρὶς ἡ πολυύμνητος Παφλαγονία ἐστίν;), see *Scripta Minora*, II, p. 284. This is corroborated by the chronicle of Michael the Syrian who explicitly states that the family of the emperor Konstantinos *12* had its roots in this region, see *Chronique* (ed. J.-B. Chabot), III (Paris, 1905), p. 165.

preserved. The house was said to belong to the eastern branch of the Doukai[1] though a corresponding western one is not known. The writers of the period, frequently in close touch with the palace, are lavish in their praise of the nobility of the Doukai and their glorious past. In particular Psellos names Andronikos, Konstantinos, and Pantherios[2] as among the ancestors of the emperor Konstantinos *12*. This should not however be taken at its face value. The father of Konstantinos *12* cannot have been a very distinguished man and he is indeed very rarely mentioned.[3]

The failure of the Doukai to establish a lasting dynasty must be seen within the historical setting of this period, during which the Byzantine polity was faced with increasing difficulties. In the first place, the crown passed to Konstantinos *12* quite accidentally, and he became emperor without the permanent support of either the army or any really influential group in the capital. It is of course true that at the outset the opposition that was instrumental in forcing the abdication of Isaakios I Komnenos had to turn to an 'anti-military' man to satisfy the civil party, so that the new emperor appeared to act in the interests of that group. Furthermore it is possible that as a close relative of the now dead patriarch

---

[1] Ἐκ τοῦ γένους τῶν ἑῴων τοῦ Δουκὸς καταγόμενοι, Kedr., II, p. 615. Isaakios I Komnenos is also described as ἑῷος by Attal., p. 53, and likewise Bryen., p. 117, calls Botaneiates one τῶν τῆς ἑῴας εὐγενεστάτων. In a similar vein Psellos praises the eastern birth of Eirene, the wife of Ioannes *13*: ἤνεγκε γοῦν αὐτὴν τῆς ἑῴας τὸ κάλλιστον, Scripta Minora, I, p. 157. On the other hand, the term ἑσπέριος (western) is almost contemptuously applied to the rebel Nikephoros Bryennios by Attal., p. 118. The contrast between the noble 'eastern' with the less noble 'western' origin (we also have τὰ ἑῷα καὶ τὰ ἑσπέρια τάγματα, Skout., p. 230) was distinctly marked in eleventh-century Byzantium. S. Vryonis, 'Byzantium: The Social Basis of Decline in the Eleventh Century', *Greek, Roman, and Byzantine Studies*, 2 (1959), 161–2, argues that the nobles of Asia Minor owed their superiority over their western counterparts to the more extensive estates they had acquired and to their insubordination towards the central government. Asia Minor had always been in a position to provide powerful feudal lords in contrast to the relatively neglected European territories. The large majority of contemporary nobles came from the east; the Bryennioi were one of the few exceptions.

[2] Τὸ μὲν ἄνω γένος ὅσον εἰς προπάππους ἁβρόν τε καὶ εὔδαιμον καὶ ὁποῖον αἱ συγγραφαὶ ᾄδουσιν διὰ στόματος γοῦν καὶ μέχρι τοῦ νῦν ἅπασιν ὁ Ἀνδρόνικος ἐκεῖνος καὶ ὁ Κωνσταντῖνος καὶ ὁ Πανθήριος, οἱ μὲν ἐξ ἄρρενος γένους οἱ δὲ ἐκ θήλεος τούτῳ (sc. the emperor Konstantinos *12*) προσήκοντες, Psellos, II, p. 140. The first two persons mentioned can be clearly identified for they are none other than Andronikos *2* and Konstantinos *3*. They are also alluded to in *Alexias*, I, p. 111, and in Kallikles, p. 322. Pantherios presents more of a problem. Psellos is careful to distinguish between the emperor's ancestors: ὁ Ἀνδρόνικος ἐκεῖνος καὶ ὁ Κωνσταντῖνος καὶ ὁ Πανθήριος, οἱ μὲν ἐξ ἄρρενος γένους οἱ δὲ ἐκ θήλεος τούτῳ προσήκοντες. This word order must be taken as implying that the emperor descended from some of them (Andronikos *2* and his son Konstantinos *3*) through a male line and from the rest (Pantherios and possibly a second unspecified Konstantinos) through a female line. In other words, it is erroneous to regard Pantherios as a member of the Doukas family as Zon., III, p. 675, does (who draws otherwise on Psellos) and some modern authorities such as the editor of Psellos, II, p. 140, n. 3; Ducange, *Familiae*, p. 161; R. Guilland, 'Etudes sur l'histoire administrative de Byzance: Le domestique des scholes', *REB*, 8 (1950), 31. The Pantherios of Psellos was in fact a relative of Romanos I Lekapenos who replaced the great general Ioannes Kourkouas as *domestikos tōn scholōn* in c. 945. See Theoph. Cont., p. 429; Georg. Cont., p. 917; Leon Gram., p. 325; Kedr., II, p. 318. The same man (called Panther) is also mentioned in the 'Vita S. Basilii Junioris' edited by A. V. Veselovskii. *Sbornik Otdeleniya Russkago Yazyka i Slovesnosti Imp. Akademii Nauk*, 46 (1889), *Prilozhenie* no. 6, 65–7, and was thence taken over by *The Russian Primary Chronicle* (translated and edited by S. Cross and O. Sherbowitz-Wetzor Cambridge, Mass., 1954), p. 72. Cf. H. Grégoire and P. Orgels, 'La guerre russo-byzantine de 941', *B*, 24 (1954), 155–6.

[3] See below, Andronikos *11*.

Michael Keroularios (Michael *14* might well have been called after him), Konstantinos *12* obtained considerable support from his clamorous partisans, but since they did not represent a group destined to survive long, their influence inevitably soon died out. Nevertheless Konstantinos *12*, a man of mediocre talents, managed to stay on his throne for more than seven eventful years and without serious challenges to his rule. His survival amid internal and external political problems may be partly attributed to the unusual absence of ambitious and experienced generals during his reign. But Konstantinos *12*, though colourless as an emperor, remained able to command a certain amount of affection and respect. His son Michael *14* had to face the same symptoms of disintegration, though by now at a more advanced stage. The appearance of this unsuitable and incapable young man on the throne had disastrous effects for the state, as well as for the entire family to which he was apparently not much attached. He constantly displayed his maliciousness towards his Doukai[1] relatives. Michael's *14* reign ended ingloriously in 1078. For a short time the rights of his son Konstantinos *23* were preserved, owing to the strong feeling for the hereditary principle. But once Alexios Komnenos assumed supreme power (1081) Doukai claims fell into the background.

The marriage of Eirene *26* to Alexios Komnenos brought the two most prominent representatives of contemporary Byzantine nobility together. From now on the Doukai occupied a secondary social position, though their numerous descendants were always proud of the name they bore. The glorification of the family (already initiated in the writings of Psellos) entered a new phase, and in the twelfth century the Doukai, together with the Komnenoi, were placed by the poets and rhetoricians at the apex of the Byzantine aristocracy.

The Doukai were wealthy, deriving their incomes largely from extensive estates scattered throughout the empire. Very little is known about these properties. Psellos vaguely speaks of a 'paternal' piece of land (it could have been in Paphlagonia) to which Konstantinos *12* retreated during a period of temporary disgrace prior to his accession.[2] We do not possess other information on that ruler's landed properties, but certain facts are known about those of his brother Ioannes *13*. The Caesar owned considerable territory near Nicomedia at the foot of Mount Sophon where the fortress of Metabole had been built. It was there that Ioannes *13* sought seclusion after the emergence of Nikephoritzes in 1073,[3] and a little later the district witnessed his adventure with the rebel Roussel.[4] In view of the virtual occupation of Bithynia by the Seljuks by c. 1080, this property must then have ceased to belong to the Caesar's family. However this may be, Ioannes *13* spent much of his later life on another important estate called τὰ Μωροβούνδου, in the more secure region of Thrace. It was there that the news of the Komnenian revolt of 1081 reached him.[5] This estate might possibly be identified with the one Psellos mentions as being in the region of Choerobacchae where the Caesar organized splendid hunting parties.[6] Andronikos

[1] Cf. Bryen., p. 101.

[2] 'Εν ἀγροῖς διέτριβε τὰ πολλὰ καὶ περὶ τὴν πατρῴαν βῶλον ἐπραγματεύετο, Psellos, ΙΙ, p. 141.

[3] Bryen., pp. 57 and 73.

[4] Bryen., pp. 77 and 81. See also below, Ioannes *13*, Andronikos *21* and Michael *24*.

[5] Cf. *Alexias*, I, pp. 81ff.

[6] 'Εν Χοιροβάκχοις ἄττων ἤ καὶ βρυχώμενος ἔνθα αἱ σαὶ θῆραι καὶ ταῦτα δὴ τὰ λαμπρὰ κυνηγέσια, Sathas, *MB*, VI, p. 306.

Doukas *21*, the Caesar's elder son, possessed considerable property bordering the river Maeander in Asia Minor. Thanks to the detailed *praktikon* which has been preserved, certain facts are known about this estate which consisted of the *episkepseis* of Miletus and Alopekai and was divided into eight *proasteia*.[1] Andronikos *21* received the land as a grant from the emperor early in 1073, but with the overrunning of Asia Minor by the Turks it is unlikely that he managed to exploit it for long. A charming and picturesque farm known as Πεντήγοστις and situated near the city of Serres in Macedonia belonged to Konstantinos *23*. It contained some houses and the owner shortly before his death entertained the emperor there.[2] The estates of Konstantinos' *23* mother, the ex-empress Maria which are referred to at the same time, were also in Macedonia near Christopolis (Kaballa).[3]

The eleventh-century Doukai entered into matrimonial relations with other distinguished families, and thus the usage of their name spread still further. The prestige of the name was to a great extent due to the marriage of Eirene *26* to Alexios Komnenos, and several of their grandchildren officially adopted it. This practice was not confined to the Komnenoi alone. The Angeloi, whose origin can also be traced to Eirene *26*, also gave birth to several Doukai and it was indeed a branch of these in Epirus that proved dynamic enough to preserve the name in western Greece until the fourteenth century. A great number of similar cases are attested in which the name of Doukas is borne along with some other noble surname, or where it completely overshadowed and replaced the patronymics. In certain families it is not difficult to find the explanation for the adoption of the name and to trace its origin, while in other cases this is impossible as it is merely mentioned.

Several Doukai were active in the twelfth century, but only a few of them can be said to be male descendants of Konstantinos *12* and Ioannes *13*. The others were most probably members of such families as the Komnenoi, the Bryennioi, the Kamateroi, the Palaiologoi, and the Angeloi who thought it more expedient to be called by the name of their distant ancestor Andronikos *21*. None of the male descendants of the emperor Konstantinos *12* lived as late as 1100 and those of his brother Ioannes *13* do not seem to have lived beyond the middle of the twelfth century. It follows then that all Doukai of the later period, even those whose genealogical position is totally untraceable, must belong to other families which inherited the name through some female ancestor.

Parts III and IV of the present work are concerned with the Doukai who belong to other families. In Part III they are sketched under the various houses from which they sprang, and in Part IV all isolated Doukai from the twelfth century up to 1453 are included. It has not proved possible to establish the provenance of these families or to show how they came to adopt the name.[4]

[1] For the estate and the relevant documents (edited in MM, vi, pp. 1–15) see P. Bezobrazov 'Patmosskaya pistsovaya kniga', *VV*, 7 (1900), 68–106; Dölger, *Regesten*, ii, p. 18, nos. 992–4; G. Rouillard, *La Vie rurale dans l'Empire byzantin* (Paris, 1953), pp. 129–33; G. Ostrogorsky, *Pour l'histoire de la féodalité byzantine* (Brussels, 1954), pp. 302–10. See also below, Andronikos *21*.

[2] *Alexias*, ii, p. 171.

[3] Τοὺς ἐν Χριστουπόλει ἀγρυὺς τῆς βασιλίσσης Μαρίας, *Alexias*, i, p. 171.

[4] It will be later seen that the word Doukas, even during the Byzantine period, was used as a first name and it must be remembered that it would be easy for it to become a surname.

The three genuine groups of Doukai, as well as the majority of families from which those of Part III stemmed, are undoubtedly included in the Byzantine upper class. Yet there are traces of another rarer usage among the common populace. It is most unlikely that those priests bearing the name in Southern Italy and Sicily and in other distant provinces had anything to do with the ambitious and cultured Doukai of Constantinople. It is possible that some of these humble Doukai became the ancestors of their namesakes who flourished after 1453.[1]

Finally it should be noted that several rather uncommon surnames derive from that of Doukas. Some forms of these are attested as early as the eleventh century, but it must be stressed that there is not the slightest evidence to link these names with the Doukai.[2]

THE DOUKAI IN BYZANTINE LIFE AND LITERATURE

The popularity of a name used for an almost uninterrupted period of at least six centuries cannot be denied. At a comparatively early date the name began to be given to children at their baptism, the earliest mention of this being in 1293.[3] The feminine form Δούκαινα was also turned into a first name.[4] Very numerous examples from the post-Byzantine and modern period of the widespread use of the name Doukas and of some of its derivatives as baptismal names[5] witness to the impact which it had made.[6] This popularity exceeded the geographical limits of the Byzantine lands. For instance, during the Arpadian period (1000–1301) the name is attested in medieval Hungary.[7]

The eleventh-century Doukai were certainly a noble and wealthy house which headed Byzantine society during the period when its members occupied the throne. But of course Byzantine notions on the aristocracy were entirely different from those of western Europe and it must not be assumed that the exceptional social standing of the Doukai was a result of their supposed nobility of

---

[1] See Appendix I.

[2] The prosopography of these families is examined in Appendix II.

[3] 'Εκοιμίθη ὁ δοῦλος τοῦ Θεοῦ Δούκας υἱός τοῦ Γριγόρι ἔτος ϛωά μηνὶ ἀπριλίῳ ιή καὶ ἔθετω ἐν τῇ ἀγήᾳ μονῇ ταύτῃ, the text being found on an inscription in the church of Ortakeni in eastern Asia Minor. See H. Grégoire, 'Rapport sur un voyage d'exploration dans le Pont et en Cappadoce', BCH, 33 (1909), 113, no. 93.

[4] No example from the Byzantine period has been found. A document of the year 1493 reads: ἡ γυναίκα του Δούκαινα τοῦ Τζατζάλη, see MM, III, p. 334. The text of an inscription, found in the church of St Theodore at Pergamos and dated in 1544/5, reads: ...δι' ἐξόδου καὶ συνδρομῆς 'Αργυροῦ ἱερέως καὶ Δουκαίνης πρεσβυτέρας; see H. Grégoire, Recueil des inscriptions grecques chrétiennes d'Asie Mineure, I (Paris, 1922), p. 17, no. 51.

[5] For some modern examples see A. Ch. Boutouras, Τὰ νεοελληνικὰ κύρια ὀνόματα ἱστορικῶς καὶ γλωσσικῶς ἑρμηνευόμενα (Athens, 1912), p. 103. cf. A. Bakalopoulos, Ἱστορία τοῦ νέου Ἑλληνισμοῦ, II, part I (Thessalonica, 1964), pp. 357–8.

[6] Certain of these later baptismal forms may however owe their origin to the Frankish title δούκας (duca), very common in Greek lands after the Fourth Crusade. It is quite probable that this title is responsible for the existence of many of the cases of the first name Δούκας. Cf. for instance the name 'Ρήγας (from rex).

[7] See Gy. Moravcsik in Cambridge Medieval History, IV, Pt. I, ed. J. M. Hussey, (Cambridge, 1966), p. 575.

birth.[1] Part of their prestige was due to the fact that some of their members were associated with the throne as emperors or empresses, but again such an association did not necessarily safeguard a family from criticism.[2] But the Doukai were generally accorded very fair treatment by the Byzantine writers.

References to the tenth-century Doukes reflect admiration for their bravery whereas the eleventh-century dynasty are mentioned in rather different terms. It is true that here we come across constant praises for the family's distinguished past, but this does not apply to the little known father of Konstantinos *12* but to the earlier Doukes from whom the imperial house was thought to descend. The imperial house itself must have encouraged the creation of the legends which linked it with the earlier Doukes and with Rome.[3] The excessive compliments for the family appear for the first time in the writings of Psellos, who may have fabricated such reports. He continually compliments the emperor for his noble ancestors.[4] Theophylaktos of Bulgaria imitates him and attached the epithets of

---

[1] The prominence and past glories of an individual family or house (γένος) were naturally much admired by the Byzantines, but as this was spontaneous and devoid of any false pretence it failed to create a class resting on an eminent past alone. Persons prided themselves in the first place on the heroic achievements of their forefathers while the element of aristocracy itself was rather subordinated to this. Hence the sudden disappearance of noble families who did not become extinct but in one way or another ceased to play the role demanded of them and thus lost their high social standing. The constant emergence throughout the Byzantine period of people of obscure and humble origin who attained the highest offices of the empire was the rule rather than the exception. Three striking cases of this were Basileios I, the family of the Kamateroi late in the eleventh century, and the rise of Theodoros Laskaris—the future emperor—in the twelfth. Laudatory praise of a family's past always remained popular, yet this was primarily meant as a compliment and was applicable to houses who, like the Doukai, had already achieved an exceptional place in society. Psellos' brief characterization of the Diogeneis clearly illustrates prevailing views about aristocracy. According to him, the family of Romanos IV was ancient and glorious with the exception of his father who by revolting unsuccessfully against the lawful government ceased to possess the hereditary noble qualities: τῷ βασιλεῖ τούτῳ φημὶ δὲ ʿΡωμανῷ τῷ τοῦ Διογένους, τὸ μὲν γένος ἀρχαῖον καὶ εὔδαιμον πλὴν τοῦ πατρός, Psellos, II, p. 157.

For the Byzantine ideas on nobility see E. Gerland, *Histoire de la Noblesse crétoise au Moyen Age* (Paris, 1907), pp. 3–5; R. Guilland, 'La noblesse de race à Byzance', BS, 9 (1947/48), 307–14 (the author cites and discusses all Greek terms used for the designation of nobility); Ph. Argenti, *Libro d'Oro de la Noblesse de Chio* (London, 1955), I, pp. 8–26 (believes that there existed a nobility of birth in Byzantium); F. Dölger in BZ, 49 (1956), 125–7. R. Guilland, 'La transmission héréditaire des titres nobiliaires à Byzance', *Palaeologia*, 8 (Osaka, 1959), 137–43 (cf. BZ, 53 [1960], 218), is inaccessible to me.

[2] For instance the Angeloi were a family still prominent and noble in the later part of the thirteenth century (cf. Pach., I, pp. 65 and 82), yet the hatred of an anonymous poet goes so far as to describe them all as a 'bastard and evil-growing family':

καὶ ταῦτα μὲν προσήνεγκε τὸ τῶν ᾿Αγγέλων γένος
τὸ νόθον καὶ κακοφυὲς τότε ʿΡωμαίοις ἄρξαν·
βασιλευσάντων γὰρ αὐτῶν τῶν ἐπὶ γῆς ᾿Αγγέλων
ἡ βασιλὶς τῶν πόλεων εἰς τέλος κατεβλήθη.

See J. Müller, 'Byzantinische Analekten', *Sitzungsberichte der kaiserlichen Akademie der Wissenschaften. Philosophisch-historische Klasse*, 9 (Vienna, 1853), 376, vv. 320–23.

[3] Cf. above p. 3, n. 1 and 2.

[4] Τὸ μὲν ἄνω γένος ὅσον εἰς προπάππους ἁβρόν τε καὶ εὔδαιμον καὶ ὁποῖον αἱ συγγραφαὶ ᾄδουσι, Psellos, II, p. 140. He also implies that the ancestral virtues have been inherited by the emperor, (τὰ ἐκ πατραγαθίας καὶ προγονικῆς εὐκλείας ἐπιδαψιλευθέντα σοι πλεονεκτήματα, Scripta Minora, I, p. 34). Even if the wife of Ioannes *13* had not belonged to the aristocracy, the nobility of her husband's family would have sufficed (κἂν μὴ τὸ γένος αὐτῇ καθεστήκει τοιοῦτον, ἀλλ᾿ ἤρκεσεν ἂν τὸ παρὰ τοῦ συζύγου, οὕτω περιφανὲς ὂν καὶ περιβόητον, Scripta Minora, I, p. 181).

'blessed'[1] and 'pious'[2] to the family, while Kallikles compares a dead Doukas of his time with the glorious tenth-century heroes.[3] Even the fifteenth-century historian Doukas *258* boasts that his grandfather Michael *241* was a scion of the famous family.[4]

With the marriage of Alexios Komnenos to Eirene Doukaina *26* in 1078 and his subsequent elevation to the throne the two most distinguished contemporary houses were united, and this union produced a new branch which proudly claimed ancestry from both families. This new branch — the Κομνηνοδοῦκαι — naturally inherited the virtues of both the Doukai and the Komnenoi.[5] In the twelfth century the two families stood poles apart, for the Komnenoi occupied the throne while the Doukai were rapidly declining, yet this did not prevent them from being frequently eulogized on an almost equal footing.[6]

But the really lasting impact of the Doukai on Byzantine literature is undoubtedly in the Acritic epic. It must however be emphasised that the references found in the poems do not relate to the Doukai as a whole but only to the tenth-century branch. Some of the heroic deeds of that period did indeed lend themselves to the creation of epic characters with prototypes in contemporary history. As early as *c.* 908 popular belief — it is not known through what medium — linked the name of Konstantinos *3* with the throne, to the evident disquiet of the reigning Leon VI.[7] The same Konstantinos *3* was reputed to have seen the Virgin in a dream. She gave him horse and arms and promised that his enemies would be crushed.[8] The popularity and the fame of this man was so great that thirty years after his death an impostor assumed his name and was accepted and supported as such by the rural populace of Bithynia.[9] This being the case, it is not strange that the names of Doukas, Andronikos, and Kon-

---

[1] *Ὦ τοῦ μακαρίου Δουκῶν γένους*, PG, 126, col. 524.

[2] *Τῆς τοῦ εὐσεβοῦς τῶν Δουκῶν γενεᾶς*, PG, 126, col. 536A.

[3] *Ἀρχαῖος Δούκας*
ὡς *Ἀνδρόνικος ἄλλος ἤ Κωνσταντῖνος*. See Kallikles, pp. 321–2.

[4] *Γένει τε καταγόμενος τῶν ἀνέκαθεν Δουκῶν κἀκ τῆς αὐτῆς σειρᾶς χρυσόκοσμος κρίκος*, Doukas, p. 47.

[5] Prodromos writes: *Δύο μὲν οὖν ἤστην σκῆπτρα Ῥωμαίοις ἀλλήλοις καλὸν ἀνταυγάζοντα· τὸ μὲν μικρῷ πρότερον τὸ Κομνηνόν, τὸ δ' εὐθὺς παρὰ πόδας τὸ Δουκικόν, ἄμφω εὐτυχῆ καὶ περιφανῆ καὶ κοσμικῆς ἀρετῆς οὐκ ἀνάξια· κἆτα ὥσπερ ἐκ συμφωνίας συνεληλυθέτην εἰς ἓν πολλῷ φανότερον καὶ λαμπρότερον τοῦτο δὴ τὸ Κομνηνοδουκικόν . . ., PG, 133, col. 1400A.* Bryennios expresses the same idea: *Ἐκ Δουκῶν γὰρ ἁρμοσάμενος* (sc. Alexios Komnenos) *τοῦ βίου τὴν κοινωνὸν εἰς μίαν συμφωνίαν ἄμφω τὰ γένη συνῆψε καὶ εἰς ἓν φυτὸν συνεδένδρωσεν· ἄμα δὲ ἐπὶ τὸ ἀρχαιότητι διαφέρον αἰδεσιμώτερον, ὥς φασί. Διὰ τοῦτο καὶ πάντες τήν τε Κομνηνικὴν ἀρχαιογονίαν καὶ Δουκικὴν αἰδούμενοι . . .,* Bryen., pp. 12–13.

[6] . . . *τὰ θεῖα γένη τὸ Κομνηνῶν καὶ τὸ Δουκῶν* . . ., Prodromos in PG, 133, col. 1253A; *ἐν δὲ ἡ τοῦ γένους φωσφορία, τὸ Κομνηνόθεν, τὸ ἐκ Δουκῶν* . . ., Eustathios in E. Kurtz, 'Evstathiya Thessalonikiiskago i Konstantina Manassi monodii na konchinu Nikifora Komnina', VV, 17 (1910), 292, v. 76; cf. ibid., 305, v. 112 (Manasses).

[7] Theoph. Cont., p. 373.

[8] The exact words, put into the mouth of Konstantinos *13*, run as follows: 'Here appeared a most glorious lady, dressed in purple, leading a fiery horse and carrying arms also emitting fire. Though I was unwilling, she urged me to put on the arms, and I became frightened. Then she persuaded me to ride the horse, saying "Those who insult God, my Son, will melt down before you like wax".' See *Vita S. Basilii Junioris*, PG, 109, col. 657B. For the epic character of this version see H. Grégoire, 'L'âge héroïque de Byzance', *Mélanges offerts à M. Nicolas Iorga* (Paris, 1933), p. 392.

[9] See below on Konstantinos *3*.

stantinos are among those most frequently met with in the epics and the ballads of the Acritic cycle.[1]

In the various versions of Digenes the name of Doukas is particularly associated with the genealogy of the main hero.[2] The maternal grandfather of Digenes is called Aaron Doukas,[3] and this latter's wife was also of the same house.[4] Their daugher Eirene, that is the mother of the hero, is of course a Δούκαινα.[5] Finally, another general Doukas became the father of Eudokia, the maiden who married Digenes.[6] Although these names are distant echoes of certain historical realities,[7] the activities of individual heroes in the epic are purely fictitious. In particular the genealogy is quite unfounded in fact and, as has been observed, when the author of the epic 'was obliged to name a Greek family he avoided the difficulty by calling everyone a Doukas'.[8]

But even so, the fact remains that such heroes of the Acritic ballads as Porphyrios, Konstantas, Xantinos, Andronikos and the like are evidently modelled upon the tenth-century Doukes. Among them Konstantinos *3* is perhaps the most popular and many of his deeds have been sung in folk poetry. His association with the throne, or rather his unsuccessful bid for the imperial power, certainly explains the name of Porphyrios and its variants. Likewise his escape to, and subsequent imprisonment in, Syria was responsible for the name of another popular hero, Αἰχμάλωτος, that is, the Prisoner.[9]

[1] On this question in general see H. Grégoire, 'Etudes sur l' Epopée byzantine', *REG*, 46 (1953), 48–55; idem, 'L'âge héroïque de Byzance', 390–7; idem, 'Ο Διγενὴς 'Ακρίτας, 22–9; S. Impelizzeri, *Il Digenis Akritas, L' Epopea di Bisanzio* (Florence, 1940), pp. 41–52.

[2] For the fictitious genealogy of Digenes see J. Mavrogordato, *Digenes Akrites* (Oxford, 1956), pp. 254–5; A. Pertusi, 'Alcune note sull'epica bizantina', *Aevum*, 36 (1962), 14–28.

[3] See the versions of Trebizond (v. 54) and Andros (v. 490). The same man is elsewhere called Andronikos Doukas (Andros v. 20), 'Ανδρόνικος ἀπὸ τῶν Κινναμάδων (Andros v. 1367), and 'Αντάκινος ἀπὸ τῶν Κινναμάδων (Grottaferrata IV, v. 54).

[4] Andros v. 30 calls her Anna while she is described as being ἐκ γένους τῶν Δουκάδων (Trebizond v. 839, Andros v. 1372) or Δούκισσα (sc. Δούκαινα) γένους τοῦ Κωνσταντίνου (Grottaferrata I, v. 267).

[5] Trebizond v. 817.

[6] Trebizond v. 1105; Oxford v. 1590.

[7] A 'revision' of the epic might have been undertaken during the Doukas dynasty (cf. Mavrogordato, p. lxvii) which could plausibly account for widespread use of the name Doukas.

[8] Ibid., p. lxxix.

[9] Grégoire, 'Ο Διγενὴς 'Ακρίτας, p. 28.

PART II

MEMBERS OF THE DOUKAS FAMILY

1. N Doux (fl. *c.* 855)

The first known member of the Doux family is a general who took part in a persecution of the Paulicians in *c.* 855. The name of Andronikos, generally given to him, is highly uncertain. The principal source for the period, Theophanes Continuatus, calls him simply 'the son of Doux',[1] and it is Kedrenos—or rather Skylitzes—who has interpolated the word 'Andronikos' into the text.[2] This later addition must be attributed to the desire of Skylitzes to be more specific when speaking of personages, and other similar examples can be found in his work. In this case he appears to have uncritically identified the persecutor of the Paulicians with Andronikos *2*. It is difficult to accept this.[3]

Whatever his first name may be, this Doux, accompanied by Leon Argyros and the otherwise unknown Soudalis, was chosen to administer a *prostagma* of Theodora, issued in *c.* 855, that ordered the forcible conversion of the Paulicians.[4] The imperial command was executed by the three men with the utmost severity, and a full-scale persecution of the heretics with grave consequences was inaugurated.[5]

2. Andronikos Doux (?–*c.* 908)

Andronikos Doux was one of the great military commanders of the early tenth century. He was perhaps related, probably as a son, to the Doux who had persecuted the Paulicians under Theodora. Very little is known of his army career and most of the available evidence relates to his revolt towards the end of his life. Nothing has been preserved on his earlier activities.

1. [1] ὁ τοῦ Δουκός, Theoph. Cont., p. 165.

[2] ὁ τοῦ Δούκα Ἀνδρόνικος, Kedr., ΙΙ, p. 154.

[3] On this question see D. I. Polemis, 'Some Cases of Erroneous Identification in the Chronicle of Skylitzes', *BS*, 26 (1965), especially pp. 75–6.

[4] Dölger, *Regesten*, I, p. 55, no. 452. The decision of Theodora to convert the Paulicians is also mentioned in an hagiographical source without however any reference to Doux or to his colleagues. Cf. the Life of St Eustratios of Augaron in Papadopoulos-Kerameus, Ἀνάλεκτα, IV, p. 382.

[5] For the persecution see C. Sathas and E. Legrand, *Les exploits de Digénis Akritas, Epopée byzantine du dixième Siècle* (Paris, 1875), pp. lxxx ff.; F. C. Conybeare, *The Key of Truth: A Manual of the Paulician Church of Armenia* (Oxford, 1898), pp. lxxix ff.; J. B. Bury, *A History of the Eastern Roman Empire from the Fall of Irene to the Accession of Basil I (A.D. 802–867)* (London, 1912), p. 278, n. 3; S. Runciman, *The Medieval Manichee: A Study of the Christian Dualist Heresy* (Cambridge, 1947), p. 40; D. Obolensky, *The Bogomils: A Study in Balkan Neo-Manichaeism* (Cambridge, 1948), pp. 196–7. It is only K. Ter-Mkrttschian, *Die Paulikianer im byzantinischen Kaiserreiche und verwandte ketzerische Erscheinungen in Armenien* (Leipzig, 1893), p. 118, who questions the authenticity of the sources in respect of this persecution.

In c. 904 Andronikos together with Eustathios Argyros was despatched to the east where both men achieved great successes against the Arabs.[1] Within this setting we must view the campaign of Andronikos against the town of Mar'ash (Germanicea) in the month of Muharram of the year of the Hegira 292 (i.e. 13 November–12 December 904). The Byzantine attackers were met by the combined Arab forces of Massisa (Mopsuestia) and Tarsus, but according to the Arab historian Tabarī, they emerged victorious and 'a certain number of Muslims were killed'.[2] In a polemical letter of Leon Choirosphaktes the values of Islamic religious belief were challenged in the face of repeated recent Byzantine victories. Among these is mentioned an extraordinary deed of Andronikos when he was said to have put to death eighteen thousand Arabs in the region of Tarsus.[3] The gross exaggeration of this statement cannot be denied, in view of the nature and the tone of Choirosphaktes' letter. But it indicates the great impact of the victories of Andronikos upon his contemporaries. The episode must also be linked with the campaigns of c. 904.

As in similar cases, the sources pay more attention to the rebellion of Andronikos Doux than to his military exploits. Yet an accurate reconstruction of the various stages in this rebellion, as well as its connection with other indirectly related events, presents many difficulties in view of chronological contradictions, different evaluations, and an unconcealed bias for or against the parties concerned.[4]

In 905 Andronikos appears to have continued to operate in eastern Asia

---

2. [1] Theoph. Cont., pp. 368–9. It should be noted that the other versions of Symeon Logothetes fail to record this expedition. But cf. Kedr., II, p. 263. The event is related concurrently with the notorious flight of Samonas which must probably be assigned to the year 903. On this dating see R. J. H. Jenkins, 'The "Flight" of Samonas', *Speculum*, 23 (1948), p. 227; M. Canard, 'Deux épisodes des relations diplomatiques arabo-byzantines au Xe siècle', *Bulletin d'Etudes Orientales* (de l'Institut Français de Damas), 13 (1949/51), 55–6; A. P. Kazhdan in Akademiya Nauk, Institut Istorii, *Dve Vizantiiskie Khroniki X Veka* (Moscow, 1959), p. 139 (historical commentary to the Russian translation of the *Vita Euthymii*); C. de Boor, *Vita Euthymii: Ein Anecdoton zur Geschichte Leo's des Weisen, A. 886–912* (Berlin, 1888), pp. 122–3; R. J. H. Jenkins, 'The Chronological Accuracy of the "Logothete" for the years A.D. 867–913', *DOP*, 19 (1965), 110.

[2] See A. A. Vasiliev, *Byzance et les Arabes*, II (2) (Brussels, 1950), p. 19; cf. Canard, op. cit., p. 56.

[3] 'Ἀλλὰ καὶ ὁ 'Ανδρόνικος, ὅτε εἰς τὰ μέρη τῆς Ταρσοῦ δεκαοκτὼ χιλιάδας εἰς ἕνα τόπον ἀπεκεφάλισεν, ποῦ ἦν ἡ καλὴ πίστις τῶν Σαρακηνῶν, ὅτε οὕτως εἰς ἕν αἷμα ἔπεσον πάντες; see P. Karlin-Hayter, 'Arethas' Letter to the Emir at Damascus', *B*, 29/30 (1959/60), 300. The letter is ascribed to Leon Choirosphaktes by R. J. H. Jenkins, 'Leo Choerosphactes and the Saracen Vizier', *Zbornik Radova Vizantoloshkog Instituta*, 8 (1963), 167–75, but cf. P. Karlin-Hayter, 'Arethas, Choirosphactes and the Saracen Vizir,' *B*, 35 (1965), 475–81. Apart from the reference to Andronikos, the letter speaks about the naval victory of Himerios in 906.

[4] There are three groups of sources that deal with the known events of Andronikos' life: the chronicles emanating from the work of Symeon Logothetes (these being practically identical in the present case, only Theoph. Cont. will be cited), the Life of St Euthymios (the edition of P. Karlin-Hayter, 'Vita S. Euthymii', *B*, 25/27 [1955/57], 1–172, is used here) and a series of Arab chronicles. The suggested chronology depends upon the relative superiority of either the *Vita Euthymii* or the versions of Logothetes' chronicle. See for instance de Boor, op. cit., pp. 126–7; V. Grumel, 'Notes chronologiques: La révolte d'Andronic Doux sous Léon VI. La victoire navale d'Himerius', *EO*, 36 (1937), 202–7; Jenkins, 'The "Flight" of Samonas', *Speculum*, 23 (1948), 235; R. H. Dolley, 'The Date of the St Mokios Attempt on the Life of the Emperor Leon VI', *Annuaire*, 10 (1950), 238; Canard, op cit., pp. 54–62, especially pp. 60–1, n. 4; Kazhdan in *Dve Khroniki*, pp. 138–9; Jenkins, 'Leo Choerosphactes and the Saracen Vizier', *Zborn. Rad. Viz. Inst.*, 8 (1963), 175. A fundamental point of disagreement between the two sources is the fact

Minor. A naval force was then in preparation under the command of Himerios in order to repel an Arab fleet[5] and he received instructions to join forces. This collaboration was prevented by the intrigues of the eunuch Samonas, a pronounced enemy of the Doux family after a recent incident with Konstantinos 3. In a letter Samonas cleverly 'revealed' to Andronikos that Himerios had secret orders to blind him. The trick worked and Doux failed to board the ship. Himerios proceeded alone and fought the naval engagement of 6 October 906,[6] in which he gained the upper hand. Andronikos then found himself in the awkward position of having disobeyed the imperial orders, and in despair he withdrew to the fortress of Kaballa,[7] accompanied by supporters and forces loyal to him.[8]

This unfortunate affair which had the appearance of a revolt by an experienced and popular general naturally caused concern at Constantinople, and the emperor quickly sent against Andronikos the latter's kinsman Gregoras Iberitzes who seems to have unsuccessfully besieged the rebel at Kaballa.[9] Andronikos was confined there for about six months,[10] hoping perhaps to obtain a pardon from the emperor. Then having heard that his friend the patriarch Nikolaos Mystikos had been deposed (February 907) and realizing his difficult position, he asked the Arabs for an *amān*, that is for a free passage to their territory. This was granted together with some military assistance to relieve the besieged from the pressure of the imperial troops. According to Tabarī, Andronikos was still at Kaballa in February–March 907, and we must suppose that soon afterwards he made his way to Tarsus and then to Bagdad where he was generously treated.[11]

---

that whereas Theoph. Cont., p. 372, presents the flight of Andronikos to Syria as a consequence of the patriarch Nikolaos' deposition (February 907), the *Vita Euthymii*, p. 82, implies that Nikolaos was still on his throne when the rebel had already crossed over to the Arabs. The author is inclined to accept the dating of the chronicles which is also in agreement with the Arab sources.

---

[5] Jenkins, 'Leo Choerosphactes and the Saracen Vizier', p. 170, suggests that Himerios was then at Attalia.

[6] Much has been written on the dating of the 'great victory' of Himerios. The date of 906 was first proposed by A. A. Vasiliev, *Vizantiya i Araby*, II (St Petersburg, 1902), p. 160.

[7] F. Babinger, 'Kavalla (Anatolien)', *Der Islam*, 29 (1950), 301–2, has with good reason identified Kaballa with the ruins of the often mentioned Turkish fortress of Kevele, lying to the west of Iconium on the foot of Takjeli Dagh.

[8] ... πολλὰ δὲ τοῦ Ἱμερίου προτρεπομένου τὸν Ἀνδρόνικον ἐν τοῖς πλοίοις εἰσελθεῖν τῶν Ἀγαρηνῶν ἐπικειμένων, ἀπεσκίρτησε, μὴ τοῦτο ποιῆσαι καταδεξάμενος. Ἱμέριος δὲ μόνος τῇ τοῦ ἁγίου ἀποστόλου Θωμᾶ μνήμῃ συμβαλὼν πόλεμον μετὰ τῶν Ἀγαρηνῶν μεγάλην νίκην εἰργάσατο. τοῦτο μαθὼν Ἀνδρόνικος, καὶ ἀπογνούς, ἅμα συγγενέσι καὶ δούλοις αὐτοῦ πόλιν κατέσχεν τὴν λεγομένην Καβάλαν εἰς ἀποστασίαν ὁρμήσας, Theoph. Cont., p. 372.

[9] Ibid.; Vasiliev, *Byzance et les Arabes*, II (2), p. 20.

[10] *Vita Euthymii*, p. 74.

[11] Μαθὼν δὲ τοῦτο Ἀνδρόνικος καὶ πῶς ὁ πατριάρχης Νικόλαος τῆς ἐκκλησίας ἐξεδιώχθη, τοῖς Ἀγαρηνοῖς ἐξέφυγεν πανοικί, τηνικαῦτα κατὰ Ῥωμαίων ἐξεληλυθόσιν· ὃν ἀμεμνουρνῆς ἐντίμως καὶ μεγαλοπρεπῶς προσεδέξατο, Theoph. Cont., p. 372. This date for his escape was proposed by Grumel, op. cit., and was subsequently accepted by R. J. H. Jenkins and B. Laourdas, 'Eight Letters of Arethas on the Fourth Marriage of Leo the Wise', Ἑλληνικά, 14 (1956), 346–7, and by Kazhdan in *Dve Khroniki* pp. 108–10. Consequently the different versions of Logothetes' chronicle together with Tabarī who both imply that Andronikos left Kaballa for Syria in the spring of 907 are preferable to *Vita Euth.*, p. 82, which makes this event prior to Nikolaos' abdication.

But the troubles of Andronikos did not end with his defection. If the chronicles are to be believed, the emperor was contemplating pardoning him, and with this in view he sent a letter bidding him to return to Byzantium.[12] Once more the reluctant fugitive was unlucky. The crafty Samonas succeeded in persuading the Arab messenger to reveal the emperor's letter to the Muslim authorities of his country. As a result Andronikos with his companions was thrown into prison and in order to save his head he was compelled to embrace Islam.[13] We are informed by Mas'ūdī that this conversion took place at the instigation of the caliph Muktafi, i.e. some time before August 908 when this caliph died.[14] No more was heard of Andronikos Doux and his death must have occurred not long afterwards. It is possible that some of his comrades, who presumably also apostatized, had successful careers among the Arabs.[15]

Apart from the possible ambitions of Andronikos, the purely defensive character of his moves was obvious and there appears to be no trace of any attempt aiming at the throne. It would be difficult not to agree with the version of Logothetes that his withdrawal to Kaballa was caused by the schemes of Samonas. The *Life* of St Euthymios which occasionally makes a vague suggestion that Andronikos entertained such high hopes is unconvincing. The seizure of Kaballa obviously had little military support and not many people followed the rebel there; most of these quickly abandoned him and did not hesitate to testify before the emperor.[16] Moreover, this affair does not indicate an ambitious

---

Nikolaos Mystikos could have written a letter to Andronikos in Kaballa, but the text given by *Vita Euth.*, pp. 74–6 (cf. Grumel, *Regesten*, II, p. 136, no. 601) is obviously not an authentic one. N. A. Popov, *Imperator Lev VI i ego pravlenie v cherkovnom otnoshenii* (Moscow, 1892), pp. 101–2, thought that it was a forgery of Samonas. Yet it is difficult to believe that this clever man could have fabricated so crude a forgery as that which makes the shrewd patriarch address the desperate rebel as 'future emperor' and beg for a reward. The very tone and content of this letter suggest that we are probably dealing with a later creation of the patriarch Euthymios' followers, always eager to slander Nikolaos.

---

[12] Theoph. Cont., p. 372; cf. Dölger, *Regesten*, I, p. 65, no. 546, who follows the chronology of de Boor. Canard op. cit., p. 59, believes that the embassy of Leon Choirosphaktes to Bagdad (Dölger, *Regesten*, no. 547) was concerned with Andronikos. It must be made clear however that the above letter of the emperor could not have been sent with Choirosphaktes, as the messenger is expressly described as an Arab.

[13] Ἐκρατήθη δὲ Ἀνδρόνικος καὶ ἐδεσμήθη μετὰ πάντων τῶν αὐτοῦ συγγενῶν· καὶ μαθὼν διὰ δόλου τοῦ Σαμωνᾶ ταῦτα γεγονέναι, ἀναγκασθεὶς τὴν ἰδίαν πίστιν αὐτός τε καὶ οἱ σὺν αὐτῷ ἐξωμόσαντο, Theoph. Cont., p. 373.

[14] Vasiliev, *Byzance et les Arabes*, II (2), p. 398; cf. Canard, op. cit. Unfortunately an 'anakreontion' on the apostasy of Andronikos by the emperor himself has not been preserved. See P. Maas, 'Literarisches zu der Vita Euthymii', *BZ*, 21 (1912), 437. Only the title of this poem has survived, 'Λέοντος τοῦ δεσπότου εἰς Ἀνδρόνικον τὸν ἀποστάτην'. See (A. Mai), *Spicilegium Romanum*, IV (Rome, 1840), p. xxxix. For the revolt see also P. Karlin-Hayter, 'The Revolt of Andronicus Ducas', *BS*, 27 (1966), 23–5, who somewhat overstresses its importance.

[15] A certain contemporary governor of Egypt (915–19) by the name of Abul-Hasan Dsukā el-Rūmi is mentioned by some of the Arab sources. Cf. F. Wüstenfeld, 'Die Statthalter von Aegypten zur Zeit der Chalifen', *Abhandlungen der königlichen Gesellschaft der Wissenschaften zu Göttingen, 4. Abteilung*, 21 (1876), 13–17; (I am indebted to Dr N. M. Panagiotakis for drawing my attention to the existence of this official). Judging from his name Dsukā el-Rumi, he must have been of Greek origin, perhaps a Doukas by family, who could have apostatized with Andronikos and remained in the service of the Arabs for the rest of his life.

[16] *Vita Euth.*, p. 94. Nine such nobles included two generals and some *protospatharioi*.

rebel with a defined objective who would undoubtedly have turned elsewhere instead of wasting time by remaining inactive in a remote fortress in Anatolia. Had the Arabs not effectively intervened, the pursuer Iberitzes would have promptly reduced Andronikos to submission. Consequently the withdrawal to Kaballa and the subsequent flight to Syria must be seen simply as the desperate move of a betrayed general with no carefully laid plans or wide support. The imperial forgiveness, so readily expressed, was presumably genuine; Konstantinos 3, the son of Andronikos, was quickly rehabilitated and received back into the service of the state.

Similarly Andronikos' implications in other contemporary events have often been overstressed. He had certainly nothing to do with the abortive attempt that nearly cost Leon VI his life in the church of St Mokios on 11 May 903.[17] Equally unfounded is the alleged connection of Andronikos with Eustathios Argyros, also suspected of plotting. Still less do his supposed dealings with the Arab fleet on the eve of Himerios' victory find even the slightest evidence in the sources. On the other hand there is a measure of truth in the allegations that Andronikos was in touch with the patriarch Nikolaos. Both the *Vita* of St Euthymios and the versions of Logothetes hint at an intimacy between the two men, and even the concluding flight to Syria is presented as being indirectly caused by the patriarch's deposition. Whatever common objective such an understanding had—and the evidence is very meagre indeed—it should probably be linked with the period of Nikolaos' mounting conflict with the emperor, that is in the months prior to February 907, when some relations with the isolated rebel of Kaballa do not appear entirely out of place. It is also possible that Andronikos was relying upon the mediation of the patriarch to obtain a pardon, and that he absconded only when he knew of his friend's own fall.

The Greek sources fail to attribute any dignity or specific military rank to Andronikos, but some information as to his official positions can be gathered from Arab accounts. Speaking of the events of Kaballa, Tabarī qualified him as *patrikios*,[18] and Mas'ūdī supplies the information that prior to his revolt Andronikos filled the post of the commander in chief.[19] This designation might

---

[17] The date is that of de Boor, op. cit., pp. 110-13, defended by V. Grumel, 'Chronologie des événements du règne de Léon VI', *EO*, 35 (1936), 40-1, by Jenkins, 'The "Flight" of Samonas', pp. 225-6, and by Kazhdan in *Dve Khroniki*, pp. 108-9, despite the objections of R. H. Dolley, 'The Date of the St Mokios Attempt on the Life of the Emperor Leon VI', *Annuaire*, 10 (1950), 231-8, in favour of 21 April 902.

Vita Euth., p. 80, hints that the patriarch Nikolaos might have known of the planned attack in the church, but this is probably a mere accusation. The fact remains that all suspicions centred in the co-emperor Alexander whose 'unbrotherly feelings' were no secret (ibid., p. 10). He hated Leon and later attempted to conspire against him (ibid., p. 60). In the attack of St Mokios, Alexander was not at the emperor's side, as had been expected but excused himself on the ground of illness. This absence was regarded as most suspicious (ibid., pp. 72 ff.; Theoph. Cont., p. 365). As Alexander was an entirely unscrupulous prince—he even thought of castrating his orphan nephew, the future Konstantinos VII Porphyrogenitus, in 912-13 and of giving the throne to his favourite Basilitzes (Theoph. Cont., p. 379) — it is not surprising that he had evil designs. For some aspects of Alexander's co-emperorship see Sp. P. Lambros, 'Leo und Alexander als Mitkaiser von Byzanz', *BZ*, 4 (1895), 92-8; cf. W. Fischer, 'Zu "Leo und Alexander als Mitkaiser von Byzanz" ', *BZ*, 5 (1896), 137-9.

[18] Vasiliev, *Byzance et les Arabes*, II (2), p. 20.

[19] Ibid., p. 398.

signify that Andronikos held the rank of *domestikos tōn scholōn*. The duties of this military official correspond at this time with those of a commander in chief, and the holders were frequently also honoured with the dignity of *patrikios*. [20]

We hear little of Andronikos' family. Tabarī speaks of 'his sons', but these remain otherwise unknown apart from Konstantinos *3*. He must however have had another son who became the father of Michael *6*.

3. Konstantinos Doux (?–913)

Like his father Andronikos *2*, Konstantinos Doux was a brilliant military commander who enjoyed widespread popularity. His known active career coincided with the later part of Leon VI's reign and ended tragically in 913.

The sources first mention Konstantinos in 903, in connection with the flight of Samonas, the notorious minister and protégé of the emperor.[1] The motives that drove this Arab eunuch to escape from Constantinople have not been satisfactorily explained, but on crossing the Halys he was recognized and sought refuge in the monastery of Timios Stauros at Siricha. There he was picked up by Konstantinos and was brought to Constantinople. The chronicles relate the story that the emperor, though told of his favourite's intentions to flee to Syria, tried to save him by inducing Konstantinos to lie before the senate and affirm that in reality Samonas had simply gone to Siricha. Nevertheless when he was formally sworn and interrogated by the emperor, he revealed the truth, as he had previously only undertaken to conceal the facts but not to lie under oath. The incident greatly annoyed Leon who in anger sent Konstantinos away.[2]

In the revolt of Andronikos *2* in 906–7 Konstantinos naturally supported and followed his father. He seems to have played an active role around Kaballa while Andronikos *2* was being besieged in the fortress.[3] Subsequently he also sought shelter in Tarsus and then in Bagdad where he presumably followed his companions in their mass apostasy.[4] It was only with a great difficulty that he managed to escape from the Arabs, and after a perilous journey through

---

[20] Cf. J. B. Bury, *The Imperial Administrative System in the Ninth Century* (London, 1911), p. 51; R. Guilland, 'Etudes sur l'histoire administrative de Byzance: Le domestique des scholes', *REB*, 8 (1950), 5–63. As this rank was then held by Gregoras Iberitzes (Theoph. Cont., p. 372), it is possible that he succeeded Andronikos as *domestikos tōn scholōn*.

3. [1] The date is still uncertain. See M. Canard, 'Deux épisodes de relations diplomatiques arabo-byzantines au Xe siècle', *Bulletin d'Etudes Orientales* (de l'Institut Français de Damas), 13 (1949/51), 55–6; A. P. Kazhdan in Akademiya Nauk, Institut Istorii, *Dve Vizantiiskie Khroniki X Veka* (Moscow, 1959), p. 112. The background and purposes of this curious journey have been reconstructed in an ingenious manner, but on insufficient evidence, by R. J. H. Jenkins, 'The "Flight" of Samonas', *Speculum*, 23 (1948), 217–35. For Samonas see also S. Kougeas, 'Κῶδιξ τοῦ πατρικίου Σαμωνᾶ', *BNJ*, 5 (1927), 198–204; R. Janin, 'Un ministre arabe à Byzance: Samonas', *EO*, 34 (1935), 307–18. Another study by P. Orgels, 'La carrière de Samonas', has been announced in *B*, 25/27 (1955/7), 660, n. 6.

[2] Theoph. Cont., pp. 369–70.

[3] Cf. Tabarī in A. A. Vasiliev, *Byzance et les Arabes*, II (2) (Brussels, 1935), p. 20, who does not name Konstantinos but refers to 'the sons' of Andronikos *2*.

[4] Theoph. Cont., p. 373; cf. Jenkins, op. cit., p. 224, n. 46.

Armenia he reached Constantinople.[5] The dating of this return of Konstantinos is not certain, but he could have come back to Byzantium in late 908.[6]

The fact that Konstantinos, on his return to Constantinople, was readily received by the emperor is an indication that the whole recent affair of Andronikos 2 had not attained so dangerous a proportion as to exclude the most prominent surviving participant from the loyal service. The government appeared willing to acknowledge that. What is not clear however is the story related to the effect that the name of Doux became in popular belief associated with the imperial throne. The sources are very scanty on this question and this particular passage does not throw adequate light upon the background. Despite the birth of Leon's son Konstantinos in May 907, widespread prophesies linked the future emperor, supposedly called Konstantinos, not with the porphyrogenitus but with Doux. Within this milieu we must also see another expression of the popularity of Doux, recounted in the *Vita S. Basilii Junioris*.[7] The vision Konstantinos is reputed to have experienced is associated of course with the revolt of 913, yet it cannot be conceived simply as an isolated instance of mass admiration, but its features, and in particular the symbolic 'purple' of the Virgin, must be interpreted as forming part of a chain of analogous manifestations, like the prophesies that frightened the emperor and the echoes in the Acritic songs in which Konstantinos is called 'Porphyrios', that is porphyrogenitus. Apparently large sections of the populace were eager to see Doux on the throne one day.

Konstantinos' dangerous popularity was inevitably viewed with much disquiet by the emperor. It is not improbable that the latter chose the name of Konstantinos for his son partly in an effort to conform with these prophesies and thus discourage some future pretender of the same name. When he received Doux in the palace on his return from Syria he warned him not to be deceived by the current rumours that a Konstantinos would reign over the Romans since the throne belonged to the emperor's son.[8] All these indications of the popularity of Konstantinos show that a legend was already beginning to grow up around the Doukes which was destined to be further developed in the epic poems.

Yet, despite imperial fears, Konstantinos Doux was fully reinstated in the army, and his new assignment appears to have been that of *strategos* of the important Charsianon theme, in succession to his father's old fellow-in-arms Eustathios Argyros.[9] He did not remain long in this post as he was shortly

[5] Theoph. Cont., p. 373; cf. Mas'ūdī in Vasiliev, op. cit., pp. 398–9, who however wrongly associates this escape of Konstantinos with the revolt of 913.

[6] H. Grégoire, 'Notes épigraphiques', *B*, 8 (1933), 34, appears to assign it in about 908; cf. Ph. Grierson and R. J. H. Jenkins, 'The Date of Constantine VII's Coronation', *B*, 22 (1962), 137. As noted, the runaways apostatized before August 908 (cf. above, Andronikos 2, n. 14), and it is therefore reasonable to date this escape to within that year.

[7] See the introduction, p. 14, n. 8.

[8] 'Μὴ πεπλάνησο καθ' ἑαυτὸν τῷ παρὰ πολλοῖς εἶναι ᾀδόμενον Κωνσταντῖνον βασιλεύσοντα 'Ρωμαίων. ὄμνυμί σοι εἰς τὴν παντέφορον δίκην καὶ εἰς τὴν τοῦ Κυρίου ἡμῶν εἰκόνα ὅτι οὐκ ἔστι σὸν τὸ βασίλειον διὰ τὸ κατονομασθῆναί σε Κωνσταντῖνον, ἀλλὰ τῷ φιλτάτῳ μου υἱῷ θεόθεν διὰ προγόνων δεδώρηται, καθὼς παρὰ πολλῶν ἁγίων ἀνδρῶν πεπληροφόρημαι. εἰ γὰρ πειραθείης τοῦτον διαχειρίσασθαι, τῇ πύλῃ ταύτῃ ἡ κεφαλή σου σώματος ἐκτὸς εἰσελεύσεται'. Ὁ καὶ γέγονεν· μετὰ γὰρ τὸ ἆραι αὐτὸν τυραννικῶς χεῖρας ἡ κεφαλὴ αὐτοῦ αἵματι καὶ λύθρῳ καὶ κόνει ἀμαυρωθεῖσα διὰ τῶν αὐτῶν πυλῶν εἰσελήλυθεν, Theoph. Cont., pp. 373–4. The other versions of Logothetes omit these words of the emperor.

[9] 'Ὁπότε καὶ προεβλήθη Κωνσταντῖνος ὁ Δοὺξ εἰς τὸ Χαρσιανόν *DAI*, I, 50/153 (p. 240); cf. II, p. 191.

afterwards promoted to the position of *domestikos tōn scholōn*, a rank by which he is referred to during the revolt of 913.[10]

In trying to reconstruct the phases of the revolt of Konstantinos, it is not easy to reconcile the unsympathetic, almost hostile, attitude[11] of Logothetes' chronicle with the apologetic version of the *Vita S. Basilii Junioris*. Although these sources agree in the broad outlines of the events related, they nevertheless fail to explain satisfactorily the patriarch Nikolaos' motives, first in summoning Konstantinos and then in turning against him and helping to put down the uprising.

Events appear to have developed as follows. When the emperor Alexander fell critically ill and every hope of recovery vanished, the patriarch Nikolaos turned to Doux. He dispatched a letter to him, urging prompt action on the sovereign's expected death. Doux was to occupy Constantinople while further support would appropriately come from Nikolaos; counting on his popularity, Konstantinos was to be proclaimed co-emperor.[12] All these plans had certainly been worked out prior to Alexander's death and presumably the patriarch had not suspected that he himself was to be appointed a member of the regency council. He took the decision to invite Doux because he trusted him and wished to see him on the throne rather than some other undesirable and unavoidable usurper taking advantage of the minority of Konstantinos Porphyrogenitus.[13] Meanwhile Alexander summoned the patriarch to his death bed and to the latter's surprise appointed him one of the guardians for the new young emperor.[14] Alexander died on 6 June 913.[15] Now that he had an assured place in the inner circle of the regency, Nikolaos must have lamented his premature letter to the ambitious general.

For his part, Konstantinos certainly welcomed the patriarch's call, though only after initial hesitation.[16] He was not in Constantinople and the news of the

---

[10] Theoph. Cont., p. 381; cf. R. Guilland, 'Etudes sur l'histoire administrative de Byzance: Le domestique des scholes', *REB*, 8 (1950), 27. The *Vita S. Basilii Junioris*, *PG*, 109, col. 657A, calls him τῆς ἀνατολῆς στρατηγοῦντι, which probably means that in 913 Konstantinos was on a military mission to the eastern frontier.

[11] Cf. F. Hirsch, *Byzantinische Studien* (Leipzig, 1876), p. 77.

[12] Theoph. Cont., p. 382. The letter was probably sent on the 4 or 5 June 913. See Grumel, *Regestes*, II, pp. 153–4, no. 640; cf. pp. 155–6, no. 644.

[13] 'Εν σπουδῇ τὴν πόλιν καταλαβεῖν πρὶν ἂν τῆς βασιλείας ἕτερος δράξοιτο, see P. Karlin-Hayter, 'Vita S. Euthymii', *B*, 25/27 (1955/7), 136. In the event of Konstantinos' success, he would have assumed the part played later by Romanos Lekapenos. Cf. S. Runciman, *The Emperor Romanus Lecapenus and his Reign* (Cambridge, 1929), pp. 49–50 and 60. *Vita Basilii*, cols 657–9, attributes the revolt of Doux to the inability of the regency to cope with the grave situation caused by the pillaging of the countryside by enemies, and the demand of the populace that Konstantinos be made co-emperor in order to expel the 'barbarians'. Actually we have no evidence of these 'barbarians' (obviously the Bulgarians) before August 913. See Theoph. Cont., p. 385; cf. S. Runciman, *A History of the First Bulgarian Empire* (London, 1930), p. 156.

[14] *Vita Euthymii*, p. 136; cf. Theoph. Cont., 382: Νικόλαος πατριάρχης ἠγνοηκὼς ὡς κατ' ἐπιτροπὴν 'Αλεξάνδρου αὐτῷ ἐγκεχείριστο τὰ τῆς ἐξουσίας ἐπιτροπεῖν.

[15] According to *Vita Basilii*, col. 657D, the patriarch and the other regents (here we have a clear anachronism) wrote to Konstantinos repeatedly, bidding him to come and obtain the crown. The regents are even reputed to have sworn on the relic of the holy cross that no harm would befall him if he came to Constantinople. Cf. A. Frolow, *La Relique de la Vraie Croix*: *Recherches sur le Développement d'un Culte* (Paris, 1961), p. 231, no. 132 (the date 912 should however be corrected to 913).

[16] *Vita Basilii*, col. 657.

emperor's death reached him a couple of days later. He began to spread word of the summons,[17] but it was probably at this stage that he realised he could no longer depend on the patriarch. Nevertheless with several trusted colleagues he rushed to Constantinople which he secretly entered by night, concealing himself in the house of his father-in-law Gregoras Iberitzes, while he waited for his partisans' signal. Two of his principal supporters, the *asecretis* Niketas and the *patrikios* Konstantinos Helladikos who was a monk, visited Doux and advised immediate action. He agreed and during the same night he made known his presence in the city. Followed by a large crowd, Konstantinos came to the gate of the Hippodrome and was there acclaimed emperor. The somewhat accidental killing of his groom disheartened him, but he continued with his plans and being loudly acclaimed by his supporters proceeded to the Chalke gate.

It is the patriarch Nikolaos to whom the hagiographical sources attribute the disaster that befell Konstantinos. Though both the *Vitae* in question are notoriously anti-Nicolaite in content, it is hardly to be believed that the total defeat of the man could have been effected without his active interference.

In any case the military backing of Konstantinos was not substantial and certainly unable to resist successfully the imperial guard under Garidas that was sent against him. A bloody fight took place in the Chalke, which quickly decided the fate of the revolt. The death of Konstantinos' son Gregoras 4, of his nephew Michael 6, and of his friend Kourtikes completely broke him; while trying to run away his horse slipped on the stone steps and he fell down. Recognized by a loyal soldier, Konstantinos was fatally hit by an arrow on his right side. He died cursing the patriarch. His head was cut off and was brought to the palace, thus fulfilling the terrible threat expressed by Leon VI five years before.[18]

In Asia Minor the fame and popularity of Konstantinos was so great that the rural populace refused to believe that he was dead. Long after his tragic end in about 932 in Bithynia a certain Basileios, originally of Macedonia, assumed his name and, incredible as it might seem, was accepted as Konstantinos Doux by the local population. The impostor was eventually caught and brought to Constantinople where he was punished by mutilation of his arm. This did not however stop Basileios. He reappeared in Bithynia, wearing a bronze arm, and repeated his old claim to be Konstantinos Doux. He gained considerable support and the offences committed by his supporters reached serious proportions. His base for operations was the castle of Plateia Petra which he had seized. Finally an army was sent against the impostor who was caught, and for the second

---

[17] Μήπω δὲ τῶν αὐτοῦ (sc. Ἀλεξάνδρου) τρίτων παρεληλυθότων, καὶ ὁ .. Κωνσταντῖνος (sc. ὁ Δούξ) παρῆν τοῖς πᾶσιν ἐπιδεικνύων τὸ τοῦ πατριάρχου γραμματεῖον, *Vita Euthymii*, p. 136. ' Τρίτα ' is the service of commemoration performed on the third day after death (cf. Ph. Koukoules, Βυζαντινῶν βίος καὶ πολιτισμός, IV [Athens, 1951], pp. 208–9), but it is not clear whether the term is here used in its proper meaning or whether it simply implies 'very shortly after Alexander's death'.

[18] See above n. 8. The partisans of Konstantinos were punished with great ruthlessness. According to the *Vita Basilii*, col. 661, more than 3000 men were put to death in addition to others who were blinded, imprisoned or exiled. Undoubtedly the *Vita Euthymii*, p. 136, which puts the number of those killed at eight hundred is nearer the truth. For the statement of Zon., III, pp. 675–76, that all male members of the Doukes were killed at this time, see the introduction, p. 7, n. 4. Theoph. Cont., p. 384, gives the names of those prominent Byzantines who had backed Doux and were then persecuted.

and last time was carried to Constantinople where he was now put to death.[19]

By his marriage to an unknown daughter of Gregoras Iberitzes,[20] Konstantinos had at least two sons, Gregoras *4* and Stephanos *5*. By custom his first-born son would have been named after his father Andronikos *2*, but as we do not hear of such a person we may assume that a probable son Andronikos may have died at an early age. After Konstantinos was killed in 913, his wife was forcibly made a nun and was sent to her home in Paphlagonia.[21]

4. Gregoras (?–913)

Gregoras was a son of Konstantinos Doux *3*. Judging from the fact that he was called after his maternal grandfather Gregoras Iberitzes, it is likely that he was the second-born son of his parents. He participated in the revolt of his father in June 913 and was killed in a clash before the Chalke gate.[1]

5. Stephanos (?–after 913)

Of Stephanos, another son of Konstantinos *3*, it is only known that after his father's death in June 913 he was castrated and together with his mother sent to their home in Paphlagonia.[1] Stephanos must then have been still a child.

6. Michael (?–913)

Michael is described as a nephew of Konstantinos Doux *3*, and this means that he was most probably a grandson of Andronikos *2*. He also participated in the revolt of June 913, but was killed together with Gregoras *4*.[1]

[19] Theoph. Cont., pp. 421–2; Ps. Sym. Mag., p. 745; Georg. Cont., p. 912; Leon Gram., pp. 321–2; Kedr., II, p. 315. Cf. Runciman, *The Emperor Romanus Lecapenus*, p. 72. For a marxist view of the revolt of pseudo-Konstantinos Doux, seen as an expression of peasant discontent after the famine of 928, see A. P. Kazhdan, ' "Velikoe vosstanie" Vasilii Mednoi ruki', *VV*, 4 (1951), 73–83. But cf. the comments of H. Grégoire in *B*, 21 (1951), 500–2.

[20] Gregoras Iberitzes who ended his days in the monastery of Stoudios (Theoph. Cont., p. 384) could have been of Georgian origin as his name indicates. For his career see Guilland, 'Le domestique des scholes', pp. 26–7. The family still existed in the mid-eleventh century (cf. Sathas, *MB*, V, pp. 197 ff.) and Anna Komnene mentions the house of Iberitzes (*Alexias*, I, p. 98).

[21] Theoph. Cont., p. 385.

4. [1] Theoph. Cont., p. 383; Ps. Sym. Mag., p. 719; Georg. Cont., p. 876; Leon Gram., p. 290; Kedr., II, p. 280; Zon., III, p. 459; P. Karlin-Hayter, 'Vita S. Euthymii', *B*, 25/27 (1955/7), 136; *Vita Basilii*, PG, 109, col. 661A.

5. [1] Theoph. Cont., p. 385; Ps. Sym. Mag., p. 721; Georg. Cont., p. 877; Leon Gram., p. 291; Kedr., II, p. 282; Zon., III, p. 461.

6. [1] Theoph. Cont., p. 383; Ps. Sym. Mag., p. 720; Georg. Cont., p. 876; Leon Gram., p. 290; Zon., III, p. 459.

N. P. Likhachev, *Istoricheskoe znachenie italo-grecheskoi ikonopisi* (St Petersburg, 1911), p. 26, no. 8

7. Nikolaos Doux (?–917)

A member of the Doux family by the name of Nikolaos is mentioned as having been one of the victims when the Bulgarians ambushed the Byzantine army at Catasyrtae near Constantinople late in 917.[1] The contemporary sources fail to specify the exact family connections of Nikolaos, only describing him as 'the son of Doux'.[2] Kedrenos makes him a son of Konstantinos *3*, but this is evidently an error.[3]

8. Andronikos Doux Lydos (?–c. 979)

It is not absolutely certain whether the word *Δούξ*, attached to the group of three people otherwise called Lydoi,[1] refers to a military rank or to a family name. As the latter appears more probable, the men in question will be treated as Doukes.

Andronikos Doux, also called Lydos,[2] was a general during the first years of Basileios II and was honoured with the dignity of *patrikios*. Little is heard of him. Together with his sons, Andronikos was among the earlier prominent supporters of the rebel Bardas Skleros to whom he surrendered after the seizure of Tzamandos late in 976.[3] He is mentioned as dead in 979/80,[4] and he perhaps died shortly before that year.

We know of two sons of Andronikos: Christophoros *9* and Bardas *10*.

gives the text of an imperfectly edited seal as follows: Θ(εοτό)κε [βοήθει τῷ σῷ] δούλῳ Μιχ (A)
Γ
ΣΠΑΘ, Κ (·) Μ ΝΟΤ, ΑΝSΚ Τȣ ΧΑΡCΙΑΝΟΥ ΤΩ ΔΟΥΚΗ. We may have here a *protospatharios* and *megas notarios* of the Charsianon theme Michael Doux who could be the same as the present one.

---

7. [1] *Τῇ δὲ νυκτὶ ἀδοκήτως ἐπιπεσόντων αὐτοῖς τῶν Βουλγάρων, καὶ τοῦ δομεστίκου φυγόντος, ἐσφάγη Νικόλαος ὁ υἱὸς τοῦ Δουκὸς καὶ πολλοὶ ἕτεροι μετ᾽ αὐτοῦ,* Theoph. Cont., p. 390; cf. Ps. Sym. Mag., p. 725; Georg. Cont., pp. 882–3; Leon Gram., p. 296; Kedr., II, p. 288. The chronology of this assault is not clear. I have followed S. Runciman, *The Emperor Romanus Lecapenus and His Reign* (Cambridge, 1929), p. 56; idem, *A History of the First Bulgarian Empire* (London, 1930), p. 161.

[2] The Byzantine army was then commanded by the *domestikos tōn scholōn* Leon Argyros, the son of Eustathios. It is to be noted that Pseudo-Symeon Magister, who often qualifies Argyros as *dux* instead of *domestikos* (cf. pp. 714 and 725), makes Nikolaos a son of this Leon, but this is only a misunderstanding.

[3] Cf. D. I. Polemis, 'Some Cases of Erroneous Identification in the Chronicle of Skylitzes', *BS*, 26 (1965), 79.

8. [1] For other bearers of that name see the introduction, p. 8, no. 1.

[2] *Ὁ πατρίκιος Ἀνδρόνικος καὶ Δοὺξ ὁ Λυδός*, Kedr., II, p. 424; *οἱ τοῦ Δούκα* (other reading *Δουκός*) *Ἀνδρονίκου τοῦ Λυδοῦ παῖδες*, Kedr., II, p. 434.

[3] Kedr., II, p. 424; cf. G. Schlumberger, *L'Epopée byzantine à la Fin du dixième Siècle*, I (Paris, 1896), pp. 374–5 (where he is called 'Antoine', but cf. II, p. 366, n. 3).

[4] Kedr., II, p. 434.

9. Christophoros (fl. *c.* 980)

Christophoros was a son of Andronikos *8*, and he bore the nickname of Epeiktes.[1] He followed his father in support of Bardas Skleros[2] to whom he remained loyal until after the rebel was defeated in combat by Bardas Phokas on 24 May 979. Then Christophoros and his brother Bardas *10* came to Bithynia where they were able to seize several remote fortresses, among them the strongholds of Armakourion and Plateia Petra, from which the two brothers repeatedly pillaged the countryside, apparently trying to compel Basileios II to give them an amnesty. When this was eventually granted, in 980/81 they were received back into imperial service.[3]

10. Bardas (?–after 1016)

Bardas, known as Mongos (the hoarse),[1] was a son of Andronikos *8* and also an active partisan of Skleros. After some experience in rebel activities,[2] he was received into loyal service and had a distinguished career in the Byzantine army. Bardas is associated with a naval expedition of which he was the leader, sent by the emperor against the Khazars in January 1016. The fleet was assisted by certain Rus' under Svenki (the 'Sphengos' of Skylitzes-Kedrenos), the brother of king Vladimir, and Bardas quickly subjugated Khazaria whose king Tzul was taken prisoner.[3]

---

9. [1] The word ἐπείκτης attached to the name of Christophoros does not signify a sort of cognomen as the editor of Kedrenos (see below) implies, but rather a nickname which might eventually become a cognomen. Ducange, *Glossarium ad scriptores mediae et infimae graecitatis* (Paris, 1688), co. 418, explains the word as meaning 'qui urget operas', which is the equivalent of the popular Greek πρωτομάστορας. Kedr., II, p. 258, speaks of a Βασίλειος ... ἐπείκτης τοῦ βασιλέως (cf. Theoph., pp. 367 and 384).

[2] Kedr., II, p. 424.

[3] Kedr., II, p. 434.

C. Sathas and E. Legrand, *Les Exploits de Digénis Akritas, Epopée byzantine du dixième Siècle* (Paris, 1875), p. cxlviii, write: 'Christophe est probablement ce Ducas, domesticus d'Orient, qui fut tué au siège d'Apamée, en 997, et dont les fils furent faits prisonniers par les Arabes d'Egypte'. This is quite without justification. The true story in the siege of Apamea is told by several oriental sources and concerns the 'dux' Damianos Dalassenos killed in 998. See for instance *The Chronography of Abu'l Faraj Commonly Known as Bar Hebraeus* (translated from the Syriac by E. A. Wallis-Budge), 1 (Oxford, 1932), pp. 180–1. The Arab historians relating the incident are discussed by M. Canard, 'Les sources arabes de l'histoire byzantine aux confins des Xe et XIe siècles', *REB*, 19 (1961), 297–8.

10. [1] Certainly a nickname in use since the fifth century, when it was attached to the name of the monophysite patriarch of Alexandria Petros III (479 and 482–9), see Theoph., p. 125.

[2] See the accounts of Andronikos *8* and Christophoros *9*.

[3] Kedr., II p. 464; cf. G. Schlumberger, *L'épopée byzantine à la fin du dixième siècle*, II (Paris, 1900), pp. 366–7. D. M. Dunlop, *The History of the Jewish Khazars* (Princeton, 1954), pp. 251–2, thinks that the expedition was directed against the region of the Caucasus. King Tzul is not otherwise known.

11. Andronikos Doukas (fl. *c.* 1020)

Information on the emperor Konstantinos' *12* father is very limited. In a speech of Psellos it is disclosed that Andronikos *21* was called after his paternal grand-father,[1] and apparently this is the only indication we possess of Andronikos' name. A seal bearing the significant inscription 'Ἀνδρόνικος πρωτοσπαθάριος καὶ στρατηγὸς τῆς Μεγάλης Πρεσθλάβας ὁ Δούκας has been found in Pliska, Bulgaria, and is assigned to the first half of the eleventh century.[2] It is quite probable that this *protospatharios* and *strategos* Andronikos Doukas is in actual fact the originator of the imperial family.

It is strange that so little has been preserved on this common ancestor of two emperors and so many patrons of literature. It may be that Andronikos, even if he were a *strategos* in Bulgaria, had been an obscure and undistinguished person.

12. Konstantinos Doukas (1006–67)

It is beyond the terms of reference of this work to examine the reign of Konstantinos X Doukas (1059–67) which in fact witnessed events of grave consequence for the later history of Byzantium. This account is concerned only with personal information, but since this particular emperor showed only a limited interest in affairs of state and especially military problems, available evidence naturally relates to the events of his unfortunate reign rather than to his own person.[1]

The emperor Konstantinos X was a son of Andronikos *11*[2] and appears to have been born, perhaps in Paphlagonia,[3] in 1006.[4] The name of Doukas is

11. [1] Τοῦ πάππου ὁμώνυμος, *Scripta Minora*, I, p. 168.

[2] See T. Gerasimov, 'Vizantiiski oloveni pechati ot Pliska', *Izvestiya na Bŭlgarskiya Arkheologicheski Institut*, 14 (1940/2), 140. The editor however has wrongly identified the owner of the seal with Andronikos *21*. But cf. the remarks of F. D(ölger) in *BZ*, 43 (1950), 236. A correction on the inscription was suggested by N. Bănescu, *Les duchés byzantinè de Paristrion (Paradounavon) et de Bulgarie* (Bucharest, 1946), p. 42, n. 1.

12. [1] The principal sources for the political history of Konstantinos' reign are the two main contemporaries, Psellos, II, pp. 138–52, and Attal., pp. 70–92. See also Skyl. Cont., pp. 651–60; Zon., III, pp. 673–81; Bryen., pp. 22–3; Glykas, pp. 604–7; Man., pp. 273–4; Skout., pp. 165–6; Ephraim, pp. 142–5. As far as I know, no special study has been exclusively devoted to these years apart from the brief accounts given in the more general textbooks. For a characterization of some aspects of Konstantinos' eventful reign see C. Neumann, *Die Weltstellung des byzantinischen Reiches vor den Kreuzzügen* (Leipzig, 1894), pp. 79–81. A theological incident of the period has been studied by G. Hofmann, 'Texte zum Religionsgespräch vor Kaiser Konstantin X. Dukas', *Miscellanea G. Galbiati*, III (=*Fontes Ambrosiani* 27, Milan, 1951), pp. 249–62.

[2] Psellos in his funeral oration for Eirene, the wife of Ioannes *13*, says that her eldest son Andronikos *21* was called after his grandfather, who was, of course, also the father of Konstantinos. See *Scripta Minora*, I, p. 168. The view of Ducange, *Familiae*, p. 161, that Andronikos *8* may have been the father of the emperor, cannot be accepted for chronological reasons.

[3] On the background of the eleventh-century Doukai see the introduction, p. 8, n. 2.

[4] According to Psellos, II, p. 151, when the emperor died in May 1067 he was just over sixty.

commonly attached to him, but some variants are also found.[5] Of his early career prior to 1057 little is known, but it does appear that by the reign of Michael IV Paphlagon, Konstantinos was a person to reckon with. He seems to have been somehow implicated in the plots of his father-in-law Konstantinos Dalassenos and after the latter was seized on 3 August 1034 and was confined to the isle of Plate in the Propontis, Konstantinos was quick to raise a voice of protest on behalf of his relative, but he himself was also arrested and imprisoned in a certain fortress. Three 'noble and wealthy' Asia Minor associates of his, Goudeles, Baianes, and Probatas, suffered the same fate, and all three had their fortunes confiscated and transferred to the emperor's brother Konstantinos.[6] There is no information as to how long he remained imprisoned, but in 1038/9 Dalassenos was still in custody and his free relatives were also seized.[7] It was perhaps this unfortunate affair that forced Konstantinos Doukas to retire for a time to the countryside and to busy himself with farming.[8]

Psellos, who certainly knew Konstantinos well and felt more affection for him than for any other contemporary ruler, relates that they became close friends during the reign of Monomachos (1042–55) and probably in the early part of it.[9] Yet the active political life of Doukas, as far as is known, only starts in 1057. In the Easter of that year (30 March) together with Ioannes *13*, he was among a number of generals from Asia Minor who came to petition the emperor Michael VI Stratiotikos for higher dignities, though their efforts proved fruitless. It is strange that Kedrenos includes the name of Konstantinos among the 'eastern generals'.[10] In fact, there is not the slightest indication that he had any military background.

By this time Konstantinos, having lost his first wife, was now married to Eudokia Makrembolitissa, a niece of the patriarch Michael Keroularios. Being honoured with the important dignity of *vestarches*, he was presumably among the first supporters of the usurper Isaakios Komnenos with whom he had been

---

[5] Most prominent among these variants is the surname of Doukitzes (cf. Appendix II), attached to Konstantinos by some minor sources. The colophon on a Messina manuscript of April 1064, written by the monk Gerasimos, informs us that it was completed ἐπὶ βασιλέως τοῦ ἐν ὀρθοδοξίᾳ λάμποντος Κωνσταντίνου τοῦ Δουκίτζη, see G. Fraccaroli, 'Dei codici greci del monastero dell SS. Salvatore', *Studi Italiani di Filologia Classica*, 5 (1897), 499–500. In a manuscript of Zonaras' *History* an explanatory gloss is found to the effect that the emperor is called by most people Doukitzes and not Doukas (διὸ καὶ τοῖς πλείοσιν οὐ Δούκας, Δουκίτζης δ'ὑποκοριζόμενος ἐπωνόμαστο), but this comes from the hand of the first modern editor Hieronymus Wolf (1516–80), see Zon., III, p. 676. The cognomen 'Ducizi' is also known from certain western sources. See Ducange, *Familiae*, p. 161; cf. H. Mädler, *Theodora, Michael Stratiotikos, Isaak Komnenos* (Plauen, 1894), p. 16, who quotes a western chronicle calling the emperor 'Constantinus Dukizzi'. An obvious derivation from it is the form 'Dioclici' found in Romualdus Salerniatnus, *Chronicon* (=*RIS*, vol. VII), pp. 182, 186, and 187, and in Andreas Dandulus, *Chronica* (=*RIS*, vol. XII), p. 213. Lupus Protospatarius in *MGH, Scriptores*, V, p. 59, calls the emperor 'Constantinus o Ducos', which may be traced to the sensible Greek Κωνσταντῖνος ὁ τοῦ Δουκός. In a poem of the following century Konstantinos is called Δουκοφυής, see K. Horna, 'Die Epigramme des Theodoros Balsamon', *Wiener Studien*, 25 (1903), 183. However this latter is a mere poetic compound very common in the twelfth-century courtly literature.

[6] Kedr., II, pp. 510–11; Zon., III, p. 589; cf. G. Schlumberger, *L'épopée byzantine à la fin du Xe siècle*, III (Paris, 1905), pp. 187–8.

[7] Cf. Kedr., II, p. 521. On the career of Dalassenos see N. Adontz, 'Notes arméno-byzantines', *B*, 10 (1935), 173–5.

[8] Psellos, II, p. 141.

[9] Psellos, II, pp. 141–2.   [10] Kedr., II, p. 615; cf. Mädler, op. cit., pp. 29–30.

associated by rank, by friendship, and by relation.[11] Psellos says that on Michael VI's fall (31 August 1057) most people looked upon Konstantinos as a prospective emperor, but he declined the honour.[12] This, however, is not supported elsewhere and is probably only a compliment to Doukas.

Konstantinos owed to the new emperor Isaakios Komnenos his promotion to the rank of *proedros*.[13] Psellos, always close to the court intrigues and partial to Konstantinos, implies that his friend was disappointed over the failure of the new emperor to fulfill promises made to him in the past, though he diplomatically ignored this unpleasant situation and avoided any clash with Isaakios. It was only on the eve of his abdication that Isaakios remembered his promises and on the advice of Psellos turned to Doukas and nominated him as his successor.[14] The story contains at least a measure of truth as the exceptional title of 'Caesar' had perhaps been promised to Doukas in 1057.[15]

The imperial change of 1059 is generally attributed to the alliance of the civil party with the influential partisans of the now dead patriarch Keroularios,[16] and the account of Psellos does not in any way hint at a voluntary and smooth abdication. He relates that the ailing Isaakios only verbally nominated his successor, but a slight improvement in his condition made him withhold the bestowal of the supreme power. It is not clear what course Konstantinos followed then but he certainly became involved in an awkward situation which was finally solved by Psellos who alone dared take the initiative. He urged the hesitating Doukas to be formally proclaimed emperor, and he himself vested the new sovereign with the insignia of his high office. Only then did Isaakios finally give in. He retired to the monastery of Stoudios and took the monastic habit.[17] Thus Konstantinos Doukas became emperor on 24 November 1059.[18] No matter what political manoeuvres had taken place, it is to the credit of the

---

11 Καὶ γὰρ τῷ Κομνηνῷ τὰ πάντα συνδιαφέρων ἦν καὶ συμπράττων καὶ τῆς πρώτης βουλῆς γινωσκόμενος, ὡς καὶ τῆς φιλίας καὶ τῆς ἀξίας καὶ τῆς ἀγχιστείας ἐγγύτατος, ὁ βεστάρχης Κωνσταντῖνος ὁ Δούκας, ἀδελφιδῆς τοῦ πατριάρχου σύνευνος καθιστάμενος, καὶ πολλὴν εὔνοιαν διδοὺς καὶ λαμβάνων ἐκεῖθεν, Attal., p. 56. It is not disclosed how the two men were related; it was certainly not a blood but an in-law relationship (ἀγχιστεία), possibly through the mother of the one of them.

12 Psellos, II, p. 142; cf. p. 136.

13 Attal. p. 69; cf. Skyl. Cont., p. 648. Up to the middle of the century the dignity of *proedros* was the highest one but was subsequently superseded by that of *protoproedros*. For its importance see Ch. Diehl, 'De la signification du titre de proèdre à Byzance', *Mélanges offerts à M. Gustave Schlumberger*, I (Paris, 1924), pp. 105–17; St. P. Kyriakides, Βυζαντιναὶ μελέται, II–V (Thessalonica, 1937), pp. 242–7; Aik. Christophilopoulou, Ἡ σύγκλητος εἰς τὸ Βυζαντινὸν κράτος (Athens, 1949), pp. 78–84 (the author enumerates all known *proedroi* and *protoproedroi*).

In describing Doukas and Isaakios, Attal., p. 69, writes: τὸν πρόεδρον Κωνσταντῖνον τὸν Δούκαν, ὃς αὐτῷ (sc. Ἰσαακίῳ τῷ Κομνηνῷ) συνίστωρ καὶ συναγωνιστὴς περὶ τὴν τῆς βασιλείας κατάκτησιν διὰ παντὸς ἐχρημάτισεν. This was taken over by Skyl. Cont., p. 648, who clearly failed to grasp the exact meaning of the words and unwillingly transformed Konstantinos into a successful official of public revenues: τὸν πρόεδρον Κωνσταντῖνον, ᾧ Δούκας τὸ πατρωνυμικὸν ἀνέκαθεν ἦν, ὡς συνίστορα καὶ συναγωνιστὴν καὶ τῶν χρημάτων ποριστὴν ἀφθονώτατον εἰς τὴν τῆς βασιλείας κατάσχεσιν.

14 Psellos, II, pp. 137–8 and 143.

15 Psellos, II, p. 136. For Doukas as an opponent of Isaakios see Mädler, op. cit., pp. 50–1.

16 Cf. Ostrogorsky, *History*, pp. 301–2.

17 Psellos, II, pp. 143–5. For a fuller account and further references see Aik. Christophilopoulou, Ἐκλογή, ἀναγόρευσις καὶ στέψις τοῦ Βυζαντινοῦ αὐτοκράτορος (Athens, 1957), p. 117.

18 For the date see D. I. Polemis, 'Notes on Eleventh-Century Chronology (1059–1081)', *BZ*, 58 (1965), 61.

new emperor that he often used to visit his fallen predecessor in his monastery cell.[19]

The elevation of Konstantinos was to some extent due to chance though he was obviously the common choice of various groups which were instrumental in ousting Isaakios. Claims that his accession was long anticipated[20] can be safely dismissed as standard Byzantine compliments. From the very beginning the new emperor appears to have failed to convince his subjects of his ability to rule. At least his alleged inefficiency is given as the primary motive behind an obscure conspiracy that very nearly succeeded. Observing a palace custom in use since the days of Monomachos, Konstantinos accompanied by his wife and children made an official pilgrimage to the famous monastery of Hagios Georgios at Mangana. He apparently went there in the evening with the intention of spending the whole of the following day of the festival at the monastery. In the meantime a plot had been formed with the objective of eliminating Doukas and putting forward a new emperor whose name was not revealed. The conspirators included men of rank with the eparch of the City at their head and the valuable assistance of certain troops and ships was also secured. The whole operation was very carefully planned and it was mere chance that saved the ruler's life. The rebellion was to start at dawn on 23 April 1061,[21] beginning in the centre of the City, and the plotters had arranged for its rapid spread at Mangana where Doukas and his family were expected to spend the day. They wisely predicted that he would naturally get alarmed by the uproar there and would quickly seek to return to his palace by sea as being safer. The crew of the imperial yacht had been drawn into the conspiracy; with the emperor aboard, they were to sail some distance from the land and then to drown him.

The rebellion started according to plan. Disturbances broke out early in the day and quickly reached Mangana. As was anticipated, the terrified emperor rushed to the sea-shore and sought a boat to return home without delay. Through a lack of co-ordination, the imperial yacht failed to arrive in time to pick up its passengers and in his haste Konstantinos embarked on another one belonging to a member of the nobility (ἀρχοντικὸν πλοιάριον) which immediately set sail. At this very moment the would-be assassins made their appearance and unsuccessfully attempted to induce the emperor to change to his own yacht. Not suspecting anything but being hard pressed by time, Konstantinos preferred to continue his trip in the less elegant boat and thus returned to his headquarters unhurt. Once the attempt on the emperor failed, the rebellion collapsed. The conspirators with the eparch and other prominent participants were arrested, but only a mild punishment was inflicted upon them. Some were forced to enter monasteries, others were jailed, banished, or had their fortunes confiscated. Unlike similar cases, no one was put to death.[22]

There is little information as to how Konstantinos personally dealt with the everyday problems facing the empire in the course of the repeated barbarian assaults both in Asia Minor and in the Balkans. Nevertheless the central government's inability to realise the seriousness of the impending danger was inevitably to a large extent a reflection of the emperor's own feelings. His reign was domin-

---

[19] Bryen., p. 23.   [20] Psellos, II, p. 135.   [21] Cf. Polemis, op. cit., pp. 61–2.
[22] The conspiracy is related by Attal., pp. 71–5, and abridged by Skyl. Cont., pp. 651–2; see also Psellos, II, pp. 148–9.

ated by civilians and represented a reaction against the more military minded Isaakios.[23] This policy was inaugurated immediately after the imperial change when the first act of the new ruler was a hasty restoration of all those who had fallen into disgrace under his soldier predecessor.[24]

This is not the place to discuss the disintegration of Byzantine power in Asia Minor and the intrusions of the Turkic hordes that within a quarter of a century were to threaten the very capital. Yet in more respects than one the emperor himself was responsible for some of these setbacks. In the first place, the inopportune measure introducing drastic cuts in military expenditure in order to economise was attributed to Konstantinos.[25] The disastrous results of such false economy were many, but contemporaries specially stressed the fall of the vital Armenian stronghold of Ani and attributed it to his unwise policy.[26]

The steps taken by the imperial government to cope with the Uze danger in the winter of 1064–65[27] only raised laughter among the Byzantines. The emperor at the head of a small band not exceeding 150 soldiers set out from Constantinople to face the barbarian swarms. He encamped not far away at Choerobacchae and the people began to wonder how the enemy was to be fought. Fortunately for all, news of the unexpected deliverance from danger arrived and so the emperor lost the only opportunity which he had had of displaying his quality in the military field; instead he rushed back to the City to offer thanksgiving to the Virgin.[28] This was the only instance in which Doukas was even remotely associated with an actual expedition.

In October 1066 the emperor, who was apparently of weak health,[29] fell ill. The disease, whose nature is unknown, proved fatal and in the following 22 May 1067[30] he died at the age of just over sixty. His dead body was carried by boat to the monastery of Hagios Nikolaos Molyboton outside the Golden Gate and buried there.[31]

Konstantinos Doukas was a person distinguished by good qualities who might have left a more favourable impression had he ruled in normal and less disturbed times. The sources are quick to stress his moderation and his love of justice. He was ready to forgive his opponents and in the conspiracy that endangered his throne he displayed a rare restraint in the punishment of the culprits.[32] He probably did not attempt any deeper study of the judicial system, but his constant efforts to see that justice was administered are well attested.[33] No one suffered mutilation during the years of his reign.[34] Equally favourable is the picture we get of the good nature of Konstantinos and his piety which was expressed in the traditional Byzantine manner by his admiration for the contemplative life and his almsgiving.[35] In addition, he really tried to improve the

---

[23] A. A. Vasiliev, *History of the Byzantine Empire, 324–1453* (Madison, Wisc., 1952), p. 352.

[24] Attal., p. 71.   [25] Attal., pp. 78–9; Psellos, II, p. 147.   [26] Attal., p. 80.

[27] For the date see Ostrogorsky, *History*, p. 303.

[28] Attal., pp. 85–86. An oration of Psellos to Konstantinos certainly refers to this incident. Needless to say, the author gives full credit to the emperor for the retreat of the Uzes and among other things he says: ἐπὶ φάλαγγος ἵστασαι καὶ χάρακα βάλλεις καὶ κατασείεις τὸ βάρβαρον καὶ πόρρωθεν ἀπελαύνεις τοῖς ἀπὸ τοῦ λόγου τοξεύμασι . . . , *Scripta Minora*, I, p. 39.

[29] Cf. Psellos, II, p. 151.   [30] See Polemis, op. cit., pp. 62–3.   [31] Attal., p. 92.

[32] Attal., p. 75; Psellos, II, pp. 140 and 149.

[33] Attal., p. 76; Psellos, II, pp. 139, 146 and 147; Bryen., p. 22.

[34] Psellos, II, p. 140.   [35] Attal., pp. 76 and 86; Skyl. Cont., p. 652; Psellos, II, p. 140.

finances of the state, especially by reductions in public expenditure.[36] This was superficially successful as a short term policy, but unfortunately in the end it seriously affected the efficiency of the armed forces on whom the burden of the austerity programme fell. Even Psellos, the greatest eulogist of the emperor, had to admit that his neglect of the army was disastrous.[37]

Konstantinos X continued the patronage of learning which was to find fuller expression under the Komnenoi.[38] Psellos addressed to him certain of his minor works. Among them are a couple of orations,[39] naturally highly eulogistic. In one of these the author warmly praises the emperor's favourable disposition towards scholars in general, something that had been entirely unknown in the course of the preceding reign when the palace was only occupied with administrative routine.[40] Moreover we possess a number of brief letters by Psellos to Doukas, none of which throws any light on the contemporary scene.[41]

Three portraits of Konstantinos are known. The first is a miniature of the 14th/15th century preserved in cod. Mutinensis gr. 122, fol. 267r, which is purely imaginary.[42] Another badly preserved miniature on cod. Par. gr. 922 shows him together with his second wife Eudokia, crowned by the Virgin.[43] The same theme is also found on an engraving of silver, but the place of the Virgin is taken by Christ.[44] Three types of seals of the emperor still survive, and they bear the legends: Κωνσταντῖνος ὁ Δούκας,[45] Κωνσταντῖνος βασιλεὺς Ῥωμαίων ὁ Δούκας,[46] and Κωνσταντῖνος βασιλεὺς ὁ Δούκας.[47]

In his brother Ioannes *13* whom he made a Caesar, Konstantinos found a trusted and valuable colleague. As already stated, he married twice. First,

---

[36] Attal., pp. 76 and 77; Skyl. Cont., pp. 652 and 655; Psellos, II, pp. 139–40.

[37] Psellos, II, pp. 146–7; cf. Attal., p. 77. It is to be noted that Psellos disassociates himself from this policy and hints that other counsellors were responsible for it. This fact contradicts the often expressed view that Psellos was the all-powerful figure in the reign of Doukas and an accomplice to the anti-militaristic measures taken.

[38] Psellos, II, p. 139. The emperor is reputed to have said that he would have wished to be distinguished by his learning rather than by his high position (ibid., p. 152).

[39] *Scripta Minora*, I, pp. 33–7 and 38–41. Both appear to have been composed after the Uze danger of 1066/7 had gone. The first is less clear, but the allusion to the invasion (p. 35), most probably refers to that event. For the other see above n. 28.

[40] *Scripta Minora*, I, p. 33.

[41] The one in *Scripta Minora*, II, pp. 41–5, no. 29, is a mere piece of extravagant praise, but another ibid., pp. 207–9, has some interest. At the imperial request, Psellos undertook the study of a marble relief containing an inscription and communicated his findings. The relief portrayed Odysseus and Circe, and the inscribed letters were interpreted as having a supposed magical meaning. Two other letters apparently accompanied a small present — fish — to the emperor, see Sathas, *MB*, v, p. 280, no. 48; and pp. 346–7, no. 104. Finally another two are of uncertain addresses, ibid., p. 283, no. 52, and p. 309, no. 74.

[42] The miniature is reproduced by Lampros, Λεύκωμα, plate 59; cf. idem in *NE*, 7 (1910), 404.

[43] A. Grabar, 'Une pyxide en ivoire à Dumbarton Oaks', *DOP*, 14 (1960), p. 128; cf. Ch. Diehl, *Manuel d'art byzantin* II (2nd ed., Paris, 1926), p. 631.

[44] See A. Goldschmidt and K. Weitzmann, *Die byzantinischen Elfenbeinskulpturen des X.–XIII. Jahrhunderts*, II (Berlin, 1934), p. 15, fig. 4; A. Grabar, *L'Empereur dans l'art byzantin* (Paris, 1936), pp. 117–18.

[45] See V. Laurent, 'Sceaux byzantins inédits', *EO*, 32 (1933), 424, no. iv.

[46] G. Schlumberger, 'Sceaux byzantins inédits', *RN*, 30 (1916), 39, no. 315.

[47] G. Schlumberger, *Sigillographie de l'Empire byzantin* (Paris, 1884), p. 422; K. Konstantopoulos, Βυζαντιακὰ Μολυβδόβουλλα (originally published in *JIAN*, 5–10 [1902–7]) nos. 281 and 281a 281γ; I. K. Sboronos in *JIAN*, 9 (1906), 297.

P.T.D.

(before 1034) to a daughter of the general Konstantinos Dalassenos whose name is unknown and who died prematurely, obviously without issue. He again married, probably before 1050, to Eudokia Makrembolitissa.[48] By his second marriage, Doukas became the father of several children: Michael *14*, N *15*, Andronikos *16*, Konstantios *17*, Anna *18*, Theodora *19* and Zoe *20*.[49] Of these Konstantios *17* and Zoe *20* were *porphyrogennetoi*.

13. Ioannes Doukas (?–c. 1088)

The Caesar Ioannes Doukas was the only brother of the emperor Konstantinos X *12* and consequently a son of Andronikos *11*, perhaps the younger one. His early life is totally unknown since any existing information on him dates after the year 1057.[1] Ioannes played a conspicuous role in the troubled period 1057–81 and continued to influence political developments up to his death in the early years of Alexios I Komnenos' reign. He was a very wealthy man, owning large estates in Thrace and in Bithynia. His close relations with Psellos are also to be noted.

There is sufficient indication pointing to a military background for Ioannes. If he is not often found taking part in actual military activities, this is because his close links with the palace tended to keep him busy in the capital. In any case,

[48] Eudokia, who was the wife in turn of Doukas and Romanos Diogenes, nearly succeeded in marrying as third husband the emperor Nikephoros III Botaneiates (Bryen., p. 127). She was a niece of the patriarch Michael Keroularios and perhaps a daughter of Ioannes Makrembolites, but her exact family background remains uncertain. Psellos was related to her family. On one occasion he says that he was 'spiritually' a brother to Eudokia's father (ἐγώ ... ἦν ἀδελφὸς τοῦ ἐκείνης πατρὸς ἐκ πνευματικῆς διαθέσεως), Psellos, II, p. 154, and elsewhere calls her his niece (see Sathas, *MB*, v, p. 347). Likewise, he describes Konstantinos Keroularios, also a nephew of the patriarch and possibly a brother of Eudokia, as his nephew (*Scripta Minora*, II, pp. 46, 48, and 254). Eudokia's portrait has also been preserved (see Lampros, Λεύκωμα, plates 59 and 61). Botaneiates granted Eudokia a very generous πρόνοια (Skyl. Cont., p. 742). When she died on an unknown date (after 1081) some verses were written which are preserved under the title 'Ἐπιτύμβιοι εἰς τὴν θανοῦσαν βασίλισσαν, see Sp. P. Lampros in *NE*, 16 (1922), 41.

In a written pledge, composed shortly before the death of Konstantinos, Eudokia solemnly took an oath not to marry again in the event of becoming a widow. The document in question (ὁ ἐγγυητικὸς ὅρκος τῆς δεσποίνης κυρίας Εὐδοκίας, ὁ γενόμενος πρὸς τὸν αὐτῆς ἄνδρα τὸν ἀοίδιμον βασιλέα κῦρ Κωνσταντῖνον τὸν Δούκαν) has been edited with an extensive commentary by N. Oikonomidès, 'Le serment de l'impératrice Eudocie (1065): Un épisode de l'histoire dynastique de Byzance', *REB*, 21 (1963), 101–28.

[49] Skout., p. 165, and a continuation of Georgios Hamartolos in *PG*, 110, col. 1237, no. 90, are wrong with regard to the daughters of the emperor.

[According to a manuscript note published by Gautier in *REB*, 24 (1966), 156, Konstantinos became emperor on 23 November 1059 and died on 23 May 1067.]

13. [1] Apart from the very many references to Ioannes Doukas in the literary sources of the period, he is mentioned in an inscription found at Synada, Bithynia, which is irreparably mutilated beyond any hope of satisfactory reconstruction. The attempts of the editors W. H. Buckler, W. M. Calder, and W. K. C. Guthrie, *Monumenta Asiae Minoris Antiqua*, IV (Manchester, 1933), p. 32, no. 96, and of H. Grégoire in *B*, 8 (1933), 758–9, though ingenious, cannot be accepted because their assumptions contradict undisputed historical data.

For Ioannes see G. Kolias, 'Ὁ καῖσαρ Ἰωάννης Δούκας ἀντιγραφεὺς τοῦ Cod. Par. 2009, *EEBΣ*, 14 (1938), 300–5; B. Leib, 'Jean Doukas, césar et moine: Son jeu politique à Byzance de 1067 à 1081', *AB*, 68 (1950), 163–79.

an active army career might have continued well into the reign of Konstantinos X *12*,[2] but on the other hand there is no reason to suppose that it was particularly successful. In 1057 Ioannes was among those generals of the east who in the Easter of that year unsuccessfully petitioned Michael VI for more favours.[3] It is reasonable to assume that he then held some responsible position on the eastern frontier; other evidence, trustworthy though perhaps inconclusive, does in fact suggest an identification of Ioannes with the *katepano* of Edessa, Ioannes Doukitzes (1059).[4]

Although Ioannes became the trusted counsellor of his brother (1059–67), he is not particularly conspicuous during this period. Nevertheless from the very beginning he is known to have been active and his part in helping to extinguish the dangerous conspiracy of 1061 is noted.[5] The sources usually refer to him as the *Caesar*. Thanks to his exceptional dignity which Konstantinos *12* conferred upon his brother,[6] Ioannes was officially the most prominent person in the state after the emperor's wife and children. However on at least one occasion he

---

[2] Psellos, II, p. 181, implies that Ioannes had both theoretical and practical knowledge of tactics. Psellos in a letter to him remarks: ἀφεὶς ἐπὶ τοῖς στρατηγήμασιν ἐγκωμιάζειν σε, καὶ οἷς πάλαι κατώρθωσας καὶ νῦν κατορθεῖς; see J. F. Boissonade, Ψελλός (Nuremberg, 1838), p. 184. Attal., p. 184, brands him as στρατηγὸς αὐτοκράτωρ in connection with a campaign. Alexios Komnenos asked the Caesar's opinion on the fortifications of Constantinople (*Alexias*, I, p. 91), something that is expected of a man with an inside knowledge of military matters. Cf. *Scripta Minora*, I, p. 164.

[3] Kedr., II, p. 615.

[4] In the first place the cognomen of Doukitzes, used instead of Doukas, is applied to Konstantinos *12* (see n. 5 in that account). The Armenian historian Matthew of Edessa in his *Chronicle* (translated by E. Dulaurier, Paris, 1858), p. 106, writes that the governor of Edessa, called Doughidz (=Doukitzes), who belonged to one of the noblest families of the empire, was invited by Isaakios I Komnenos to Constantinople and was given the throne on the latter's abdication. The name of this governor is also supplied by a well-known and reliable manuscript notice, written on 4 April 1059, which mentions Ioannes Doukitzes as the *katepano* of Edessa at that time; see R. Devreesse, *Bibliothèque Nationale. Catalogue des Manuscrits grecs*. II. — *Les Fonds Coislin* (Paris, 1945), p. 242. The emperor Konstantinos *12* must of course be clearly distinguished from the governor of Edessa (cf. E. Honigmann, *Die Ostgrenze des byzantinischen Reiches von 363 bis 1071* [Brussels, 1935], pp. 138–9), but it might be asked whether Matthew, who certainly drew upon a distorted local tradition, did not actually confuse the two brothers, thus making them one person, and identifying Ioannes Doukas with the governor of his home town who was called to the imperial throne. V. N. Zlatarski, 'Edna datirana pripiska na grŭtski ot sredata na XI. vek', *BS*, I (1929), 23–4, who edited and commented upon the notice in question, assumed that the *katepano* Ioannes Doukitzes is in fact Ioannes Doukas the future Caesar. Apart from all this, there is further evidence to the effect that Ioannes (perhaps during the early years of his brother's reign) was for a time at Edessa and in nearby Syria on official assignment. This information is derived from a letter which Psellos wrote to Ioannes referring to a previous letter written by Ioannes and sent to Psellos from Edessa (ἀναμνήσθητί μοι καὶ τοῦ ἐξ Ἐδέσσης γράμματος καὶ τῶν μετὰ ταῦτα λόγων, Boissonade, op. cit., p. 186).

[5] Attal., p. 74.

[6] Psellos, II, p. 150; cf. R. Guilland, 'Etudes sur l'histoire administrative de l'empire byzantin: Le césarat', *OCP*, 13 (1947), 176. See also the brilliant but highly eulogistic remarks of Psellos on this title of Ioannes in *Scripta Minora*, I, p. 172; cf. Boissonade, op. cit., p. 184. Although the sources are silent, the elevation to this dignity must be presumably dated shortly after Konstantinos *12* ascended the throne. Certainly it was for Ioannes Doukas that Psellos wrote the still unpublished essay Τὸ τοῦ καίσαρος ὄνομα κατὰ διαφόρους σημασίας, found in cod. Vat. gr. 672 fol. 272r–272v, see R. Devreesse, *Codices Vaticani Graeci*. III.–*Codices 604–866* (Vatican, 1950), p. 125. This short work, which I have examined in microfilm, does not contain any information on Ioannes.

seems to have fallen into imperial disfavour and he solicited the intervention of Psellos.[7] Of the positions entrusted to the Caesar, only one is known, namely an uncertain assignment in Antioch in the course of Konstantinos' *12* early years.[8] After his brother's death, the Caesar remained unreservedly attached to the imperial family. Previously during a serious illness Konstantinos *12* had not hesitated to place the fate of his wife and his children into Ioannes' hands.[9]

It is strange that Ioannes Doukas does not figure prominently during the regency of the dowager empress Eudokia (22 May–31 December 1067). The empress apparently had little difficulty in deceiving him over her plans. She married Romanos Diogenes and it is rather surprising that the Caesar apparently had neither the power nor the will to cope effectively with this development which he could hardly have favoured. Despite his strong hostility towards Romanos, he reacted in a comparatively mild way. Nevertheless he tried to safeguard the rights of his nephew Michael *14* but only somewhat vaguely.[10]

Officially the new emperor Romanos IV appeared to accept the advice of Ioannes,[11] but in fact he quickly pushed him into the background together with the other members of the Doukas family. All the same, the mutual hatred of the two men was sufficiently controlled to prevent a violent outbreak. At least the Caesar was prudent enough to leave Constantinople and go into involuntary retirement on his estates in Bithynia,[12] where he was at the time of the disaster of Mantzikert (19 August 1071). He must have been informed about the situation in the east by his son Andronikos *21* who had deserted from the emperor before the battle started.

In the turmoil and the palace intrigues that followed, the Caesar assumed a decisive if evil role. Eudokia, who for the second time found herself as regent,

---

[7] The Caesar wrote to Psellos expressing the fear that the emperor no longer favoured him and Psellos in reply took pains to assure his friend that this was not the case (σοὶ δ'ἄρα τίς δαίμων ἐβάσκηνε, καὶ νοήματά τινα δυσελπιστίας μεστὰ τῇ ψυχῇ σου παρέφθειρε, καὶ ὑπείληφας ὅτι σοι ὁ ἀδελφός, ἵν᾽οὕτως εἴποιμι καὶ πατήρ, ἠλάττωσέ σοι τὴν πρώτην εὐμένειαν καὶ μέχρι τῶν παρασήμων τῆς εὐτυχίας προαγαγών τῆς πρὸς σὲ εὐνοίας ἐπαύσατο; Boissonade, op. cit., p. 185; cf. n. 8). It was perhaps for this reason that Psellos seized the opportunity to extol the ὁμόνοια and the συμφυία of the two brothers, *Scripta Minora*, I, p. 165.

[8] In the same letter Psellos informs the Caesar that he had shown the latter's letter to the emperor (i.e. Konstantinos *12*) who 'explained the affair of Antioch and under solemn oath added that it was not against your will that the order had been issued but only because he (sc. the emperor) was anxious to know from you certain of the most confidential matters there (sc. in Antioch)', see Boissonade, op. cit., p. 187. It is useless to speculate what the order (πρόσταξις) in question was about. It certainly does not correspond to the only known imperial order relating to Antioch (Dölger, *Regesten*, II, p. 15, no. 959; no. 962, also referring to that city, belongs to the regency of Eudokia; see Attal., p. 181).

[9] Psellos, II, p. 151.

[10] Psellos, II, pp. 156–7, openly derides the Caesar's soft attitude towards this marriage. He says that Ioannes φωνάς τινας ὑπὲρ ἐκείνου (sc. Michael *14*) ἀφείς, συμπανηγυρίζει τοῖς βασιλεύουσι, καὶ μονονοὺ τὸν ὑμέναιον ᾄδει καὶ τῶν ἐπιγαμίων ἐμφορεῖται κρατήρων. Matthew of Edessa, op. cit., p. 160, implies that the Caesar willingly accepted Romanos as the new emperor. According to Skout., p. 167, Eudokia put her brother-in-law aside and assumed all state responsibilities herself.

[11] Attal., pp. 101–2.

[12] Bryen., p. 43. See also Psellos, II, p. 161, who adds that if Romanos were not bound by oath, he would have put Ioannes to death.

immediately recalled him from his semi-exile in Bithynia, and in Constantinople Ioannes once more sided with Psellos in favour of a joint rule of Michael *14* and his mother.[13] This dynastic arrangement proved of a short duration as the unexpected news of Romanos' liberation completely altered the scene. Ioannes was shrewd enough to realise the implications arising out of Eudokia's known sympathies with Romanos. She was still in an active position capable of opposing Ioannes' designs. The anti-Romanos party which together with the Caesar counted on Psellos' advice, reacted promptly. Being supported by the Varangian guard it forced Eudokia to take the veil and proclaimed Michael *14* as sole emperor (end October 1071).[14] Anna Dalassene, the mother of the future Alexios I, who was a bitter personal enemy of Ioannes Doukas, was suspected of scheming with Romanos and was banished to the isle of Prinkipo together with some of her children.[15]

There can be no doubt that the real instigator of all these drastic measures was the Caesar himself who for the first and only time became the driving force behind a weak ruler. Actively assisted by his two sons, he made sure that the resistance offered by Romanos in Asia Minor was crushed. The sources are explicit in condemning the Caesar as wholly to blame for the deplorable blinding of Romanos.[16] His predominant influence in the court was however only of brief duration and was unexpectedly brought to an end.

Ioannes had introduced to the palace a eunuch, commonly known as Nikephoritzes, who was soon raised to the position of *logothetēs tou dromou* and completely captivated Michael *14*. Such was the impact of this crafty and unscrupulous man on the feeble emperor that the latter unhesitatingly sacrificed the Caesar at his request, as well as Psellos and another trusted counsellor Ioannes bishop of Side. It appears that the Caesar with his sons contemplated some sort of action to get rid of Nikephoritzes and a second withdrawal to Bithynia with Andronikos *21* in the autumn of 1073 must probably be seen in this context. Presumably nothing came of these plans and after the winter was over Ioannes returned to the capital.[17]

The Caesar was no match for the eunuch. Nikephoritzes had cleverly induced Michael *14* to view his uncle not only with dislike but also with suspicion.[18] He then conceived the idea of eliminating him completely from the scene and persuaded the emperor to entrust Ioannes with the warfare about to be conducted against the Norman mercenary Roussel de Bailleul who had recently revolted in Asia Minor. Ioannes had to obey. At the head of an army he crossed to Asia, passed the Bithynian mountains and on hearing that the rebel was encamped in the region of the Sangarios sources, proceeded via Dorylaion to meet Roussel. The two armies, ready for battle, faced one another near the Zompou bridge of

[13] Psellos, II, p. 164; Bryen., pp. 43–4.
[14] Psellos, II, p. 166; Attal., pp. 168–9.
[15] Bryen., p. 50; cf. Chalandon, *Les Comnène*, I, pp. 26–7.
[16] See Bryen., p. 55; Zon., III, p. 707. An oriental source whose account is not however entirely accurate, presents the 'Kisarios' (the Caesar) as acting contrary to the imperial orders. See *The Chronography of Abū'l Faraj Known as Bar Hebraeus* (translated by E. A. Wallis-Budge, Oxford, 1932), I, pp. 222–3.
[17] Bryen., pp. 57 and 73; for the date see D. I. Polemis, 'Notes on Eleventh-Century Chronology (1059–1081)', *BZ*, 58 (1965), 66–7.
[18] Attal., p. 182; Skyl. Cont., p. 707.

the river.[19] The right wing of the imperial troops was occupied by western mercenaries headed by the Frank Papas.[20] Botaneiates, the future emperor, was in charge of the Asia Minor regiments which were posted in the rear, while Andronikos 21 commanded the left wing. The Caesar, besides having the overall command, also had under his direct orders the Varangian guard which occupied the centre of the imperial phalanx. These loosely composed forces completely failed in their task. The quick mass defection of the western mercenaries to their fellow countryman Roussel, followed by the withdrawal of Botaneiates, gave the upper hand to the rebel. The loyal troops were miserably routed, the Caesar was taken prisoner and a gallant but desperate attempt by Andronikos 21 to free him ended in failure.[21]

This astounding victory left Roussel in virtual control of a large area. With his important prisoner, whom he nevertheless treated well, the rebel came to Bithynia and encamped in the region east of Nicomedia where the Caesar's estates lay. There he seized the commanding fortress of Metabole on Mount Sophon (now Sabandja Dagh) which enabled him to exercise his authority over the plains below.[22] The distressed government of Constantinople hastily prepared a haphazard new expedition against Roussel, but the sudden death of its commander Konstantinos 22 held up any immediate action against the rebel.[23]

It was sometime after this that an understanding was reached between Ioannes Doukas and his captor. Roussel's unexpected proclamation of Ioannes Doukas co-emperor cannot be entirely explained as due to his own initiative and it is unlikely that this step was taken against the will of the Caesar. It must of course always be borne in mind that the self interest of the Frankish rebel came first, yet the dissatisfaction of Ioannes with the emperor and with his right-hand Nikephoritzes would naturally have made him view Roussel's aims with some favour. Bryennios, who stood close to the Doukas family, describes him as being reluctant in the face of the rebel's bold gesture, but does not omit to point out that the newly proclaimed Ioannes after an *initial* hesitation came to view the whole affair with a measure of realism.[24]

In spite of the inefficiency of Michael's 14 government, the adventure of Roussel and the Caesar ended in disaster. Nikephoritzes secured the collaboration of the Seljuks who were promised large sums if they would agree to combat the rebel.[25] Their general Artouch was dispatched with a substantial force to Mount Sophon which appears to have become the headquarters of Roussel.

---

[19] The bridge was on the military road from Dorylaion to Sebastea on the large bend of the Sangarios, some 60 miles to the south-west of Ancyra. See W. M. Ramsey, *The Historical Geography of Asia Minor* (London, 1890), map facing p. 197. In connection with this campaign, Glykas, p. 614, calls Ioannes a '*stratopedarches*', but this does not mean that he carried this specific rank; the author simply implies that he was the commander-in-chief.

[20] For the name see H. Grégoire in *B*, 23 (1953), 514, n. 1.

[21] The expedition and the Caesar's defeat are related at some length by Bryen., pp. 73–7, and in more condensed form by Attal., pp. 184–6. Attal., p. 184, attributes the defeat to a tactical error, namely Ioannes' failure to comply with the suggestion of Botaneiates that they should wait for reinforcements before attacking.

[22] Bryen., p. 77.   [23] Bryen., p. 80.

[24] Bryen., pp. 80–1; cf. Attal., pp. 188–9. Bryennios relates the incident with unusual sympathy and comments that the Caesar (who happened to be his wife's great-grandfather), but for God's will, could easily have succeeded in obtaining the crown.

[25] Dölger, *Regesten*, II, p. 19, no. 997.

Without delay Artouch reached the peak of the mountain (called Maroxos) and was able to spy out the movements of the Franks encamped in the village of Trisea below. The Turks made their attack cleverly so that the surprised Franks were put to flight while Roussel and the Caesar fell into the enemy's hands. The Norman chieftain was soon ransomed by his wife, but the Caesar was kept in custody by the victorious Artouch who subsequently moved to the interior. Eventually the emperor, fearing perhaps another understanding between his uncle and the Turks paid heavily to have him set free. Ioannes, however, remembering his recent impious proclamation and not without reason anticipating unpleasant repercussions, first came to Trachonesion in the Propontis where he wisely chose to embrace the monastic life. Only then did he dare enter Constantinople and appear before the emperor.[26]

Ioannes Doukas—a monk from now on—does not seem to have taken any further part in the political life of Michael's *14* reign. Yet he helped to arrange the marriage of his granddaughter Eirene *26* with the promising young Alexios Komnenos despite opposition from both the palace and the bridegroom's forceful mother.[27]

The revolt of Botaneiates which started in October 1077 brought secret rejoicing to the Caesar. Although he pretended not to encourage any actions against his nephew,[28] he must have welcomed the imperial change. He was quick to advise Michael *14* to abdicate and enter a monastery.[29] After the accession of Botaneiates, in the face of much canonical irregularity, Ioannes was instrumental in assisting the new emperor to marry the ex-empress Maria, the wife of Michael *14*.[30]

The Caesar was staying in his estates Ta Moroboundou in Thrace in the spring of 1081. There he was caught by surprise at the news of Alexios Komnenos' revolt. The Komnenoi, aware of his inclinations and sympathies, jokingly invited him to their cause: 'We on our side', so their message ran, 'have prepared a right good meal, not wanting in rich condiments, but if you on your side wish to share this banquet, you must come with all speed to partake of it.'[31] Ioannes did not waver. Immediately he set out to meet Alexios. On his way he succeeded in rendering two important services to the rebel, first by acquiring for him a large amount of money carried by an imperial tax collector and then on crossing the Hebrus by persuading a band of Turkish mercenaries, originally employed by Botaneiates, to change sides.

The Komnenoi with the rebel troops on their way to Constantinople were happy to welcome the Caesar who was accompanied by his young grandsons Michael *24* and Ioannes *25*. At the village of Schiza a crucial conference took place which formulated policy and tactics, and still more important, agreed upon the imperial candidacy of Alexios rather than that of his elder brother Isaakios, thanks to the persuasive intervention of the Caesar in his favour.[32]

---

[26] Bryen., pp. 77–83; Attal., pp. 188–93; Zon., III, p. 711. For the dating of those events cf. Polemis, op. cit., pp. 66–8.

[27] Bryen., pp. 106–8.   [28] Bryen., p. 121.   [29] Bryen., p. 125; *Alexias*, I, p. 44.

[30] Bryen., pp. 126–7. The intervention of the Caesar on behalf of Maria must be partly explained by his hostility towards Eudokia Makrembolitissa who was also a candidate in the bridal stakes. Had he not intervened, Eudokia would probably have married for the third time.

[31] *Alexias*, I, p. 82; trans. E. A. S. Dawes, *Anna Comnena: The Alexiad* (London, 1928), p. 57.

[32] *Alexias*, I, pp. 82–5.

From then on, probably until his death, Ioannes Doukas acted as a counsellor to Alexios. He first urged the rebel to proceed with all speed to the capital and later advised him to turn down the almost desperate overtures of Botaneiates. When the army stood before the walls of Constantinople, Alexios asked him to inspect the fortifications and give him his opinion. As Ioannes wore the monk's garb, it was only with reluctance that he agreed openly to assume a military expert's role. His fears proved justified for the soldiers of the imperial guard did not refrain from uttering insulting jokes against the 'abbot'. Nevertheless he suggested to the would-be emperor to befriend the loyal mercenaries and it was actually through this policy that Alexios managed to enter the City.[33]

After the successful outcome of the Komnenian revolt, the Caesar enjoyed an honoured treatment. Together with his relatives, curiously enough including the young empress Eirene 26, he lodged at the 'lower palace' while the Komnenoi with their mother and the ex-empress Maria lived in the palace of Boukeleon.[34] The sources do not provide sufficient information to enable us to see more clearly the court intrigues in which the Caesar was a central figure. The expulsion of Maria from the palace and the coronation of Eirene 26 could only have been effected by his decisive interference.[35] The year of his death is unknown, but since Anna Komnene (born on 2 December 1083) writes that she saw Ioannes for a little while,[36] it might be approximately fixed to around 1088.

There is hardly an important event in Byzantium between the years 1067–81 in which Ioannes Doukas was not associated directly or indirectly. This however must not create the false impression that he was a policy maker behind ineffective rulers. By nature the Caesar does not seem to have been very much different from his brother Konstantinos 12 or from his nephew Michael 14, both notoriously uninspiring personalities. The power and the influence he exerted were to a large extent due to high social position and to great wealth rather than to personal talents for which Ioannes was not particularly conspicuous. In vain one looks for any constructive element in the policies which he had inspired. On the contrary, he made numerous blunders and experienced many setbacks. Though he could have taken the reins of government into his hands after his brother's death in May 1067, he allowed himself to be elbowed aside by Eudokia who easily deceived him in her intention to marry Romanos. The latter in turn completely ignored the Caesar and this was again repeated a few years later by Nikephoritzes. The incident with Roussel which culminated in the untimely proclamation again indicates Ioannes' lack of judgement.

Among the voluminous correspondence of Psellos we find about twenty-five letters addressed to Ioannes Doukas, in addition to others whose inscription is uncertain. Those which can be dated belong to the period 1059–67, but before that time the two men were already on intimate terms.[37] The letters provide

---

[33] *Alexias*, 1, pp. 98–9.   [34] *Alexias*, 1, p. 105.

[35] Cf. *Alexias*, 1, pp. 106–10. For his influence during the early years of Alexios see G. Buckler, *Anna Comnena: A Study* (London, 1929), p. 125. The Caesar, especially during the later period of his life, had to face the utmost hostility from the emperor's mother Anna Dalassene, cf. ibid., p. 248.

[36] ὃν κἀγὼ ἐπ' ὀλίγον φθάσασα τεθέαμαι, *Alexias*, 1, p. 84. As the editor observes (p. 179), apart from this there is a complete lack of evidence about this event.

[37] Ioannes had described the virtues of Konstantinos 12 to Psellos before 1067 (ὃς καὶ πρὸ τοῦ κράτους τὸν ἄνδρα μοι πολλάκις ὑπεζωγράφησας), Boissonade, op. cit., p. 185.

useful information on Ioannes. Several of them contain compliments about his horsemanship and remarks on his love of hunting,[38] but all the same Psellos disapproved of his friend's neglect of books for the sake of sport of this kind.[39] Still, on another occasion he did not hesitate to praise the Caesar's alleged interest in learning.[40] Certain questions on anatomy are answered in another letter.[41] Equally notable is one in which Psellos congratulates him on the birth of a grandson who on account of his inability to speak properly is called 'a second Psellos'.[42] It is also known that Ioannes himself wrote a number of highly complimentary letters to Psellos,[43] none of which survive. Moreover Psellos gives us the extremely interesting information that the Caesar took pains to have the scholar's own letters copied and preserved.[44] This is not in fact the only instance of his activity in having manuscripts copied. The famous cod. Par. gr. 2009, which contains the *De Administrando Imperio*, was written by his secretary Michael Rozaites.[45] It should also be noted that Ioannes Doukas himself made some literary efforts. A fifteenth-century manuscript appears to ascribe to him a hymn to St Basil.[46]

Ioannes Doukas married, probably about 1045, Eirene, a daughter of the brave general Niketas Pegonites.[47] Thanks to the long funeral oration Psellos devoted to her death (Eirene died in 1060–66), some incidents of her life are known.[48] By this marriage, Ioannes became the father of two sons, Andronikos *21* and Konstantinos *22*. He survived both.

---

[38] Apparently Ioannes' favourite hunting was over his estates at Choerobacchae (see one o Psellos' letters in Sathas, *MB*, v, pp. 306–7, no. 71), most probably to be identified with the estate called Ta Moroboundou. See also two other letters of Psellos in *Scripta Minora*, II, pp. 205–6, no. 186, and pp. 278–81, no. 232. In the second of these the author thanks the Caesar for a horse which had been presented to him and adds that Andronikos *21* had recently described a hunting game to Psellos (ibid., p. 280).

[39] Sathas, *MB*, v, pp. 406–9, no. 156.

[40] *Scripta Minora*, II, pp. 276–8, no. 231. Psellos, II, pp. 181–2, says that Ioannes divided his interests between books and hunting, and in Boissonade, op cit., p. 184, he compliments him as being λογιώτατος and σοφώτατος.

[41] *Scripta Minora*, II, pp. 129–30, no. 101.

[42] Sathas, *MB*, v, pp. 307–8, no. 72.

[43] ... ἐγὼ δὲ τὰ σὰ γράμματα τοῖς ἐμοῖς ἐγχαράττω στέρνοις, καὶ ἀναγινώσκω πυκνότερον· καὶ ἐμαυτὸν ἄγαμαι καὶ πέπεισμαι εἶναι σοφός, καὶ ἐπαινῶ σε τῆς μαρτυρίας, Boissonade, op. cit., p. 176; ... ἀποβλέπων εἰς τὸν σκοπὸν τῶν πρὸς ἐμέ σου γραμμάτων, ibid., p. 171.

[44] Καὶ σὺ μὲν τὰς ἐμὰς ἐπιστολὰς βιβλία ποιεῖς, Boissonade, op. cit., p. 176. An investigation into the manuscript tradition of Psellos' letters might throw some light on this question.

[45] See Gy. Moravcsik, 'La provenance du manuscrit byzantin du "De Administrando Imperio" ', *Izvestiya na Bŭlgarskoto Istorichesko Druzhestvo*, 16/18 (1940), 333; cf. *DAI*, I, p. 15. The scribe Rozaites calls himself a 'domestic servant' (οἰκογενὴς οἰκέτης) to Ioannes.

[46] It is found on cod. Λαύρας 1661, fols. 132r–134v, under the title Κανὼν ἰαμβικὸς εἰς τὸν ἅγιον καὶ μέγαν Βασίλειον, ὃς καὶ ἀπεδώθη τῷ εὐτυχεστάτῳ καίσαρι Ἰωάννῃ, οὗ ἡ ἀκροστιχὶς αὕτη δι' ἡρωικοῦ στίχου " καίσαρος ἠγαθέου (read ἠγάθεε) Βασίλειε δέχοιο ἀοιδήν ", see Spyridon Lauriotes and S. Eustratiades, *Catalogue of the Greek Manuscripts in the Library of the Laura on Mount Athos* (Cambridge, Mass., 1925), p. 293.

[47] The family name and the career of Eirene's father have been established by H. Grégoire, 'Du nouveau sur l'histoire bulgaro-byzantine: Nicétas Pégonitès vainqueur du roi bulgar Jean Vladislav', *B*, 12 (1937), 282–91.

[48] The oration is in *Scripta Minora*, II, pp. 155–89. Eirene was the eldest child (p. 162), of a prominent family (p. 157) and her father had fought bravely in the Bulgarian war under Basileios II (p. 160). She had suffered once from hepatitis which however subsided (p. 171); she died probably of another prolonged illness (pp. 173–4).

14. Michael Doukas (?–c. 1090)

Despite the fact that Michael VII Doukas had been associated with the throne, first as junior co-emperor and then as sole emperor for more than fifteen years, the information which has come down to us about his person is comparatively limited. This is to be explained by the ruler's lack of personality, which not only had a disastrous impact on politics but inevitably created a most unfavourable impression on his contemporaries. It is with rare unanimity that the sources pass judgement on the unfortunate emperor. The epigrammatic but appropriate comment of Attaleiates is well known. He described Michael, on account of his flabby and tiresome nature, as being 'old among the young'.[1] Psellos, who as teacher and adviser knew him intimately, has devoted a character sketch to Michael which is understandably noted for its enthusiasm,[2] but although biased towards the Doukas family, the author does not conceal the emperor's short-comings and weaknesses. Michael's complete indifference to the affairs of the imperial administration,[3] as well as his blind dependence upon the will of his mother at a time when he was already of age, could not but strike Psellos.[4] Still more severe are criticisms drawn from other sources.[5]

Michael VII Doukas was the eldest[6] son of the emperor Konstantinos *12* and his second wife Eudokia Makrembolitissa. The year of his birth is not known, but as Psellos says that in 1067 'he had long since passed his youth ($\ddot{\eta}\beta\eta$)'[7] Michael could have been born well before 1050. He would then have been of age at his father's death, and his inability to assume the imperial responsibilities, which instead went to his mother and subsequently to Romanos IV, perhaps suggests that his natural powers were less than average. Konstantinos *12*, soon after he ascended the throne (1059), had indeed taken the preliminary step of having Michael crowned co-emperor.[8]

In the seven months that elapsed between the death of Konstantinos *12* (22 May 1067) and the accession of Romanos IV (1 January 1068) Michael shared the supreme power with his mother and his youngest brother Konstantios *17*.[9] Contrary to what might have been expected, he does not seem to

---

14. [1] Γέρων ἐν νέοις διὰ τὸ παρακείμενον καὶ ἀπαλὸν ἐλογίζετο, Attal., p. 180; cf. Skyl. Cont., p. 705; Man., p. 284, v. 6679.

[2] Psellos, II, pp. 172–8. This section is misleadingly captioned Ἡ βασιλεία Μιχαὴλ τοῦ Δούκα; it does not go beyond a mere description of the emperor's character and habits.

[3] Psellos, II, p. 153.   [4] Psellos, II, pp. 163–4.

[5] Skyl. Cont., p. 706, says that Michael was lacking in a manly and resolute spirit. Bryennios openly dislikes him. He has harsh words to say and concludes that the emperor's unstable nature was made up of two opposing vices: vanity and wickedness (Bryen., p. 57). Elsewhere he supplies the information that Michael was stammering in speech (βραδύγλωσσος, ibid., p. 73). Zon., III, p. 707, describes him as foolish, soft and entirely incompetent to rule. Cf. Glykas, pp. 613–14; Ephraim, p. 147, vv. 3399–3402. Matthew of Edessa, *Chronique* (translation by E. Dulaurier, Paris, 1858), p. 177, alone of all sources finds words of compliment for Michael, but surely no credence should be given to his judgement which was swayed by religious considerations.

[6] Psellos, II, p. 141.   [7] Psellos, II, p. 153.   [8] Psellos, II, p. 148.

[9] Psellos, II, pp. 152–3; Bryen., p. 23; Skout., p. 166 (who makes a clear distinction between Michael and Konstantios *17* who had been crowned by their father and Andronikos *16* who had not). Less precise are Attal., p. 92, and Skyl. Cont., p. 660, who write that Eudokia and her children assumed governmental responsibilities. The information of the former group is also

have held the highest position of the three but simply the secondary and subordinate one, which was in actual fact practically equal to that of his brother.[10] On the eve of Eudokia's marriage to Romanos, Michael was told of the imminent developments but apparently failed to realise their serious implications.[11]

Although care was taken to safeguard the threatened rights of Michael at the accession of Romanos,[12] he entered another period of eclipse in spite of the fact that officially together with both his brothers, he still continued to enjoy a nominal and, of course, an entirely inactive, co-emperorship.[13] The disastrous outcome of Romanos' last campaign at Mantzikert on 19 August 1071,[14] completely changed the picture and enabled Michael to come to the fore and to obtain the crown which would have most probably otherwise remained beyond his grasp.

At the instigation of Psellos and Ioannes *13*, Michael appeared in September 1071 as a joint ruler with his mother and a month later, following the removal of Eudokia, he was proclaimed as sole emperor[15] although for at least the next few years, he continued to recognise his brothers Andronikos *16* and Konstantios *17* as junior co-emperors,[16] even though their role was purely decorative.

Always incapable of taking independent action, Michael fell under the direct control of men more experienced in public affairs than he was. At first his uncle Ioannes *13* together with Psellos remained in close contact with him, but the real authority appears to have rested with the prudent eunuch Ioannes bishop of Side. But none of these enjoyed the imperial confidence for long. The inopportune efforts of the Caesar to support and promote the unscrupulous Nikephoritzes in palace affairs not only brought about the eclipse of the traditional advisors of the dynasty but meant the concentration of all power in the hands of this crafty eunuch. Indeed from then on (1073) Michael sunk deeper into the

supported by the evidence of a nomisma, presumably dating from this period. It portrays Eudokia in the centre with Michael on the left and Konstantios *17* on the right. See W. Wroth, *Catalogue of the Imperial Byzantine Coins in the British Museum* (London, 1908), II, p. 521; cf. H. Goodacre, *A Handbook of the Coinage of the Byzantine Empire* (London, 1957), p. 249.

---

[10] This becomes evident not only from the arrangement of the three figures in the above mentioned coin with Eudokia in the centre but also from the fact that all sources consider the empress both as the guardian and the real ruler during this brief period.

[11] Psellos, II, p. 156; cf. Skyl. Cont., p. 666.

[12] Psellos, II, p. 157.

[13] The sole evidence is likewise a coin, showing Romanos with Eudokia (obv.) and Michael with Andronikos *16* and Konstantios *17* on either side (rev.). See Wroth, op. cit., p. 523; Goodacre, op. cit., p. 254. For a seal with an identical portraiture see Laurent, *Médaillier Vatican*, p. 9, no. 12.

[14] For the date see J. Laurent, *Byzance et les Turcs Seldjoucides dans l'Asie occidentale jusqu'en 1081* (Paris, 1913), p. 43 n. 10.

[15] For the dating see D. I. Polemis, 'Notes on Eleventh-Century Chronology (1059–1081)', *BZ*, 58 (1965), 63–5.

[16] The difference in the titles of the three men can be seen in a chrysobull in *Scripta Minora*, I, p. 334 (cf. Dölger, *Regesten*, II, p. 19, no. 1003) which bears the signatures of Michael as βασιλεὺς καὶ αὐτοκράτωρ ῾Ρωμαίων and of each of his brothers as βασιλεὺς ῾Ρωμαίων. For the distinction see F. Dölger, 'Das byzantinische Mitkaisertum in den Urkunden', *BZ*, 36 (1936), especially p. 137 (=*Byzantinische Diplomatik* [Ettal, 1956], p. 119).

eunuch's clutches, and he is mentioned only as an instrument of Nikephoritzes[17] whose intensely unpopular measures caused widespread dissatisfaction. In particular the increase in the price of wheat gained for Michael the curious nickname of *Parapinaki(o)s*, as a nomisma could no longer purchase a medimnus of grain but only a medimnus less a pinakion (= quarter).[18]

The ineffective rule of Michael was further shaken by several military revolts such as those of Roussel de Bailleul, Nestor, Bryennios, and finally Botaneiates who proved victorious. His revolt originated in Asia Minor in October 1077, but he did not enter the capital until 3 April 1078. Michael had abdicated on 31 March and took the monastic vows in the monastery of Stoudios.[19] Sometime afterwards, perhaps at the suggestion of Botaneiates,[20] the former emperor consented to the unique honour of being given the metropolitan see of Ephesus.[21] But this appointment was in name only. Michael visited his distant metropolis once and then lived as an ordinary monk in the monastery of Manuel in Constantinople[22] where he probably died in around 1090.[23] Late in 1081 he had been shown to the Norman ambassadors in an effort to demonstrate that a pretender in Epirus, put forward by Robert Guiscard, had nothing to do with the former emperor of Byzantium.[24]

Michael Doukas is often praised for his literary interests,[25] but it is probable that these were rather superficial and pedantic, undoubtedly the result of Psellos' concentrated but nevertheless rather fruitless labours. The latter stood very close to the young prince for about fifteen formative years and took meticulous pains to instruct him in the various branches of knowledge of which Psellos himself was a master. He addressed numerous writings to Michael, most of which are educative in character and content. Among what were probably the earliest is a long poem in iambic and political verse, attempting to explain to Michael certain legal concepts, which was composed at the command of Konstantinos *12*.[26] A similar work is concerned with the explanation of church doctrine.[27]

---

[17] Cf. Attal., p. 184. Nikephoritzes even succeeded in convincing Michael that his own mother, brothers, and other relatives were scheming against him (ἀπετείχιζε δὲ τῆς τοῦ βασιλέως ἀγάπης τήν τε μητέρα καὶ τοὺς ὁμαίμονας καὶ τοὺς λοιποὺς συγγενεῖς ὡς βασιλειῶντας δῆθεν καὶ τὸ συνοῖσον αὐτῷ μὴ θέλοντας, Attal., p. 200). Very characteristically, Zon., III, p. 708, says that Nikephoritzes used the emperor as a slave (ἀνδράποδον).

[18] Skyl. Cont., p. 714; Zon., III, p. 712; cf. Ostrogorsky, *History*, p. 306.

[19] For the circumstances and the dating of these events see Polemis, op. cit., pp. 69–71.

[20] Attal., p. 303. Skout., p. 171, says that Michael was reluctantly made metropolitan of Ephesus and banished by Botaneiates to the island of Lesbos.

[21] For references see Grumel, *Regestes*, III, p. 29, no. 909.   [22] Skyl. Cont., pp. 738–9.

[23] Zon., III, p. 723, relates how Michael on his death bed was implored by his former wife Maria (now being a nun) to forgive her for her uncanonical marriage to Botaneiates. Chalandon, *Les Comnène*, I, p. 63, no. 4, dates this incident in c. 1091.

[24] *Alexias*, I, p. 54. Some western sources such as G. Malaterra, *De rebus gestis Rogerii Calabriae et Siciliae comitis et Roberti Guiscardi ducis fratris eius* (ed. E. Pontieri, *RIS*, v), p. 64, and *Platynae Historici* (ed. G. Gaida, *RIS*, III), p. 191, subscribe to the Norman tale that Michael after his expulsion travelled to Italy and begged the Pope and Guiscard to help him recover the throne.

[25] Psellos, II, pp. 174–5; *Alexias*, II, p. 34; Zon., III, p. 708.

[26] Σύνοψις τῶν νόμων διὰ στίχων ἰάμβων καὶ πολιτικῶν πρὸς τὸν βασιλέα καίσαρα Μιχαὴλ τὸν Δούκαν ἐκ προστάξεως τοῦ πατρὸς αὐτοῦ καὶ βασιλέως, PG, 122, cols 925–73. The word καίσαρα is obviously an error for κύριον. Another legal work is found ibid., cols. 919–24.

[27] Στίχοι πολιτικοὶ πρὸς τὸν βασιλέα κύριον Μιχαὴλ τὸν Δούκαν περὶ δόγματος, PG, 122, cols. 811–17.

And in addition to some chapters on theology,[28] apparently unpublished, there exist two other pieces on the titles of the Psalms,[29] identical in content but the first in prose and the second in political verse. A work on physics,[30] as well as the comprehensive Διδασκαλία Παντοδαπή,[31] was written for Michael's intellectual instruction. A collection of riddles[32] belongs to the same category.

Different from this type of didactic literature is a short Προσφωνηματικὸς λόγος to Michael,[33] obviously later than the year 1071, which appears to have been composed during the period of the author's disgrace. At the command of the same Michael, Psellos wrote in 1075 a piece on the famous miracle at the Blachernae.[34] Finally mention should be made of official documents written by Psellos in the name of the emperor.[35]

It is well known that apart from Psellos the other noted philosopher of the age Ioannes Italos also found much support and encouragement at court from both Michael and his two brothers.[36] At least one of Italos' writings, namely that concerning the immortality of the soul, was addressed to Michael.[37]

A few portraits of Michael as emperor survive. A miniature of the 14/15th century is purely imaginary,[38] but another one in cod. Athous 1268 (Pantokratoros 234) depicts him together with Psellos.[39] A third portrait shows the emperor with his wife being crowned by Christ.[40] The Holy Crown of Hungary, dated about 1075, includes among its several portraits in enamel one of Michael.[41]

[28] Cf. PG, 122, col. 510A. This must be different from a similar work entitled Πρὸς τὸν αὐτοκράτορα Μιχαὴλ κεφάλαια θεολογικὰ ἔνδεκα edited by Dositheos, Τόμος Ἀγάπης (Jassy, 1698), pp. 490–93.

[29] Scripta Minora, I, pp. 372–85 and 389–400.

[30] Πρὸς τὸν βασιλέα κύριον Μιχαὴλ τὸν Δούκαν ἐπιλύσεις σύντομοι φυσικῶν ζητημάτων, PG, 122, cols. 783–809.

[31] Michael Psellos, De Omnifaria Doctrina (ed. L. G. Westerink, Utrecht, 1948), p. 3; cf. Hussey, Church and Learning, pp. 78–9.

[32] Cf. PG, 122, col. 520C. In cod. Panteleemonos 141 (Athous 5647), fol. 128v, there are found Στίχοι πρὸς τὸν βασιλέα κῦρ Μιχαὴλ τοῦ Δούκα; see Sp. P. Lampros, Κατάλογος τῶν ἐν ταῖς βιβλιοθήκαις τοῦ Ἁγίου Ὄρους Ἑλληνικῶν κωδίκων (Cambridge, 1900), II, p. 300, who cites the opening line. These verses, seven altogether, have been published from another manuscript by Sophronios (Eustratiades), Πανδέκτη Νικολάου Καρατζᾶ λογοθέτου γενικοῦ τῆς τοῦ Χριστοῦ Μεγάλης Ἐκκλησίας, Ἐκκλησιαστικὸς Φάρος, 6 (1910), 85, under the title Τοῦ κυροῦ Μιχαὴλ τοῦ Ψελλοῦ πρὸς τὸν βασιλέα Μιχαήλ. Psellos informs Michael on the church's position with regard to the marriage between a man and his second cousin's daughter.

[33] Scripta Minora, I, pp. 42–4. Here Psellos expresses his joy at seeing the slanderings pronounced against him exposed.

[34] Edited by J. Bidez, Catalogue des Manuscrits alchimiques grecs, VI (Brussels, 1928), pp. 192–210.

[35] These are three chrysobulls to be found in Sathas, MB, IV, pp. 385–8 (Dölger, Regesten, II, p. 18, no. 989), pp. 388–92 (Dölger, Regesten, II, p. 18, no. 990), and in Scripta Minora, I, pp. 329–34 (Dölger, Regesten, II, p. 19, no. 1003) and a selention, also in Scripta Minora, I, pp. 351–55.

[36] Alexias, II, p. 34; cf. P. E. Stephanou, Jean Italos, Philosophe et Humaniste (Rome, 1949), p. 17; J. M. Hussey, Ascetics and Humanists in Eleventh-Century Byzantium (London, 1960), pp. 8–9.

[37] Ioannes Italos, Quaestiones Quodlibetales (ed. P. Joannou, Ettal, 1956), p. 63.

[38] It is one of a series devoted to Byzantine emperors in Cod. Estense (Modena) 122, fol. 274v, reproduced by Lampros, Λεύκωμα, plate 62.

[39] Ibid.

[40] Ibid. The portrait which is on enamel once belonged to the monastery of Gelati in Georgia. It bears the inscription Στέφω Μιχαὴλ σὺν Μαριὰμ χερσί μου. Cf. A. Grabar, L'Empereur dans l'Art byzantin (Paris, 1936), p. 118.

[41] It is accompanied by the traditional inscription Μιχαὴλ ἐν Χριστῷ πιστὸς βασιλεὺς Ῥωμαίων ὁ Δούκας. See Gy. Moravcsik, 'A magyar szent korona görög feliratai', Egyetemes Philológiai Közlöny, 59 (1935), 125 and plate VI; P. J. Kelleher, The Holy Crown of Hungary (Rome, 1951), p. 35 and plate XI, no. 23.

His seal bears the inscription 'Μιχαὴλ αὐτοκράτωρ 'Ρωμαίων ὁ Δούκας'.[42]
After he became emperor, Michael Doukas married a Caucasian princess
who took the name of Maria.[43] She bore him a son, Konstantinos 23.

15. N   (?--after 1059)

A son of Konstantinos 12 and Eudokia, younger than Michael 14 but older than
Andronikos 16, of unknown name died at an early age shortly after his father's
accession to the throne (24 November 1059). Psellos who provides the information praises his beauty.[1]

16. Andronikos Doukas (c. 1057–after 1081)

Andronikos was the third son of the emperor Konstantinos 12 and Eudokia
Makrembolitissa; he was born in about 1057.[1] Although standing very close
to the imperial government for perhaps the greater part of his life, he appears
to have played little part in either military or political affairs. Certainly the
sources pay little attention to him. Whenever he figures, it is mostly in a casual

[42] See G. Schlumberger, *Mélanges d'archéologie byzantine* (Paris, 1895), p. 262, no. 118; W. de
Gray Birch, *Catalogue of Seals in the Department of Mss. in the British Museum* (London, 1898), v,
p. 3, no. 17456.

[43] Matthew of Edessa, op. cit., p. 178, says that she was a daughter of the Georgian king
'Kourke' (George II, 1072–89). However, the authority on Georgian history M. Brosset,
Histoire de la Georgie depuis l'Antiquité jusqu'au XIXe Siècle, 1 (St Petersburg, 1849), pp. 330–1, n. 2,
believes that Maria was originally called Martha and was in fact a daughter of king Bagrat IV
(1027–72), but he wrongly dates her marriage in 1065. Tzetzes in his *Chiliades* (ed. Th. Kiessling,
Leipzig, 1825), v, vv. 590–1, speaks of her

σὺν τῇ δεσποίνῃ Μαριὰμ τῇ 'Αβασγίσσῃ λέγω
ἣν οἱ πολλοὶ 'Αλάνισσαν φασὶν οὐκ ἀκριβοῦντες

Cf. Bryen., p. 56. A description of Maria's rare beauty is found in *Alexias*, 1, pp. 107–8. It has
already been noted that after the abdication of Michael she uncanonically married Botaneiates
(cf. B. Leib, 'Nicéphore III Botaneiatès (1078–1081) et Marie d'Alanie', *Actes du VIe Congrès
International d'Etudes Byzantines*, I [Paris, 1950], pp. 129–40), and after 1081 she enjoyed for a while
the highly suspicious favours and affection of Alexios I Komnenos. Maria died as a nun in
obscurity sometime after 1090 (cf. Zon., III, p. 723, see above n.23). A miniature of her together
with Botaneiates has been preserved in cod. Coisl. 79, fol. IV (see the coloured reproduction in
Lampros Λεύκωμα, plate 63). It has also been established that cod. Athous 129 (Hagiou Paulou
2), which bears the supplication Σταυρέ, φύλαττε βασίλισσαν Μαρίαν, once belonged to her.
See A. Papadopoulos-Kerameus, , 'Ανύπαρκτος κῶδιξ Μαρίας βασιλίσσης τοῦ 8000ῦ ἔτους,
BZ, 14 (1905), 269–70. A third miniature of Maria, holding her infant son, was known to
Papadopoulos-Kerameus from another manuscript (psalterion). In the Παιδεία Βασιλική
(Institutio Regia) of Theophylaktos Hephaistos, written for Konstantinos 23 at the request of
Maria, a chapter is devoted to her piety and her noble ancestry, see *PG*, 126, col. 260B.

15. [1] Psellos, II, p. 148.

16. [1] Psellos, II, p. 148. When Psellos wrote the concluding part of his *Chronographia*, that is in
c. 1075, Andronikos 'had just entered his manhood' (ibid., p. 179), which might point to c. 1057.
In Psellos' monody (see n. 2) it is asserted that the prince had ἐκ σπαργάνων σχεδὸν τὸ βασιλεύειν
λαχών (cod. Par. gr. 1182, fol. 179v), a remark which only makes sense if it is borne in mind that
Andronikos was born very shortly before his father's accession.

or decorative fashion.[2] Despite the laudatory descriptions of Psellos, he appears to have been an insignificant and incompetent person who even in his own milieu failed to make his presence felt.

Strangely enough and in contrast to his two other sons, the emperor never crowned Andronikos. Thus he did not participate as a junior co-emperor in the interim regency of Eudokia after the death of his father Konstantinos *12*. It was Romanos IV Diogenes who placed Andronikos on an equal footing with his brothers[3] soon after he came to the throne. Yet in contrast to Konstantios *17*, the co-emperorship of Andronikos evidently made an impression on the popular mind, and his name is included in some lists of Byzantine emperors.[4] Romanos himself was undoubtedly moved by pure expediency. In his expedition to eastern Asia Minor in the summer of 1068, he kept Andronikos as a hostage,[5] obviously to prevent possible movements against him by other members of the Doukas family who were staying in Constantinople. Andronikos continued as co-emperor during the early years of Michael's *14* reign; he even seems to have been promoted at the expense of Konstantios *17*.[6]

Andronikos had studied under Psellos.[7] In a little personal sketch Psellos praises his dexterity in horsemanship and in hunting, sports which other members of the family also enjoyed.[8] Apart from this monody, other works exist which were written especially for Andronikos and in particular for his education. Psellos composed a brief treatise on geometry for him[9] and Ioannes Italos two philosophical essays, one concerning dialectic[10] and the other dealing with the interpretation of an Homeric passage on dreams.[11]

[2] Principal references are Psellos, ii, pp. 148 and 179–80; Attal., p. 106; Skyl. Cont., p. 670; Skout., pp. 166–8. In addition there is an unpublished fragmentary monody on Andronikos by Psellos, entitled Ἑτέρα μονῳδία εἰς τὸν βασιλέα κῦρ ᾿Ανδρόνικον τὸν Δούκαν for which cf. D. I. Polemis, 'Notes on Eleventh-Century Chronology (1059–1081)', *BZ*, 58 (1965), 74.

[3] Attal., p. 106; Skyl. Cont., p. 670; Skout., p. 167; cf. F. Dölger in *Paraspora* (Ettal, 1961), p. 216. In a coin depicting Romanos and Eudokia with the three Doukas brothers (for references see above Michael *14*, n. 13) Andronikos appears on Michael's *14* left, and this position may indicate that as the youngest βασιλεύς of the three he gave precedence to the other two.

[4] His name appears between those of Romanos IV and Michael VII *14* in the lists of emperors commemorated in the synodica of the unknown bishopric suffragan of Athens (Euripos ?), of Cyprus (12th century), and of Rhodes (13th century). See S. Eustratiades, Τὸ συνοδικὸν τῆς ᾿Εκκλησίας τῆς ῾Ελλάδος, *EEBΣ*, 13 (1937), p. 14; N. Cappuyns, 'Le Synodicon de Chypre au XIIe siècle', *B*, 10 (1935), p. 491; idem., 'Le Synodicon de l'église de Rhodes au XIIIe siècle', *EO*, 33 (1934), 200.

[5] Attal., p. 106; Skyl. Cont., p. 670.

[6] For references see the sketch on Konstantios *17*, n. 8.

[7] In the above mentioned monody Psellos exclaims: Ὤμοι τοῦ καλλίστου τῶν φοιτητῶν, μᾶλλον δὲ τοῦ κορυφαίου τῆς περὶ ἐμὲ μουσικῆς χορείας, fol. 41r. He also remarks that Andronikos' personal interests were directed towards the study of philosophy and sports. In both he distinguished himself.

[8] Psellos, ii, pp. 179–80; cf. the monody, fol. 179v.

[9] ᾿Απόκρισις σχεδιασθεῖσα πρὸς τὸν κυρὸν ᾿Ανδρόνικον ἐρωτήσαντα περὶ τοῦ τῆς γεωμετρίας μαθήματος ποῖον τὸ τέλος αὐτῆς, edited in J. F. Boissonade, Ψελλός (Nuremberg, 1838), pp. 159–63. Here Andronikos is called αὐτοκράτωρ (p. 159).

[10] ᾿Ιωάννου τοῦ ᾿Ιταλοῦ πρὸς τὸν βασιλέα κῦρ ᾿Ανδρόνικον ἐρωτήσαντα περὶ διαλεκτικῆς, edited by G. Cereteli, *Iohannis Itali Opuscula Selecta*, i, (Tiflis, 1942), pp. 1–28; cf. Hussey, *Church and Learning*, p. 92.

[11] Εἰς τὸν βασιλέα ᾿Ανδρόνικον ἀπορήσαντα, τί ἐστιν ὅ φησιν ῞Ομηρος τῶν ὀνείρων τοὺς μὲν ἐκ κεράτων, τοὺς δὲ ἐξ ἐλεφάντων εἶναι, Cereteli, op. cit., pp. 29–31; cf. P. Joannou, *Ioannes Italos, Quaestiones Quodlibetales* (Ettal, 1956), p. 53.

Andronikos married an unknown woman who died very shortly after his death.[12]

17. Konstantios Doukas (1060–81)

Konstantios was the youngest son of the emperor Konstantinos X *12*, born late in 1060, less than a year after his father had ascended the throne.[1] He was therefore a porphyrogenitus and was known as such to his contemporaries. His Christian name has been preserved in two forms: some sources call him Konstantinos while others employ the variant Konstantios. A reference to the form Konstantios exists in a manuscript colophon of 1060/1, that is less than a year after he had been born.[2] This appears to support that particular form of the name, especially as it was also extremely unusual for children in Byzantium to be named after living parents.

Zonaras says that Konstantios was crowned by his father immediately after his birth and treated so before his brothers were.[3] Zonaras does of course largely draw on Psellos but it is not clear whether this particular information can be traced to him, as is often thought.[4] Yet most probably Konstantinos X *12* did

---

[12] Ἡ μὲν γὰρ γαμετή . . . εὐθὺς μετὰ σὲ ἐπὶ σὲ μεταβέβηκε, cod. Par. gr. 1182, fol. 41r. This passage indicates that in spite of its character the monody, at least in its surviving form, was not written for Andronikos' funeral. It is hard to imagine that these words could have been spoken over the dead man's coffin. Some period, however short, must have elapsed between husband and wife's deaths. But on the other hand, the repeated rhetorical phrase 'Here lies an emperor' excludes the possibility of regarding the work as a mere expression of the author's grief or simply as a means of consoling Eudokia. It was pronounced by Psellos himself—the autobiographical element provides ample proof of this—most probably in the course of a commemoration service (μνημόσυνον) on Andronikos' grave sometime after his death.

Since writing this, the monody has been published by P. Gautier, 'Monodie inédite de Michel Psellos sur le basileus Andronic Doucas,' *REB*, 24 (1966), 153–70, who argues that the two fragments belong to two different monodies of Psellos.

17. [1] For references see D. I. Polemis, 'Notes on Eleventh-Century Chronology (1059–1081)', *BZ*, 58 (1965), 72, n. 71.

[2] Ibid., n. 70. For references to the two forms see N. Oikonomidès, 'Le serment de l'impératrice Eudocie (1067): Un épisode de l'histoire dynastique de Byzance', *REB*, 21 (1963), 116–17.

[3] Ὅθεν οὗτος (sc. Konstantios) καὶ πορφυρογέννητος ἦν, ὃν αὐτίκα καὶ πρὸ τῶν ἄλλων τοῖς βασιλικοῖς παρασήμοις ἐκόσμησεν, εἶτα καὶ τοὺς λοιποὺς ἀνηγόρευσε, Zon., III, p. 681. In this passage Zonaras wrongly implies that Andronikos *16* was also crowned by his father. This is not so.

[4] In describing the birth of Konstantios, Psellos writes: Μετὰ δὲ τὴν βασιλείαν, οὔπω ἡλίου τὸν ἐνιαύσιον κύκλον περιοδεύσαντος ὁμοῦ δὲ τίκτεται παιδίον τῷ βασιλεῖ, καὶ τοῦ βασιλείου εὐθὺς καταξιοῦται ὀνόματος, Psellos, II, p. 148. The phrase τοῦ βασιλείου εὐθὺς καταξιοῦται ὀνόματος is rather ambiguous. The modern translators of the *Chronographia* take it as referring to a coronation and render that Konstantios 'fut aussitôt jugé digne de l'empire' (Renauld, ibid.) or he was 'at once dignified with the imperial title' (*The Chronographia of Michael Psellos*, translated from the Greek by E. R. A. Sewter [London, 1953], p. 260). See also J. Seger, *Byzantinische Historiker des zehnten und elften Jahrhunderts. 1.–Nikephoros Bryennios* (Munich, 1888), p. 122; Aik. Christophilopoulou, Ἐκλογή, ἀναγόρευσις καὶ στέψις τοῦ Βυζαντινοῦ αὐτοκράτορος (Athens, 1955), p. 117; H. Bibicou in *B*, 29/30 (1959/60), 55, n. 3, who also assume that Konstantios received the imperial dignity before Michael *14*. The unprecedented act of designating a youngest son as heir apparent—since the supposed coronation cannot mean anything else in the case of the infant Konstantios—in complete disregard of the rights of two elder sons, presumably for no other reason than simply because he happened to be a porphyrogenitus, would have constituted a novel conception in the Byzantine tradition of imperial succession.

treat his porphyrogenitus son in a special manner and after he had crowned Michael *14* it is likely that he also bestowed the imperial dignity upon Konstantios.[5] Consequently in the first regency of Eudokia (22 May–31 December 1067) Konstantios officially appears as sharing the throne together with Michael *14* and their mother,[6] but we must assume that he occupied the lowest in the imperial hierarchy. He continued to enjoy the same position during the reign of Romanos IV (1068–71) the only difference being that the lowest place in this nominal co-emperorship was now occupied by Andronikos *16*.[7]

Information concerning the position of Konstantios in the reign of Michael VII *14* (1071–8) is somewhat confused. In the first place, at least during the early years, he acted as junior co-emperor together with Andronikos *16*. The signatures of both appear in an imperial document, and since that of Konstantios comes last[8] it might with some justification be inferred that, in contrast to his earlier higher position, he was now demoted to the third place. Some support for this view is found in Konstantios' own allegations, made a few years

When thinking of a younger son's elevation to the throne, the case of Manuel I Komnenos naturally comes to mind. He became emperor at his dying father's wish and in disregard of the seniority of his brother Isaakios. See Kinn., pp. 23–5, and Chon., pp. 61–2, but cf. R. Browning, 'The Death of John II Comnenus', *B*, 31 (1961), especially pp. 234–5. But the fact remains that the rights of an elder surviving son were as a rule respected, even if this happened to be contrary to the sovereign's own wish. Some two hundred years after the birth of Konstantios Doukas, Michael VIII Palaiologos greatly desired to leave the throne to his favourite youngest son Konstantinos *148*, likewise a porphyrogenitus, but the junior position of the prince proved an insurmountable obstacle. Greg., I, p. 187, makes the point perfectly clear: ... εἰ μὴ τὸ ὑστερογενὲς μέγα πρὸ ποδῶν ἔκειτο κώλυμα, αὐτὸν (sc. Κωνσταντῖνον) ἂν μάλα ἀσμένως τῶν βασιλικῶν σκήπτρων ἐδείκνυ διάδοχον ὁ πατήρ (sc. Michael).

To return to Psellos, I do not believe that by βασίλειον ὄνομα he meant a coronation. Whenever he speaks of such ceremonies, he is explicit and more detailed. See his references to the imperial nominations of Romanos III Argyros (I, pp. 31–2), Michael IV Paphlagon (I, p. 54), Michael V Kalaphates (I, p. 88), and Michael VII Doukas (II, p. 148). Βασίλειον ὄνομα can also be the baptismal name of the βασιλεύς and in this case the name of the reigning emperor, that is Konstantinos. It seems then that what Psellos intended to convey was that Konstantinos *12* baptized his newly-born son with the 'imperial name', that is called him Konstantinos-Konstantios. Zonaras, otherwise confused in this description (cf. above n. 3), probably misunderstood Psellos.

---

[5] Anna in *Alexias*, I, p. 161, mentions him as ταινίας τῷ τότε καιρῷ βασιλικῆς παρὰ τοῦ πατρὸς ἀξιωθείς: Cf. Skout., p. 165.

[6] For references see above Michael *14*, n. 9.

[7] This is evident from Konstantios' position in a coin of the period where he is placed on Michael's *14* right. See above Michael *14*, n. 13.

[8] *Scripta Minora*, I, p. 334. H. Bibicou 'Une page d'histoire diplomatique de Byzance au XIe siècle: Michel VII Doukas, Robert Guiscard et la pension des dignitaires', *B*, 29/30 (1959/60), 56–7, considers the signature Κωνσταντῖνος ἐν Χριστῷ τῷ Θεῷ πιστὸς βασιλεὺς Ῥωμαίων ὁ Δούκας of this chrysobull as being not Konstantios but Konstantinos *23*. This is hardly acceptable. In the first place the form Κωνσταντῖνος is inaccurate for the sole manuscript of the document has Κωνστάντιος. Furthermore, Psellos writing his history in *c*. 1075 (for the date see J. M. Hussey, 'Michael Psellus, the Byzantine Historian', *Speculum*, 10 [1935], 83), that is after the chrysobull was drawn up, still calls Konstantios a βασιλεύς (Psellos, II, p. 180). Similarly, William of Apulia, III, 1–3 (ed. M. Matthieu, Palermo, 1961, p. 164) also regards him as co-emperor:

' ... Michael Romani iura regebat
imperii cum fratre suo, qui nomine dictus
Constantinus erat.'

But cf. H. Antoniadi-Bibicou, 'Note sur l'un des signataires du chrysobulle de Michael VII Doukas en faveur de Robert Guiscard', *REB*, 23 (1965), 244–51.

later, that he had been badly treated by Michael *14*,[9] although this may of course refer to some other incident. Despite these apparent ill favours, Konstantios may have occasionally been regarded as successor to the throne prior to the birth of the emperor's son Konstantinos *23*. He, rather than the elder Andronikos *16*, had been suggested by the emperor to Robert Guiscard as prospective bridegroom for one of the Norman chief's daughters. Two letters with similar content, written by Psellos, put forward the respective matrimonial proposals.[10] Although these plans fell through, they do nevertheless indicate that Konstantios' official position was such that his marriage would be considered as an effective means of appeasing Byzantium's most formidable enemy. Two years later, after Michael's *14* son was born, similar propositions were made to Guiscard, but Konstantios was no longer the topic of the new and delicate negotiations. Apparently his own position at court had now been taken by the younger porphyrogenitus whom his father hoped to marry to another of the Norman leader's daughters.

Konstantios Doukas is again heard of in 1077 as the friend and associate of Alexios Komnenos. Much as he was wished to see Alexios married to his sister Zoe *20*, Konstantios was unable to achieve this.[11] The two men appear as comrades-in-arms late in 1077 during the siege of Constantinople by the forces of Ioannes Bryennios. With a handful of men, both were entrusted with the responsibility of guarding the land walls of the city. A timely and courageous surprise sally by Alexios resulted in a spectacular capture of some twenty soldiers of the enemy and won him high praise from the Byzantines, including the emperor himself. Konstantios, we are told, unable to share in this triumph, became both annoyed and envious and blamed his friend for not having invited him to join him in the successful ambush.[12]

A few months later, when the final stage in the revolt of Nikephoros Botaneiates was reached, Michael *14*, being about to abdicate, seriously thought of offering his crumbling throne to Konstantios. No doubt he had already lost all hope of securing it for his own son. Presumably without his brother's knowledge,

---

[9] Bryen., pp. 124–5. Attal., p. 305, claim that Konstantios τῆς βασιλευούσης πόλεως καὶ τῶν ἀνακτόρων παρὰ τοῦ συγγόνου (sc. Michael *14*) ἀπείργετο καὶ πρὸς τὴν ἀντίπεραν ἠλαύνετο θάλασσαν certainly refers to a possible semi-exile of his some years later.

[10] The letters were edited for the first time by K. N. Sathas, 'Deux lettres inédites de l'empereur Michel Doukas Parapinace à Robert Guiscard rédigées par M. Psellus', *Annuaire de l'Association pour l'Encouragement des Etudes Grecques*, 8 (1874), 193–221, and again in *MB*, v, pp. 385–92, who correctly considered them to be addressed to the Norman chief. This attribution was immediately challenged by V. G. Vasilievskii, 'Dva pis'ma vizantiiskago imperatora Mikhaila VII Duki k Vsevolodu Yaroslavichu', *Zhurnal Ministerstva Narodnogo Prosveshcheniya*, 182 (December 1875), 270–315, in favour of the Kievan prince. E. Kurtz, reviewing the article in *BZ*, 3 (1894), 630–33, accepted Vasilievskii's opinion, but Chalandon, *Les Comnène*, i, pp. 61–2, and *Histoire de la Domination normande en Italie et en Sicile* (Paris, 1907), i pp. 260–64, reverted to the original view of Sathas. This is also accepted by Dölger, *Regesten*, ii, p. 18, nos. 989–90, who dates the letters in 1072–3, by L. Bréhier, *Vie et mort de Byzance* (Paris, 1947), p. 241, by M. Matthieu, 'Les faux Diogènes', *B*, 22 (1952), 141–3, and again in *Guillaume de Pouille, La Geste de Robert Guiscard* (Palermo, 1961), p. 306, and by Bibicou, op. cit., p. 56, no. 3. On the other hand, the old theory of Vasilievskii still finds some favour, mainly among students of Russian history. See F. Drexl in *BZ*, 41 (1941), 299, n. 1; G. Vernadsky, *A History of Russia*. ii. — *Kievan Russia* (New Haven, 1948), p. 351; *The Russian Primary Chronicle*. Laurentian text translated and edited by S. H. Cross and O. P. Sherbowitz-Wetzor (Cambridge, Mass., 1953), pp. 273–4.

[11] Bryen., p. 107.   [12] Bryen., pp. 115–16.

the emperor expressed this wish to Alexios Komnenos, who for his part seemed to favour such a change and at once tried to secure a written pledge from Michael *14*. This was immediately granted, and Alexios rushed to Konstantios urging him to hurry to the palace and take possession of the throne as Michael *14* was now preparing to enter a monastery. Konstantios could not however be persuaded. Knowing that Botaneiates' arrival was imminent and hoping to secure certain favours from him, he decided to turn down the risky offer. He thought it wiser to proceed to the camp of the rebel and salute him as the new emperor.[13] Therefore, on the eve of Botaneiates' entrance to Constantinople, i.e. on 2 April 1078,[14] Konstantios accompanied by Alexios crossed the Bosphorus and came to the headquarters of the rebel at Prainetos (now Kara Mürsel) on the southern shores of the Gulf of Nicomedia.[15] Botaneiates received the unexpected newcomers coolly. Alexios spoke first and began to explain how badly his friend had fared at the hands of Michael *14* and added that Konstantios was now hoping for better times and looking forward to being shown some paternal kindness. Seizing the opportunity, Konstantios himself stressed that no matter how his brother disliked him, he could never entertain any thought of being unfaithful to him as emperor, and he promised a similar 'unshaken loyalty' to the new sovereign.[16]

Botaneiates was satisfied with this profession of loyalty, and once on the throne he did not disappoint Konstantios whom he treated, if not in a fatherly manner, at least with friendship. According to Attaleiates, he had him regularly invited in the palace as a companion at his table, and still more important, he left his properties and revenues untouched.[17]

But this good relationship did not last. Konstantios could not forget his background and especially the fact that he had once been so close to the throne and

[13] Bryen., pp. 124–5; cf. Dölger, *Regesten*, II, p. 20, no. 1009.
[14] Botaneiates arrived on 3 April 1078, cf. Polemis, op. cit., p. 71.
[15] On Botaneiates' itinerary I have preferred the evidence of the better informed Attaleiates to that of Bryennios who makes him stop at the palace of Rufinianai in the suburbs of Chalcedon and puts Konstantios' encounter with him there.
[16] Bryen., pp. 124–5.
[17] Cf. Attal., p. 305. The explicit statement that Konstantios' fortune remained intact raises the question as to whether Botaneiates actually laid a hand on the properties of the other members of the Doukas family.
It is difficult, in view of the available evidence, to accept what Bryennios has to say in his introduction (especially pp. 6–11) on the efforts of Alexios Komnenos to do justice to Konstantios and to have him received as the lawful successor of Botaneiates. The beginning of this introduction is missing and in addition the text suffers from several lacunae. Moreover, the author's confusion of Konstantios with the son of Michael *14* (in p. 11 it is said that the porphyrogenitus concerned was betrothed to the daughter of Alexios) makes one doubt traditional interpretations of this passage (for instance see G. Buckler, *Anna Comnena: A Study* [London, 1929], p. 30; H. Grégoire in the translation of Bryennios in *B*, 23 [1953], 469–73). I believe that the author here had Konstantinos *23* in mind throughout (cf. *Alexias*, I, pp. 66–8). It is hardly conceivable that a person of nearly twenty years, such as Konstantios, could be referred to as παιδίον (Bryen., p. 7), or that the φυσικῶς ἐπὶ ταύτην (sc. βασιλείαν) δικαιούμενος (ibid., p. 6) is the brother and not the son of the former emperor. Besides there is also an obvious inconsistency. The account of Bryennios presupposes unfriendly relations between Botaneiates and Konstantios, whereas, up to the revolt of the latter, this was not so. Seger, op. cit., p. 96, writes: 'Der Verfasser der Vorrede kennt also offenbar nur einen Konstantin Porphyrogennetos, den er für den Bruder Michaels hält, aber mit vielen Zügen aus dem Leben des anderen (sc. Konstantinos *23*)'. But it is rather the opposite which is true.

he began to have new aspirations. Consequently when opportunity arose, he did not hesitate to make use of this.

Probably in the spring of 1079[18] Botaneiates despatched a small army to Nicaea for the purpose of proceeding further inland against the Seljuks. This expeditionary force, being limited in strength, refused to start military operations unless it was reinforced. The emperor was therefore compelled to enlarge it with a number of ἀθάνατοι[19] well-trained for warfare but undisciplined and of questionable loyalty. These crossed to Chrysopolis, and were expected to join the forces already on their way. Konstantios Doukas was assigned to this campaign but certainly not as commander in chief.[20] He joined the army at Chrysopolis and in some way or another succeeded in inducing some of the troops to proclaim him emperor. But this act, far from gaining general support in the army, immediately caused a fierce fight among the soldiers; Konstantios' backers only prevailed after a nine-hour struggle. The alarming news quickly reached Constantinople, and Botaneiates made hurried efforts to cope with this disturbing development. Fortunately for him the revolt did not spread to the capital. All available soldiers in Constantinople were mustered and special precautions were taken to prevent the rebel from crossing into Europe and entering the City. Yet the rebellion was only extinguished after Botaneiates had managed to win over some of the participants. These, after having been promised a pardon, renounced allegiance to Konstantios and handed him over to the emperor. He was forcibly made a monk and was then banished to an unspecified island.[21]

Obviously Konstantios' confinement to his unknown monastery came to an end with Botaneiates' fall. After Alexios Komnenos won the crown (1 April 1081), he was at once transferred from his island of exile to a responsible position in the army. He is mentioned among those military commanders who in the Norman war advised Alexios to continue the incessant fight against Guiscard.[22]

---

[18] For the date see Polemis, op. cit., pp. 72–3.

[19] For the ἀθάνατοι see Bryen., pp. 133–4.

[20] This becomes evident from Attal., p. 307, who says that in the disturbances that followed the leader of the army happened to be still in Constantinople. The information of Skyl. Cont., p. 742 and Zon., III, p. 724, who respectively call Konstantios στρατηγὸς and στρατάρχης of these forces, is probably due to a misunderstanding.

[21] The whole affair is related at some length by Attal., pp. 305–9, who uses it as an excuse to praise Botaneiates, and it is repeated in an abridged form by Skyl. Cont., p. 742, and Zon., III, p. 724. The last two sources report a rumour according to which Konstantios, after being confined to his monastery, was eventually ordained priest. This, however, cannot be accepted since two years later he is found in the army.

It is hard to believe that Konstantios when barely nineteen years old would have ventured to revolt alone without some sort of encouragement from others, more responsible and more experienced than himself. Who were these πονηρότατοι σύμβουλοι (Attal., p. 307) who incited him to follow the dangerous course? In the absence of more information it is useless to speculate on their identity. But one cannot overlook the fact that Alexios Komnenos had by that time already turned his ambitions towards the crown. Konstantios was a friend of his and once Alexios had ascended the throne he had him quickly rescued from the monastery. Konstantios, himself a former junior co-emperor and a recent candidate, undeniably had substantial claims which could not be ignored. Could the curious proclamation at Chrysopolis have been cleverly engineered by Alexios for the sole purpose of discrediting Konstantios, thus removing a potential rival?

[22] Alexias, I, p. 155. For temporary confinements in Byzantine monasteries see especially Hussey, Church and Learning, pp. 162–3 and 180.

But he did not survive this war. Very shortly afterwards, on 18 October 1081, in a bloody engagement before Dyrrachion he was killed together with another valiant comrade, Nikephoros Synadenos, who was betrothed to Konstantios' sister Zoe *20*.[23] Speaking of his death, William of Apulia adds that he was buried with 'the proper honours'.[24]

Konstantios Doukas died young, but his brief life does at least indicate that as a person he had more admirable qualities than either of his brothers. Psellos, who knew him intimately, devotes a character sketch to him,[25] in which he praises him for his dexterity in horsemanship and in hunting. The same author also wrote a medical treatise for his instruction.[26]

No known portrait or seal of Konstantios appear to have been preserved.[27] There is also no evidence that he married.

18. Anna (before 1057–after 1075)

Anna was the eldest daughter of the emperor Konstantinos X *12* and his second wife Eudokia.[1] She entered a monastery and was still there when Psellos wrote his *Chronographia*.[2]

---

[23] *Alexias*, I, p. 161.

[24]   'Occidit hoc bello regni spoliatus honore
        Constantinus et est subhumatus honore decenti', *La Geste de Robert Guiscard*, IV, vv. 432–3 (p. 226). His death is also reported by other western sources, which confuse him with Konstantinos *23*. Cf. Matthieu, ibid., p. 323, and in *B*, 22 (1952), 137, n. 4.

[25] Psellos, II, p. 180.

[26] Ἰατρικόν πρὸς Κωνσταντῖνον τὸν Πορφυρογέννητον, see L. Allatius, 'De Psellis et eorum scriptis diatriba', *PG*, 122, col. 523A.

[27] E. Darkó, 'Der Konstantinos der ungarischen heiligen Krone', *Hoffilerov Zbornik* (= *Serta Hoffilleriana*, Zagreb, 1940), pp. 437–41, has attempted to show that the co-emperor Konstantinos portrayed in the Holy Crown of Hungary is Konstantios, but in my opinion this cannot be so. See the chapter on Konstantinos *23*, n. 26.

18. [1] Skyl. Cont., p. 659; Glykas, p. 607; Skout., p. 165 (wrong account); Ioel (Bonn), p. 65.

[2] Psellos, II, p. 148. At first glance, Psellos' account of the female issue of Konstantinos *12* might appear inconsistent with the information supplied by the other sources (cf. the editor ibid., p. 148, n. 1). However, a closer examination of his narrative shows that this is not precisely so. He (ch. XX) speaks of the children born to Konstantinos *12 prior* to his accession and rightly alludes to the three sons and the two daughters whom he fails to name, but he adds that the younger daughter was already married (presumably Theodora *19*) while the elder had taken the veil. In the following section (ch. XXI) Psellos begins to speak of the children born to the emperor *after* he received the crown. He refers to the birth of Konstantios *17* but then abruptly turns to Michael's *14* coronation without any mention of the child born afterwards, i.e. Zoe *20*. Having missed his opportunity here, Psellos omits any reference to her at all. That Zoe *20* is not one of the daughters already mentioned is also supported by the fact that she was neither a nun nor was she married when the second part of the *Chronographia* was composed, i.e. in *c*. 1075. Indeed she is called παρθένος . . . καὶ τῷ εἴδει εὐπρεπής (Skyl. Cont., p. 738) in 1078, and it was a few years later that she married Adrianos Komnenos (see the relevant account).

Psellos, loc. cit., does not name Anna but calls her ἀρετῆς φερώνυμος which is of course wrong if taken to denote the Hebrew name of Hannah. Yet it is possible that he took the word as meaning 'virtue' instead of the correct 'grace'. On the other hand, the word ἀρετή used as a first name in Byzantium is very rare (some examples of it dating from the fourteenth century can be found in L. Petit, *Actes de Xénophon* [St Petersburg, 1903], pp. 44 and 50, and Bompaire, *Actes de Xeropotamou, passim*), but it may have been Anna's name in monastic life.

19. Theodora (before 1059–after 1075)

Theodora was the second-born daughter of Konstantinos X *12* and Eudokia,[1] but very little is heard of her. After 1071 she was given in marriage to the Venetian doge Domenico Silvio (1070–84) who on the occasion received the high Byzantine dignity of *protoproedros*.[2] She was still alive when Psellos wrote his account of her father in his history.[3] It is not known whether she had any children.

20. Zoe (*c.* 1062–before 1136)

Zoe, the third daughter of Konstantinos *12* and Eudokia,[1] is explicitly called a πορφυρογέννητος[2] and was presumably the youngest child of the imperial couple.[3] In 1077 her brother Konstantios *17* tried to induce Alexios Komnenos to marry her, but the latter chose Eirene *26*.[4] Again after the accession of Botaneiates (1078), Zoe was among the bridal candidates (including her mother) for the aged and widowed emperor who however selected the ex-empress Maria.[5] Then she seems to have been betrothed to Nikephoros Synadenos, but his death in October 1081 left her once more without a prospective husband.[6]

19. [1] Skyl. Cont., p. 659; Glykas, p. 607; Skout., p. 165 (wrong account); Ioel (Bonn) p. 65.

[2] Ducange, *Familiae*, p. 165; cf. P. Kretschmayr, *Geschichte von Venedig*, 1 (Gotha, 1905), p. 156; S. Romanin, *Storia documentata di Venezia*, 1 (Venice, 1912²), pp. 310–11.

[3] Psellos, II, p. 148. Cf. above Anna *18*, n. 2.

In his *Opuscula varia* Peter Damianus devotes a chapter to an unnamed Byzantine wife of a Venetian doge who on account of her voluptuous way of life ended her days miserably ('De Veneti ducis uxore, quae prius nimium delicata, demum toto corpore computruit', *PL*, 145, col. 744). The story is repeated by such later chroniclers as Andrea Dandulo, *Chronicon* (RIS, XII), p. 215 and Marino Sanudo, *Le vite dei dogi* (RIS, XXII), p. 155. This Byzantine princess is occasionally thought to be Theodora, see for instance Ph. Koukoules, Βυζαντινῶν βίος καὶ πολιτισμός, v (Athens, 1952), p. 148. But this cannot be so, as Peter Damianus died on 22/23 February 1072, and thus could not have written on the death of Theodora, who certainly passed away some years later. The 'Opusculum quinquagesimum' which includes the section on the doge's wife is thought to have been composed in 1059 long before the author's death (cf. F. Dressler, *Petrus Damiani: Leben und Werk* [Rome, 1954], p. 240) and must refer to another Byzantine princess, Maria, a sister of the emperor Romanos III Argyros, who was married to the doge Pietro Orseolo earlier in the century.

20. [1] Skyl. Cont., p. 659; Glykas, p. 607; Skout., p. 165 (wrong account); Ioel (Bonn), p. 65.

[2] *Alexias*, I, p. 108.

[3] Konstantios *17* was born less than a year after his father became emperor, and it is therefore extremely unlikely that Zoe was his senior. Speaking of Alexios' betrothal to Eirene *26*, Bryen., p. 107, says, ἦν γὰρ αὐτῷ (sc. Κωνσταντίῳ *17*) ἀδελφὴ πρεσβυτέρα, Ζωὴ τὸ ὄνομα, which implies that she was older than her porphyrogenitus brother. However, in view of Anna Komnene's evidence that Zoe was a porphyrogenita (also somewhat supported by Psellos' account, cf. above Anna *18*, n. 2) the information of Bryennios must be discounted as inexact. Yet the author could have *originally* meant that Zoe was older than Eirene *26*, but this interpretation is impossible in the present wording of the text.

[4] Bryen., p. 107; cf. Chalandon, *Les Comnène*, I, p. 33.

[5] Skyl. Cont., p. 738, who on the occasion extols her beauty; cf. *Alexias*, I, p. 108.

[6] *Alexias*, I, p. 161.

A little later Zoe, thanks to the efforts of her half brother Nikephoros Diogenes, finally married the emperor's younger brother Adrianos Komnenos.[7] Adrianos who was created *protosebastos* and acted as *megas domestikos tēs Dyseōs* became a well-known military figure. At the end of his life he took the monastic habit with the name of Ioannes and died on 19 April 1105.[8] The date of Zoe's death is not known, but it was certainly before 1136.[9]

By her marriage to Adrianos Komnenos, Zoe appears to have become the mother of at least one daughter of unknown name.[10]

21. Andronikos Doukas (before 1045–1077)

Of the two sons of the Caesar Ioannes *13* and his wife Eirene, Andronikos was the elder[1] as well as the more outstanding. Born sometime before 1045,[2] he was named after his paternal grandfather Andronikos *11*.[3] He appears to have devoted himself exclusively to a military career and in the course of his life took part in many campaigns. In the sources he is occasionally called a *protovestiarios*,[4] but by this period the designation no longer implied specific responsibilities;[5] consequently it must be regarded as a highly honorary title conferred upon a trusted relative of the imperial family. In addition, Andronikos also carried the equally important senatorial dignity of *protoproedros*.[6]

We do not hear of Andronikos' activities prior to 1071. In that year he accompanied Romanos IV Diogenes in his last disastrous campaign in Asia Minor and at Mantzikert the command of the rear imperial regiments, consisting of the

---

[7] *Alexias*, I, p. 176.

[8] See a manuscript notice edited by B. de Montfaucon, *Palaeographia Graeca* (Paris, 1708), p. 47.

[9] She is mentioned as dead in the *Typikon* of the Pantokrator monastery which was written in 1136. See Dmitrievskii, *Typika*, p. 662.

[10] In a letter of Theophylaktos of Bulgaria in *PG*, 126, col. 405, reference is made to a dead son-in-law (γαμβρός) of Adrianos. It is possible that this daughter of Zoe became the wife of Andronikos *136*.

21. [1] Psellos, II, p. 168; Bryen., pp. 51 and 100; *Alexias*, I, p. 11.

[2] When his mother Eirene died (1060/66), Andronikos was already married and had two sons, see *Scripta Minora*, II, pp. 179 and 188.

[3] Ibid., p. 168.

[4] Bryen., p. 107; Skout., p. 177; MM, v, p. 376 (=*PG*, 127, col. 1093C); MM, vi, pp. 4 and 5; seal (see below). Cf. R. Guilland, 'Fonctions et dignités des eunuques', *EB*, 2 (1944), 210–11. Needless to say, a clearcut distinction should be made between the titles of *protovestiarios* and *protovestiarites* (cf. F. Dölger, *Beiträge zur byzantinischen Finanzverwaltung, besonders des 10. und 11. Jahrhunderts* [Leipzig, 1927], p. 32); it is therefore through either a corrupted text or a misprint that the latter qualification is attached to Andronikos in MM, vi, p. 15.

[5] Dölger, *Beiträge*, pp. 32–3; G. Buckler, *Anna Comnena: A Study* (London, 1929), p. 277.

[6] Attal., p. 173; MM, v, p. 376 (=*PG*, 127, col. 1093C); MM, vi, pp. 1, 4, 5, and 15; seal (see below). Bryen., p. 41, and Skyl. Cont., p. 703, call him instead a *proedros* which should be rejected in view of the more abundant and more concrete evidence found elsewhere. It is possible however that the title of *proedros* was borne by Andronikos prior to his elevation to the higher dignity. For the two titles see Ch. Diehl, 'De la signification du titre de "Proèdre" à Byzance', *Mélanges offerts à M. Gustave Schlumberger*, I (Paris, 1924), especially p. 115; Aik. Christophilopoulou, Ἡ σύγκλητος εἰς τὸ Βυζαντινὸν κράτος (Athens, 1949), pp. 85–8. Andronikos' offices and dignities gave him the privilege of being addressed as πανυπέρλαμπρος, see MM, vi, p. 15.

Varangian guard and the troops raised by the nobles, was entrusted to him.[7] He was thus in charge of a vital post, but his burning hostility towards the emperor caused him to adopt a subversive role during the critical hour. Not only did Andronikos spread words of panic among the ranks but chose to withdraw with his own troops just before the battle started, thus setting the example for the subsequent mass desertions which followed.[8] He thus escaped possible captivity, or even death, but his treacherous conduct largely contributed to the rout and defeat of the imperial forces. Andronikos eventually returned to Constantinople,[9] probably visiting on the way his father, then in semi-exile in Bithynia. In the palace intrigues that culminated in Eudokia's expulsion from the capital, Andronikos, in conformity with family policy, actively assisted the Caesar in his plans to eliminate the emperor Romanos.

It was in fact Andronikos who directed the final stage of the expedition against the unfortunate Romanos. It was probably on this occasion that he was created *domestikos tōn scholōn*,[10] and in the spring of 1072 he continued the offensive taking over from his brother Konstantinos *22* who had already been recalled to Constantinople. In this capacity he crossed to Chrysopolis where for six days he was busy making the necessary preparation before setting out. On his way through Asia Minor, Andronikos collected more troops, and being thus reinforced proceeded without further delay towards Cilicia where Romanos was desperately trying to organize resistance. Unopposed he passed the Cilician Gates and surprised the enemy. Romanos largely relied on the assistance of the Armenian Chatatourios who commanded a substantial part of his forces.[11] The Doukas troops were also jointly commanded by Crispin, a Frank mercenary chieftain who had formerly been a supporter of Romanos; it was he who gained the upper hand and put the adversaries to flight. Chatatourios was captured, and his forces defeated. In gratitude for the humane treatment he received, the noble Armenian presented Andronikos with a magnificent precious stone which the latter in turn offered to the empress Maria.[12]

---

[7] Τὰς τῶν ἑταίρων τάξεις ἔχων καὶ τὰς τῶν ἀρχόντων Bryen., p. 41. The phrase τῶν ἀρχόντων is rather ambiguous; I take it as referring not to regiments composed of nobles but to those raised by them which however seems somewhat unconvincing for this period. Bryennios' warm praise for Andronikos and his silence over Doukas' deplorable desertion are understandable since the ῞Υλη Ἱστορίας was written for Eirene *26*.

[8] Attal., pp. 161–2; Skyl. Cont. p. 698.   [9] Attal., p. 168.

[10] Andronikos is mentioned with this rank by Bryen., p. 52, but the other sources give slightly different designations. Thus we find: δομέστικος τῆς Ἀνατολῆς (Attal., p. 173), μέγας δομέστικος (MM, VI, pp. 4, 5, and 15), δομέστικος τῶν σχολῶν τῆς Ἀνατολῆς (seal, see below), and μέγας δοὺξ τῶν σχολῶν τῆς Ἀνατολῆς (MM, V, p. 376 [= PG, 127, col. 1093C]). Psellos, II, p. 168, says that Michael *14* had ξυμπάσης τε τῆς ἔω τὴν ἀρχὴν πιστεύσας to Andronikos. But all these variants denote one and the same rank, that of the δομέστικος τῶν σχολῶν τῆς Ἀνατολῆς or as it was called by then, μέγας δομέστικος, which was the senior commander in chief, being in charge of the Asia Minor regiments. See Stein, 'Untersuchungen', pp. 50–51; R. Guilland, 'Etudes sur l'histoire administrative de Byzance: Le domestique des scholes', REB, 8 (1950), especially p. 48. An obscure reference to Andronikos as the father of Anna *27* and as a most distinguished general is found in the dialogue *Timarion*. See A. Ellissen, *Analekten der mittel– und neugriechische Literatur*, IV (Leipzig, 1860), p. 50.

[11] For his career see J.-F. Laurent, 'Le duc d'Antioche Khatchatour (1063–72), *BZ*, 30 (1929/30), pp. 405–11; H. Grégoire, 'Héros épiques méconnus', *Annuaire*, 2 (1934), 459–63; V. Laurent, 'La chronologie des gouverneurs d'Antioche sous la seconde domination byzantine', *Mélanges de l'Université Saint Joseph*, 38 (1962), 248.

[12] Bryen., p. 53.

The cause of Romanos was now lost. The former emperor shut himself up in the fortress of Adana whence he made an ineffective attempt to win over his old ally Crispin. Nothing remained but his surrender, made only after a solemn promise of pardon and safety. According to some accounts, Andronikos was touched by a sincere pity for his defeated adversary and treated Romanos in a manner befitting his former high position.[13] On the homeward journey orders came to blind the captive; Andronikos seems to have raised his voice on behalf of Romanos and wrote to his father — the real instigator of the measure — urging clemency. His entreaties, if really ever made, were ignored,[14] and at Kotyaion the former emperor was mercilessly blinded on 29 June 1072.[15]

However successful his dealings with Romanos may have been, Andronikos never had a really influential position in the palace. He consistently followed his father and in the fall of 1073 (after the first clashes with Nikephoritzes) he went into temporary seclusion with him in Bithynia.[16] They both returned to the capital in the following spring, but in the meantime the revolt of Roussel had broken out in Asia Minor. It was suggested to the emperor Michael *14* that Andronikos should be sent against Roussel, a proposal which he turned down on the advice of Nikephoritzes. Eventually Ioannes *13* assumed the overall command, and Andronikos, still continuing as *domestikos tōn scholōn*, took part in the expedition. In the decisive battle that was fought on the Zompou bridge of Sangarios he was in charge of the left wing of the imperial phalanx.[17] Andronikos fought bravely, but his soldiers fled before the enemy, and he himself was wounded. Hearing that his father had been taken prisoner, he rushed forward to rescue him. In spite of his wounds, on horseback and with sword in hand, he succeeded in cutting a way through the enemy lines, killing several of his opponents. But the attempt was beyond his power. He reached the spot where the Caesar was held, but surrounded and fiercely attacked he only escaped death through his father's intervention at the last moment. Consequently he too was captured.[18]

The two prisoners enjoyed honorable captivity in Roussel's hands and were moved to Bithynia. On account of his wounds, Andronikos' condition deteriorated despite the attention he received from the Franks. After considerable effort, the Caesar persuaded Roussel to allow him to travel to Constantinople in order that he might receive proper medical treatment there. The rebel consented only on condition that the sons of Andronikos should be kept by the Franks as hostages. After reaching the capital he recovered but he only enjoyed good health for a brief period. He again fell ill, this time with dropsy, and the doctors were unable to save him.[19] Andronikos embraced the monastic life with the name of Antonios and died on 14 October 1077.[20]

---

[13] See Psellos, II, p. 171; Bryen., p. 54. Yet there is a story that Romanos was given poison by his captors (Attal., pp. 175–6; Skyl. Cont., p. 707) which contradicts Psellos and Bryennios.

[14] Bryen., p. 55.

[15] For this date, as well as that of Romanos' death, see D. I. Polemis, 'Notes on Eleventh-Century Chronology (1059–1081)', *BZ*, 58 (1965), 65 and 76.

[16] Bryen., p. 55. See also above on Ioannes *13*.

[17] Bryen., p. 74.   [18] Bryen., pp. 75–7.   [19] Bryen., p. 100.

[20] Cf. Polemis, op. cit., p. 68. The commemoration (μνημόσυνον) of Andronikos is prescribed in the *Typikon τῆς Κεχαριτωμένης* as follows: Μηνὶ ὀκτωβρίῳ ιδ´ τελείσθωσαν τὰ μνημόσυνα τοῦ μακαρίτου ἁγίου αὐθέντου καὶ πατρὸς τῆς βασιλείας μου, τοῦ πρωτοπροέδρου καὶ πρωτοβεστιαρίου καὶ μεγάλου

The name of Andronikos Doukas is linked with the so-called *praktikon* of Patmos, an important document for the understanding of the administrative processes of feudal land management in Byzantium. The imperial act bears the date of February 1073,[21] that is after the defeat of Romanos. If any special reason lies behind this generous grant by the emperor, it may possibly be an expression of the imperial favour and satisfaction at the handling of the crisis.[22] It would appear then that Andronikos was presented with this reward after his return to Constantinople.

Like his father, Andronikos was on intimate terms with Psellos. There exists a letter of the scholar addressed to him, which is in fact an exhortation prompted by his first military successes over Romanos (spring 1072).[23] He is also known to have taken part in the Caesar's hunting expeditions.[24] A seal definitely attributable to Andronikos has been preserved bearing the inscription: Θεοτόκε, βοήθει ᾿Ανδρονίκῳ πρωτοπροέδρῳ, πρωτοβεστιαρίῳ καὶ δομεστίκῳ τῶν σχολῶν τῆς ᾿Ανατολῆς τῷ Δούκα.[25]

Well before 1066 Andronikos married Maria, a lady of Bulgarian origin who was a daughter of prince Trojan and claimed ancestry from king Samuel (976–1014).[26] Maria, frequently called by her husband's title as *protovestiaria*,[27] was a forceful woman who exerted some influence in the court of Alexios I Komnenos. She rebuilt the church of the Chora monastery[28] and was on close terms with the famous panoplist Euthymios Zygabenos.[29] Prior to her death, Maria took the veil and the monastic name of Xene; she died on 21 November of an unknown year during the reign of Alexios.[30]

By his marriage to Maria, Andronikos Doukas became the father of five children: Michael *24*, Ioannes *25*, Eirene *26*, Anna *27*, and Theodora *28*. The first three were born before 1067.[31] It is interesting to note that the name 'Andronikos', so common among the families of Komnenos, Palaiologos,

---

δουκὸς τῶν σχολῶν τῆς ᾿Ανατολῆς κυροῦ ᾿Ανδρονίκου τοῦ Δούκα, τοῦ μετονομασθέντος τῷ ἁγίῳ καὶ ἀγγελικῷ μεγάλῳ σχήματι κυροῦ ᾿Αντωνίου. See MM, v, p. 376 (=PG, 127, col. 1093C).

[21] Cf. Dölger, *Regesten*, II, p. 18, no. 992. The *praktikon* itself can be found in MM, VI, pp. 4–15.

[22] For the date cf. Polemis, op. cit., p. 66.

[23] See Sathas, *MB*, v, pp. 392–4. The address has been lost, but there is no reason to doubt the editor's attribution. There is a reference to Chatatourios (p. 395), specially associated with Andronikos (cf. Bryen., pp. 51–3).

[24] Cf. *Scripta Minora*, I, p. 280.

[25] It has been edited at least twice: A. Mordtmann, 'Περὶ Βυζαντινῶν μολυβδοβούλλων', Περιοδικὸν τοῦ ῾Ελληνικοῦ Φιλολογικοῦ Συλλόγου Κωνσταντινουπόλεως, 7 (1872/3), 77, no. 28; G. Schlumberger, *Sigillographie Byzantine* (Paris, 1881), p. 335.

[26] *Scripta Minora*, I, p. 169. Bryen., p. 106, adds that on her mother's side Maria descended from the illustrious Byzantine families of Kontostephanos, Aballantes, and Phokas. Anna *107* in *Alexias*, II, p. 138, speaks of a noble Bulgarian Radomir who was related to Maria on his mother's side.

[27] *Alexias*, I, pp. 79 and 80; II, p. 61.

[28] *Greg.*, I, p. 459; cf. R. Janin, *Les Eglises et les Monastères* (Paris, 1953), p. 549.

[29] *Alexias*, III, p. 223.

[30] Eirene *26* in her typikon writes: Μηνὶ νοεμβρίῳ κά τελείσθωσαν τὰ μνημόσυνα τῆς ἡγιασμένης αὐθεντρίας καὶ μητρὸς τῆς βασιλείας μου κυρᾶς Μαρίας, τῆς διὰ τοῦ ἁγίου καὶ ἀγγελικοῦ μεγάλου σχήματος μετονομασθείσης κυρᾶς Ξένης, MM, v, p. 376 (=PG, 127, col. 1096A).

[31] Thus when the kaisarissa Eirene, his mother, died (1060/66), Andronikos' two elder sons had already been born. See *Scripta Minora*, I, pp. 169, 179, and 188. Eirene *26* was born in 1066.

Angelos, Kamateros, and other, passed to them from this Doukas through the Greek custom of naming children after their grandparents.

22. Konstantinos Doukas (before 1050–1075/76)

Konstantinos Doukas was the younger[1] son of Ioannes *13* and Eirene Pegonitissa. Though he was said to have been called after the emperor Konstantinos X *12*,[2] it is hard to imagine that he could have been born as late as his uncle's reign (1059–67).[3] Like his elder brother, Konstantinos carried the high senatorial dignity of *protoproedros*.[4]

In the palace revolt in October 1071 which resulted in Eudokia's elimination from all influence in imperial affairs Konstantinos, together with other members of his family, played an active part.[5] It was also to him that the first campaign against Romanos was shortly afterwards entrusted. Contrary to expectation, the former emperor was liberated by the Turks and after learning of the hostile developments in Constantinople, he managed to raise an heterogeneous army. At the head of this he marched westward to Dokeia which he occupied and he then prepared to make his stand there. Konstantinos Doukas was ordered to set out to check Romanos' further advance. He collected a few troops in the capital and then crossed to Asia Minor where he recruited his main force. He had the advantage of being joined by Crispin, an experienced Frankish chieftain who after being degraded and exiled by the emperor Romanos IV had then been restored to favour by the new government. It was to him rather than to the two Doukas brothers that the retreat and subsequent defeat of Romanos was due.

Romanos, for his part, largely counted on the services of other Frankish mercenaries. He was also assisted by Theodoros Alyattes, an old and distinguished comrade of his. Konstantinos came to Dokeia, but the initial occasional skirmishes between the two opponents there proved indecisive. Romanos left his defence to Alyattes who tried to repel the attackers, but as soon as the engagement began his Franks changed sides joining their kinsman Crispin. Alyattes' soldiers were routed and himself was captured and blinded. This was the first serious setback for Romanos since he had been freed from captivity, and it raised high hopes in Constantinople. In disappointment Romanos withdrew to his native Cappadocia where for the moment he confined himself in the stronghold of Tyropoion,[6] and his cause was temporarily strengthened by the arrival of Chatatourios. On account of the winter (1071–2) Konstantinos was

---

22. [1] Psellos, II, p. 167; Bryen., pp. and 80 and 100.

[2] *Scripta Minora*, I, pp. 168–9.

[3] When he was despatched in 1071 to Asia Minor at the head of an army to fight Romanos, Konstantinos could hardly have been less than twenty. He was named after Konstantinos *12* probably as a compliment towards a distinguished close relative.

[4] Attal., p. 169; Skyl. Cont., pp. 702 and 703, calls him a *proedros*. Cf. above Andronikos *21*, n. 6.

[5] Psellos, II, p. 165; Attal., pp. 168–9; Bryen., pp. 45–6.

[6] Tyropoion has been identified with Τρυπία in Cappadocia and is located between Melitene and Lykandos; see H. Grégoire, 'Notes de géographie byzantine. Les forteresses cappadociennes d'Antigu-Nigde et de Tyropoion-Trypia', *B*, 10 (1935), 254–6.

recalled to Constantinople. The command of the next expedition was given to Andronikos *21*.[7]

In 1073 Konstantinos Doukas was created *protostrator*,[8] and after the Caesar and Andronikos *21* had gone to Bithynia he stayed behind, close to the emperor in the hope that he might detach him from the influence of Nikephoritzes. A little later (perhaps in the autumn 1074) after his father and brother had fallen into Roussel's hands Konstantinos was about to lead another campaign in an attempt to free them. However on the night before he was to depart, he was seized by an acute pain and despite the doctors' efforts he died early in the following morning. As a result the expedition was called off.[9]

An extant seal of Konstantinos reads: Κύριε, βοήθει Κωνσταντίνῳ πρωτοπροέδρῳ τῷ Δούκᾳ.[10]

It appears that Konstantinos Doukas became the father of at least one son N *29*.

23. Konstantinos Doukas (1074–c. 1095)

The porphyrogenitus Konstantinos Doukas was the only[1] son of the emperor Michael VII *14* and Maria the Caucasian. He appears to have been born in 1074 and certainly before August in that year.[2] Those who stood close to him were particularly impressed by his exceptional beauty both as an infant and as

---

[7] In general I have followed the version of Attal., pp. 169–70 and 172. Bryen., pp. 47–51, largely drawing on Psellos, II, pp. 166–8, differs in some details, particularly in making Romanos IV seize not Dokeia but Amaseia. No precise indication is given as to Konstantinos' military position. Attal., p. 169, calls him στρατηγὸς αὐτοκράτωρ, the usual designation for the supreme commander in similar cases.

[8] Bryen., p. 59; cf. R. Guilland, 'Etudes de titulature et de prosopographie byzantines: Le protostrator', *REB*, 7 (1949/50), 160.

[9] Bryen., pp. 80 and 100. G. Buckler, *Anna Comnena: A Study* (London, 1929), p. 216, n. 9, thinks that Konstantinos probably died of appendicitis. For the date see D. I. Polemis, 'Notes on Eleventh-Century Chronology (1059–1081)', *BZ*, 58 (1965), 67.

It should be noted that a contemporary *protoproedros* and *drungarios tēs viglēs* Konstantinos, regarded with some reservations as Doukas by Dölger, *Regesten*, II, p. 19, no. 1004, is actually Konstantinos Keroularios, perhaps a brother of Eudokia Makrembolitissa, for whom see R. Guilland, 'Contribution à l'histoire administrative de l'empire byzantin. Le drongaire et le grand drongaire de la veille', *BZ*, 43 (1950), 352.

[10] It has been edited by B. A. Panchenko, 'Kollektsii Russkago Arkeologicheskago Instituta v Konstantinopole. Katalog molivdovul', *Izvestiya Russkago Arkeologicheskago Instituta v Konstantinopole*, 13 (1908), 141, no. 467, and by K. Konstantopoulos, '*Βυζαντιακὰ μολυβδόβουλλα*' (originally in *JIAN*, 5–10 [1902–7]), no. 477. The fact that the seal omits the title *protostrator* for Konstantinos suggests that it dates from before 1073.

23. [1] Anna in *Alexias*, II, p. 172, calls him μονογενής. For Konstantinos see B. Leib, 'A Byzance. L'Aiglon avant l'Aiglon: Constantin Doucas Porphyrogenète (v. 1074–v. 1094)', *Bulletin de l'Association Guillaume Budé*, IV sér., No. 2 (1954), p. 83–100, and especially the expanded form of this 'Un basileus ignoré: Constantin Doucas (v. 1074–94)', *BS*, 17 (1956), 341–59.

[2] The only clue as to his age is supplied in *Alexias*, I, p. 104, where the authoress notes that in 1081 Konstantinos had not yet passed his seventh year (οὔπω τὸν ἕβδομον ὑπερελάσαν χρόνον). Psellos, II, pp. 178–9, in his sole reference to him (written in *c.* 1075) supports this in observing that the infant had not yet spoken and was still being suckled. H. Bibicou, 'Une page d'histoire diplomatique de Byzance au XIe siècle: Michael VII Doukas, Robert Guiscard et la pension des dignitaires', *B*, 29/30 (1959/60), 53, puts Konstantinos' birth early in 1074.

a child.[3] Whatever information on Konstantinos' life is recorded by the sources is almost always invariably connected with his high position as an imperial prince and more specifically with the prolonged though vain efforts to safeguard his hereditary rights to the throne.

At a very early age Konstantinos received the imperial insignia, that is, he was designated as heir apparent.[4] Thus at a difficult period in August 1074 the hard pressed government endeavoured to appease the Normans by proposing the betrothal of the infant to one of Robert Guiscard's daughters.[5] This was agreed upon. The girl came to Constantinople and became known to the Greeks as Helene. Until Michael's *14* fall in 1078 she was regarded as the future wife of a future emperor.[6] The dissolution of the betrothal after Botaneiates' accession and the confinement of Helene to a convent served as the pretext for Guiscard's attack on Byzantium.[7]

As a natural consequence of Michael's *14* fall the young prince, despite his mother's second marriage to the new emperor Botaneiates, had to renounce all his rights and prerogatives.[8] This gave rise to certain misstatements found in non-Greek sources to the effect that Botaneiates had Konstantinos castrated.[9] The empress Maria made persistent attempts to have her son recognised as the lawful heir,[10] but she failed since the aged and childless Botaneiates finally decided to support the candidature of another of his relatives.[11]

In spite of favour during the first years of Alexios I's reign and of Maria's strong influence at that time, the rights of Konstantinos were finally quashed.

[3] Cf. Psellos, II, pp. 178–9; *Alexias*, I, p. 104; Theophylaktos of Bulgaria in *PG*, 126, col. 256D.

[4] Psellos, II, p. 178, saw him as ταινίᾳ βασιλικῇ ἀναδεδεμένον τὴν κεφαλήν. Cf. Zon., III, p. 733, and Skout., p. 168. In the chrysobull of his father to Guiscard he is called βασιλεύς, *Scripta Minora*, I, p. 330. Similarly Konstantinos' portrait in the Holy Crown of Hungary is accompanied by the inscription Κωνσταντῖνος βασιλεὺς 'Ρωμαίων ὁ πορφυρογέννητος; for references see below n. 26.

[5] Skyl. Cont., pp. 720 and 724; cf. *Alexias*, I, p. 37. The proposals were put forward in a chrysobull (Dölger, *Regesten*, p. 19, no. 1003) written by Psellos which can be found in *Scripta Minora*, I, pp. 329–34. The document is especially noted for the bestowal of honorary Byzantine titles on the Norman nobility as a result of the betrothal. For an analysis of this see H. Bibicou, op. cit., pp. 43–75. For the betrothal and its political repercussions see F. Chalandon, *Histoire de la Domination normande en Italie et en Sicile* (Paris, 1912), I, p. 264; P. Charanis, 'Byzantium, the West, and the Origin of the First Crusade', *B*, 19 (1949), especially pp. 19–20; idem in K. M. Setton (gen. ed.) and M. W. Baldwin (ed.), *A History of the Crusades*, I (Philadelphia, 1955), pp. 187–8; M. Matthieu, *Guillaume de Pouille, Le Geste de Robert Guiscard* (Palermo, 1961), p. 306.

[6] Anna Komnene, out of hatred for this matrimonial project (for this bias of hers see G. Buckler, *Anna Comnena: A Study* [London, 1929], p. 263), claims that Konstantinos, then only a child less than four years old, shunned and abhorred his fiancée from the very beginning (*Alexias*, I, p. 46).

[7] Cf. Chalandon, *Les Comnène*, I, p. 63; G. Kolias, 'Κίνητρα καὶ προσχήματα τῆς εἰσβολῆς τοῦ Ροβέρτου Γυϊσκάρδου εἰς τὸ Βυζάντιον (1081)', *Πλάτων*, 10 (1958), 115–25.

[8] *Alexias*, I, p. 115.

[9] The translation of Bar-Hebraeus reads: 'Then Nicephorus (sc. Botaneiates) castrated the two sons (sic) of Michael and took his wife', see E. A. Wallis-Budge (translator), *The Chronography of Abul' Faraj Known as Bar-Hebraeus* (Oxford-London, 1932), I, p. 227. According to G. Malaterra, *De rebus gestis Rogerii Calabriae et Siciliae comitis et Roberti Guiscardi ducis fratris ejus* (ed. E. Pontieri, *RIS*, v), p. 64, the child on his father's abdication was 'turpiter eunuchizatus'. As Chalandon, *Les Comnène*, I, p. 63, n. 1, maintains, this is not acceptable on account of Konstantinos' subsequent betrothal to Anna.

[10] According to Bryen., pp. 6 ff., it was Alexios Komnenos who openly championed the rights of Konstantinos. See above Konstantios *17*, n. 17.

[11] *Alexias*, I, p. 66.

There is no doubt that the intimacy of the emperor with Maria, regardless of its nature, was largely responsible for the promises and the lavish honours which the child received. From the outset he was lodged at the imperial palace together with the Komnenoi,[12] and on the advice of Ioannes *13*, Maria induced Alexios to issue a chrysobull and solemnly confirm the special privileges granted to Konstantinos. Consequently for a few years he acted as junior co-emperor. His signature used to appear in state documents, and on public occasions he accompanied the emperor in an official, though purely nominal, capacity.[13] The climax came a few days after the birth of Alexios I's eldest child Anna *107* (born on 2 December 1083) when Konstantinos was betrothed to her. The two children were looked upon as the future rulers, and their names were included in acclamations.[14] It is hard to tell how sincere these acts of Alexios were, for to a great extent they were due to political considerations. However one cannot simply dismiss them as hypocritical or even provisional. Should the emperor have failed to have a male heir, the betrothal of Anna *107* to Konstantinos would have offered an ideal solution.

It is generally assumed that the birth of Ioannes Komnenos in 1087 was the reason why Konstantinos was deprived of his rights. This sounds reasonable enough, but the fact remains that no source supports such an hypothesis. On the contrary, the only author who touches on the question implies that the betrothal only ended with Konstantinos' death.[15] Always sensitive to anything connected with her unfortunate fiancé, Anna *107* hints that she was too young to remember the honours which they both enjoyed.[16] Apparently this was already a thing of the past by 6 January 1088, the date for a speech of Theophylaktos of Bulgaria.[17] Only Bryennios gives a reason for Alexios' decision. According to him, this deprivation was due to a grave disease that befell the porphyrogenitus, thus preventing his future elevation to the throne. This disease whose nature is not revealed eventually led to the young man's death.[18] Now, the demotion certainly occurred before 1088 and Konstantinos did not die until after 1094; it is therefore somewhat unlikely that a 'grave' illness, as Bryennios describes it, could have taken more than six years to carry off the porphyrogenitus. However it is possible that Konstantinos lost his privileges because of some minor disease, which the clever emperor was quick to exploit

[12] *Alexias*, I, pp. 104–5.

[13] *Alexias*, I, pp. 115–16; cf. Dölger, Regesten, II, p. 24, no. 1064. Theophylaktos of Bulgaria in his Παιδεία Βασιλική, certainly written after 1081, keeps addressing Konstantinos as a βασιλεύς. See *PG*, 126 cols. 253A, 253B, 257D etc.

[14] Bryen., p. 11; Zon., III, p. 738; *Alexias*, II, p. 62. As Buckler, *Anna Comnena*, pp. 40–41, observes, Anna *107* only by implication tells us that she was betrothed to Konstantinos whom she otherwise treats in a most cherished manner.

[15] Zon., III, p. 738.   [16] *Alexias*, II, p. 62.

[17] Although Theophylaktos finds words of praise for almost every member of the imperial house, he is conspicuously silent in respect of Konstantinos who would not have been so neglected if he were still a junior co-emperor. On the contrary, the author 'reproaches' Alexios for not yet having crowned his newly-born son (Ioannes *108*). See P. Gautier, 'Le discours de Théophylacte de Bulgarie à l'autocrator Alexis Ier Comnène', *REB*, 20 (1962), 117[15]. Cf. the editor's comments ibid., pp. 105–6. The year of the speech, formerly thought to be 1090, is now convincingly shown to be 1088 (ibid., p. 105).

[18] . . . εἰ μὴ βαρεῖα νόσος πρότερον τῷ πορφυρογεννήτῳ εἰσφρήσασα μὴ συγχωροῦσα τούτῳ τῆς τοιαύτης ἀρχῆς, μετ'οὐ πολὺ τῶν ἐνταῦθα προήρπασεν, Bryen., p. 12.

immediately after Ioannes' *108* birth. Bryennios is frequently inexact on Konstantinos, and he could purposely or unwillingly have linked a possible early disease in 1087 with the fatal one some six years later.

But even if this were so, Konstantinos continued to receive imperial favour up to the end, and Alexios is reputed to have continued to show fatherly affection.[19] When the emperor stopped at Serres on his march against the Serbs early in 1094, Konstantinos invited and entertained him in his own extensive and picturesque estates nearby called Pentegostis.[20] For the first time he was intending to participate in a military campaign, but the magnanimous Alexios promptly excused him.[21] For his part he remained loyal to Alexios and refused to lend his house to the rebel Nikephoros Diogenes,[22] in spite of his mother's implication in the plot.[23] Then he is heard of no more and he must have died shortly afterwards.

At the suggestion of Maria, Theophylaktos Hephaistos wrote (1081/8) his Παιδεία βασιλικὴ πρὸς τὸν πορφυρογέννητον Κωνσταντῖνον (Institutio regia).[24] The work aimed at preparing the young prince for the high office he never attained and it contains little personal information. It passes almost in silence over his father, but it contains a long section in praise of Maria. In addition, the child is complimented for his beauty and his intelligence as well as his ability in manly sports such as hunting, horsemanship and the bow.[25]

The portrait of Konstantinos Doukas has been preserved in the Holy Crown of Hungary which dates from *c.* 1075.[26]

24. Michael Doukas (*c.* 1061–1108/18)

The *protostrator* Michael Doukas was the elder[1] son of Andronikos *21* and consequently a close relative of the emperor Alexios I Komnenos through the latter's wife Eirene *26*. His birth apparently falls within the early years of Konstantinos

---

[19] *Alexias*, II, p. 172   [20] *Alexias*, II, p. 171.   [21] *Alexias*, II, p. 172.
[22] *Alexias*, II, p. 175.   [23] *Alexias*, II, p. 179.

[24] Edited in *PG*, 126, cols. 253–85. For an analysis of the work see B. Leib, 'La Παιδεία Βασιλικὴ de Théophylacte, archevêque de Bulgarie, et sa contribution à l'histoire de la fin du XIe siècle', *REB*, 11 (1953), 197–204. Leib (p. 203) dates the treatise in 1088/9, but in view of Gautier's work (cited above n. 17), it must be probably assigned to an earlier period. A paraphrase in modern Greek has been preserved in cod. Μετοχίου Παναγιου Τάφου 299, fol. 229r ff., see Papadopoulos-Kerameus, Ἱεροσολυμιτικὴ Βιβλιοθήκη, IV, p. 270.

[25] *PG*, 126, cols. 256–7.

[26] See Gy. Moravcsik, 'A magyar szent korona görög feliratai', *Egyetemes Philologiai Közlöny*, 59 (1935), 131–4. E. Darkó, 'Der Konstantinos der ungarischen heiligen Krone', *Hoffillerov Zbornik* (= *Serta Hoffilleriana*, Zagreb, 1940), pp. 437–41, on the grounds that the pictured figure represents a man of about fifteen, attributes the portrait to Konstantios *17*. However, this is extremely unlikely since Konstantinos held a position similar to that of Andronikos *16* whose picture would have also been expected to be included on the crown. As P. J. Kelleher, *The Holy Crown of Hungary* (Rome, 1951), p. 58, points out, imperial children were normally represented as older than in actual fact in Byzantine art. The portrait which is on enamel is reproduced in Moravcsik, op. cit., plate vii; Darkó op. cit., p. 439; Kelleher, op. cit., plate xi no. 24.

24. [1] Bryen., p. 78.

X's *12* reign.[2] As a child, Michael, together with his brother, was handed over to the rebel Roussel (*c.* 1075) as hostage so that his father Andronikos who was seriously ill could be allowed to go to Constantinople for proper medical attention. The Frank held the two boys imprisoned in a fortress in Bithynia. There Michael's and Ioannes' *25* slave attendants were successful in winning over a local peasant with thorough knowledge of the surrounding countryside to help the boys escape to Nicomedia. They chose a moonless night for their attempt, but although the plan had been carefully worked out, only Michael with his attendant, the eunuch Leontakios, was lucky enough to slip out of the fortress; thus, after a whole night's arduous walk he was brought safely to Nicomedia[3] and thence undoubtedly to Constantinople. As a young man, Michael is mentioned again. In the process of the highly uncanonical marriage of the newly created emperor Nikephoros III Botaneiates to the ex-empress Maria he played a delicate part. Following the Caesar's instructions, he promptly produced a priest at the right time to bless the irregular ceremony.[4] Three years later, he accompanied his grandfather at the crucial conference at Schiza in Thrace in which the candidature of Alexios Komnenos as an emperor was finally agreed upon.[5]

As a man close to the palace both by relationship and by partisanship, Michael not only received various honours but also actively participated in several military engagements.[6] He held the civil dignity of *sebastos*,[7] and from at least 1083 onwards he filled the important rank of *protostrator*.[8] In the warfare between the attacking Normans led by Bohemund and the Byzantines in Thessaly in

---

[2] In *c.* 1075 Michael is described as being still a child (παῖς, Bryen., pp. 77 ff.), but in 1078 he was already a young man (νεανίας, Bryen., p. 127). When Psellos wrote his epitaph for the kaisarissa Eirene Pegonitissa (1060/66), Michael was still an infant (*Scripta Minora*, I, p. 179). Psellos' congratulations to Ioannes *13* on the birth of a grandson (Sathas, *MB*, v, pp. 307–8) could refer to Michael; (cf. Ioannes *13*, n. 42). The name he bore is presumably that of the emperor Konstantinos X's *12* eldest son who was at that time crowned as co-emperor (Psellos, II, p. 148). It is therefore reasonable to suppose that his birth coincided approximately with Michael VII's crowning, but neither of these events can be dated. Eirene *26* was born in 1066, and in addition to Michael she was also preceded by another brother Ioannes *25*. Michael's birth appears then most probably to have been in the early sixties.

[3] Bryen., pp. 77–80.

[4] Bryen., pp. 126–7; cf. B. Leib, 'Nicéphore III Botaneiatès (1078–81) et Marie d'Alanie', *Actes du VIIe Congrès International d'Etudes Byzantines*, I (Paris, 1950), especially p. 134.

[5] *Alexias*, I, p. 84.

[6] Anna *107* in *Alexias*, I, p. 103, speaks of a certain Michael, qualified as ἐπ'ἀνεψιᾷ γαμβρός of the Komnenoi who later became λογοθέτης τῶν σεκρέτων. The editor (pp. 173–4), disagreeing with Ch. Diehl, 'Un haut fonctionnaire byzantin: Le logothète τῶν σεκρέτων', *Mélanges offerts à N. Jorga* (Paris, 1933), p. 218, n. 1, identifies him with Michael Doukas. This is also the view of F. Dölger, 'Der Kodikellos des Christodulos in Palermo', *Archiv für Urkundeforschung*, 11 (1929), 26 (=*Byzantinische Diplomatik* [Ettal, 1956], p. 29), but this cannot be so. S. De Jongh in her unpublished thesis *La Généalogie des Comnène à Byzance*, p. 10, has with good reason identified this inadequately described Michael with Michael Keroularios who became the husband of an unknown daughter of Alexios I's sister Maria and Michael Taronites. Both Michael Doukas and Michael Keroularios were present in the synod of 1092; the latter's name appears in the form: τοῦ σεβαστοῦ καὶ λογοθέτου κυροῦ Μιχαήλ, *PG*, 127, col. 972C.

[7] Ibid.

[8] *Alexias*, II, pp. 31, 98, and 100; *PG*, 127 cols. 972C and 1096B; Lampros, 'Μαρκιανὸς 524', p. 155; cf. R. Guilland, 'Etudes de titulature et de prosopographie byzantines: Le protostrator', *REB*, 7 (1949), 160.

1083, Michael was in charge of the heavily armed infantry which included also Turkic and other barbarian mercenaries. He had occupied the defiles called 'Domenikou palation', not far from Larissa, but as he could not conform to the emperor's planned strategy, his troops were badly routed by the enemy.[9] He also accompanied Alexios during the ill-fated campaign against the Patzinaks in Bulgaria in 1087. Belonging to the inner circle of the emperor's advisors, Michael, in the face of the overwhelming pressure of the enemy attacks, suggested that Alexios should flee. This the emperor actually did, though only after some initial hesitation. In the ensuing flight Michael's horse slipped down, but happily for him an attendant offered his own and thus Doukas was once more able to rejoin the emperor.[10]

Shortly afterwards Michael Doukas reappears in the field for the last time. Just before the famous battle of Mt Levunion (29 April 1091) in which the Patzinak swarms were annihilated, he, together with Adrianos Komnenos, was entrusted with supervising the orderly crossing of a bridge, newly built over the river Hebrus by the Byzantine army.[11]

Once more the name of Michael is met in connection with official duties. He was present in an important synod in 1092 that discussed certain theological aspects of image worship.[12] His name seems to occur in a letter written in 1108,[13] and he probably died shortly afterwards. We only hear that he died on 9 January of an unknown year, but certainly before his sister Eirene *26* wrote the *Typikon* for her convent τῆς Κεχαριτωμένης.[14]

By an unknown marriage or marriages, Michael Doukas became the father of many children.[15] Some of them are mentioned by their names: Konstantinos

[9] *Alexias*, II, pp. 30–31. Anna *107* who does not spare words in praise of her uncle's balanced judgement and impressive stature, calls him on this occasion a *phalangarches*. However this cannot imply a specific military rank or position; it simply denotes that Michael was in command of all the forces the authoress speaks of. Cf. ibid., p. 28, where the same term is applied to an official of Latin origin called Bryenne. An anonymous poem of the twelfth century calls Ioannes *99* an *archiphalangarches*; see Lampros, 'Μαρκιανὸς 524', pp. 178–9.

[10] *Alexias*, II, pp. 98–100.

[11] *Alexias*, II, p. 137.

[12] *PG*, 172, col. 972C. His high senatorial position can be seen from the fact that his name occurs second in the list after that of the *megas domestikos* (i.e. Adrianos Komnenos, the emperor's younger brother) among some fifty officials. The date is uncertain, cf. Grumel, *Regestes*, III, p. 55, no. 967.

[13] A letter of Theophylaktos to Ioannes Pantechnes speaks of a usurper in the region of Ochrida whom Michael was sent to fight (ὁ γάρ τοι πανσέβαστος σεβαστὸς καὶ πρωτοστράτωρ, κύριος Μιχαήλ, παρὰ τοῦ βασιλέως ἐστάλη, *PG*, 126, col. 484D). This is thought to refer to Bohemond's campaign in 1108, see P. Gautier, 'Le dossier d'un haut fonctionnaire d'Alexis I Comnène, Manuel Straboromanos', *REB*, 23 (1965), 170. There exists a speech of consolation by Straboromanos Πρὸς τὴν δέσποιναν Εἰρήνην τὴν Δούκαιναν παραμυθητικὸς ἐπὶ τῷ θανάτῳ τοῦ ἀδελφοῦ αὐτῆς Μιχαὴλ σεβαστοῦ τοῦ πρωτοστράτορος (edited by Gautier, ibid., pp. 195–201, the end, however, is missing). Little concrete personal information on Michael is preserved in this work. He succumbed to an illness in the course of which Eirene *26* had nursed him and his death caused her great grief (ibid., p. 198).

[14] Μηνὶ ἰανουαρίῳ θ' τελείσθωσαν τὰ μνημόσυνα τοῦ περιποθήτου αὐταδέλφου τῆς βασιλείας μου καὶ πρωτοστράτορος κυροῦ Μιχαὴλ τοῦ Δούκα, MM, v, p. 376 (=*PG*, 127, col. 1096B). His commemoration is also prescribed in the *Typikon* of the Pantokrator monastery where he is not named but simply called *protostrator*, uncle of the founder (that is, of the emperor Ioannes II Komnenos). See Dmitrievskii, *Typika*, p. 662.

[15] In the above mentioned *logos* Straboromanos says: παῖδες αὐτῷ πολλοί τε καὶ καλοὶ καὶ ποθούμενοι, οἱ μὲν ἀπῆσαν οἱ δὲ παρῆσαν ἐπιθρηνοῦντες αὐτόν, Gautier, op. cit., p. 198.

30, Theodora *31* and perhaps Eirene *32*. There was also another daughter Na *31a*. Another (?) son is referred to in a poem by the physician Nikolaos Kallikles.[16]

25. Ioannes Doukas (*c.* 1064–before 1136)

Among the Byzantine military commanders of the late eleventh century the name of Ioannes Doukas occupies an outstanding place, both by virtue of the nature of the missions he supervised and by the brilliant successes he achieved. He was the second-born son of Andronikos *21* and Maria the Bulgarian. The year of his birth should be placed in about 1064,[1] and the infant was called after his grandfather the Caesar. At the age of about ten he was handed over to the rebel Roussel in exchange for his father, but unlike Michael *24* who succeeded in forcing his escape Ioannes was unlucky and had to remain under guard,[2] presumably up to the time of Roussel's defeat and capture by the Turks. Being left an orphan at an early age, Ioannes was cared for and brought up by his grandfather with whom he was staying in the latter's estates Ta Moroboundou in Thrace in 1081. It was he who rushed to the Caesar with the unexpected news of the Komnenian revolt against Botaneiates, much to the old man's amazement and disbelief.[3] Subsequently he went with the Caesar to the meeting at Schiza,[4] but it is unlikely that he was old enough to contribute to the decisions taken there.

After Dyrrachion was recovered from the Normans in 1085, Ioannes appears to have been sent there as the new governor at the head of a large force. He stayed in the region for a number of years and directed the Byzantine offensive against the Serbs. In a series of campaigns he gained the upper hand and captured several towns and fortresses of both Zeta and Rascia; the climax came when the ruler of Zeta, Vodin, fell into his hands. Little is heard of this warfare waged from Dyrrachion which served as a base for the military operations in the area. Even the dating is uncertain. However, Ioannes stayed there up to spring of 1092 when he was recalled to Constantinople and was given command of a new assignment against Tzachas, the ambitious emir of Smyrna.[5]

---

[16] *Εἰς τὸν Σμυρναῖον ἐκφράσαντα τὸν τελευτήσαντα υἱὸν τοῦ πρωτοστράτορος*, Kallikles, p. 347, no. xxix. The *protostrator* in question is presumably Michael Doukas, but there is no clue as to whether this son of his can be identified with Konstantinos *30*. Cf. the remarks of the editor ibid., pp. 374–5.

Michael (*Μιχαὴλ ὁ σεβαστὸς καὶ πρωτοστράτωρ*) is also mentioned in an hagiographical source as having visited St Kyrillos towards the end of the eleventh century and is there described as *φιλομόναχος*; see E. Sargologos, *La Vie de Saint Cyrille le Philéote, moine byzantin (d. 1110)* (Brussels, 1964), p. 212.

25. [1] He was older than Eirene *26* (born in 1066) as may be seen from the fact that whereas Ioannes is mentioned in Psellos' epitaph for the kaisarissa Eirene, she is not. See *Scripta Minora*, I, pp. 179 and 188, where the author speaks of Andronikos' *21* 'infant sons', obviously Michael *24* who was the eldest and our Ioannes. In 1081, while staying with his grandfather, he is described as *νέος ἔτι ὢν καὶ μήπω μειράκιον*, *Alexias*, I, p. 81.

[2] Bryen., pp. 78–9; cf. above on Michael *24*.   [3] *Alexias*, I, pp. 81–2.   [4] *Alexias*, I, p. 84.

[5] *Alexias*, II, pp. 115 and 158; cf. K. Jireček, *Geschichte der Serben*, I (Gotha, 1911), p. 238. Anna *107* observes that her uncle had remained at Dyrrachion for eleven years, but this cannot be right

Tzachas, who had been threatening the capital with his fleet, had eventually retreated to his headquarters in Smyrna where the imperial commander Konstantinos Dalassenos pursued him. In order to assist Dalassenos, Ioannes Doukas was dispatched by the emperor in command of a large force consisting of troops and ships with instructions to proceed to the island of Lesbos. Anna Komnene says that on this occasion he received the new title of *megas dux* which from then on came to denote the head of the Byzantine fleet.[6] Ioannes was to retain the command over the land forces and hand over the navy to Dalassenos. Mitylene, the capital of Lesbos, was already occupied by Tzachas, and Doukas crossed to the island without delay. His first act there was to erect wooden towers which served a double purpose both as fortifications and as watchtowers. The enemy defences had been entrusted to Tzachas' brother. The ensuing warfare which was only conducted in daytime proved indecisive. Anna *107* would like us to believe that it was the strategic genius of the emperor which perceived from afar that his troops could take advantage of the sun rays in the afternoon and thus make their attack at a time when the enemy soldiers had to face a blinding sun in their efforts to watch the Byzantines and hit back. Alexios sent a letter to his general with this shrewd advice.[7] The imperial strategy was promptly followed, and the Turks were utterly routed. Tzachas gave up the important island and only asked for a safe passage to Smyrna. The Byzantines consented to this, but the crafty Turk was anxious to carry off many of the islanders. Thereupon Dalassenos urged Doukas to let him attempt another attack by sea while the Turks were sailing to Smyrna. This actually took place, and all Christian captives were liberated, though Tzachas succeeded in escaping. Doukas concluded his mission by strengthening the fortifications of Mitylene. The Byzantines were also able to recapture from the Turks several Aegean islands including Samos. The commanders then returned to Constantinople.[8]

Ioannes only stayed in the capital for a few days. News came of two usurpations, one in Crete by Karykes, the other in Cyprus by Rapsomates, both obscure

as Chalandon, *Les Comnène*, I, p. 143, n. 1, and G. Buckler, *Anna Comnena: A Study* (London, 1929), p. 402, n. 5, maintain. It is also unlikely that in these eleven years a sojourn before 1085 is included, as Ioannes, born in *c.* 1064, was still too young to be given the overall command of this vital post, though he could have first gone there as a subordinate. His successor was the emperor's nephew Ioannes Komnenos, and it is in error that Doukas is mentioned in Dölger, *Regesten*, II, p. 40, nos. 1159–60. In any case, the name of Ioannes Doukas is attested in the synod of 1092 (Grumel, *Regestes*, III, p. 55, no. 967) where it follows those of Adrianos Komnenos and Michael 24. See *PG*, 127, col. 972C.

---

[6] *Alexias*, II, pp. 115 and 158; cf. Stein, 'Untersuchungen', p. 57; R. Guilland, 'Etudes de titulature et de prosopographie byzantines. Les chefs de la marine byzantine: Drongaire de la flotte, grand drongaire de la flotte, duc de la flotte, mégaduc', *BZ*, 44 (1951), 223.
It is thought that Ioannes Doukas is the first bearer of this title. Recently a document, dated December 1085, has been published which bears the signature: Νικήτας ὁ ἐλάχιστος μοναχὸς καὶ τῆς τοῦ Θεοῦ Μεγάλης Ἐκκλησίας πρωτοσύγκελος προνοητὴς τῶν κτημάτων τοῦ μεγάλου δουκὸς ὑπέγραψα; see Bompaire, *Actes de Xéropotamou*, p. 67. Who is this μέγας δούξ? Ioannes' association with the title only begins in 1092 although he might have received it a year or two earlier. But in 1085 he was at Dyrrachion and it seems unlikely that he was so honoured then. The document of Xeropotamou may possibly refer to another *megas dux*, perhaps the first actually known, so far unidentified by name.

[7] Dölger, *Regesten*, II, p. 41, no. 1166.

[8] The expedition is related at some length in *Alexias*, II, pp. 158–62.

and almost unknown figures. Doukas was given the task of re-establishing imperial authority in these two large islands. At the head of a considerable naval force, he set out and before landing on Crete he stopped at the nearby island of Karpathos, intending perhaps to muster his ships and make the final preparations prior to the decisive assault. His imminent landing created such widespread confusion that it caused a new coup in Crete, this time against the rebel Karykes who was assassinated before Doukas set his foot on the island. Crete then submitted without further bloodshed.[9]

The subjugation of Cyprus turned out to be a more complicated process. Having adequately garrisoned Crete, Doukas proceeded to Cyprus and on his first attack captured the stronghold of Kyrenia. The local usurper Rapsomates, who according to Anna *107*, had little fighting experience, hurried from Nicosia to face the imperial troops but dared not venture an open clash with them. His spasmodic resistance soon completely collapsed, and not long after-wards he was captured by Boutoumites, a general under Doukas. Thus the imperial control was once again effectively asserted and a new governor Eumathios Philokales[10] was appointed on this strategic island. Ioannes then returned to Constantinople.[11]

In the reconquest of western Asia Minor following the storming of Nicaea (19 June 1097) by the knights of the First Crusade, Ioannes Doukas played an equally conspicuous role. In a measure aimed at frightening the Seljuk emirs of the maritime principalities, he was ordered to spread word of Nicaea's capture and also to display Tzachas' daughter who had been taken prisoner there. Once more he had the supreme command of the army and the fleet, but at the head of the latter he placed a certain Kaspax to whom the governorship of Smyrna was promised in the event of its recapture. Ioannes besieged the town, still held

---

[9] *Alexias*, II, p. 162; cf. E. Gerland, *Histoire de la Noblesse crétoise au Moyen Age* (Paris, 1907); originally published in *Revue d'Orient Latin*, 10–11 (1904–9), 22–4; H. Glykatzi-Ahrweiler, 'L'administration militaire de la Crète byzantine', *B*, 31 (1961), 224–6. The Cretan naval cam-paign is also dealt with in a well-known passage of the *Vita S. Meletii Junioris* written by Nikolaos, bishop of Methone, in 1141. See the edition of Vasilievskii in *Pravoslavnii Palestinskii Sbornik*, 6 (1886), 27–8. This account supplements what *Alexias* has to say and to some extent differs from it. The hagiographer makes Doukas direct his fleet 'to the ports of Euripos' (Euboea) where it is maintained that he sought a meeting with Saint Meletios who advised moderation and avoid-ance of bloodshed; the news of Karykes' death reached him there, and only then did he proceed and establish control over Crete. The version of the *Vita* makes it difficult, if not impossible, to imagine another call of the fleet at Karpathos on its way south. One of the letters of Theophylaktos of Bulgaria, addressed to Ioannes, might support the fact that Doukas stayed at Euboea. The eminent metropolitan expresses his appreciation of the favourable disposition of the addressee towards him and begs Doukas to continue it both with regard to the writer and also towards the latter's kinsmen in his native Euboea. See the text in *PG*, 126, cols. 309–12 (= cols. 509–12). Now it is possible that Theophylaktos solicited his protector on behalf of his relatives on the occasion of Doukas' call at Euboea. In actual fact we have no evidence of any previous or subsequent association of Ioannes with the administration of the island that could explain the reference in the letter of Theophylaktos. Bearing in mind the account of the *Vita Meletii*, it is reasonable to conceive the letter as having been received just before, or during, the Byzantine fleet's stay there.

[10] For the career of this distinguished general see Sp. N. Marinatos, 'Εὐμάθιος Φιλοκάλης, τελευταῖος στρατηγὸς τοῦ βυζαντινοῦ θέματος Κρήτης', *EEBΣ*, 7 (1930), 388–93; Laurent, *Médaillier Vatican*, pp. 55–9; C. Mango and E. J. W. Hawkins in *DOP*, 18 (1964), 335–9.

[11] *Alexias*, II, pp. 162–4. The references to this expedition by Zon., III, p. 737; Glykas, p. 620; Ephraim, pp. 151–2, are of no value. For the incident of Cyprus cf. G. Hill, *A History of Cyprus*, I (Cambridge, 1949), pp. 297–9.

by Tzachas, from the land, while the fleet did the same from the sea. Unable to resist the combined assault, Tzachas came to terms and agreed to hand over Smyrna and in return be free to move out with his troops. Thus Kaspax became the new governor, but shortly afterwards he was accidentally assassinated by an Arab. This resulted in a terrible massacre of the city's population by his sailors, and his vacant post was filled by another experienced general, Hyaleas.

Ioannes continued his campaign in the neighbouring districts. He left the fleet to garrison Smyrna, and with the army he himself moved to Ephesus which he recovered. Thence he proceeded to the valley of the Maeander river where Byzantine power quickly replaced that of the Seljuks. Doukas gained repeated successes and captured many prisoners and plenty of booty. Most important of all, the well-known towns of Sardes, Philadelphia, Laodicea, Lampe, and Polyboton passed under Byzantine control.[12] Doukas apparently advanced further than this, but no information is available.

At this point the active career of Ioannes seems to come to a close. Although he lived for some years to come, he never again appears in an official capacity. This may possibly be due to some illness or perhaps to his participation in one of those obscure conspiracies that were frequent during Alexios I's reign. Otherwise his premature retirement seems difficult to account for.[13]

In the course of his life Ioannes Doukas is mentioned as holding the senatorial ranks of *sebastos*[14] and *pansebastos sebastos*.[15] If these are distinguishable, it is obvious that up to at least 1092 he held the dignity of *sebastos*, and only afterwards was promoted to the higher title.[16] When Eirene 26 wrote the *Typikon* of Kecharitomene (1110/18), Ioannes was alive but had embraced monastic life with the name of Antonios,[17] which his father had also chosen. He must have died between this unknown date and 1136 as he is enumerated among the deceased uncles of the emperor Ioannes *108* in the *Typikon* of the Pantokrator monastery.[18]

No evidence in respect of Ioannes' family has come down to us. As to his personal relations, we know that he was on close terms with Theophylaktos of

---

[12] *Alexias*, III, pp. 24–7; cf. Chalandon, *Les Comnène*, I, pp. 196–8. J. Griffiths, *Travels in Europe, Asia Minor and Arabia* (London, 1805), p.44, writes that in Smyrna 'are still visible the ruins of a citadel said to have been rebuilt by the celebrated Greek admiral John Ducas, who took Smyrna in 1097'. Can this be based on an otherwise unknown inscription?

[13] It is true that the *Alexias* is somewhat restrained in its treatment of Ioannes Doukas. It is not that blame is actually cast upon him, yet the authoress refrains from giving full credit for what he had achieved. It is true that on one occasion Anna *107* calls him μαχιμώτατος (*Alexias*, I, p. 115), but this is the only compliment he gets. The defeat of Tzachas, in reality an exceptional military success, is presented in such a manner that the absent emperor gets all credit for it (*Alexias*, II, pp. 159–60). All this is in contrast to the abundant credit showered on another uncle of the authoress, the less significant Michael *24*. It looks as though Anna *107* must have felt some resentment towards Ioannes when she wrote her account forty years later.

[14] *Vita Meletii* in op cit., p. 27; *PG*, 127, col. 9726 (*c.* 1092); *PG*, 126, col. 532A.

[15] *PG*, 127, col. 1096B. In the address of one of Theophylaktos' letters Ioannes is called *sebastos* but in the text of the same *pansebastos*. *PG*, 126, cols. 309–12 (=cols. 509–12).

[16] A similar case is offered by the *cursus honorum* of Eumathios Philokales who at different times held the two dignities in question. See Laurent, *Médaillier Vatican*, p. 57.

[17] Τελείσθωσαν τὰ μνημόσυνα τοῦ περιποθήτου αὐταδέλφου τῆς βασιλείας μου τοῦ πανσεβάστου σεβαστοῦ κυροῦ Ἰωάννου τοῦ Δούκα, τοῦ διὰ τοῦ ἀγγελικοῦ μεγάλου σχήματος μετονομασθέντος κυροῦ Ἀντωνίου, καθ' ἣν ἂν ἡμέραν ἐκδημήσῃ, *PG*, 127, col. 1096B.

[18] See Dmitrievskii, *Typika*, p. 662. Ioannes is not named but simply called '*megas dux*, the emperor's uncle'.

Bulgaria who addressed at least two letters to him. The two men apparently became acquainted in the period when Ioannes' headquarters were at Dyrrachion (before 1092) and he could easily have come into contact with the metropolitan of Ochrida. Reference has already been made to one of these letters, which is in fact a complimentary piece. The other is similar in content and was written after Doukas was transferred from the region, but Theophylaktos continued to beg for his assistance, especially in matters of local administration.[19] In addition, Ioannes was also mentioned in another letter of the learned prelate.[20]

26. Eirene Doukaina (1066–1123 ?)

The empress Eirene Doukaina who became the wife of Alexios I Komnenos[1] was the first-born daughter of Andronikos *21* and Maria. She was born, presumably in Constantinople, in 1066.[2] Shortly before her father's death in October 1077, Eirene, through the initiative of her clever mother, was betrothed to Alexios whose first wife had recently died; the marriage which was obviously the result of diplomatic considerations appears to have been celebrated early in the following year.[3] The married life of the imperial couple is depicted by their daughter Anna *107* as a most happy one, but it is probable that at least during the early years Eirene's position in the palace was far from secure and was repeatedly threatened by the open hostility of her mother-in-law Anna Dalassene, a bitter enemy of the entire Doukas family, and also by the highly suspicious attachment of her husband to the ex-empress Maria. After the accession of Alexios (1 April 1081), for unexplained reasons Eirene stayed away from the emperor for a few days and lodged at the 'lower palace' together with her only protector at that time, the still active Caesar Ioannes *13*, her own grandfather, while Alexios with all his blood relations, including his brothers, occupied the palace proper of Boukeleon.[4] Intrigues behind the scenes and strong pressure upon Alexios brought about Eirene's official crowning by the patriarch Kosmas a week after the new emperor ascended the throne.[5]

From then on Eirene frequently comes into Anna's narrative. Although she exerted but little influence at the beginning, her position was gradually strengthened and eventually she managed to make her presence felt.[6] When

---

[19] The letter in *PG*, 126, cols. 521–4.

[20] *PG*, 126, col. 532A.

26. [1] For Eirene see the lively sketch of Ch. Diehl in *Figures byzantines* Deuxième série (Paris, 1903³), pp. 53–85 (=idem, *Impératrices de Byzance* [Paris, 1959], pp. 189–215). Cf. the uncritical chapter in J. McCabe, *The Empresses of Constantinople* (London, 1913), pp. 197–217.

[2] The only indication as to this date is provided in *Alexias*, I, pp. 105 and 111, where Anna says that her mother was hardly fifteen in 1081.

[3] For the date see D. I. Polemis, 'Notes on Eleventh-Century Chronology (1059–1081)', *BZ*, 58 (1965), 68–9. The marriage resulted in a wide and decisive support for Alexios on the part of the Doukai who were the first to acclaim him as emperor, see *Alexias*, I, p. 87.

[4] *Alexias*, I, p. 105.

[5] *Alexias*, I, p. 110; Zon., III, p. 733; cf. Chalandon, *Les Comnène*, I, pp. 53–4; G. Buckler, *Anna Comnena: A Study* (London, 1929), p. 122.

[6] Sources other than Anna *107*, as might be expected, supply more interesting details on this question. According to Zon., III, p. 747, the emperor at first neglected Eirene but later came to love her and subsequently she had a great influence over him. Cf. Glykas, p. 622.

Alexios was trying to collect money, after the loss of Dyrrachion to the Normans (October 1081), the empress was the first to contribute.[7] On several occasions she accompanied her husband in his various campaigns. Thus in September 1105 Alexios, facing an invasion by Bohemund, came to Thessalonica and asked Eirene to join him there. The emperor was at that time suffering from arthritis and she humbly nursed him.[8] Similarly on another campaign against Bohemund in November 1107 the empress followed Alexios, but despite his entreaties she was unwilling to proceed any further, and the next spring she returned from Thessalonica to Constantinople.[9] Again in 1116 she was brought to Nicomedia from the island of Prinkipo where she had been staying, and once more took care of her husband in his poor health.[10] Indeed the empress repeatedly performed the functions of a nurse in her efforts to relieve her ailing husband and particularly during his last fatal illness.[11]

It would have been too much to expect from Anna *107*, the principal authority for Eirene's life, an unbiased and balanced account of her mother's character and activities. The vivid description of Eirene where she is compared to Athena[12] can be read as a specimen of the authoress' tendency to idealise. The generosity and the benevolence of the empress often found expression in characteristic acts of piety and clemency. After the suppression of the dangerous conspiracy of the Anemas brothers, the emperor presented his wife with the luxurious house of one of the prominent participants called Ioannes Solomon. Eirene however felt a deep sorrow for Solomon's wife and instead decided to decline the gift and leave the house to the disgraced family.[13] Equally merciful, together with her daughter Anna *107*, she succeeded in persuading the indignant Alexios to refrain from the blinding of Michael Anemas and the other leading plotters.[14]

Eirene's influence and power at the Byzantine court ended with the death of her husband in 1118. The story of her support for her beloved Anna *107* at the expense of the lawful heir Ioannes II *108* and of her vain efforts to elevate the reluctant Bryennios is still far from clear.[15] Soon afterwards she must have assumed the monastic habit[16] and subsequently lived a quiet life in the convent of Kecharitomene until her death which in all probability occurred on 19 February 1123.[17]

---

[7] *Alexias*, II, p. 10.

[8] *Alexias*, III, p. 60. On the nature of this and of the other frequent illness of Alexios see now K. Alexandrides, 'Ueber die Krankheiten des Kaisers Alexios I. Komnenos', *BZ*, 55 (1962), 68–75.

[9] *Alexias*, III, pp. 88 and 106.

[10] *Alexias*, III, pp. 190–6.   [11] *Alexias*, III, pp. 163–4, 171–2, and 233; cf. Glykas, p. 622.

[12] *Alexias*, I, pp. 111–12.   [13] *Alexias*, III, p. 72.

[14] *Alexias*, III, p. 74. On this conspiracy see B. Leib, 'Complots à Byzance contre Alexis I Comnène (1081–1118)', *BS*, 23 (1962), especially pp. 267–9.

[15] Zon., III, pp. 760–62; Chon., pp. 8–12 and 17; Skout., p. 187; cf. Chalandon, *Les Comnène*, I, pp. 273–6; II, pp. 2–8. Some minor sources such as Glykas, p. 622, and Ephraim, p. 161 (vv. 3770–80) record that the empress did in fact hate her son.

[16] Cf. Skout., p. 186.

[17] To begin with, Eirene is spoken of as being dead in the *Typikon* of the Pantokrator monastery written in 1136, see Dmitrievskii, *Typika*, p. 662. Similarly the empress's youngest son Isaakios Komnenos (father of the future emperor Andronikos I) in the *Typikon* of the Kosmosoteira monastery (written in 1152) refers to his dead mother and adds that she passed away on 19

The consort of the first Komnenos was a cultured woman, a true representative of her times, a patron of learning and on intimate terms with the contemporary scholars. Like her husband, she was well-versed in theology and especially acquainted with the writings of St Maximos the Confessor.[18] The eminent dogmatist Euthymios Zygabenos, the author of the Δογματικὴ Πανοπλία, knew her and her mother well, even before he was commissioned by the emperor to compose his extensive work.[19]

Perhaps no other Byzantine empress or princess had a greater impact on contemporary literature than Eirene to whom a considerable number of diverse works were either dedicated or written at her personal request. The most important of these latter is undoubtedly the "Υλη Ἱστορίας of her son-in-law Nikephoros Bryennios.[20] It should not be forgotten that of all her children the empress was particularly attached to her daughter Anna *107*. Theodoros Prodromos wrote some verses of consolation for Eirene on the occasion of the death of her son Andronikos.[21] Moreover numerous references to her are found in the laudatory poetry of the same Prodromos.[22] The other prominent contemporary, the physician Nikolaos Kallikles, also composed a poem for Eirene.[23]

February of the first indiction. Isaakios also relates two extraordinary happenings associated with his pious mother. First, she miraculously closed her own eyes at the moment of her death in the presence of all her relatives and subsequently fragrant oil (μύρον) sprang out from her grave. See L. Petit, 'Typicon du monastère de Kosmosoteira près d'Aenos (1152)', *Izvestiya Russkago Arkheologicheskago Instituta v Konstantinopole*, 13 (1908), 65. As E. Kurtz, 'Unedierte Texte aus der Zeit des Kaisers Johannes Komnenos', *BZ*, 16 (1907), 74, argues, the only appropriate year for the first indiction cited in the *Typikon* is 1123. This has not however passed unchallenged. Chalandon, *Les Comnène*, II, p. 15, n. 2, draws attention to the fact that Eirene survived to witness the death of her son Andronikos who may have died after 1123. This leads Chalandon to the conclusion that there must be a copyist's error in the indiction given in the *Typikon* of Kosmosoteira and he is inclined to correct it to eleven (= 1133). Yet it should be pointed out that both the excerpt given by M. Gedeon in Ἐκκλησιαστικὴ Ἀλήθεια, 18 (1898), 145, and the complete text of Petit, loc. cit., have the indiction and the month's day written in full and not expressed by the customary letter-numbers of the Greek alphabet.

It is also to be noted that a misleading reference to 'the emperor Alexios' wife' in *c.* 1143 (Kinn., p. 36) in actual fact applies to the wife of Alexios Komnenos, the eldest brother of Manuel I, who had been crowned by his father.

---

[18] *Alexias*, II, p. 38.   [19] *Alexias*, III, p. 223.   [20] *Alexias*, I, p. 5; II, p. 9, cf. Bryen., p. 15.

[21] Στίχοι ἡρῷοι εἰς τὴν βασίλισσαν κυρὰν Εἰρήνην τὴν Δούκαιναν ἐπὶ τῷ θανάτῳ τοῦ σεβαστοκράτορος υἱοῦ αὐτῆς. The complete text has been edited by A. Majuri, 'Anecdota Prodromea dal Vat. gr. 305', *Rendiconti della Reale Accademia dei Lincei. Classe di scienze morali, storiche e filologiche*. Serie v. 17 (1908), 541–4. Some excerpts in S. Papademetriou, *Theodor Prodrom* (Odessa, 1905), p. 170.

[22] In a poem written for the wedding of one of Eirene's grandsons Prodromos acclaims her as 'the best of all empresses' (Papademetriou, op. cit., p. 413 [=*PG*, 133, col. 1077]). Similarly in the epitaph for Theodora, a daughter-in-law of Anna *107*, the same poet calls her μεγίστη ἄνασσα (Kurtz, op. cit., p. 92, vv. 169–70) and in an epithalamium for the sons of the same Anna, Eirene is described as the 'divine empress' (τὴν ἱερὰν ταυτηνὶ βασιλίδα, τὴν φερώνυμον Εἰρήνην, τὸν Δουκικὸν ὄρπηκα, *PG*, 133, col. 1400B). Eirene is also seen as 'the head of the family (= the Doukai), the most great empress' (τὴν ἀρχηγὸν τοῦ γένους καὶ μεγίστην βασίλισσαν) in the monody for Gregorios Kamateros (see Majuri, op. cit., p. 548; Papademetriou, p. 175, n. 71). A similar apostrophe is used by Psellos in his epitaph for the kaisarissa Eirene where the empress Eudokia Makrembolitissa is described as κοινὴ βασιλὶς τοῦ γένους ἡμῶν σύμπαντος (*Scripta Minora*, I, p. 189). Eudokia was of course related to Psellos, see Konstantinos *12*, n. 48.

[23] It is entitled Εἰς τὸ ξύλον τὸ κοσμηθὲν ὑπὸ τῆς δεσποίνης, Kallikles, p. 319, no. II. In the text of the poem Eirene is called Δουκῶν λαμπτήρ.

The teacher of rhetoric Michael Italikos, who later became archbishop of Philippopolis, was likewise on intimate terms with her. At least two pieces of his are addressed to Eirene. The first is a short speech,[24] published from an imperfect manuscript,[25] and the other a letter still unpublished.[26] Manuel Straboromanos also stood close to the empress. We possess two works which this scholar wrote for her. The more important is a rather long but unfortunately incomplete speech of consolation for the death of Eirene's brother Michael 24,[27] and the other a mere three-line epigram to St Demetrios on her behalf.[28] In addition, a number of letters, some of them anonymous, were written to Eirene and are still preserved.[29] Finally an anonymous poem is inscribed on a cross, now at St Mark's in Venice, once dedicated by the empress and dating from the period of her retirement to the convent.[30]

Eirene's name is linked with the foundation, or rather the restoration, of the Constantinopolitan convent known as Θεοτόκου τῆς Κεχαριτωμένης and more especially with the detailed *Typikon* which she provided for it.[31] The document, in its original form dating from before 1118, besides its importance for the knowledge of monastic life and administration[32] is also valuable for the section of the

[24] Λόγος αὐτοσχέδιος ῥηθεὶς εἰς τὴν δέσποιναν κυρὰν Εἰρήνην, edited by J. A. Cramer, *Anecdota Graeca e Codd. Manuscriptis Bibliothecarum Oxoniensium*, III (Oxford, 1836), pp. 164–5 (cf. M. Treu, 'Michael Italikos', *BZ*, 4 [1895], 8–10). The author calls Eirene 'the most learned of all empresses' (p. 164) and from what he has to say on her two modes of life, the 'imperial' and the 'contemplative' (p. 165), it appears that the *logos* was written after Eirene had taken the veil, that is, after 1118.

[25] G. Mercati, 'Gli aneddoti d'un codice bolognese', *BZ*, 6 (1897), 130 ff., has observed that cod. 2412 of the University of Bologna, fol. 73v–74r, includes one folio missing from the manuscript used by Cramer. The missing section is not indicated in the edition of Italikos.

[26] It is preserved in cod. Barocci 131, fol. 229v–30v. See R. Browning, 'The Patriarchal School at Constantinople in the Twelfth Century', *B*, 32 (1962), 195; idem, 'Unpublished Correspondence between Michael Italicus, Archbishop of Philippopolis, and Theodoros Prodromos', *Byzantinobulgarica*, 1 (1962), 280 and 282.

[27] See P. Gautier, 'Le dossier d'un haut fonctionnaire d'Alexis Ier Comnène, Manuel Straboromanos', *REB*, 23 (1965), 195–201.

[28] Ibid., p. 201.

[29] Thus we have a brief letter of Theophylaktos of Bulgaria (τῇ δεσποίνῃ ἐπισκεψαμένῃ αὐτῷ ἀρρωστήσαντι) expressing his gratitude for Eirene's visit during his illness (*PG*, 126, col. 469). Another anonymous letter of puzzling content (the empress addressed is not named and a brother of hers, is referred to as bishop of Kitros) has been edited by Mercati, op. cit., pp. 138–40. The monk Nikolaos Kataskepenos also wrote a letter to Eirene, published in M. I. Gedeon, 'Νικολάου μοναχοῦ Κατασκεπηνοῦ ἐπιστολαὶ καὶ στιχηρὰ μετὰ τῶν τοῦ Συμεὼν Λογοθέτου τοῦ Μεταφραστοῦ', Ἀρχεῖον Ἐκκλησιαστικῆς Ἱστορίας, 1 (1911), 70–72. Another anonymous letter addressed τῇ βασιλίσσῃ μοναχῇ Εἰρήνῃ (Sp. P. Lampros, Κατάλογος τῶν ἐν ταῖς Βιβλιοθήκαις τοῦ Ἁγίου Ὄρους Ἑλληνικῶν Κωδίκων, 1 [Cambridge 1895], p. 105) most probably refers to her.

[30] The text is easily accessible in A. Frolow, *La Relique de la Vraie Croix: Recherches sur le Développement d'un Culte* (Paris, 1961), pp. 315–16, no. 308, where the older editions and the relevant literature are cited.

[31] Published in MM, v, pp. 327–91, and in *PG*, 127, cols. 985–1128. The founder signs the *Typikon* as Εἰρήνη ἐν Χριστῷ τῷ Θεῷ πιστὴ βασίλισσα Ῥωμαίων ἡ Δούκαινα. For a facsimile of the beautiful signature see B. de Montfaucon, *Palaeographia Graeca* (Paris, 1708), p. 301. The retaining of the family name of Eirene after her marriage (in fact, she is never, to my knowledge, called a Κομνηνή) need not be regarded as peculiar. Married women in twelfth-century Byzantium as a rule kept their maiden surnames and it was only in the following century that the modern usage began to gain ground. See Introduction, p. 2, n. 2.

[32] On this important document see K. Krumbacher, *Geschichte der byzantinischen Literatur* (Munich, 1897²), pp. 315 and 317; Kurtz, op. cit., pp. 95 and 104; Diehl, loc. cit.; L. Oeconomos,

μνημόσυνα (church services of commemoration of the dead) which preserve a number of dates important for contemporary prosopography.

One portrait of Eirene in enamel (XII cent.) has been preserved in Pala d'Oro in St Mark's in Venice and it bears the inscription Εἰρήνη εὐσεβεστάτη αὐγοῦστα.[33] Eirene is also shown on a very rare type of coin, preserved in gold and in billon, together with her husband Alexios and their son Ioannes.[34]

By her marriage to Alexios Komnenos, Eirene became the mother of seven children born in the following order: Anna *107* (the historian, 1083), Maria (1085), Ioannes *108* (the future emperor, 1087), Eudokia (*c.* 1092), Theodora (*c.* 1095), Andronikos (1098), and Isaakios (1100?).[35]

27. Anna Doukaina (*c.* 1068–before 1136)

Anna Doukaina was the second daughter of Andronikos *21* and was born in about 1068. Little is known of her. At an early age, presumably shortly before the accession of Alexios I Komnenos (1 April 1081), she was given in marriage to the distinguished general Georgios Palaiologos[1] who henceforth as a close and trusted relative of the imperial family was destined to play a prominent role, especially in Dyrrachion during the war with the Normans.

When Eirene *26* wrote the *Typikon* of Kecharitomene (1110/18), Anna, who is referred to there by her husband's dignity as *pansebastos sebaste*, was still alive,[2] but in 1136 she was already dead.[3]

Two seals bearing the legends Θεοτόκε, βοήθει τῇ σῇ δούλῃ Ἄννῃ Δουκαίνῃ[4] and Κύριε, βοήθει τῇ σῇ δούλῃ Ἄννῃ σεβαστῇ τῇ Δουκαίνῃ[5] could belong to her.

Almost all the subsequent Palaiologoi were offspring of the marriage of Anna

La Vie religieuse dans l'Empire byzantin au Temps des Comnènes et des Anges (Paris, 1918), pp. 166–92; Hussey, *Church and Learning*, pp. 186–9; Grumel, *Regestes*, III, p. 50, no. 957; R. Janin, *Les Eglises et les Monastères* (Paris, 1951), pp. 196–9; H.-G. Beck, *Kirche und theologische Literatur im byzantinischen Reich* (Munich, 1959), p. 647. R. Janin, 'Le monachisme byzantin au Moyen Age commende et typica (Xe–XIVe siècle)', *REB*, 22 (1964), 36–8.

---

[33] See the coloured reproduction in Lampros, Λεύκωμα, plate 66. Its attribution to our Eirene is not certain; the portrait might respresent the homonymous wife of Ioannes II. See A. Grabar, *L'Empereur dans l'Art byzantin* (Paris, 1936), p. 21.

[34] W. Wroth, *Catalogue of the Imperial Byzantine Coins in the British Museum* (London, 1908), II, p. 544, no. 23; cf. H. Goodacre, 'Irene Doukaina, Wife of the Emperor Alexius I', *Numismatic Chronicle*, 19 (1939), 105–11.

[35] For their dates of birth, indicated in brackets, I am indebted to De Jongh, *Généalogie des Comnène*, pp. 26–42.

27. [1] *Alexias*, I, pp. 80 and 84. An obscure reference to this union is found in *Timarion*; see A. Ellissen, *Analekten der mittel- und neugriechischen Literatur*, IV (Leipzig, 1860), p. 50. See also Kallikles, pp. 321–2.

[2] Τελείσθωσαν τὰ μνημόσυνα τῆς περιποθήτου αὐταδέλφης τῆς βασιλείας μου, τῆς πανσεβάστου σεβαστῆς κυρᾶς Ἄννης τῆς Δουκαίνης, καθ' ἣν ἂν ἡμέραν ἐκδημήσῃ πρὸς Κύριον, see *PG*, 127, col. 1096C.

[3] Dmitrievskii, *Typika*, p. 663. Anna is spoken of as 'the emperor's (= Ioannes *108*) aunt, the wife of Palaiologos'.

[4] See J. Ebersolt, 'Sceaux byzantins du Musée de Constantinople', *RN*, 18 (1914), 214–15, no. 163.

[5] See K. Konstantopoulos, Βυζαντιακὰ Μολυβδόβουλλα (Athens, 1917), no. 294.

Doukaina to Georgios. Yet the couple's immediate descendants are far from well established. The union appears to have produced at least two sons, Nikephoros *135* and Andronikos *136*. These were called after their respective grandfathers, Nikephoros Palaiologos and Andronikos *21*, and may have employed the novel compound surname Doukas-Palaiologos which came into vogue during the twelfth century.

●

28. Theodora (*c.* 1070–before 1110/18)

Theodora was the youngest daughter of Andronikos *21*, and she must therefore have been born in about 1070. She had been 'promised' to God by her parents since her infancy[1] and lived in a convent under the monastic name of Eirene. Theodora died on 20 February of an unknown year before the *Typikon* of Kecharitomene was written (1110/18).[2]

29. N

Theodoros Prodromos wrote iambic verses for Zoe *33* which give certain information, not to be found elsewhere, on her parentage. The poet explicitly says that Zoe's *33* father was a member of the Doukas family, in fact a grandson of the Caesar, and her mother was the first-born daughter of the *sebastokrator* Isaakios Komnenos. Neither of the parents is named.[1]

The *sebastokrator* Isaakios certainly refers to the elder brother of Alexios I Komnenos. The unknown father of Zoe *33* (N) should be sought among the grandsons of the Caesar Ioannes *13*, namely in the sons of either Andronikos *21*

28. [1] Bryen., p. 106.

[2] Μηνὶ Φεβρουαρίῳ κ΄ τελείσθωσαν τὰ μνημόσυνα τῆς περιποθήτου αὐταδέλφης τῆς βασιλείας μου, τῆς πανεντίμου καὶ παντίμου κυρᾶς Θεοδώρας τῆς διὰ τοῦ ἁγίου καὶ ἀγγελικοῦ μεγάλου σχήματος μετονομασθείσης κυρᾶς Εἰρήνης, PG, 127, col. 1096B. Theodora is also mentioned as the emperor's aunt 'the *pantimos*' (an appellation also used in her sister's *Typikon*) in the *Typikon* of the Pantokrator monastery (1136), see Dmitrievskii, *Typika*, p. 662.

It is hard to see how a contemporary(?) seal, bearing the iambic inscription Σκέποις, πάναγνε, Δούκαιναν Θεοδώραν, could belong to this Theodora. She had already assumed the name of Eirene since her early days, and in no circumstance could she have employed her lay name. The seal was originally attributed to a non-existent Ioannes Doukas by G. P. Galavaris, 'The Mother of God of the Kanikleion', *Greek, Roman, and Byzantine Studies*, 2 (1959), 177-82, but the reading was corrected by V. L(aurent) in *BZ*, 53 (1960), 504-5.

29. [1] The poet makes the husband of Zoe *33* say:

> ἡ σύζυγος γάρ, ἥν μοι σὺ ξυνηρμόσω,
> Δουκὸς πατρὸς προῆλθε καισαρεγγόνου
> καὶ Κομνηνὴν ἔσχηκε λαμπρὰν μητέρα,
> σεβαστοκρατοῦς τέκνον Ἰσαακίου
> καὶ τοῦτο πρωτόρριζον ἐν θυγατράσι.

See C. Gallavotti, 'Laurentiani codicis altera analecta', *Atti della Accademia Nazionale dei Lincei.* Serie VIII *Rendiconti. Classe di scienze morali, storiche e filologiche*, 4. (1949), 355–6. Cf. below Zoe *33*, n. 2.

or Konstantinos *22*. As it is hard to imagine that a marriage was ever concluded between a daughter of Isaakios Komnenos (whose brother Alexios had already taken Eirene *26*) and one of Eirene's *26* brothers, it is safer to assume that N must have been an otherwise unheard of son of Konstantinos *22*.

There appears to be no evidence as to whether Zoe *33* had any brothers or sisters.

30. Konstantinos Doukas (fl. *c.* 1118)

Konstantinos Doukas is the only known son of the *protostrator* Michael *24*, and most of the information about him is derived from the letters of Theophylaktos of Bulgaria. The archbishop makes a couple of passing references to him on the occasion of Konstantinos' appointment as administrator of the Vardar district in Macedonia.[1] His occupation of that post is confirmed by a clear passage in a later document which speaks of Konstantinos as having been *dux* and *praktor* of Strymon and Thessalonica in December 1118.[2]

Theophylaktos addressed Konstantinos, who carried the dignity of *sebastos*, in two of his letters. The first of these is a complimentary piece which appears to have been dispatched shortly after Doukas took up his duties in Macedonia; the second is shorter and presumably accompanied a gift of fish sent by the prelate together with his blessing.[3]

An undated seal which bears the metrical inscription

Σφράγισμα Δούκα σεβαστοῦ Κωνσταντίνου
ὅνπερ, ἀθλητά, ἐκ πάσης βλάβης ῥύου[4]

probably belongs to this Konstantinos.

There is no information about Konstantinos' wife or possible children.[5]

---

30. [1] See *PG*, 126, cols. 432D and 492B. The second passage contains a compliment to the effect that Konstantinos resembled his father in his love of letters (ἐπειθόμην τοῖς Βαρδαριώταις ἐπαφεθῆναι τὸν πανσέβαστον υἱὸν τοῦ πρωτοστράτορος, τά τε ἄλλα πατρῴζοντα, καὶ τὴν πρὸς τοὺς λόγους διάθεσιν . . .).

[2] See G. Rouillard and P. Collomp, *Actes de Lavra. Edition diplomatique et critique* (Paris, 1937), p. 161, no. 57/82. The Greek text runs as follows: τοῦ γεγονότος δουκὸς καὶ πράκτορος Στρυμῶνος καὶ Θεσσαλονίκης κυροῦ Κωνσταντίνου τοῦ Δούκα κτλ. St. P. Kyriakides who examined the original has observed that there is a lacuna between the words πράκτορος and Στρυμῶνος which is not indicated by the editors. He therefore proposed to insert the word Βολεροῦ which appropriately makes Doukas the administrator of Boleron, Strymon, and Thessalonica. See his Βυζαντιναὶ Μελέται (Thessalonica, 1937), pp. 211–12; cf. P. Lemerle, *Philippes et la Macédonie orientale à l'époque chrétienne et byzantine* (Paris, 1945), p. 158.

[3] The letters in *PG*, 126, cols. 480–81.

[4] Laurent, *Bulles métriques*, p. 172, no. 482. The invocation is to St George.

[5] For a reference to a son of Michael *24* who might well be identical with the present Konstantinos see Michael *24*, n. 16.

31. Theodora Doukaina (fl. c. 1125)

In a couple of anonymous dedicatory epigrams reference is made to Euphrosyne, the wife of the *protonobilissimos* Nikolaos Maurokatakalon. The poems speak of her as Doukoblastos[1] or as a 'scion of the Doukas branch',[2] and one of them provides some additional facts on her ancestry. Euphrosyne was a grand-daughter of the *protostrator* Michael 24, and her father who carried the dignity of *pansebastos* (*pansebastos sebastos?*) was called Theodoros. By her marriage to Maurokatakalon, Euphrosyne became the mother of two children, Theodoros[3] and Maria.[4]

Euphrosyne might have been the granddaughter of Michael 24 either through her father Theodoros or through her unknown mother. I would support the second hypothesis. In another epigram of the same collection a certain Theodora Doukaina and her husband Theodoros are mentioned.[5] These could be the parents of Euphrosyne.

31a. Na (fl. c. 1100)

A daughter of Michael 24, of unknown name is alluded to in an hagiographical source. In fact only her husband Ioannes, a nephew of Alexios I, is referred to as a γαμβρός (presumably son-in-law) of Michael 24.[1]

31. [1] Lampros, 'Μαρκιανὸς 524', p. 134.

[2] Ibid., p. 155.

[3] Ibid. Theodoros is possibly to be identified with a Theodoros *doukophyes*, known from another epigram of the same collection, ibid., p. 22.

[4]
> Νικόλαός σοι ταῦτα πιστὸς οἰκέτης
> πρωτονοβελίσσιμος ἐκ τῆς ἀξίας,
> Μαυροκατακαλὼν δὲ πατρὸς ἐκ γένους,
> Εὐφροσύνη δὲ Δουκικῆς ῥίζης κλάδος
> πρωτοστράτορος Μιχαὴλ τὸ παππόθεν,
> ὃς αὐτανάσσης ἦν σύναιμος Εἰρήνης,
> Θεοδώρου δὲ πανσεβάστου πατρόθεν,
> ἃς σῷζε, Σῶτερ, πρὸς τρυφῆς φέρων χλόην
> Θεοδώρῳ συνάμα καὶ τῇ Μαρίᾳ,
> τέκνοις συνάπτων εὐφροσύνης ἐν τόποις.

See Lampros, 'Μαρκιανὸς 524', p. 155.

[5]
> Θεοδώρα Δούκαινα σοῦ κράτους λάτρις.
> Σὺ δ'ἀλλὰ μακροὺς ἡλίους μοι τοῦ βίου
> σὺν Θεοδώρῳ συνευνέτῃ νέμοις
> λύτρον νόσου, εὔροιαν εὐπραγημάτων,

Ibid., p. 40.

31a. [1] ... Ἰωάννης ὁ σεβαστὸς καὶ ἀνεψιὸς τοῦ παμμακαρίστου βασιλέως καὶ γαμβρὸς τοῦ πρωτοστράτορος see E. Sargologos, *La Vie de Saint Cyrille le Philéote, moine byzantin* (d. *1110*) (Brussels, 1964), p. 249. The only *protostrator* mentioned in the *Vita* is Michael 24. As the editor says (ibid., p. 476, n. 157) there are two nephews of Alexios I with the name of Ioannes. One is the eldest son of Isaakios Komnenos and the other is Ioannes Taronites, the son of the emperor's sister Maria. For the latter see A. Leroy-Molinghen, 'Les deux Jean Taronite de l'Alexiade', *B*, 14 (1939), 147–53.

32. Eirene (fl. 1093/1123)

Although not explicitly referred to as *Δούκαινα*, Eirene was certainly a member of the family and possibly a daughter of Michael *24*.[1] She is known through the writings of Prodromos and Kallikles. At the end of the eleventh century Eirene became the wife of Gregorios Kamateros, an educated man of humble origin who held high office under Alexios I and during the early years of Ioannes II.[2]

Gregorios and Eirene who became the ancestors of the Doukai-Kamateroi

---

32. [1] Prodromos describes Eirene as a daughter of the Doukai and as related to Eirene *26*: 'Αλλ' ἔδει σε πάντως, ἀρίστη μοι σεβαστῶν, Δουκῶν ὑπάρχουσαν θυγατέρα, καὶ τῆς Δουκικῆς μοίρας μεταλαχεῖν καὶ τῷ γένει κοινωνῆσαι τῶν συμφορῶν καὶ τὸν χορὸν συναναπληρῶσαι τοῖς ἀμφὶ τὴν ἀρχηγὸν τοῦ γένους καὶ μεγίστην βασίλισσαν see A. Majuri, 'Anecdota Prodromea dal Vat. gr. 305', *Rendiconti della Reale Accademia dei Lincei*. Serie v. *Classe di scienze morali, storiche e filologiche* 18 (1908), 531. In addition, Eirene had a son Michael (Kallikles, p. 334) who could have been called after his maternal grandfather.

[2] In fact, we find several references to the man at the end of the eleventh and the early twelfth centuries in addition to a couple of seals edited by G. Schlumberger in *Sigillographie de l'Empire byzantin* (Paris, 1884), p. 628, and in *Mélanges d'archéologie byzantine* (Paris, 1895), p. 199. The seals were also edited and commented upon by N. A. Bees, 'Zur Sigillographie der byzantinischen Themen Peloponnes und Hellas', *VV*, 21 part iv (1914), 217–59, who came to the conclusion that all literary, documentary, and sigillographic references pertaining to the name of Gregorios Kamateros belong to one and the same person. V. Laurent, 'Un sceau inédit du protonotaire Basile Kamateros', *B*, 6 (1931), 264–6, is rather sceptical about this attribution, but it should be noted that a certain coherence appears to link all references. In a document of the year 1088 (Dölger, *Regesten*, III, p. 38, no. 1148) specific mention is made to Gregorios Kamateros, son of Basileios, who carried the title of λογαριαστὴς τοῦ σεκρέτου τοῦ γενικοῦ (MM, VI, p. 50). In *c.* 1093 Anna *107* speaks of a Gregorios Kamateros as recently having been engaged as secretary to the emperor (νεωστὶ προσληφθεὶς καὶ ὑπογραμματεύων τῷ αὐτοκράτορι, Alexias, II, p. 178). Chon., pp. 13–14 (cf. Skout., p. 188) adds some other details. Gregorios was a learned man of inconspicuous background who was made a secretary to the emperor (τῷ βασιλεῖ δὲ προσληφθεὶς Ἀλεξίῳ καὶ τοῖς ὑπογραμματευομένοις καταλεγείς). He was afterwards sent to the provinces as a tax collector in which capacity he accumulated substantial wealth that helped him to marry one of the emperor's relatives; then he was created λογοθέτης τῶν σεκρέτων. Gregorios Kamateros then acted as λογαριαστὴς τοῦ σεκρέτου τοῦ γενικοῦ (for the office see F. Dölger, *Beiträge zur byzantinischen Finanzverwaltung, besonders des 10. und 11. Jahrhunderts* [Leipzig, 1927], p. 19, n. 8) in 1088, imperial secretary in *c.* 1093, subsequently tax collector, and ended as λογοθέτης τῶν σεκρέτων. To his post as a tax collector in Greece must be assigned one of his seals reading Θεοτόκε, βοήθει Γρηγορίῳ πραίτορι Πελοποννήσου καὶ Ἑλλάδος τῷ Καματηρῷ. This qualification as πραίτωρ supports Choniates' statement that Gregorios became rich through tax farming in the provinces. For the office of *praitor* see N. Banescu, 'La signification des titres de πραίτωρ et de προνοητὴς à Byzance aux XIe et XIIe siècles', *Miscellanea Giovanni Mercati*, III (=*Studi e Testi*, 123 [1946]), especially p. 394, where the author concludes that a holder 'fût un chef du cadastre' (cf. the accusations which were raised against such officials by Michael Choniates later in the century, quoted ibid., p. 391). Theophylaktos of Bulgaria was on friendly terms with Kamateros and addressed five of his letters to him (in *PG*, 126, cols. 325–9, 368–9, 489–97, 537–40, and 549–52) and possibly a sixth (ibid. cols. 384–5; it bears the caption Τῷ Καματηροπούλῳ, and in it the author introduces a young grandson of Psellos). One of these letters includes a passage to the effect that the emperor raised Gregorios to the office of *logothetes* which entitled him to sit in council with the sovereign and also to the office of *protasecretis*, that is, imperial secretary (ἡλίκον αὐτόν σε τό τε τοῦ λογοθέτου ἀξίωμα τέθεικε, τοῦ πάλαι βασιλεῖ συνεδρεύοντος, καὶ τὸ τοῦ πρωτασηκρῆτις ὀφφίκιον τοῦ ἀεὶ τοῖς αὐτοκράτορσιν ὑπογραμματεύοντος, ibid., col. 492A). In another letter it is disclosed that Kamateros had great power with the emperor (ibid., col. 368C). At least one of these letters of Theophylaktos alludes to the fact that Gregorios had become a monk. This is actually consistent with what we learn from a poem entitled: Εἰς τὸν Χριστὸν ἱστάμενον ἐπὶ τῷ τάφῳ ὡς ἐκ προσώπου ἀμφοτέρων τοῦ τε

eventually embraced monastic life.[3] They appear to have left a number of children, mostly unknown. Their son Michael, 'a beautiful scion of the Doukai and the Kamateroi', died young.[4] The distinguished high official and theologian Andronikos Doukas Kamateros *98* was also one of their sons.[5]

33. Zoe (fl. *c.* 1120)

The *sebaste* Zoe was a daughter of N Doukas *29* and his wife the daughter of Isaakios Komnenos. She married the *sebastos* Georgios Botaneiates,[1] a relative but apparently not a descendant of the emperor, who however died shortly afterwards. By this marriage, Zoe had a daughter.[2]

λογοθέτου καὶ τῆς συμβίου αὐτοῦ κυρᾶς Εἰρήνης μετὰ μοναχικοῦ σχήματος ἱσταμένων, see Kallikles, p.332, no. XIX.

Gregorios Kamateros, who was also honoured with the senatorial dignity of *sebastos*, on his death became the subject of a monody by Prodromos which is edited by A. Majuri, op. cit., pp. 528–35. Both the editor (p. 548) and S. Papademetriou, *Theodor Prodrom* (Odessa, 1905), p. 175, n. 71, assign the text to 1123. Kallikles also composed a poem Εἰς τὸν τάφον τοῦ Καματηροῦ λογοθέτου, pp. 333–4, no. XXI. For Gregorios see also V. S. Shandrovskaya, 'Grigorii Kamatir i ego pechat v sobranii Gosudarstvennogo Ermitazha', *VV*, 16 (1959), 173–82.

---

[3] Kallikles, pp. 332–4; cf. G. Stadmüller, 'Zur Geschichte der Familie Kamateros', *BZ*, 34 (1934), 354.

[4] Δουκῶν Καματηρῶν τε πάγκαλον κλάδον, Kallikles, p. 334.

[5] An epitaph, probably written by Tzetzes, laments the death of a certain Theodoros Kamateros who was Δουκικῆς κλὼν ὀσφύος καὶ τῆς Καματηρῶν εὐγενοῦς ῥιζουχίας; see S. Pétridès, 'Epitaphe de Théodore Kamatéros', *BZ*, 19 (1910), 9, vv. 51–2. The information supplied by the poem is limited; we learn that Theodoros was of a good family but was attacked by dysentery as a result of which he entered a monastery where he died young. Some additional details on the man are also available. Tzetzes sent him a couple of letters and calls Theodoros a *sebastos*; see Th. Pressel (ed), *Joannis Tzetzae Epistolae* (Tübingen, 1851), p. 78. Another letter of the archbishop Theophylaktos to Gregorios Kamateros makes a passing reference to the 'sweet' (γλυκύς) Theodoros (*PG*, 126, col. 497B), a term appropriate for a small child. It is quite possible that this Theodoros was also a son of Gregorios and Eirene.

A letter of Tzetzes bears the caption Τοῖς σεβαστοῖς τοῖς υἱοῖς τοῦ Καματηροῦ (Pressel, op. cit., p. 79), but their identity remains unknown.

33. [1] A seal of a certain Georgios Botaneiates (edited by Laurent, *Bulles métriques*, p. 223, no. 660) probably belongs to him.

[2] The information is derived from two poems, ostensibly spoken by Zoe and her husband, published by C. Gallavotti, 'Laurentiani codicis altera analecta', *Atti dell'Accademia Nazionale dei Lincei. Serie VIII. Rendiconti. Classe di scienze morali, storiche e filologiche*, 4 (1949), 355–6. They are also in S. Papademetriou, *Theodor Prodrom* (Odessa, 1905), pp. 381–2 and 385–6. Cf. above N *29*, n. 1. On her background Zoe says

ἐκ Δουκικῆς προῆλθον εἰς φῶς ὀσφύος,
Κομνηνικὴ δὲ νηδὺς ἐξήνεγκέ με.

The daughter of Zoe may have become the mother of Konstantinos Doukas Kalamanos *96*.

PART III

THE NAME OF DOUKAS IN
OTHER FAMILIES

In this part persons who have borne the name of Doukas, either as their only known surname or as an alternative one or even in compound form, have been grouped under the families to which they appropriately belong. Some seventy such families have been traced. Many of them are only represented by a single name while others include more than twenty. Wherever possible, an attempt has been made to explain the appearance of the name of Doukas in these families. Needless to say, the cases examined here are but a fraction of the very great number of Byzantines who adopted and used the name of Doukas. With the publication of new documents, epigrams, seals and other sources the relevant prosopography will doubtless be further illuminated.

The introductory lines to each family, some of them quite brief and far from adequate, have been written solely to acquaint the reader with the family background in so far as it relates to the Doukas family. With this in view occasional prosopographical information has been added. In the absence of more systematic treatment of the majority of the families concerned, this may be of some use though it is necessarily incomplete. Only persons who are called Doukai by the sources have been included here. This has of course its disadvantages. It means that once a different surname is attached to their children, brothers, or even parents, these have to be omitted from consideration. But the alternative would have been beyond the scope of this study which is only concerned with the prosopography of the Doukai.

ADRIANOS

Adrianos ('Αδριανός, 'Αδριανός) is an unusual family name and does not seem to be attested before the fourteenth century. In October 1392 a certain Adrianos, now dead, spoken of as γαμβρὸς to Demetrios ὁ Τζηρίγγης, left some estates to a monastery.[1] Cod. Vat. gr. 336 once belonged to a member of the family who wrote down some notes of personal interest.[2] Nikolaos Adrianos was protoierus Moreae in 1495.[3]

---

[1] F. Dölger, *Aus den Schatzkammern des Heiligen Berges* (Munich, 1948), p. 311.

[2] According to them, the unnamed writer had a brother Demetrios Adrianos who was born in 1413 and in the following year he himself was married. Their mother died in 1419. See R. Devreesse, *Codices Vaticani Graeci*, II (Vatican, 1937), p. 8.

[3] See D. A. Zakythinos, *Le Despotat grec de Morée*, II (Athens, 1953), p. 122.

34. Petros Doukas Adrianos: Two documents of July 1349 are signed by an imperial official (κουράτωρ) Petros Doukas Adrianos.[1] They concern a dispute between Philippa Asanina and the monastery of Xeropotamou over an estate in Macedonia. Petros appears to have been a nobleman for he is called εὐγενέστατος,[2] and he had also been created οἰκεῖος by the emperor. One of the documents describes him as a relative of Philippa Asanina[3] and this may account for the name of Doukas, borne by him, which could have been passed on by the family of Asan.

AGALLON

The Agallones were a family active during the last period of Byzantium's existence. The name ('Αγάλλων and in a vulgar form 'Αγάλλος) possibly derives from the verb ἀγάλλω (to honour, to glorify). Several members of the house are known: Konstantinos Agallon in c. 1280,[4] Manuel Agallon in 1330,[5] Georgios Agallon in c. 1400.[6] Sometime after 1444 Ioannes Argyropoulos was said to have taught among others Agallon ('Αγάλλωνα τὸν τοῦ Μόσχου).[7] Nikolaos Boullotes Agallon is attested both as a scribe and as *katholikos krites* of Morea in 1447.[8] Certain other references to unspecified Agallones date from the fourteenth century. An Agallos (sic) was among the *archons* of Constantinople who were arrested on 5 December 1371.[9] Another Agallon is mentioned in a letter of Manuel Raoul to Laskaris Metochites (1366/9).[10] An unknown writer of the same period addressed a letter to an Agallon.[11] Of course these last references do not necessarily imply three different persons; one or more of them may apply to a member of the Doukai-Agallones mentioned below.

A branch of the family styled as Doukai-Agallones flourished in the fourteenth century, but what is known of them derives solely from the will of Ioannes Laskaris Kalopheros, an active unionist of the time,[12] written in Latin in Venice on 5 July 1388. One cannot tell how the name of Doukas passed into the family.

---

[1] *Actes de Xéropotamou*, pp. 193–6.

[2] Ibid., p. 194.

[3] τὸν οἰκεῖον τῷ κραταιῷ καὶ ἁγίῳ ἡμῶν αὐθέντῃ καὶ βασιλεῖ Δούκαν κῦρ Πέτρον τὸν 'Αδριανόν, προσγενῆ τε ὄντα αὐτῆς (sc. Φιλίππας), ibid., p. 195. The documents state that Philippa Asanina was a daughter of Demetrios Asanes and the wife of the priest Michael ὁ Κοντοπετρῆς.

[4] MM, IV, p. 265.

[5] Regel et al., *Actes de Zographou*, p. 67.

[6] MM, II, p. 416.

[7] F. Fuchs, *Die höheren Schulen von Konstantinopel im Mittelalter* (Berlin, 1926), p. 71.

[8] Sp. P. Lampros, ' Λακεδαιμόνιοι βιβλιογράφοι καὶ κτήτορες κωδίκων κατὰ τοὺς μέσους αἰῶνας καὶ ἐπὶ Τουρκοκρατίας', *NE*, 4 (1097), 303–5; P. Lemerle, 'Le juge général des Grecs et la réforme judiciaire d'Andronic III', *Memorial Louis Petit* (Bucharest, 1948), p. 315; D. A. Zakythinos, *Le Despotat grec de Morée*, II (Athens, 1953), p. 130.

[9] Sp. P. Lampros and K. I. Amantos, *Βραχέα Χρονικά* (Athens, 1932), p. 81.

[10] R.-J. Loenertz, 'Emmanuelis Raul epistulae XII', *EEBΣ*, 26 (1956), 145.

[11] Sp. P. Lampros, ' Κατάλογος τῶν κωδίκων τῶν ἐν 'Αθήναις βιβλιοθηκῶν πλὴν τῆς 'Εθνικῆς ' *NE*, 4 (1907), 232.

[12] Bibliography on the man can be found in R.-J. Loenertz, *Correspondance de Manuel Calecas* (Vatican, 1950), p. 21, n. 2.

P.T.D.

35. Eudokia Doukaina Agallonissa: She was a sister of Ioannes Laskaris Kalopheros and lived in Constantinople in 1388. Kalopheros bequeathed to her five hundred 'bisantia alba de Cipro' from the revenues of his estates in Cyprus. This sum was to be given to Eudokia ('domine Efdokie Duchine Agalonisse, sorori dicti testatoris') on condition that she distributed part of it to the testator's poor relatives.[1] Eudokia must have inherited the name of Doukas-Agallon from her husband who is never heard of. She had a son Ioannes *36*.

36. Ioannes Doukas Agallon: Ioannes is the only known son of Eudokia *35*. The bequest made to his mother in the will of Kalopheros was to pass to him on the same terms after her death ('post vero mortem ipsius domine Efdochye . . . quingenta bisantia dari debere omni anno durantibus redditibus predictis domino Iohanni Duci Agalo, filio domine Efdochie legitimo . . .').[2] Ioannes also seems to be mentioned simply as Ἀγάλλων in a couple of letters of Demetrios Kydones to Kalopheros (1377–82).[3]

In the same will an already deceased Andronikos Agallon is referred to. He had an illegitimate son Iakobos who was to receive a bequest of one hundred bezants.[4] The connection of this Andronikos with Eudokia's family remains unspecified; it is unlikely that he was another son of hers. He could have been her husband's brother or even her husband himself.

AKROPOLITES

The first reference to a member of the Akropolites family is probably the one relating to the house of Iberitzes, situated near the Acropolis of Constantinople, which was said to have belonged to an Akropolites in the tenth century.[5] Nikolaos Akropolites was a βεστάρχης καὶ χαρτουλάριος τοῦ στρατιωτικοῦ λογοθέτου in 1088,[6] and in the middle of the twelfth century a μέγας χαρτουλάριος τοῦ γενικοῦ λογοθέτου Michael Akropolites lived.[7] Contemporary with him is the monk Gregorios Akropolites, recipient of one of Glykas' theological letters.[8] But the most distinguished member of the family is Georgios Akropolites, the active diplomat and historian who managed to attain the high office of *megas logothetes*.[9] In the thirteenth century the Akropolitai entered into matrimonial relations with such prominent representatives of the Byzantine aristocracy as the Tornikioi,[10] the Philanthropenoi,[11] and the Kontostephanoi.[12]

[1] R.-J. Loenertz, *Démétrius Cydonès, Correspondance* (Vatican, 1956–60), I, p. 188.
[2] Ibid.   [3] Ibid., II, pp. 110, 113, 374.   [4] Ibid., p. 190.
[5] R. Janin, *Constantinople byzantine. Développement urbain et répertoire topographique* (Paris, 1950), p. 334.
[6] MM, VI, p. 50.
[7] Laurent, *Médaillier Vatican*, pp. 70–71, no. 81.
[8] Gerasimos Mikragiannanites, ' Κατάλογος χειρογράφων κωδίκων τῆς βιβλιοθήκης τοῦ Κυριακοῦ τῆς κατὰ τὸ ῾Αγιώνυμον ῎Ορος τοῦ ῎Αθω ῾Ιερᾶς καὶ Μεγαλωνύμου Σκήτης τῆς ῾Αγίας Θεομήτορος ῎Αννης ', *ΕΕΒΣ*, 29 (1959), 155.
[9] For the descendants of Georgios see the not entirely reliable account in M. Treu, *Maximi monachi Planudis Epistulae* (Breslau, 1890), pp. 248–50.
[10] Cf. Nicol in *DOP*, 19 (1965), 252.   [11] Treu, op. cit., p. 249.
[12] See below, p. 84.

37. Maria Doukaina Akropolitissa: A single mention of her is made in a patriarchal document of 1351, referring to the purchase of the land of the Mougoulion convent made by Maria Palaiologina[1] from Maria Doukaina Akropolitissa and her son-in-law Demetrios Kontostephanos (... ἐξωνησα-μένη ἀπὸ τῆς κυρᾶς Μαρίας Δουκαίνης τῆς ᾿Ακροπολιτίσσης ἐκείνης καὶ τοῦ ἐπὶ θυγατρὶ γαμβροῦ αὐτῆς κὺρ Δημητρίου τοῦ Κοντοστεφάνου ἐκείνου).[2] Maria Palaiologina returned to Constantinople after 1281, and this purchase was certainly concluded shortly afterwards.

This information should be coupled with a notice found in the Paris codex of Suidas which mentions the foundation of the convent of Mougoulion[3] but makes it clear that the original small church had been built in 1261 by the father-in-law of the unnamed owner of the manuscript (ἐκτίσθη δὲ ἡ Παναγία τῶν Μαγουλίων χαμηλὴ παρὰ τοῦ πενθεροῦ μου). These two references to the well-known convent have led to the identification of the owner of the manuscript as the historian Georgios Akropolites whose wife Maria Doukaina Akropolitissa is thought to be.[4] This appears possible, but the assumption that Isaakios Doukas 73, a brother of Ioannes III Batazes 72, was in fact the father of Maria[5] is open to question.

Kougeas makes Isaakios Doukas a maternal uncle of Michael VIII *142*; actually Isaakios was the grandfather of that emperor's wife Theodora *74*.[6] Had Akropolites married a daughter of Isaakios *73*, he would have been, properly speaking, an uncle of Michael VIII *142* and not a γαμβρός as he is explicitly described.[7] Assuming that Maria Doukaina Akropolitissa was the wife of Georgios, as a close relative of Michael VIII *142*, she could have inherited the name of Doukas either from the Palaiologoi or from the Batatzai. The second alternative may be the more probable. Maria could have been related to Isaakios Doukas *73* but not as his daughter; two children of Isaakios *73* are known: Ioannes the father of Theodora *74* who died young and does not appear to have left other children,[8] and the εὐγενὴς γραῦς Στρατηγοπουλῖνα[9] who could hardly have been the mother of Maria. Still Isaakios *73* may have left other children, and an unheard of son or daughter of his could have become the parent-in-law of Georgios Akropolites and the builder of the original church of Mougoulion.

[1] Papadopulos, *Genealogie der Palaiologen*, p. 33, no. 54.

[2] MM, I, p. 312.

[3] The notice was edited by F. Dölger, 'Der Titel des sogenannten Suidaslexikons', *SBBAW*, 1936, pp. 30–31.

[4] S. B. Kougeas, ''Ο Γεώργιος ᾿Ακροπολίτης κτήτωρ τοῦ Παρισινοῦ κώδικος τοῦ Σουΐδα', *Byzantina-Metabyzantina*, I, II (1949), especially pp. 70–1; cf. H. Grégoire in *B*, 21 (1952), 259, n. 1. However, it must be pointed out that the wife of Georgios Akropolites is called Eudokia by her son Konstantinos; see H. Delehaye, 'Constantini Acropolitae hagiographi byzantini epistularum manipulus,' *AB*, 51 (1933), 282; cf. D. M. Nicol, 'Constantine Acropolites; A Prosopographical Note,' *DOP*, 19 (1965), 251. If this is not a monastic name, identification of Maria Doukaina Akropolitissa as the wife of Georgios must be abandoned.

[5] Kougeas, op. cit., pp. 71–3; R. Janin, *Les Eglises et les Monastères* (Paris, 1951), p. 222.

[6] See Akrop., p. 101.

[7] MM, III, p. 96; cf. Akrop., p. 164.

[8] Akrop., p. 101.

[9] Pach., II, pp. 154–5.

An unpublished seal, belonging to a *kouropalatissa* Maria Akropolitissa, has been preserved.[1] As the historian is never mentioned with the rank of *kouropalates*, it is unlikely that the seal belongs to his wife Maria.

Georgios Akropolites and Maria Doukaina Akropolitissa became the parents of at least three children: the *megas logothetes* Konstantinos Akropolites,[2] the monk Melchisedek[3] and a daughter Theodora *38*.

38. Theodora Doukaina Akropolitissa: An interesting note on cod. Vat. gr. 307 preserves the names of two members of the Akropolites family and their spouses. Ioannes Komnenos Akropolites married Theodora Doukaina Philanthropene *167* and Theodora Doukaina Akropolitissa married Demetrios Komnenos Kontostephanos.[4] These lines were apparently written on the occasion of the two marriages which could have been simultaneous, and I believe that the two Akropolitai mentioned were most probably brother and sister. The additional reference to Demetrios Kontostephanos as a γαμβρός of Maria Doukaina Akropolitissa (see above) leaves no doubt that the present Theodora was Maria's daughter.

Ioannes Komnenos[5] Akropolites could be an unknown son of the historian, or even of Melchisedek before he took monastic vows.

---

[1] Laurent, *Médaillier Vatican*, p. 71, n. 5.

[2] For Konstantinos and his family see Nicol, op. cit., pp. 249–56.

[3] Cf. Treu, loc. cit.

[4]   *I.*   Ἀκροπολίτης Κομνηνὸς Ἰωάννης
              Φιλανθρωπηνῇ Δουκαίνῃ Θεοδώρᾳ.
         Θεὸς χαριτόκλητον εἰς Θεοδώραν
              Φιλανθρωπηνὴν Ἀκροπολίτην ἄγει.

        II.   Χριστὸς Κομνηνῷ τὴν Δούκαιναν συνδέει
              τὴν Ἀκροπολίτισσαν Κοντοστεφάνῳ.
         Κοντοστεφάνῳ Κομνηνῷ Δημητρίῳ
              Θεὸς συνάπτει Δούκαιναν Θεοδώραν.

See G. Mercati and P. Franchi de 'Cavalieri, *Codices Vaticani Graeci*, 1 (Rome, 1923), p. 456. I have corrected Δούκαιν(α) to Δουκαίνῃ and συνδεῖ (?) to συνδέει.

[5] The surname Komnenos in the thirteenth century is almost meaningless. Any of the noble families, including the Palaiologoi and the Batatzai, could claim it.

ANGELOS

The Angeloi, an inconspicuous family originally from Philadelphia in Asia
Minor, owed their rapid social advancement to the rather unexpected marriage
of their kinsman Konstantinos to Theodora, the youngest daughter of Alexios I
Komnenos and Eirene Doukaina *26*. This union might have been distasteful
to the imperial couple. Its lineage nevertheless proved significant enough to
produce three emperors (true, no particular asset to their house[1]) as well as
establishing one of its branches in Epirus, where it showed itself, with the
possible exception of the rulers of Trebizond, as the most dynamic of all the
descendants of the Komnenoi.[2]

Konstantinos Angelos and Theodora Komnene, married in 1110/15, became
the parents of four sons and three daughters,[3] at least two of whom officially
assumed as their distinctive cognomen their maternal grandmother's family
name of Doukas. This need not cause surprise. The name of Angelos, as a less
noble and less significant one, had to give way before the more pretentious
appelations of Doukas and Komnenos which naturally had a greater appeal to
the Byzantine nobility of the twelfth century. The Angeloi, as is well-known,
almost cease to exist as a prominent family after 1204, but the name of Doukas,
either in itself or in various compound forms, passed on to the Greek, and later
to the Serbian, rulers of Epirus and Thessaly and was preserved there up to the
fifteenth century.

---

[1] Τὸ τῶν ἀνάκτων χιμαιρῶδες τρικάρηνον as Nikolaos Mesarites describes the Angelos dynasty.
See A. Heisenberg, 'Neue Quellen zur Geschichte des lateinischen Kaisertums und der Kir-
chenunion', I, *SBBAW*, 1922, p. 25. An anonymous chronicle calls the Angeloi

... τὸ τῶν 'Αγγέλων γένος
τὸ νόθον καὶ κακοφυὲς τότε 'Ρωμαίοις ἄρξαν,

for reference see the introduction p. 13, n. 2.

[2] No satisfactory modern work dealing the entire family with its western branches exists.
There is of course the old account of Ducange, *Familiae*, pp. 201–11, which can still be profitably
used. The emergence of the house and its fortunes during the twelfth century have been studied
by G. Ostrogorsky, 'Vozvyshenie roda Angelov', *Yubileinyi Sbornik Russkago Arkheologicheskago
Obshchestva* (Belgrade, 1936), pp. 111–29, which should however now be amended by L. Stiernon's 'Les origines du Despotat d'Epire', *REB*, 17 (1959), 90–126, and 'Notes de prosopographie
et de titulature byzantines: Constantin Ange (pan)sebastohypertate', *REB*, 19 (1961), 373–83.
A detailed, but not entirely accurate, genealogy of the Epirote and Thessalian branches
of the Angeloi was compiled by C. Hopf, *Chroniques gréco-romanes* (Berlin, 1873), pp. 529–30.
On this cf. N. A. Bees, 'Sur les tables généalogiques des despotes et dynastes médievaux
d'Epire et de Thessalie', *Zeitschrift für osteuropäische Geschichte*, 3 (1913), 209–15. Certain heraldic
works mentioned in *BZ*, 47 (1954), 479–80, are of no value to the historian of this Byzantine
house.

[3] Of his sons, Andronikos *39* and especially Ioannes *40* were the more active while Alexios
and Isaakios are only rarely mentioned. The daughters were Maria the wife of Konstantinos
Kamytzes (S. Papademetriou, ''Ο Πρόδρομος τοῦ Μαρκιανοῦ κώδικος XI. 22', *VV*, 10 [1903],
111), Eudokia who married Goudelios Tzykandeles (cf. Lampros, ' Μαρκιανὸς 524 ', pp. 123–4),
and Zoe who became the wife of Andronikos Synadenos (for his career see V. Laurent, 'Andronic
Synadenos', *REB*, 20 [1962,] 210–14).

39. Andronikos Doukas (or **Angelos**): Called either Angelos[1] or Doukas,[2] Andronikos was one of the sons of Konstantinos Angelos and Theodora Komnene. He took part in the campaign of Myriokephalon (1176)[3] as well as in other unfortunate expeditions against the Turks.[4] In 1177 he was a member of the embassy that travelled to Jerusalem to renew an alliance with king Baldwin IV.[5] He was an enemy of Andronikos Komnenos but was unsuccessful in attempting to prevent him from entering the City (1182),[6] and afterwards he stood in opposition to his regime. Consequently, he faced violent persecution and was compelled to flee together with his sons.[7] Andronikos sought refuge in Acre in Syria where he appears to have died,[8] certainly before the accession of his son Isaakios (12 September 1185).

A seal bearing the metrical inscription

$$\text{"}Aνανδρε\ μῆτερ,\ πορφυροβλάστου\ κλάδον$$
$$\text{'}Aνδρόνικον\ Δούκαν\ με,\ παρθένε,\ σκέποις$$

probably belongs to him.[9]

Andronikos, sometime before 1155, married Euphrosyne Kastamonitissa[10] and became the father of six sons—among them Isaakios II, Alexios III, and Konstantinos,[11] the others' names being uncertain or unknown—and two daughters, Eirene[12] and Theodora.[13] As far as it can be ascertained, none of his children is ever mentioned as having the name of Doukas.

---

[1] Chon., pp. 254 and 319; Skout., p. 318; William of Tyre in *PL*, 201, col. 830B.

[2] In a document of 2 March 1166 (*PG*, 140, col. 236B), where he is described as a 'cousin' to the emperor (Manuel I Komnenos). See also Skout., p. 296. Elsewhere (*PG*, 140, col. 253B), the name of Andronikos appears together with those of his brothers but without family designations. Note that a manuscript of Choniates refers to him as Δούκας, see Chon., p. 254. An inscription of 1192/3 mentions him without family name, see H. Grégoire, 'Hellenica et byzantina', *B*, 32 (1962), 44.

[3] Chon., p. 233; Skout., p. 285; cf. Chalandon, *Les Comnène*, II, pp. 507 ff.

[4] Chon., p. 254; Skout., pp. 296–7, relates that following his desertion the emperor almost reached the decision to make him wear woman's clothes and expose him publicly.

[5] William of Tyre in *PL*, 201, col. 830B; cf. Dölger, *Regesten*, II, p. 86, no. 1526.

[6] Chon., p. 319; Skout., pp. 318–19; cf. F. Cognasso, 'Partiti politici e lotte dinastiche in Bisanzio alla morte di Manuele Comneno', *Memorie della Reale Accademia delle Scienze di Torino. Scienze morali, storiche e filologiche*, 62 (1912), 249.   [7] Chon., pp. 344–6.

[8] See 'Chronicon Magni Presbyteri' in *MGH*, Scriptores XVII, p. 511; cf. Cognasso, loc. cit.

[9] The last edition of the seal is by Laurent, *Bulles métriques*, p. 17, no. 20, who cautiously attributes it to Andronikos *21*; cf. idem, 'Bulletin de sigillographie byzantine. 1930', *B*, 6 (1931), 815. In actual fact, we must look for the owner of the seal among the sons of a porphyrogenitus parent (πορφυροβλάστου κλάδον), and the present Andronikos is apparently the only one that fits in.

[10] His son Isaakios, who was not the eldest, is described as less than forty when he lost his throne in 1195 (Chon., p. 596). The same Chon., p. 365, calls the mother of this emperor Euphrosyne and elsewhere (p .574) refers to Theodoros Kastamonites as a maternal uncle of Isaakios. Euphrosyne died in 1185/95 while accompanying Isaakios in a campaign against Dyrrachion. See J. Darrouzès, 'Notice sur Grégoire Antiochos (1160 à 1196)', *REB*, 20 (1962), 67.

[11] For the career of Konstantinos see M. Bachmann and F. Dölger, 'Die Rede des Megas Drungarios Gregorios Antiochos auf den Sebastokrator Konstantinos Angelos', *BZ*, 40 (1940), especially pp. 361–2. To this Konstantinos an inscription of an altar cloth published by M. S. Theochare, ' 'Η ἐνδυτὴ τοῦ 'Αγίου Μάρκου ', *EEBΣ*, 29 (1959), 194, certainly belongs as V. Laurent, 'Le sébastocrator Constantin Ange et le péplum du musée de Saint-Marc à Venise', *REB*, 18 (1960), 208–13, has convincingly shown despite the editor's rejoinder 'Sur le sébastocrator Constantin Comnène Ange et l'endyté du Musée de Saint Marc à Venise', *BZ*, 56 (1963), 273–83.

[12] Chon., p. 489. She became the wife of Ioannes Kantakouzenos.

[13] Chon., pp. 497–8. Theodora married Conrad of Montferrat.

40. Ioannes Doukas: Ioannes, the son of Konstantinos Angelos and Theodora Komnene is always called Doukas by the sources.[1] The dignity of *sebastokrator* was apparently conferred upon him shortly after Isaakios II ascended the throne.[2] The date of Ioannes' birth is not known, and the conventional reference to him as an 'old man' in 1185[3] does not help to fix it. In any case, his name is met for the first time on 2 March 1166, in an imperial document.[4] Ten years later Ioannes commanded a section of the army at the battle of Myriokephalon[5] but failed to repel the Seljuks when ordered to do so.[6]

Like his other close relatives, Ioannes Doukas opposed the regime of Andronikos I and he naturally joined hands with his nephew Isaakios in the desperate effort that overthrew the last Komnenos.[7] In the coronation ceremony, seeing the hesitation of Isaakios in accepting the still insecure crown, he raised a laugh by offering his own bald head to be crowned instead, but this gesture was violently opposed by the people who shouted that they did not wish to be ruled by an old man.[8] Despite his age, Ioannes took part in several campaigns fought by the new emperor against the rebelling Bulgarians, and at least on one occasion it was said that he commanded the Byzantine forces admirably.[9] However the distrustful emperor suspected him of having his eyes on the throne and in particular feared Ioannes' close associations with the rebel Alexios Branas.[10] There appears to be some truth in this as Ioannes was quick to support his other nephew Alexios III in the coup of 1195 and his conspicuous presence is attested in the procession that escorted the newly created emperor to the palace.[11]

By an unspecified marriage,[12] Ioannes Doukas became the father of

[1] For references see Stiernon, 'Les origines du Despotat d'Epire', pp. 102 ff.

[2] He is called by this title for the first time in 1186 by Chon., p. 482.

[3] Chon., p. 450. Similarly during the reign of Alexios III (1195–1203) he is spoken of as being 'very mature in age' (πεπαίτερος ὢν τὴν ἡλικίαν, Chon., p. 604).

[4] *PG*, 140, col. 236B. He also participated in the synod of 6 March 1166, *PG*, 140, col. 253B.

[5] Chon., p. 233; Skout., p. 285.   [6] Chon., p. 245.

[7] Chon., p. 447.

[8] Chon., p. 450; Skout., p. 357; cf. Cognasso, op. cit., pp. 314–15.

[9] Chon., p. 489; cf. R. L. Wolff, 'The Second Bulgarian Empire', *Speculum*, 24 (1949), p 184. He also accompanied Isaakios in the disastrous campaign of 1191 in which he managed to escape unharmed with his troops (Chon., p. 562).

[10] Chon., pp. 489 and 502; cf. F. Cognasso, 'Un imperatore bisantino della decadenza: Isacco II Angelo', *Bessarione*, 31 (1915), 279. Judging from a document of 10 September 1191 (Grumel, *Regestes*, III, p. 181, no. 1178), where Ioannes' name comes directly after that of the emperor (Papadopoulos-Kerameus, 'Ἀνάλεκτα, II, p. 362), one can regard him as the second most prominent man in the empire at that time.

[11] Once again the baldness of Ioannes became the target of derision when his σεβαστοκρατορικὸς στέφανος fell to the ground when the mule on which he was riding gave a sudden jump (Chon., pp. 604–5; Skout., p. 415). Subsequently he appears as a personal enemy of his nephew Manuel Kamytzes (Chon., p. 660). Ioannes also figures in an imperial document wrongly assigned to Alexios I Komnenos by the editors in G. Rouillard and P. Collomp, *Actes de Lavra* (Paris, 1937), p. 122, no. 45. For the dating of this document see F. Dölger, 'Zur Textgestaltung der Lavra-Urkunden und zur geschichtlichen Auswertung', *BZ*, 39 (1939), 34; G. Ostrogorsky, 'Urum–Despotes: die Anfänge der Despoteswürde in Byzanz', *BZ*, 44 (1951), 451, n. 3; idem, *Pour l'histoire de la féodalité byzantine* (Brussels, 1953), pp. 45–6.

[12] P. d'Outreman, *Constantinopolis Belgica* (Tournai, 1643), p. 288, writes: '. . . Ioannes sebasto-crator frater Andronici Angeli fuit, atque adeo Isaaci et Alexij Imperatorum patruus, qui ducta Zoe Constantini Ducae ex Anna Comnena filia, uxoris gratia, in Ducarum familiam per

Isaakios,[1] Alexios *41*, Theodoros *42*, Manuel *43*, Konstantinos *44*, and one or more daughters of unknown name.[2] He had also an illegitimate son Michael *45*.

41. Alexios: A seal bearing the legend

$$'E\gamma\grave{\omega} \; \kappa\rho\alpha\tau\acute{\nu}\nu\omega \; \tau\grave{\alpha}s \; \gamma\rho\alpha\phi\grave{\alpha}s \; 'A\lambda\epsilon\xi\acute{\iota}o\upsilon$$
$$\varDelta o\upsilon\kappa\hat{\omega}\nu \; Ko\mu\nu\eta\nu\hat{\omega}\nu \; 'A\gamma\gamma\epsilon\lambda\omega\nu\acute{\upsilon}\mu\omega\nu \; \kappa\lambda\acute{\alpha}\delta o\upsilon^3$$

should certainly be dated to the second half of the twelfth century. It is possible that the owner is Alexios, a son of Ioannes *40* whom Choniates calls Komnenos and who was blinded by Andronikos.[4]

---

adoptionem transijt'. Ducange, *Familiae*, p. 206, could find no trace of such a marriage which is indeed not confirmed by any source. Nevertheless, this statement that Ioannes Doukas married a certain Zoe Doukaina is found in the secondary literature with various attempts (some chronologically and genealogically impossible) to define the family connections and the ancestry of this Zoe. Cf. for instance A. Meliarakis, Ἱστορία τοῦ Βασιλείου τῆς Νικαίας καὶ τοῦ Δεσποτάτου τῆς Ἠπείρου (*1204–1261*) (Athens, 1898), p. 49; S. Cirac Estopañan, *Bizancio y España* (Barcelona, 1943), i, p. 181, and ii, table viii; P. Lemerle, 'Trois actes du Despote d'Epire Michel ii concernant Corfou, connus en traduction latine', Προσφορὰ εἰς Στίλπωνα Π. Κυριακίδην (Thessalonica, 1953), p. 407; D. M. Nicol, *The Despotate of Epiros* (Oxford, 1957), p. 11; V. Grumel *La chronologie* (Paris, 1958), p. 364. But after all the information of d'Outreman might be correct. A seal belonging to a Zoe, νύμφη of the porphyrogenita Theodora Komnene (see Laurent, *Bulles métriques*, p. 53, no. 149), who can be no other than the daughter of Alexios I, could in fact refer to the wife of Ioannes Doukas.

---

[1] He married a daughter of Alexios Branas, cf. Chon., pp. 447 and 502.

[2] Ioannes Kantakouzenos who in about 1240 became the husband of Eirene Palaiologina (cf. Papadopulos, *Genealogie der Palaiologen*, pp. 18–19, no. 29) is described in epigrams of Planudes as being a son of a daughter of the present Ioannes Doukas; see Sp. P. Lampros, ''Ἐπιγράμματα Μαξίμου Πλανούδη', *NE*, 13 (1916), especially pp. 416 and 418. The name of Kantakouzenos' mother is not known nor that of his father; the latter might have been Michael Kantakouzenos who is called a συγγενὴς of Alexios III Angelos by Chon., p. 593. In a letter of Bardanes a twin sister of Theodoros *42* is mentioned; see E. Kurtz, 'Georgios Bardanes, Metropolit von Kerkyra', *BZ*, 15 (1906), 604. She might be identical with the mother of Kantakouzenos or be distinguished from her as Kurtz, op. cit., p. 611, believes.

There is a third, indirect, reference to a daughter of Ioannes. A count of Cephalonia, thought to be Maio Orsini (1194–1238), is called by a western source a *sororius* of Theodoros *42*, see 'Chronica Alberti monachi trium fontium', *MGH*, Scriptores, 23 (1874), 938. This means of course that his wife was a daughter of Ioannes, but Orsini is known to have been married after 1216 and perhaps only a little before 1228; see I. Romanos, ' Γρατιανὸς Ζώρζης ' in Κερκυραϊκὰ Χρονικά 7 (1959), 214, and especially N. A. Bees, 'Ein politisches Treubekenntnis von Benedictus dem römisch-katholischen Bischof von Kefalonia (1228)', *BNJ*, 3 (1922), 172. The name of this woman is variously given as Anna or Theodora (see Bees, op. cit., pp. 171–2 where the older literature is cited and discussed). But it is almost impossible to explain how Ioannes, already an old man in 1185 (see above p. 87, n. 3), could have a daughter bearing children as late as forty years later. Could she have been a niece of Theodoros *42*? Whoever her father was, in a Greek document of 1228 she is called Κομνηνή (Bees, op. cit., p. 166) and she appears to have become the mother of four children: Theodoros who died young, Richard who succeeded his father, and two daughters (Romanos, op. cit., pp. 218–19; Hopf, *Chroniques gréco-romaines*, p. 529).

[3] Laurent, *Bulles métriques*, pp. 42–3, no. 114.

[4] Chon., p. 483. The parentage of Alexios has been established by E. L. Vranoussi, Τὰ ἁγιολογικὰ κείμενα τοῦ ὁσίου Χριστοδούλου (Athens, 1966), pp. 162–4, citing evidence from an encomium of St Christodoulos.

42. Theodoros Doukas Komnenos (Angelos): Theodoros, the dangerous rival of the Nicaean emperors, was a son of Ioannes *40*.[1] Like his father and his brothers, he preferred to employ in his official acts the name of Doukas, especially in its compound form Κομνηνὸς ὁ Δούκας. Yet the cognomens Angelos and Komnenos are frequently attached to his person.[2]

The early career of Theodoros is obscure. He succeeded his half-brother Michael *45* in *c.* 1215 and the capture of Thessalonica between October and December 1224[3] was his greatest achievement leading to his coronation by Chomatianos in 1227/8.[4] Henceforth Theodoros signs as *basileus kai autokratōr Rōmaiōn*.[5] His defeat by the Bulgarian tzar Ivan II Asen at Klokotniča in April 1230[6] resulted in his captivity in the course of which he was blinded after being implicated in a conspiracy against his victor.[7] Released in *c.* 1237,[8] he returned to Thessalonica where he was once more the real power behind his weak sons. He died a captive in Nicaea shortly after 1253.[9]

No known seals of Theodoros exist. He issued some types of coinage which

[1] He is referred to by the sources throughout as a brother of Michael *45*. See Akrop., p. 24; Greg., I, p. 25; Skout., p. 454; Ephraim, v. 7639. An inscription on the walls of Dyrrachion commemorates him as follows:

παῖς οὗτος ἀνδρὸς εὐτυχοῦς Ἰωάννου
σεβαστοκρατοροῦντος, ἄνθους πορφύρας,
Θεόδωρος μέγιστος ἐν στρατηγίαις
Δούκας Κομνηνὸς εὐσθενὴς βριαρόχειρ.

See A. Boeckh, *Corpus Inscriptionum Graecarum*, IV, p. 99.

[2] Theodoros himself appears to have used both forms interchangeably. Thus a document of May 1228 is signed by Θεόδωρος ... ὁ Δούκας (B. Vasilievskii, 'Epirotica sacculi XIII', *VV*, 3 [1896], 299; cf. Chomatianos in J. B. Pitra, *Analecta Sacra et Classica*, VI [Rome, 1891], pp. 94, 261) while another dated June of the same year bears the signature Θεόδωρος ... Κομνηνὸς ὁ Δούκας (MM, V, p. 15). In a letter to Apokaukos from September 1219 he signs Θεόδωρος ὁ Δούκας, but in the text he calls himself Θεόδωρος Κομνηνὸς ὁ Δούκας (Vasilievskii, 'Epirotica', p. 253). The same inconsistency is observed in the contemporary sources. The patriarch Manuel and his regular correspondent Apokaukos refer to him either as Δούκας (ibid., pp. 264 and 280; S. Pétridès, 'Jean Apokaukos, lettres et autres documents inédits', *Izvestiya Russk. Arkh. Instituta v Konstantinopole*, 14 [1909], 9, 10, 13, 14, 16, 22) or as Κομνηνός (Vasilievskii, 'Epirotica', pp. 268–9 and *passim*; Pétridès, 'Jean Apokaukos', pp. 23, 26, 31; A. Papadopoulos-Kerameus, ' Συνοδικὰ γράμματα Ἰωάννου τοῦ Ἀποκαύκου, μητροπολίτου Ναυπάκτου ', *Βυζαντίς*, I [1909], 10). Similarly Chomatianos, op. cit., in addressing or mentioning Theodoros, uses the appelations Δούκας (pp. 109, 488, 526), Κομνηνὸς ὁ Δούκας (pp. 53, 468), Κομνηνός (pp. 53, 92, 127, 135, 335, 336, 473), or even μέγας Κομνηνός (pp. 90, 153, 393). As Stiernon, 'Les origines du Despotat d'Epire', p. 117, has observed, Akropolites speaking of Theodoros before 1230 calls him Κομνηνὸς and only after his fall refers to him as Ἄγγελος. Greg., I, pp. 26, 27, 28, and Skout., pp. 475, 484, call him Ἄγγελος. Michael Choniates addresses him as Theodoros Doukas and as καλλώπισμα Κομνηνῶν Δουκάδων δόξα, Ῥωμαίων καύχημα, see Sp. P. Lampros, *Μιχαὴλ Ἀκομινάτου τοῦ Χωνιάτου Τά Σωζόμενα*, I (Athens, 1879), pp. 326 and 329.

[3] For the date see J. Longnon, 'La reprise de Salonique par les Grecs en 1224', *Actes du VIe Congrès International d'Etudes Byzantines*, I (Paris, 1950), pp. 141–6; B. Sinogowitz, 'Zur Eroberung Thessalonikes im Herbst 1224', *BZ*, 45 (1952), 28; G. Ostrogorsky, *History of the Byzantine State* (Oxford, 1956), p. 384, n. 1; Nicol, *The Despotate of Epiros*, pp. 63 and 73–4.

[4] L. Stiernon, 'Les origines du Despotat d'Epire', *Actes du XIIe Congrès d'Etudes Byzantines* (Belgrade, 1964), II, pp. 197–202, maintains that the coronation took place between November 1227 and April 1228.

[5] Cf. his documents listed by Lemerle, 'Trois actes', pp. 408–9.

[6] Akrop., p. 42; cf. Nicol, op. cit., p. 110.

[7] Akrop., p. 42; Pach., I, p. 82. Apparently this punishment was inflicted upon Theodoros long after his capture as Asen is reputed to have treated him well for some time (ἐπὶ πολύ).

[8] Akrop., pp. 60–61; cf. Nicol, op. cit., p. 134.   [9] Akrop., p. 92; cf. Nicol, op. cit., p. 153.

do not however bear the title of *basileus* but that of *despotes* which no source attaches to him. His name in the coins appears in the forms Θεόδωρος Δούκας or Θεόδωρος δεσπότης ὁ Δούκας.[1]

Theodoros married, undoubtedly before he acquired power in Epirus, Maria Petraliphina (Doukaina) *160*. They had four children: Ioannes, Demetrios *46*, Anna *47* and Eirene.[2]

43. Manuel Doukas: Manuel, the son of Ioannes *40*, is commonly known as Doukas[3] and only rarely is he referred to as Angelos.[4] Sometime after 1215 (or more likely after 1227/8) Theodoros conferred upon Manuel the dignity of a *despotes*, and it was with this title that he governed Thessalonica during his brother's captivity (1230–*c.* 1237).[5] After his expulsion from this city, he eventually succeeded in establishing himself for a brief period in Thessaly where he died in 1241.[6]

In *c.* 1216, through the efforts of Theodoros *42*, Manuel married a Serbian princess who was a sister of king Stephen II Nemanja.[7] She could not have lived long as in 1225 Manuel married again, this time with Maria, an illegitimate daughter of Ivan II Asen of Bulgaria.[8] We do not hear of any of his children. After his expulsion from Thessalonica in *c.* 1237, his wife was sent back to her father.[9] During his rule in Thessalonica Manuel issued some coinage with the inscription Μανουὴλ δεσπότης ὁ Δούκας.[10]

His seal bears the legend Μανουὴλ δεσπότης Κομνηνοδούκας.[11]

[1] W. Wroth, *Catalogue of the Coins of the Vandals, Ostrogoths and Lombards and of the Empires of Thessalonica, Nicaea and Trebizond in the British Museum* (London, 1911), pp. 16–93; cf. Nicol, op. cit., pp. 204–5.

[2] Akrop., p. 60; Skout., p. 484. Of these only Demetrios *46* and Anna *47* are referred to as Doukai. Ioannes, a gentle and ascetic man, held Thessalonica as *basileus* (*c.* 1238–42) and as *despotes* (1242–4) until his premature death. Eirene became the wife of Ivan II Asen of Bulgaria and gave him several children. See some verses for their marriage edited by S. G. Mercati in *Isvestiya na Arkheologicheskiya Institut*, 9 (1935), 34.

[3] In the only genuine document of his with a signature he signs Μανουὴλ δεσπότης ὁ Δούκας, MM, III, p. 67. In a letter of the patriarch Germanos II it is said τοῦ Κομνηνοῦ κυροῦ Μανουὴλ τοῦ Δούκα, BZ, 16 (1907), 137. Chomatianos, op. cit., p. 525, calls him simply Μανουὴλ Δούκας.

[4] Akrop., p. 43; Skout., p. 475.

[5] Akrop., p. 43, says that both before and during his rule in Thessalonica he was styling himself as *despotes*. Cf. R. Guilland, 'Etudes sur l'histoire administrative de l'empire byzantin: le despote', REB, 17 (1959), 74. In a *prostagma* of his Theodoros *42* mentions Manuel as follows: τὸν πανευτυχέστατον δεσπότην καὶ περιπόθητον αὐτάδελφον τῆς βασιλείας μου κῦριν Μανουὴλ τὸν Δούκαν, Papadopoulos-Kerameus, 'Ανάλεκτα, IV, p. 119. This document which is dated November indiction VIII is assigned by the editor to the year 1234, i.e. in a period when Theodoros was certainly captive in Bulgaria. The alternative year 1219 likewise presents a difficulty due to the mention of the word βασίλεια in the document before Theodoros' *42* coronation. The supposed reference to Manuel as αὐτοκράτωρ in a much mutilated inscription at the church of Panagia Βλαχερνῶν in Arta (so A. K. Orlandos, ' Βυζαντινὰ μνημεῖα τῆς "Αρτης', 'Αρχεῖον τῶν Βυζαντινῶν Μνημείων τῆς Ἑλλάδος, 2 [1936], 45–7) is hard to explain.

[6] Akrop., pp. 62 and 64; cf. Meliarakis, op. cit., p. 33.   [7] Chomatianos, op. cit., pp. 50–51.

[8] Akrop., pp. 41, 44, and 60; cf. Meliarakis, op. cit., p. 251; Nicol, op. cit., p. 114.

[9] Akrop., p. 61.

[10] See Wroth, op. cit., pp. 197–9; Dr Longuet, 'Deux monnaies de Manuel l'Ange Comnène Ducas empereur de Thessalonique (1230–1262 [sic])', RN, v series, 7 (1943), 137–44; Nicol, op. cit., pp. 205–6.

[11] The reading was proposed by Lemerle, 'Trois actes', p. 410, n. 20. Another seal reading Μάρτυς, Μανουὴλ Κομνηνοδούκαν σκέποις (Laurent, *Bulles métriques*, pp. 86–7, no. 243) may belong to Manuel.

44. Konstantinos Doukas (Komnenos): Konstantinos was a son of Ioannes Doukas *40*.[1] He is mostly designated as Doukas[2] and only rarely as Komnenos.[3] Presumably after his coronation Theodoros made Konstantinos a *despotes*,[4] and it appears that he was entrusted with the administration of the district of Naupaktos which might have been extended to the whole of Epirus. This could have lasted till the advent of Michael *48*, sometime after 1230. Nevertheless Konstantinos continued to be active during the period afterwards and is met with for the last time in 1242, still bearing the dignity of *despotes*.[5] It is not known whether he left any children.

45. Michael Doukas (Komnenos, Angelos): Michael, the creator of the separatist state of Epirus,[6] was an illegitimate son of Ioannes *40*.[7] Consequently the Greek sources mostly call him Doukas[8] and also Komnenos and Angelos.[9] The year of his birth is not known; Choniates speaks of him as being young in 1201.[10]

[1] Cf. Akrop., p. 24. For the man see especially Nicol, op. cit., pp. 54–7. It is possible that he is identical with another Konstantinos Doukas *235* mentioned by Chon., p. 756, and Skout., p. 448, as a rival of Konstantinos Laskaris at Constantinople in the night of 12 April 1204.

[2] Apokaukos in his letters speaks of him as ὁ πανευγενέστατος Δούκας κυρὸς Κωνσταντῖνος (Pétridès, op. cit., p. 28) or τὸν πανευτυχέστατον αὐτάδελφον τοῦ τῶν ἡμετέρων κράτορος καὶ νικητοῦ Κομνηνοῦ (sc. Θεοδώρου *42*), κῦρ Κωνσταντῖνον τὸν Δούκαν (Vasilievskii, op. cit., p. 271) or ὁ πανευτυχέστατος κύριός μου κῦρ Κωνσταντῖνος ὁ Δούκας (ibid., p. 281). His brother Theodoros *42* refers to him (in 1228) as τοῦ πανευτυχεστάτου δεσπότου καὶ περιποθήτου αὐταδέλφου τῆς βασιλείας μου κῦρ Κωνσταντίνου τοῦ Δούκα (ibid., p. 298). Cf. Papadopoulos-Kerameus, Ἀνάλεκτα, IV, p. 122.

[3] E.g. in a letter of the patriarch Germanos II, dated in April 1229, it is said τοῦ πανιερωτάτου Κομνηνοῦ κυρίου Κωνσταντίνου; see G. A. Ralles and M. Potles, Σύνταγμα τῶν θείων καὶ ἱερῶν κανόνων, v (Athens, 1958), p. 106; cf. Orlandos, op. cit., p. 58.

[4] Akrop., pp. 37 and 65; cf. Nicol, op. cit., pp. 54 and 67; Guilland, op. cit., p. 75.

[5] Akrop., p. 65; cf. Nicol, op. cit., p. 140, n.12.
According to an eighteenth-century note Konstantinos built the church of the monastery of Βαρνακόβας, near Naupaktos, in 1228/9. See Sp. P. Lampros, ' Ἡ μονὴ Βαρνακόβας καὶ οἱ ἐν αὐτῇ ὑποτιθέμενοι τάφοι τῶν αὐτοκρατόρων Ἀλεξίου καὶ Μανουὴλ τῶν Κομνηνῶν', ΝΕ, 6 (1909), 383. Among the inscriptions of the same monastery there are two mutilated ones which may refer to members of the Doukas-Angelos family, the second mentioning an unidentifiable Komnenodoukas; see A. K. Orlandos, Ἡ μονὴ Βαρνακόβας (Athens, 1922), pp. 12–14.

[6] For references to him see especially L. Stiernon, 'Les origines du Despotat d'Epire', REB, 17 (1959), 120–26.

[7] Chon., pp. 700 and 841. In one of his documents, preserved in Latin, he says, 'ego Michael Comnanus Dux, filius quondam sevastocratoris Ioannis Ducis', TT, II, p. 119. Several other contemporary sources speak of Michael as a cousin (ἐξάδελφος) of the emperors Isaakios II and Alexios III or as an uncle (θεῖος) of Alexios IV. For references see Stiernon, 'Les origines', pp. 103–5.

[8] In a διαγνωστικὸν σημείωμα of his, dating from the reign of Isaakios II, he signs himself Μιχαὴλ ὁ Δούκας, MM, IV, p. 327; cf. p. 328. Another document, assigned by the editors to June 1206 (ibid., III, p. 59), in reality belongs to Michael *48*. See M. Marković, 'Vizantiske povelje Dubrovačkog arkhiva', Zbornik Rad. Viz. Inst., I (1952), 260–61; Lemerle, 'Trois actes', p. 413, n. 28; Nicol, op. cit., pp. 22–3, n. 22. No Greek document from his rule in Epirus survives (Lemerle, op. cit., p. 407), and in the only Latin one Michael styles himself 'Michael Comnanus Dux' (see above n. 7) which is obviously a rendering of the Greek Μιχαὴλ Κομνηνὸς ὁ Δούκας. His son Michael *48* refers to him as τοῦ ἀοιδίμου αὐθέντου καὶ πατρός μου τοῦ Κομνηνοῦ κῦρ Μιχαὴλ τοῦ Δούκα, MM, III, p. 67.

[9] Chomatianos, op. cit., pp. 50 and 51, calls him Κομνηνός. Similarly Apokaukos: τοῦ ἀοιδίμου κῦρ Μιχαὴλ τοῦ Κομνηνοῦ, see Vasilievskii, op. cit., p. 270. Greg., I, p. 13, says ὁ ἐξ Ἀγγέλων ... Κομνηνὸς Μιχαήλ but elsewhere (pp. 25 and 27) refers to him simply as Angelos. Neither Choniates nor Akropolites, the two most important sources for the period, attach any family name to Michael.   [10] Νέος ὢν καὶ αὐθάδης, Chon., p. 700.

For a period during the last years of Isaakios II (1185–95) Michael was in command of the theme of Mylassa and Melanoudion in Asia Minor with the rank of *dux kai anagrapheus*,[1] and he held the same post under Alexios IV (1204).[2] The antecedents of his establishment in Epirus in 1205[3] have not yet been satisfactorily explained, but his appearance in Greece in the aftermath of the Fourth Crusade was in keeping with Michael's adventurous nature. Contrary to what has been sometimes affirmed by scholars, it does not appear that he ever adopted or was given the dignity of *despotes* during his rule in Epirus (1205–*c.* 1215); neither do the Greek sources name him as such.[4] Indeed it seems that he refrained from assuming any particular title during his ten-year rule there. The motives behind, and the exact date of, Michael's assassination in *c.* 1215,[5] according to a tradition at Bellegrada (Berat),[6] are likewise obscure.

Two seals of Michael are preserved which date from before 1205. They bear the legends

$$\Sigma\phi\rho\acute{a}\gamma\iota\sigma\mu\alpha \ \gamma\rho\alpha\phi\ \hat{\omega}\nu \ M\iota\chi\alpha\grave{\eta}\lambda \ \Delta o\acute{\upsilon}\kappa\alpha \ \phi\acute{\epsilon}\rho\omega$$

and

$$\Sigma\phi\rho\acute{a}\gamma\iota\sigma\mu\alpha \ \gamma\rho\alpha\phi\ \hat{\omega}\nu \ M\iota\chi\alpha\grave{\eta}\lambda \ \Delta o\acute{\upsilon}\kappa\alpha \ \phi\acute{\epsilon}\rho\omega$$
$$\sigma\epsilon\beta\alpha\sigma\tau\sigma\kappa\rho\alpha\tau\sigma\rho\sigma\hat{\upsilon}\nu\tau\sigma\varsigma \ \epsilon\mathring{\upsilon}\theta\alpha\lambda o\hat{\upsilon}\varsigma \ \kappa\lambda\acute{a}\delta o\upsilon.[7]$$

The *Life* of St Theodora *162* claims that Michael had married a lady of the Melissenos family, and after her death he took a cousin of hers who had recently become a widow after the assassination of her husband Senachereim, a local governor.[8] The story if not entirely correct is at least based on a historical incident, as a contemporary source informs us that Michael, after his coming to Arta, married the daughter of an Epirote magnate.[9] In any case Michael is referred to as the father of three daughters — Theodora, Maria, and one unnamed — probably a son Konstantinos,[10] and in addition an illegitimate son Michael *48*.

---

[1] MM, IV, pp. 321 and 322; cf. Dölger, *Regesten*, II, pp. 102–3, no. 1633; Stiernon, 'Les origines', pp. 120–21.

[2] MM, IV, p. 328. Chon., p. 700, calls him φορολόγος, a term which is probably equivalent to ἀναγραφεύς. See Stiernon, 'Les origines', p. 121, but cf. Stein, 'Untersuchungen', p. 28.

[3] For the date see Nicol, op. cit., pp. 13 ff.

[4] On this question see Stiernon, 'Les origines', pp. 122 ff; Guilland, op. cit., p. 73.

[5] Akrop., p. 25. For some different views on this dating see Nicol, op. cit., p. 45, n. 34.

[6] Ibid., p. 42.

[7] See MM, IV, p. 327, and Laurent, *Bulles métriques*, pp. 168–9, nos. 474–5. A third seal reading
$$\Sigma\phi\rho\alpha\gamma\hat{\iota}\delta\alpha \ \tau\grave{\eta}\nu \ \sigma\acute{\eta}\nu, \ M\iota\chi\alpha\grave{\eta}\lambda \ \pi\rho\omega\tau\sigma\sigma\tau\acute{a}\tau\alpha,$$
$$\pi\sigma\theta\epsilon\hat{\iota} \ \sigma\epsilon\beta\alpha\sigma\tau\grave{\sigma}\varsigma \ M\iota\chi\alpha\grave{\eta}\lambda \ \acute{\sigma} \ \tau\sigma\hat{\upsilon} \ \Delta o\acute{\upsilon}\kappa\alpha$$
(ibid., p. 132, no. 375) could also belong to him. Yet he is never mentioned as *sebastos*.

[8] *PG*, 127, cols 904–5. The account is extremely confused for, among other errors, Theodoros *42*, Manuel *43*, and Konstantinos *44* are included among the sons of Michael. Yet the *Vita* was composed late in the thirteenth century, see L. Vranoussis, Χρονικὰ Ἠπείρου, I (Jannina, 1962), pp. 49–54.

[9] 'Michalis (common designation of him by western sources) prist la file a un riche Grieu, qui tenoit la terre de par l'empereor', Villehardouin, *La Conquête de Constantinople* (ed. E. Faral), II (Paris, 1961²), p. 110, no. 301.

[10] Theodora is mentioned by Chomatianos, op. cit., p. 51, in 1216; Maria became the wife of Konstantinos *121* Maliassenos; Na was the eldest daughter and in 1209 was given in marriage to Eustace of Flanders, a brother of king Henry of Constantinople, see *PL*, 216, col. 353D; Henri de Valenciennes, *Histoire de l'Empereur Henri de Constantinople* (ed. J. Longnon, Paris, 1948), 694, (p. 121). As for Konstantinos, he is mentioned in a document, preserved in Latin, of his

46. Demetrios Angelos Doukas: He was the younger son of Theodoros *42* and Maria *160*,[1] and in a manuscript notice written on 25 September 1244, his name is given in the form 'Αγγελοδούκας.[2] As a young and irresponsible man, Demetrios succeeded his brother Ioannes in Thessalonica in 1244 with the rank of *despotes*.[3] His rule was brought to an end late in 1246[4] by Batatzes who imprisoned Demetrios in the fortress of Lentiana in Bithynia[5] where he apparently died. At his fall he could not have been much above twenty years of age.[6]

47. Anna Doukaina: Anna, called Doukaina,[7] was the elder daughter of Theodoros *42*.[8] In *c.* 1224 she married Stephen Doukas *102* the future king of Serbia (1227–34) and their betrothal ring has been preserved.[9] After the fall of her husband, Anna sought refuge at Ragusa,[10] but eventually returned to Serbia where she died in about 1258.[11]

48. Michael (Komnenos) Doukas: Michael of Epirus was a bastard son of Michael I *45*,[12] probably born during the early years of his father's rule. He officially bore the name of Doukas, often in the compound form Κομνηνὸς ὁ Δούκας,[13] but like other members of his house he is sometimes referred to as

---

father (*promissio*) and it appears that he had been designated as successor, see TT, II, p. 123. Konstantinos could have been the only legitimate son of Michael but may have died before *c.* 1215, as a child.

---

[1] Akrop., pp. 60 and 70.

[2] See L. Politis, 'Eine Schreiberschule im Kloster τῶν 'Οδηγῶν ', *BZ*, 51 (1958), 271.

[3] Akrop., p. 79; cf. Guilland, op. cit., p. 75. Apparently the title was confirmed by Batatzes: ἡ γὰρ Θεσσαλονίκη . . . τὸν Δημήτριον ἐγνώριζέ τε δεσπότην καὶ κατωνόμαζε· δεσπότης γὰρ ἦν καὶ πρὸς τοῦ βασιλέως τετιμημένος, Akrop., p. 79.

[4] Meliarakis, op. cit., pp. 373–4; Nicol, op. cit., pp. 146–7.

[5] Akrop., p. 84.

[6] *Ἦν δὲ φέρων οὗτος τὴν ἡλικίαν τοῦ μείρακος, προσεχῶς εἰς αὐτὴν παραγγείλας καὶ μήπω χνοάζων τὸ γένειον*, Akrop., p. 83; cf. p. 79.

[7] MM, III, p. 66.

[8] Akrop., p. 60. For Anna see K. Jireček, *Geschichte der Serben*, I (Gotha, 1911), pp. 303–5; M. Laskaris, *Vizantiske Princeze u srednjevekovnoj Srbiji* (Belgrade, 1926), pp. 38–52.

[9] The inscription on the ring reads
> Μνῆστρον Στεφάνου Δουκικῆς ῥίζης κλάδου,
> Κομνηνοφυής τ' ἐν χερσὶν "Αννα δέχου.

K. Krumbacher, 'Ein serbisch-byzantinischer Verlobungsring', *SBBAW*, 1906, pp. 421–52, rightly attributed it to the daughter of Theodoros *42*. See also C. Weyman in *BZ*, 16 (1907), 745; S. Kougeas, ' 'Ο δακτύλιος τοῦ ἀρραβῶνος μιᾶς Κομνηνῆς ', *Παναθήναια*, no. 159 (1907), 73–9; N. A. Bees in *Βυζαντίς*, I (1909), 504–5. For another view see S. Papademetriou, 'Serbo-vizantiiskoe obruchalnoe koltso', *379 Zasedanie Imperatorskago Odesskago Obshchestva Istorii i Drevnostei 30-to Yanvarya 1907 goda*, but cf. V. Čajkanović, 'Über die Echtheit eines serbisch-byzantinischen Verlobungsrings', *BZ*, 19 (1910), 111–14.

[10] Cf. B. Krekić, *Dubrovnik (Raguse) et le Levant au Moyen Age* (Paris, 1961), p. 167, no. 3.

[11] M. A. Purković, 'Two Notes on Mediaeval Serbian History', *Slavonic Review*, 29 (1950/51), 545–7.

[12] Most contemporary sources refer to Michael as a νόθος (bastard). Akrop., p. 24, says that he ἐκ παλλακῆς ἐκείνῳ (sc. Michael I) γεγένηται. However elsewhere (p. 25) the source observes that on the night of his murder Michael *45* was in bed with his wife (νύκτωρ ἐπὶ τῆς κλίνης συγκαθεύδων τῇ γυναικί). Should this γυνή be distinguished from the παλλακή?

[13] Cf. his signature Μιχαὴλ ὁ Δούκας in MM, III, pp. 59 and 68 (for the attribution of the first document to him see above p. 91, n. 8). His signature can also be seen in two documents, preserved in Latin, in the forms 'Michael despota dux' and 'Michael despotus Comninus dux'. The first

Angelos[1] by the Greek sources. From after 1230[2] until his death, which seems to have occurred before August 1268,[3] he directed the affairs of Epirus as an independent ruler. In c. 1249, on the occasion of the betrothal of his son Nikephoros 49 to the granddaughter of Batatzes, Michael was honoured by the Nicaean emperor with the dignity of *despotes*.[4]

Perhaps after his establishment in Epirus, Michael married Theodora Petraliphina *162*.[5] They had three sons: Nikephoros 49, Ioannes 50, and Demetrios-Michael 51 and three daughters.[6] Michael was also the father of two illegitimate sons, Theodoros[7] and Ioannes 52 who appears to have been born before his other children. The *Life* of St Theodora ascribed a mistress, a lady of the Gangrenos family, to him, and she could have been the mother of his bastard sons.

49. Nikephoros: He was the eldest son of Michael 48 and Theodora *162*.[8] His birth can be only approximately dated to c. 1240.[9] His sole extant document bears no signature,[10] and the Greek sources fail to attribute any cognomen to him.[11] Nikephoros ruled Epirus from the death of his father (before August 1268) till he died in c. 1290.[12]

---

of them is obviously the rendering of the Greek Μιχαὴλ δεσπότης ὁ Δούκας (Lemerle, 'Trois actes', pp. 420–21), but whether the second form can be traced to an original Μιχαὴλ δεσπότης Κομνηνοδούκας (ibid., p. 423) is doubtful. The form Μιχαὴλ δεσπότης Κομνηνὸς ὁ Δούκας seems more likely.

---

[1] Pach., i, p. 21; Greg., i, pp. 48 and 74.

[2] Nicol, op. cit., p. 128.

[3] See A. Nikarouses, ' Χρονολογικαὶ ἔρευναι. Β'. — Πότε ἀπέθανε Μιχαὴλ Β' ῎Αγγελος ὁ δεσπότης τῆς 'Ηπείρου ', ΔΙΕΕΕ, new series, i, part iv (1928), pp. 136–41.

[4] Akrop., p. 88; Greg., i, p. 49; cf. Dölger, *Regesten*, iii, p. 21, no. 1799; Guilland, op. cit., p. 75.

[5] Akrop., p. 88; Pach., i, p. 107; Greg., i, pp. 47, 48, 57, and 110.

[6] Helene (1242–71) became the wife of king Manfred and died in prison; for her tragic fate see M. A. Dendias, ''Ελένη 'Αγγελῖνα Δούκαινα βασίλισσα Σικελίας καὶ Νεαπόλεως ', 'Ηπειρωτικὰ Χρονικά, 1 (1926), 219–94. Anna (died c. 1284) married the prince of Achaia William Ville-hardouin and after his death the lord of Thebes Nicholas St Omer (cf. Meliarakis, op. cit., pp. 520–21). Another unnamed daughter is mentioned by Pach., ii, p. 319, as having become the wife of Alexios Raoul (ὃν ἐν ἀκμῇ ἡλικίας ὄντα ὁ δεσπότης Μιχαὴλ γαμβρὸν ἠγάγετο, τῆς δεσποίνης Θεοδώρας ζηλωτὸν ἐκτόπως ποιούσης τὸ κῆδος).

[7] Theodoros was probably the elder and was killed at the battle of Vodena in 1257 (Akrop., pp. 146 and 148; Pach., i, p. 26, wrongly calls him Manuel).

[8] Akrop., pp. 134 and 169; Pach., i, pp. 85, 89, and 243; Greg., i, pp. 47 and 110.

[9] It appears that when he was betrothed in c. 1249 Nikephoros was still a child, and his pro-longed engagement was probably due to his being unable to marry before the permissible age.

[10] Lemerle, 'Trois actes', p. 413.

[11] Pach., ii, p. 200, refers to him as ὁ ἐξ 'Αγγέλων Νικηφόρος. The reading Κομνηνοδούκας δεσπότης Νι[κηφόρο]ς, found in a mutilated inscription (A. K. Orlandos, 'Η Παρηγορήτισσα τῆς ῎Αρτης [Athens, 1921], p. 79) is open to question in the opinion of the present writer.

[12] The traditional date, based on inexact western sources, is c. 1296. See for instance Hopf, loc. cit.; Romanos, op. cit., p. 46; Papadopulos, *Genealogie der Palaiologen*, p. 19, no. 30; Lemerle, 'Trois actes', p. 413, n. 29. However, I. K. Bogiatzides, 'Τὸ Χρονικὸν τῶν Μετεώρων ', ΕΕΒΣ, 1 (1924), 148, had drawn attention to a passage in Pach., ii, p. 200 (already cited by Romanos), where it is implied that the death of Nikephoros is chronologically little removed from that of Ioannes 50. Now, as Bogiatzides has convincingly shown, Ioannes 50 certainly died before 1289, and he rightly puts Nikephoros' death around that date. That Nikephoros died before 1294 is also inferred from the fact that his daughter Thamar who is known to have married in 1294/5

In *c.* 1249 Nikephoros was brought to the East by his mother, and at Pegai he was betrothed to Maria, the eldest daughter of the future Theodoros II *75* of Nicaea; on this occasion Batatzes conferred upon Nikephoros the dignity of *despotes*.[1] The marriage was celebrated in Thessalonica in October 1256.[2] It appears that Maria gave birth to a daughter, also called Maria, and died of ill-treatment in 1258.[3] Nikephoros was married again in the summer/autumn 1264, this time to Anna, the third daughter of Ioannes Kantakouzenos and Eirene (Eulogia) Palaiologina.[4] By this marriage, he became the father of two children, Thamar and Thomas *53*.[5]

50. Ioannes Doukas: Ioannes called Doukas[6] was a son of Michael *48*.[7] In 1261 his mother Theodora *162* brought him as hostage to Constantinople, and shortly thereafter Michael VIII gave him as husband to the second-born daughter of the *sebastokrator* Konstantinos Tornikios.[8] Ioannes appears to have despised his wife, and as a result he was imprisoned by the emperor in 1280.[9] The year of his death is not known.[10] There is evidence that he had at least one daughter, Helene.

(see E. G. Léonard, *Les Angevins de Naples* [Paris, 1954], p. 210) is mentioned as still unmarried and unprotected at her father's death (Pach., II, p. 201). Moreover Thamar's mother unsuccessfully attempted to secure Michael IX Palaiologos as her daughter's husband (Pach., II, p. 202), and only after her failure there did she turn to the Angevins. Certainly some time must have lapsed between Nikephoros' death and Thamar's wedding.

---

[1] Akrop., pp. 88 and 92; Pach., I, p. 36; Greg., I, pp. 47–9 and 57; cf. Meliarakis, op. cit., p. 376; Dölger, *Regesten*, III, p. 21, no. 1799; Guilland, op. cit., p. 76. His title was confirmed on his marriage to Maria (Akrop., p. 134) and again by Michael VIII *142* when Nikephoros married for the second time (Pach., I, p. 243).   [2] Akrop., p. 134; cf. Nicol, op. cit., p. 160.
[3] Akrop., p. 154; cf. P. A. Arabantinos, Χρονογραφία τῆς Ἠπείρου (Athens, 1856), I, p. 76; Meliarakis, op. cit., p. 483. For their daughter see Romanos, op. cit., pp. 230 and 234. She was sent to Cephalonia and was persuaded to marry Giovanni Orsini, the future count (1304–17), cf. Ducange, *Familiae*, p. 210; see also *The Chronicle of Morea*, v. 8867 (ed. P.P. Kalonaros, p. 357). Among the children of Orsini and Maria were Nikolaos and Ioannes *56* the future rulers of Epirus.
[4] Pach., I, p. 243; Greg., I, pp. 92 and 130; cf. Dölger, *Regesten*, III, pp. 47–8, no. 1931; Papadopulos, *Genealogie der Palaiologen*, p. 19, no. 30. The Byzantine sources (cf. Pach., II, pp. 59, 67, 72, and 450) refer to Anna as ' βασίλισσα ', but this implies neither an empress nor a queen but only a princess. Pach., I, p. 180, uses the word when referring to the daughters of Theodoros II, while Kant., I, p. 274, speaks of the wife of the *despotes* Demetrios Palaiologos as *basilissa*. The chronicle of Epirus repeatedly uses the term to refer to Epirote princesses. For Anna, the wife of Nikephoros, see Sp. P. Lampros, ' "Αννα ἡ Καντακουζηνή. Βυζαντιακὴ ἐπιγραφὴ ἐξ Αἰτωλίας ', *NE*, I (1904), 37–42.
[5] Pach., II, p. 201. Thamar married in 1294/5 Philippe d'Anjou, a son of Charles II, who was the prince of Tarento (Romanos, op. cit., p. 235; Hopf, op. cit., p. 529; Léonard, op. cit., p. 201), but despite previous assurances (Pach., II, p. 450), she was forced to renounce her faith and adopt the name of Caterina (Romanos, op. cit., p. 251). This marriage was dissolved in 1309 (cf. Léonard, op. cit., p. 202), and Thamar died in 1311.
[6] In some verses on the death of Ioannes' daughter Helene, Philes (Miller), I, p. 253, writes:
Δούκας δὲ πατὴρ ὧπερ ἡ κλῆσις χάρις.
[7] Pach., I, p. 243; Greg., I, pp. 47 and 110.
[8] Pach., I, pp. 107–8 and 243. Greg., I, p. 110, is certainly wrong in claiming that Ioannes was still a minor and unmarried on his father's death.   [9] Pach., I, p. 485.
[10] The view of Lampros in *NE*, 15 (1921), 25–7, and Orlandos, ' Βυζαντινὰ μνημεῖα τῆς "Αρτης ', p. 43, based on a very fragmentary inscription, that Ioannes and Demetrios-Michael *51* were murdered after their father died cannot be accepted in the face of Pach., I, p. 485, and other sources.

51. Demetrios-Michael Doukas: Demetrios, the youngest son of Michael *48*, changed his name to Michael after his father's death to honour him.[1] He appears to have been officially called Doukas[2] although the nickname Koutroules is also attached to him.[3] In 1278 he came to Constantinople and married Anna, the daughter of Michael VIII; on this occasion he was created *despotes*.[4] Of this union two sons were born, Konstantinos and Andronikos, both of whom assumed the name of Palaiologos.[5] Michael made a career in the Byzantine army; in 1281 he fought with the Byzantine forces against Charles of Anjou in Epirus,[6] and he also participated with the Alans in 1301 in a campaign against the Turks of Menteshe in Asia Minor.[7]

His wife Anna died before 1299, and in the following year Michael married the former wife of king Milutin; she was a daughter of the Bulgarian ruler Terter.[8] There seem to have been children from this marriage but no details are known. In 1304 Michael was suspected of plotting and together with his wife and children was thrown into prison. His rich lands, which had been given to him as dowry by Michael VIII, went to Michael IX as compensation for the loss of his πρόνοιαι in Asia Minor. His house was also confiscated and was given to the despot Ioannes Palaiologos.[9] The year of his death remains unknown.[10]

---

[1] Pach., I, pp. 243 and 439; Greg., I, p. 47.

[2] Kant., I, p. 211; II, p. 196. The archaic form *Δούξ*, used by the author, does not refer to a rank, as the editor implies, but simply to Michael's cognomen. But he is also called Komnenos, see below n. 4.

[3] Greg., I, pp. 204 ff. *The Chronicle of Morea* (v. 3470, ed. Kalonaros, p. 150) attributes the nickname of Koutroules to Nikephoros *49*. This name is in fact met with as a surname. An Ioannes Koutroules is mentioned in 1394 (MM, II, pp. 210–11) and in 1338 we have a reference to a χωράφιον τοῦ Κουτρούλλη (Bompaire, *Actes de Xéropotamou*, p. 75). A Nicola Cutrulopulo lived in 1299, see K. D. Mertzios, ''Η συνθήκη Ἐνετῶν-Καλλέργη καὶ οἱ συνοδεύοντες αὐτὴν κατάλογοι', *Κρητικὰ Χρονικά*, 3 (1949), 281. In 1705 an Anastasios Koutroules is active as a church painter in Zakynthos, see D. Sisilianos, Ἕλληνες Ἁγιογράφοι μετὰ τὴν Ἅλωσιν (Athens, 1935), pp. 122–3.

[4] Pach., I, p. 441; Greg., I, p. 204; cf. Papadopulos, *Genealogie der Palaiologen*, p. 29, no. 47; Dölger, *Regesten*, III, p. 71, no. 2032; Guilland, 'Despot', p. 76. There has been preserved a Τόμος ὁ ἐκτεθεὶς ἐπὶ τῷ συνοικεσίῳ τοῦ δεσπότου κυροῦ Μιχαὴλ καὶ τῆς βασιλίσσης Ἄννης, θυγατρὸς τοῦ ἁγίου βασιλέως, edited by M. I. Gedeon, ''Ιωάννου Βέκκου τοῦ οἰκουμενικοῦ πατριάρχου συνοδικὰ γράμματα', 'Αρχεῖον 'Εκκλησιαστικῆς 'Ιστορίας, I (1911), 48–50, which allows the marriage of sixth degree ἐξ ἀγχιστείας as Nikephoros *49*, the brother of Demetrios-Michael, had previously married Anna's first cousin. The synodal document is dated November 1278 and the spouses are referred to as τῇ περιποθήτῳ θυγατρὶ τοῦ κραταιοῦ καὶ ἁγίου ἡμῶν δεσπότου καὶ βασιλέως κυρᾷ Ἄννῃ Κομνηνῇ τῇ Παλαιολογίνῃ καὶ τῷ τοῦ μακαρίτου δεσπότου ἐκείνου κυροῦ Μιχαὴλ τοῦ Δουκὸς γνησίῳ υἱῷ τῷ Κομνηνῷ κυρῷ Μιχαήλ (ibid., p. 48).

[5] For these and their families see Papadopulos, *Genealogie der Palaiologen*, pp. 29–32, nos. 47–51.

[6] Pach., I, p. 512; cf. D. J. Geanakoplos, *Emperor Michael Palaeologus and the West* (Cambridge, Mass., 1959), p. 331.

[7] Pach., II, p. 315. While Michael was in Asia Minor, Planudes addressed to him at least two letters. See *Maximi monachi Planudis Epistulae* (ed. M. Treu, Breslau, 1892), pp. 228–9.

[8] Pach., II, p. 304; Greg., I, p. 204; cf. Dölger, *Regesten*, IV, p. 30, no. 2216.

[9] Pach., II, pp. 407–9; cf. Dölger, *Regesten*, IV, pp. 60–61, nos. 2260 and 2262; G. Ostrogorsky, *Pour l'histoire de la féodalité byzantine* (Brussels, 1953), p. 100.

[10] A short poem Πρὸς τὸν τοῦ βασιλέως ἐξάδελφον κυρὸν Μιχαὴλ τὸν Παλαιολόγον is wrongly thought to refer to this Michael by the editor in Philes (Martini), p. 83. Papadopulos, *Genealogie der Palaiologen*, p. 29, no. 47, went further and claimed that Michael was identical with the leader of the zealots, Michael Palaiologos, whom Kant., II, pp. 569–71, mentions without hint as to his family connections. In the present writer's opinion, this is unjustified, as no references to Michael

52. Ioannes Doukas: Ioannes, the energetic ruler of Neopatras, was a bastard son of Michael 48.[1] The sources always call him Doukas[2] or refer to him with his dignity of *sebastokrator* which he received from Michael VIII in c. 1272.[3] Ioannes Doukas ruled Thessaly and central Greece from c. 1268 until his death which occurred sometime — perhaps shortly — before 1289.[4]

Prior to 1259 Ioannes had married a daughter of Taronas, a Vlach chieftain in Thessaly.[5] His wife who is called Komnene Doukaina outlived him and became a nun with the name of Hypomone.[6] She bore him several children: three sons, Michael, Konstantinos 54, and Theodoros who were known by the surnames of Komnenos, Doukas, and Angelos respectively[7] and four daughters.[8]

53. Thomas Komnenos Doukas: Thomas was a son of Nikephoros 49[9] whom he succeeded as ruler of Epirus in c. 1290. His surname does not appear to have been preserved in the Greek sources; it may have been Κομνηνὸς ὁ Δούκας.[10] With the dignity of *despotes*, given to him by Andronikos II,[11] he ruled

after 1304 exist and he is certainly nowhere called Palaiologos. Moreover Michael who was probably born around 1260 could hardly have been active as late as 1346, the year when Michael Palaiologos was killed.

---

[1] Akrop., pp. 170 and 171; Pach., I, pp. 83, 85, 243, 307, 412; II, p. 201; Greg., I, pp. 47 and 110.

[2] E.g. Pach., I, pp. 84, 85, 322, 323; II, p. 67. A notice of the year 1788, written on cod. Παντελεήμονος 793 (Athous 6300), gives the text of an inscription, now lost, of the church of Porta Panagia of Thessaly to the effect that it was constructed παρὰ συνδρομῆς καὶ ἐξόδου τοῦ πανευτυχεστάτου σεβαστοκράτορος Κομνηνοῦ Ἰωάννου Ἀγγέλου τοῦ Δούκα ἔτει ͵ϛψϟαʹἰνδ. ιαʹ (=1282/3); see A. K. Orlandos, ''Η Πόρτα-Παναγιὰ τῆς Θεσσαλίας ', Ἀρχεῖον τῶν Βυζαντινῶν Μνημείων τῆς Ἑλλάδος, I (1935), 8. Due to a confusion with his name, the Latins knew Ioannes as the 'Duke' of Neopatras; cf. W. Miller, *The Latins in the Levant: A History of Frankish Greece (1204–1566)* (London, 1908), p. 132.   [3] Pach., I, p. 308; Greg., I, p. 111.

[4] As I. K. Bogiatzides, ' Τὸ Χρονικὸν τῶν Μετεώρων ', ΕΕΒΣ, I (1924), 146–7, has shown, a document of Andronikos II, dated March 1289 (cf. Dölger, *Regesten*, IV, p. 13, no. 2131) implies that Ioannes was dead by then. The traditional date of his death is 1296 and is based on inexact western sources. Hopf, op. cit., p. 529, first proposed it and it was then taken over by most modern authorities without regard to Bogiatzides' correction.

[5] His wife is the cause of a quarrel on the eve of the battle of Pelagonia, Pach., I, pp. 83–4.

[6] Τὸν μοναδικὸν ζυγὸν ὑποδῦσα Κομνηνὴ κυρὰ Ὑπομονὴ ἡ Δούκαινα, MM, V, p. 254; cf. Bees, 'Sur les tables généalogiques', p. 210. Her lay name is not preserved, but she is called the daughter of the Vlach Taronas. For some other references to that surname see M. I. Gedeon, ' Βυζαντινὰ συμβόλαια ', ΒΖ, 5 (1896), 114.

[7] Pach., II, p. 201. Michael was the eldest and was killed in prison in Constantinople in 1307; for him see Arabantinos, op. cit., I, pp. 102–5. For Theodoros see M. Th. Laskaris, ' Θεόδωρος Ἄγγελος, υἱὸς τοῦ σεβαστοκράτορος τῆς Θεσσαλίας Ἰωάννου ', ΕΕΒΣ, 3 (1926), 223–4.

[8] Of these daughters only the name of Helene is known. She became the wife of the Duke of Athens William de la Roche (1280–87), and after his death married Hugues de Brienne; see Hopf, op. cit., p. 473; F. Gregorovius — Sp. P. Lampros, Ἱστορία τῆς πόλεως Ἀθηνῶν κατὰ τοὺς Μέσους Αἰῶνας, I (Athens, 1904), p. 510; Miller, op. cit., p. 134. Another daughter became the wife of Andronikos Tarchaneiotes, see Pach., I, pp. 308 and 322; cf. Papadopulos, *Genealogie der Palaiologen*, p. 14, no. 23. The third daughter married king Milutin of Serbia (Pach., II, p. 273), and a fourth one was in prison with her brother Michael in Constantinople in 1299 (Pach., II, p. 73).   [9] Pach., II, p. 201.

[10] A document of his, preserved in Latin, bears the signature 'Thomas despoti Comnino Ducha' which is traced to Θωμᾶς δεσπότης Κομνηνοδούκας by P. Lemerle, 'Le privilège du Despot d'Epire Thomas pour le venitien Jacques Contareno', ΒΖ, 44 (1951), 391. The form Κομνηνὸς ὁ Δούκας appears more convincing.

[11] Pach., II, p. 202; cf. Kant., I, p. 13; Guilland, op. cit., p. 76.

H   P.T.D.

Epirus until he was assassinated by his nephew and successor Nikolaos Orsini at Jannina in 1318.[1]

In 1304 Thomas was betrothed to Anna Palaiologina, a daughter of Michael IX.[2] The marriage was celebrated in 1313[3] but remained without issue.

54. Konstantinos Doukas: He was a son of Ioannes *52* whom he succeeded as the ruler of Neopatras sometime before 1289. Konstantinos was known as Doukas[4] and carried the dignity of *sebastokrator*.[5] Little is mentioned about him. According to Hopf, his wife was called Anna Evagionissa and died in 1317.[6] Konstantinos became the father of a son Ioannes *55* and died in 1303.[7]

55. Ioannes Angelos Doukas: Ioannes, the ineffective last ruler of Neopatras, was a son of Konstantinos *54* and the sources speak of him as Doukas and Angelos.[8] Like his father and grandfather, he seems to have assumed the dignity of *sebastokrator*.[9] Ioannes was a man of feeble nature and seeing his domain threatened by the local magnates, in 1315 he married Eirene, an illegitimate daughter of Andronikos II. There were no issue, and he died after three years of married life, still a young man, in 1318.[10]

56. Ioannes Doukas: Ioannes was not properly a Doukas but an Orsini, being the son of Giovanni Orsini, the palatinate count of Cephalonia, and Maria, the daughter of Nikephoros *49* of Epirus. Nevertheless, he employed the more impressive surname of Doukas and he is sometimes referred to as such.[11] Some Greek sources persist in calling him κόντος,[12] that is the count, despite the fact that the government of Constantinople had already conferred upon him the dignity of *despotes*.[13] Ioannes, after murdering his brother Nikolaos in *c.* 1323,

---

[1] Greg., I, p. 318.   [2] Pach., II, pp. 450–51.

[3] Greg., I, p. 283; cf. Papadopulos, *Genealogie der Palaiologen*, p. 19, no. 31; p. 44, no. 70. After her husband's death, Anna married his murderer but died in 1320. Nikolaos was actually a nephew of Thomas (see above p. 95, n. 3), was made a *despotes* (MM, I, p. 171), and was in turn assassinated by his brother Ioannes *56* in 1323.

[4] Pach., II, p. 201.   [5] Pach., II, pp. 206 and 284.

[6] Op. cit., p. 529.   [7] Ibid.

[8] Gregoras calls him Doukas (I, p. 278) and as ᾿Αγγελωνύμων ἀπόγονος (I, p. 318). Philes wrote a poem Εἰς τὸν τάφον ᾿Αγγέλου τοῦ υἱοῦ τοῦ σεβαστοκράτορος, Philes (Martini), pp. 123–5, no. 87.

[9] Greg., I, p. 249, says that he succeeded τῶν προγόνων καὶ σεβαστοκρατόρων ἀρχῆς. As neither he nor the poem of Philes clearly name him as *sebastokrator*, his title may not have been confirmed by the imperial government.

[10] Greg., I, pp. 278–9; cf. K. M. Setton, *Catalan Domination of Athens, 1311–1388* (Cambridge, Mass., 1948), p. 29; Papadopulos, *Genealogie der Palaiologen*, p. 42, no. 67. Philes (Martini), p. 126, says that his wife ἵστησιν ἀντίτυμβον/λιποῦσα τὸν χθὲς ἐννεάμηνον γάμον, but this nine-month marriage is certainly not correct in view of Gregoras' clear statement.

[11] MM, I, p. 171; Kant., I, p. 474, uses the archaic form Δοὺξ which is obviously Ioannes' surname and not his title as the editor thinks. Konstantinos Hermoniakos who lived at his court composed the vulgar paraphrase of the Iliad

εἰς ἀξίωσιν δεσπότου
Κομνηνοῦ ᾿Αγγελοδούκα
᾿Ιωάννου τοῦ ἡρῴου
τοῦ τὴν δύσιν δεσποτεύων.

See Constantin Hermoniacos, *La Guerre de Troie* (ed. E. Legrand, Paris 1890), p. 3.

[12] Greg., I, pp. 536 and 657; II, pp. 100, 249, and 557.

[13] Greg., I, p. 544; Kant., I, pp. 479 and 499; MM, I, p. 171; *Epirotica* in S. Cirac Estopañan, *Bizancio y España* (Barcelona, 1943), II, p. 36; N. A. Bees, ' Σερβικὰ καὶ βυζαντιακὰ γράμματα Μετεώρου', *Βυζαντίς*, 2 (1911/12), 76; Guilland, op. cit., p. 68.

established himself as the ruler of Epirus until he was in turn poisoned by his own wife in 1335.[1] By his marriage to Anna, a daughter of Andronikos Palaiologos the son of Demetrios-Michael *51*, he became the father of two children, Nikephoros *57* and Thomais.[2]

57. Nikephoros Doukas: Nikephoros was a son of Ioannes *56* and his wife Anna, being born in 1328/9.[3] He was generally known by the name of Doukas.[4] His brief life was a stormy one. After some early unsuccessful attempts to acquire his paternal dominions in Epirus, Nikephoros was made a *panypersebastos* in 1339[5] and was taken to Constantinople. In the civil war he followed his father-in-law Kantakouzenos who after his final success in 1347 honoured him with the dignity of *despotes*.[6] After 1350 Nikephoros governed the towns of the Hellespont and Ainos,[7] and in late 1355, taking advantage of the turbulent situation in Epirus, went there and was able to gain control of affairs. This, however, did not last long as in 1358 Nikephoros was killed near the village of Acheloos while fighting against the Albanians.[8]

In 1337 Anna arranged the marriage of Nikephoros with Maria, the daughter of Ioannes Kantakouzenos.[9] The marriage was not celebrated until sometime during 1341–2.[10] During his early years there had been a move to marry him to the daughter of the princess of Tarento.[11] After his establishment in Epirus, Nikephoros expelled his wife and married Helene, the sister of the Serbian kral. This step, taken for political reasons, proved extremely unpopular and soon Nikephoros recalled Maria who in the meantime had taken refuge near her brother Manuel at Mystras. However, before she returned to Epirus her husband was dead.[12] Their marriage remained childless[13] and Maria eventually went to

[1] Greg., I, p. 536.

[2] For references see Papadopulos, *Genealogie der Palaiologen*, pp. 31–2, no. 51. Hopf, op. cit., p. 529, mentions another daughter and adds that she died at an early age. Thomais in *c.* 1350 married the Serbian prince Symeon Urosh Palaiologos who ruled Thessaly for a period in 1350–1357 and became the mother of Ioannes *58*, Maria and possibly another son Stephanos, cf. *Epirotica*, p. 36; Greg., III, p. 557; Papadopulos, *Genealogie der Palaiologen*, pp. 25–6, no. 40; Bees, 'Sur les tables généalogiques', p. 211; M. Laskaris, 'Deux chartes de Jean Uroš, dernier némanide', *B*, 25/27 (1955/57), 310–23; D. M. Nicol, *Meteora: The Rock Monasteries of Thessaly* (London, 1963), p. 64

[3] Kant., I, p. 500, describes Nikephoros in *c.* 1335/6 as being οὔπω ἔτη ἑπτὰ γεγενημένου. This is probably confirmed by what he says in 1342 to the effect that owing to his youthfulness Nikephoros could not participate in a campaign (ἀδυνάτως ἔχοντι στρατεύεσθαι διὰ τὴν ἡλικίαν — ἔτι γὰρ παρήμοιβε τὴν παιδικήν, ibid., II, p. 195). On the other hand, Greg., I, p. 545, says that in *c.* 1339 he was fourteen years old. This obviously contradicts the statement of Kantakouzenos who must have known better as he made Nikephoros the husband of his daughter.

[4] Kant., I, pp. 503, 511, 534; II, pp. 195 and 321; III, pp. 33 and 315; *Epirotica*, p. 38; Bees, ' Σερβικὰ καὶ βυζαντιακὰ γράμματα Μετεώρου ', p. 74.   [5] Kant., I, p. 534.

[6] Kant., III, p. 33. In 1339 Kantakouzenos, speaking to the people of Arta, referred to Νικηφόρῳ τῷ ὑμῶν δεσπότῃ, ibid., I, p. 532. Guilland, op. cit., p. 77, maintains that Nikephoros had inherited this title. This may have been true for all rulers of Epirus were then called δεσπόται, but it must not be forgotten that in every case the title had to be confirmed by Constantinople.

[7] Kant., III, pp. 211 and 310; Greg., III, p. 249.

[8] Kant., III, pp. 315–19; *Epirotica*, p. 37. The duration of Nikephoros' rule in Epirus, given by this last source as three years and two months is certainly wrong as Romanos, op. cit., p. 306, n. 4, has observed.

[9] Kant., I, pp. 500–1; *Epirotica*, p. 36.   [10] Kant., II, p. 321; Greg., III, p. 557.

[11] Kant., I, p. 510.   [12] Kant., III, pp. 317–19.

[13] Romanos, op. cit., p. 299, mentions a son Manuel.

Constantinople where she ended her days as a nun in the monastery of the Kyra Martha in Constantinople.[1]

58. Ioannes Doukas (Uresis Palaiologos): Ioannes,[2] called either Doukas[3] or Uresis Palaiologos[4] was a son of Symeon Urosh and Thomais, the daughter of Ioannes *56*. He is called a *basileus* in the inscriptions of Meteora and ruled in Thessaly in November 1372, becoming a monk before 1381 with the name of Ioasaph.[5] Ioannes became the second founder of the monastic community of Meteora where he was much revered. After his death he was proclaimed a saint,[6] his portrait adorns many frescoes, and his skull is preserved as a holy relic. Ioannes died in Meteora before 24 February 1423.[7]

59. Maria Angelina Doukaina Palaiologina: Maria who signed a document as Μαρία βασίλισσα 'Αγγελῖνα Δούκαινα ἡ Παλαιολογῖνα[8] was a daughter of Symeon Urosh and Thomais.[9] In 1366 she married the cruel despot of Jannina Thomas Preljubović[10] for whose death (occurring on 23 December 1385) she was probably responsible. Early in 1386 Maria took as second husband the new despot Esau Buondelmonti.[11] Both her marriages were without issue.[12] She died on 28 December 1394.[13]

A portrait of Maria, bearing the inscription Μαρία εὐσεβεστάτη βασίλισσα 'Αγγελῖνα Κομνηνὴ Δούκαινα ἡ Παλαιολογῖνα, has been preserved on an ikon in the monastery of Meteoron.[14]

---

[1] Kant., III, p. 319; see R. Janin, *Les Eglises et les Monastères* (Paris, 1953), pp. 336 f.

[2] For this man see T. B. Neroutsos, ''O βασιλεὺς μοναχὸς 'Ιωάσαφ', 'Εστία, 2 (1891), 61–2; N. A. Bees, ' Συμβολὴ εἰς τὴν ἱστορίαν τῶν μονῶν τῶν Μετεώρων ', Βυζαντίς, 1 (1909), 236κζ'–236κθ'; idem, 'Geschichtliche Forschungsresultate und Mönchs- und Volkssagen über die Gründer der Meteorenklöster ', *BNJ*, 3 (1922), 269–95; Papadopulos, *Genealogie der Palaiologen*, pp. 26–7, no. 42; M. Laskaris, 'Deux chartes de Jean Uroš, dernier némanide', pp. 277–328; Nicol, *Meteora*, pp. 101–12.

[3] See the document of Maria *59* in Cirac, op. cit., II, p. 31 (also in Bees, ' Σερβικὰ καὶ βυζαντιακὰ γράμματα Μετεώρου ', p. 21); cf. the mutilated inscription of Kastoria: καὶ τοῦ υἱοῦ αὐτοῦ ['Ιωάννου τοῦ Δ]ούκα in A. K. Orlandos, ' Τὰ Βυζαντινὰ μνημεῖα τῆς Καστορίας ', 'Αρχεῖον τῶν Βυζαντινῶν μνημείων τῆς 'Ελλάδος, 4 (1936), 97 (cf. Lascaris, op. cit., p. 283).

[4] Bees, 'Geschichtliche Forschungsresultate', p. 371.

[5] Lascaris, op. cit., pp. 293–4. See his portrait, plates I–III.

[6] Cf. S. Eustratiades, 'Αγιολόγιον τῆς 'Ορθοδόξου 'Εκκλησίας (Athens, n.d.), p. 240.

[7] Bees, 'Geschichtliche Forschungsresultate', p. 379, with full references.

[8] Cirac, op. cit., II, p. 31. The document is also in Bees, ' Σερβικὰ καὶ βυζαντιακὰ γράμματα Μετεώρου ', pp. 20–23.

[9] Papadopulos, *Genealogie der Palaiologen*, p. 26, no. 41.   [10] *Epirotica*, p. 39.

[11] *Epirotica*, p. 49. For the marriages of Esau who died in 1403 see C. Jireček, 'Die Witwe und die Söhne des Despoten Esau von Epirus', *BNJ*, 1 (1920), 1–16.

[12] A daughter of Thomas, Eirene, who married the son of Petros Lyosh and died during the plague of 1374–5 (*Epirotica*, pp. 42–3) must have been the offspring of an earlier marriage of the despot.

[13] *Epirotica*, p. 52.

[14] See N. A. Bees, ' Μετεώρου πίναξ ἀφιερωθεὶς ὑπὸ τῆς βασιλίσσης Παλαιολογίνης ', 'Αρχαιολογικὴ 'Εφημερίς, 1911, pp. 177–85; A. Xyngopoulos, ' Βυζαντιναὶ εἰκόνες ἐν Μετεώροις,' 'Αρχαιολογικὸν Δελτίον, 10 (1926), 44–5; idem, 'Νέαι προσωπογραφαί τῆς Παλαιολογίνας καὶ τοῦ Θωμᾶ Πρελιούμποβιτς,' Δελτίον τῆς Χριστιανικῆς 'Αρχαιολογικῆς 'Εταιρείας, 4 (1964–5), 53–67.

APOKAUKOS

From the late tenth century onwards the surname of Apokaukos ('Ἀπόκαυκος, less common form 'Ἀπόκαυχος) was borne by various active Byzantines.[1] In c. 990 Basileios Apokaukos was the *strategos* of the Peloponnesus.[2] Two Apokaukoi became metropolitans, Konstantinos in Dyrrachion[3] and the far more famous Ioannes in Naupactus. The *sebastohypertatos* Ioannes Apokaukos is mentioned in 1277.[4] Among the many other members of the house the priests Konstantinos Apokaukos (1381)[5] and Manuel Apokaukos (1399)[6] and the nobleman Andronikos Apokaukos Melissenos (1406)[7] can be mentioned. Very conspicuous is the family of the *megas dux* Alexios Apokaukos (murdered in 1345) who was the actual power behind the imperial regency in 1341–5.[8] Alexios had been of humble background, and his childhood was spent in poverty but eventually he acquired both power and wealth.[9] He may occasionally have been called Doukas.[10] Two of his brothers are mentioned in 1362.[11] Alexios was apparently married twice. The *megas primikerios* Ioannes Apokaukos (killed by the Zealots in Thessalonica in 1345) was his first son.[12] He had also three daughters.[13]

60. Georgios Doukas Apokaukos: We know of only one person styled as Doukas Apokaukos. He was a *megas drungarios* (τῆς βίγλης ?) and is mentioned only once, namely in a document of Ioannes V dated on 25 March 1342 (κυροῦ Γεωργίου Δούκα μεγάλου δρουγγαρίου τοῦ 'Ἀποκαύκου).[14] Georgios Doukas Apokaukos may have been a son of the *megas dux* Alexios.

[1] Individuals with this name are listed by N. B. Tomadakis in 'Ο Ἰωσὴφ Βρυέννιος καὶ ἡ Κρήτη κατὰ τό 1400 (Athens, 1947), pp. 122–3, and in ' Οἱ λόγιοι τοῦ δεσποτάτου τῆς 'Ηπείρου', ΕΕΒΣ, 27 (1957), 8.

[2] Sp. P. Lampros, ''Ο βίος Νίκωνος τοῦ Μετανοεῖτε ', ΝΕ, 3 (1906), 174–5; cf. A. Bon, Le Péloponnèse byzantin jusqu'en 1204 (Paris, 1951), p. 186.

[3] V. Laurent, Le Corpus des Sceaux de l'Empire Byzantin v.–L'Eglise (Paris, 1963), pp. 562–6 no. 738.

[4] MM, III, p. 96.

[5] MM, II, p. 21.

[6] MM, II, pp. 297, 392, and 487.

[7] MM, III, p. 153; cf. MM, II, p. 566.

[8] For the man see R. Guilland, 'Etudes de civilisation et de littérature byzantines: Alexis Apocaucos', Revue des Lyonnais, 1921, pp. 523–41 (inaccessible to me); idem, Correspondance de Nicéphore Grégoras (Paris, 1927), pp. 299–301.

[9] Γένους γὰρ τῶν ἀδόξων ὑπάρχων ἐκ νέου καὶ πενίᾳ συντεθραμμένος, Greg., III. p. 577; cf. p. 585.

[10] See (his?) monogram in S. Eyice, 'Alexis Apocauque et l'église byzantine de Sélymbria (Silivri)', B, 34 (1964), 90.

[11] They were called Ioannes and Nikephoros, see Kant., II, p. 556; III, p. 364.

[12] 'Ο ἐκ τῆς προτέρας συζύγου πρῶτος 'Ἀποκαύκου υἱός, Greg., II, p. 740.

[13] Their names remain unknown. One of them married Ioannes Gabalas (Greg., II, p. 701), another Andronikos Palaiologos (Papadopulos, Genealogie der Palaiologen, p. 30, no. 49), and the third Ioannes Asan (Greg., II, p. 797).

[14] MM, III, p. 114; cf. R. Guilland in BZ, 43 (1950), 356, and 44 (1951), 222; Dölger, Regesten, v, p. 5, no. 2876.

APRENOS

'Απρηνός (also called "Απριος[1] and 'Απραῖος[2]) is an inhabitant of the Thracian town of Apros. The family of that name was already included among the nobles of the Empire of Nicaea in 1258.[3] As a native of Apros, Ioannes Kalekas, the patriarch of Constantinople (1334–47) is occasionally called 'Απρηνός.[4] A *protovestiarites* Aprenos, of unknown first name, was killed while fighting against the Bulgarian leader Ivajlo in 1277.[5]

From the thirteenth century onwards a few people are styled Doukai-Aprenoi; it is not clear how the name of Doukas entered the onomatology of the family. Although one Aprenos carried the compound Palaiologos-Doukas and could have been descendant of a union with a member of the reigning house, it is more reasonable to suppose that the form Doukas-Aprenos owed its existence to a marriage concluded between the Aprenoi and a noble Nicaean family which had in the meantime employed the name of Doukas.

61. Doukas Aprenos: In a διαθηκῷον γράμμα, written by Theodoros Komnenos Branas and dated to June 1285, among the witnesses the name of Λέων ὁ Μανίκης, ὁ γραμματικὸς τοῦ Δεύκα τοῦ 'Απρηνοῦ is included.[6] Δεύκα is obviously a (typographic ?) error for Δούκα. This Doukas Aprenos, of unspecified first name, might be Manuel 62.

62. Manuel Doukas Aprenos: A document dated in May 1293 and signed by the *domestikos* τῶν ἀνατολικῶν θεμάτων Manuel Sgouropoulos[7] mentions Manuel and refers to him as τοῦ οἰκείου τῷ κραταιῷ καὶ ἁγίῳ ἡμῶν αὐθέντῃ καὶ βασιλεῖ πανευγενεστάτου Δούκα κυροῦ Μανουὴλ τοῦ 'Απρηνοῦ.[8] At that time the *oikeios* Manuel Doukas Aprenos was at odds with the monks of Lembiotissa.

One is tempted to identify Manuel Doukas Aprenos with a Manuel Doukas who is also known from the documents of Lembiotissa. He was a wealthy land-owner in Asia Minor, and three of his letters are preserved.[9] One of these dis-

---

[1] Kant., I, pp. 140, 142, and 143.

[2] See B. A. Mystakides, 'Μητρόπολις "Απρω καὶ μητροπολίτης "Απρω ', Θρακικά, 2 (1929), 42.

[3] Pach., I, p. 65.

[4] J. Müller, 'Byzantinische Analekten', *Sitzungsberichte der kaiserlichen Akademie der Wissenschaften. Philosophisch-historische Klasse*, 9 (Vienna, 1853), p. 391; Sp. P. Lampros and K. I. Amantos, Βραχέα Χρονικά (Athens, 1932), pp. 31 and 88. Another short chronicle calls him ὁ ἀπὸ τῆς "Απρου ἱερεύς, see R.-J. Loenertz, 'La chronique brève de 1352', *OCP*, 30 (1964), 41.

[5] Pach., I, p. 466.

[6] MM, IV, p. 115. The will bears the date June, A. M. 6793, indiction X. The indiction, however, does not correspond to the year 1285; I have accepted the editor's date.

[7] Cf. Dölger, *Regesten*, IV, p. 17, no. 2153.   [8] MM, IV, p. 229; cf. p. 230.

[9] See MM, pp. IV, 104–5, 105, and 141–2. All bear the signature 'Ο δοῦλος τοῦ κραταιοῦ καὶ ἁγίου ἡμῶν αὐθέντου καὶ βασιλέως Μανουὴλ ὁ Δούκας. The letters are dated indiction II, and one of them contains the passage Κατὰ τὴν σήμερον ἡμέραν, ὅπερ ἐστὶ σάββατον θ' τοῦ φεβρουαρίου μηνὸς τῆς νῦν τρεχούσης δευτέρας ἰνδικτιῶνος, MM, IV, p. 142. As no Saturday of the second indiction corresponds to a 9 February in the thirteenth century, one may safely consider either the σάββατον or the θ' (φεβρουαρίου) as wrong. In the dating of the documents the fact that one of them mentions an ἡγούμενος Kallistos may also help. But the date of Kallistos himself is not known; see the passages on him cited by A. M. Fontrier, 'Le monastère de Lembos près de Smyrne et ses possessions au XIII siècle', *BCH*, 16 (1892), 410.

closes that Manuel's πάροικοι had unlawfully occupied certain estates belonging to the monastery of Lembiotissa.[1]

63. Andronikos Doukas Aprenos: The *protostrator* Andronikos Doukas Aprenos lived under Michael VIII and had a daughter who became the first wife of the *megas domestikos* Michael Tarchaneiotes and the mother of the so-called Νοστογγόνισσα.[2]

64. Philippos Doukas Aprenos: A patriarchal document dated August 1400[3] is concerned with a suit brought against Philippos Doukas Aprenos by Anna Laskarina Tagarina. Philippos had long ago borrowed 45 hyperpyra on condition that if he failed to pay back his debt within two years, Laskarina was to acquire his right of protection (ἀδελφᾶτον) over the monastery of Theotokos τοῦ Μαρούλη. Aprenos was unable to meet his obligation and several years before 1400 Laskarina was legally granted this protection by three *katholikoi kritai*. Their decision was later confirmed by others. Philippos Doukas Aprenos had a daughter called Iakobina. In 1400 she submitted to the patriarch that the ἀδελφᾶτον actually belonged to her, having been given directly to Iakobina by her paternal grandfather and she claimed that her father could not cede it to Laskarina. The patriarch, however, upheld the previous decisions in favour of the latter.

It is possible that a reference to a vineyard of a Doukas Aprenos (ἄρχεται ἀπὸ τῆς γωνίας τοῦ ἀμπελίου Δούκα τοῦ Ἀπρηνοῦ... καταντᾶ εἰς τὸ σύνορον Δούκα τοῦ Ἀπρηνοῦ)[4] in 1400 relates to the present Philippos.

65. Demetrios Palaiologos Doukas Aprenos: He appears in a document of June 1400 as a witness, together with a Michael Sardenos, in a case of a divorce.[5] Demetrios probably came from, or lived at, Sylebria.

ARIANITES

The name Arianites ('Ἀριανίτης) has been seen as ethnikon, denoting one who comes from Ariane (Iran).[6] The Arianitai were a noble family, associated with the army since about 1000. David Arianites was an able commander under Basileios II[7] and Konstantinos Arianites fought against the Patzinaks under Monomachos.[8] In the fifteenth century the Komnenoi Arianitai were chieftains in Albania.[9]

---

[1] MM, IV, pp. 141–2.

[2] 'Η δὲ Νοστογγόνισσα θυγάτηρ ἦν τοῦ μεγάλου δομεστίκου ἐξ ἑτέρας γυναικὸς γεννηθεῖσα αὐτῷ, τῆς τοῦ πρωτοστράτορος Ἀνδρονίκου τοῦ Δούκα θυγατρός, ὃν καὶ Ἀπρηνὸν οἱ πολλοὶ ἔλεγον. This is part of an explanatory gloss on Pach., I, p. 294[14], found in cod. Monac. 442 (written in c. 1350) and it was edited by A. Heisenberg, 'Aus der Geschichte und Literatur der Palaiologenzeit', *SBBAW*, 1920, p. 11.

[3] MM, II, pp. 424–6. On certain aspects of this document see P. Lemerle, 'Recherches sur les institutions judiciaires à l'époque des Paléologues', *Annuaire*, 9 (1949), 380–82.

[4] MM, II, p. 384.

[5] MM, II, p. 403; cf. Papadopulos, *Genealogie der Palaiologen*, p. 81, no. 134.

[6] See Moritz, *Zunamen*, II, p. 34.

[7] V. Laurent, 'Les thèmes byzantines de Serbie au XIe siècle', *REB*, 15 (1957), 189.

[8] Kedr., II p. 596.   [9] Ducange, *Familiae*, pp. 196–8.

66. Michael Doukas Arianites: Michael Doukas Arianites was a fourteenth-century nobleman,[1] perhaps of Macedonia, who is mentioned in the will of Theodoros Sarantenos (October 1326). He married the only daughter of Theodoros Sarantenos who died before 1326. They had several children.

ASAN

The Byzantine family of Asan or Asanes (*'Ασάν*, *'Ασάνης*) came into being with the marriage of the Bulgarian tzar Ivan III Asen with Eirene Palaiologina the daughter of Michael VIII in 1278.[2] One of their sons adopted the name of Doukas Angelos Komnenos Palaiologos. The Asanaioi, frequently designated as Palaiologoi, continued to appear even after 1453.

67. Andronikos Doukas Angelos Komnenos Palaiologos: Philes wrote a number of poems for the man[3] whom he calls by the above appelations.[4] Andronikos was a son of Eirene, a daughter of Michael VIII, by her marriage to the Bulgarian tzar Ivan III Asen.[5] He was born in the last quarter of the thirteenth century and died after 1355. The surname Asan is very frequently attached to him and to his children. He married the daughter of Michael *89* and Maria *153*[6] and had two sons, Ioannes and Manuel, and a daughter Eirene who became the wife of Ioannes VI Kantakouzenos.

68. Ioannes Doukas Asan: A seal bears the inscription: [*Γρ*]*αφὰς σφρα-γί*[*ζω 'Iω*]*άννου Δού*[*κα*] *τοῦ 'Ασάν*.[7] The word *Δούκα* is not certain but appears quite probable. In view of the many persons called *'Iωάννης 'Ασάν(ης)* it is difficult to determine who this particular Ioannes Doukas Asan is.

69. Ioannes Doukas Angelos Palaiologos Raoul Laskaris Tornikes Philanthropenos Asanes: His name which includes some of the most famous Byzantine surnames, is preserved on a fifteenth-century ikon, now in the monastery of Mega Spelaion near Kalabryta.[8] The letters had become almost

---

[1] *τοῦ εὐγενεστάτου Δούκα κυροῦ Μιχαὴλ τοῦ 'Αριανίτου*; see G. I. Theocharides, *Μία διαθήκη καὶ μία δίκη Βυζαντινή* (Thessalonica, 1962), p. 19. See below Eudokia *158*, p. 164.

[2] Cf. Papadopulos, *Genealogie der Palaiologen*, pp. 27–8, no. 44, and family tree on p. 29. Yet there is an earlier reference to a Byzantine family of Asanes, for a document of March 1235 speaks of a *προάστειον τὸ ποτὲ ἐπιλεγόμενον τοῦ 'Ασάνη*, see MM, IV, p. 10. For fuller references to members of the family see Gy. Moravcsik, *Byzantinoturcica* (Berlin, 1958), II, p. 74.

[3] *Τῷ ἀνεψιῷ τοῦ αὐτοκράτορος τῷ Παλαιολόγῳ κυρῷ 'Ανδρονίκῳ*, Philes (Martini), pp. 21–3; cf. 23–5; *'Επιτάφιοι τῇ γυναικὶ τοῦ ἀνεψιοῦ τοῦ αὐτοκράτορος κυροῦ 'Ανδρονίκου τοῦ Παλαιολόγου*, ibid., pp. 63–8; also some other poems.

[4] Philes (Miller), II, p. 19; Philes (Martini), p. 66.

[5] For references see Papadopulos, *Genealogie der Palaiologen*, p. 28, no. 46.

[6] For references see below Michael *89*, p. 121, n. 17.

[7] K. M. Konstantopoulos, *'Νέα προσκτήματα τοῦ 'Εθνικοῦ Νομισματικοῦ Μουσείου. B' Βυζαντιακὰ μολυβδόβουλλα '*, *JIAN*, 3 (1900), 184, no. 39.

[8] See G. A. Sotiriou, *' Ἡ εἰκὼν τοῦ Παλαιολόγου τῆς μονῆς τοῦ Μεγάλου Σπηλαίου '*, *'Αρχαιολογικὸν Δελτίον*, 4 (1918), 31; cf. Papadopulos, *Genealogie der Palaiologen*, p. 96, no. 193. The name of Ioannes is written in capital letters as follows: *ΙΩΑΝΝΗΣ ΔΟΥΚΑΣ ΑΓΓΕΛΟΣ ΠΑΛΑΙΟΛΟΓΟΣ ΡΑΟΥΛ ΛΑΣΚΑΡΗΣ ΤΟΡΝΙΤΖΗΣ ΦΙΛΑΝΘΡΩΠΙΟΣ Ο ΑΣΑΝΗΣ*. The form *Τορνίτζης* (instead of *Τορνίκης*) should be noted. It does not seem to be attested elsewhere and an explanation may be found in the widespread pronunciation of -*κι* as- *τσι*(-*τζι*) in local dialect.

illegible but in the middle of the last century they were restored by a local painter (one cannot tell how accurately).

ATRAPES

The surname of Atrapes (Ἀτράπης) is rare in Byzantium. Apart from Manuel 70 I have found only one other Leon Atrapes who was a scribe in 1423.[1] It is possible that the two were related.

70. Manuel Doukas Atrapes: He was a scribe who lived in the fifteenth century, perhaps around 1445/6, and apparently specialized in copying medical works. Two manuscripts of his, both predominantly medical, survive. In cod. Reg. Suec. 182 he signs himself as Μανουὴλ Δούκας ὁ Ἀτράπης καὶ καθολικὸς γραμματικός and also notes that Ἐγράφη παρ᾽ ἐμοῦ Μανουὴλ τοῦ Ἀτράπη ζητηθεῖσα δὲ παρὰ Μιχαὴλ τοῦ Λεσβίου.[2] In cod. Laur. Conv. Soppr. App. 2, fol. 218r, his signature is simply as Μανουὴλ ὁ Ἀτράπης.[3]

BALSAMON

The surname of Balsamon (Βαλσαμών) is borne by very many Byzantines frequently active in ecclesiastical administration. Perhaps the first of them is the famous canonist Theodoros Balsamon, patriarch of Antioch (c. 1190). Balsamon ὁ Ξυλέας is mentioned in a document of c. 1280[4] and Georgios Balsamon was dux of the island of Cos at the same period.[5] Of the numerous church dignitaries of that name I only mention the μέγας σκευοφύλαξ πρεσβύτερος Michael Balsamon in 1380,[6] the μέγας σακελλάριος διάκονος Demetrios Balsamon in 1400,[7] the λογοθέτης διάκονος Manuel Balsamon in 1400,[8] and the μέγας χαρτοφύλαξ καὶ ἀρχιδιάκονος Michael Balsamon in 1440.[9]

71. Theodora Doukaina Balsamina: Theodora (Δούκαινα κυρὰ Θεοδώρα ἡ Βαλσαμῖνα) was the daughter of an Angelos from whom she may have inherited the name of Doukaina. She had a brother who had married Eudokia Philanthropene, and he became the father of a daughter Na. Na was about to marry a certain Cheilas. A piece of land, given by Angelos directly to his granddaughter Na, was then claimed by Theodora. The synodal court, whose act was dated December 1315, rejected Theodora's claim and confirmed the original bestowal.[10]

---

[1] Cf. Voger-Gardthausen, *Schreiber*, p. 261.

[2] H. Stevenson, *Codices manuscripti graeci Reginae Suecorum et Pii PP. II Bibliothecae Vaticanae descripti* (Rome, 1888), p. 125. The manuscript contains a few folios by another scribe written in 1445/6.

[3] E. Rostagno and N. Festa, 'Indice dei codici greci laurenziani non compresi nel catalogo del Bandini', *Studi Italiani di Filologia Classica*, 1 (1893), 215.

[4] MM, IV, p. 260.

[5] MM, VI, p. 246; cf. Dölger, *Regesten*, IV, p. 15, no. 2142a.

[6] MM, II, p. 16.   [7] MM, II, p. 354.   [8] MM, II, p. 385

[9] J. Gill, *The Council of Florence* (Cambridge, 1959), index s.v.   [10] MM, I, pp. 32–3.

BATATZES

The name of *Βατάτζης* has been explained as being derived either from the word *βάτος* (bush) or the word *βατάκι* (ray-fish).[1] The Batatzai were a distinguished Byzantine house who from the late tenth century onwards played an active part in serving the state, particularly in the army.[2] From early times the family appears to have been established in Thrace;[3] even at a later period Ioannes III *72* was said to have his roots in that region.[4] An intermarriage between two distant branches of the family created the house of Diplobatatzes (cf. *Διπλοπαλαιολόγος*), attested in the thirteenth century and later and still in existence at Constantinople in the sixteenth century.[5] In the eleventh century the Batatzai became related to the Bryennioi,[6] and the bonds between the two families continued for some time.[7]

Although the emperor Ioannes III *72* chose to use the name of Doukas, it is obvious that his patronymic proper was Batatzes.[8] Despite the fact that the Batatzai were an ancient house, it is rather peculiar that the emperor himself ignored this and only boasted of being descended from the Komnenoi and the Doukai.[9] In the same vein, contemporary poets complimented him with the familiar epithets *Δουκογενής*,[10] *Δουκόφυτος*,[11] *Δουκόβλαστος*,[12] and *Δουκοφυής*,[13]

---

[1] See the note of K. I. Amantos in *Ἑλληνικά*, 4 (1931), 492. Cf. the cryptic verse καὶ ἡ βάτος ἀπὸ πέρα which is explained as βάτος ἐστὶν ὁ Βατάτζης; see A. Heisenberg, 'Kaiser Johannes Batatzes der Barmherzige: eine mittelgriechische Legende', *BZ*, 14 (1905), 176.

[2] For the family see Ducange, *Familiae*, pp. 222–4; K. I. Amantos, ''Η οἰκογένεια Βατάτζη', *ΕΕΒΣ*, 21 (1951), 174–8.

[3] Καί τινες τῶν ἐκ τῆς Ἀνδριανουπόλεως ἰλλούστριοι καὶ στρατηγικαῖς ἀρχαῖς διαπρέψαντες, ὁ μὲν Βατάτζης πανοικί . . . (c. 1000), Kedr., II, pp. 451–2; Kedr., II, p. 565, also speaks of an ἐγχωρίου δυνάστου τοῦ λεγομένου Βατάτζη, συγγενοῦς ὄντος τοῦ Τορνικίου in Thrace in 1049.

[4] Akrop., p. 26; Skout., p. 462; Ephraim, v. 7846 (p. 316) all agree that Ioannes came from Didymoteichon. His *Vita* calls him 'Ἰωάννης ὁ Θρᾷξ (Heisenberg, op. cit., p. 195[14]) and describes his ancestors as being εὐπατρίδαι τε ὄντως—'Ὀρεστιὰς γὰρ ἡ πατρίς σφισι (ibid., p. 198[1, 2]).

[5] Cf. M. Crusius, *Turcograecia* (Basel, 1584), p. 91.

[6] The relationship of a Batatzes and a Batatzaina with the rebel Nikephoros Bryennios in 1078 is noted by Attal., pp. 244–8, and Skyl. Cont., p. 729.

[7] The *Life* of St Meletios speaks of a Bryennios, *dux* of Thebes, who had a relative Batatzes; see V. G. Vasilievskii, 'Vita S. Meletii', *Pravoslavnii Palestinskii Sbornik*, 17 (1886), 29. A twelfth-century seal belongs to a Bryennios Batatzes; see V. Laurent, 'Bulletin de Sigillographie byzantine', *B*, 5 (1930), 587; N. A. Mouchmov, 'Un nouveau boullotirion byzantin', *B*, 4 (1927/28), 190.

[8] . . . 'Ἰωάννην τὸν Δούκαν, οὗ Βατάτζης τοὐπίκλην, Akrop., p. 26.

[9] Οἱ τῆς βασιλείας μου γενάρχαι, οἱ ἀπὸ τοῦ γένους τῶν Δουκῶν τε καὶ Κομνηνῶν ἵνα μὴ τοὺς ἑτέρους λέγω, see I. Sakellion, ''Ἀνέκδοτος ἐπιστολὴ τοῦ αὐτοκράτορος 'Ἰωάννου Δούκα Βατάτση πρὸς τὸν πάπαν Γρηγόριον ἀνευρεθεῖσα ἐν Πάτμῳ', 'Ἀθήναιον, I (1872), 374.

[10] Τῆς δουκογενοῦς βασιλίδος ὀσφύος, Akrop., II, p. 43[1].

[11] Πᾶϊς δουκοφύτων ἐρικυδῶν βασιλήων; see H. Grégoire, *Recueil des Inscriptions grecques chrétiennes d'Asie Mineure*, I (Paris, 1922), p. 22, no. 81, v. 11. The entire poetical inscription is now more readily accessible in C. A. Trypanis, *Medieval and Modern Greek Poetry* (Oxford, 1951) p. 50.

[12] Δουκόβλαστος 'Ἰωάννης; see A. Heisenberg, *Nicephori Blemmydae Curriculum Vitae et Carmina* (Leipzig, 1896), p. 112[4].

[13] Τοῦ δουκοφυοῦς παγκλεοῦς 'Ἰωάννου, ibid., p. 115[11].

but never found a word of praise for the Batatzai. Only the emperor's *Vita*, written late in the fourteenth century, was aware that Ioannes 72 was above all a scion of the Batatzes family, but the hagiographer's lavish praise of the hero's forefathers, whose description flatly contradicts the contemporary Choniates, should not overshadow the conspicuous silence of more reliable sources. The answer to all this is perhaps not difficult to find. The father of Ioannes III was certainly a Batatzes but not necessarily a noble one. During the reign of Isaakios Angelos (1185–95) Choniates speaks of a Basileios Batatzes, a man of humble origin, who married the emperor's cousin and was made δομέστικος τῆς 'Ανατολῆς.[1] Basileios was killed while fighting against the Bulgarians in *c.* 1193[2], and his wife had a brother Konstantinos who acted as δούξ τοῦ στόλου and is described as a cousin (ἐξάδελφος) of Isaakios.[3] It is very probable that Basileios Batatzes was in fact the father of Ioannes III. He had married in about 1189, while Ioannes was born in 1192. His wife was an Angelina,[4] but like other members of her house might have preferred the greater prestige of the names of Doukas and Komnenos which her children promptly inherited and used. Consequently the humble background and the person of Basileios Batatzes were easily forgotten.

72. Ioannes Doukas: The Byzantine emperor Ioannes III was probably a son of Basileios Batatzes[5] and his wife the Angelina. He himself preferred to sign himself as 'Ιωάννης ὁ Δούκας[6] and most contemporary sources call him so,[7]

---

[1] Βασίλειος ὁ Βατάτζης γένους μὲν ἀσήμου βλαστών, διὰ δὲ τὸ εἰς γυναῖκα οἱ γαμετὴν συναφθῆναι τὴν τοῦ βασιλέως πρὸς πατρὸς ἐξανεψιὰν δομέστικος τῆς ἀνατολῆς τιμηθεὶς καὶ τὴν δουκικὴν ἀρχὴν τῶν Θρακησίων ἀναζωσάμενος, Chon., pp. 522–3; cf. Skout., p. 388. A document which he issued in the capacity of δούξ καὶ ἀναγραφεὺς τοῦ θέματος Μυλάσσης καὶ Μελανουδίου, dated to August 1189, as well as the reading on his seal, are preserved; see MM, IV, p. 330.

[2] Chon., pp. 587–8.

[3] Chon., pp. 570–1.

[4] Possibly a daughter of Isaakios, the son of Konstantinos Angelos and Theodora Komnene. A brother of Ioannes III, called Isaakios 73, might easily have been called after him.

[5] In the family tree of the Laskareis in V. Grumel, *La chronologie* (Paris, 1958), p. 565, the name of Ioannes' father is indicated as Basileios. The *Vita* calls the emperor's grandfather Konstantinos (Heisenberg, 'Kaiser Johannes Batatzes', p. 200[12]) and adds that he had two sons Nikephoros and Theodoros who were persecuted by Andronikos Komnenos and had to flee first to Iconium and then via Crete to Italy where they were seized and blinded (ibid., p. 205). This is evidently the same story related by Chon., pp. 340–43, which concerns the *megas domestikos* Ioannes Batatzes Komnenos and his sons Manuel and Alexios. These people who were closely related to the imperial house can in no way be regarded as the immediate forefathers of Ioannes III. His hagiographer, writing more than two centuries after the events, seems to have been confused; in particular, influenced by the fact that Ioannes III had a son Theodoros, he may have imagined that the emperor's father was also called Theodoros.

[6] All his documents that bear a signature are signed in this manner.

[7] Akrop., pp. 26, 32 and 50; Pach., I, pp. 64, 68, 117, 134, 349, 368, and 374; II, p. 154 etc.; Greg., I, pp. 24, 35, and 92; *B*, 10 (1935), 491; N. Festa, *Theodori Ducae Lascaris Epistulae CCXVII* (Florence, 1892), pp. 1, 67, 117, 150, and 159; Skout., pp. 467, 469 etc.; Sp. P. Lampros and K. I. Amantos, Βραχέα Χρονικά (Athens, 1932), p. 7; Papadopoulos-Kerameus, Ἱεροσολυμιτικὴ Βιβλιοθήκη, IV, p. 339; J. Moravcsik, 'Der Verfasser der Legende von Johannes des Barmherzigen', *BZ*, 27 (1927), 38; Sp. P. Lampros, 'Κυπριακὰ καὶ ἄλλα ἔγγραφα ἐκ τοῦ Παλατίνου κώδικος 367 τῆς Βιβλιοθήκης τοῦ Βατικανοῦ', *NE*, 14 (1917), 39 and 40; MM, IV, pp. 27, 29, 48 etc. and numerous other references.

while the epithets of Βατάτζης[1] and Δούκας Βατάτζης[2] are comparatively rare. A unique form is 'Ιωάννης Δούκας ὁ Βριανός.[3]

Ioannes was born in c. 1192[4] and in the early years of his career was dignified by the title of *protovestiarites*.[5] He became emperor in January 1222[6] and reigned for thirty-two years until his death at Nymphaeum on 4 November 1254.[7] He was buried at the monastery τῶν Σωσάνδρων in Magnesia. Some fifty years after his death, Ioannes Doukas, though not formally canonised by the Greek Church, began to be venerated as a saint — ἅγιος 'Ιωάννης ὁ 'Ελεήμων[8] — and his feast was especially observed in the region of Magnesia.

Ioannes III married twice. In 1212 he was chosen by the emperor Theodoros I Laskaris as the bridegroom for his eldest daughter Eirene *115*.[9] She bore to him only one son Theodoros *75* and died in 1239. Ioannes married again in 1244, this time Constance, the fourteen-year-old daughter of the emperor Frederick II Hohenstaufen, who was called Anna by the Greeks.[10] Ioannes, however, was hardly attracted by his young bride. Her German companion, the so-called Μαρκεσῖνα (marchioness), became his mistress and had some influence over him.[11]

---

[1] Kant., I, p. 11; Sphrantzes, p. 7 (Papadopulos, p. 10); R.-J. Loenertz, 'La chronique brève de 1352. Texte, traduction et commentaire', *OCP*, 29 (1963), 332, § 2; a poem bears the title Στίχοι τοῦ κυροῦ Γεωργίου τοῦ χαρτοφύλακος Καλλιπόλεως πρὸς 'Ιωάννην τὸν Βατάτζην ἐλθόντα εἰς τὴν Καλλίπολιν, see M. Gigante, *Poeti Italobizantini del secolo XIII* (Naples, 1958), p. 70.

[2] Skout., p. 462; R.-J. Loenertz, 'Chronicon breve de Graecorum imperatoribus', *ΕΕΒΣ*, (28 1958), 206, § 1; K. D. Mertzios, Μνημεῖα Μακεδονικῆς 'Ιστορίας (Thessalonica, 1947), p. 29; G. I. Theocharides, ' Οἱ Τζαμπλάκωνες. Συμβολὴ εἰς τὴν βυζαντινὴν μακεδονικὴν προσωπογραφίαν τοῦ ΙΔ′ αἰῶνος ', Μακεδονικά, 5 (1961/63), 131.

[3] Lampros–Amantos, Βραχέα Χρονικά, p. 54; it may stand for βριαρός.

[4] When he died in 1254, he is described as being either sixty-two (Akrop., p. 103), or sixty (Greg., I, p. 50). The first appears nearer the truth.

[5] Akrop., p. 26; Ephraim, v. 7847 (p. 316).

[6] According to the short chronicle, Loenertz, 'Chronicon breve', p. 206, he reigned for thirty-two years and ten months.

[7] The traditional date is 3 November 1254, and is given by Akrop., p. 103, and by an *enthymesis* in Papadopoulos-Kerameus, 'Ιεροσολυμιτικὴ Βιβλιοθήκη, IV, p. 339; cf. V. Laurent, 'Notes de chronographie et d'histoire byzantine,' *EO*, 36 (1937), 162–5. On the other hand, another *enthymesis* dates his death to 4 November (Moravcsik, loc. cit.), and this is confirmed by the fact that his μνήμη has subsequently been celebrated on that particular day; 4 November, therefore, seems more likely; cf. K. I. Amantos, ' 'Ο βίος 'Ιωάννου Βατάτζη τοῦ 'Ελεήμονος', Προσφορὰ εἰς Στίλπωνα Π.Κυριακίδην (Thessalonica, 1953), pp. 32–4.

[8] Halkin, *BHG*, II, pp. 34–5; S. Eustratiades, 'Αγιολόγιον τῆς 'Ορθοδόξου 'Εκκλησίας (Athens, n.d.), p. 229. In cod. Burney (British Museum) 54 (XVI s.), fol. 219v, there are to be found a τροπάριον, a κοντάκιον, and the οἶκος in celebration Τοῦ ἁγίου ἐνδόξου καὶ εἰς ἀποστόλους βασιλέως 'Ιωάννου τοῦ νέου ἐλεήμονος, τοῦ ἐν Μαγνησίᾳ καὶ Βατάτζη. The τροπάριον praises him for having spread the faith among the barbarians ('Ιωάννη ἀοίδιμε, εἵλκυσας σὺ πρὸς πίστιν τῶν βαρβάρων τὰ πλήθη). Could this mean that he was somehow concerned in trying to propagate Christianity among the Seljuks?

[9] Akrop., p. 26; Pach., I, p. 317; Greg., I, p. 24; Kant., I, pp. 11 and 83.

[10] Pach., I, p. 181; Greg., I, p. 92. The poet Nikolaos Eirenikos wrote on this occasion Τετράστιχα εἰς τὸν ἀρραβῶνα τῶν εὐσεβεστάτων καὶ ἐκ Θεοῦ ἐστεμμένων μεγάλων βασιλέων 'Ιωάννου τοῦ Δούκα καὶ "Αννης τῆς εὐγενεστάτης αὐγούστης, printed in A. Heisenberg, 'Aus der Geschichte und Literatur der Palaiologenzeit', *SBBAW*, 1920, pp. 99–105. Constance-Anna died as a nun in Valencia in 1313; bibliography on her in D. J. Geanakoplos, *Emperor Michael Palaeologus and the West* (Cambridge, Mass., 1958), p. 144, n. 25.

[11] Akrop., p. 104; Greg., I, pp. 45–6.

The emperor appears to have tried his hand at hymn writing.[1] His seal reads: 'Ἰωάννης δεσπότης ὁ Δούκας.[2]

73. Isaakios Doukas: The *sebastokrator* Isaakios Doukas was a brother of Ioannes III Doukas but is only rarely mentioned. He had the title of *pansebastos sebastos* and as such was present while the treaty of Nymphaeum on 13 March 1261, was being signed.[3] Isaakios became the father of at least two children, Ioannes[4] and a daughter who married Konstantinos Strategopoulos.[5]

Apart from Isaakios, the emperor Ioannes also had another brother of unknown name. The latter had a daughter who married the *protovestiarios* Alexios Raoul (1253)[6] and became the mother of Ioannes *181*.

74. Theodora Doukaina Komnene Palaiologina: The empress Theodora who became the wife of Michael VIII *142* was a daughter of Ioannes, the son of Isaakios *73*, and Eudokia[7] and appears to have been born in *c.* 1240. The names she carried[8] were those of her husband. At a young age in 1253[9] Theodora married the future emperor Michael Palaiologos. She died on 4 March 1303.[10] Her extant seals bear the inscription Θεοδώρα εὐσεβεστάτη αὐγοῦστα Δούκαινα ἡ Παλαιολογῖνα.[11]

75. Theodoros Doukas Laskaris: Theodoros II of Nicaea was the only son of Ioannes III *72* and his wife Eirene *115*. He preferred to sign himself as Θεόδωρος Δούκας ὁ Λάσκαρις and some contemporary sources call him so.[12]

---

[1] See G. I. Papadopoulos, Συμβολαὶ εἰς τὴν ἱστορίαν τῆς παρ' ἡμῖν ἐκκλησιαστικῆς μουσικῆς (Athens, 1890), pp. 267–8.

[2] K. M. Konstantopoulos, ' Ἡ σφραγὶς Ἰωάννου Δούκα Βατάτζη ', *JIAN*, 16 (1914), 28–31; Laurent, *Médaillier Vatican*, p. 10, no. 14.

[3] '. . . et des nobles homes, Isaach, duc et pansebastis et sebastis, famillier du dit treserin empereor '; see J. A. C. Buchon, *Recherches et Matériaux pour servir à une Histoire de la Domination française à la Suite de la quatrième Croisade*, 1 (Paris, 1840), p. 468. The word 'duc' is presumably not a title but an inexact rendering of the surname Δούκας ascribed to Isaakios by Akrop., p. 101. 'Famillier' is of course the equivalent of the Greek οἰκεῖος.

[4] Ioannes married an Eudokia Angelina and died young. He was the father of Theodora *74* (ὁ τοῦ σεβαστοκράτορος υἱὸς Ἰωάννης ἔτι ἐν μείραξιν ὢν τὸ χρεὼν ἐξεμέτρησε, χήραν μὲν τὴν αὐτοῦ γαμετὴν Εὐδοκίαν ἀφείς, τὴν τοῦ Ἀγγέλου Ἰωάννου θυγατέρα, ὀρφανὴν δὲ τὴν θυγατέρα αὐτοῦ Θεοδώραν, ἥτις εὐτυχῶς τῷ Κομνηνῷ τότε συνέζευκτο Μιχαήλ· ἡ γὰρ μήτηρ αὐτῆς Εὐδοκία καίτοι γε νέα οὖσα πάνυ τὴν χηρείαν φέρειν ἠσπάσατο, Akrop., p. 101).

[5] Cf. Pach., I, pp. 24 and 64–5; II, pp. 154–5.

[6] Akrop., pp. 92 and 99; Pach., II, pp. 154–5.   [7] See above n. 4; cf. Skout., p. 504.

[8] Her ὁμολογία πίστεως begins with the words Θεοδώρα ἐν Χριστῷ τῷ Θεῷ πιστὴ αὐγοῦστα καὶ αὐτοκρατόρισσα Ῥωμαίων Δούκαινα Κομνηνὴ ἡ Παλαιολογῖνα; see J. Dräseke, 'Der kircheneinigungsversuch des Kaisers Michael VIII Paläologos', *Zeitschrift für Wissenschaftliche Theologie*, 34 (1891), 353; for this document cf. L. Petit, 'La profession de foi de l'impératrice Theodora (1283)', *EO*, 18 (1916/18), 286–7. Theodora also issued another document in MM, VI, pp. 225–6, and also the *Typikon* of the monastery of Lips (Delehaye, 'Deux typica', pp. 106–40). An inscription refers to her as Θεοδώρα ἐν Χριστῷ τῷ Θεῷ πιστὴ βασίλισσα καὶ αὐτοκρατόρισσα Ῥωμαίων ἡ Κομνηνή; see A. Boeckh, *Corpus Inscriptionum Graecarum*, IV (Berlin, 1877), p. 346, no. 8754.

[9] Papadopulos, *Genealogie der Palaiologen*, p. 2, no. 1.

[10] Ibid., p. 2, no. 1. On her death Theodoros Metochites wrote a Μονῳδία ἐπὶ τῇ βασιλίδι Θεοδώρᾳ τῇ τοῦ βασιλέως μητρί, in cod. Vind. phil. gr. 95, fol. 179r–189r; see H. Hunger, *Katalog der griechischen Handschriften der Österreichischen Nationalbibliothek*, I (Vienna, 1961), p. 203.

[11] Laurent, *Médaillier Vatican*, pp. 10–12, nos. 15–16.

[12] For instance MM, IV, p. 221; Loenertz, 'La chronique brève de 1352', p. 332, § 3.

Elsewhere his name is given as Komnenos Laskaris,[1] or more often simply Laskaris.[2] He was born early in 1222, approximately at the time when his father became emperor,[3] but since he is never called porphyrogenitus, we may suppose that his birth preceded his father's accession. He was called after his paternal grandfather Theodoros I Laskaris.[4]

Ioannes III failed to crown his son during his lifetime[5] and so Theodoros was proclaimed emperor by the army and the nobility at Nymphaeum following his father's death on 4 November 1254, and was symbolically raised on a shield.[6] His coronation, however, had to wait for the election of a new patriarch[7] and was presumably performed early in 1255. Like his father, Theodoros was subject to epileptic attacks and succumbed to a severe one in August 1258[8] at the early age of thirty-six. On his death bed he took monastic vows[9] retaining the name of Theodoros.[10] He was buried at the monastery τῶν Σωσάνδρων.[11]

As a boy of eleven, Theodoros was betrothed to the nine-year-old Helene, a daughter of the Bulgarian tzar Ivan II Asen in 1233.[12] They were married in 1235.[13] This marriage produced five children: Ioannes 76, Eirene,[14] Maria,[15] Theodora[16] and Eudokia.[17]

The emperor Theodoros II occupies an outstanding place in the literature of the thirteenth century. His theological writings are numerous[18] and he was

---

[1] Boeckh, op. cit., pp. 342–3.

[2] Pach., I, pp. 21, 65, 68, 82 etc.; Greg., I, pp. 53, 92, 95 etc.; Lampros–Amantos, Βραχέα Χρονικά, p. 54; Festa, Epistulae, pp. 1, 67, 117, and 159.

[3] Τοιοῦτος γὰρ ὁ χρόνος αὐτῷ ὁπόσος τῆς πατρικῆς βασιλείας ἐτύγχανε· σχεδὸν γὰρ τῇ πατρικῇ ἀναρρήσει καὶ ἡ γέννησις ἐκείνου συνέδραμεν, Akrop., p. 104.

[4] Cf. Akrop., p. 49.

[5] Greg., I, p. 53.

[6] Akrop., p. 104; Greg., I., p. 55.

[7] Akrop., p. 106; Greg., I, p. 55.

[8] Κατὰ νοέμβριον γὰρ ἄρξας ἐν αὐγούστῳ μηνὶ τὸ τέλος ἔσχηκε τῆς ζωῆς, Akrop., p. 153.

[9] Akrop., p. 153; Pach., I, p. 39; Greg., I, p. 61.

[10] An addition to the synodicon of Cyprus reads: Θεοδώρου τοῦ ἐν εὐσεβεῖ τῇ μνήμῃ γενομένου ἀοιδίμου βασιλέως ἡμῶν τοῦ Δούκα, τοῦ διὰ τοῦ θείου καὶ ἀγγελικοῦ σχήματος μετονομασθέντος πάλιν Θεοδώρου μοναχοῦ, αἰωνία ἡ μνήμη; see N. Cappuyns, 'Le synodicon de Chypre au XIIe siècle', B, 10 (1935), 491. The editor (pp. 493–4) believes that this commemoration refers to Theodoros 42 of Thessalonica, but this is hardly acceptable.

[11] Akrop., p. 153; Greg., I, p. 65; Loenertz, 'La chronique brève de 1352', p. 332, § 3.

[12] Akrop., pp. 49 and 52–3; Greg., I, p. 30.

[13] Akrop., p. 50. The marriage took place at Gallipoli; see Ph. Meyer, Die Haupturkunden für die Geschichte der Athosklöster (Leipzig, 1894), p. 188.

[14] In early 1258 Eirene married the Bulgarian tzar Constantine Tich, (Akrop., p. 152; Pach., I, pp. 36, 138, and 183), whom she continuously pressed to avenge the blinding of Ioannes 76 (Pach., I, pp. 138, 183, 210, and 342).

[15] Maria became the wife of Nikephoros 49 of Epirus; see Akrop., pp. 88, 133, and 134; Pach., I, p. 36; Greg., I, p. 63.

[16] Theodora married in c. 1261 the French nobleman Valincourt, Greg., I, p. 92.

[17] She appears to have been the youngest daughter of the emperor and was given in marriage to the Count of Ventimiglia, Akrop., p. 154; Greg., I, p. 93 (calls her Eirene). Pach., I, p. 181, seems to mention another daughter of Theodoros whom Michael VIII married to the Bulgarian Sviatoslav. Ducange, Familiae, p. 224, considers her illegitimate.

[18] Cf. H.-G. Beck, Kirche und theologische Literatur im byzantinischen Reich (Munich, 1959), pp. 673–4. For Theodoros as an author see also N. B. Tomadakis, Βυζαντινὴ Γραμματολογία (1204–1453), I (Athens, 1957), pp. 106–13.

especially successful in hymn writing.[1] His numerous letters to such men as Akropolites, Blemmydes, and Mouzalon are very important.[2] His seal reads:

> Ἀνακτόπαιδα Δούκαν, ἀθλητά, σκέποις
> Θεόδωρον Λάσκαριν τὸν βασιλέα.[3]

Some portraits of him have been preserved.[4]

76. Ioannes Doukas Laskaris: The unfortunate child emperor Ioannes IV was the only son of Theodoros II *75* and Helene the Bulgarian. The sources mostly call him Laskaris[5] and only occasionally Δούκας ὁ Λάσκαρις.[6] He appears to have been born on 25 December 1250.[7] On the death of Theodoros *75* in August 1258 Ioannes was recognised as emperor, but his rights were gradually suppressed by the usurper Michael Palaiologos *142* who finally deprived him of the imperial insignia.[8] By the time Constantinople was regained, Ioannes had lost all his prerogatives; he was finally blinded on 25 December 1261[9] and was subsequently confined to a fortress in Bithynia. He was still there when the new emperor Andronikos II visited him in 1284.[10] He must have died by 1305.[11]

Ioannes IV seems to have died as the monk Ioasaph and to have been regarded as a saint.[12]

---

[1] Papadopoulos, *Συμβολαί*, pp. 168–9; C. Emereau, 'Hymnographi Byzantini', *EO*, 24 (1925), 177.

[2] Festa, *Epistulae*; idem, 'Noterelle alle epistole di Teodoro Lascaris', *Studi Italiani di Filologia Classica*, 7 (1899), 204.

[3] Laurent, *Bulles métriques*, p. 16, no. 19.   [4] Lampros, *Λεύκωμα*, pl. 73–4.

[5] Greg., I, pp. 80, 173, and 174; Sphrantzes, p. 26 (Papadopulos, p. 30); cf. p. 41 (Papadopulos, p. 46).

[6] Loenertz, 'La chronique brève de 1352', p. 332, § 4.

[7] Akrop., p. 154, observes that ἀφῆλιξ ἐτύγχανεν ὢν ἐν τῷ καιρῷ τῆς τελευτῆς τοῦ βασιλέως καὶ πατρός (sc. in August 1258)· οὔπω γὰρ τελείων ἐνιαυτῶν ὑπῆρχεν ὀκτώ. The anonymous chronicle agrees with this: αὐγούστῳ ἰνδικτιῶνος αʹ ἀνηγορεύθη βασιλεὺς ὢν ἐτῶν οὔπω ηʹ, see Loenertz, 'La chronique brève de 1352', p. 332, § 4. This evidence establishes that Ioannes was born in 1250. But other sources do not agree. Pach., I, p. 35, makes him nine in 1258 and Greg., I, p. 62 (cf. Sphrantzes, p. 12) six (ἦν γὰρ ἕκτον τηνικαῦτα διανύων ἀπὸ γενέσεως ἔτος ἐκεῖνος). This points to 1252 as the year of his birth, but elsewhere the same Gregoras states that when blinded in 1261 Ioannes was ten years old (δεκαετῆ ἤδη τυγχάνοντα, Greg., I, p. 93). According to Pach. I, p. 192, the child was deprived of his sight κατὰ τὴν ἡμέραν τῆς ἑορτῆς τοῦ Σωτῆρος καθ᾿ ἣν ἄρα καὶ ἐγεννήθη. This seems to imply Christmas.
On the occasion of his birth, Blemmydes dedicated a few verses to Ioannes

> Τῷ νεογνῷ μου βασιλεῖ, τῷ βασιλείας ἄνθει
> εὔχεται σὸς πρεσβύτερος μονάζων Νικηφόρος.

See Heisenberg, *Blemmydae vita*, pp. 110–11.

[8] Pach., I, p. 127.

[9] Pach., I, p. 192; Greg., I, p. 93.

[10] Pach., I, p. 103–4; Greg., I, pp. 173–4. For the false Angevin claims alleging that Ioannes went to Italy cf. Geanakoplos, *Michael Palaeologus*, pp. 217–18.

[11] Cf. I. Ševčenko, 'The Imprisonment of Manuel Moschopulos in the year 1305 or 1306', *Speculum*, 27 (1962), 149 and 156, n. 93.

[12] In 1349 a Russian monk prayed at his grave in the monastery of St Demetrios in Constantinople. He speaks of him as 'svjatago carja Laskarijasafa'; see I. Ševčenko, 'Notes on Stephen, the Novgorodian Pilgrim to Constantinople in the XIV Century', *Südostforschungen*, 12 (1953), 173–5.
Likewise a post-Byzantine list of saints, compiled by the monk Silvestros of Constantinople, regards Ioannes IV as a νεοφανὴς ἅγιος. His name appears in the form Ὁ ἀπὸ βασιλέων Ἰωάσαφ Λάσκαρις μοναχός, see the book Ἐπιστολὴ Εὐγενίου τοῦ Βουλγάρεως πρὸς Πέτρον τὸν Κλαίρκιον περὶ τῶν μετὰ τὸ σχίσμα Ἁγίων τῆς Ὀρθοδόξου Ἀνατολικῆς Ἐκκλησίας καὶ τῶν γινομένων ἐν αὐτῇ

BOUMBALIS

77. Maria Doukaina: The family of Boumbalis (*Μπουμπάλης, Πούμπαλις, Μπούπαλις*) is one of *πάροικοι* in the katepanikion of Revenikia (*χωρίον τοῦ Συμεών*) in Macedonia. Michael Boumbalis was a son of the widow Maria Doukaina and had a wife Maria and a son Ioannes (*c.* 1300).[1] A few years later (1315/20) Michael Boumbalis is mentioned as having two sons Stanos and Georgios and two daughters Eirene and Kale.[2] At the same time a Nikolaos Boumbalis and his brother Ioannes appear.[3]

BRYENNIOS

No convincing etymology of the name Bryennios (the traditional orthography *Βρυέννιος* may not be correct) has been offered,[4] but there is probably a common root with the female name *Βρύαινα* which was in use during the early Byzantine period.[5] The earliest known member of the house is the *patrikios* Bryennios who lived at Constantinople during the reign of Leon III (717–41),[6] and up to the end of the Empire the Bryennioi are frequently met with.[7] It may be suggested that some of the Byzantines of the later period who bore the name of Bryennios might have owed their existence to a Norman chieftain in the service of Alexios I called Brienne.[8] In the eleventh century the Bryennioi were not a numerous family but belonged to the military aristocracy in which they occupied a distinguished place. The marriage of Nikephoros Bryennios to Anna Komnene *107*

θαυμάτων (Athens, 1844), p. 26. To be sure, the relative part of the list is given as follows: Μιχαὴλ Καπίνος ὁ ἀπὸ βασιλέων. Ἰωάσαφ Λάσκαρις μοναχός. Ἰωάννης Βατάτζης οὗ τὸ λείψανον ἐν τῇ Μαγνησίᾳ κτλ., but there can be no doubt that there is a misplacement of the fullstop and the phrase ὁ ἀπὸ βασιλέων really belongs to Ioasaph Laskaris and not to Michael Kapinos.

---

[1] Bompaire, *Actes de Xéropotamou*, p. 144; cf. p. 148.
[2] Ibid., p. 156.   [3] Ibid., p. 155; cf. p. 160.
[4] K. I. Amantos, ' *Κεφαλληνιακὰ ἐπώνυμα* ', *Ἑλληνικά*, 10 (1937/8), 119–20, is inclined to see the name as composed by the prefix *Βρι-* and the word *αἶνος*, meaning 'much-renowned'. N. B. Tomadakis, *Ὁ Ἰωσὴφ Βρυέννιος καὶ ἡ Κρήτη κατὰ τὸ 1400* (Athens, 1947), p. 20, thinks that the original form may have been *Εὐρυγένης*, that is 'he with a broad beard', inasmuch as the popular form *Βρυγένης* is attested. The Byzantines themselves connected the name with the phrase *βρύειν ἐννοίας*; cf. an epigram published by Tomadakis, ibid. The female form of the name is always *Βρυέννισσα*, whereas a derivative of it is certainly *Βριαινίτης* mentioned in *c.* 1270, Bompaire, *Actes de Xéropotamou*, p. 71.
[5] St Fantinos was *Γεωργίου καὶ Βρυαίνης γέννημα*, see H. Delehaye, *Synaxarium Ecclesiae Constantinopolitanae* (Brussels, 1902), col. 224. An abbess of a convent in Nisibis was also called *Βρύαινα* (ibid., cols. 769–70). S. Eustratiades, *Ἁγιολόγιον τῆς Ὀρθοδόξου Ἐκκλησίας* (Athens, n.d.), p. 84, mentions a saint *Βρυαίνη*.
[6] Delehaye, op. cit., col. 347.
[7] For the family see Ducange, *Familiae*, pp. 176–7, and the family tree in the notes of Bryen., p. 196; see also S. Wittek–De Jongh, 'Le césar Nicéphore Bryennios, l'historien, et ses ascendants', *B*, 23 (1953), 463–8.
[8] In *Alexias*, ii, pp. 28 ff., he is called *Βρυέννιος*.

(1097) shows the exceptional standing of the family, despite the recent revolt by some of its members. Yet the couple's immediate descendants chose to bear the names of Doukas and Komnenos and by so doing their surname proper of Bryennios passed into the background during the twelfth century.

78. Ioannes Doukas: Ioannes, always called Doukas, was a son probably the younger one, of Nikephoros Bryennios and Anna *107*. He made a career in the army and according to Manasses, who also praises his literary inclinations, he distinguished himself in the wars against the Italians, the Seljuks and other barbarians, and also in the Caucasus.[1] Ioannes' presence is attested in the synod of 6 March 1166.[2] Moreover we possess an epigram, originally composed for a dedication to Christ on his behalf.[3]

In *c.* 1122 Ioannes married a Caucasian princess who assumed the Greek name of Theodora. She died in 1138 and had already become the mother of a son Nikephoros who also appears to have passed away shortly afterwards.[4] Ioannes married again, this time to an unknown lady, and became the father of four other sons. Of these we know the names of the eldest Nikephoros Komnenos—presumably the first Nikephoros had died in the meantime—and of the youngest Manuel.[5]

[1] Τοῦτο δὲ οὐ μόνον ʽΡωμαῖοι καὶ Σκύθαι καὶ Ἰταλοὶ καὶ οἴδασι καὶ κηρύττουσιν, ἀλλὰ καὶ Κόλχοι καὶ Σαυρομάται καὶ οἱ τὰς ὑπωρείας τοῦ Καυκάσου νεμόμενοι καὶ οἱ τῶν Φάσιδος ῥείθρων τοῦ βαθυχεύμονος πίνοντες; see E. Kurtz, 'Efstathiya Thessalonikiiskago i Konstantina Manassi monodii na konchinu Nikifora Komnina', *VV*, 17 (1910), 308-9. Prodromos speaks of an expedition against the Seljuks of the Sangarios, taking place in 1138, in which Ioannes participated; see E. Kurtz, 'Unedierte Texte aus der Zeit des Kaisers Johannes Komnenos', *BZ*, 16 (1907), 89, vv. 67 ff. Ioannes appears to be the Ioannes Doukas whom Kinn., p. 128, calls a cousin of Manuel I and who intervened in a quarrel between the emperor's brother Isaakios and Andronikos Komnenos.

[2] Τοῦ περιποθήτου ἐξαδέλφου τοῦ βασιλέως ἡμῶν τοῦ ἁγίου, κυροῦ Ἰωάννου τοῦ Δούκα τοῦ υἱοῦ τοῦ ἀοιδίμου καίσαρος τοῦ Βρυεννίου, *PG*, 140, col. 253 A.

[3] Ἐπὶ ἐγχειρίῳ τοῦ κυρίου καὶ Θεοῦ ἡμῶν Ἰησοῦ Χριστοῦ γεγονότι παρὰ τοῦ Δούκα κυροῦ Ἰωάννου τοῦ υἱοῦ τοῦ καίσαρος ἐκείνου κυροῦ Νικηφόρου τοῦ Βρυεννίου, Lampros, 'Μαρκιανὸς 524', p. 30.

[4] Ioannes married at the same time as his elder brother Alexios Komnenos, and Prodromos composed for the occasion an Ἐπιθαλάμιος τοῖς τοῦ πανευτυχεστάτου καίσαρος υἱοῖς, edited in *PG*, 133, cols. 1397-1406. In it Ioannes is poetically called ὁ τῆς Δουκικῆς ῥίζης ὄρπηξ ὁ χαριτώνυμος (ibid., col. 1399 B). Both the brides were Caucasian in origin. Zon., III, p. 761, states that very soon after the death of Alexios I (15 August 1118) Ioannes II *108* rode to the Mangana in order to welcome the Abasgian embassy that escorted the bride of the Caesar's (i.e. Bryennios') elder son. At the time of the wedding Eirene *26* was still alive (*PG*, 133, col. 1400B), and Kurtz, 'Unedierte Texte', p. 86, dated it shortly before her death in 1123. Prodromos also wrote an epitaph for Theodora (ibid., pp. 88-93) which provides some information about her. She was of a foreign but noble house (p. 88, vv. 25-6), and after coming to Constantinople she was educated under the direct care of Eirene *26* and Anna *107* (p. 88, vv. 36 ff.). While her husband was on the Sangarios campaign, Theodora fell fatally ill and before her death assumed the monastic habit with the name of Aikaterina (p. 92, v. 176). Kurtz, ibid., p. 85, has with a good reason placed her death in 1138. Apparently Nikephoros was Theodora's only child (cf. pp. 93, v. 190, and 89, vv. 60-2).

[5] Nikephoros Komnenos, *sebastos* and ἐπὶ τῶν δεήσεων, is the subject of a μονῳδία by Eustathios of Thessalonica and of a λόγος ἐπικήδειος by Konstantinos Manasses, both edited by Kurtz, 'Monodii', pp. 290-302 and 302-22, respectively. The editor (p. 286), dates Nikephoros' death in about 1173, and many hints in both speeches support the view that he died aged about thirty (cf. pp. 291⁴¹, 299³²⁴, and 300³⁴²). The fact that this Nikephoros is not the son of Theodora becomes clear from the remark that in contrast to the elder one, he had brothers (p. 298) and also that his mother outlived him (pp. 294-5). In the speeches we find some references to Ioannes who was still alive (cf. pp. 295¹⁹⁵, 297²⁴⁸, and 303³⁰). Nikephoros Komnenos left behind two sons whom Manasses addresses as βλαστήματα Δουκικά, ῥιζουχίας Κομνηνικῆς (ibid., p. 297²⁵⁴ ff.).

79. Eirene Doukaina: Eirene Doukaina was the eldest daughter of the historians Nikephoros Bryennios and Anna *107* and the beloved granddaughter of Eirene *26*. She is mentioned several times in the *Typikon* of the Κεχαριτωμένης and particularly in connection with the ἐφορεία of the convent which was to pass to her after the deaths of the empress's daughters Anna *107* and Maria.[1] Alone of all the founder's grandchildren, Eirene's name is included among the persons for whom commemoration services after death are laid down.[2] Prodromos speaks of her in the epithalamium of her brothers (*c.* 1122) but calls Eirene a 'premature widow'.[3]

A still unpublished letter of Georgios Tornikes addressed to Eirene has been preserved.[4] It probably dates from the middle of the century. Moreover, the same writer in his funeral oration for Anna *107*, composed in about 1148, makes reference to a daughter of Anna who may well be Eirene.[5]

80. Alexios Doukas: Alexios Doukas who is mentioned in a couple of poems by Konstantinos Manasses and in an inscription on the relic of Grandmont must be certainly distinguished from Alexios, the elder son of Anna *107*, who is invariably called Komnenos.[6] Still he appears to have been a descendant of the historians. An unpublished letter of Georgios Tornikes is addressed to 'the *sebastos* Alexios, the grandson of the Caesar Bryennios, being dux of Dyrrachion and Ochrida'.[7] It is therefore tempting to identify this Alexios with Alexios Doukas who is mentioned as having as maternal great grandmother the empress Eirene *26*[8] and is also spoken of as being a 'grandson of the Caesar, descendant

A certain *sebastos* Nikephoros ἐκ τῶν Βρυεννίων who was married in 1161 to a niece of Manuel I (Kinn., p. 210) could not have been a descendant of Nikephoros and Anna *107* as it would be impossible to imagine a marriage between two second cousins.

---

[1] *PG*, 127, cols. 1109C, 1116C, and 1117C.

[2] Τελείσθωσαν τὰ μνημόσυνα τῆς περιποθήτου ἐγγονῆς τῆς βασιλείας μου κυρᾶς Εἰρήνης τῆς Δουκαίνης, τῆς θυγατρός τῆς πορφυρογεννήτου καὶ καισαρίσσης κυρᾶς Ἄννης, καθ᾽ ἣν ἂν ἡμέραν ἐκδημήσῃ, ibid., col. 1093A.   [3] *PG*, 133, col. 1403C.

[4] The letter bears the address Τῇ θυγατρὶ τῆς πορφυρογεννήτου καὶ καισαρίσσης κυρᾶς Ἄννης κυρᾷ Εἰρήνῃ, and it is preserved in cod. Vind. phil. gr. 321, fol. 11v–12r. See Sp. P. Lampros, ''Ο Βιενναῖος κῶδιξ Phil. graecus CCCXXI', *NE*, 13 (1916), 7; cf. H. Hunger, *Katalog der griechischen Handschriften der Österreichischen Nationalbibliothek*, i (Vienna, 1961), p. 410.

[5] See R. Browning, 'An Unpublished Funeral Oration on Anna Comnena', *Proceedings of the Cambridge Philological Society*, no. 188, new series no. 8 (1962), 4.

[6] Kinn., pp. 168 and 172; Chon., p. 215; letter of Michael Italikos to him in J. B. Cramer, *Anecdota Oxoniensia*, III (Oxford, 1836), p. 192, no. 24. For the career of Alexios Komnenos see briefly R. Guilland, 'Études de titulature et de prosopographie byzantines: Les chefs de la marine byzantine', *BZ*, 44 (1951), 226.

[7] Τοῦ αὐτοῦ (sc. Γεωργίου τοῦ Τορνίκη) πρὸς τὸν σεβαστὸν κῦρ 'Αλέξιον τὸν ἔγγονον τοῦ καίσαρος Βρυεννίου ὄντα δοῦκα τοῦ Δυρραχίου καὶ τῆς 'Αχρίδος, see Lampros, ' 'Ο Βιενναῖος κῶδιξ ', p. 10.

[8] The inscription is on a σταυροθήκη, no longer extant but formerly in the Abbey of Grandmont (Haut-Garonne), and the text is easily accessible in A. Frolow, *La Relique de la Vraie Croix: Recherches sur le développement d'un culte* (Paris, 1961), pp. 329–32, no. 319. The verses referring to Alexios read as follows:

> ἐκ Δουκικῆς φυέντι καλλιδενδρίας
> ἧς ῥιζοπρέμνον ἡ βασιλὶς Εἰρήνη,
> ἡ μητρομάμμη, τῶν ἀνάκτων τὸ κλέος,
> 'Αλεξίου κρατοῦντος Αὐσόνων δάμαρ.
> Ναί, ναὶ δυσωπῶ τὸν μόνον φύλακά μου,
> σὸς δοῦλος 'Αλέξιος ἐκ γένους Δούκας.

of emperors'.[1] Consequently he must have been a son of Eirene *79* or of some other unknown daughter of Anna *107*. In 1160 Manasses found Alexios Doukas in charge of the administration of Cyprus and was entertained by him there.[2]

CHANDRENOS

The family name of Χανδρηνός (or Χαντρηνός) is not particularly common. The *chartophylax* of the Patriarchate Eustathios Chantrenos, mentioned between the years 1172 and 1192,[3] is perhaps the best known. A Georgios Chandrenos is met with in 1357.[4] Thomas Magister wrote a speech to the emperor in support of a Chandrenos.[5] The name survived during the later period. A Theodoros μουσελίμης ὁ Χανδρινός is known from a sigillion of 1702.[6]

81. Doukas Chandrenos: He is mentioned only in the epitaph written by Philes for the death of his wife Theodote *91*: Ἐπιτάφιοι εἰς τὴν σύζυγον τοῦ Δούκα τοῦ Χανδρηνοῦ.[7] It is not improbable that he could be identified with the Chandrenos of Thomas Magister.

The editor attributes the poem to Kallikles and considers Alexios Doukas as 'le fils de Jean Doukas, cousin germain de Manuel I Comnène'. Eirene *26* is, of course, described as μητρομάμμη to Alexios, a term which I do not take in its usual connotation of 'maternal grandmother', but I interpret it as implying his 'mother's grandmother'.

---

[1] A relevant fragmentary text edited by L. Sternbach, 'Analecta Manassea', *Eos*, 7 (1902), 180–94, remains inaccessible to me. K. K(rumbacher) in a note on the article in *BZ*, 11 (1902), 581, quotes the line καισάρων θυγατριδοῦς, βασιλέων ἀπόγονος and says that the editor regards the man so described as a nephew of Nikephoros Bryennios. However, the word θυγατριδοῦς can only mean a daughter's son, and this coupled with the phrase βασιλέων ἀπόγονος would fit a grandson of Anna *107*.

[2] K. Horna, 'Das Hodoiporikon des Konstantin Manasses', *BZ*, 13 (1904), pp. 313–55. The author gratefully expresses his appreciation for the services Alexios rendered to him while in Cyprus. Manasses describes him as ὁ Δουκόβλαστος εὐκλεὴς Ἀλέξιος ὁ τηνικαῦτα κυριαρχῶν Κυπρίων (p. 336, vv. 57–8), Δουκῶν ὁ κλάδος (p. 326, v. 68), and ὁ χρυσοῦς Δούκας (p. 338, v. 129). The editor (pp. 350–1) identifies him with the son of Anna *107*, and this is also the opinion of Chalandon, *Les Comnène*, II, p. 219, but the two should in fact be regarded as different, as maintained by De Jongh, *Généalogie des Comnène*, pp. 34–5.

[3] Grumel, *Regestes*, III, p. 155 no. 1125; p. 182 no. 1179 and p. 183 no. 1180. Two seals of Eustathios are published by V. Laurent, *Le Corpus des Sceaux de l'Empire byzantin*. v. — *L'Eglise* (Paris, 1963), pp. 83–4 no. 104, and pp. 89–90 no. 110.

[4] MM, I, p. 375.

[5] F. Boissonade, *Anecdota Graeca*, II (Paris, 1830), pp. 188–211. Chandrenos came from Asia Minor (p. 192), and it was there that he was especially successful as a general (pp. 193–4). Moreover he fought in Thrace against the Turks and the Italians (p. 194) and also in other places.

[6] D. A. Zakythinos, 'Ἀνέκδοτα πατριαρχικὰ ἔγγραφα τῶν χρόνων τῆς Τουρκοκρατίας (1593–1798)', Ἑλληνικά, 2 (1929), 398³¹.

[7] Philes (Martini), pp. 74–5; cf. Papadopulos, *Genealogie der Palaiologen*, p. 16, no. 25.

CHOUMNOS

The family of Choumnos (Χοῦμνος), active since the eleventh century, rose to a very high position in the fourteenth century, thanks to the prestige of its illustrious representative Nikephoros Choumnos. The Choumnoi[1] contracted marriages with such prominent families as the Palaiologoi, the Strategopouloi, the Tarchaneiotai, and the Philanthropenoi.

82. Michael Doux Choumnos: He was a priest (πρεσβύτερος), and we possess the text of one of his letters, addressed to the patriarch, in which he gives a promise to behave properly.[2] This document is dated in June 1391, but another reference to a πρεσβύτερος Μιχαὴλ ὁ Χοῦμνος, undoubtedly the same person, is found in June 1400.[3]

CHRYSAPHES

83. Manuel Doukas Chrysaphes: Under the name of Μανουὴλ Χρυσάφης two ecclesiastical musicians are known: the first was active immediately after 1453[4] and the second flourished in c. 1600.[5] The former is also called Doukas and obviously held the church office of *lampadarios*. In addition to being a musician, he is also a known scribe whose two extant manuscripts were written in 1458 and 1463.[6]

---

[1] The members of the family have been traced by J. Verpeaux, 'Notes prosopographiques sur la famille Choumnos', *BS*, 20 (1959), 252–66.

[2] MM, II, pp. 153–4; cf. Verpeaux, op. cit., p. 264. The letter is signed by πρεσβύτερος Μιχαὴλ ὁ Χοῦμνος, but in the text his full name is given ('Εγὼ πρεσβύτερος Μιχαὴλ Δοὺξ ὁ Χοῦμνος). Δοὺξ is of course the archaic form of the surname Δούκας.

[3] MM, II, p. 401.

[4] G. I. Papadopoulos, Συμβολαὶ εἰς τὴν ἱστορίαν τῆς παρ' ἡμῖν ἐκκλησιαστικῆς μουσικῆς (Athens, 1890), p. 292; Spyridon Lauriotes and S. Eustratiades, Κατάλογος τῶν κωδίκων τῆς Μεγίστης Λαύρας (Paris, 1925), p. 455.

[5] Papadopoulos, op. cit., p. 302.

[6] Vogel–Gardthausen, *Schreiber*, p. 282. Cf. his notice on cod. 'Ιβήρων 1120 (Athous 1120) containing church music: 'Ετελειώθη τὸ παρὸν βιβλίον αἱ ἀκολουθίαι πᾶσαι τῆς ψαλτικῆς διὰ χειρὸς Μανουὴλ Δούκα λαμπαδαρίου τοῦ Χρυσάφη. 'Εν ἔτει ͵ϛ λ ξϛ' ἰνδ. ϛ' ἰουλλίου, see Sp. P. Lampros, Κατάλογος τῶν ἐν ταῖς βιβλιοθήκαις τοῦ 'Αγίου "Ορους ἑλληνικῶν κωδίκων, II (Cambridge, 1895), p. 252. D. I. Pallas, Κατάλογος χειρογράφων τοῦ Βυζαντινοῦ Μουσείου 'Αθηνῶν, II (Athens, 1933), p. κβ', calls him 'Εμμανουὴλ Χρυσολωρᾶς Δούκας ὁ Χρυσάφης.

For the musical output of Manuel see A. Papadopoulos-Kerameus, ' Μανουὴλ Χρυσάφης, λαμπαδάριος τοῦ βασιλικοῦ κλήρου ', *VV*, 8 (1901), 526–45.

DALASSENOS

The Dalassenoi (Δαλασσηνοί) were a distinguished family prominent in eleventh-century military life. Perhaps the most conspicuous of their members was Anna Dalassene, the forceful mother of Alexios I Komnenos, who however belonged to the family only on her mother's side.[1] The family owed its name to the village of Δάλασσα,[2] and this prompted Adontz who wrote its history[3] to identify the village with the Armenian locality Dalash and to argue that the Dalassenoi were Armenians.[4] But this has not been proved. After the eleventh century the family almost disappears from history.

84. Konstantinos Doukas Dalassenos: His name survives in a seal bearing the inscription

$$\Gamma\rho\alpha\phi\grave{\alpha}\varsigma\ \sigma\phi\rho\alpha\gamma\acute{\iota}\zeta\omega\ K\omega\nu\sigma\tau\alpha\nu\tau\acute{\iota}\nu o\upsilon\ \Delta\alpha\lambda\alpha\sigma\sigma\eta\nu o\hat{\upsilon}\ \tau o\hat{\upsilon}\ \Delta o\acute{\upsilon}\kappa\alpha.^{[5]}$$

This is thought to date from the eleventh century, and two identifications for the owner of the seal have been proposed. Schlumberger is inclined to see in him the general Konstantinos Dalassenos who distinguished himself in the war against the Turks in 1092.[6] According to Adontz, Konstantinos Dalassenos Doukas was a supposed son of the first marriage of the emperor Konstantinos X *12* to the daughter of Konstantinos Dalassenos in 1034.[7] Both these opinions lack documentary evidence.

[1] Bryen., p. 19; *Alexias*, I, p. 163. For Anna see S. Runciman, 'The End of Anna Dalassena', *Annuaire*, 9 (1949), 517- 24; D. Papachryssanthou, 'La date de la mort du sébastocrator Isaac Comnène, frère d'Alexis Ier, et de quelques événements contemporains', *REB*, 21 (1963), 252–3.

[2] Psellos, I, p. 122; II, p. 141.

[3] N. Adontz, 'Notes arméno-byzantines', *B*, 10 (1935), 171–85; cf. P. Charanis, 'The Armenians in the Byzantine Empire', *BS*, 22 (1961), 229. Some Dalassenoi unknown to Adontz: Theodoros *proedros* and δούξ Θεσσαλονίκης καὶ Σερρῶν (1062/3), F. Dölger, *Aus den Schatzkammern des Heiligen Berges* (Munich, 1948), pp. 105, 162, and 330; and *protonobilissimos* (1067), idem, *Byzantinische Diplomatik* (Ettal, 1956), p. 28; the 'Caesar' Ioannes Rogerios was called Dalassenos, L. Stiernon, 'Notes de titulature et de prosopographie byzantines', *REB*, 22 (1964), 185–7; Ioannes Dalassenos, scribe (1217/21), cf. *EEBΣ*, 11 (1935), 476; Eustratios Dalassenos, πάροικος in Lemnos (1331), MM, VI, p. 252.

[4] Adontz, op. cit., pp. 180 ff.

[5] G. Schlumberger, *Sigillographie byzantine* (Paris, 1881), p. 651; K. Konstantopoulos, Βυζαντιακὰ μολυβδόβουλλα, no. 618β.

[6] *Alexias*, II, pp. 66 ff.

[7] Adontz, op. cit., p. 178.

DIASORENOS

The surname of Diasorenos derives from the Διὸς ἱερόν, found in several places in western Asia Minor. The earliest form appears to have been Διοσιερηνός[1] which in the course of time became first Διοσορηνός[2] and then Διασορηνός. The same locality also gave rise to the names of Διοσιερίτης[3] and Διασορίτης.[4] A church of St George in Phrygia, situated in a former Διὸς ἱερόν,[5] gave the distinctive appelation of Diasorites to the saint.[6]

Neilos Diasorenos was a fourteenth-century follower of Palamas and a canonist.[7] Iakobos Diasorenos was a well-known Renaissance scribe.[8] Georgios Diasorenos lived in 1511.[9] The branch of Doukas-Diasorenos remains unconnected with any other family of the period.

85. Doukas Diasorenos: He is the recipient of a patriarchal letter, dated not long after 1388.[10] Although he is simply addressed as Doukas Diasorenos (ἐν ἁγίῳ πνεύματι υἱὲ τῆς ἡμῶν μετριότητος, κῦρ Δούκα Διασωρηνέ), it cannot be supposed that the appelation of Doukas is used here as a first name since this could in no circumstance be inherited by another person. Diasorenos had been associated with a hideous crime in the past. He was accomplice in some treason (τὸ κινῆσάν σε πρὸς προδοσίαν τὴν αὐτῶν, καὶ οὐκ ἔχεις τοῦτο ἀρνήσασθαι, ὡς οὐκ ἄλλως ἔχει) which resulted in the death of ten persons, in addition to misfortunes befalling others who were exiled or deprived of their properties (τὸ μυστήριον ἐξήγγειλας, καὶ ἀπέθανον ἄνθρωποι . . . δέκα . . . ὅτι δὲ ὁ φόνος τῶν δέκα ἀνδρῶν ἀπὸ συνεργίας γέγονε τῆς σῆς καὶ ἡ δήμευσις καὶ ἡ ἐξορία τῶν ἄλλων, τοῦτο πᾶσιν ἐστὶ φανερόν.[11]

These things had happened long before the extant letter was written (τοῦτο πρὸ πολλῶν συνέβη τῶν χρόνων). Subsequently Diasorenos approached the patriarch Neilos (1379–88), and begged for forgiveness. Neilos had by then died but ecclesiastical pardon was promptly given. Diasorenos however was still not satisfied and wrote to one of Neilos' successors (Antonios ? Τὰ γράμματά σου διεκομίσθησαν εἰς τὴν ἡμῶν μετριότητα) and once more asked for the absolution of his sin which apparently still tormented him. The preserved patriarchal letter is a reply to his request. Diasorenos is forgiven by the church, but he is reminded not to attempt to minimize his guilt and is exhorted to adhere to the

---

[1] Georgios Diosierenos in 1316, MM, I, pp. 53–5.

[2] Κωνσταντῖνος Διοσορηνοῦ (XIV century) in MM, IV, p. 104; Γεώργιος Διοσορηνός (XIV century) in MM, IV, p. 129; cf. K. I. Amantos, ' Γλωσσικὰ ἐκ Χίου ', Λαογραφία, 7 (1923), 337, n. 3.

[3] Petit, Actes de Chilandar, I, p. 17. The form Διοσιερίτης dates from ancient times, cf. Amantos, loc. cit.

[4] Petit, Actes de Chilandar, I, p. 17.   [5] Pach., II, p. 260.

[6] K. I. Amantos, ' Ἅγιος Γεώργιος ὁ Διασορίτης ', Ἑλληνικά, 11 (1939), 330–1.

[7] H.-G. Beck, Kirche und theologische Literatur im byzantinischen Reich (Munich, 1958), p. 787.

[8] Vogel–Gardthausen, Schreiber, pp. 152–4; cf. Ch. G. Patrineles, ' Ἕλληνες κωδικογράφοι τῶν χρόνων τῆς Ἀναγεννήσεως ', Ἐπετηρὶς τοῦ Μεσαιωνικοῦ Ἀρχείου, 8 (1958/9), 79.

[9] MM, III, p. 263.

For some other Diasorenoi see MM, IV, pp. 115 and 175.

[10] MM, II, pp. 314–20.   [11] Ibid., p. 315.

Christian principles and to make an effort to compensate the relatives of those who had lost their lives through his action.

86. Pantoleon Doukas Diasorenos: The same document mentions Pantoleon Doukas Diasorenos as having brought Diasorenos' letter of supplication to the patriarch (τὰ γράμματα σου διεκομίσθησαν μετὰ τοῦ κατὰ πνεῦμα υἱοῦ αὐτῆς Δούκα Διασωρηνοῦ τοῦ Παντολέοντος).[1] The phrase κατὰ πνεῦμα υἱοῦ is rather puzzling. It would be appropiate for a spiritual relationship, but it would be hard to consider the elder Doukas Diasorenos as an ecclesiastic. I am inclined to regard him as a godfather of Pantoleon.

EXAZENOS

87. Konstantinos Exazenos Doukas: The name of Exazenos (᾽Εξαζηνός) is very rare in Byzantium,[2] yet its bearers in the early twelfth century undoubtedly belonged to the nobility. Anna Komnene speaks of two cousins 'the so-called Exazenoi', and she also attributes a second distinctive cognomen to each of them; one is called Doukas and the other Hyaleas. Nikephoros Exazenos Hyaleas and his cousin Konstantinos Exazenos 'so-called Doukas', men experienced in warfare, were implicated in the conspiracy of the Anemas brothers,[3] but thanks to the humane sentiments of the empress and Anna *107* they were spared blinding. [4] The Exazenoi were however soon restored to imperial favour and in 1107 they gained a significant victory over the Normans in Epirus.[5] Late in the same year they were sent to prevent reinforcements from reaching Bohemund from Italy.[6]

It appears that the names of Doukas and Hyaleas, as borne by these two members of the Exazenos family, were acquired through their mothers who presumably belonged to the respective houses. Anna *107*, closely related to all known Doukai of the period does not hint at any connections with this Konstantinos Exazenos Doukas. All the same, Konstantinos may have been associated with some other branch of the family, unknown to us so far and perhaps only distantly related to the imperial house.

---

[1] Ibid., p. 314.

[2] The only other instances known to me where it is mentioned, are in the references to the monastery called τοῦ ᾽Εξαζηνοῦ in Thessalonica in 1304 and 1401. See Petit, *Actes de Chilandar*, p. 48; MM, II, p. 521.

[3] *Alexias*, III, pp. 69–70.

[4] *Alexias*, III, pp. 73–4.

[5] *Alexias*, III, p. 80.

[6] *Alexias*, III, p. 88; cf. Dölger, *Regesten*, II, p. 51, no. 1237.

GABRAS

The common name Gabras ($\Gamma\alpha\beta\rho\hat{\alpha}s$)[1] is attested since the eleventh century, and its first bearers came from Chaldia. The numerous people who bore it belonged to different classes of Byzantine society. Some of the wealthier branches contracted marriages with other houses of the nobility.

88. Manuel Doukas Komnenos Gabras: His name appears on a marble inscription of Mystras dated in 1300/1. He had bought a piece of land from the monks of an unknown monastery for forty hyperpyra which he subsequently donated to the same.[2]

GLABAS

The name of Glabas ($\Gamma\lambda\alpha\beta\hat{\alpha}s$) is certainly derived from the popular word $\gamma\kappa\lambda\acute{\alpha}\beta\alpha$ of Slavic origin, meaning 'head'. Consequently $\Gamma\lambda\alpha\beta\hat{\alpha}s$ has the same connotation as the widespread surname $K\epsilon\phi\alpha\lambda\hat{\alpha}s$.[3] The first member of the family is met with as early as 977,[4] but the Glabades did not emerge as a distinguished family until the thirteenth century.[5] It was sometime during the period of the first Palaiologoi that they attained high social standing and entered into matrimonial relations with other leading aristocrats and in particular with the Tarchaneiotai.[6] It seems very probable that through these latter the Glabades acquired the name of Doukas.

[1] J. Ph. Fallmerayer, *Geschichte des Kaisertums von Trapezunt* (Munich, 1827), pp. 18–19, considers the word as being Chaldaic and signifying the hero. K. I. Amantos, $\Sigma\chi\acute{\epsilon}\sigma\epsilon\iota s$ $\dot{E}\lambda\lambda\acute{\eta}\nu\omega\nu$ $\kappa\alpha\grave{\iota}$ $To\acute{\upsilon}\rho\kappa\omega\nu$, I (Athens, 1955), p. 140, n. 5, thinks that $\Gamma\alpha\beta\rho\hat{\alpha}s$ may have been shortened from $\Gamma\alpha\beta\rho\iota\acute{\eta}\lambda$.

[2] $A\ddot{\upsilon}\tau\eta$ $\dot{\eta}$ $\ddot{\alpha}\mu\pi\epsilon\lambda os$ $\dot{\eta}$ $\epsilon\dot{\upsilon}\rho\iota\sigma\kappa o\mu\acute{\epsilon}\nu\eta$ $\gamma\acute{\upsilon}\rho\omega\theta\epsilon\nu$ $\tauo\hat{\upsilon}$ $\tauo\iotao\acute{\upsilon}\tauo\upsilon$ $\kappao\iota\mu\eta\tau\eta\rho\acuteίou$ $\mu\epsilon\tau\grave{\alpha}$ $\tau\hat{\omega}\nu$ $\dot{o}\pi\omega\rhoo\phi\acute{o}\rho\omega\nu$ $\delta\acute{\epsilon}\nu\delta\rho\omega\nu$ $\dot{\epsilon}\pi\rho\acute{\alpha}\theta\eta$ $\pi\alpha\rho\grave{\alpha}$ $\tauo\hat{\upsilon}$ $\kappa\alpha\theta\eta\gammaou\mu\acute{\epsilon}\nuou$ $\kappa\upsilon\rhoo\hat{\upsilon}$ $'A\gamma\acute{\alpha}\theta\omega\nuos$ $\iota\epsilon\rhoo\mu o\nu\acute{\alpha}\chiou$ $\kappa\alpha\grave{\iota}$ $\pi\acute{\alpha}\nu\tau\omega\nu$ $\epsilon\dot{\upsilon}\rho\iota\sigma\kappa o\mu\acute{\epsilon}\nu\omega\nu$ $\dot{\alpha}\delta\epsilon\lambda\phi\hat{\omega}\nu$ $\pi\rho\grave{o}s$ $\tau\grave{o}\nu$ $\sigma\kappao\lambda\iota\kappa\hat{\alpha}\nu$ $\kappa\acute{\upsilon}\rho\iuoν$ $M\alpha\nuou\grave{\eta}\lambda$ $\Deltao\acute{\upsilon}\kappa\alpha\nu$ $K o\mu\nu\eta\nu\grave{o}\nu$ $\tau\grave{o}\nu$ $\Gamma\alpha\beta\rho\hat{\alpha}\nu$ (text $\Gamma\alpha\upsilon\rho\hat{\alpha}\nu$) $\epsilon\iotas$ $\dot{\upsilon}\pi\acute{\epsilon}\rho\pi\upsilon\rho\alpha$ μ' $\kappa\alpha\grave{\iota}$ $\pi\acute{\alpha}\lambda\iota\nu$ $\delta\acute{\epsilon}\delta o\kappa\epsilon\nu$ $\pi\rho\grave{o}s$ $\tau\grave{\eta}\nu$ $\muo\nu\grave{\eta}\nu$ $\ddot{\epsilon}\nu\epsilon\kappa\alpha$ $\psi\upsilon\chi\iota\kappa\hat{\eta}s$ $\sigma\omega\tau\eta\rhoίas$. $'E\nu$ $\ddot{\epsilon}\tau\epsilon\iota$ $,s\omega\theta'$ $\iota\nu\delta.$ $\iota\delta'$. See A. Boeckh and J. Franz, *Corpus Inscriptionum Graecarum*, IV (Berlin, 1877), p. 350, no. 8763. The word $\sigma\kappao\lambda\iota\kappa\hat{\alpha}\nu$ is not clear. It does not look as if it is part of Gabras' name though an $oἴ\kappa\eta\mu\alpha$ $\tauo\hat{\upsilon}$ $Kou\lambda\iota\kappa\hat{\alpha}$ is mentioned in 1202 (cf. MM, III, p. 49). Can $\sigma\kappa\omega\lambda\eta\kappa\hat{\alpha}s$ signify the man who cultivates silkworms?

[3] Philes is already fully aware of the meaning of Michael *89*'s surname

$T\acute{\iota}s$, $\hat{\omega}$ $\sigma\tau\rho\alpha\tau\eta\gamma\acute{\epsilon}$, $\kappa\alpha\grave{\iota}$ $\Gamma\lambda\alpha\beta\hat{\alpha}\nu$ $\kappa\acute{\epsilon}\kappa\lambda\eta\kappa\acute{\epsilon}$ $\sigma\epsilon$;
$\sigma\eta\mu\alpha\acute{\iota}\nu\epsilon\tau\alpha\iota$ $\gamma\grave{\alpha}\rho$ $\dot{\eta}$ $\kappa\epsilon\phi\alpha\lambda\grave{\eta}$ $\tau\hat{\eta}$ $\phi\rho\acute{\alpha}\sigma\epsilon\iota$.

Philes (Miller), II, p. 107, vv. 74–5.

The form $\Gamma\lambda\alpha\beta\hat{\alpha}s$ is really the more hellenized version of the proper one $\Gamma\kappa\lambda\alpha\beta\hat{\alpha}s$. The name must always have being pronounced — as today — as though it were written $\Gamma\kappa\lambda\alpha\beta\hat{\alpha}s$.

[4] Basileios Glabas mentioned by Kedr., II, p. 452.

[5] Their family history has still to be written. But see the following useful notices: X. A. Siderides, ' $\Pi\epsilon\rho\grave{\iota}$ $\tau\hat{\eta}s$ $\dot{\epsilon}\nu$ $K\omega\nu\sigma\tau\alpha\nu\tau\iuo\upsilon\pi\acute{o}\lambda\epsilon\iota$ $\muo\nu\hat{\eta}s$ $\tau\hat{\eta}s$ $\Pi\alpha\mu\mu\alpha\kappa\alpha\rhoίστου$ $\kappa\alpha\grave{\iota}$ $\tau\hat{\omega}\nu$ $\kappa\tau\eta\tau\acute{o}\rho\omega\nu$ $\alpha\dot{\upsilon}\tau\hat{\eta}s$', $\dot{E}\lambda\lambda\eta\nu\iota\kappa\grave{o}s$ $\Phi\iota\lambdao\lambdao\gamma\iota\kappa\grave{o}s$ $\Sigma\acute{\upsilon}\lambda\lambdao\gammaos$ $K\omega\nu\sigma\tau\alpha\nu\tau\iuo\upsilon\pi\acute{o}\lambda\epsilon\omega s$, $\pi\alpha\rho\acute{\alpha}\rho\tau\eta\mu\alpha$, 20/22 (1892), 20–21; N. A. Bees, ' $A\dot{\iota}$ $\pi\alpha\sigma\chi\acute{\alpha}\lambda\iota\alpha\iota$ $\dot{\epsilon}\pi\iota\gamma\rho\alpha\phi\alpha\grave{\iota}$ $\tauo\hat{\upsilon}$ $'A\gammaίou$ $\Delta\eta\mu\eta\tau\rhoίou$ $\Theta\epsilon\sigma\sigma\alpha\lambdaoνίκης$ $\kappa\alpha\grave{\iota}$ $\dot{o}$ $\mu\eta\tau\rhoo\pi o\lambdaίτης$ $\alpha\dot{\upsilon}\tau\hat{\eta}s$ $'I\sigmaίδωρos$ $\Gamma\lambda\alpha\beta\hat{\alpha}s$ (+1396) ', *BNJ*, 7 (1928/9), 142, n. 3; G. I. Theocharides, ' $M\iota\chi\alpha\grave{\eta}\lambda$ $\Deltao\acute{\upsilon}\kappa\alpha s$ $\Gamma\lambda\alpha\beta\hat{\alpha}s$ $T\alpha\rho\chi\alpha\nu\epsilon\iota\acute{\omega}\tau\eta s$ ($\pi\rhoo\sigma\omega\pi o\gamma\rho\alpha\phi\iota\kappa\acute{\alpha}$) ', $'E\pi\iota\sigma\tau\eta\muo\nu\iota\kappa\grave{\eta}$ $'E\pi\epsilon\tau\eta\rho\grave{\iota}s$ $\tau\hat{\eta}s$ $\Phi\iotaλosophικῆς$ $\Sigma\chio\lambda\hat{\eta}s$ $\tauo\hat{\upsilon}$ $\Pi\alpha\nu\epsilon\pi\iota\sigma\tau\eta\mu\acuteίou$ $\Theta\epsilon\sigma\sigma\alpha\lambdaoνίκης$, 7 (1957), 193–4; Laurent, *Médaillier Vatican*, pp. 53–4.

[6] In addition to Doukai Tarchaneiotai Glabades mentioned in this section, we know of the *protostrator* Makarios Glabas Tarchaneiotes, a relative of the emperor, in 1347. See H. Hunger, 'Kaiser Johannes V. Palaiologos und der Heilige Berg ', *BZ*, 45 (1952), 369 ff.

89. Michael Doukas Glabas Tarchaneiotes: He was one of the few successful generals during the reign of Andronikos II, but his career has been frequently confused in the past with that of the *protovestiarios* Michael Tarchaneiotes.[1] The full name of Michael, together with that of his wife, appears on an inscription, no longer extant, of Pammakaristos which was seen and copied by Gerlach (1578).[2] Otherwise, contemporary sources refer to him as Glabas,[3] Doukas Glabas,[4] or Tarchaneiotes Glabas.[5] Michael's career fills the last two decades of the thirteenth century and the first years of the fourteenth century.[6] He could have been born in 1250/60,[7] but his parents remain totally unknown. In *c.* 1273 he was a *kouropalates* and subsequently he was created *megas papias*,[8] *pinkernes*, *megas kontostaulos*,[9] and finally *protostrator*.[10] He died shortly before 1315.[11]

Michael Glabas is the subject of several poems by Philes, some of them dedicatory to holy objects. He himself was the author of an exegetical catena[12] and of a work on strategy[13]. He is also associated with the restoration of two monasteries: the Pammakaristos at Constantinople in 1293[14] and St John the Baptist at Sozopolis.[15]

Michael's wife was Maria Doukaina Komnene Palaiologina Branaina *153*. Although a poem of Philes is an entreaty to the Theotokos on behalf of Maria who desired to be given the joy of children,[16] it appears that later in life the couple became the parents of a daughter[17] who afterwards married Andronikos *67*.

90. Konstantinos Tarchaneiotes Doukas Glabas: He is known only from a short poem of Philes written on his behalf. Konstantinos had been suffer-

---

[1] The problem has now been admirably elucidated by Theocharides, op. cit., who gives sketches of the careers of both Michaels (see especially pp. 186–91 and 191–202).

[2] Μιχαὴλ Δούκας Γλαβᾶς Ταρχανειώτης; see the text in V. Laurent, 'Kyra Martha: Essai de topographie et de prosopographie byzantine', *EO*, 38 (1939), 299; the inscription is also given by A. M. Schneider, *Byzanz* (Berlin, 1936), p. 61; Theocharides, op. cit., p. 192.

[3] Pach., I, p. 350; II, p. 271; Greg., I, pp. 159 and 484; Philes (Miller), I, pp. 91, 280, and 432; II, pp. 14, 103, 107, 139 and 241; Philes (Martini), p. 76.

[4] Philes (Miller), I, pp. 36, 80, and 432; II, pp. 230, 241, and 413; Philes (Martini), p. 65.

[5] Pach., I, p. 183; II, p. 12; cf. II, p. 445.

[6] A poem of Philes in 337 iambic trimeters, entitled Εἰς τὰ τοῦ πρωτοστράτορος ἐκείνου τοῦ θαυμαστοῦ στρατηγήματα, contains valuable historical information on Michael who fought successively in Bulgaria, Albania, Thessaly, and Serbia; see Philes (Miller), II, pp. 240–55.

[7] Theocharides, op. cit., p. 199.

[8] Τὸν Γλαβᾶν κουροπαλάτην καὶ μέγαν παπίαν ἐσύστερον, Pach., I, p. 350.

[9] Ἐκ μεγάλου παπίου, εἶτα δὲ καὶ πιγκέρνην, εἰς μέγαν κονοσταῦλον τὸν Ταρχανειώτην τιμήσας Γλαβᾶν, Pach., II, p. 12.

[10] Ὁ . . . μέγας κονοσταῦλος ὁ Ταρχανειώτης Γλαβᾶς ὃν καὶ πρωτοστράτορα ὁ κρατῶν μετὰ ταῦτα ἐποίει, Pach., I, p. 183. Both Pach., II, p. 445, and Greg., I, p. 159, highly praise the military talents of Michael.   [11] Theocharides, op. cit., p. 202.

[12] Cf. the poem of Philes Περὶ τῶν τοῦ θαυμαστοῦ πρωτοστράτορος κεφαλαίων ἅπερ ἀπὸ τῆς θείας γραφῆς ἠρανίσατο in Philes (Miller), II, pp. 230–3; see H.-G. Beck, *Kirche und theologische Literatur im byzantinischen Reich* (Munich, 1959), p. 711.

[13] Ἐπίγραμμα εἰς τὸ βιβλίον ὃ συντέταχεν ὁ πρωτοστράτωρ ἐκεῖνος ὁ Γλαβᾶς ἐν διαφόροις κεφαλαίοις στρατηγικοῖς; see E. Martini, 'A proposito d'una poesia inedita di Manuel File', *Reale Istituto Lombardo di Scienze e Lettere. Rendiconti*, serie II, 29 (Milan, 1896), pp. 470–1, vv. 46. Michael had left the manuscript of his work to his daughter's husband Andronikos *67* (ibid., p. 471).

[14] Cf. R. Janin, *Les Eglises et Les Monastères* (Paris, 1953), p. 218.

[15] Philes (Miller), II, p. 245, vv. 103–7.   [16] Philes (Miller), I, p. 76.

[17] Philes (Martini), pp. 65–6; cf. the convincing arguments of Theocharides, op. cit., pp. 202–3.

ing from bad haemorrhage of the bowels and now gives his thanks to the Mother of God for his miraculous recovery.[1]

91. Theodote Glabaina (Doukaina) Tarchaneiotissa: Theodote was of unknown parentage and apart from a poem of Philes, written on the occasion of her death, no other information on her survives. She died at the age of sixteen after a three-year marriage to Doukas Chandrenos *81* and was buried with her father and her brother.[2]

92. Markos Doukas Glabas syr Mourinos: He is known from a document which he issued in *c.* 1370 and which concerns a piece of land containing a mill in Macedonia, sold by Markos to the monastery of Docheiariou but then claimed by the monks of Xeropotamou.[3] One of his ancestors (Μουρῖνος, Murino) was obviously of Italian background[4] and it appears that his father, perhaps a Mourinos, married a lady of the Doukas Glabas branch.

IAGARIS

The name Iagaris ('Ἰάγαρις) appears in the fifteenth century. An Iagaris is the addressee of a letter by Manuel Palaiologos.[5] In 1436 Andronikos Iagaris was sent by the emperor as ambassador to Trebizond.[6] During the same period Manuel Palaiologos Iagaris[7] and the *megas stratopedarches* Markos Palaiologos Iagaris[8] are mentioned.

93. Manuel Iagaris Doukas Tyris: Manuel Iagaris Doukas, called Tyris (i.e. 'cheese', certainly a nickname), was a scribe[9] who wrote the cod. Par. gr. 2305, containing medical works of Ioannes Aktouarios, in 1418.[10]

---

[1]   Κωνσταντῖνός σοι Ταρχανειώτης Δούκας
         Κομνηνοφυὴς καὶ Γλαβᾶς τάδε γράφει,
Philes (Miller), i, p. 37.

[2] 'Ἐπιτάφιοι εἰς τὴν σύζυγον τοῦ Δούκα τοῦ Χανδρηνοῦ, Philes (Martini), pp. 74–5. The poet refers to her as follows:

          πλήν, ὦ θεατά, τὴν Θεοδότην βλέπων
          (οὕτω γὰρ ἡ κλῆσις αὐτῆς ἐκ βρέφους),
          ἔτι δὲ καὶ Γλάβαιναν ἐκ Δουκῶν γένους
          καὶ Ταρχανειώτισσαν (ὦ κτύπων μόνων).

Papadopulos, *Genealogie der Palaiologen*, p. 16, no. 25, wrongly considers her to be a daughter of Michael Doukas Glabas.

[3] The text in F. Dölger, *Aus den Schatzkammern des Heiligen Berges* (Munich, 1948), pp. 313–14.

[4] Cf. the note of Dölger, ibid., p. 314, and idem, 'Neues zu Alexios Metochites und zu Theodoros Meliteniotes', *Byzantinische Diplomatik* (Ettal, 1956), pp. 332–3. Dölger thinks that the father of Markos was the *protovestiarites* Demetrios Mourinos; cf. Dölger, *Regesten*, IV, p. 62, no. 2357 (*c.* 1315).

[5] E. Legrand, *Lettres de l'empereur Manuel Paléologue* (Paris, 1893), p. 48.

[6] Dölger, *Regesten*, v, p. 121, no. 3458.

[7] Papadopulos, *Genealogie der Palaiologen*, p. 94, no. 184.

[8] R. Guilland, 'Etudes sur l'histoire administrative de l'empire byzantin: Le Stratopédarque et le Grand Stratopédarque', *BZ*, 36 (1953), 84.   [9] Cf. Vogel-Gardthausen, *Schreiber*, p. 276.

[10] The colophon, in red letters, reads: 'Ἐτελειώθη ἡ παροῦσα βίβλος ἐν ἔτει ͵ϛ ᾽λκϛ' μηνὶ φεβρουαρίῳ κϛ' ἰνδ. ια' γραφεῖσα διὰ χειρὸς Μανουὴλ 'Ἰάγαρι Δούκα τοῦ Τυρὶ καὶ οἱ ἀναγινώσκοντες αὐτὴν εὔχεσθέ με διὰ τὸν κύριον ἵνα εὕρω ἔλεος ἐν τῇ ἡμέρᾳ τῆς κρίσεως; see cod. Par. gr. 2305, fol. 399v.

KABASILAS

In the fourteenth century the ancient family[1] of Kabasilas (Καβάσιλας) was especially active in Macedonia. Two members of it bore the name of Doukas but it is not possible to trace the origin of this.

94. Demetrios Doukas Kabasilas: The *megas papias* Demetrios Kabasilas[2] is also called Demetrios Doukas Kabasilas.[3] During the civil wars (1341–7) he was a loyal supporter of Kantakouzenos who promptly rewarded him for his services with the grant of extensive lands in Macedonia. Demetrios, whose father was probably a Georgios Kabasilas, appears to have been associated with the army.[4] He is also mentioned in other documents of the years 1351,[5] 1367,[6] and 1368.[7] Kydones addressed him with one of his letters in 1386/7.[8] The view that Demetrios acquired the name of Doukas from his wife[9] seems unlikely.

95. Doukas Kabasilas: He was a nobleman in Thessalonica, and in 1425 Venice decided to increase his monthly allowance.[10] Doukas Kabasilas might have been a descendant of Demetrios *94*.

KALAMANOS

The Hungarian prince Boritz, a son of king Kaloman, sought refuge at the Byzantine court and was much honoured by the emperor Ioannes II Komnenos. Through his wife who was presumably a member of the Doukas family he became related to the imperial house.[11] Boritz was called Καλαμᾶνος by the Byzantines,[12] and became the father of Konstantinos *96*. The origin of the family

---

[1] Information about the family and its members can be found in K. D. Mertzios, Μνημεῖα Μακεδονικῆς Ἱστορίας (Thessalonica, 1947), p. 51, n. 4; S. Salaville, 'Quelques précisions pour la biographie de Nicolas Cabasilas', Πεπραγμένα τοῦ Θ′ Βυζαντινολογικοῦ Συνεδρίου, III (Thessalonica, 1958), pp. 217–18; D. B. Bagiakakos, ' Βυζαντινὰ ὀνόματα καὶ ἐπώνυμα ἐκ Μάνης', Πελοποννησιακά, 3/4 (1960), 200–3; Theocharides, article cited below, p. 6, n. 1.

[2] G. I. Theocharides, ' Δημήτριος Δούκας Καβάσιλας καὶ ἄλλα προσωπογραφικὰ ἐξ ἀνεκδότου χρυσοβούλλου τοῦ Καντακουζηνοῦ', Ἑλληνικά, 17 (1962), 4 and 5.

[3] Regel et al., *Actes de Zographou*, p. 104; V. Laurent in *EO*, 30 (1931), 347, n. 7.

[4] See the chrysobull of Kantakouzenos in Theocharides, op. cit., pp. 4-6. For the career of Demetrios cf. ibid, pp. 14–18.

[5] F. Dölger, *Aus den Schatzkammern des Heiligen Berges* (Munich, 1948), no. 19[11].

[6] Regel et al., *Actes de Zographou*, p. 104.

[7] Laurent in *EO*, 30 (1931), 347, no. 7.

[8] R.-J. Loenertz, *Démétrius Cydonès, Correspondance*, II (Rome, 1960), pp. 260–1. Demetrios must be distinguished from the homonymous addressee of letters by Choumnos, Gregoras, and Gabras, cf. Theocharides, op. cit., pp. 8–10.

[9] Theocharides, op. cit., p. 16.

[10] Mertzios, op. cit., p. 51.

[11] Kinn., p. 117. William of Tyre in *PL*, 201, col. 755D, calls Konstantinos *96* a relative (*consanguineus*) of the emperor; cf. the notes of Ducange in Kinn., pp. 340–41 and 365–6; Chalandon, *Les Comnène*, II, p. 62.

[12] He was defeated and killed by the Hungarians in 1156, see Chon., p. 123; Skout., p. 239.

of Kalamanos which survived many years thereafter[1] should perhaps be traced to this Hungarian nobleman.

96. Konstantinos Doukas Kalamanos: The *sebastos* Konstantinos Doukas Kalamanos was a son of the Hungarian Boritz and his wife the unknown lady of the Doukas family.[2] In 1162 Konstantinos, although still young, held the post of the *dux* of Cilicia and distinguished himself in campaigns against the Muslims. Together with the Franks of Syria, he attacked Nur ad Din, the emir of Aleppo, but although he fought with fierce courage he was finally taken prisoner.[3] However ten years later he is once more active in the same district of Asia Minor.[4]

A plate in gold, commemorating the victories of Manuel I Komnenos over the Hungarians, was presented to him by Konstantinos Doukas Kalamanos. The accompanying inscription has survived. It speaks of the 'sebastos Doukas-offspring Kalamanos, a scion of Paeonian royal roots' who 'brings forward a Doukan gift to the emperor'.[5]

A seal of Konstantinos bearing the legend

$$\Sigma\phi\rho\alpha\gamma\grave{\iota}\varsigma\ \sigma\epsilon\beta\alpha\sigma\tauο\hat{υ}\ Δο\acute{υ}κα\ το\hat{υ}\ Καλαμ\acute{α}νου$$

is known.[6]

---

[1] A document of 1192 mentions τὸν ἐν τῇ τοποθεσίᾳ τῶν Καλυβίων οἶκον τοῦ Καλαμάνου ἤτοι τοῦ Βοτανειάτου, MM, III, p. 28; cf. p. 31. An unnamed Kalamanos is referred to in an undated document in MM, IV, pp. 292 and 294. Other members are cited by Gy. Moravcsik, *Byzantino-turcica* (Berlin, 1958), II, p. 147.

[2] If the reference to Καλαμάνου ἤτοι τοῦ Βοτανειάτου relates to the family of Konstantinos, or even to Konstantinos himself, it is possible that the name of Botaneiates might have been that of one of his maternal ancestors. Combining that with the name of Doukas we come to Zoe *33* whose husband was Georgios Botaneiates and who had a daughter. She may have become the wife of Boritz and the mother of Konstantinos.

[3] Kinn, p. 216; cf. Chalandon, *Les Comnène*, II, pp. 525–8. The campaign of Kalamanos is likewise recorded by non-Greek historians such as Ibn-al-Athir in *Recueil des Historiens des Croisades. Historiens orientaux* (Paris, 1872), p. 531, and Michael the Syrian (ed. J. B. Chabot), III (Paris 1910), p. 324. Chon., p. 183, relates an amusing incident which must be dated about this time. The emperor Manuel I much annoyed by the scandalous elopement of his wife's sister Philippa with his cousin Andronikos (the future emperor), instructed Kalamanos to rush to Antioch and attempt to detach Philippa from the seducer under the pretence of wishing to marry her himself. The scheme completely failed. The young princess was so much fascinated by Andronikos that she showed only contempt for the unfortunate Kalamanos. This being the case, Choniates continues, Konstantinos occupied Tarsus on his way home and waged war against the Armenians. However, he was captured and the emperor paid a heavy ransom to free him.

[4] Kinn., p. 286.

[5] Ἐπὶ πατελίῳ χρυσῷ ἐν ᾧ εἰκονίσθησαν τὰ κατὰ τὴν Οὐγγρίαν τρόπαια τοῦ βασιλέως, Lampros, ' Μαρκιανὸς 524 ', pp. 175–6; cf. Gy. Moravcsik, ' Σημειώσεις εἰς τὰ καλλιτεχνικὰ μνημεῖα τῶν οὐγγροβυζαντινῶν σχέσεων', Χαριστήριον εἰς 'Αναστάσιον Κ. 'Ορλάνδον, I (Athens, 1964), pp. 30–31. In the same collection and in another dedicatory epigram the name of Kalamanos is also included (Lampros, ' Μαρκιανὸς 524 ', p. 120).

[6] Edited by Laurent, *Bulles métriques*, p. 153, no. 439 (cf. p. 251). See also G. Schlumberger, 'Un sceau de plomb au nom d'un prince de la famille royale de Hongrie, au XIIe siècle, au service de l'empire byzantin en Asie', *REG*, 32 (1919), 490–4, who gives a sketch of Kalamanos' career. Another seal, owned simply by a Kalamanos, might have belonged to the same man; see Laurent, *Bulles métriques*, pp. 226–7, no. 671.

KALOTHETOS

The name Kalothetos (Καλόθετος; the form Καλοθέτης is wrong[1]) is common during the last centuries of Byzantium, being borne by noblemen and commoners alike.[2] It is not known how the name of Doukas passed into the family.[3]

97. Ioannes Kalothetos Doukas: He was the possessor of the fourteenth century cod. Par. gr. 2954 which contains works of Lucian and other ancient texts.[4] In December 1357 an Ioannes Kalothetos is met with,[5] but there is no evidence to identify him with the present Ioannes Kalothetos Doukas.

KAMATEROS

The family of Kamateros (Καματηρός) is known to Byzantine sources from the ninth century onwards, but it does not become distinguished until the twelfth century in the course of which its members occupied high office in state and church and contracted marital ties with the imperial house and other noble Byzantine families. Still, the predominance of the Kamateroi was comparatively short and it appears that the family rapidly declined after the Fourth Crusade.[6]

The marriage of Eirene Doukaina *32* to Gregorios Kamateros gave rise to the branch of Doukai Kamateroi which comprises most of the more important members of the family in the twelfth century.

---

[1] Cf. Th. Bolides in *EEBΣ*, 1 (1924), 351.

[2] Information on the family can be found in N. A. Bees, ''Ἀνέκδοτα βυζαντιακὰ μολυβδόβουλλα', *JIAN*, 9 (1906), 51–2; idem, ' Ἰωσὴφ Καλοθέτης καὶ ἀναγραφὴ τῶν ἔργων αὐτοῦ', *BZ*, 17 (1908), 86–7, n. 4; Alexandros Lauriotes, ' Περὶ τῆς Χιακῆς οἰκογενείας Καλοθέτου', *Νεολόγου* Ἑβδομαδιαία Ἐπιθεώρησις, 2 (1893), 401–3; G. I. Zolotas, Ἱστορία τῆς νήσου Χίου, II (Athens, 1923), pp. 371 ff.; St. Binon, *Les origines légendaires et l'histoire de Xéropotamou et de Saint-Paul de l'Athos* (Louvain, 1942), p. 280; K. I. Amantos, ' Γενεαλογικὰ ἐκ Χίου', *EEBΣ*, 26 (1956), 38–40.

[3] It may have been derived from a branch of the Komnenoi, perhaps the Angeloi, as in 1390 a συγκλητικὸς ἄρχων Andreas Komnenos Kalothetos is found (MM, III, p. 143). In 1361 a *parakoimomenos* Angelos Kalothetos is mentioned; cf. R.-J. Loenertz, 'Emmanuelis Raul epistulae XII', *EEBΣ*, 26 (1956), 145.

[4] As such he is mentioned by Vogel–Gardthausen, *Schreiber*, p. 173. The relevant notice reads: Ταύτη ἡ βίβλος ὑπάρχει ἐμὴ ἐγὼ δὲ εἰμὶ Ἰωάννης Καλόθετος ὁ Δούκας. τέλος, see cod. Par. gr. 2954, fol. 337v.   [5] MM, I, p. 374.

[6] For the family and its members see V. Laurent, 'Un sceau inédit du protonotaire Basile Kamateros', *B*, 6 (1931), 261–71; G. Stadtmüller, 'Zur Geschichte der Familie Kamateros', *BZ*, 34 (1934), 352–8; G. G. Ladas, ' Βιογραφικαί τινες σημειώσεις περὶ τῶν Καματηρῶν καὶ τῶν ἐν τῷ πατριαρχικῷ σιγιλλίῳ τῆς μονῆς τοῦ Παντοκράτορος τῆς Ταὼ ἀναφερομένων ἀττικῶν ἀνδρῶν,' Συλλέκτης, 2 (1952/8), 64–74; V. S. Shandrovskaya, 'Grigorii Kamatir i ego pechat v sobranii Gosudarstvennogo Ermitazha', *VV*, 16 (1959), 173–82. One of the last noble Kamateroi was certainly the mother of the patriarch Arsenios Autoreianos (1255–9 and 1261–5); cf. Skout., p. 511. The Kamateroi of the later period are poor peasants. A locality Καματερὸ in Attica (cf. P. A. Phourikes, 'Συμβολὴ εἰς τὸ τοπωνυμικὸν τῆς Ἀττικῆς', Ἀθηνᾶ, 41 [1929], 84–5) is linked by Stadtmüller, op. cit., with the family, but this is doubtful as the word can mean, among other things, the pine tree.

98. Andronikos Doukas Kamateros: Called 'Doukas and Kamateros'[1] or more often simply Kamateros,[2] Andronikos was a son of Gregorios and Eirene *32*.[3] He flourished during the reign of Manuel I and apart from having been honoured with the dignities of *sebastos*[4] and *pansebastos sebastos*,[5] he also at one time or another filled the high posts of *eparchos* of the City,[6] *megas drungarios tēs viglēs*,[7] and *epi tōn deēseōn*.[8] In 1161 Andronikos was a member of the embassy that travelled to Antioch in order to escort to Constantinople the imperial bride Maria, a daughter of prince Raymond.[9]

Andronikos was a learned man who was in close touch with contemporary scholars. Reference has already been made to Prodromos and the anonymous of cod. Marc. gr. 524. In addition, we possess two orations of Gregorios

---

[1] Th. Pressel, *Ioannes Tzetzae Epistolae* (Tubingen, 1851), p. 90; cf. below n. 4.

[2] E.g. Kinn., p. 210; *PG*, 140, cols. 177D and 253C; 141, col. 397A; *VV*, 11 (1904), 479; *NE*, 13 (1916), 11; Pressel, op. cit., pp. 80 and 91.

[3] We are not explicitly informed that Andronikos was the son of Gregorios, but this can be deduced from scattered references. Kinn., p. 210, calls him a relative (συγγενής) to Manuel I, and Prodromos says that on his mother's side Andronikos was a Doukas while his father was the *logothetes* Kamateros; see S. Papademetriou, *Theodor Prodrom* (Odessa, 1905), p. 376. In the same vein the anonymous poet of cod. Marc. gr. 524 in a series of dedicatory epigrams gives the family names of Andronikos' parents. See Lampros, ' Μαρκιανὸς 524 ', pp. 44, 48-9, 50, 52, 53, and 54. He is also described in a like manner in a poem on the Ἱερὰ Ὁπλοθήκη by Georgios Skylitzes:

> ... Ἀνδρόνικος ἐκ μητρὸς Δούκας
> ὁ πανσέβαστος Καματηρὸς πατρόθεν
> μέγας τε δρουγγάριος ἐκ τῆς ἀξίας.

See A. K. Demetrakopoulos, Ὀρθόδοξος Ἑλλάς (Leipzig, 1872), p. 29.

[4] Lampros, ' Μαρκιανὸς 524 ', pp. 44, 48, 50, 52, 53, and 54; Pressel, op. cit., pp. 80 and 90; Papademetriou, loc. cit.

[5] *PG*, 140, cols. 177D and 253C; Pressel, op. cit., p. 91; L. Petit, 'Documents inédits sur le concile de 1166 et ses derniers adversaires', *VV*, 11 (1904), 479. The references (except that in Pressel) correspond to the years 1157, 1166, and 1170 respectively. Kinn., p. 210, in 1161 speaks of him as ἀνὴρ σεβαστότητι μὲν ἀξιωθείς which must necessarily be taken as implying the dignity of *pansebastos sebastos* rather than the lower one of *sebastos*. With the former rank Andronikos is also referred to in the often quoted title of Eustathios of Thessalonica's commentary to Dionysios Periegetes; see C. Müller, *Geographi Graeci Minores*, 1 (Paris, 1855), p. 201. L. Stiernon, 'Notes de titulature et de prosopographie byzantines. Sébaste et gambros', *REB*, 23 (1965), especially pp. 231-2, argues that the titles *sebastos* and *pansebastos sebastos* are not indistinguishable.

[6] Kinn., p. 210 (1161); *PG*, 140, col. 177D (1157). Andronikos, therefore, acted in this capacity from 1157 until up to at least 1161.

[7] Bekkos in *PG*, 141, col. 397A; *PG*, 140, col. 253D (1166); Petit, loc. cit. (1170); Demetrakopoulos, loc. cit.; E. L. Vranoussi, ' Πατμιακὰ Β'. Πρόσταξις Μανουὴλ Α' Κομνηνοῦ ὑπὲρ τῆς ἐν Πάτμῳ μονῆς Ἰωάννου τοῦ Θεολόγου ', Χαριστήριον εἰς Ἀναστάσιον Κ. Ὀρλάνδον, 11 (Athens, 1964), p. 84 (1176); cf. R. Guilland, 'Contribution à l'histoire administrative de l'empire byzantin: Le drongaire et le grand drongaire de la veille', *BZ*, 43 (1950), 353. It is therefore evident that he assumed this position following his relinquishment of that of *eparchos* (1161/6) and held it until after 1176. Andronikos is also mentioned as holding that office by Lampros, ' Μαρκιανὸς 524 ', pp. 49, 50, 52, 53, and 54.

[8] The address of a letter by Tornikes reads: ' Τῷ σεβαστῷ τῷ ἐπὶ τῶν δεήσεων κυρῷ Ἀνδρονίκῳ τῷ Καματηρῷ; see Sp. P. Lampros, ' Ὁ Βιενναῖος κῶδιξ Phil. graecus CCCXXI', *NE*, 13 (1916), 11; cf. H. Hunger, *Katalog der griechischen Handschriften der Österreichischen Nationalbibliothek*, 1 (Vienna, 1961), p. 410; R. Guilland, 'Etudes sur l'histoire administrative de l'Empire byzantin. Le Maître des Requêtes,' *B*, 35 (1965), 105. As Andronikos was still only a *sebastos* (that is prior to 1157), he apparently held that position before that year. See also below on Ioannes 99, p. 128, n. 9.

[9] Kinn., p. 210; cf. Dölger, *Regesten*, 11, p. 75, no. 1442.

Antiochos[1] as well as letters of Georgios Tornikes,[2] Euthymios Malakes[3] and Theodoros Balsamon[4] addressed to him. Tzetzes in particular was on intimate terms with him and in the *Chiliades* often speaks of or alludes to Andronikos;[5] he also sent him a couple of letters.[6] Being a skilled theologian himself, Andronikos is largely remembered for his Ἱερὰ Ὁπλοθήκη, an extensive dogmatic and theological exposition on various heresies, modelled upon a similar work of Zygabenos but re-inforced by fresh arguments against the teaching of the Latins and the Armenians.[7] He also wrote an epigram on the procession of the holy spirit.[8]

A seal of Andronikos with the inscription Θεοτόκε, βοήθει Ἀνδρονίκῳ τῷ Καματηρῷ has been preserved.[9]

Tzetzes speaks of an unnamed brother of Andronikos.[10] Of his children, Ioannes *99*, Basileios *100*, Euphrosyne *101*,[11] and Theodora[12] are known.

99. Ioannes Doukas: He was almost always called Doukas[13] and only rarely Doukas Kamateros,[14] or simply Kamateros,[15] Ioannes was a son of Andronikos *98*.[16] By virtue of the various high ranks he held and the frequent

[1] Both are still unpublished. For analyses see J. Darrouzès, 'Notice sur Grégoire Antiochos (1160 à 1196)', *REB*, 20 (1962), 68–9.

[2] Also unpublished. See Lampros, ' Ὁ Βιενναῖος κῶδιξ CCCXXI ', p. 11; Hunger, op. cit., p. 410.

[3] See A. Papadopoulos-Kerameus, ' Εὐθύμιος Μαλάκης, μητροπολίτης Νέων Πατρῶν ', Ἐπετηρὶς Παρνασσοῦ, 7 (1903), 20–21. It bears the address Τῷ σεβαστῷ καὶ μεγάλῳ δρουγγαρίῳ κῦρ Ἀνδρονίκῳ τῷ Καματηρῷ.

[4] Τῷ Καματηρῷ κυρῷ Ἀνδρονίκῳ τῷ μεγάλῳ δρουγγαρίῳ, edited by E. Miller, 'Poèmes astro-nomiques de Théodore Prodrome et Jean Camatère', *Notices et Extraits des Manuscrits de la Biblio-thèque Nationale*, 23, 11 (1872), 42.

[5] Cf. G. Hart, 'De Tzetzarum nomine, vitis, scriptis', *Jahrbücher für Classische Philologie*, Sup-plementband 12 (1881), 23, n. 43; C. Wendel, 'Tzetzes', in Pauly–Wissowa–Kroll, *RE*, 70 (1948), col. 1996.

[6] Pressel, op. cit., pp. 80 and 91.

[7] For Andronikos as a theologian and for his work which has only in part been published see H.-G. Beck, *Kirche und theologische Literatur im byzantinischen Reich* (Munich, 1959), pp. 626–7. The stylistic qualities of the Ἱερὰ Ὁπλοθήκη were held in high esteem by its dogmatic opponent Ioannes Bekkos who thought that τὸ μὲν ἐπὶ κάλλει λόγου καὶ φράσει ταύτης θαυμάσιον ἐπαινέσαι καὶ ἀποδέξασθαι, see *PG*, 141, col. 397A.

[8] Cf. Papadopoulos-Kerameus, Ἱεροσολυμιτικὴ Βιβλιοθήκη, IV, p. 180.

[9] It is edited by N. P. Likhachev, *Istoricheskoe Znachenie Italo-grecheskoi Ikonopisi* (St Petersburg, 1911), p. 124, no. 2.

[10] Τῷ ἐμῷ μὲν αὐθέντῃ τῷ σῷ ἀδελφῷ συντόμως σταλήτω ἡ ἐπιστολὴ καὶ τὰ βράχιστά μοι στιχίδια, Pressel, op. cit., p. 80.

[11] Vranoussi, op. cit., p. 95.

[12] Theodora became the wife of the *megas dux* Michael Stryphnos, see Chon., p. 716; cf. Laurent, *Médaillier Vatican*, pp. 66–9, no. 79.

[13] E.g. Kinn., pp. 109, 135–72, 260, and 269; Eust., p. 20; Chon., pp. 125, 313, and 318; Skout., pp. 239, 318 and 389; MM, III, p. 2; *PG*, 140, col. 236B; *NE*, 8 (1911), 179; Michael Choniates (for reference see below p. 128, n. 8); letters of Glykas (see below p. 128, n. 1); W. Regel, *Fontes Rerum Byzantinarum*, 1 (St Petersburg, 1892), p. 16.

[14] Skout., p. 311.

[15] Chon., p. 301, and some manuscripts of his, cf. J. A. J. van Dieten, 'Noch einmal über Niketas Choniates', *BZ*, 57 (1964), 311; Skout., p. 247; address of a letter of Tornikes (see below p. 130, n. 2).

[16] This becomes evident from the address of Eustathios' commentary to Dionysios Periegetes where it is explicitly recorded that Ioannes Doukas was the son of the *megas drungarios* Andronikos Kamateros *98*. See C. Müller, *Geographi Graeci Minores*, 1 (Paris, 1855), p. 201.

important missions of both military and diplomatic nature which he undertook, Ioannes Doukas occupies an outstanding — perhaps the most outstanding — place among the officials of his time.[1] He was related to the imperial house, and Kinnamos calls him ἐξάδελφος of Manuel I.[2]

In the course of his public career which almost fills the second half of the twelfth century Ioannes is referred to as *sebastos*,[3] *pansebastos sebastos*,[4] and *oikeios* of the emperor.[5] Among the various posts he held were those of *megas hetaireiarches*,[6] *eparchos* of the City,[7] and *logothetes tou dromou*.[8] It appears unlikely that he ever had been *epi tōn deēseōn*,[9] and he was definitely never a *krites tou vēlou*, as has been suggested.[10]

Ioannes Doukas participated in the Serbian campaign of *c*. 1150,[11] and a few years later (1155/6), together with Michael Palaiologos, he was despatched to Ancona with the task of attempting to drag Frederick Barbarossa into an anti-Norman coalition.[12] Then he led the Byzantine forces (with Alexios Komnenos

---

[1] A fair amount of information on his public activities has been preserved which may eventually be further illuminated by other evidence in the still unpublished speeches and letters that were written for Ioannes. Brief sketches, mostly inadequate and occasionally confused, can be found in Regel, op. cit., pp. viii–x; K. Krumbacher, 'Michael Glykas: Eine Skizze seiner Biographie und seiner litterarischen Thätigkeit nebst einem unedierten Gedichte und Briefe desselben', *SBBAW*, 1894, pp. 424–5; Laurent, 'Un sceau inédit', pp. 367–8; Stadtmüller, 'Familie Kamateros', pp. 356–8.

[2] Kinn., p. 125; cf. p. 109. As a Kamateros, Ioannes could not have been a cousin of Manuel **if** it is assumed that Eirene *29* was a niece of Eirene *26*. But he could have married a Komnene and through his wife become the emperor's cousin.

[3] Kinn., p. 135 (1155); *PG*, 140, col. 236B (1166); Regel, op. cit., p. 16 (1168/75); Krumbacher, op. cit., p. 422; Lampros, 'Μαρκιανὸς 524 ', p. 179.

[4] *VV*, 11 (1904), 479 (1170); MM, III, p. 2 (1188).   [5] Of Isaakios II in 1188, MM, III, p. 2.

[6] *VV*, 11 (1904), 479 **(1170)**; *PL*, 201, col. 830B (1177); Chon., p. 313 (1182). As such he is also referred to in a λαλιὰ καὶ προσφώνησις by Eustathios when Doukas was sent by the emperor to Thessalonica (Regel, op. cit., p. 16). The speech is dated by the editor (p.x) to 1168/75. Similarly Ioannes is named as *megas hetaireiarches* in two letters of Glykas (Krumbacher, op. cit., p. 421, no. 8 and p. 422, no. 17) thought to have been written after 1181.

[7] He is described as *eparchos* during the turbulent years that followed Manuel's death. Cf. Eust., p. 20; Chon., p. 301; Skout., p. 311.

[8] It was obviously Isaakios II who raised Doukas to this position. See Chon., p. 141 and 525 (1189); Skout., p. 389 (1189); MM, III, p. 2 (1188); Michael Choniates, Ὑπομνηστικὸν to Alexios III lastly edited by G. Stadtmüller, *Michael Choniates, Metropolit von Athen (ca. 1138– ca. 1222)* (Rome, 1934), p. 164; letter of Tornikes (see below p. 130, n. 2).

[9] The sole evidence is found in the address of Eustathios' commentary to Dionysios Periegetes where certain manuscripts associate the rank with Doukas' name, while others attribute it to the author, and this shows that it might have originated from a gloss; see R. Browning, 'The Patriarchal School at Constantinople in the Twelfth Century', *B*, 32 (1962), 192, n. 1. Furthermore it should be noted that the passage includes the name Andronikos *99*, who, as we definitely know from another source, acted for a period as ἐπὶ τῶν δεήσεων (see above p. 126, n. 8); as neither Eustathios nor Ioannes are otherwise recorded occupants of this office, it is very probable that the marginal addition was originally meant to apply to Andronikos *99*.

[10] See Stadtmüller, 'Familie Kamateros', p. 357, who cites Kinn., p. 269. This passage however, far from supporting this, merely links the office in question with the name of an entirely different person, Nikephoros Kaspax.

[11] Kinn., pp. 109–12; cf. Chalandon, *Les Comnène*, II, p. 390. The other Byzantine commander was Ioannes Kantakouzenos.

[12] Kinn., p. 135; cf. Dölger, *Regesten*, II, p. 70, no. 1396. In the summer of 1147 Doukas, together with Demetrios Makrembolites, had gone on another mission to king Louis VII in Regensburg. Cf. Dölger, *Regesten*, II, p. 65, no. 1354. The embassy is known from western sources who refer to

Bryennios) which invaded and temporarily occupied a large part of Italy but at their decisive defeat at Brindisi (28 May 1156) he was taken prisoner.[1] Eventually he returned to Constantinople, and in 1164 he led the army in Serbia. Two years later he took a leading part in a new Hungarian campaign, and Doukas' distinction and prominence in this war found expression in the symbolic erection of a monumental cross, bearing a commemorative inscription, deep in the distant Magyar territory.[2] Manuel used his distinguished relative once more. In 1077 he sent him to Jerusalem to renew an alliance against Egypt with king Baldwin IV.[3]

After the death of that emperor, Ioannes found himself in opposition to the unpopular *protosebastos* Alexios Komnenos,[4] but in 1182 he used his influence to smooth out the civil disturbances that occurred.[5] Despite the attempts of Andronikos I to win over Doukas (who was then the commander of Nicaea), he nevertheless remained hostile to his regime.[6] However, he enjoyed the confidence of Isaakios II, and in 1188–9 he was twice sent as ambassador to Barbarossa in an effort to make sure that the Crusade that was to travel across Byzantine territory would pass through without unpleasant incidents.[7]

Prominent as he was in public affairs, Ioannes was no less conspicuous in his private life. Choniates relates that he was a heavy drinker but still finds words of praise for the man.[8] Two works of Eustathios of Thessalonica were written for him: the commentary of Dionysios Periegetes[9] and the above-mentioned speech.[10] Michael Glykas addressed two of his letters, purely theological in

---

Ioannes as 'Maurus' or 'Mauroducas', see W. Ohnsorge, 'Ein Beitrag zur Geschichte Manuels I. von Byzanz' in *Abendland und Byzanz* (Darmstadt, 1958), pp. 395–7. 'Maurodoukas' was probably a nickname of Ioannes.

---

[1] Kinn., pp. 147 ff.; for this campaign and for Ioannes' role see Chalandon, *Les Comnène*, II, pp. 363–70, and especially P. Lamma, *Comneni e Staufer*, I (Rome, 1955), pp. 149 ff. His successes there and especially in Ancona have given rise to the epic *La Chanson de Jean de Lancon* (=Ioannes Doukas); see H. Grégoire, 'Nouvelles notes épiques', *B*, 25/27 (1955/57), 781.

[2] Kinn., pp. 260–61. The planting of the cross by Doukas forms the subject of some verses: ''Επίγραμμα γεγονὸς ἐπὶ τῷ ἐμπαγέντι μέσον τῆς οὐγγρικῆς χώρας Τιμίῳ Σταυρῷ', in Lampros, ' Μαρκιανὸς 524 ', pp. 178–9; cf. Gy. Moravcsik, ' Σημειώσεις εἰς τὰ καλλιτεχνικὰ μνημεῖα τῶν οὐγγροβυζαντινῶν σχέσεων', Χαριστήριον εἰς 'Αναστάσιον Κ. 'Ορλάνδον, I (Athens, 1964), pp. 27–9, who believes that the cross was planted in Transylvania.

[3] William of Tyre in *PL*, 201, col. 820B; cf. Dölger, *Regesten*, II, p. 86, no. 1526. William calls Doukas 'Ioannes vir magnificus megaltriarca'.

[4] Eust., p. 20; Chon., p. 33; Skout., p. 311.

[5] Chon., p. 312.

[6] Chon., p. 318.

[7] Chon., pp. 525–6; MM, III, p. 2; Skout., p. 389; cf. Dölger, *Regesten*, II, p. 94, nos 1581–2 and 1587. Another probable reference to Ioannes dates from 1188. He appears to have 'edited' the chrysobull of Alexios I of 1082 (Dölger, *Regesten*, II, no. 1150), see MM, VI, p. 53; cf. F. Dölger, 'Die Kaiserurkunden des Ioannes-Theologos-Klosters auf Patmos', *BZ*, 28 (1928), 341–2.

[8] Chon., p. 149; Stadtmüller, 'Familie Kamateros', p. 356.

[9] See above p. 127, n. 16.

[10] Εἶδος λαλιᾶς τινὸς καὶ προσφωνήσεως ὅτε ὁ πάνσεπτος σεβαστὸς καὶ μέγας ἑταιρειάρχης κῦρ 'Ιωάννης ὁ Δούκας ἦλθεν εἰς Θεσσαλονίκην ἐρευνήσων τὸν Λεπενδρηνὸν κατὰ θεῖον καὶ βασιλικὸν ὁρισμόν, edited by Regel, op. cit., pp. 16–24. Eustathios praises Doukas' experiences in the wars in Asia Minor, on the Danube, and in Italy (pp. 18–21).

content, to him,[1] and Georgios Tornikes some more, all unpublished.[2] A certain philosopher Konstantinos of Nicaea wrote a speech for Doukas[3] and the anonymous epigram for the erection of the cross in Hungary has already been referred to.[4] Finally it appears that Ioannes Doukas himself tried his hand at literature.[5]

100. Basileios Kamateros Doukas: Basileios Kamateros,[6] only once referred to as 'Doukas and Kamateros' (in his seal), was a brother of Euphrosyne *101*[7] and, therefore, a son of Andronikos *98*. He held the dignities of *sebastos*[8] and *pansebastos sebastos*[9] and since at least 1166 acted as a *protonotarios*.[10] In 1182 he was *logothetēs tou dromou* but being an opponent of Andronikos I he was blinded[11] and then banished to Russia.[12] Nevertheless he was again very active during the reign of Alexios III and even after 1204.[13]

Basileios was on friendly terms with the Choniatai who addressed several of their letters to him.[14]

---

[1] Krumbacher, op. cit., p. 421, no. 8, and p. 422, no. 17. Krumbacher dates them after 1181 (p. 425).

[2] One letter bears the caption ' Τῷ σεβαστῷ καὶ λογοθέτῃ τοῦ δρόμου κῦρ Ἰωάννῃ τῷ Καματηρῷ ὅτε ἦν ἔτι ὑποψήφιος (sc. ὁ Τορνίκης) Ἐφέσου' see Lampros, ''Ο Βιενναῖος κῶδιξ CCCXXI ', p. 8; cf. Stadtmüller, 'Familie Kamateros', p. 358. In fact, three other letters, preserved in the same manuscript, appear to be addressed to Ioannes, but all of them call him Kamateros; see Hunger, op. cit., p. 410.

[3] K. Krumbacher, *Geschichte der byzantinischen Literatur* (Munich, 1897²), p. 474.

[4] Cf. above p. 129, n. 2. The poem speaks of Ioannes as ἀρχιφαλαγγάρχης, a rather poetic designation for the military commander.

[5] H. Omont, *Inventaire sommaire des manuscrits grecs de la Bibliothèque Nationale* (Paris, 1888), III, p. 295, and Krumbacher, *Geschichte*, p. 786, mention a certain Ioannes Doukas as having written two poems in political verse preserved in cod. Par. suppl. gr. 675 (XIV s.). I have consulted photographs of these texts which seem to belong to the twelfth century and may have been written by our Ioannes. The first poem bears the title Στίχοι τοῦ σεβαστοῦ κυροῦ Ἰωάννου τοῦ Δούκα εἰς ἑαυτὸν καὶ κατὰ τῆς τῶν ἀνθρώπων ἀβελτερίας ἐν οἷς καὶ περὶ ψυχῆς ζήτησις (fol. 267r–267v) and the second (fol. 267v–268r) Μονῳδία τοῦ αὐτοῦ διὰ πολιτικῶν στίχων εἰς τὴν κραταιὰν ἡμῶν δεσποίνην. This latter could refer to Manuel's I first wife Bertha-Eirene who died in 1160.

[6] This surname is given to him by the sources. See Chon., p. 641; PG, 140, col. 253C; Sp. P. Lampros, Μιχαὴλ Ἀκομινάτου τοῦ Χωνιάτου τὰ Σωζόμενα (Athens, 1879–80), I, p. 312; II, pp. 62 and 257; E. Miller, *Recueil des Historiens des Croisades. Historiens grecs*, II (Paris, 1881), p. 664.

[7] Chon., p. 641.   [8] Seal; Miller, loc. cit.   [9] PG, 140, col. 253C (1166).

[10] In his seal and also in PG, 140, col. 253C, where in the same document and a few lines below the name of an homonymous, Basileios Kamateros *prōtonobilissimos* and *eparchos* occurs. This latter whose seal was published by Laurent, *Bulles métriques*, p. 236, no. 710, is probably the future patriarch.

[11] Chon., pp. 345–6; Lampros, Χωνιάτου τὰ Σωζόμενα, I, p. 312, and II, p. 62. It appears that the blinding affected the one eye only, cf. the notes of Lampros, ibid., II, p. 522.

[12] Ibid., I, p. 321, and II, p. 528.

[13] Chon., p. 641. In 1209/10 he was sent to Leon II of Armenia, cf. Dölger, *Regesten*, III, p. 3, no. 1680.

[14] To begin with there are two letters of Niketas published by Miller, op. cit., pp. 664–5, and in 'Poèmes astronomiques de Théodore Prodrome et de Jean Camatère', *Notices et Extraits des Manuscrits de la Bibliothèque Nationale*, 23, II (1872), p. 112. These call Basileios 'an uncle of the emperor', presumably Theodoros I Laskaris who was married to one of Euphrosyne's daughters, and they apparently date from after 1204. A similar address is borne by a letter by Michael Choniates Τῷ γυναικοθείῳ τοῦ βασιλέως τοῦ Λάσκαρι κῦρ Βασιλείῳ τῷ Καματηρῷ (Lampros, Χωνιάτου τὰ Σωζόμενα, II, pp. 257–61; cf. the commentary pp. 632–3) which was written in 1208; for the date see Stadtmüller, *Michael Choniates*, pp. 134 and 138. Another letter of Michael to him deals with the blinding of Basileios (Lampros, Χωνιάτου τὰ Σωζόμενα, II, pp. 62–4)

His surviving seal bears the legend

Σφραγὶς σεβαστοῦ τοῦ πρωτονοταρίου
τοῦ Καματηροῦ καὶ Δούκα Βασιλείου.[1]

101. Euphrosyne Doukaina: Euphrosyne called Doukaina[2] who became (long before 1195) the wife of Alexios III Angelos was a daughter of Andronikos 98.[3] In contrast to her worthless husband, she was a courageous and clever woman who did not remain indifferent to state affairs and court intrigues. Having meddled in conspiracies more than once, she had to quit the palace for a while.[4] At the fall of Alexios (18 August 1203) Euphrosyne was arrested with some of her relatives,[5] but a few months later on the eve of the City's capture by the Latins she succeeded in making her escape with Alexios 126 and her daughter Eudokia.[6] She subsequently spent some years accompanying her wandering husband and finally lived for a period in Arta where she died in around 1211.[7] We are informed that Euphrosyne owned large tracts of land in southern Thessaly.[8]

By her marriage to Alexios, Euphrosyne became the mother of three daughters, Eirene,[9] Anna,[10] and Eudokia,[11] all of whom married before 1195.

and was apparently sent shortly after the fall of Andronikos (cf. Stadtmüller, *Michael Choniates*, p. 124). Finally we possess from the same pen a *Προσφώνημα εἰς τὸν γυναικάδελφον τοῦ βασιλέως καὶ λογοθέτην κῦρ Βασίλειον τὸν Καματηρόν* (Lampros, *Χωνιάτου τὰ Σωζόμενα*, I, pp. 312–23) which contains some historical information (cf. the editor's commentary, ibid., II, pp. 519–30) and was written under Alexios III (Stadtmüller, *Michael Choniates*, p. 131).

---

[1] Laurent, 'Un sceau inédit'.
[2] Chon., p. 600; Skout., p. 414. There is an inadequate sketch on Euphrosyne in J. McCabe, *The Empresses of Constantinople* (London, 1913), pp. 238–56.
[3] This is implied in a passage from the life of St Leontios, patriarch of Jerusalem (Halkin, *BHG*, II, p. 55, no. 985), quoted and discussed by Vranoussi, op. cit., p. 93.
[4] Chon., pp. 647 and 687.
[5] Chon., p. 727.   [6] Chon., p. 755.   [7] Akrop., p. 17.
[8] The *Partitio Romaniae* states: 'Pertinentia imperatricis (sc. Euphrosynae) scilicet Verna, Fersala, Domocos, Revenica, duo Almiri, cum Demetriadi', TT, I, p. 487; cf. the Greek translation ibid., p. 493.
[9] Eirene married twice, first to Andronikos Kontostephanos who died in *c.* 1197 (Chon., pp. 604, 641, and 660) and shortly afterwards to Alexios Palaiologos who had divorced his wife for Eirene's sake (Chon., pp. 673, 696, 703, and 709). By her second husband who died before 1204 (Akrop., p. 9), she had a daughter Theodora who became the mother of Michael VIII (Greg., I, p. 96; Dmitrievskii, *Typika*, p. 787). In 1203 Eirene followed her father in his exile (Chon., p. 723).
[10] She also married twice. First (before 1190) to Isaakios Komnenos (Chon., pp. 562, 604, and 613), later created *sebastokrator*, who commanded the Byzantine forces in the Bulgarian war but was defeated, taken prisoner (1196), and died in captivity (Chon., pp. 616, 620, and 660). Anna bore him a daughter Theodora who became the wife of the Bulgarian adventurer, the boyar Ivanko (Chon., pp. 676–7). Anna married again, this time Theodoros Laskaris (Chon., p. 674; Akrop., p. 9; Kant., I, p. 11), the future emperor of Nicaea, by whom she became the mother of three daughters: Eirene 115, Maria, and Eudokia.
[11] Eudokia married three times. At first her uncle Isaakios II gave her to king Stephen of Serbia to whom she bore a number of children, including Stephanos 102. In Serbia she was accused of adultery, was humiliated, and sent back to her father (1202) who in the meantime had secured the throne (Chon., pp. 703–4 and 804; Akrop., p. 9). A. Meliarakis, ' Τὸ νόσημα μιᾶς βασιλίσσης παραμορφούμενον ἐν τῇ ἱστορίᾳ ', Ἑστία Εἰκονογραφημένη, no. 1 (1 January 1895), pp. 2–4, and no. 2 (8 January 1895), pp. 10–12 (cf. idem, Ἱστορία τοῦ Βασιλείου τῇ

102. Stephanos Doukas: The Serbian king Stephen Radoslav was a son of king Stephen the 'First-crowned' and Eudokia the daughter of Euphrosyne *101*. In several Greek documents[1] and in his coins[2] he is called Στέφανος ὁ Δούκας, a surname which he presumably inherited from his grandmother Euphrosyne *101*. He also uses this form in his signature at least once.[3] Stephanos held the throne for a brief period (1228–34) and became the husband of Anna *47*. Their betrothal ring has been preserved.[4]

103. (Doukas): A seal believed to belong to Isaakios Komnenos, the usurper and 'tyrant' of Cyprus (1185), bears the metrical invocation to St George

Κομνηνοδουκόπαιδα μητροπατρόθεν
Ἰσαάκιον ὃς σεβαστοκρατόρων
θυγατρόπαις γαμβρός τε, μάρτυς με σκέποις[5]

According to this, Isaakios was a Komnenos on his mother's side and a Doukas on that of his father. His maternal grandfather and his father-in-law (or perhaps his wife's brother instead[6]) were both *sebastokratores*. Some of this information can be corroborated for Isaakios was in fact the son of an unknown daughter of the *sebastokrator* Isaakios Komnenos, a brother of Manuel I.[7] Moreover he is also described as being a close relative of Euphrosyne *101*[8] and Andronikos *104*,[9] a fact which makes sense only if it is assumed that the father of Isaakios belonged to the Doukai Kamateroi and, as is revealed in the seal, that he officially employed the name of Doukas.[10]

Isaakios Doukas of Cyprus is the only known son of this N Doukas; he married an Armenian lady,[11] but the inscription of the seal cannot refer to this marriage. It is of course quite possible that he had previously taken as wife the daughter (or the sister) of an unknown *sebastokrator*.

104. Andronikos Doukas: He belonged to the notorious entourage of Andronikos I which became infamous through their excesses in dealing with the emperor's enemies or suspects.[12] Falling into disgrace on account of his relation-

---

Νικαίας καὶ τοῦ Δεσποτάτου τῆς Ἠπείρου [Athens, 1898], pp. 630–40), has attempted to show that Eudokia's expulsion was due to a contagious skin disease she was alleged to suffer from. Eudokia remained at Constantinople up to the City's fall whereupon she escaped with Alexios *126* who married her shortly afterwards (Chon., pp. 755, and 804). After the tragic end of her second husband, her father gave her in marriage to Leon Sgouros, the ruthless lord of Argos (Chon., pp. 804–5; Akrop., p. 13). For Eudokia and especially her function as queen of Serbia, see M. Laskaris, *Vizantiske Printseze u Srednijevekovnoi Srbiji* (Belgrade, 1926), pp. 5–37.

---

[1] MM, III, p. 66; Chomatianos in J. B. Pitra, *Analecta Sacra et Classica Spicilegio Solesmensi parata*, VI (Rome, 1891), col. 686.   [2] Laskaris, op. cit., p. 45.
[3] F. Miklosich, *Monumenta Serbica* (Vienna, 1860), p. 52.   [4] See above on Anna *47*.
[5] The inscription has been edited by V. Laurent, 'Mélanges d'épigraphie grecque et de sigillographie byzantine', *EO*, 31 (1932), 434–5, and again in *Bulles métriques*, p. 218, no. 693.
[6] Γαμβρός in Greek can imply both.
[7] Cf. Chon., pp. 376, 377, and 379. An anonymous chronicle speaks of Isaakios as τὸ γένος ἐκ τοῦ Μανουὴλ τοῦ Κομνηνοῦ κατάγων, see J. Müller, 'Byzantinische Analekten', *Sitzungsberichte der Kaiserlichen Akademie der Wissenschaften. Philosophisch-historische Klasse*, 9 (Vienna, 1853), p. 368, v.53.
[8] Chon., p. 611.   [9] Chon., p. 377.
[10] Ducange, *Familiae*, op. 183–4, had already recognised that the father of Isaakios might have been a Doukas.
[11] Laurent, 'Mélanges', pp. 434–5.   [12] Chon., p. 380.

ship and former support for Isaakios of Cyprus he suffered a terrible death on 30 May 1185, together with Konstantinos *226*. His body was then carried to a Jewish cemetery on the Asiatic shores of the Bosphorus and was cut into pieces.[1]

Andronikos was related to the 'tyrant' of Cyprus Isaakios Komnenos,[2] and his surname of Doukas could thus have been inherited from the Doukai Kamateroi.

KATRARES

105. Ioannes Doukas Katrares: The name of Ioannes Doukas Katrares appears in a document of Chios dated 28 July 1446, which he signs as a witness. He was a brother of the *notarios* Stephanos Katrarios.[3]

KAUKADENOS

The first reference to a member of the Kaukadenos (*Καυκαδηνός*) family probably dates from the twelfth century.[4] The name is not particularly widespread. In the fourteenth century Theodoros Kaukadenos was a man of letters and a friend of Demetrios Kydones[5] and Manuel Palaiologos.[6]

106. Doukas Kaukadenos: A synodal act of March 1394 speaks of a Doukas Kaukadenos who had attempted to conclude a marriage (*ἐπεχείρησε ποιῆσαι συνοικέσιον*) which was against canon law and as a result he was anathematized. Now he asks for forgiveness. This was promptly granted on the condition that he would never enter into such a marriage.[7]

Another document of April 1400 refers to a vineyard of Doukas Kaukadenos which was now owned by Manuel Philanthropenos, a cousin of the emperor (*τοῦ ἀμπελίου Δούκα τοῦ Καυκαδηνοῦ, ὅπερ νῦν κέκτηται ὁ περιπόθητος ἐξάδελφ τοῦ . . . αὐτοκράτορος κῦρ Μανουὴλ ὁ Φιλανθρωπηνός*).[8]

---

[1] Chon., pp. 381–2, 384, and 407; Skout., pp. 341–3.

[2] Chon., p. 377; Skout., says that he had been *συνήθης ἐκ παίδων τυγχάνων καὶ κατὰ γένος ἔγγιστα* to Andronikos.

[3] See M. I. Manousakas, ' *Στέφανος Κατράριος ὁ πρῶτος γνωστὸς Ἕλληνας νοτάριος τῆς Χίου* ', *Εἰς Μνήμην Κωνσταντίνου 'Ι. 'Αμάντου, 1874–1960* (Athens, 1960), p. 271.

[4] Sp. P. Lampros, ' *Τοῦ Θεολογάκη ὡς ἐκ προσώπου τῶν καλουμένων τζύρων* ', *ΝΕ*, 7 (1910), 356: *Ἐλέῳ βασιλικῷ καὶ καυκαδηνικῇ προχειρίσει τιμηθεὶς δικτάτωρ καὶ ἀρχιστράτηγος τῆς ἡμῶν τῶν ἰχθύων πληθύος*.

[5] R.-J. Loenertz, *Démétrius Cydonès, Correspondance* (Rome, 1960), pp. 88, 93, and 300.

[6] E. Legrand, *Lettres de l'Empereur Manuel Paléologue* (Paris, 1893), p. 35.

[7] MM, II, p. 204.

[8] MM, II, p. 379.

KOMNENOS

The family of Komnenos (Κομνηνός) appears for the first time towards the tenth century, but up to the accession of Alexios I in 1081 it could not equal the Doukai for social prestige. Nevertheless their predominantly military background seemed to give them a superior vitality which continued uninterrupted until the fall of their dynasty, and even afterwards it was their descendants who established themselves in Epirus and in Trebizond.[1]

The marriage of Eirene 26 to Alexios Komnenos in 1079 caused the name of Doukas to be adopted by some of their immediate descendants. Two of their children[2] and at least one of their grandsons, all properly speaking Komnenoi, are sometimes found with the name of Doukas and as such will receive a brief treatment here. The compound Κομνηνοδούκας was also coined in the twelfth century, but it was a purely poetic form.[3]

107. Anna Komnene (Doukaina): Anna Komnene, the famous historian,[4] and first-born daughter of Alexios I and Eirene 26, is at least once referred to

---

[1] For the Komnenoi as a whole and for their origin see Ducange, *Familiae*, pp. 169–206; A. Komnenos Hypselantes, Τὰ μετὰ τὴν Ἅλωσιν (ed. G. Aphthonides, Constantinople, 1870), pp. 8–11; G. Murnu, 'L'origine des Comnène', Academie Roumaine, *Bulletin de la Section Historique*, 11 (1924), 212–16; Chalandon, *Les Comnène*, 1, pp. 21 ff.; G. Buckler, *Anna Comnena: A Study* (London, 1929), pp. 264–5; K. I. Amantos, ''Η καταγωγὴ τῶν Κομνηνῶν', Θρακικά, 10 (1938), 232–3; A. Papadopoulos-Kerameus, ''Ο τελευταῖος Κομνηνὸς κατ'ἔγγραφον ἐπίσημον τοῦ μητροπολίτου 'Ηρακλείας Νεοφύτου', ΔΙΕΕΕ, 2 (1885), 667–79. Very important for the period up to 1204 but occasionally incomplete is the genealogical survey of S. De Jongh, *La Généalogie des Comnène à Byzance* (unpublished doctoral dissertation at the University of Brussels, 1937). The content of two older books on the family [Demetrius Stephanopoli Comnène], *Précis historique de la maison impériale des Comnène où l'on trouve l'origine, les moeurs et les usages des Maniotes* (Amsterdam, 1784) and E. F. Baron Henin de Cuvillers, *Coup d'oeil historique et généalogique sur l'origine de la maison impériale des Comnène* (Venice, 1798) is purely fantastic.

[2] A metrical seal inscription supposedly mentions a certain Isaakios Komnenodoukas, and is attributed to the youngest son of Alexios I (who became the father of Andronikos I) who could have inherited the name of Doukas from his mother Eirene 26. See Laurent, *Bulles métriques*, pp. 72–3, no. 201; R. Guilland, 'Etudes sur l'histoire administrative de l'empire byzantin: Le stratopédarque et le grand stratopédarque', *BZ*, 46 (1953), 68–9; P. Joannou, *Christliche Metaphysik in Byzanz*. I. — *Die Illuminationslehre des Michael Psellos und Joannes Italos* (Ettal, 1956), p. 25. However the seal's inscription is only fragmentary but the still legible letters bear a startling resemblance to a text published by Laurent, *Bulles métriques*, p. 218, no. 639, coming from a seal belonging to Isaakios Komnenos, the 'tyrant' of Cyprus (see Doukas Kamateros 103). In both cases the invocation is made to St George who in the first seal is addressed as προστάτης and in the second as μάρτυς. In fact, all words but one coincide, and the reconstruction of the complete text of the first seal, however ingenious, cannot be accepted. In my opinion, both seals definitely belong to Isaakios of Cyprus.

[3] See for instance Lampros, ' Μαρκιανὸς 524 ', *passim*.

[4] Recent bibliographies on Anna can be found in M. E. Colonna, *Gli storici bizantini dal IV al XV secolo*. I. — *Storici profani* (Naples, 1956), pp. 23–6, and in Gy. Moravcsik, *Byzantinoturcica* (Berlin, 1958), 1, pp. 219–23. Some subsequent additions: R. Katičić, ' "Αννα ἡ Κομνηνὴ κα ὁ 'Ομηρος ', *EEBΣ*, 27 (1957), 213–23; idem, ' 'Η ἀρχαιομάθεια καὶ τὸ ἐπικὸν πνεῦμα εἰς τὴν 'Αλεξιάδα τῆς "Αννης Κομνηνῆς', *EEBΣ*, 29 (1959), 81–6; B. Leib, 'Les silences d'Anna Comnène ou ce que n'a pas dit l'Alexiade', *BS*, 19 (1958), 1–11; idem, 'Complots à Byzance contre Alexis I Comnène (1081–1118)', *BS*, 23 (1962), 250–75; E. L. Vranoussi, Κομισκόρτης ὁ ἐξ 'Αρβάνων. Σχόλια εἰς χωρίον τῆς "Αννης Κομνηνῆς, Jannina, 1962; R. Browning, 'An Unpublished

as Doukaina,[1] a designation which is partly explained by the special attachment which she felt for her mother. Anna was born on 2 December 1083,[2] and as an infant and child she was for some years betrothed to Konstantinos *23*. In 1097[3] she married Nikephoros Bryennios, subsequently created 'Caesar', who died in 1136/7.[4] Anna herself died in comparative obscurity a little after 1148.[5]

The attribution of three well-known seals to Anna[6] is, in my opinion, possible but not established above all doubt.

By her marriage to Bryennios, Anna became the mother of at least four children: Alexios Komnenos, Ioannes *78*, Eirene *79*, and another daughter (or daughters) of unknown name.

108. Ioannes Komnenos (Doukas): The emperor Ioannes II Komnenos is included here because at least once in an inscription of the fourteenth century he is mentioned as Komnenos Doukas.[7] Ioannes, a porphyrogenitus prince, was

---

Funeral Oration on Anna Comnena', *Proceedings of the Cambridge Philological Society*, no. 188, new series no. 8 (1962), 1–12; P. Wirth, 'Eine Lakune im Logos Epitaphios des Georgios Tornikes auf Anna Komnene?', *BZ*, 56 (1963), 234; Y. N. Liubarskii, 'Mirovozzrenie Anny Komninoi', *Uchenie Zapiski Velikolukskogo Pedagogicheskogo Instituta*, 24 (1964), 152–76; idem, 'Ob istochnikakh Aleksiyadi Anny Komninoi', *VV*, 25 (1964), 99–120; E. L. Vranoussi, 'Le mont des Kellia. Note sur un passage d'Anne Comnène', *Zbornik Radova Vizantoloshkog Instituta*, 8/2 (1964), 459–64.

---

[1] Prodromos addresses a poem to her as follows: Εἰς τὴν σοφωτάτην πορφυρογέννητον καὶ καισάρισσαν κυρὰν "Ανναν τὴν Δούκαιναν περὶ τῶν ἑαυτοῦ; see the text in S. Papademetriou, *Theodor Prodrom* (Odessa, 1905), pp. 115–18. In the epitaph for Anna's daughter-in-law Theodora the same poet calls the historian τὸ Δουκικὸν θρύλλημα, τὴν σοφὴν "Ανναν; see E. Kurtz, 'Unedierte Texte aus der Zeit des Kaisers Johannes Komnenos', *BZ*, 16 (1907), 88, v. 43.

[2] *Alexias*, II, pp. 60–61; cf. Buckler, op. cit., pp. 39–40.

[3] Ibid., pp. 32–3 and 42; S. Wittek–De Jongh, 'Le césar Nicéphore Bryennios, l'historien, et ses ascendants', *B*, 23 (1953), 468.

[4] Chalandon, *Les Comnène*, II, p. 17.

[5] Cf. Browning, op. cit., p. 4.

[6] The three inscriptions read as follows:

(a) Δι'εὐλάβειαν οὐ φέρει θείους τύπους
"Αννης Κομνηνῆς ἡ σφραγὶς ἀλλὰ στίχους.

(b) Κομνηνοδουκῶν ἐκ γένους σφραγὶς "Αννης.

(c) Σφραγὶς τύπος πέφυκε Κομνηνῆς "Αννης.

See Laurent, *Bulles métriques*, pp. 38–9 no. 106, pp. 71–2 no. 200, and p. 162 no. 462; cf. F. Tailliez, 'Le sceau d'Anne Comnène et deux corrections', *OCP*, 14 (1948), 176–9. Buckler, op. cit., pp. 6–7, also assigns them to the historian. However the existence of another Anna Komnene *230*, perhaps also a Doukaina on her mother's side, makes the traditional attribution, far from certain.

[7] See A. Boeckh and J. Franz, *Corpus Inscriptionum Graecarum*, IV (Berlin, 1877), p. 335, no. 8722. The inscription belonged to the Pantokrator monastery at Constantinople and refers to Ioannes as

"Αναξ χαριτώνυμος, ἀριστεὺς μέγας,
'Αλεξίου παῖς, Μανουὴλ φυτοσπόρος,
Κομνηνὸς Δούκας, πορφυρόβλαστος κλάδος.

Prodromos (in *PG*, 133, col. 1396B; cf. 1393A) speaks of him as ὅρπηξ Κομνηνῶν, εὐθαλὴς Δουκῶν κλάδος. Another poet addresses the emperor

"Ηλιε πορφυρογέννητε, 'Ρώμης ἀστὴρ τῆς νέας
κοσμολαμπές, Δουκολαμπές, δέσποτα μονοκράτωρ,

the eldest son of Alexios I and Eirene *26*, born in September/December 1087.[1] Shortly afterwards he was proclaimed emperor. Ioannes succeeded his father on 15 August 1118,[2] and reigned until 8 April 1143,[3] when he was probably assassinated.[4]

In perhaps 1104/5[5] Ioannes married the Hungarian princess Pyriska, a daughter of king Ladislav, who was called Eirene by the Greeks. She died as the nun Xene on 13 August 1134,[6] and was canonized by the Byzantine church.[7] By this marriage, Ioannes became the father of eight children: Alexios (1106), Andronikos (1108), Isaakios (1113), Manuel (the future emperor, 1122), Maria (twin sister of Alexios, 1106), Anna (1110), Theodora (1116), and Eudokia (1119).[8]

109. Ioannes Doukas: He was a son of the *sebastokrator* Andronikos Komnenos, a son of Alexios I and Eirene *26*. He is mentioned only once, in connection with the synod of 6 March 1166.[9]

110. Komnenos Doukas: A certain Komnenos Doukas who cannot be further identified paid for the copying of cod. Coisl. gr. 5 in 1263/4. The manuscript was written by Theodoros Lampetes and contains books of the Old Testament.[10]

111. Alexios Komnenos (Angelos Doukas): There are certain poems by a *protonotarios* of Trebizond, Stephanos Sgouropoulos, which are addressed to

---

see C. Gallavotti, 'Laurentiani codicis altera analecta', *Atti della Accademia Nazionale dei Lincei*, Serie VIII. *Rendiconti*, 4 (1949), 356. The anonymous author of cod. Marc. gr. 524 speaking of Manuel I says:

ὅρπηξ Μανουὴλ διπλοφυοῦς πορφύρας
Κομνηνοδουκῶν ἐξ ἀνάκτων αὐτάναξ,

see Lampros, ' *Μαρκιανὸς* 524 ', p. 51. Manuel is also called *Κομνηνοδούκας* in an inscription of Manuel Kamytzes' seal, see Laurent, *Bulles métriques*, p. 112, no. 319.

---

[1] *Alexias*, II, pp. 62–3; cf. P. Gautier, 'Le discours de Théophylacte de Bulgarie à l'autocrator Alexis I Comnène (6 Janvier 1088)', *REB*, 20 (1962), 107.

[2] *Alexias*, III, p. 236.

[3] Kinn., p. 29.

[4] Cf. R. Browning, 'The Death of John II Comnenus', *B*, 31 (1961), 229–35.

[5] De Jongh, *Généalogie des Comnène*, p. 44.

[6] Chalandon, *Les Comnène*, II, pp. 83 and 88.

[7] See H. Delehaye, *Synaxarium Ecclesiae Constantinopolitanae* (Brussels, 1902), cols. 887–90. For other editions of the *Vita* and bibliography see Moravcsik, op. cit., p. 568; see also M. Živojinović, 'Slovenski prolog žitija carice Irine', *Zbornik Radova Vizantoloshkog Instituta*, 8 II (1964), 483–92.

[8] For their approximate dates of birth, indicated in brackets, I am indebted to De Jongh, op. cit. The children of Ioannes are all enumerated by the emperor in the *Typikon* of Pantokrator, see Dmitrievskii, *Typika*, p. 663.

[9] Τοῦ περιποθήτου ἐξαδέλφου τοῦ κραταιοῦ καὶ ἁγίου ἡμῶν βασιλέως κυροῦ Ἰωάννου τοῦ Δούκα, τοῦ υἱοῦ τοῦ ἀοιδίμου πορφυρογεννήτου καὶ σεβαστοκράτορος κυροῦ Ἀνδρονίκου τοῦ περιποθήτου θείου τῆς ἁγίας αὐτοῦ βασιλείας, PG, 140, col. 252D.

[10] See R. Devreesse, *Bibliothèque Nationale. Catalogue des manuscrits grecs*. II. — *Les Fonds Coislin* (Paris, 1945), p. 5. The relevant notice which is now hardly legible has been edited by B. de Montfaucon, *Bibliotheca Coisliana olim Segueriana* (Paris, 1715), p. 41.

an emperor Alexios Komnenos[1] who seems to be Alexios III the ruler of Trebizond. The sixth poem addresses Ioannes as

'Αγγελώνυμε καὶ Δούκα
κορυφὴ ποθεινοτάτη[2]

This appears to be the only instance of an emperor of Trebizond being thus designated[3] for these μεγάλοι Κομνηνοί had of course nothing to do with the Angeloi. One can only attribute the poet's words to the influence of the compound "Αγγελος Δούκας Κομνηνός which was much in use.

Ioannes, later called Alexios, was the second-born son of the emperor Basileios of Trebizond and his mistress Eirene, being born on 5 October 1338.[4] Together with his mother he became emperor on 12 December 1349, and was crowned on 21 January 1350.[5] On 28 September 1351, he married Theodora, a daughter of Nikephoros Kantakouzenos, cousin of the emperor.[6] Alexios died on 20 March 1390,[7] Theodora on 12 November 1426.[8] He became the father of Andronikos (illegitimate),[9] Anna,[10] Basileios,[11] Manuel,[12] Eudokia,[13] and Maria.[14]

KORESSES

The family of Koresses (Κορέσσης and the more archaic Κορέσσιος) often appears in Byzantium. A twelfth-century seal belongs to a Konstantinos Koresses,[15] and a document of July 1262 speaks of a χωράφιον τοῦ Μακροκορέση in Cephalonia.[16] In 1401 Nikolaos Koreses and his son Manuel are mentioned.[17] The Koressioi established themselves in Chios from the fourteenth century onwards and became one of the most prominent houses there.[18] We do not know how the name of Doukas came to be adopted by the family.

112. Doukas Koresses: Doukas Koresses (ὁ Δούκας ὁ Κορέσης) is mentioned in a document of Chilandar dated in November 1360. He was at odds with that monastery.[19] It is possible that the man might be identified with a Koresses mentioned in the years 1341 and 1375 as inhabiting Serres.[20]

---

[1] Τοῦ πρωτονοταρίου Τραπεζοῦντος Στεφάνου τοῦ Σγουροπούλου πρὸς τὸν βασιλέα κυρὸν 'Αλέξιον τὸν Κομνηνὸν στίχοι ἐγκωμιαστικοί; see the texts in T. Papatheodorides, ''Ανέκδοτοι στίχοι Στεφάνου τοῦ Σγουροπούλου ', 'Αρχεῖον Πόντου, 19 (1954), 262–82.

[2] Ibid., p. 281.

[3] The rulers of Trebizond always employed the surname μέγας Κομνηνὸς in their signature; cf. the signature of Alexios III himself in D. A. Zakythinos, Le Chrysobulle d'Alexis III Comnène, empereur de Trébizond, en faveur des Vénitiens (Paris, 1932), p. 37.

[4] Sp. P. Lampros, ' Τὸ Τραπεζουντιακὸν χρονικὸν τοῦ πρωτοσεβαστοῦ καὶ πρωτονοταρίου Μιχαὴλ Παναρέτου ', NE, 4 (1907), 271.

[5] Ibid., p. 276.   [6] Ibid., pp. 277–8.   [7] Ibid., pp. 292–3.

[8] Ibid., p. 293.   [9] Ibid., p. 280.   [10] Ibid.

[11] Ibid., p. 281.   [12] Ibid., p. 285.   [13] Ibid., p. 290.

[14] Ibid., 294.   [15] Laurent, Collection Orghidan, p. 225, no. 444.

[16] MM, v, p. 24.   [17] MM, II, p. 546.

[18] For the branch of Chios see G. I. Zolatas, 'Ιστορία τῆς Χίου, II (Athens, 1923) pp. 355 ff.; Ph. Argenti, Libro d'Oro de la Noblesse de Chio (London, 1955), I, pp. 73–4; II, pp. 59–60; K. I. Amantos, ' Γενεαλογικὰ ἐκ Χίου ', ΕΕΒΣ, 26 (1956), 40.

[19] L. Petit, Actes de Chilandar, pp. 308–9.

[20] P. Lemerle, Actes de Kutlumus (Paris, 1946), pp. 89, 128, and 131.

KOURTIKES

The family of Kourtikes (Κουρτίκης, originally Κουρτίκιος) was of Armenian background[1] and owes its existence in Byzantine society to the chieftain Kourtikios who in 872 entered the imperial service together with his men.[2] It was probably he who fell against the Bulgarians several years later.[3] Another Kourtikes, still branded as Armenian, was associated with the revolt of Konstantinos *3* and was killed in 913.[4] In 944 Manuel Kourtikes helped Konstantinos Porphyrogenitus dethrone Romanos Lekapenos and was made *drungarios tēs viglēs*.[5] Later on Michael Kourtikes is mentioned as a partisan of Skleros (976).[6] In the eleventh century a Basileios Kourtikes, nicknamed Ioannikios, who originally came from Adrianople, fought against the Normans.[7] He is probably the same as the one whom Bryennios calls a cousin of Nikephoros Palaiologos.[8] Another Kourtikes was implicated in the conspiracy of Anemas in c. 1103.[9] In 1237 we meet a Theodoros Kourtikes.[10] In c. 1200 there is a *proto-proedros* Nikolaos Kourtikes,[11] and in the fifteenth century a scribe Ἰωάννης ἀναγνώστης υἱὸς τοῦ Κουρτίκη.[12] Kantakouzenos speaks of τὸν Ταρχανειώτην Μανουήλ, τὸν καὶ Κουρτίκην προσαγορευόμενον.[13] Finally some Kourtikai are known from sigillography.[14]

112a. Doukaina Kourtikina: A seal bears the inscription: Θεοτόκε, βοήθει Δουκαίνᾳ μοναχῇ τῇ Κουρτικίνᾳ.[15] It is not possible to tell how this nun Doukaina Kourtikina was related to the Doukai.

113. Ioannes Doukas Kourtikes: Ioannes Doukas Kourtikes is mentioned in a number of imperial documents of the years 1233–4, and at that time he filled the post of *dux* of the theme of Thrakesion (δοὺξ τοῦ θέματος τῶν Θρᾳκησίων).[16] Ioannes is qualified as a σύγγαμβρος of the emperor Ioannes III.[17]

---

[1] P. Charanis, 'The Armenians in the Byzantine Empire', *BS*, 22 (1961), 227–8.

[2] Theoph. Cont., p. 268.   [3] Theoph. Cont., p. 358.

[4] Theoph. Cont., p. 383; Ps. Sym. Mag., p. 720; Georg. Cont., p. 876.

[5] R. Guilland, 'Contribution à l'histoire administrative de l'empire byzantin: Le drongaire et le grand drongaire de la veille', *BZ*, 43 (1950), 351.

[6] Kedr., II, pp. 424 and 427.

[7] Bryen., pp. 112 and 154; *Alexias*, I, pp. 34–5; II, pp. 26 and 76.

[8] Bryen., p. 160.   [9] *Alexias*, III, p. 69.

[10] MM, IV, pp. 89–90. Two other references in MM, IV, pp. 8 and 17, belong either to him or to Ioannes *112*.

[11] MM, IV, p. 329. He is probably to be identified with an homonymous in Cos for whom see MM, VI, p. 228.

[12] Vogel–Gardthausen, *Schreiber*, p. 175.

[13] Kant., II, p. 71.

[14] See Laurent, *Bulles métriques*, p. 210, no. 604; Laurent, *Collection Orghidan*, p. 225, no. 445 (Michael Kourtikes).

[15] See V. Laurent, *Le corpus des sceaux de l'Empire byzantin*, V2 (Paris, 1965), p. 295, no. 1464. The editor assigns it to the end of the eleventh century, but this may be too early. Even if a nephew or a niece of Eirene *26* had married a member of the Kourtikes family, his or her daughter (a Doukaina Kourtikina) could not have been active as a nun before 1100.

[16] Dölger, *Regesten*, III, pp. 11–12, nos. 1731–3 and 1736–7; cf. idem, 'Chronologisches und Prosopographisches zur byzantinischen Geschichte des 13. Jahrhunderts', *BZ*, 27 (1927), 307.

[17] MM, IV, pp. 146, 147, 214, and 240.

Properly speaking, a σύγγαμβρος of that emperor would have been the husband of one of his wife's sisters.[1] But it is definitely known that the daughters of Theodoros I Laskaris were married to other men and Ioannes could not have been the husband of one of these. Another official of the same period is also called a σύγγαμβρος of Ioannes III.[2] Σύγγαμβρος must indicate a different relationship here which it is not possible to determine.

114. Georgios Doukas Maniates Kourtikes: He was an official of the empire of Trebizond and signs a document, dated November 1343, as ὁ δοῦλος τοῦ κραταιοῦ καὶ ἁγίου ἡμῶν αὐθεντὸς καὶ βασιλέως Γεώργιος Δούκας Μανιάτης ὁ Κουρτίκης.[3]

LASKARIS

The name Λάσκαρις (or Λάσκαρης) is thought to have been derived from a word in Cappadocian dialect δάσκαρης (teacher).[4] The first member of the Laskaris family known to the sources is the emperor of Nicaea Theodoros I who, judging from his marriage to a lady of the reigning house, must have been a person of some repute in the last quarter of the twelfth century. The origin and the background of Theodoros are entirely unknown and in all probability they were humble. Nevertheless he is called Komnenos,[5] and this may indicate a distant relationship with the imperial house. The Laskareis, that is the close relatives of Theodoros I, are not particularly active during the years of the Nicaean empire. Even though that emperor did not leave behind any adult male descendants, the surname itself is quite common in the later period of Byzantium and has continued to be ever since.[6]

115. Eirene Doukaina Komnene: Eirene was the eldest of the three daughters of Theodoros I Laskaris and his wife Anna, the daughter of Alexios III and Euphrosyne *101*.[7] She was born in the first years of the thirteenth century.[8]

---

[1] Michael Stryphnos, for instance, is called σύγγαμβρος of Alexios III, see *REB*, 19 (1961), 266. We know that their wives (Euphrosyne *101* and Theodora) were sisters.

[2] MM, IV, p. 179.

[3] Papadopoulos-Kerameus, 'Ἀνάλεκτα, II, p. 257; cf. Chrysanthos, 'Η 'Εκκλησία Τραπεζοῦντος (Athens, 1933), pp. 514–15. The editor has Κουρτίκας which I correct to Κουρτίκης.

[4] See Ph. Koukoules, ' Βυζαντινῶν τινων ἐπιθέτων σημασία καὶ ὀρθογραφία ', *ΕΕΒΣ*, 5 (1928), 11–12; cf. D. B. Bagiakakos, ' Βυζαντινὰ ὀνόματα καὶ ἐπώνυμα ἐκ Μάνης ', *Πελοποννησιακά*, 3/4 (1960), 208.

[5] ... πρὸς τὸν βασιλέα 'Ρωμαίων τὸν Κομνηνὸν κυρὸν Θεόδωρον τὸν Λάσκαριν; see A. Heisenberg, *Analecta. Mitteilungen aus italienischen Handschriften byzantinischer Chronographen* (Munich, 1901), p. 23.

[6] For the Laskareis see Ducange, *Familiae*, pp. 218–21. The later history of the family has been examined by B. A. Mystakides, ' Λασκάρεις 1400–1869', *ΕΕΒΣ*, 5 (1928), 130–68. A copyist's error has resulted in the appearance of a non-existent emperor Manuel Doukas Laskaris in a document of 1300; cf. Dölger, *Regesten*, IV, p. 31, no. 2224.

[7] Akrop., pp. 10 and 26; cf. Pach., I, p. 317.

[8] Chon., p. 674; Akrop., p. 9.

Eirene is called Komnene[1] and also Doukaina.[2] Eirene's first marriage (after 1212) to Konstantinos *140* was blessed by the learned metropolitan of Ephesus Nikolaos Mesarites.[3] Konstantinos *140*, however, died very soon, and she married again to the future emperor Ioannes III *72*[4] to whom she bore a son Theodoros *75*. Then while hunting Eirene fell from her horse and suffered injuries to her womb which prevented her from giving birth to other children.[5] She died, perhaps in the summer of 1239,[6] as a nun[7] with the name of Eugenia.[8]

116. Manuel Doukas Laskaris: Manuel, *oikeios* of the emperor, is mentioned as *domestikos tōn dytikōn scholōn* in a document of 1320.[9]

LIMPIDARES

117. Konstantinos Doukas Limpidares: A letter addressed to Charles de Valois, written in very bad Greek and signed by a certain Konstantinos Doukas Limpidares (Κωνσταντῖνος Δούκας ὁ Λημπηδάρης), is in fact a request for help on behalf of an Asia Minor commander in the face of Turkish pressure and the inefficiency of the Byzantine government.[10] The letter is dated in 1308.[11]

Other information on Konstantinos, or on other bearers of the name Limpidares, appears to be lacking.

---

[1] Akropolites wrote on her death Στίχοι ἐπιτύμβιοι εἰς τὴν δέσποιναν Κομνηνὴν κυρὰν Εἰρήνην in Akrop., ΙΙ, pp. 3–6; see also Sp. P. Lampros, ' Κυπριακὰ καὶ ἄλλα ἔγγραφα ἐκ τοῦ Παλατίνου κώδικος 367 τῆς Βιβλιοθήκης τοῦ Βατικανοῦ ', ΝΕ, 14 (1917), 41 (εἰς βασίλισσαν ... κλῆρον πατρῷον τὴν βασιλείαν ἀπολαβοῦσα ... κυρᾷ Εἰρήνῃ Κομνηνῇ).

[2] ... τῆς θυγατρὸς τοῦ βασιλέως κῦρ Θεοδώρου τοῦ Λάσκαρι κυρᾶς Εἰρήνης τῆς Δουκαίνης; see A. Heisenberg, *Nikolaos Mesarites, Die Palastrevolution des Johannes Komnenos* (Würtzburg, 1907), p. 10.

[3] Ibid. Akrop., p. 26, and Skout., p. 461, call her husband Andronikos Palaiologos.

[4] Akrop., p. 26; Pach., I, p. 317; Greg., I, p. 24; Kant., I, pp. 11 and 83.

[5] Greg., I, p. 44.

[6] Akrop., pp. 62–4, and Skout., p. 485, state that her death was signalled by two phenomena: first, a comet made its appearance six months before she died and was visible for three months, and then a solar eclipse occurred while ἡλίου τὸν καρκίνον διοδεύοντος περὶ μεσημβρίαν. Consequently a year must be sought in which a total eclipse occurred in June, preceded by the appearance of a comet. In 1239 there was such an eclipse on 3 June and a comet is also attested on the very same day; cf. V. Grumel, *La chronologie* (Paris, 1958), pp. 467 and 474.

[7] Akrop., ΙΙ, p. 6, vv. 104–8.

[8] Many years later her niece Theodora *74* spoke of Eirene as τῆς περιποθήτου θείας τῆς βασιλείας μου, τῆς ἀοιδίμου δεσποίνης κυρᾶς Εἰρήνης καὶ ἐν μακαρίᾳ τῇ λήξει γενομένης Εὐγενίας μοναχῆς, MM, VI, p. 225.

[9] L. Petit, *Actes de Chilandar*, pp. 131 and 134; cf. R. Guilland, 'Etudes sur l'histoire administrative de Byzance: Le domestique des scholes', *REB*, 8 (1950), 51.

[10] See H. Constantinidi–Bibicou, ' Documents concernant l'histoire byzantine déposés aux archives nationales de France ', *Mélanges offerts à Octave et Melpo Merlier*, I (Athens, 1956), p. 127; the text is also found in MM, ΙΙΙ, p. 244

[11] Constantinidi–Bibicou, op. cit., p. 128.

MACHONEOS

118. Doukas Machoneos: A document dated November 1376 is signed among others by ὁ δοῦλος τοῦ κραταιοῦ καὶ ἁγίου ἡμῶν βασιλέως Δούκας Μαχωνέος.[1] The form Μαχωνέος is peculiar and in all probability wrong.

MALAKES

Several bearers of the name Malakes (Μαλάκης) are known. Euthymios Malakes occupies a prominent place in the theological literature of the period of the Angeloi. A Malakes was a supporter of the late thirteenth-century revolt of Philanthropenos in Asia Minor.[2] An ᾿Αντώνιος Μαλάκης τάχα καὶ μοναχός (XIII s.) was a scribe.[3] Another scribe Demetrios Skylitzes Malakes, active in 1370, came from Corfu.[4] An *oikodomos* Theodoros Malakes flourished in 1296[5] and Demetrios Malakes is met with in 1314.[6] In 1374 there was ὁ τῆς πόλεως τῶν Κορυφῶν καὶ τῆς ὅλης νήσου νομικὸς σεβαστὸς Δημήτριος ὁ Μαλάκης.[7] The surname continued to be used during the Turkish occupation.[8]

The branch of Doukas Malakes is represented by two members. The name of Palaiologos is included in the compound surname of one of them, and this may perhaps suggest that the name of Doukas passed over to the Malakai through a marriage with a member of the thirteenth-century Palaiologoi. It appears that the name of Doukas proved popular in the family and eventually came to be used as a first name. A Doukas Malakes, together with others of his house, signs an archiepiscopal document of the year 1569.[9]

119. Ioannes Doukas Malakes: He was a scribe who flourished in the mid-fourteenth century. Only one manuscript of his survives, the cod. Monacensis 216 containing works of Gregorios Nazianzenos, which was written in November 1348. The colophon reads: Χεὶρ ἁμαρτωλοῦ ᾿Ιωάννου Δούκα τοῦ Μαλάκη. ῾Η παροῦσα θεολογικὴ βίβλος ἐτελειώθη κατὰ μῆνα νοέμβριον τῆς πρώτης ἰνδικτιῶνος τοῦ ͵ϛωνζ´ ἔτους.[10]

---

[1] W. Regel, E. Kurtz, and B. Korablev, *Actes de Philothée* (St Petersburg, 1913), p. 33.
[2] Pach., II, p. 299. [3] Vogel–Gardthausen, *Schreiber*, p. 38.
[4] J. Bick, *Die Schreiber der Wiener griechischen Handschriften* (Vienna, 1920), pp. 36–7, no. 25.
[5] Petit, *Actes de Chilandar*, p. 30. [6] Ibid., p. 60.
[7] MM, III, p. 248.
[8] At Thessalonica the name of χατζῆ Μαλάκης τοῦ Δήμου is included among the witnesses in a document of 1766; see K. D. Mertzios, Μνημεῖα Μακεδονικῆς ῾Ιστορίας (Thessalonica, 1947), p. 400.
[9] See P. N. Papageorgiou, ‘ ῾Η ἐν Θεσσαλονίκῃ μονὴ τῶν Βλαταίων καὶ τὰ μετόχια αὐτῆς’, ΒΖ, 8 (1899), 412.
[10] I. Hardt, *Catalogus codicum manuscriptorum graecorum Bibliothecae Regiae Bavaricae*, II (Munich, 1808); cf. Sp. P. Lampros, ‘ Λακεδαιμόνιοι βιβλιογράφοι καὶ κτήτορες κωδίκων κατὰ τοὺς μέσους αἰῶνας καὶ ἐπὶ Τουρκοκρατίας ’, ΝΕ, 4 (1907), 182. It should be noted that the first indiction does not correspond to November of the year A.M. 6857 (=1348) but to A.D. 1347. Vogel–Gardthausen, *Schreiber*, p. 176, confuse the present Ioannes with Ioannes Doukas Neokaisareites *130*.

120. Nikephoros Doukas Palaiologos Malakes: He lived in the early fifteenth century. He was a physician who left his native Mystras and settled in Constantinople. On 16 October 1415, Manuel Holobolos sent him a letter (Μανουὴλ ῾Ολοβώλου σὺν τοῖς ἁρμάτοις τῷ ἀρίστῳ καὶ λαμπροτάτῳ ᾿Ασκληπιαδῶν, κυρῷ Νικηφόρῳ Δούκα Παλαιολόγῳ τῷ Μαλάκῃ) to which Nikephoros replied on 21 October 1415 (Παλαιολόγου Δούκα τοῦ Μαλάκη ἀμοιβαῖα πρὸς κυρὸν Μανουὴλ τὸν ῾Ολόβωλον).[1] Nikephoros appears also to have been either the scribe or the possessor of cod. Bononiensis Bibl. Univ. 1808 on which (fol. 310r) the note is written: Νικηφόρος Δούκας ὁ Μαλάκης.[2]

MALIASENOS

The Maliasenoi (Μαλιασηνοί), not to be confused with the Melissenoi,[3] were wealthy and powerful landlords in thirteenth-century Thessaly where they built their family monasteries of ᾿Οξείας ᾿Επισκέψεως at Makrinitza and Νέας Πέτρας near Portaria.[4] It is through the preserved archives of these foundations that most of our information on the Maliasenoi has been transmitted. Not many of their members are known, but these few became closely related by marriages both with the imperial family of Constantinople and with the Doukai-Angeloi of Epirus.

Not much has been preserved on the background of the family. In a σημείωμα dated 10 September 1191,[5] a *pansebastos sebastos* Nikolaos Maliases is mentioned.[6] This man might well have been the founder of the family and the father of Konstantinos *121*. The form Μαλιάσης — its existence is apparently not attested elsewhere — might be the result of a palaeographical error in place of Μαλιασηνός.

121. Konstantinos Komnenos Maliasenos Doukas Bryennios: Konstantinos is mostly called Komnenos Maliasenos,[7] but the names of Doukas[8] and Bryennios[9] are occasionally attached to him, while the full four-name

---

[1] See M. Treu, 'Mazaris und Holobolos', *BZ*, 1 (1892), 88–9.

[2] V. Puntoni, 'Indice dei codici greci delle biblioteche Universitaria e Comunale di Bologna', *Studi Italiani di Filologia Classica*, 3 (1895), 396.

On Nikephoros see also Vogel–Gardthausen, *Schreiber*, p. 338; Lampros, op. cit., p. 181; Papadopulos, *Genealogie der Palaiologen*, p. 95, no. 190.

[3] For the persistent confusion concerning the two families see P. Lemerle, *L'Emirat d'Aydin* (Paris, 1957), p. 119, n. 1. For the Maliasenoi see especially De Jongh, *Généalogie des Comnène*, pp. 87–93, and B. Ferjančić, 'Porodica Maliasina u Tesaliji', *Zbornik Filozofskog Fakulteta* (of the University of Belgrade), 7 (1963), 241–9.

[4] Cf. N. A. Giannopoulos, ῾ Αἱ παρὰ τὴν Δημητριάδα βυζαντιναὶ μοναί ᾿, *EEBΣ*, 1 (1924), 210–40, and 2 (1925), 227–41; F. Stählin, E. Meyer and A. Heidner, *Pagasai und Demetrias* (Berlin-Leipzig, 1934), pp. 221–4.

[5] Grumel, *Regestes*, iii, p. 181, no. 1178.

[6] Τοῦ πανσεβάστου σεβαστοῦ κυροῦ Νικολάου τοῦ Μαλιάση; see Papadopoulos-Kerameus, ᾿Ανάλεκτα, ii, p. 363. Another reference to a member of the Maliasenos family is found in cod. Coisl. gr. 29 (XII s.): ἡ παροῦσα θεία δέλτος περιῆλθε τῷ ἁμαρτωλῷ Μαλιασήνῳ ἐξονησθεῖσα παρὰ τοῦ ⟨. . .⟩ εἰς ὑπέρπυρα κδ᾿; see R. Devreesse, *Bibliothèque Nationale, Catalogue des Manuscrits grecs*, ii. — *Les Fonds Coislin* (Paris, 1945), p. 25. It cannot be determined who this Maliasenos is.

[7] MM, iv, pp. 342 ff.

[8] MM, iv, p. 375.   [9] MM, iv, pp. 373 and 375.

compound occurs only once.[1] His epitaph was written by Manuel Holobolos who praises him as being

ῥίζης Κομνηνῶν εὐφυὴς μέγας κλάδος
καισαρόπαιδος πορφυροβλάστου τόκος.[2]

This ancestor then of Konstantinos had parents who were born in the πορφύρα and also bore the dignity of Caesar. Coupled with the name of Bryennios, often attached to the Maliasenoi, this description points to Nikephoros Bryennios and his wife Anna *107*. Apparently one of their children was claimed as the ancestor of the Thessalian magnates. The name of Doukas, borne by the family, could be plausibly explained by this connection with the Doukai-Bryennioi.

Konstantinos Maliasenos is mentioned for the last time in *c.* 1252 when Michael II of Epirus entrusted a mission to him. He had long before married Maria Komnene Angelina, a daughter of Michael I *45* of Epirus.[3] They had at least one son Nikolaos *122*. Konstantinos assumed the monastic habit without changing his name[4] and died sometime before October 1256.[5]

122. Nikolaos Komnenos Maliasenos Doukas Angelos (Bryennios):

Like his father Konstantinos *121*, Nikolaos is mostly called Komnenos Maliasenos,[6] but on several occasions the names of Doukas[7] and Bryennios[8] are included in his compound. The name of Angelos, frequently used,[9] was presumably inherited from his mother.

Nikolaos married Anna Palaiologina *154*, a niece of Michael VIII, sometime around 1255. They had at least one son Ioannes who is likewise called Komnenos Maliasenos, and only rarely does he use the names of Palaiologos and Angelos.[10] In the seventies of the thirteenth century Nikolaos and his wife assumed the monastic habit with the names of Ioasaph and Anthousa and retired to Nea Petra where they died after 1280.[11]

It is not perfectly clear who the monk Neilos Maliasenos was. He is mentioned in two inscriptions of 'Οξεία 'Επίσκεψις, the first calling him κτήτωρ δεύτερος of the monastery[12] and the other

τὸ δουκόβλαστον μοναχῶν κλέος
Μαλιασηνὸν ἐκ Βρυεννίων ἔρνος
Νεῖλον μοναχόν . . .[13]

The contention that Neilos was a second monastic name of Nikolaos[14] remains to be proved. It is possible that he was another son of Konstantinos.

---

[1] MM, IV, p. 375.
[2] See M. Treu, 'Manuel Holobolos', *BZ*, 5 (1896), 550, vv. 6–7.
[3] Skout., p. 502; MM, IV, pp. 345 and 346; Treu, op. cit., p. 550, v. 3.
[4] Cf. Treu, op. cit., p. 551, n. 1.
[5] An ὑπόμνημα of the patriarch Arsenios, dated October 1256, refers to him as τοῦ μακαρίτου ἐκείνου Κομνηνοῦ κυροῦ Κωνσταντίνου τοῦ Μαλιασηνοῦ, MM, IV, p. 354; cf. Stählin et al., op. cit., p. 222, n. 7.
[6] MM, IV, pp. 330 ff.
[7] MM, IV, pp. 362, 408, 415, and 420.
[8] MM, IV, pp. 369 and 372.   [9] MM, IV, pp. 357 ff.
[10] Cf. De Jongh, *Généalogie des Comnène*, p. 89.
[11] They are mentioned for the last time in that year in MM, IV, p. 424.
[12] Giannopoulos in *ΕΕΒΣ*, 2 (1925), 229.
[13] Ibid., p. 235.
[14] Giannopoulos in *ΕΕΒΣ*, 1 (1924), 224; Stählin et al., op. cit., p. 224.

MAMALIS

The surname Mamalis (*Μάμαλις*) has been traced to the word *μάμαλον* (small wave).[1] The family of that name was certainly included among the aristocracy. Alexios *ὁ Μάμαλος* (sic) was blinded by Andronikos I in 1185.[2] In *c.* 1400 the brothers Theodoros and Ioannes Mamalis are mentioned,[3] and in 1459 the noble Constantinopolitan Ioannes Mamalis appears in Ragusa.[4] In the sixteenth century some members of the family, still classed as noble, continued to reside at Constantinople.[5]

123. Andreas Doukas Mamalis: He is mentioned in a patriarchal document of November 1401 where he is described as οἰκεῖος τῷ κρατίστῳ καὶ ἁγίῳ μου αὐτοκράτορι, κατὰ πνεῦμα υἱὸς τῆς ἡμῶν μετριότητος. Andreas Doukas Mamalis had a dispute with his brother Georgios Mamalis over an undivided garden (κηπικὸν περιβόλιον). Other brothers mentioned in the same document are Nikolaos Mamalis and Konstantinos Mamalis as well as a sister Μαμαλῖνα ἡ ἀρχόντισσα.[6]

MANDROMENOS

124. Demetrios Doukas Mandromenos (*Μανδρομηνός*): He appears to have been a local merchant in Mesembria. We have three of his letters. One of them, dated 26 September 1453, is addressed to the *krites* Nikolaos Isidoros, and deals with the transportation of salt.[7]

MELACHRINOS

There are numerous bearers of the name Melachrinos (*Μελαχρινός*, dark-complexioned; originally *Μελαγχρ(ο)ινός*)[8] and only a few can be cited here: Meletios Melachrinos paid for cod. *Δοχειαρίου* 45 (Athous 2719) in 1272/3;[9] the *vestiarites* Nikolaos Melachrinos was a scribe who flourished in 1449;[10] Makarios Melachrinos was a monk of Laura in 1430;[11] Ioannes Melachrinos is

---

[1] G. Petropoulos in *EEBΣ*, 23 (1953), 536.   [2] Skout., p. 347.   [3] MM, II, p. 375.

[4] B. Krekić, *Dubrovnik (Raguse) et le Levant au Moyen Age* (Paris, 1961), p. 402, no. 1390.

[5] M. Crusius, *Turcograecia* (Basel, 1584), p. 91.   [6] MM, II, pp. 543-6.

[7] See the text in J. Darrouzès, 'Lettres de 1453', *REB*, 22 (1964), 85-6; cf. the editor's comments ibid., pp. 113-14.

Chalkokondyles (ed. Darkò), II, p. 197, speaks of a Μεχμέτης ὁ Μανδρομηνοῦ παῖς, a man of Greek origin who became commandant of Ancyra and then of Pisidia.

[8] Cf. F. Dölger, *Aus den Schatzkammern des Heiligen Berges* (Munich, 1948), p. 167: τῆς γυναικὸς τοῦ Μελαγχρηνοῦ Λέοντος.

[9] Sp. P. Lampros, Κατάλογοι τῶν ἐν ταῖς Βιβλιοθήκαις τοῦ Ἁγίου Ὄρους Ἑλληνικῶν Κωδίκων, I (Cambridge, 1895), p. 238.

[10] Sp. P. Lampros, ' Λακεδαιμόνιοι βιβλιογράφοι καὶ κτήτορες κωδίκων κατὰ τοὺς μέσους αἰῶνας καὶ ἐπὶ Τουρκοκρατίας ', *NE*, 4 (1907), 308-9.

[11] Bompaire, *Actes de Xéropotamou*, p. 241; Petit, *Actes de Chilandar*, p. 72.

mentioned in 1371;[1] Manuel Melachrinos was a priest of Philadelphia.[2] A priest from Corfu, Petros Melachrinos, appears in a local document of 1447.[3] In a Venetian document of 1430 several Melachrinoi (Demetrios, Ioannes, Georgios) are included among the more distinguished citizens of Thessalonica,[4] while some πάροικοι of the same name are known in the fourteenth century.[5]

125. Ioannes Doukas Melachrinos: A document of the year 1415 concerning the employees of the salina in the district of Thessalonica bears the signature: Ὁ δοῦλος τοῦ κραταιοῦ καὶ ἁγίου ἡμῶν αὐθέντου καὶ βασιλέως Ἰωάννης δοὺξ ὁ Μελαχρινός μαρτυρῶν ὑπέγραψα.[6] The editor considers the word δοὺξ as referring to the rank of Ioannes Melachrinos, ostensibly a governor of Thessalonica at that time. This cannot be accepted.

A near contemporary Venetian document refers to a Doukas Melachrinos, a noble resident of Thessalonica in 1425, whose monthly allowance was increased from 70 to 100 aspra by the Venetian senate.[7] Surely the word Doukas is here a name. The word δοὺξ in the Greek document cannot be anything but the surname of Melachrinos in an archaic form. It is very likely that both references speak of one and the same man, Ioannes Doukas Melachrinos.

MOURTZOUPHLOS

Mourtzouphlos (Μούρτζουφλος) was originally a mocking nickname which was given to Alexios V *126*. Choniates has preserved its meaning by stating that Alexios was so called because he used to contract his eyebrows in such a way that they appeared to meet over his eyes.[8] The nickname was later used as a surname. In 1313 we meet Manuel Mourtzouphlos[9] and in 1374 the priest Andronikos Mourtzouphlos.[10] Μούρτζουφλο is also a geographical name in the north Aegean Sea.[11]

The two Doukai who are also called Mourtzouphloi bear that name definitely as a nickname. It is not clear who their ancestors were.

126. Alexios Doukas: The unfortunate Byzantine emperor Alexios V Doukas is usually referred to by the contemptuous nickname of Mourtzouphlos.[12]

---

[1] MM, I, p. 372.

[2] R. Devreesse, *Codices Vaticani Graeci*. II. — *Codices 330–603* (Vatican, 1937), p. 369.

[3] Θεολογία, 3 (1925), 50.

[4] K. D. Mertzios, Μνημεῖα Μακεδονικῆς Ἱστορίας (Thessalonica, 1947), p. 50.

[5] Bompaire, *Actes de Xéropotamou*, index s.v.

[6] Euthymios Dionysiates and St. P. Kyriakides, ' "Εγγραφα τῆς ἱερᾶς μονῆς τοῦ Ἁγίου Διονυσίου ἀφορῶντα εἰς ἀγνώστους ναοὺς τῆς Θεσσαλονίκης ', Μακεδονικά, 3 (1953/5), 365.

[7] Mertzios, loc. cit.

[8] Ἐκ τοῦ συνεσπάσθαι τὰς ὀφρῦς καὶ οἷον τοῖς ὀφθαλμοῖς ἐπικρέμασθαι πρὸς τῶν ἐφήβων ἐπωνόμαστο Μούρτζουφλος, Chon., p. 742; cf. Akrop., p. 153; Skout., p. 443; Moritz, *Zunamen*, I, pp. 25–6; Ph. Koukoules, 'Βυζαντινῶν τινων ἐπιθέτων σημασία καὶ ὀρθογραφία ', EEBΣ, 5 (1928), 14–15.

[9] P. Lemerle, *Actes de Kutlumus* (Paris, 1945), p. 53.

[10] Petit, *Actes de Chilandar*, p. 326.

[11] A. Delatte, *Les Portulans grecs*. II. — *Compléments* (in Académie Royale de Belgique, Classe des Lettres et de Sciences morales et politiques, *Mémoires* 53, Brussels, 1958), p. 53.

[12] Western sources generally employ the word 'Morchufle' or variants of it.

No allusion to a supposed noble ancestry appears to have been preserved, but this silence may probably be due to the invariable hostility shown to him by both Greek and western chroniclers.[1]

Little information on Mourtzouphlos prior to 28 January 1204, has survived.[2] On that day he managed to overthrow Alexios IV Angelos, whom he put into prison and quietly disposed of a few days later,[3] while he himself became emperor. Under his predecessor, Mourtzouphlos was held in high esteem and confidence and exerted some influence. He also carried the dignity of *protovestiarios*.[4] An anonymous Greek chronicle claims that before his accession, Alexios filled the post of *megas dux*,[5] but this is certainly wrong and could have arisen through a misunderstanding of the cognomen Doukas. The same source describes him as an 'old man and decrepit, having grown thick hair and a thick beard'.[6] A week after his coup, Mourtzouphlos was crowned in the church of St Sophia.[7] He remained in his high office until the eve of Constantinople's fall to the Franks.[8]

Before he became emperor, Mourtzouphlos had married a daughter of Philokales[9] whom he seems to have deserted for the sake of Eudokia the daughter of Alexios III and Euphrosyne *101*. In the evening of 12 April 1204, Mourtzouphlos made his way out of Constantinople taking with him Eudokia and her mother. At Mosynopolis he married Eudokia, but his subsequent adventures proved tragic. Alexios III, now father-in-law to Mourtzouphlos, hated him and in the presence of Eudokia had him blinded in a bath. Deserted by all, the former emperor wandered around in Mosynopolis until the end of the year when he was caught by the crusaders. One of their captains, Thierry de Loos,

---

[1] The bias of the crusader sources is understandable. Equally unfavourable towards him is Choniates who however had good reason to be dissatisfied with the emperor, as he had deprived the historian of his office as *logothetēs tōn sekretōn* and promoted Philokales in his place (Chon., p. 749). Despite its hostility, the Chronicle of Morea (v. 732), calls him πλούσιος ἄνθρωπος, ἄρχων ἀπὸ τὴν Πόλιν. But this source is much confused in respect of contemporary Greek rulers.

[2] The chronicle of Robert de Clari contains some information on Alexios not found elsewhere. According to him, when Isaakios II and his son Alexios IV were reinstated by the Crusaders (18 August 1203), Mourtzouphlos had been in prison for seven years (this probably indicates that he had been close to Isaakios II before 1195) and was then liberated at their command. See 'La Prise de Constantinople' in C. Hopf, *Chroniques gréco-romanes* (Berlin, 1873), p. 44. A little later Mourtzouphlos advised Alexios IV to resist Frankish pressure and demands (ibid., p. 48).

[3] Chon., pp. 744-5; Akrop., p. 7; Skout., p. 444; Villehardouin, *La Conquête de Constantinople* (ed. E. Faral), II (Paris, 1961²), pp. 20-22 (nos. 221-3); cf. J. Longnon, *L'Empire latin de Constantinople et la Principauté de Morée* (Paris, 1949), pp. 43-4.

[4] Chon., p. 745; Akrop., p. 7; Skout., p. 444; cf. R. Guilland, 'Fonctions et dignités des eunuques', *EB*, 2 (1944), 213.

[5] J. Müller, 'Byzantinische Analekten', *Sitzungsberichte der kaiserlichen Akademie der Wissenschaften. Philosophisch-historische Klasse*, 9 (Vienna, 1853), p. 373, v. 227.

[6] Γέρων τριπέμπελος, δασὺς πώγωνα καὶ τὴν κάραν, ibid., v. 230. Chon., p. 750, describes Alexios as hollow by nature, having a hard voice and being hoarse in speech (ἦν γὰρ καὶ φύσει κοῖλος καὶ βαρὺς τὴν φωνὴν καὶ τὸν φάρυγγα βραγχιῶν).

[7] Villehardouin, op. cit., II, p. 20, no. 222; *Chronicle of Morea*, v. 741.

[8] Chon., p. 755, remarks that he reigned for two months and sixteen days, that is up to 12 April 1204. Cf. another chronicle published by Müller, op. cit., p. 390.

[9] Chon., p. 749 (cf. Skout., p. 445) calls him the emperor's father-in-law. This Philokales should be perhaps identified with Eumathios, an official frequently met with during the period of the Angeloi.

brought him back to Constantinople, and there an inhuman punishment was inflicted upon Mourtzouphlos, ostensibly for his treason towards the 'lawful' emperor Alexios IV. The blind man was thrown down from a high column and was killed instantly.[1]

A couple of miniatures of Alexios V Doukas have been preserved.[2]

127. Isaakios Doukas: The *primikerios* Isaakios Doukas, nicknamed Mourtzouphlos, was an official during the last years of the Nicaean empire. In *c.* 1253 he was sent as ambassador to Michael II *48* of Epirus,[3] and four years later he was put in command of an army against the Bulgarians.[4]

MOUZAKIOS

The common name Mouzakes (Μουζάκης, older form Μουζάκιος) is generally regarded as being of Albanian origin.[5] Several bearers of it are active during the Byzantine period and are encountered in sources from the eleventh century onwards. It is difficult, if not impossible, to explain the Albanian derivation of the word during that early period. The later Μουζάκηδες were certainly of Albanian background, yet this in no way proves that the Byzantine families of that name were of the same ethnic descent.

Only a few of the many Mouzakai can be mentioned here. Anna Komnene speaks of a Mouzakes of unknown first name in *c.* 1092.[6] A monk Leon Mouzakes lived in *c.* 1160,[7] and Ἀναστάσης ὁ Μουζάκης in the fourteenth century.[8] The estate of another Mouzakes is referred to in a document of 1346.[9] A manuscript notice of the year 1441/2 mentions a Theodoros Mouzakes.[10] There is also a seal

---

[1] Chon., pp. 755 and 804; Akrop., pp. 8–10; Skout., pp. 448–51; Villehardouin, op. cit., II, p. 74 no. 266, p. 78 no. 270; p. 80 no. 271; p. 114 no. 306, and pp. 114–16 nos. 307–8. Faral, ibid., p. 115, n. 3, assigns his death late in November 1204. According to Robert de Clari (op. cit., p. 81), the cruel death of Mourtzouphlos was due to the intervention of the Venetian doge Enrico Dandolo.

[2] See J. A. J. van Dieten, 'Wurden aus dem Codex Vindobonensis Historicus Graecus 53 fünf Miniaturen entfernt?' *BZ*, 55 (1962), 229; a miniature of a later period has been reproduced by Lampros, ' Λεύκωμα ', plate 72.

[3] Akrop., p. 92; Skout., p. 502.

[4] Ἡγεμόνα δὲ τοῦ στρατεύματος τὸν Ἰσαάκιον Δούκαν κατέστησεν, ὃν καὶ Μούρτζουφλον ὠνόμαζον, τῷ γένει τούτου τοὐπίκλην τινῶν ἐπιθέντων τῶν παίζειν εἰωθότων ἐπὶ τὰς κλήσεις, πριμμική-ριον ὄντα τότε τῆς βασιλικῆς αὐλῆς, Akrop., p. 144.

[5] Cf. L. Ch. Zoes, ' Βιογραφικὰ σημειώματα περὶ τῆς οἰκογενείας Μουζάκη ', ΕΕΒΣ, 3 (1926), 254–6. In the sixteenth century a Giovanni Musachi wrote the fantastic 'Breve memoria de li discendenti di nostra casa Musachi', edited by C. Hopf, *Chroniques Gréco-romanes* (Berlin, 1873), pp. 270–340; genealogy ibid., p. 532. However the word μουζάκιον is found in a source as early as the tenth century and has been interpreted as deriving from the Armenian and signifying a kind of shoe, cf. N. M. Panagiotakis, ' Λέων ὁ Διάκονος. Βιογραφικά. Χειρόγραφα καὶ ἐκδόσεις ', reprinted from ΕΕΒΣ, 34 (1965), 105, n. 3.

[6] *Alexias*, II, pp. 178–9.

[7] *PG*, 137, col. 669B.

[8] C. Giannelli, *Codices Vaticani Graeci. Codices 1684–1744* (Vatican, 1961), p. 146.

[9] W. Regel, Χρυσόβουλλα καὶ γράμματα τῆς ἐν τῷ Ἁγίῳ Ὄρει Ἄθω ἱερᾶς καὶ σεβασμίας μεγίστης μονῆς τοῦ Βατοπεδίου (St Petersburg, 1898), p. 23.

[10] A. Alexoudes, ' Δύο σημειώματα ἐκ χειρογράφων ', ΔIEEE, 4 (1892), 279.

belonging to Niketas Mouzakes.[1] In the later period the name Mouzakes becomes very common in many parts of the Greek world.[2]

128. Theodoros Doukas Mouzakios: He lived in the thirteenth century and died as the monk Theodoretos on 24 December of an unknown year.[3] Theodoros Doukas Mouzakios had given an ornamented icon of St Onouphrios and 100 hyperpyra to the monastery of Theotokos τῆς Βεβαίας 'Ελπίδος in Constantinople. He had been *epi tou stratou*.

Nothing is known on the family connections of Theodoros. The marriage of his daughter to a member of the reigning house, as well as the word εὐγενέστατος which is applied to him, indicate that his background was not a humble one. Theodoros' known daughter was Eudokia *197*, and she became the wife of Theodoros Komnenos Doukas Synadenos *196*.[4]

MOUZALON

The surname Mouzalon (*Μουζάλων*) is met with in the sources from the eleventh century[5] and in the period of the Palaiologoi becomes comparatively widespread. Several Mouzalones occupied high state and church offices. Nikolaos Mouzalon was the patriarch of Constantinople in 1147–51, and a namesake of his became bishop of Amyklai soon afterwards.[6] At approximately the same time a μαΐστωρ τῶν ῥητόρων Mouzalon flourished.[7] Georgios Mouzalon and his two brothers became powerful and much hated during the reign of Theodoros II (1254–8). They were men of humble origin from Adramytion,[8] and very shortly after the death of that emperor they all came to a violent end. Georgios had married the learned Theodora Palaiologina[9] and became the father of another distinguished official and author Theodoros Mouzalon.[10] In 1275 a Manuel Mouzalon is mentioned[11] and later in the century the *drungarios tou plōimou* Stephanos Mouzalon.[12] The *sebastos* Konstantinos Mouzalon came from

---

[1] K. Konstantopoulos, ' Βυζαντιακὰ μολυβδόβουλλα ', *JIAN*, 9 (1906), 140, no. 662b.

[2] For some place names deriving from it as well as for some *stradioti* bearing the name Mouzakes see K. E. Biris, 'Αρβανῖτες. Οἱ Δωριεῖς τοῦ νεωτέρου 'Ελληνισμοῦ (Athens, 1960), p. 197.

[3] Μηνὶ δεκεμβρίῳ κδ' τελείσθωσαν τὰ μνημόσυνα τοῦ εὐγενεστάτου συμπενθεροῦ μου ... κυροῦ Θεοδώρου Δούκα Μουζακίου τοῦ ἐπὶ τοῦ στρατοῦ, τοῦ διὰ τοῦ θείου καὶ ἀγγελικοῦ σχήματος μετονομασθέντος Θεοδωρήτου μοναχοῦ, Delehaye, *Deux Typica*, p. 94.

[4] Eudokia is called Δούκαινα Κομνηνὴ Συναδηνὴ Παλαιολογίνα (Delehaye, *Deux Typica*, p. 13) in the manner of her husband's name. She is described under the Synadenoi (no. *197*).

[5] Theophylaktos of Bulgaria wrote a poem Εἰς μοναχὸν Μουζάλωνα σιωπῶντα, see S. G. Mercati, 'Poesie di Teofilatto di Bulgaria', *SB*, 1 (1924), 177.

[6] Grumel, *Regestes*, III, p. 136, no. 1096, and p. 163, no. 1137.

[7] R. Browning, 'The Patriarchal School at Constantinople in the Twelfth Century', *B*, 23 (1963), 14.

[8] Cf. Akrop., p. 124.

[9] Papadopulos, *Genealogie der Palaiologen*, p. 20, no. 34.

[10] See M. Treu, *Maximi monachi Planudis Epistulae* (Breslau, 1890), pp. 241–3; H.-G. Beck, *Kirche und theologische Literatur im byzantinischen Reich* (Munich, 1959), pp. 679–80.

[11] Pach., I, p. 426. [12] Pach., II, p. 398.

Thessalonica (1324).[1] Kydones wrote a letter to a Mouzalon (1383/6)[2] who might possibly be identified with a wealthy nobleman of those times[3] Ioannes Mouzalon ὁ Τορνίκης lived in 1370,[4] and the ἰατροφιλόσοφος Demetrios Mouzalon is mentioned as dead in a spurious document of 1441.[5]

129. Ioannes Doukas Mouzalon: He lived in the first half of the fourteenth century and is only known from the poems of Philes. He is called *megas drungarios*,[6] and this probably means that Ioannes Doukas Mouzalon was a *megas drungarios tēs viglēs*.[7] It is not clear how he acquired the name of Doukas.

NEOKAISAREITES

The designation Neokaisareites (Νεοκαισαρείτης), that is a native of the Pontic town of Neocaesarea, served as a family name during the thirteenth and fourteenth centuries.[8] Michael Neokaisareites is mentioned in 1274[9] and is described as one of the notables of his time (τις τῶν ἐπιφανῶν).[10] He had a daughter Eudokia who became the wife of one of Andronikos II's sons.[11] Another Michael Neokaisareites was *apographeus* in 1318.[12]

130. Ioannes Doukas Neokaisareites: A considerable number of manuscripts, several of them now in the National Library of Athens, were written by a certain Ioannes Doukas Neokaisareites whose family connections and background remain totally unknown. The dated ones belong to the period 1334–66.

---

[1] MM, I, p. 100.

[2] R.-J. Loenertz, *Démétrius Cydonès, Correspondance*, II (Rome, 1960), pp. 251–2.

[3] Μουζάλων πλούσιος καὶ ἐπίσημος ὁρᾶται ἀκμάζων ἐπὶ τῶν ἡμερῶν Ἰωάννου τοῦ Α' ἐκ τῶν Παλαιολόγων, P. Lemerle, *Actes de Kutlumus* (Paris, 1945), p. 243.

[4] G. Ferrari dalle Spade, 'Registro Vaticano degli atti bizantini di diritto privato', *SB* 4 (1935), 267.

[5] Bompaire, *Actes de Xéropotamou*, p. 237.

[6] Ἐκ προσώπου τοῦ μεγάλου δρουγγαρίου εἰς τὸν Τίμιον Πρόδρομον, Philes (Miller), II, pp. 187–8. The poet concludes

ὁμώνυμός σοι ταῦτα Δούκας Μουζάλων,
ὦ λύχνε φωτός, καὶ μέγας δρουγγάριος.

Another short poem Τῷ μεγάλῳ δρουγγαρίῳ διὰ χαλινόν, Philes (Martini), p. 41, is certainly addressed to the same man, and this probably applies to two other poems to an unspecified *megas drungarios* in Philes (Miller), I, pp. 227–8, and II, pp. 167–8.

[7] Cf. R. Guilland, 'Contribution à l'histoire administrative de l'empire byzantin: Le drongaire et le grand drongaire de la veille', *BZ*, 43 (1950), 355; idem, 'Études de titulature et de prosopographie byzantines. Les chefs de la marine byzantine: Drongaire de la flotte, grand drongaire de la flotte, duc de la flotte, mégaduc', *BZ*, 44 (1951), 221.

[8] In Psellos, *Scripta Minora*, II, pp. 89–91, a letter bears the caption Τῷ Νεοκαισαρείτῃ, but this must not be taken as a surname; it only refers to the archbishop of Neocaesarea, cf. F. Drexl, 'Nachträge zur Ausgabe der Psellosbriefe von Kurtz-Drexl', *BZ*, 41 (1941), 309.

[9] Pach., I, p. 395; cf. Dölger, *Regesten*, III, p. 65, no. 2013.

[10] Greg., I, p. 293.

[11] Papadopulos, *Genealogie der Palaiologen*, p. 37, no. 60.

[12] Dölger, *Regesten*, IV, p. 71, nos. 2401–2.

Politis has observed that most of Neokaisareites' manuscripts contain one of, or both, the following verses:

(a) Τῷ τερατουργῷ τῶν καλῶν Θεῷ χάρις,
     ὕμνος, αἶνος ἄπαυστος πρέπει καὶ δόξα

(b) Χεὶρ ἁμαρτωλοῦ Ἰωάννου τοῦ Δούκα
     καὶ κακογράφου τοῦ Νεοκαισαρείτου[1]

NESTONGOS

The Byzantine family of Νεστόγγος — it also occurs in the forms Νεοστόγγος, Νεστώγκων, and Νοστόγγος[2] — owes its name to a Bulgarian prince Nestong, mentioned in c. 1018.[3] The earliest reference to a Greek family Nestongos appears to be in 1136 when the *Typikon* of the Pantokrator monastery speaks of the house of Nestogios.[4] In the thirteenth century the Nestongoi are sufficiently wealthy and prominent to be included among the noblest houses in 1258.[5] Several of them became related to the Batatzai, the Palaiologoi, the Tarchaneiotai and other leading families of the time.

Andronikos Nestongos was a first cousin of Ioannes III Batatzes, but during that emperor's early years he organized a conspiracy which, however, was foiled and was himself imprisoned at Magnesia whence he escaped to the Turks and died among them. He also had a brother Isaakios, likewise involved in the plot, who was as a result blinded and had his arm amputated.[6] In 1255 a Theodoros Nestongos was in command of the fortress of Melnik.[7] A second Isaakios Nestongos was ἐπὶ τῆς βασιλικῆς τραπέζης in 1257.[8] Pachymeres writes that Georgios Nestongos was so dear to Theodoros II that, had the emperor lived a little longer, he would have made him a son-in-law.[9] In 1259 Michael Nestongos, described as a nephew of Michael VIII, was created *protosebastos*.[10] Nikephoros Tarchaneiotes, the husband of Maria (Martha) Palaiologina,[11] had earlier (before 1237) been married to a lady of the Nestongos family. Their daughter

---

[1] In Vogel–Gardthausen, *Schreiber*, p. 176, he is confused with Ioannes Doukas Malakes *119*. For Neokaisareites see especially L. Politis, ' Σημείωμα περὶ τοῦ βιβλιογράφου Ἰωάννου Δούκα τοῦ Νεοκαισαρείτου ', Εἰς Μνήμην Σπυρίδωνος Π. Λάμπρου (Athens, 1935), pp. 587–95, where two specimens of his handwriting are given; cf. idem, 'Eine Schreiberschule im Kloster τῶν 'Οδηγῶν ', *BZ*, 51 (1958), 18–19.

[2] The correct version is Νεστόγγος; see F. Dölger, 'Chronologisches und Prosopographisches zur byzantinischen Geschichte des 13. Jahrhunderts', *BZ*, 27 (1927), 318, n. 11.

[3] Ὁ τοῦ Σιρμίου κρατῶν ἀδελφὸς τοῦ Νεστόγγου Σέρμην, Kedr., ii, p. 476; cf. Gy. Moravcsik, *Byzantinoturcica* (Berlin, 1958), ii, p. 210.

[4] Ὁ οἶκος τοῦ Νεστογίου [Νεστόγγου?] μετὰ τῶν δύο ξενοδοχείων καὶ χωραφίων, Dmitrievskii, *Typika*, p. 697.

[5] Cf. Pach., i, p. 65.

[6] Akrop., pp. 36–7.

[7] Akrop., p. 115; cf. F. Dölger, 'Zwei byzantinische Reiterheroen erobern die Festung Melnik', Παρασπορά (Ettal, 1961), p. 301, n. 6.

[8] Akrop., pp. 142 and 151.

[9] Pach., i, pp. 65 and 75.

[10] Pach., i, p. 109.

[11] Papadopulos, *Genealogie der Palaiologen*, pp. 13–14, no. 22.

was the particularly active Nostongonissa of Pachymeres.[1] Finally a Nestongos was the son-in-law of Eustathios Kinnamos (1316?).[2]

Several Nestongoi assumed the name of Doukas in the second half of the thirteenth century and later. Some of them were related to the Palaiologoi. This relationship could have come about as a result of the earlier attested bond with the family of Batatzes. But it is also possible that the name of Doukas passed to the family through a marriage concluded between the Nestongoi and an unknown cousin of Michael VIII.

131. Alexios Doukas Nestongos: In September 1267 Alexios Doukas Nestongos signed a document; he then bore the dignity of *pinkernes* and was governor of Thessalonica.[3] In the text he is referred to as cousin (ἐξάδελφος) to the emperor.[4]

132. Konstantinos Doukas Nestongos: The name of Konstantinos Doukas Nestongos who bore the dignity of *parakoimōmenos tēs megalēs sphendonēs* is given in the text of the treaty with the Venetians of 15 June 1285, which he witnessed.[5] There are also other references to him. An official γράμμα, bearing the date February indiction IV (probably 1291) is signed by Konstantinos.[6] He is also mentioned in another document of April 1292.[7]

An imperial *prostagma* bearing the date March indiction V (thought to be 1292[8]) speaks of the emperor's uncle Ioannes Doukas Nestongos as a *parakoimōmenos tēs megalēs sphendonēs*.[9] It is hard to believe that in that very short period two uncles of the emperor belonging to the branch of Doukas Nestongos held this unusual dignity. The full name of Konstantinos is attested both in the Greek and in the Latin documents, while that of Ioannes is only found in the document of 1292 and might, therefore, be a mistake. Under the circumstances, only one such *parakoimōmenos* could have existed: Konstantinos Doukas Nestongos.

Without first name, Konstantinos is mentioned by Pachymeres in connection with the visit of Andronikos Palaiologos to Tralles and the refounding of the city

---

[1] He calls her τὴν ἐκ Νοστόγγων Ταρχανειώτισσαν (Pach., II, p. 354), and this shows that she had inherited the name Νοστόγγισσα (Pach., I, pp. 292–6; II, p. 38) not from her husband but from her mother; indeed Nostongonissa is described as a daughter of Tarchaneiotes ἐκ προτέρας γυναικός (Pach., I, p. 296), who was a daughter of Andronikos 63 (A. Heisenberg, 'Aus der Geschichte und Literatur der Palaiologenzeit', *SBBAW*, 1920, p. 11).

[2] MM, I, pp. 56–7.

[3] His signature appears in the form ὁ δοῦλος τοῦ κραταιοῦ καὶ ἁγίου ἡμῶν αὐθέντου καὶ βασιλέως κεφαλὴ τῆς Θεσσαλονίκης Ἀλέξιος Δούκας Νεστώγκων πιγκέρνης; see Regel et al., *Actes Zographou*, p. 24; cf. E. Kourilas, ''Ο κατάλογος τῶν ἐπισήμων Ἀθωνικῶν ἐγγράφων τοῦ Οὐσπένσκη ', *ΕΕΒΣ*, 8 (1931), 68.

[4] Regel et al., *Actes Zographou*, p. 22.

[5] 'Avunculo imperij nostri parachimumeno magnesfendonis domino Constantino Duca Nestingo', TT, III, p. 339; cf. Dölger, *Regesten*, IV, p. 7, no. 2104.

[6] Γράμμα τοῦ παρακοιμωμένου τῆς μεγάλης σφενδόνης στέργον τὸ ἐκδοτήριον τοῦ σὺρ Ἀδάμ, issued by ὁ δοῦλος τοῦ κραταιοῦ καὶ ἁγίου ἡμῶν αὐθέντου καὶ βασιλέως Κωνσταντῖνος Δούκας ὁ Νεστόγγος, MM, IV, pp. 103–4.

[7] MM, IV, p. 258.

[8] Dölger, *Regesten*, IV, p. 16, no. 2147.

[9] Τοῦ θείου τῆς βασιλείας μου τοῦ παρακοιμωμένου τῆς μεγάλης σφενδόνης κυροῦ Ἰωάννου Δούκα τοῦ Νεστόγγου, MM, IV, p. 257.

under the new name of Andronikopolis in 1280.[1] He appears to have been made governor of it, but with the sacking of the city by the Turks he was taken prisoner.[2]

As an uncle of Andronikos II,[3] Konstantinos Doukas Nestongos may well have been a brother of Alexios *131* who is described as a cousin of Michael VIII.[4]

133. Doukas Nestongos: The first name of this active official who flourished early in the fourteenth century has not been preserved. Pachymeres calls him Doukas,[5] Nestongos Doukas,[6] or simply Nestongos.[7] In the early part of 1304 he had been governor ($\kappa\epsilon\phi\alpha\lambda\dot\eta$) of Magnesia and carried the dignity of *primikērios tēs aulēs* but the emperor made him *megas hetaireiarchēs*.[8] He was a bitter enemy of the Catalan leader Roger de Flor and being suspect he sought asylum at the monastery of Peribleptos. As soon as he dared to move out, Doukas Nestongos was caught, deprived of his titles, and thrown into prison (14 June 1304).[9] In the following year he was released and restored to his positions.[10] Then he played a leading part in the warfare against the Catalans.[11] Of the other specific ranks he held, we are informed that he acted as *epi tou stratou*.[12]

134. Doukas Nestongos: The *megas papias* Doukas Nestongos (also of unknown first name) was a Greek official in the service of the Serbian king Stephen Dušan, and in 1354 he was sent on a mission to Avignon.[13]

PALAIOLOGOS

According to a late tradition, the Palaiologoi, like the Doukai, were brought to Constantinople by Constantine the Great.[14] From its first appearance around 1080 the family emerges as quite distinguished, and the highly successful careers of its members[15] quickly brought them marriage alliances with the leading aristocracy of the day, such as the Doukai, the Komnenoi, and later the Angeloi. Frequent intermarriage among these groups created a new branch which

---

[1] $T\grave{o}\nu$ $\pi\alpha\rho\alpha\kappa\omega\iota\mu\dot\omega\mu\epsilon\nu\omega\nu$ $\tau\hat\eta\varsigma$ $\mu\epsilon\gamma\dot\alpha\lambda\eta\varsigma$ $\sigma\phi\epsilon\nu\delta\dot\omega\nu\eta\varsigma$ $Nо\sigma\tau\dot\omega\gamma\gamma\omega\nu$, Pach., I, p. 469; for the date of this incident cf. I. Ševčenko, *Etudes sur la polémique entre Théodore Métochite et Nicéphore Choumnos* (Brussels, 1962) p. 137, n. 6.

[2] Pach., I, p. 474.   [3] Cf. above p. 151, n. 5.

[4] Philes wrote a poem $\Pi\rho\grave{o}\varsigma$ $\tau\grave{o}\nu$ $\ddot\alpha\gamma\iota\omega\nu$ $\Sigma\tau\dot\epsilon\phi\alpha\nu\omega\nu$ $\tau\grave{o}\nu$ $\pi\rho\omega\tau\omega\mu\dot\alpha\rho\tau\upsilon\rho\alpha$ $\pi\epsilon\rho\grave{\iota}$ $\tau\omega\hat\upsilon$ $\kappa\tau\dot\eta\tau\omega\rho\omega\varsigma$ $\tau\hat\eta\varsigma$ $\mu\omega\nu\hat\eta\varsigma$ $\alpha\dot\upsilon\tau\omega\hat\upsilon$ $\tau\omega\hat\upsilon$ $\pi\alpha\rho\alpha\kappa\omega\iota\mu\omega\mu\dot\epsilon\nu\omega\upsilon$ $\dot\epsilon\kappa\epsilon\dot\iota\nu\omega\upsilon$, Philes (Miller), II, pp. 260–63. The man is not named; he was $\pi\alpha\rho\alpha\kappa\omega\iota\mu\dot\omega\mu\epsilon\nu\omega\varsigma$ $\tau\hat\eta\varsigma$ $\mu\epsilon\gamma\dot\alpha\lambda\eta\varsigma$ $\sigma\phi\epsilon\nu\delta\dot\omega\nu\eta\varsigma$ (p. 261, vv. 32–3), fought against the Turks, and became a monk $\Delta\iota\omega\nu\dot\upsilon\sigma\iota\omega\varsigma$ $\tau\dot\eta\nu$ $\kappa\upsilon\rho\iota\omega\nu\upsilon\mu\dot\iota\alpha\nu$ (p. 262, v. 53). He was buried in the monastery. R. Janin, *Les églises et les monastères* (Paris, 1953), p. 493, identifies him with Konstantinos Doukas Nestongos.

[5] Pach., II, pp. 502, 524, 543, 624, and 627.   [6] Pach., II, pp. 428 and 429.

[7] Pach., II, pp. 431 and 433.   [8] Pach., II, p. 429; cf. Dölger, *Regesten*, IV, p. 20, no. 2166.

[9] Pach., II, pp. 431–3.   [10] Pach., II, p. 502.

[11] Pach., II, pp. 524, 543, 549, 624, and 627.

[12] $T\iota\nu\grave{\alpha}$ $\tau\hat\omega\nu$ $\psi\iota\lambda\iota\kappa\hat\omega\nu$ $\tau\alpha\gamma\mu\dot\alpha\tau\omega\nu$ $\pi\epsilon\rho\grave{\iota}$ $\tau\grave{o}\nu$ $\mu\dot\epsilon\gamma\alpha\nu$ $\dot\epsilon\tau\alpha\iota\rho\epsilon\iota\dot\alpha\rho\chi\eta\nu$ $\hat\eta\sigma\alpha\nu$ $\tau\grave{o}\nu$ $\Delta\omega\dot\upsilon\kappa\alpha\nu$, $о\dot\upsilon\varsigma$ $\hat\eta\gamma\epsilon\nu$ $\hat\omega\nu$ $\dot\epsilon\pi\grave{\iota}$ $\tau\omega\hat\upsilon$ $\sigma\tau\rho\alpha\tau\omega\hat\upsilon$ $\pi\rho\dot\omega\tau\epsilon\rho\omega\nu$, Pach., II, p. 624.

[13] See A. V. Solovjev, 'Grecheskie arkhonti v Serbskom tsarstve XIV veka', *BS*, 2 (1930), 282.

[14] See *commentariidi I Theodoro Spandugino Cantacusino, gentilhuomo Constantinopolitano, dell' origine de principi Turchi et de costumi di quella natione* (Florence, 1551), p. 129.

[15] For some echoes of the early Palaiologoi in the Acritic epic cf. H. Grégoire, 'La carrière du premier Nicéphore Phocas', $\Pi\rho\omega\sigma\phi\omega\rho\grave{\alpha}$ $\epsilon\dot\iota\varsigma$ $\Sigma\tau\dot\iota\lambda\pi\omega\nu\alpha$ Π. $K\upsilon\rho\iota\alpha\kappa\dot\iota\delta\eta\nu$ (Thessalonica, 1953), p. 233.

derived its ancestry from all four eminent houses, and it should be remembered that both Michael VIII throughout the whole of his reign and Andronikos II up to 1315 officially signed themselves as Δούκας Ἄγγελος Κομνηνὸς ὁ Παλαιολόγος, though eventually only the last cognomen prevailed. However the double genealogical chain leading from Georgios Palaiologos (1081) to the emperor Michael VIII (born in 1224/5) who was said to have been a Διπλοπαλαιολόγος[1] cannot be established beyond dispute.[2]

The marriage of Georgios Palaiologos to Anna Doukaina 27 explains the name of Doukas which proved so popular among the Palaiologoi. In addition, there were other marriages between the two families, at least one of which (that of Alexios 138 to Anna 217) is known to us. According to the terms of reference of this work, only those Palaiologoi who are at least once called, or in any way clearly described as, Doukai are included here. There are other cases in which ancestry with the Doukai is otherwise attested[3] but these have been omitted.

135. Nikephoros Doukas Palaiologos: The *sebastos* Nikephoros Doukas Palaiologos, known from a seal reading

Γραφῶν σφράγισμα καὶ κῦρος Νικηφόρου
Δούκα σεβαστοῦ Παλαιολόγου φέρω,[4]

appears to have been the eldest son of Georgios Palaiologos and Anna 27.[5] He bears the name of his paternal grandfather. It is very likely that he should be

---

[1] Greg., I, p. 60; H. Grégoire, 'Imperatoris Michaelis Palaeologi de vita sua', *B*, 29/30 (1959/60), 449.

[2] The early Palaiologoi, that is those of the late eleventh and the twelfth centuries, are enumerated by Ducange, *Familiae*, pp. 230–32. However, the standard work for them is V. Laurent, 'La généalogie des premiers Paléologues', *B*, 8 (1933), 125–49, in which a skeleton genealogy, linking the more prominent members, is successfully established. This was further enriched and amended by the additional contributions of De Jongh, *Généalogie des Comnène*, pp. 94–105. The present writer has slightly differed from both these scholars on the genealogical position of Georgios *139*. For the suspect references to the alleged Italian origin of the Palaiologoi see D. J. Geanakoplos, *Emperor Michael Palaeologus and the West, 1258–1282* (Cambridge, Mass., 1959), pp. 17–18, n. 5. The fundamental study for the genealogical history of the house is A. Th. Papadopulos, *Versuch einer Genealogie der Palaiologen, 1259–1453* (Munich, 1938). For the descendants of the Palaiologoi after 1453 see G. E. Typaldos, 'Οἱ ἀπόγονοι τῶν Παλαιολόγων μετὰ τὴν ἅλωσιν', *ΔIEEE*, 8 (1923), 129–57, and D. A. Zakythinos, *Le Despotat grec de Morée*, I (Paris, 1932), pp. 285–97.

[3] For instance, in an epithalamium of Prodromos, published by E. Miller, *Recueil des Historiens des Croisades. Historiens grecs*, II (Paris, 1881), pp. 764–5, celebrating the wedding of a niece of Manuel I, the bridegroom is repeatedly described as a son of a dead and glorious Palaiologos (identified by Laurent, op. cit., pp. 138 ff., as Michael *137*) and as a scion of the Doukas family. As late as 1802 a document mentions a χ(ατζῆ) Παλαιολόγος Δούκας as being ἐπίτροπος in Lemnos for the school of Mount Athos, see K. Th. Demaras, ' 'Η σχολὴ τοῦ 'Αγίου Ὄρους στὰ 1800 ', 'Ελληνικά, 15 (1957), 155. [4] Laurent, *Bulles métriques*, p. 35, no. 95.

[5] In the *Timarion* in A. Ellissen, *Analekten der mittel- und neugriechischen Literatur*, IV (Leipzig, 1860), p. 50, it is implied that a son of Georgios Palaiologos and Anna *27* acted as *dux* of Thessalonica. Laurent, 'Premiers Paléologues', pp. 142–3, saw in him a certain *kouropalates* Romanos 'the son of Palaiologos', mentioned in 1092 (*PG*, 127, col. 973A), but, as De Jongh, *Généalogie des Comnène*, p. 95, points out, this is chronologically impossible as Anna *27*, born in *c*. 1068, could certainly not have been the mother of a son active only twenty-four years later. This Romanos was in fact a son of the *protonobilissimos* Georgios Palaiologos (*PG*, 127, col. 973D), perhaps a cousin of his illustrious namesake. De Jongh thinks that either Nikephoros or an unknown brother of his should be identified as this *Dux* of Thessalonica. On the contrary, Chalandon, *Les Comnène*, II, pp. 218–19, sees in him Michael Palaiologos *137*.

identified with 'Nikephoros, the nephew of the empress' (sc. Eirene *26*) who in 1117 performed an impressive act of bravery in the war against the Turks near Philomelion in Asia Minor and thus earned the emperor's warm compliments. He is described as a young man (νεανίας) at that time.[1]

136. Andronikos: Andronikos carried the dignity of *sebastos* and seems to have been called Doukas.[2] He was the second-born son of Georgios Palaiologos and Anna *27*, named after his maternal grandfather Andronikos *21*. He died early of heart failure. He preceded his parents to the grave, but eventually they were buried with him.[3] Andronikos left behind a wife (possibly a daughter of Zoe *20*) and was perhaps the father of Georgios *139*.[4]

137. Michael Palaiologos Doukas: Michael Palaiologos Doukas was active as a general during the twelfth century, but his relation to the other Palaiologoi remains unspecified. In all probability he was a grandson of Georgios and Anna *27*.[5] Michael carried the dignity of *sebastos*,[6] and during the Italian invasion of Manuel he commanded the Byzantine forces but died in Bari in 1156[7] after having become a monk. A couple of anonymous poems, written on the occasion of his death, refer to him as

> . . . Παλαιολόγου
> Δουκὸς σεβαστοῦ Μιχαήλ, . . .

and

> . . . Μιχαήλ, θαῦμα τῆς στρατηγίας,
> ἄγαλμα Δουκῶν, δόξα Παλαιολόγων.[8]

138. Alexios Palaiologos Komnenodoukas: He lived during the first half of the twelfth century and was the husband of Anna Doukaina *217*.[9] It is not possible to tell who this Alexios Palaiologos was.[10]

---

[1] *Alexias*, III, p. 203.

[2]   Σεβαστὸς ᾿Ανδρόνικος ἐκ Δουκῶν γένους,
Kallikles, p. 322.

[3] Andronikos is the subject of a moving epitaph in iambic verses by Nikolaos Kallikles. See Kallikles, pp. 321–2, no. vi (poems vii–x are likewise dedicated to Andronikos' memory). The text is now readily accessible in R. Cantarella, *Poeti Bizantini* (Milan, 1948), I, pp. 175–6, no. LXXVII. In his speech of consolation to Eirene *26* (written in 1108/18) Manuel Straboromanos alludes to the recent death of that empress's nephew (. . . λύπη δὲ αὕτη νοσεῖ, ἣν ἔχει μὲν ἐπ᾿ἀδελφῇ καλὸν παῖδα θρηνούσῃ, see P. Gautier, 'Le dossier d'un haut fonctionnaire d'Alexis I Comnène, Manuel Straboromanos', *REB*, 23 (1965), 195. This certainly refers to a son of Anna *27* and most probably to Andronikos.

[4] See below p. 155, n. 5. For a daughter of Andronikos (or Nikephoros *135*) see D. I. Polemis, ''Ανεπίγραφοι στίχοι εἰς τὸν θάνατον ᾿Ιωάννου Βρυεννίου τοῦ Κατακαλών,' *ΕΕΒΣ*, 35 (1966), especially pp. 112–14.   [5] Cf. Laurent, 'Premiers Paléologues', *passim*.

[6] Kinn., pp. 70 and 82. The poet (see below n. 8), addresses him as πανσέβαστε.

[7] Kinn., p. 151. For the part he played in Italy see Chalandon, *Les Comnène*, II, pp. 352–64.

[8] C. Gallavotti, 'Laurentiani codicis altera analecta', *Atti della Accademia Nazionale dei Lincei*. Serie VIII. *Rendiconti. Classe di scienze morali, storiche e filologiche*, 4 (1949), 361–2. The editor wrote δουκός, believing apparently that the word referred to Michael's title.

[9]   Πλὴν ἀλλ᾿ἄναξ ᾿Ανναν με σὺν ᾿Αλεξίῳ
                    τῷ συζυγοῦντι Παλαιολόγῳ σκέποις
                    Κομνηνοδούκα κλάδον ἐκ Δουκῶν γένους,
Kallikles, p. 337.

[10] Of the known persons who were called Alexios Palaiologos in the twelfth century, one was a son of Georgios *139* (Lampros, ' Μαρκιανὸς 524 ', p. 133), another was present in the synod

139. Georgios Palaiologos Doukas Komnenos: Georgios called Doukas,[1] Palaiologos,[2] (Palaiologos) Doukas Komnenos,[3] and in poetry Komnenodoukas[4] was probably the son of a son of Georgios Palaiologos and Anna *27*, possibly of Andronikos *136* through his marriage to the unknown daughter of Zoe *20*.[5] Georgios, being successively *sebastos*[6] and *pansebastos sebastos*,[7] acted in the capacity of *megas hetaireiarches*.[8] In 1162 he was dispatched on a diplomatic mission to Hungary[9] and in 1167 escorted an imperial princess to her bridegrom king Amaury of Jerusalem.[10]

of 6 March 1166 (*PG*, 140, col. 252C), and a third was the maternal grandfather of Michael VIII (Dmitrievskii, *Typika*, p. 787). The second of them might have been the present Alexios.

---

[1] In a poem of Prodromos, see S. Papademetriou, *Theodor Prodrom* (Odessa, 1905), p. 90 (cf. ibid., p. 104).
[2] Kinn., p. 215; *PG*, 140, col. 236D and 252C; Lampros, ' Μαρκιανὸς 524 ', p. 28.
[3] Ibid., pp. 28, 141, and 145.   [4] Ibid., p. 28; in his seal (see the following note).
[5] Both Laurent, 'Premiers Paléologues', p. 146, and De Jongh, *Généalogie des Comnène*, pp. 100–3, consider Georgios as a great grandson of Anna *27*, a view which is not shared by the present writer. De Jongh, op cit., pp. 104–5, has recognised that in order to explain the chain of compound family names and other minor points, we must assume a marriage between a son of Anna *27* and the unknown daughter of Zoe *20*. This is plausible enough, but whereas by a series of ingenious assumptions she concludes that Georgios was a grandson of that union, I am inclined to see him as a son for the following reasons: (1) The name itself of Georgios, according to the popular Greek custom, ought to be that of the grandfather; it is obvious that it was given in honour of the elder Georgios Palaiologos. (2) For all their flamboyance, the anonymous poems published by Lampros appear to give an indication of Georgios' parents. There is a clearcut distinction between his father who was a Palaiologos and his mother a 'Komnenodoukaina', who was an emperor's granddaughter (cf. Lampros, ' Μαρκιανὸς 524', pp. 138 and 143). Leaving aside the Komnenian emperors (who were very closely related to Georgios), the grandfather of Georgios' mother ought necessarily to be Konstantinos *12*. (3) A seal published by Laurent, *Bulles métriques*, pp. 163–4, no. 466, and bearing the legend
Σφραγὶς τῶν γραφῶν σεβαστοῦ Γεωργίου
πορφυροβλαστόπαιδος Κομνηνοδούκα,
is dated by its learned editor to the thirteenth century and is cautiously assigned to an untraced prince of the Trapezountian court. I believe it belongs to our Georgios. Its inscription can be compared with a parallel text concerning the same man:
Σὺν γοῦν σεβαστὸν μέγαν ἑταιρειάρχην
Γεώργιόν με Κομνηνοδούκαν σκέποις,
see Lampros, ' Μαρκιανὸς 524 ', p. 28 (I have corrected Κομνηνὸν Δούκαν to Κομνηνοδούκαν). What is of interest here is the word πορφυροβλαστόπαιδος, the reading of which seems certain. Properly speaking, the compound means 'the son of a *porphyroblastos*', which I take as implying the grandson of a *porphyrogennetos* as neither of Georgios' parents could possibly have been son or daughter of an emperor. In fact (again excluding the Komnenoi), we are once more led to the two children of Konstantinos *12*, namely Konstantios *17* and Zoe *20*. As the former died childless, only Zoe *20*, as the wife of Adrianos Komnenos, corresponds to the description of Georgios' grandmother.
[6] Kinn., p. 215 (1162); *PG*, 140, col. 236D (1166); Lampros, ' Μαρκιανὸς 524 ', pp. 28, 138, 141, and 145; see the preceding note.
[7] *PG*, 140, col. 252C (1166). However, there might be a misunderstanding in respect of this dignity. Several persons, including Georgios, are described as *sebastoi* in a document of 2 March 1166, and as *pansebastoi sebastoi* in another of 6 March of the same year. If these dignities are distinguishable it is difficult to imagine that all were promoted during the short interval of four days.
[8] Kinn., p. 215 (1162); *PG*, 140, cols. 236D and 252C (1166); Lampros, ' Μαρκιανὸς 524 ', p. 28.
[9] Kinn., p. 215; cf. Chalandon, *Les Comnène*, II, pp. 474–5.
[10] William of Tyre in *PL*, 201, col. 779C; cf. Dölger, *Regesten*, II, p. 81, no. 1477.

We know of one of Georgios' brothers, Konstantinos Palaiologos by name.[1] By a marriage to an unidentified wife, Georgios had a son Alexios.[2]

140. Konstantinos Doukas Palaiologos: The *despotes* Konstantinos Doukas Palaiologos lived during the early thirteenth century, but his parentage remains unspecified. He became the first husband of Eirene Doukaina *115* — their marriage was blessed by Nikolaos Mesarites at Nicaea[3] — in *c.* 1212. Konstantinos, however, died shortly afterwards,[4] apparently without issue.

141. Andronikos Doukas Komnenos Palaiologos: A seal which bears the metrical inscription

Σφράγισμα γραφῶν ᾿Ανδρονίκου τοῦ Δούκα
Κομνηνοφυοῦς Παλαιολόγου γένους

has been assigned to the father of Michael VIII.[5] Akropolites calls him Komnenos Palaiologos.[6] His son claimed that Andronikos descended from imperial princesses.[7]

Andronikos flourished as a general under Batatzes. He died shortly after 1246[8] having assumed the monastic habit with the name of Arsenios.[9] In the course of his career he had acted as *megas domestikos*.[10]

It seems that Andronikos married twice. His first wife Theodora (she also

---

[1] *PG*, 140, col. 252C.

[2] Lampros, ' Μαρκιανὸς 524 ', p. 133 (cf. above p. 154, n. 10).
The so-called autobiography of Michael VIII mentions an ancestor of his called Georgios Palaiologos who had built the monastery of St Demetrios in Constantinople, see Grégoire, op. cit., p. 463. It is not clear whether he is meant to be our Georgios or the elder one.

[3] Φθάνει γὰρ ὁ Μεσαρίτης Νικόλαος ὁ τῆς ᾿Εφέσου ἀρχιεπίσκοπος ἱερολογῆσαι τὸν δεσπότην κῦρ Κωνσταντῖνον τὸν Δούκαν τὸν καὶ Παλαιολόγον μετὰ τῆς θυγατρὸς τοῦ βασιλέως κῦρ Θεοδώρου τοῦ Λάσκαρι τῆς κυρᾶς Εἰρήνης τῆς Δουκαίνης ἐν τῷ περιόπτῳ κάστρῳ Νικαίας, σάκκον περιβληθεὶς μετὰ καὶ τῆς λοιπῆς ἀρχιερατικῆς στολῆς; see A. Heisenberg, *Nikolaos Mesarites, Die Palastrevolution des Johannes Komnenos* (Würtzburg, 1907), p. 10.

[4] Akrop., p. 26, calls him Andronikos Palaiologos (cf. Skout., p. 461), and he relates two different versions on the circumstances of his death. In one passage the author claims that Andronikos met his end as a result of some love adventure (μετ᾿οὐ πολὺ δὲ ὁ δεσπότης Παλαιολόγος θνῄσκει, ὡς μὲν τινὲς ἔφασκον ἐξ ἐρωτικῶν διαθέσεων, Akrop., p. 26), and a few pages below it is alleged that the same Palaiologos was killed at the battle of Lentiana (Akrop., p. 29; Skout., p. 464). This inconsistency, coupled with the fact that Akropolites himself was not yet born while these events were taking place, makes the other source, which calls the man Konstantinos, more credible.

[5] Laurent, *Bulles métriques*, p. 165, no. 469. Another seal reading

Παλαιολόγος ᾿Ανδρόνικός με γράφει
Κομνηνοδουκῶν ἐξ ἀνάκτων ὀσφύος
ὁ πρωτοπανσέβαστος ἐξυπέρτατος

(ibid., p. 224, no. 661) may also belong to him.

[6] Akrop., p. 83.

[7] ᾿Ο μὲν οὖν πατὴρ εἰς βασιλίδων καὶ βασιλέως γαμβροὺς ἀναφέρει τὸ γένος προγόνους, see Grégoire, op. cit., p. 449.

[8] Akrop., p. 86; Skout., p. 498.

[9] Dmitrievskii, *Typika*, p. 787. There is a monody on the death of Andronikos by Iakobos of Bulgaria. He addresses the dead as follows:

᾿Ανδρόνικε μέγιστε ἐν στρατηγίαις
ῥίζης Κομνηνῶν εὐερνέστατον πρέμνον

and also refers to his monastic name Arsenios; see S. G. Mercati, 'Sulla vita e sulle opere di Giacomo di Bulgaria', *Izvestiya Bulgarskago Arkheologicheskago Instituta*, 9 (1935), 175.

[10] Akrop., p. 84; Greg., I, p. 69 (says that Theodoros I gave him the position); Dimitrievskii, *Typika*, p. 787.

became a nun with the name of Theodosia) was a daughter of Alexios Palaiologos and Eirene (the daughter of Alexios III and Euphrosyne *101*)[1] by whom he became the father of Michael *142*, Ioannes, Maria (Martha), and Eirene (Eulogia). After Theodora's death, Andronikos married again and this time became the father of Konstantinos *149*.

142. Michael Doukas Angelos Komnenos Palaiologos: The official name of the founder of the last dynasty of Byzantium was Michael Doukas Angelos Komnenos Palaiologos.[2] More common are the names Komnenos[3] and Palaiologos[4] used by the narrative sources. Michael was the eldest[5] son of Andronikos *141* and his first wife Theodora and was born, presumably in Asia Minor, in 1224/5.[6]

Under Batatzes, Michael had already achieved distinction and held various military posts. In 1252/3 he was made *megas kontostablos*[7] and shortly after the assassination of Mouzalon (September 1258) *megas dux*.[8] It seems that approximately at the same time he was named *basileopatōr*,[9] and a little later (13 November 1258) he attained the very high dignity of *despotes*.[10] Michael's meteoric rise to power simply paved his way to the throne. It has now been established that he was first proclaimed emperor at the palace of Nymphaeum on 1 January 1259.[11] Sometime afterwards he was crowned at Nicaea,[12] and this was repeated at Constantinople at the end of August 1261.[13] Michael reigned until his death which occurred in a village in Thrace on 11 December 1282.[14]

---

[1] Greg., I, p. 69; Dmitrievskii, *Typika*, p. 787.

[2] Cf. the pattern used consistently in his signature, e.g. in MM, III, pp. 84 and 96; IV, p. 28; V, pp. 13 and 20; VI, p. 201. See also an inscription in A. Boeckh–J. Franz, *Corpus Inscriptionum Graecarum*, IV (Berlin, 1877), p. 346, no. 8754. An introductory poem to the *Typikon* of the monastery of Ἀρχαγγέλου Μιχαὴλ calls him

Ὁ Μιχαὴλ σοι ταῦτα Ῥωμαίων ἄναξ
Κομνηνοφυής, Δουκοφυής, ἐκ γένους
Παλαιολόγος Ἄγγελος εὔνουν τρέφων,

see P. N. Papageorgiu, 'Zwei iambische Gedichte saec. XIV und XIII', *BZ*, 8 (1899), 677. The double name Komnenos Palaiologos is employed by Greg., I, pp. 49, 68, 70, and 72.

[3] Akrop., pp. 84, 93 etc.; Greg., I, p. 70; Skout., pp. 503 and 528; Sphrantzes, pp. 7, 10, 14, and 16.

[4] Akrop., p. 90; Greg., I, pp. 57 ff.; Skout., pp. 501 ff.; Pach., I, pp. 18 ff.; Sphrantzes, pp. 11 and 15. [5] Akrop., p. 84.

[6] The date is based on the calculations of Akrop., p. 98, who makes him twenty-seven in *c.* 1252 and of Pach., I, p. 531, who puts Michael's age at fifty-eight on his death in 1282; cf. Papadopulos, *Genealogie der Palaiologen*, p. 3, no. 1; Geanakoplos, op. cit., p. 17.

[7] Akrop., p. 134; Pach., I, p. 21; cf. R. Guilland, 'Etudes sur l'histoire administrative de l'empire byzantin: Le Grand Connétable', *B*, 19 (1949), 104.

[8] Pach., I, p. 68; cf. R. Guilland, 'Etudes de titulature et de prosopographie byzantines: Les chefs de la marine byzantine. Drongaire de la flotte, grand drongaire de la flotte, duc de la flotte, mégaduc', *BZ*, 44 (1951), 229. [9] Pach., I, p. 75.

[10] Pach., I, p. 79; Akrop., p. 169; Greg., I, p. 71; cf. R. Guilland, 'Etudes sur l'histoire administrative de l'empire byzantin: Le Despote', *REB*, 17 (1959), 57–8. The exact date is given by an anonymous chronicle published by R.-J. Loenertz, 'La chronique brève de 1352', *OCP*, 29 (1963), 333; cf. the editor's comments, ibid., p. 341 and P. Wirth, 'Die Begründung der Kaisermacht Michaels VIII Palaiologos', *JÖBG*, 10 (1961), 89–90.

[11] The date is given by Pach., I, pp. 81 and 96, and is confirmed by the chronicle of 1352 (Loenertz, op. cit., cf. p. 333), see Wirth, op. cit., pp. 85–9. For a summary of earlier views cf. Ostrogorsky, *History*, p. 397, n. 2, and Geanakoplos, op. cit., p. 46, n. 67.

[12] Wirth, op. cit., p. 91.   [13] Ibid.; Geanakoplos, op. cit., pp. 121–2.

[14] Pach., I, p. 531; Gregoras, I, p. 159; cf. Geanakoplos, op. cit., p. 370.

He was buried without any ecclesiastical rites, and his remains appear to have been transferred to the monastery of Christ at Selybria.[1]

In 1253 Michael married Theodora 74[2] by whom he became the father of the following children: Manuel, Andronikos 143, Konstantinos 148, Theodoros, Eirene, Anna, and Eudokia. He also had two illegitimate daughters Euphrosyne and Maria, the second by his mistress Diplobatatzaina.[3]

Some portraits of Michael survive.[4] So does his seal bearing the legend: Μιχαὴλ ἐν Χριστῷ τῷ Θεῷ πιστὸς βασιλεὺς καὶ αὐτοκράτωρ Ῥωμαίων Δούκας Ἄγγελος Κομνηνὸς ὁ Παλαιολόγος καὶ νέος Κωνσταντῖνος.[5]

143. Andronikos Doukas Angelos Komnenos Palaiologos: The Byzantine emperor Andronikos II employed the signature Ἀνδρόνικος Δούκας Ἄγγελος Κομνηνὸς ὁ Παλαιολόγος up to 1314, and then simply Ἀνδρόνικος ὁ Παλαιολόγος during the period afterwards.[6] He was the second son of Michael 142 and Theodora 74, being born on 25 March 1259[7], probably at Nicaea. Together with his parents he was crowned at St Sophia at the end of August 1261[8] and on the death of his father on 11 December 1282, he succeeded him. Andronikos was forced to abdicate on 23/24 May 1328,[9] and assumed the monastic habit with the name of Antonios on 30 January 1330.[10] He died in the night of 12/13 February 1332,[11] and was buried in the monastery of Lips.[12]

[1] Loenertz, op. cit., p. 33.   [2] Akrop., p. 101.

[3] Cf. Papadopulos, *Genealogie der Palaiologen*, pp. 3–4, no. 1.

[4] Lampros, Λεύκωμα, pl. 75–6.

[5] K. M. Konstantopoulos, ''Η δίκη τοῦ σεκρέτου', ΕΕΒΣ, 10 (1933), 293. For other references to the formula νέος Κωνσταντῖνος, used by Michael, cf. Geanakoplos, op. cit., p. 121, n. 8.

[6] It has been observed by F. Dölger in *BZ*, 34 (1934), 126, n. 1; 35 (1935), 258 and 505; 39 (1939), 333, n. 3; *Regesten*, IV, p. 68, no. 2383, that all signed documents of Andronikos bear the long compound up to February 1314 and his patronymic proper after January 1316. For the year 1315 there are no records. On one occasion Pach., II, p. 433, calls him ὁ Δούκας καὶ βασιλεὺς while Akrop., p. 188, calls him Komnenos. Philes says

> πρὸς τὸν κραταιότατον αὐτάνακτά μου
> Κομνηνὸν Ἀνδρόνικον Ἄγγελον Δούκαν
> Παλαιολόγον τὴν πνοὴν τῶν Αὐσόνων

or

> . . . ὁ κρατάρχης Αὐσόνων
> Κομνηνὸς Ἀνδρόνικος Ἄγγελος Δούκας
> Παλαιολόγος . . .

see Philes (Martini), pp. 2 and 15. A contemporary inscription refers to him as τοῦ μεγάλου βασιλέως Ἀνδρονίκου Κομνηνοῦ τοῦ Παλαιολόγου; see S. K. Kougeas, ' Βυζαντινὴ ἐπιγραφὴ ἐκ Βερροίας ', Ἑλληνικά, 7 (1934), 104.

[7] There are several indications about Andronikos' age in the narrative sources (cf. Papadopulos, *Genealogie der Palaiologen*, p. 35, n. 2 and 4; F. Dölger, Παρασπορά [Ettal, 1961], p. 186, n. 32), but these fail to establish the exact date of his birth. A manuscript notice, edited by I. Ševčenko, *Etudes sur la polémique entre Théodore Métochite et Nicéphore Choumnos* (Brussels, 1962), p. 137, n. 6, discloses that on 25 March 1326, the emperor's years were calculated and found to be exactly sixty-six 'for on the day of the Annunciation (i.e. 25 March) he was born'. This conclusively points to 25 March 1259.   [8] Dölger, Παρασπορά, p. 186.

[9] Greg., I, pp. 419–20; Loenertz, op. cit., p. 39, no. 19 (cf. his comments ibid., p. 43); cf. Ševčenko, op. cit., p. 8, n. 2.   [10] Loenertz, op. cit., p. 40, no. 22; cf. his comments ibid., p. 48.

[11] Greg., I, p. 472; Loenertz, op. cit., p. 40, no. 26 (cf. his comments ibid., pp. 50–1). Greg., I, pp. 465–72, gives the text of a funeral speech he delivered on the occasion. For another one written by Theodoros Kabasilas on Andronikos' death see I. Ševčenko, 'Nicolaus Cabasilas' Correspondence and the Treatment of Late Byzantine Literary Texts', *BZ*, 47 (1954), 56, n. 5.

[12] Greg., I, p. 463.

Andronikos was married twice, both times to western princesses. His first wife was Anna, a daughter of the Hungarian king Stephen IV whom he married on 8 November 1273.[1] Anna became the mother of two sons, Michael *145* and Konstantinos and died in 1281/2. In *c.* 1285 Andronikos married Yolande of Montferrat who assumed the Greek name of Eirene *144*. She bore him several children: Ioannes, Theodoros *146*, Demetrios *147*, and Simonis. Besides these, Andronikos had two illegitimate daughters: Maria and Eirene.[2]

Several miniatures of Andronikos are known.[3]

144. Eirene Komnene Doukaina Palaiologina: There is a seal which bears the inscription: Εἰρήνη εὐσεβεστάτη αὐγοῦστα Κομνηνὴ Δούκαινα ἡ Παλαιολογῖνα.[4] The editor attributes it with reason to the second wife of Andronikos II *143*. Eirene was the daughter of William, marquis of Montferrat, and his wife Beatrice, a Spanish princess. Her original name was Yolande which was changed to Eirene after her marriage to Andronikos in *c.* 1285. She died at Drama in Macedonia in 1317 and her remains were brought to Constantinople and buried in the monastery of Pantokrator.[5]

145. Michael Doukas Angelos Komnenos Palaiologos: Michael, the elder son of Andronikos *143* and his first wife Anna, employed the usual pattern of compound names in his signature as a co-emperor.[6] He was born in 1277.[7] He was already crowned by his grandfather in 1281,[8] and there was another more significant coronation on 21 May 1295, which gave extensive prerogatives to Michael.[9] He died on 12 October 1320.[10]

---

[1] Pach., I, p. 318; cf. Greg., I, p. 109.

[2] Papadopulos, *Genealogie der Palaiologen*, p. 35, no. 58.

[3] See the reproductions in Lampros, Λεύκωμα, pl. 77–80.

[4] N. P. Likhachev, *Istoricheskoe znachenie Italo-grecheskoi ikonopisi* (St Petersburg, 1911), p. 35, no. 19. For Eirene see Ch. Diehl, *Figures byzantines*, II (Paris, 1927), pp. 226–45; H. Constantinidi-Bibicou, 'Yolande de Montferrat, impératrice de Byzance', *L'Hellénisme Contemporain* 4 (1950), 425–42.

[5] Greg., I, p. 273. Philes wrote a poem on her death (ἐπιτάφιοι δεσποινικοί, Martini, pp. 13–17, vv. 65) in which he enumerates Eirene's children by their order of birth: Ioannes, Simonis, Theodoros *146*, Theodora, Isaakios, Demetrios *147*, and Bartholomaios. Another Μονῳδία ἐπὶ τῇ μακαρίτιδι καὶ ἀοιδίμῳ δεσποίνῃ Κομνηνῇ κυρᾷ Εἰρήνῃ τῇ Παλαιολογίνῃ by Alexios Lampenos was edited by Sp. P. Lampros, ' Αἱ μονῳδίαι Ἀλεξίου τοῦ Λαμπηνοῦ καὶ ὁ οἶκος τοῦ Ἀνδρονίκου Α' Παλαιολόγου ', *NE*, 11 (1914), 377–82.

[6] Μιχαὴλ ἐν Χριστῷ τῷ Θεῷ πιστὸς βασιλεὺς καὶ αὐτοκράτωρ Ῥωμαίων Δούκας Ἄγγελος Κομνηνὸς ὁ Παλαιόλογος; see F. Dölger, *Facsimiles byzantinischer Kaiserurkunden* (Munich, 1931), p. 35; idem, *Aus den Schatzkammern des Heiligen Berges* (Munich, 1948), p. 39. Philes (Martini), p. 83, vv. 18–19, calls him

> ἄναξ Μιχαὴλ Παλαιολόγος Δούκας
> Κομνηνοφυὴς εὐσεβὴς αὐτοκράτωρ.

Cf. Philes (Miller), II, p. 261.

[7] When he died in 1320, he was forty-three, Kant., I, p. 13.

[8] Cf. Dölger, *Paraspora*, p. 187.

[9] Pach., II, p. 195; cf. J. Verpeaux, 'Notes chronologiques sur les livres II et III du De Andronico Palaeologo de Georges Pachymère', *REB*, 17 (1959), 170–73.

[10] Greg., I, p. 277; Kant., I, p. 13; Sphrantzes, p. 33. Choumnos wrote three poems on his death; see E. Martini, 'Spigolature bizantine. I versi inediti di Niceforo Chumno', *Nota letta all'Accademia d'Archeologia, Lettere e Belle Arti della Società Reale di Napoli*, 9 An. 3 (1900), 121–9; Michael Gabras also wrote (a now lost) funeral oration on him; see R. Guilland, *Nicéphore Grégoras, Correspondance* (Paris, 1927), pp. 334–5.

On 16 January 1295,[1] Michael married the Armenian princess Rita who assumed the Greek name of Maria. They became the parents of four children: Andronikos III, Manuel, Anna, and Theodora.[2]

146. Theodoros Komnenos Doukas Angelos Palaiologos: The *porphyrogenitus* Theodoros, the son of Andronikos *143* and Eirene *144*, in a document of his half-brother Michael *145*, dated December 1316, is referred to as Komnenos Doukas Angelos Palaiologos.[3] Theodoros was born in about 1288 and since 1305 acted as the marquis of Montferrat where he founded a long-lasting dynasty.[4] In 1326 he wrote a didactic work which is preserved only in a French translation.[5] He died in 1338.

147. Demetrios Angelos Doukas Palaiologos: These names appear in a poem on a Menologion.[6] The editor assigns them to the son of Andronikos *143* and Eirene *144*[7] who is known to have carried the dignity of *despotes*.[8] Demetrios was born after 1294—he was, therefore, a porphyrogenitus—and died after 1343.[9]

Demetrios married, perhaps a certain Theodora,[10] and had a daughter Eirene and perhaps two other children.

148. Konstantinos Doukas Palaiologos: A seal reading:

Σφραγὶς ὁ Χριστὸς καὶ φυλακτὴρ καὶ σκέπη
ἀνακτόπαιδος δεσπότου Κωνσταντίνου
καὶ πορφυρανθοῦς Δούκα Παλαιολόγου[11]

may belong to Konstantinos, the third son of Michael *142* and Theodora *74*. He was a porphyrogenitus, born after 1260, but in spite of his prerogatives in the court he is never mentioned by other sources as *despotes*.[12] Konstantinos married

---

[1] The references are cited by Papadopulos, *Genealogie der Palaiologen*, p. 36, n. 19; cf. Ševčenko, *Etudes*, p. 129, n. 6.

[2] Papadopulos, *Genealogie der Palaiologen*, pp. 36–7, no. 59.

[3] Τοῦ ὑψηλοτάτου μαρκέση Μοντεφεράντη πορφυρογεννήτου Κομνηνοῦ κυρίου Θεοδώρου Δούκα Ἀγγέλου τοῦ Παλαιολόγου; see F. Cognasso, 'Una crisobolla di Michele IX Paleologo per Teodoro I di Monferrato', *SB*, 2 (1927), 46; cf. p. 47.

[4] Cf. Papadopulos, *Genealogie der Palaiologen*, pp. 39–40, no. 62. For some aspects of his rule in Italy see D. A. Zakythinos, ''Ο μαρκίων τοῦ Μομφερράτου Θεόδωρος Α' Παλαιολόγος καὶ ὁ βασιλεὺς τῆς Γαλλίας Φίλιππος ὁ ϛ' ', *EEBΣ*, 11 (1935), 16–28.

[5] Ševčenko, op. cit., pp. 163–6.

[6]   Παλαιολόγος Ἄγγελος Δούκας τάδε
βασιλέως παῖς εὐσεβὴς καὶ δεσπότης
Δημήτριος τὴν κλῆσιν ἐκ Δημητρίου,
see P. Joannou, 'Das Menologion des Despoten Demetrios I. Palaiologos', *BZ*, 50 (1957), 308.

[7] Papadopulos, *Genealogie der Palaiologen*, pp. 40–1, no. 63.

[8] Cf. Guilland, 'Le despote', p. 61.

[9] F. Dölger, *Byzantinische Diplomatik* (Ettal, 1956), p. 95.

[10] Papadopulos, *Genealogie der Palaiologen*, p. 40, no. 63, says that his wife was of unknown name. Philes (Miller), II, p. 154, speaks of a Κομνηνοφυὴς Θεοδώρα as the wife of an unnamed porphyrogenitus. Now of the porphyrogeniti sons of Michael VIII only Theodoros (Papadopulos, p. 27, no. 43) had a wife of unknown name who could have been called Theodora. Of the wives of the porphyrogeniti sons of Andronikos only that of Demetrios is never mentioned. Consequently she may be the Theodora of Philes.

[11] Laurent, *Bulles métriques*, pp. 149–50, no. 424, who attributes it to the last emperor of Byzantium. The only other porphyrogenitus Konstantinos to whom the seal may belong is the son of Michael VIII.

[12] Cf. Guilland, 'Le despote', pp. 58–9.

Eirene, a daughter of Ioannes Raoul *181* and became the father of a son Ioannes. He died as the monk Athanasios on 5 May 1306.[1]

149. Konstantinos Angelos Komnenos Doukas Palaiologos: Konstantinos was a junior half-brother of Michael VIII, being a son of Andronikos *141* and his second unknown wife.[2] He may have been born in *c.* 1230. His full name is found in the *Typikon* of the convent of *Βεβαίας Ἐλπίδος*.[3] Konstantinos was honoured with two high dignities by his emperor brother being made *caesar* in 1259[4] and *sebastokrator* shortly afterwards.[5] In 1263–4 he was sent to the Peloponnese in a drive against the Frankish strongholds but was not particularly successful.[6]

In 1260 Konstantinos married Eirene Branaina Komnene Laskarina Kantakouzene.[7] Both died at approximately the same time in *c.* 1270 after having taken monastic vows with the names of Kallinikos and Maria.[8] Konstantinos was the father of five children: Michael, Andronikos *150*, Maria *151*, Na, and Theodora.[9]

150. Andronikos Komnenos Branas Doukas Angelos Palaiologos: He was the son of Konstantinos *149* and his wife Eirene.[10] His full name is given in the *Typikon* of *Βεβαίας Ἐλπίδος*.[11] Andronikos appears to have followed a military career[12] and died as the monk Arsenios on 28 June of an unknown year before 1310/46.[13]

[1] Papadopulos, *Genealogie der Palaiologen*, p. 23, no. 37.

[2] There are two passages which make it clear that Michael and Konstantinos were the sons of Andronikos *141* but by different mothers. Akrop., p. 161, remarks τὸν δὲ αὐτάδελφον αὐτοῦ (sc. Μιχαήλ) Κωνσταντῖνον ἐξ ἑτέρας ὄντα τούτῳ μητρός, and Greg., I, p. 72 (cf. p. 80), refers to him as ἀμφιμήτριος ἀδελφὸς of Michael *142*. Papadopulos, *Genealogie der Palaiologen*, p. 6, no. 5, does not differentiate.

[3] . . . τοῦ πανευτυχεστάτου σεβαστοκράτορος Κομνηνοῦ τοῦ Παλαιολόγου Δούκα τοῦ Ἀγγέλου κυροῦ Κωνσταντίνου τοῦ διὰ τοῦ θείου καὶ ἀγγελικοῦ σχήματος μετονομασθέντος Καλλινίκου μοναχοῦ, Delehaye, *Deux Typica*, p. 81. In a slightly different form his name is found in the inscription below his portrait in the same document: Κωνσταντῖνος Κομνηνὸς Παλαιολόγος ὁ παν⟨ευ⟩τυχέστατος σεβαστοκράτωρ καὶ πατὴρ τῆς ἐκτητορίσσης, ibid., p. 12.

[4] Akrop., p. 161; Pach., I, p. 97; cf. R. Guilland, 'Etudes sur l'histoire administrative de l'empire byzantin: le Césarat', *OCP*, 13 (1947) 182–3.

[5] Akrop., p. 173; Pach., I, p. 108.

[6] Pach., I, pp. 205–9; Zakythinos, *Despotat*, I, pp. 33–9; Geanakoplos, op. cit., pp. 158–9 and 171–3.

[7] So in Delehaye, *Deux Typica*, p. 81 (cf. p. 12, inscription on her portrait). Eirene was, strictly speaking, a Branaina (ibid., p. 23).   [8] Ibid., p. 81.

[9] Cf. Papadopulos, *Genealogie der Palaiologen*, p. 6, no. 5. Andronikos *150* and Maria *151* are mentioned with the name of Doukas.   [10] Cf. Papadopulos, *Genealogie der Palaiologen*, p. 6, no. 5.

[11] . . . Ἀνδρόνικος Κομνηνὸς Βρανᾶς Δούκας Ἄγγελος ὁ Παλαιολόγος ὁ διὰ τοῦ θείου καὶ ἀγγελικοῦ σχήματος μετονομασθεὶς Ἀρσένιος μοναχός . . . καὶ τὰ τούτου μνημόσυνα γίνεσθαι κατὰ τὴν εἰκοστὴν ὀγδόην τοῦ ἰουνίου μηνός, Delehaye, *Deux Typica*, p. 92. Philes (Martini), p. 86, vv. 50–51 refers to him

" Κομνηνοφυοῦς Ἀγγελωνύμου " φράσον
" Παλαιολόγου Δούκα τοῦ νοῦ τοῦ ξένου ".

[12] Cf. the verses of Philes (Martini), p. 84, vv. 9–13:

ὁ λαμπρὸς Ἀνδρόνικος ἐξεῦρε, ξένε,
ὃς γίνεται μὲν ἐκ σεβαστοκράτορος,
ἀνδρὸς μαχητοῦ δεξιὸς παῖς ἐν μάχαις,
σοφοῦ στρατηγοῦ ταγματάρχης ἀγχίνους
ἀριστέως ἥρωος ὁπλίτης γίγα

[13] See above n. 11.

M   P.T.D.

Andronikos Branas Doukas Palaiologos has a place in Byzantine literature for he composed a number of works three of which are known:

1. A polemical tract against the Jews.[1]
2. A romance in verse which might be the *Kallimachos and Chrysorrhoe*.[2]
3. Chapters on virtues and vices.[3]

151. Maria Komnene Branaina Laskarina Doukaina Tornikina Palaiologina: Maria was a daughter of Konstantinos *149* and Eirene, and her only mention is found in the Typikon of Βεβαίας Ἐλπίδος where it is said that she died as the nun Mariamne on 16 September of an unknown year.[4] She had previously become the wife of Isaakios Tornikes *209* to whom she bore a son Andronikos *210*. The name Laskarina was inherited from her mother.

152. Ioannes Komnenos Doukas Angelos Branas Palaiologos: Ioannes was a son of the Bulgarian tzar Smilec (1292–3) and Na, the daughter of Konstantinos *149*. He died as the monk Ioasaph on 8 August of an unknown year.[5]

[1] Only published in Latin in *PG*, 133, cols. 796–924, where it is wrongly attributed to the emperor Andronikos I Komnenos. There is an introductory epigram which unambiguously points to the real author

> Ἔγραψα δ᾽αὐτὴν Ἀνδρόνικος ἐκ πόθου
> ἀδελφόπαις ἄνακτος Αὐσόνων γένους
> Κομνηνοφυοῦς ἐκ σεβαστοκράτορος,

PG, 133, col. 793. In addition Philes wrote a poem Εἰς τὸ βιβλίον τὸ παρὰ τοῦ ἐξαδέλφου τοῦ αὐτοκράτορος συντεθὲν κατὰ Ἰουδαίων, Philes (Martini), pp. 84–6, vv. 53, which equally leaves no doubt that the present Andronikos wrote the work.

[2] Philes wrote an Ἐπίγραμμα εἰς ἐρωτικὸν βιβλίον τοῦ ἐξαδέλφου τοῦ αὐτοκράτορος in 161 verses which in conclusion describes the author (Andronikos) in these words:

> ἴσως μαθεῖν, βέλτιστε, τὸν πλάστην θέλεις;
> Κομνηνοφυὴς Ἀνδρόνικος γεννάδας·
> πλήρης χαρίτων οὗτος· ἥρως ἐν μάχαις,
> ῥήτωρ φυσικός, ἐν γραφαῖς φλόγα πνέων,
> ἐν συλλογισμοῖς, ἐν στρατηγικοῖς πόνοις,
> ἐν ταῖς πολιτικαῖς τε καὶ δειναῖς δίκαις
> ἐν πᾶσιν ἁπλῶς τοῖς καλοῖς ὄλβος βρύων·
> ὃς τίκτεται μὲν ἐκ σεβαστοκράτορος
> ἀνακταδέλφου σώφρονος Κωνσταντίνου
> φρονήσεως δὲ πᾶν ὑποσπάσας γάλα
> τοῦ συμφυοῦς ἔμεινε κοσμήτωρ γένους.

See E. Martini, 'A proposito d'una poesia inedita di Manuel File', *Reale Istituto Lombardo di Scienze e Lettere. Rendiconti*, serie II, 29 (Milan, 1896), p. 469. For the authorship of the romance see B. Knös, 'Qui est l'auteur du roman de Callimaque et de Chrysorrhoe?' Ἑλληνικά, 17 (1962), 274–95, who summarizes all earlier views and concludes that the data given by Philes do not permit of the identification of *Kallimachos and Chrysorrhoe* with the romance written by Andronikos and leaves the question undecided.

[3] Κεφάλαια περὶ ἀρετῆς καὶ κακίας τοῦ Παλαιολόγου κυροῦ Ἀνδρονίκου τοῦ Κομνηνοῦ, τοῦ υἱοῦ τοῦ τρισμακαρίστου ἀοιδίμου σεβαστοκράτορος; cf. K. Krumbacher, *Geschichte der byzantinischen Literatur* (Munich, 1897²), p. 780.

[4] Μηνὶ σεπτεμβρίῳ ις´ τελείσθωσαν τὰ μνημόσυνα τῆς περιποθήτου μου αὐταδέλφης κυρᾶς Μαρίας Κομνηνῆς Βραναίνης Λασκαρίνης Δουκαίνης Τορνικίνης τῆς Παλαιολογίνης, τῆς διὰ τοῦ θείου καὶ ἀγγελικοῦ σχήματος μετονομασθείσης Μαριάμνης μοναχῆς, Delehaye, *Deux Typica*, p. 92; cf. Papadopulos, *Genealogie der Palaiologen*, p. 8, no. 8.

[5] Μηνὶ αὐγούστῳ ὀγδόῃ ὀφείλουσι γίνεσθαι τὰ μνημόσυνα τοῦ περιποθήτου μου ἀνεψιοῦ κυροῦ Ἰωάννου Κομνηνοῦ Δούκα Ἀγγέλου τοῦ Παλαιολόγου, υἱοῦ τῆς ὑψηλοτάτης δεσποίνης τῶν Βουλγάρων, τοῦ διὰ τοῦ θείου κα ἰαγγελικοῦ σχήματος μετονομασθέντος Ἰωάσαφ μοναχοῦ, Delehaye, *Deux Typica*, p. 93; Papadopulos, *Genealogie der Palaiologen*, pp. 8–9, no. 10.

153. Maria Doukaina Komnene Palaiologina Branaina: The *proto-stratorissa* Maria was certainly a member of the Branas-Palaiologos family, but her parentage cannot be traced. Her full name is given in the now lost inscription of Pammakaristos.[1] She became the wife of the *protostrator* Michael Doukas Glabas *89* and is the subject of several poems by Philes who assigns all the above appelations to her.[2] At a comparatively late period Maria became the mother of a daughter[3] and must have died after 1315.

154. Anna (Angelina) Komnene Doukaina Palaiologina Philanthropene Maliasene: The full name of Anna appears only once,[4] and the appellation Angelina is found on a fragmentary inscription.[5] She is called a niece (ἀνεψιά) of Michael VIII,[6] but this probably indicates that she was the daughter of one of this emperor's cousins and a Philanthropene.[7] In *c.* 1255 Anna became the wife of Nikolaos Maliasenos *122* to whom she bore a son Ioannes. She died after 1280 after having taken the monastic habit with the name of Anthousa.[8]

155. Euphrosyne Doukaina (Palaiologina?): A much mutilated inscription, perhaps of the early fourteenth century, preserves the name of Eudokia Doukaina (Palaiologina?) who had taken the veil with the name of Eugenia. The legible text reads: Εὐφροσύνη Δούκαινα ἡ Βαλε[ανη ἡ] μετονομασθεῖσα Εὐγενία κ.[9] It might, however, be more likely to read ἡ Παλεο[λογῖνα ἡ] μετονομασθεῖσα Εὐγενία (μοναχή).

156. Manuel Komnenos (Doukas) Palaiologos: A seal bears the inscription

Σφραγὶς Μανουὴλ Κομνηνοῦ πανσεβάστου
ῥίζης Δουκικῆς Παλαιολόγων κλάδος.[10]

It is not possible to identify this *pansebastos sebastos* Manuel Komnenos (Doukas) Palaiologos.

157. Doukas Palaiologos: A manuscript note which seems to be chronologically confused preserves the name of a Doukas Palaiologos who apparently lived at Mystras during the last years of Byzantium.[11]

---

[1] Μαρία Δούκαινα Κομνηνὴ Παλαιολογῖνα Βράναινα ἡ πρωτοστρατόρισσα καὶ κτητόρισσα; cf. R. Janin, *Les églises et les monastères* (Paris, 1953), p. 220.

[2] Philes (Miller), I, pp. 76 and 280; Philes (Martini), p. 65.

[3] G. I. Theocharides, 'Μιχαὴλ Δούκας Γλαβᾶς Ταρχανειώτης (προσωπογραφικά)', 'Ἐπιστημονικὴ Ἐπετηρὶς τῆς Φιλοσοφικῆς Σχολῆς τοῦ Πανεπιστημίου Θεσσαλονίκης, 7 (1957), 197–8.

[4] MM, IV, p. 369.　　　　　[5] Giannopoulos in *ΕΕΒΣ*, 4 (1927), 46.

[6] MM, IV, p. 357 and *passim*.

[7] It would be difficult to imagine that Anna was the daughter of one of Michael VIII's brothers.

[8] See above Nikolaos *122*; on Anna cf. Papadopulos, *Genealogie der Palaiologen*, p. 72, no. 106.

[9] W. H. Buckler, 'Three Inscriptions', *B*, 8 (1933), 176. The inscription comes from the monastery of Myrelaion at Constantinople, and the editor comments: 'The date is lost; the style of lettering would seem to place it about the beginning of the 14th century'.

[10] Laurent, *Bulles métriques*, p. 145, no. 409.

[11] An ἀργυρόβουλλον of one of the last despots of Mystras grants the village of Potamia to Thomas Pyropoulos and Ioannes Basilikos; a note on it reads: "Ἄνωθεν κῦρ Θωμᾶς Πυρόπουλος εἶχεν γυναῖκα τὴν ἀδελφὴν τοῦ Μισιχπασιᾶ τοῦ Δοῦκα τοῦ Παλαιολόγου Μέγεθου ἐκ τὸν Μυζηθρᾶν; see Sp. P. Lampros, Κατάλογοι τῶν ἐν ταῖς μοναῖς τοῦ Ἁγίου Ὄρους Ἑλληνικῶν κωδίκων, II (Cambridge, 1900), p. 432. This grant appears to have been made about the middle of the fifteenth century, Mesich Pasha may be Manuel Palaiologos born in 1455 (Papadopulos, *Genealogie der Palaiologen*, p. 68, no. 101). None of his three sisters could have married Thomas Pyropoulos.

158. Eudokia Doukaina Angelina Komnene: Eudokia[1] was a daughter of Athanasios Soultanos (Palaiologos).[2] She became the wife of Theodoros Skouterios Sarantenos, a nobleman of Berrhoia in Macedonia. Eudokia became the mother of some sons and a daughter who became the wife of Michael Doukas Arianites *66*. She and all her children died before 1326.[3]

PARASPONDYLOS

The family of Paraspondylos (Παρασπόνδυλος), though never numerous, is attested from at least the eleventh century. Two letters of Psellos are addressed to a *protosynkellos* Paraspondylos.[4] Ioannes Parasphondylos (Paraspondylos?) was a *megas archon* in 1342,[5] and in 1345 a certain Paraspondylos was governor of Adrianople.[6] In 1437 another member of the family was *megas dux*.[7] An unfrocked priest Ioannes Paraspondylos is mentioned in 1371.[8] Finally Zotikos Paraspondylos, probably a monk, on the eve of the fall of Constantinople wrote his poem on the battle of Varna.[9]

159. Doukaina Paraspondylina Angelina: An iambic poem in 62 verses of Philes, entitled Ἐπιτάφιοι, was written on the occasion of the death of a noble lady of the Paraspondylos family.[10] She is not named, but the poet praises her aristocratic stock as she belonged to the Doukai Paraspondyloi Angeloi and was also descended from the Komnenoi.[11] She came from Constantinople.[12] Her husband was the army man Gabras Komnenos who was perhaps originally of Trebizond and was made κριτὴς τοῦ φοσσάτου by the emperor.[13] They became

---

[1] ... τῆς εὐγενεστάτου Κομνηνῆς Ἀγγελίνης κυρᾶς Εὐδοκίας, see G. I. Theocharides, Μία διαθήκη καὶ μία δίκη Βυζαντινή (Thessalonica, 1962), p. 18; ἡ μακαρῖτις ἐκείνη εὐγενεστάτη Δούκαινα Ἀγγελῖνα, ibid., p. 24.

[2] Ibid., p. 21. It is possible that Athanasios is the monastic name of Alexios Soultanos Palaiologos, perhaps a son of Melane *202* (Papadopulos, *Genealogie der Palaiologen*, p. 74, no. 110).

[3] Theocharides, op. cit., p. 55.   [4] *Scripta Minora*, II, pp. 104–5 and 115–16.

[5] MM, III, p. 114.   [6] Kant., II, p. 525.

[7] Cf. Guilland in *BZ*, 44 (1951), 233.   [8] MM, I, pp. 540–41.

[9] K. Krumbacher, *Geschichte der byzantinischen Literatur* (Munich, 1897²), pp. 838–9; Gy. Moravcsik, *Byzantinoturcica* (Berlin, 1958), I, pp. 579–80.

[10] Philes (Miller), I, pp. 291–4.

[11]   Δουκῶν γὰρ ἦν τοῦτο καὶ Παρασπονδύλων
            Κομνηνοφυῶν ὁπλιτικῶν Ἀγγέλων,
Philes (Miller), I, p. 292, vv. 31–2.

[12]   ἦν γὰρ ἐκείνης ἥδε πατρὶς ἡ πόλις
Philes (Miller), I, p. 292, v. 24.

[13]   ἡ Κολχὶς ηὐπρέπιζε καὶ τὸν νύμφιον,
            καὶ γίνεται δὴ συμφυὴς οὗτος γάμος
            ἀρθρῶν παρ' ἀμφοῖν καὶ ψυχὰς καὶ σαρκία.
            Γαβρᾶς γὰρ αὐτὴν ὁ σφαγεὺς τῶν βαρβάρων
            ἐκεῖθεν ἐλθὼν εὐκλεῶς ἠγάγετο,
            Κομνηνὸς ἡδύς, ἀρετῶν παῖς ἀγχίνους,
            ὃν αὐτάναξ ἄριστος εὐνοίας χάριν
            ἔδειξε τιμῶν καὶ κριτὴν τοῦ φοσσάτου,
Philes (Miller), I, p. 293, vv. 34–41.

the parents of an unspecified number of daughters who apparently took the veil.[1]

PETRALIPHAS

The Byzantine house of Petraliphas (Πετραλίφας) owes its origin to a Norman nobleman of the time of the First Crusade—the Πέτρος τοῦ ᾿Αλίφα of Anna Komnene—who went over to the service of Alexios I, remained in Byzantium, and settled at Didymoteichon in Thrace in c. 1107.[2] This Peter of Alifa seems to have married into the aristocracy, and it is very probable that the four Petraliphas brothers from Didymoteichon who distinguished themselves in the siege of Corfu by Manuel Komnenos in 1149[3] were his sons. The family of Petraliphas continued to appear until the fifteenth century[4] and contracted marriages with the Komnenoi,[5] the Tornikai,[6] the Branades[7] and, of course, the Doukai. It seems that the name of Doukas was passed to Andronikos *161* through the Komnenoi.

160. Maria Doukaina Komnene: Maria was a sister of Ioannes Petraliphas,[8] her parents being unknown. She is never called Petraliphina but only Doukaina[9] and Komnene[10] on a few occasions. It would appear that Maria assumed these names from her husband after marriage, though the possibility that she inherited them from her father cannot be excluded.

It was most probably during the first decade of the thirteenth century that Maria married Theodoros *42* the future ruler of Epirus and emperor of Thessalonica (for their children see above Theodoros *42*). The year of her death is unknown. We have three letters of Apokaukos and fragment of a fourth one addressed to Maria.[11]

[1]   τὰς γὰρ ἑαυτῆς φιλτάτας ἡ καλλίπαις
        εἰς τὸν βυθὸν καθῆκε τῆς ἀμνηστίας,
Philes (Miller), I, p. 293, vv. 46–7.

[2] See *Alexias*, I, p. 161; II, pp. 22 and 32; cf. Marquis de la Force, 'Les conseillers latins d'Alexis Comnène', *B*, 11 (1936), 158–60. A family tree, showing both the Greek and the Latin branches, was published by E. Miller in *Recueil des Historiens des Croisades*. II. — *Historiens grecs* (Paris, 1881), p. 49. The Greek side is incomplete and unreliable. For some indications on the family see D. M. Nicol, *The Despotate of Epiros* (Oxford, 1957), pp. 215–16.

[3] Πετραλεῖφαί τινες αὐτάδελφοι τέσσαρες ἐκ τῶν Φράγκων γένους ὁρμώμενοι καὶ κατὰ τὸ Διδυμότειχον τὴν οἴκησιν ἔχοντές, Chon., p. 110; cf. Skout., p. 233.

[4] A nun Petraliphina, γυναικαδέλφη of Markos Palaiologos Iagaris is mentioned in 1400, see MM, II, p. 497.

[5] In c. 1200 we meet the *sebastokrator* Nikephoros Komnenos Petraliphas, see Bompaire, *Actes de Xéropotamou*, p. 70.

[6] Akrop., pp. 39 and 90; Skout., p. 501.

[7] MM, I, p. 150.

[8] Akrop., p. 39, calls him a γυναικάδελφος of Maria's husband Theodoros *42*.

[9] A letter of Apokaukos to her bears the address Πρὸς τὴν κραταιὰν Δούκαιναν, see V. Vasilievskii, 'Epirotica saeculi XIII', *VV*, 3 (1896), 282.

[10] See A. Papadopoulos-Kerameus, ' Συνοδικὰ γράμματα ᾿Ιωάννου τοῦ ᾿Αποκαύκου, μητροπολίτου Ναυπάκτου ', *Βυζαντίς*, I (1909), 14; Chomatianos in J. B. Pitra, *Analecta sacra et Classica Spicilegio Solesmeni parata*, VI (Roma, 1891), p. 306, addresses her τῇ κραταιᾷ κυρίᾳ ἡμῶν τῇ μεγάλῃ Κομνηνῇ.

[11] For editions see N. B. Tomadakis, ' Οἱ λόγιοι τοῦ Δεσποτάτου τῆς ᾿Ηπείρου ', *ΕΕΒΣ*, 27 (1957), 28 and 33, nos. 12, 16–17, and 33.

161. Andronikos Komnenos Doukas Petraliphas: He is only mentioned in a Serbian document of 11 April 1227. As an official, Andronikos orders that the *dikaios* Mandoukas gives his estate of Mounziani to the monastery of Chilandar.[1]

162. Theodora Doukaina: The so-called *basilissa* Theodora who became the wife of Michael II of Epirus[2] was a daughter of Ioannes Petraliphas and a certain Helene.[3] The name of Doukaina by which she is referred to[4] is presumably that of her married life. Theodora married Michael II *48* in about 1230 and thereafter spent her life in Arta (for her children see above Michael *48*). She was repeatedly used by her husband in his dealing with the court of Nicaea in order to smooth out the differences between the two Greek states. After Michael's *48* death (before 1267) Theodora became a nun and was eventually buried in the monastery of St George (the present-day church of St Theodora) in Arta where her tomb with a relief portrait of her still survives.[5]

Theodora's pious and virtuous life assured her of a place in the Greek ἁγιολόγιον. She was officially canonized and her feast is commemorated on 11 March.[6] Her *acoluthia*, together with a short *Life*, was composed towards the end of the thirteenth century by the monk Iakobos Meles Iasites.[7]

163. Anna Doukaina Petraliphina: An inscription on marble, originally at the Latin church of St Paul in Galata but now in the Museum of Constantinople, speaks of Anna Doukaina Petraliphina as having died on 8 October, Indiction II, of an unknown year between 1391 and 1490.[8]

---

[1] See A. V. Solovjev, 'Un inventaire des documents byzantins de Chilandar', *Annaly Instituta imeni N. P. Kondakova*, 10 (1938), 46–7.

[2] For the significant part she played in the affairs of Epirus see Nicol, op. cit., *passim*. There is also a recent publication on her by K. Strates, Θεοδώρα, ἡ βασίλισσα τοῦ Δεσποτάτου τῆς Ἠπείρου (Arta, 1960) (inaccessible to me).

[3] Cf. her *Life* in *PG*, 127, col. 904A. Akrop., pp. 91 and 166, calls Theodoros Petraliphas, the brother of Theodora, a γυναικάδελφος of Michael II.

[4] It is preserved in the form ἡ βασίλισσα Δούκαινα Θεοδώρα in a fragmentary inscription of Arta, see A. K. Orlandos, ' Βυζαντινὰ μνημεῖα τῆς "Άρτης', 'Αρχεῖον τῶν Βυζαντινῶν Μνημείων τῆς 'Ελλάδος, 2 (1936), 43.

[5] Idem, ' 'Ο τάφος τῆς 'Αγίας Θεοδώρας ', ibid., especially p. 109. The relief shows beside Theodora a smaller male figure in high official garb on her left. This may be her son Nikephoros *49*.

[6] Cf. S. Eustratiades, 'Αγιολόγιον τῆς 'Ορθοδόξου 'Εκκλησίας (Athens, n.d.), p. 180. A small church, commemorating Theodora, was recently built at Servia in Macedonia, supposedly her birth place, see the volume 'Ακολουθίαι τῆς ὁσίας μητρὸς ἡμῶν Θεοδώρας βασιλίσσης "Άρτης τῆς ἐκ Σερβίων Μακεδονίας, edited by Dionysios L. Psarianos (metropolitan of Servia and Kozane) (Athens, 1965), which also includes the *Life* (pp. 31–5).

[7] See especially L. Vranoussis, Χρονικὰ 'Ηπείρου (Jannina, 1962), pp. 49–54, who discusses the date and the editions of the *Life* and calls attention to its importance as a source for some later local chronicles of western Greece.

[8] See V. Laurent, 'Inscriptions grecques d'époque romaine et byzantine', *EO*, 35 (1936), 221. The inscription reads: ['E]κοιμήθη ἡ δούλη τοῦ [Θεοῦ "Α]ννα Δούκενα ἡ Πετ[ραλ]ιφήνα, ἐν ἔτη [. . . i]νδικτιῶνος β′ ἐν μηνὶ ὀκτωβρίῳ η′. The unknown year must be one of the following: 1393, 1408, 1423, 1438, 1453, 1468, 1483.

PETZIKOPOULOS

Two members of the family of Petzikopoulos (*Πετζικόπουλος*) carry the name of Doukas.

164. Demetrios Doukas Petzikopoulos: He signed a document dated 22 January 1327, which deals with the sale of three houses and a piece of land to the monastery of Chilandar.[1] Demetrios was the son of a *stratopedarches* Petzikopoulos, already dead at that time, and Martha who was then a nun under the name of Melane. Demetrios had a sister Eulogia (a nun) and two brothers, Ioannes Senachereim and Konstantinos.[2]

165. Maria Doukaina Petzikopoulina: She may have been a sister of the *stratopedarches* Petzikopoulos and had a daughter Kale who is mentioned as the wife of Alexandros Doukas Sarantenos *183* on 9 November 1322.[3]

PHILANTHROPENOS

The family name of Philanthropenos is etymologically connected with the Constantinopolitan monastery of *Χριστοῦ τοῦ Φιλανθρώπου* — *Φιλανθρωπηνός* being any monk dwelling there. Thus in November 1158 the abbot of St Mamas, Athanasios Philanthropenos, is expressly described as originally belonging to the monastery of *Χριστοῦ τοῦ Φιλανθρώπου*.[4] But Athanasios was probably unrelated to the noble family whose existence is not attested in the twelfth century. The Philanthropenoi emerge in about the middle of the thirteenth century and continue to be encountered frequently in high military and administrative affairs up to the fall of Constantinople, and even for sometime afterwards.[5]

The Philanthropenoi married into other aristocratic houses, and their name often appears in compound forms. Several of them — they may constitute a distinctive branch of the family — frequently used the name of Doukas which must have been adopted during the period of the Nicaean Empire.

---

[1] Petit, *Actes de Chilandar*, pp. 230–5.

[2] Εὐδοκία μοναχὴ ἡ κατὰ σάρκα γνησία θυγάτηρ τοῦ στρατοπεδάρχου ἐκείνου τοῦ Πετζικοπούλου, Μάρθα μοναχὴ ἡ μήτηρ αὐτῆς ἡ μετονομασθεῖσα Μελάνη, ὁ δοῦλος τοῦ κραταιοῦ καὶ ἁγίου ἡμῶν αὐθέντου καὶ βασιλέως καὶ γνήσιος υἱὸς τῆς Μελάνης Δημήτριος Δούκας ὁ Πετζικόπουλος, Ἰωάννης ὁ Σεναχερείμ καὶ Κωνσταντῖνος οἱ γνήσιοι τούτου αὐτάδελφοι, ibid., p. 231. A Petzikopoulos, who together with a Sarantenos inflicted damages upon the properties of Chilandar (F. Dölger, *Aus den Schatzkammern des Heiligen Berges* [Munich, 1948], p. 84), was probably the *stratopedarches*.

[3] Petit, op. cit., p. 84.

[4] S. Eustratiades, ' Τυπικὸν τῆς ἐν Κωνσταντινουπόλει μονῆς τοῦ ἁγίου μεγαλομάρτυρος Μάμαντος', Ἑλληνικά, 1 (1928), 303, 309, and *passim*.

[5] For the prosopography of the family see M. Treu, *Maximi monachi Planudis, Epistulae* (Breslau, 1892), pp. 235–8; N. A. Bees, 'Geschichtliche Forschungsresultate und Mönchs- und Volkssagen über die Gründer der Meteorenklöster', *BNJ*, 3 (1922), 376–7, n. 5; Athenagoras, ' Συμβολαὶ εἰς τὴν ἱστορίαν τοῦ Βυζαντινοῦ οἴκου τῶν Φιλανθρωπηνῶν', *ΔΙΕΕΕ*, 10 iv (1928), 61–74; V. Laurent in *EO*, 29 (1930), 495–7, and 31 (1932), 177–81; P. Lemerle, *Actes de Kutlumus* (Paris, 1945), p. 127; Laurent, *Bulles métriques*, p. 190.

166. Alexios Doukas Philanthropenos: In the Bulgarian war of 1255 a fortress of the enemy near Ochrida was stormed by the troops commanded by Alexios Doukas Philanthropenos.[1] Chronologically Alexios is the first important Philanthropenos to be mentioned, and it is quite possible that he is identical with the *protostrator* and later *megas dux* Alexios Philanthropenos, an able and successful naval commander who flourished between the years 1263 and 1271.[2] This Alexios who seems to have been dead by 1275[3] had a daughter Maria who married Michael Tarchaneiotes and became the mother of several children including the *pinkernes* Alexios Doukas Philanthropenos *171*.[4]

167. Michael Doukas Philanthropenos: A number of references to this name occur during the period 1286–1304 and most likely relate to a single person. A σεκρετικὴ δικαίωσις of June 1286 speaks of him as *epi tēs trapezēs* and *oikeios* to the emperor.[5] In *c.* 1303, described as an old and noble man, Philanthropenos was sent by the emperor to defend Magnesia against the Turks.[6] On 11 November 1304, Michael, now called an uncle of the emperor, became a monk and took the name of Alypios.[7]

Assuming that Michael Doukas Philanthropenos was an uncle of Andronikos II, we have to suppose that either he or his unknown wife was a cousin of Michael VIII or perhaps a cousin of the latter's wife Theodora *74*. Otherwise it is difficult to explain the relationship.

168. Theodora Doukaina Philanthropene: She lived in the second half of the thirteenth century and became the wife of Ioannes Komnenos Akropolites,[8] probably a son of the historian.

169. Eirene Komnene Doukaina Philanthropene Kantakouzene: Eirene is only known from a manuscript notice, recording her death which occurred on 8 August 1292. Previously she had taken monastic vows with the name of Euphrosyne.[9]

---

[1] ʿΟ Φιλανθρωπηνὸς ʾΑλέξιος εἷλεν ὁ Δούκας, Akrop., p. 119; cf. Skout., p. 519.

[2] See Pach., I, pp. 109, 206, 209, 309, 325, 333–4, and 337, who consistently calls him ʾΑλέξιος Φιλανθρωπηνός. For his career see the accounts of R. Guilland in *REB*, 7 (1949), 165 (as *protostrator*) and in *BZ*, 44 (1951), 231 (as *megas dux*).   [3] Cf. Pach., I, p. 411.

[4] Pach., I, p. 206; cf. Papadopulos, *Genealogie der Palaiologen*, pp. 14–16, no. 24; G. I. Theocharides, ' Μιχαὴλ Δούκας Γλαβᾶς Ταρχανειώτης (προσωπογραφικά) ', ʾΕπιστημονικὴ ʾΕπετηρὶς τῆς Φιλοσοφικῆς Σχολῆς τοῦ Πανεπιστημίου Θεσσαλονίκης, 7 (1957), 187.

[5] . . . οἵ τε οἰκεῖοι τῷ κραταιῷ καὶ ἁγίῳ ἡμῶν αὐθέντῃ καὶ βασιλεῖ, ὁ ἐπὶ τῆς τραπέζης κῦρ Μιχαὴλ Δούκας ὁ Φιλανθρωπηνός . . . , MM, IV, p. 276.

[6] ʾΗν δὲ ὁ ἐπὶ τῆς τραπέζης Φιλανθρωπηνός, ἀνὴρ εὐγενείᾳ καὶ γήρᾳ συνέσει τε καὶ ἐμπειρίαις στρατηγικαῖς ἐς ἅπαν κοσμούμενος, Pach., II, p. 400.

[7] Μηνὶ νοεμβρίῳ ιαʹ ἰνδ. γʹ ἔτει ͵ϛωιγʹ (= 1304) ἠξιώθη ὁ περιπόθητος θεῖος τοῦ κραταιοῦ καὶ ἁγίου ἡμῶν αὐθέντου καὶ βασιλέως Μιχαὴλ Δούκας ὁ Φιλανθρωπηνὸς τοῦ θείου καὶ ἀγγελικοῦ σχήματος μετονομασθεὶς ʾΑλύπιος μοναχός. The notice is found in cod. Batopediou 760, fol. 294r, and is badly edited by S. Eustratiades and Arcadios Batopedenos, *Catalogue of the Greek Manuscripts in the Library of the Monastery of Vatopedi on Mount Athos* (Cambridge, Mass., 1924), p. 149.

[8] This is implied in the following verses found in cod. Vat. gr. 307

> ʾΑκροπολίτης Κομνηνὸς ʾΙωάννης
> Φιλανθρωπηνῇ Δουκαίνῃ Θεοδώρᾳ·
> Θεὸς χαριτόκλητον εἰς Θεοδώραν
> Φιλανθρωπηνὴν ʾΑκροπολίτην ἄγει.

See G. Mercati and P. Franchi de'Cavalieri, *Codices Vaticani Graeci*, I (Rome, 1323), p. 376; cf. above p. 84, n. 4.

[9] Μηνὶ αὐγούστῳ ηʹ ἡμέρᾳ Σαββάτῳ ἰνδ. εʹ ἔτει ͵ϛψιʹ ἐκοιμήθη ἡ πανευγενεστάτη Κομνηνὴ κυρία Εἰρήνη Δούκαινα ἡ Φιλανθρωπηνὴ ἡ Κατακουζηνή, ἡ διὰ τοῦ θείου καὶ ἀγγελικοῦ σχήματος

170. Eirene Komnene Philanthropene Doukaina: She died as the nun Euphrosyne on 7 September 1303.[1]

171. Alexios Doukas Philanthropenos: Alexios was the second-born son of Michael Tarchaneiotes (a nephew of Michael VIII) and Maria the daughter of Alexios *166*. Appropriately speaking, he was a Tarchaneiotes but chose to be called after his maternal grandfather.[2] Consequently the sources refer to him as Philanthropenos[3] and less frequently as Doukas.[4] Alexios was born in about 1270[5] and is much praised for his military skill. He had been honoured with the dignity of *pinkernes*,[6] and in the early nineties of the thirteenth century he was sent by the emperor to Asia Minor where he gained impressive successes against the Turks. But in 1296 he revolted and was blinded.[7] In his old age he was once more used by the emperor when in 1333 he was despatched to besiege Mitylene.[8] He died shortly afterwards.

Alexios Doukas Philanthropenos married a daughter of Konstantinos Akropolites in 1295.[9] He had at least one son, Michael, born in 1296.[10] Alexios was an intimate friend of many scholars of his age. Planudes, Gregoras, Michael Gabras, and Matthaios of Ephesus wrote him letters.[11] Philes also sent him a poem begging for assistance.[12]

172. Doukas Philanthropenos: A couple of short poems by Manuel Philes are in the form of prayer, ostensibly addressed by a Doukas Philanthropenos and his wife to Christ and the Theotokos, begging to be blessed with children.[13] It is not possible to identify them.

μετονομασθεῖσα Εὐφροσύνη μοναχή, Eustratiades and Arcadios, op. cit., p. 149. As printed, the date must be wrong. The year of the creation 6710 corresponds to the fifth indiction and is A.D. 1202 (but 8 August was not Saturday then). Yet this is too early for a member of the Philanthropenos family. I have corrected ,ϛψι' to ,ϛω (=A.M. 6800 = A.D. 1292). Again 8 August 1292, was not Saturday but Friday.

---

[1] Μηνὶ σεπτεμβρίῳ ζ' ἰνδ. β' ἔτει ,ϛωιβ' ἡμέρᾳ Κυριακῇ ἐκοιμήθη ἡ πανευγενεστάτη Κομνηνὴ κυρία Εἰρήνη ἡ Φιλανθρωπηνὴ ἡ Δούκαινα, ἡ διὰ τοῦ θείου καὶ ἀγγελικοῦ σχήματος μετονομασθεῖσα Εὐφροσύνη μοναχή Eustratiades and Arcadios, op. cit., p. 149. 7 September 1303, was Saturday and not Sunday.

It is rather curious that the two obituary notices, almost contemporary, concerning two women of the same name are found on the same folio of the manuscript (cf. above p. 168, n. 9). One has to consider the existence of two near contemporary homonymous ladies, unless one could go as far as to suggest emending the first text to read: Μηνὶ αὐγούστῳ η' . . . ἠξιώθη ἡ πανευγενεστάτη . . . Κατακουζηνὴ τοῦ θείου καὶ ἀγγελικοῦ σχήματος etc.

[2] . . . τοῦ Ταρχανειώτου δεύτερος παῖς ὁ Φιλανθρωπηνὸς 'Αλέξιος ἐκ τοῦ πρὸς μητρὸς πάππου 'Αλέξιος, Pach., II, p. 210.

[3] Cf. Greg., I, pp. 195, 361, 534; Kant., I, p. 479; Planudes in Treu, op. cit., pp. 60, 93, 95, 114, 135, and 164.   [4] Ibid., pp. 111[94], 123, 166[52].

[5] In 1295 he was ἐν ταῖς ἀκμαῖς ἤδη τῆς νεότητος ἀνθῶν, Greg., I, p. 361.

[6] Pach., II, p. 210; Greg., I, p. 195; Kant., I, p. 479.

[7] Pach., II, pp. 210–29; Greg., I, pp. 195–202.

[8] Greg., I, p. 534; Kant., I, p. 479.

[9] See Treu, op. cit., p. 249; Pach., II, p. 214, speaks of 'Ακροπολίτης Μελχισεδέκ, θεῖος ὢν τῆς αὐτοῦ (sc. 'Αλεξίου) γυναικός.   [10] Treu, op. cit., pp. 238 and 249.

[11] For Alexios' career see R. Guilland, 'Alexios Philanthropène', *Revue des Lyonnais*, 1922, pp. 47–59 (inaccessible to me) and idem, *Nicéphore Grégoras, Correspondance* (Paris, 1927), pp. 372–4.

[12] Πρὸς τὸν Φιλανθρωπηνὸν τὸν πιγκέρνην, Philes (Miller), I, pp. 262–4.

[13] Φιλανθρωπηνὸς ταῦτα σὸς λάτρης Δούκας; see Philes (Miller), I, p. 319. Both the editor (n. 2) and Athenagoras, op. cit., p. 63, identify him with Alexios *171*, but this seems unlikely.

173. Georgios Doukas Philanthropenos: Two documents, one undated and the other of May 1346, speak of Georgios Doukas Philanthropenos as *archon* of the island of Lemnos. He carried the dignity of *megas hetaireiarches*.[1] His seal bears the inscription:

Φιλανθρωπηνοῦ τὰς γραφὰς Γεωργίου
φύλαττε, Γεώργιε, καὶ κῦρος νέμε.[2]

174. Nikephoros Doukas Philanthropenos: The name of Nikephoros Doukas Philanthropenos is known only from a notice written on a fourteenth-century manuscript which he had paid to be copied.[3]

175. Komnene(?) Doukaina Philanthropene: The name of this lady has not been preserved in its entirety. In January 1397 she paid to have cod. Xeropotamou 234 (Athous 2567) copied.[4]

176. Zoe Doukaina Philanthropene Mouriskissa: Zoe signs an undated document, perhaps of the fourteenth century, which takes up a complaint raised by the monks of St John Theologos in Patmos. She promises that in future neither her men (πάροικοι) nor those of her relatives will inflict damages upon the properties of the monastery.[5]

PRASOMALES

The unusual name Πρασομάλης, i.e. the 'leek-haired' (the one with straight hair) is found in a compound form with that of Doukas.

177. Doukas Prasomales: In February 1421 the unknown possessor of what is now cod. Par. suppl. gr. 1202 had paid two nomismata to Doukas Prasomales in order to purchase the manuscript.[6]

---

[1] Ὁ δοῦλος τοῦ κραταιοῦ καὶ ἁγίου ἡμῶν αὐθέντου καὶ βασιλέως Γεώργιος Δούκας ὁ Φιλανθρωπηνὸς καὶ μέγας ἑταιρειάρχης, S. Eustratiades, ''Ἱστορικὰ μνημεῖα τοῦ ''Αθω '', Ἑλληνικά, 2 (1929), 382. In the other document, which is a chrysobull, he is simply called Georgios Philanthropenos, ibid., p. 359.

[2] See V. Laurent, 'Légendes sigillographiques et familles byzantines', *EO*, 31 (1932), 177–81; idem, *Bulles métriques*, p. 190, no. 544.

[3] It reads: Βίβλος ὁ Κλῖμαξ. Τὼ παρὼν βιβλίον διὰ συνδρομῆς καὶ ἐξόδου τοῦ πανευγενεστάτου(?) κυροῦ Νικηφόρου Δούκα τοῦ Φιλανθρωπηνοῦ ἐγράφη καὶ . . . , see Th. D. Moschonas, 'Κρυπτογραφικὸν σημείωμα τοῦ ὑπ'ἀριθ. χειρογράφου 160 (138) τῆς Πατριαρχικῆς Βιβλιοθήκης 'Αλεξανδρείας', *Tome Commémoratif du Millénaire de la Bibliothèque Patriarcale d'Alexandrie* (Alexandria, 1953), p. 328.

[4] . . . συνδρομῇ τῆς πάντα καλῆς Κ[ομ]νηνῆς τῆς καὶ Δουκένας καὶ Φιλανθρωπηνῆς, see Bompaire, *Actes de Xéropotamou*, p. 29. L. Politis, 'Paläographische Miszellen vom Heiligen Berg', *BZ*, 50 (1957), 315, reads Κ[υρι]ανένης.

[5] See MM, VI, pp. 247–8. Her signature reads Ζωη Δουκηνα Φιλανθρωπινη η Μ(υ)ρισκησα. Μουρίσκος (Moresco) was a Genoese pirate who was made *protovestiarios* in 1305, Dölger, *Regesten*, IV, p. 44, no. 2276.

[6] Ἠγόρασα τὸ παρὸν βιβλίον παρὰ Δούκα τοῦ Πρασομάλου διὰ νομισμάτων β' ἐπὶ τῆς βασιλείας κυροῦ Μανουὴλ τοῦ Παλαιολόγου καὶ Ἑλένης ἐν μηνὶ φεβρουαρίῳ ἰνδ. ιδ' τοῦ ἔτους ͵ϛ ϡκθ'; see S. Kugéas 'Notizbuch eines Beamten der Metropolis in Thessalonike aus dem Anfang des XV. Jahrhunderts', *BZ*, 23 (1914/19), 160, n. 4; Ch. Astruc and M.-L. Concasty, *Bibliothèque Nationale. Catalogue des Manuscrits grecs. Le Supplément grec*, III (Paris, 1960), p 380.

PRINKIPS

The *Πρίγκιπες Χειλᾶδες* were a noble family of the southern Peloponnese in the last centuries of Byzantium. The patriarch of Antioch Theodosios V Prinkips (1275–83/4) was not a son of prince William Villehardouin, as is often asserted, but a scion of this prominent house.[1] Pachymeres describes him as *εὐγενεῖ μὲν τὰ ἐς γένος, ἐκ Πριγκίπων δὲ τῶν κατὰ Πελοπόννησον κατάγοντι τὸ ἀνέκαθεν.*[2] In 1343 Kantakouzenos mentions another Prinkips,[3] while Nikephoros Prinkips Cheilas is a fifteenth-century writer.[4] In 1394 we meet Georgios Prinkips and his father *Κωνσταντῖνος ἐκεῖνος ὁ τοῦ Πρίγγιπος.*[5] Esaias Prinkips is a monk in 1407,[6] and Demetrios Palaiologos Prinkips is mentioned in a document of 1421.[7] Likewise the name Cheilas is not uncommon during these times.[8]

178. Ioannes Doukas Prinkips Cheilas: He was an *apographeus*, mentioned in a chrysobull of August 1393 as an *oikeios* to the emperor.[9]

RADENOS

The common name Radenos (*'Ραδηνός*) appears in the Byzantine sources from at least the tenth century onwards, and according to the etymology of Pseudo-Symeon Magister it derives from the village of Rade in the Anatolikon theme.[10] Of the very many bearers of it only a few can be mentioned here: Theodoros, *πρωτοσπαθάριος κριτὴς ἐπὶ τοῦ ἱπποδρόμου* (1020);[11] Anna, sister of Radenos;[12] Ioannes, *πρόεδρος καὶ ἐπὶ τῆς βασιλικῆς σακέλλης* (1088);[13] Konstantinos, *sebastos* and *parathalassites* (1188);[14] Konstantinos (1286);[15] Ioannes (1312);[16] Michael

---

[1] For the family see I. K. Bogiatzides, ' *Οἱ Πρίγκιπες Χειλᾶδες τῆς Λακεδαίμονος*', *NE*, 19 (1925), 192–209; cf. Ducange, *Glossarium ad scriptores mediae et infimae graecitatis* (Paris, 1688), col. 1227; F. Dölger, *Aus den Schatzkammern des Heiligen Berges* (Munich, 1948), pp. 269–70; Bompaire, *Actes de Xéropotamou*, p. 210.

[2] Pach., I, p. 402.

[3] Kant., II, p. 383.

[4] Bogiatzides, op. cit., pp. 197–209.

[5] MM, II, p. 221.

[6] Bompaire, *Actes de Xéropotamou*, p. 213.

[7] Dölger, *Schatzkammern*, p. 266.

[8] Some bearers of it are cited by D. B. Bagiakakos, ' *Βυζαντινὰ ὀνόματα καὶ ἐπώνυμα ἐκ Μάνης*', *Πελοποννησιακά*, 3/4 (1960), 217–19.

[9] Dölger, *Schatzkammern*, p. 51; cf. Dölger, *Regesten*, v, p. 80, no. 3239.
The editor however gives his name as *Χαλᾶς* and not *Χειλᾶς*. But the former does not seem to be found during the Byzantine period, while Cheilas is a common name, and in addition it is found as a compound with the surname Prinkips.

[10] *'Ραδηνὸς ἀπὸ 'Ράδης κώμης τοῦ τῶν Ἀνατολικῶν θέματος (κέκληται)*, Ps. Sym. Mag., p. 707. For a brief note on the family see K. Amantos in *Ἑλληνικά*, 3 (1930), 538–9.

[11] G. Ficker, *Erlasse des Patriarchen von Konstantinopel Alexios Studites* (Keil, 1921), p. 21.

[12] Psellos, *Scripta Minora*, II, p. 93.

[13] MM., VI, p. 51.

[14] MM, VI., p. 124; cf. Skout., p. 424.

[15] MM, IV, p. 227.

[16] Bompaire, *Actes de Xéropotamou*, p. 119.

(1337);[1] Nikolaos (1371);[2] several Radenoi in Thessalonica (c. 1425);[3] Philippos (1500).[4]

179. Stephanos Doukas Radenos: He is the only person of the Radenos family who is also referred to as Doukas. His signature appears in a number of documents of Mount Athos:

1. Document of Batopedi dated March 1415 which he signs together with Ioannes Radenos.[5]
2. Document of Docheiariou dated September 1418.[6]
3. Document of Rossikon dated May 1419 in which Stephanos is called *kephale* of Kassandreia.[7]
4. Document of Lavra dated January 1420 in which the name of Ioannes Radenos once more occurs.[8]
5. Document of Batopedi dated April 1421.[9]

RAOUL

The family of Raoul (*'Ραούλ*), originally of Norman stock, owes its existence to a western soldier who came over to the side of Byzantium (1080). In the twelfth century these Raoul became completely hellenized, and afterwards they were included among the nobility. The contracted form *'Ράλ* occurs from 1391 onwards and was soon transformed into *'Ράλης* and as such the name is still quite common.[10] In the thirteenth century the Raoul became related to other distinguished families, including the Laskareis and the Palaiologoi.

180. Konstantinos Raoul Doukas: His name is preserved in a seal which is dated to the late twelfth century:

'Ραοὺλ σεβαστοῦ Δούκα τοῦ Κωνσταντίνου
σφράγισμα καὶ κύρωσις ἀσφαλεστάτη.[11]

---

[1] MM, IV, p. 90.

[2] MM, I, p. 372.

[3] K. D. Mertzios, Μνημεῖα Μακεδονικῆς Ἱστορίας (Thessalonica, 1947), pp. 46, 50, and 52.

[4] Sathas, MB, V, p. 675.

[5] Arkadios Batopedenos, '΄Αγιορειτικὰ ἀνάλεκτα ἐκ τοῦ ἀρχείου τῆς μονῆς Βατοπεδίου', Γρηγόριος ὁ Παλαμᾶς, 3 (1919), 336.

[6] Chr. Ktenas, 'Τὰ κειμηλιαρχεῖα τῆς ἐν ᾽Αγίῳ ῎Ορει ἱερᾶς μονῆς τοῦ Δοχειαρίου', ΕΕΒΣ, 7 (1930), 11; cf. E. Kourilas, '΄Ο κατάλογος τῶν ἐπισήμων ᾽Αθωνικῶν ἐγγράφων τοῦ Οὐσπένσκη ', ΕΕΒΣ, 8 (1931), 72.

[7] St. P. Kyriakides, Βυζαντιναὶ μελέται II–V (Thessalonica, 1937), pp. 214–15; cf. S. Eustratiades, ' Ἱστορικὰ μνημεῖα τοῦ ῎Αθω ', Ἑλληνικά, 2 (1929), 379.

[8] Dölger, Regesten, V, p. 106, no. 3376.

[9] Arkadios, op. cit., p. 335.

[10] There is a study on the family by A. Ch. Chatzes, Οἱ 'Ραούλ, 'Ράλ, 'Ράλαι (1080–1800) (Kirchhain, 1908) which is not always entirely satisfactory. This is reviewed with addenda by N. A. Bees in Βυζαντίς, 2 (1911/12), 250–55. See also B. A. Mystakides, ' Οἱ 'Ράλ(λ)αι,' ΕΕΒΣ, 5 (1928), 256–82. For the Ralai of Chios (first appearance in 1511) see especially Ph. P. Argenti, Libro d'Oro de la Noblesse de Chio (London, 1955), I, pp. 101–4; II, pp. 139–41 (family trees).

[11] Laurent, Bulles métriques, p. 172, no. 483.

The editor is inclined to identify this *sebastos* Konstantinos Raoul Doukas with a Konstantinos Raoul who is mentioned in 1191[1] and was also among those who proclaimed Alexios Angelos emperor in 1195.[2] Choniates includes him among that emperor's relatives.[3] If the owner of the seal is identical with the man of 1191/5, it is likely that the name of Doukas passed to him through the Angeloi. His father could have married a Doukaina Angelina.

181. Ioannes Komnenos Raoul Doukas Angelos Petraliphas: Ioannes was the eldest son of the *protovestiarios* Alexios Raoul who had married the daughter of an unnamed brother of Batatzes.[4] His long compound name[5] gives an indication of his ancestors. His father was a Raoul, the names of Komnenos, Doukas, and Angelos were obviously inherited from the brother of Batatzes who may have married a lady of the Petraliphas family.[6]

In 1258 Ioannes Raoul was imprisoned together with his brothers by Theodoros II.[7] Shortly afterwards, however, he was restored and given the command in the war against Epiros by Michael VIII.[8] Following the assassination of Georgios Mouzalon (September 1258), Ioannes took over his position as *protovestiarios* and also married his widow Theodora, a daughter of Ioannes Kantakouzenos and Eirene (Eulogia) Palaiologina the emperor's sister.[9] This marriage produced some daughters, only one of whom, Eirene, is mentioned by name. She became the wife of Konstantinos *148*.[10]

Ioannes Raoul appears to have been dead by 1284. His wife Theodora who

---

[1] Papadopoulos-Kerameus, *Ἀνάλεκτα*, II, p. 362.

[2] Chon., 593.

[3] . . . ἄνθρωποι κατὰ γένος τῷ βασιλεῖ συναπτόμενοι; ibid.

[4] Akrop., pp. 160–71; Pach., I, p. 108; Greg., I, p. 167; Sp. P. Lampros, ' *Ἐπιγράμματα Μαξίμου Πλανούδη* ', *NE*, 13 (1916), 416, 417, and 418; S. Kougeas, 'Zur Geschichte der Münchener Thukydideshandschrift Augustanus F', *BZ*, 16 (1907), 594.

References to Alexios Raoul occur between the years 1253 and 1303. Akrop., p. 92 (cf. pp. 155, 160) calls the *protovestiarios* Alexios Raoul γαμβρὸν ὄντα ἐπ' ἀδελφόπαιδι τοῦ βασιλέως (sc. 'Ιωάννου Βατάτζη); Pach., II, p. 69, speaks of an Alexios Raoul as being a γαμβρός of *protovestiarios* Tarchaneiotes Philanthropenos (c. 1284) and elsewhere (II, p. 320) of a *megas domestikos* Alexios Raoul ὃν ἐν ἀκμῇ ἡλικίας ὄντα ὁ δεσπότης Μιχαήλ (sc. Michael II of Epiros) γαμβρὸν ἠγάγετο τῆς δεσποίνης Θεοδώρας ζηλωτὸν ἐκτόπως ποιούσης τὸ κῆδος in 1303. Evidently we are dealing with more than one person called Alexios Raoul, and the contention of Chatzes, op. cit., pp. 13–15, that all these references belong to the father of Ioannes Raoul is unacceptable. In any case, the *protovestiarios* Alexios Raoul had, besides Ioannes, three more sons: Isaakios, Manuel, and an unnamed one (cf. Akrop., p. 155; Pach., I, p. 484; II, p. 207) as well as a daughter who figures in the text of Pachymeres as Κλοϊστά (presumably a corrupted form) and married Andronikos Mouzalon and then Andronikos Palaiologos (Papadopulos, *Genealogie der Palaiologen*, pp. 71–2, no. 105).

[5] . . . Κομνηνὸς 'Ιωάννης
'Ραοὺλ ὁ Δούκας, "Αγγελος Πετραλίφης,
Lampros, op. cit., p. 417.

[6] It is also possible that Petraliphas represents instead the name of Ioannes' paternal grandmother.

[7] Akrop., p. 155.

[8] Akrop., p. 160

[9] Pach., I, p. 108; cf. Papadopulos, *Genealogie der Palaiologen*, pp. 20–21, no. 34; R. Guilland, 'Fonctions et dignités des eunuques', *EB*, 2 (1944), 214.

[10] Pach., I, pp. 154–5; Greg., I, p. 190 (γυναῖκα τῶν 'Ραοὺλ θυγατέρων); cf. Papadopulos, *Genealogie der Palaiologen*, p. 23, no. 37.

was a learned woman much interested in theology[1] became a nun with the name of Kyriake and restored the monastery of St Andreas ἐν τῇ Κρίσει; she died on 6 December 1300.[2]

SARANTENOS

Some members of the family of Sarantenos (Σαραντηνός)[3] are also mentioned with the name of Doukas. They may have adopted it through the Angeloi.

182. Angelos Doukas Sarantenos: A poem of Philes is written for and addressed to 'Αγγέλῳ Δούκᾳ τῷ Σαραντηνῷ.[4] This man could also claim the Komnenoi as his ancestors.[5] His first name is not given. N Doukas Sarantenos had a successful career in the army and married a noble lady by whom he had eight children.[6] But his life turned out tragically since he lost all his children, and at the time when Philes was writing Sarantenos had founded and entered a monastery.

183. Alexandros Doukas Sarantenos: Alexandros Doukas Sarantenos was the husband of Kale, a daughter of Maria Doukaina Petzikopoulina *165*. There is a document of 9 November 1322, which confirms the sale of three of their houses to the monastery of Chilandar.[7] He seems to have had other dealings, not always amicable, with the monks of that monastery.[8] Alexandros is also mentioned in another document of July 1335, issued by the δομέστικος τῶν θεμάτων Konstantinos Makrenos, which refers to three of his brothers, the monk Ignatios Sarantenos, Diomedes and Nikolaos *184*.[9]

---

[1] For Theodora see M. Treu, *Maximi monachi Planudis Epistulae* (Breslau, 1892), pp. 245–7; Chatzes, op. cit., pp. 17–22; H.-G. Beck, *Kirche und theologische Literatur im byzantinischen Reich* (Munich, 1958), p. 698. A manuscript notice describes her as

> 'Ρώμης νέας ἄνακτος ἀδελφῆς τέκους
> Καντακουζηνῆς ἐξ ἀνάκτων 'Αγγέλων
> Δουκῶν φυείσης Παλαιολόγων φύτλης
> 'Ραοὺλ δάμαρτος χαριτωνύμου
> Κομνηνοφυοῦς πρωτοβεστιαρίου,

Kugeas, loc. cit.

[2] The monastery was restored in 1284 (cf. R. Janin, *Les églises et les monastères* [Paris, 1953], p. 32), and Planudes who composed Εἰς τὸν ναὸν τοῦ 'Αγίου 'Ανδρέου ἡρωοελεγεῖοι ὃν ἀνήγειρεν αὐτῷ πρωτοβεστιαρία remarks that to Theodora

> κοινωνὸς βιότου δὲ 'Ραοὺλ πέλεν 'Ιωάννης
> τιμὴν εἰληφὼς πρωτοβεστιαρίου
> αὕτη χηροσύνην ἔστερξεν ἀμέμπτως,

see Lampros, op. cit., p. 416. This χηροσύνη of Theodora probably predates the restoration of the church.

[3] On the Sarantenoi who appear chiefly in Macedonia in the fourteenth century see G. I. Theocharides, *Μία διαθήκη καὶ μία δίκη Βυζαντινή* (Thessalonica, 1962), pp. 51–60.

[4] Philes (Miller), 1, pp. 247–9, in sixty iambic verses.

[5]
> Κομνηνοφυὴς 'Αγγελώνυμος Δούκας
> Σαραντηνός τὸ θαῦμα τῆς πανοπλίας,

Philes (Miller), 1, p. 247, vv. 4–5.

[6]
> Κήδους δὲ τυχὼν ὁ χρυσοῦς τρισολβίου,
> καὶ τέτταρας δὶς ἐξενεγκὼν φιλτάτους,

Philes (Miller), 1, p. 247, vv. 10–11.

[7] Petit, *Actes de Chilandar*, pp. 178–81.

[8] Ibid., pp. 186 and 202.   [9] L. Petit, *Actes de Xénophon* (St Petersburg, 1903), p. 68.

184. Nikolaos Doukas Sarantenos: He was a brother of Alexandros and is only mentioned in the document of 1335.[1] He was by then dead.

185. Anna Doukaina Sarantene Intanina: Anna[2] is referred to in an ecclesiastical document of December 1348.[3] Much earlier she had become the wife of an unnamed man by whom she gave birth to two sons and one daughter. After the death of her first husband and some years of widowhood, Anna married a certain Devlitzenos (εἰς δεύτερον συνοικέσιον τῷ Δευλητζηνῷ συζευχθῆναι) and then died. Her second husband appropriated her dowry in spite of the fact that her three children were poor. The synodal court decided in favour of the children. Anna had a sister (by that time a nun) Elaiodora of Thessalonica (᾿Ελαιοδώρα ἡ Σαραντηνὴ ἡ Τζυμυπίνισσα).

The unusual name ᾿Ιντανῖνα seems to be the feminine form of the name of Anna's first husband.

SEBASTOPOULOS

The surname Sebastopoulos (Σεβαστόπουλος) derives from the dignity of σεβαστός (cf. Domestikopoulos, Tourmarchopoulos and the like).[4] Almost contemporary with Helene *186* were Andronikos Sebastopoulos whose name often occurs in the correspondence of Kydones[5] and Phokas Sebastopoulos (fl. 1396).[6]

186. Helene Doukaina Sebastopoulina: The only reference to this lady is found in a manuscript notice which records her death. Helene Doukaina Sebastopoulina died as the nun Hypomone on 20 December 1407.[7]

SGOUROPOULOS

Of the many Sgouropouloi (Σγουρόπουλοι) mentioned in the fourteenth and fifteenth centuries only a few are enumerated here: Michael, Andreas, and Georgios (1357);[8] the priest Ioannes Sgouropoulos (1371);[9] the *hypodiakonos*

---

[1] Τοῦ τε ἐκείνου κυροῦ Νικολάου Δούκα τοῦ Σαραντηνοῦ, ibid.

[2] Δούκαινα κυρὰ ῎Αννα Σαραντηνὴ ἡ ᾿Ιντανῖνα, MM, I, p. 283.

[3] MM, I, pp. 283–4.

E. Kourilas, ' Τὰ ἁγιορειτικὰ ἀρχεῖα καὶ ὁ κατάλογος Πορφυρίου Οὐσπένσκη ', EEBΣ, 7 (1930), 222, mentions a Stephanos Doukas Sarantenos (Στέφανον Δούκαν τὸν Σαρανδηνόν), apparently in a document of 1422. This is certainly wrong. The man should be Stephanos Doukas Radenos *179*.

[4] After 1453 the family is found in Chios; see Ph. P. Argenti, *Libro d'Oro de la Noblesse de Chio* (London, 1955), II, pp. 125–6; II, pp. 249–52 (family trees).

[5] R.-J. Loenertz, *Démétrius Cydonès, Correspondance*, II (Rome, 1960), p. 89 and *passim*.

[6] L. Petit, *Actes du Pantocrator* (St Petersburg, 1903), p. 31.

[7] Τῷ αὐτῷ ἔτει (= ‚ϛ᾿λιϛ´) κατὰ τὸν δεκέ(μβ)ριον τῇ κ´ ἀπέθανεν ῾Ελένη Δούκαινα ἡ Σεβαστοπουλῖνα, μετονομασθεῖσα ῾Υπομονὴ μοναχή, see A. Gonzato, 'Il codice Marciano greco 408 e la data del romanzo bizantino di Alessandro con una ipotesi sull'autore', BΖ, 56 (1963), 248.

[8] MM, I, pp. 371, 374, and 375.

[9] G. I. Theocharides, ' Οἱ Τζαμπλάκωνες. Συμβολὴ εἰς τὴν Μακεδονικὴν προσωπογραφίαν τοῦ ΙΔ´ αἰῶνος ', Μακεδονικά, 5 (1961/3), 153.

Manuel Sgouropoulos (1387);[1] the priest Michael Sgouropoulos (1390/1400);[2] Iakobos (1400);[3] Manuel (1446);[4] the priests Nikolaos and Christophoros (1314).[5] During the earlier period the name is not so common. In 1286 there is the *pansebastos sebastos* δομέστικος τῶν ἀνατολικῶν θεμάτων Manuel Sgouropoulos.[6]

187. Doukas Sgouropoulos: The fourteenth-century cod. Marc. gr. App. Cl. V, 8, containing medical works, was thought to have been written by an Argyropoulos Doukas.[7] But this is a bad reading of the scribe's true name which is Doukas Sgouropoulos: Πόνημα χειρὸς Δούκα τοῦ Σγουροπούλου.[8]

SGOUROS

The common word σγουρός (curly)[9] was a popular surname among the Greeks. The surname is met in the forms Σγοῦρος and Σγουρός. The earliest bearer of it is perhaps Leon Sgouros who in 1088 was χαρτουλάριος τοῦ σεκρέτου τοῦ γενικοῦ λογοθέτου.[10] Some other Sgouroi are: the *sebastos* Ioannes Sgouros (1188/99);[11] the *megas logariastes* Michael Sgouros (1192/7);[12] Leon Sgouros the cruel ruler of Argos (1204), perhaps the most famous of all; Michael Sgouros (1357);[13] στρατιώτης Σγοῦρος;[14] Theodoros Sgoures in Thessalonica (1415);[15] Petros and Georgios (1453).[16]

188. Andronikos Doukas Sgouros: Andronikos Doukas Sgouros who presumably lived during the last years of the empire is said to have composed a polemical work against the Latins.[17] Some other writings have been preserved under his name:

1. A schematic diaeresis of divine providence and the pre-destination of men, cod. Laur. Conv. soppr. 117 (s. xv), fol. 147v.[18]

---

[1] MM, II, p. 98.   [2] MM, II, pp. 141, 345, and 357.   [3] MM, II, p. 344.

[4] M. I. Manousakas, ' Στέφανος Κατράριος ὁ πρῶτος γνωστὸς Ἕλληνας νοτάριος τῆς Χίου ', *Εἰς Μνήμην Κ. Ἀμάντου 1874–1960* (Athens, 1960), p. 271.

[5] Petit, *Actes de Chilandar* pp. 59–60.

[6] Dölger, *Regesten*, IV, p. 9, no. 2115.   [7] Vogel–Gardthausen, *Schreiber*, p. 113.

[8] Sp. P. Lampros, 'Ἀργυροπούλεια (Athens, 1910), p. πς'.

[9] For the connotations of the word see D. I. Georgakas, ' Περὶ τῆς λέξεως σγουρὸς καὶ τῶν συγγενῶν ', *Ἀθηνᾶ*, 47 (1937), 37–52.   [10] MM, I, p. 373.

[11] MM, VI, pp. 124, 129, and 143. This is probably to be identified with an Ioannes Sgouros mentioned in Lampros, ' Μαρκιανὸς 524 ', p. 143.

[12] MM, III, p. 37; IV, p. 141.   [13] MM, I, p. 373.

[14] R.-J. Loenertz, *Démétrius Cydonès, Correspondance*, II (Rome, 1960), p. 123.

[15] Euthymios Dionysiates and St. P. Kyriakides, ' Ἔγγραφα τῆς ἱερᾶς μονῆς τοῦ Ἁγίου Διονυσίου ἀφορῶντα εἰς ἀγνώστους ναοὺς τῆς Θεσσαλονίκης ', *Μακεδονικά*, 3 (1953/5), 364.

[16] M. Manoussakas, 'Les derniers défenseurs crétois de Constantinople d'après les documents vénitiens', *Akten des XI. Internationalen Byzantinistenkongress München 1958* (Munich, 1960), p. 337.

[17] A. Demetrakopoulos, Ὀρθόδοξος Ἑλλάς (Leipzig, 1872), p. 96; K. Krumbacher, *Geschichte der byzantinischen Literatur* (Munich, 1897²), p. 114; H.-G. Beck, *Kirche und theologische Literatur im byzantinischen Reich* (Munich, 1959), p. 753.

[18] Ἀνδρονίκου Δούκα τοῦ Σγούρου ἡ διαίρεσις αὕτη. See E. Rostagno and N. Festa, 'Indice dei codici greci laurenziani non compresi nel catalogo del Bandini', *Studi Italiani di Filologia Classica*, 1 (1893), 156; cf. H. Beck, *Vorsehung und Vorherbestimmung in der theologischen Literatur der Byzantiner* (Rome, 1937), pp. 147–9.

2. A poem on the Holy Trinity, cod. Oxon. Cromwell 10 (s.xvi), fol. 472v–473r.[1]

3. Church hymns, cod. *Ἀλεξίου Κολυβᾶ* 71 (s.xv), fol. 23r.[2]

4. Other hymns, cod. Ambr. 294 (s.xv-xvi), fol. 173–9.[3]

5. A poem on St Gregorios of Nazianzus, cod. Oxon. Cromwell 10 (s.xvi).[4]

SPARTENOS

Spartenos (*Σπαρτηνός*) is the inhabitant or the man who comes from the town of Sparta, not necessarily that of the Peloponnese. Several Spartenoi are known: a Spartenos in Thessalonica (1246);[5] Demetrios Spartenos (as a monk David) and his sons Ioannes, Konstantinos, and Michael (1265);[6] Konstantinos Spartenos (1295);[7] Demetrios Spartenos;[8] the brothers *pansebastoi sebastoi* Ioannes and Pothos (1295);[9] the *primikērios tōn taboulariōn* Petros Spartenos;[10] the *megas hetaireiarches* Georgios Spartenos and the *megas tzaousios* Ioannes Spartenos (1330);[11] the priest Sabbas Spartenos (1383);[12] Theodoros Spartenos (1400).[13]

189. Theodoros Doukas Spartenos: A *πωλητήριον γράμμα*, dated 4 July 1341, issued by the nun Agape Angelina Sphrantzaina Palaiologina speaks of her brother Theodoros Doukas Spartenos as *oikeios* to the emperor.[14] Theodoros and Agape had a sister of unknown name who was married to Manuel Phakenos.[15] It appears that this branch of Doukas-Spartenos, like some other Spartenoi, belonged to the nobility of the time.

The same document mentions a piece of land *τῆς Δουκαίνης*,[16] but it is not clear to whom this reference applies.

---

[1] H. O. Coxe, *Catalogi codicum mss. Bibliothecae Bodleianae*, 1 (Oxford, 1853), col. 431, no. 21, describes it 'Andronici Ducae Siguri carmen de S. Trinitate; per quaesitum et responsum'. I was able to check the manuscript for the author's name, and it is indeed given in the form *Ἀνδρονίκου Δούκα τοῦ Σιγούρου*, yet it can be no doubt that the surname should be corrected to read ' *Σγούρου* '. The poem consists of fifty seventeen-syllable verses.

[2] *Κατανυκτικῶν. Τὰ γράμματα κυροῦ Ἀνδρονίκου ῥήτορος τοῦ Σγούρου*; see Sp. P. Lampros, ' *Κώδικες τῆς Βιβλιοθήκης Ἀλεξίου Κολυβᾶ*', *NE*, 13 (1916), 254.

[3] *Κανόνια νέα ὀρθωθέντα παρὰ Ἀνδρονίκου Δούκα τοῦ Σγούρου*; see Ae. Martini and D. Bassi, *Catalogus codicum graecorum Bibliothecae Ambrosianae* (Milan, 1906), 1, p. 294.

[4] H. O. Coxe, op. cit., col. 432; cf. I. Sajdak, *Historia critica scholiastarum et commentatorum Gregorii Nazianzeni* (Cracow, 1914), p. 268.

[5] Skout., pp. 495–6.

[6] Petit, *Actes de Chilandar*, p. 15.

[7] Bompaire, *Actes de Xéropotamou*, pp. 100–1.

[8] F. Dölger, *Aus den Schatzkammern des Heiligen Berges* (Munich, 1948), p. 331.

[9] Ibid., p. 167.　　　　　[10] Ibid.　　　　　[11] Regel et al., *Actes de Zographou*, p. 68.

[12] MM, ii, p. 50; cf. p. 299.

[13] MM, ii, p. 303.

[14] *Τὸν ἀδελφόν μου, οἰκεῖον τῷ κραταιῷ καὶ ἁγίῳ ἡμῶν αὐθέντῃ καὶ βασιλεῖ κῦριν Θεόδωρον Δούκαν τὸν Σπαρτηνόν*, see Alexandros Lauriotes, ' *Ἀθωΐτις στοά* ', *VV*, 9 (1902), 132.

[15] Ibid. In the text *Φαξηνόν*, but since this form does not seem to be attested elsewhere it should probably be corrected to *Φακηνόν*. This last name is found in *VV*, 5 (1898), 493; P. Lemerle *Actes de Kutlumus* (Paris, 1945), p. 57.

[16] Alexandros, ' *Ἀθωΐτις στοά* ', p. 133.

N   P.T.D.

SPHRANTZES

190. Gabriel(?) Sphrantzes Doukas: His name appears in cod. Par. gr. 1348 (s. xiv), fol. 365v, which contains the Βασιλικὰ accompanied by scholia: καὶ τόδε(?) τοῦ Σφρατζὴ Γαυριὴλ(?) τοῦ Δούκα ἔχ(ων) φύλλ(α) γεγραμμ(έν)α τνς'.[1]

STRABOMYTES

Στραβομύτης means 'wry-nosed'[2] and has been used as a family name since the eleventh century. Theodoros Strabomytes was a relative and supporter of the rebel Leon Tornikios in 1048.[3] A Strabomytes Kantakouzenos lived in the fifteenth century.[4]

191. Doukas Strabomytes: A document of June 1407,[5] concerning a dispute between the monastery of the Lavra and the archbishopric of Imbros, is signed by the *oikeios* to the emperor Doukas Strabomytes.[6] Further information on the man appears to be lacking.

SYNADENOS

The name Synadenos (Συναδηνός) is a geographical designation denoting the inhabitant of the Phrygian town of Synada. The family of Synadenos appears in history early in the eleventh century, and it was always included in the nobility though many of the later Synadenoi were of lower status. Several letters survive by an official described ἀπὸ κριτῶν Philetos Synadenos and are thought to have been written in 1000–6.[7] In 1040 Basileios Synadenos was *strategos* of Dyrrachion,[8] and the emperor Botaneiates was related to a nobleman of the east, called Synadenos, to whom he wished to bequeath the throne.[9] The Synadenoi became especially prominent during the thirteenth and

[1] V. Laurent, ' Σφραντζῆς et non Φραντζῆς ', *BZ*, 44 (1951), 375, in his enumeration of the bearers of the name Sphrantzes includes the present one as 'Sphrantzès Gavrinos Ducas'. I have consulted the manuscript and I prefer to read Γαυριήλ (Gabriel) though this is also by no means certain.

[2] Cf. the surnames Strabotrichares, Strabospondylos, Strabopodos etc.

[3] Kedr., ii, pp. 564–5.

[4] Doukas, p. 239.

[5] For the date see P. Lemerle, 'Le juge général des grecs et la réforme judiciaire d'Andronic III ', *Mémorial Louis Petit* (Paris, 1948), p. 314.

[6] Οἰκεῖοι τῷ κραταιῷ καὶ ἁγίῳ ἡμῶν αὐθέντῃ καὶ βασιλεῖ ἄρχοντες δεφένσορες ὑπηρέται ἀπό τε Δούκα τοῦ Στραβομύτου καὶ Λάσκαρι τοῦ Ἀλεξανδρῆ; see S. Eustratiades, ' Ἱστορικὰ μνημεῖα τοῦ Ἄθω', Ἑλληνικά, 2 (1929), 381.

[7] J. Darrouzès, *Epistoliers byzantins du Xe siècle* (Paris, 1960), pp. 48–9.

[8] Kedr., ii, p. 527. He is the 'Sinodianus' of William of Apulia, i, v. 406 (ed. M. Mathieu, p. 120; cf. p. 273).

[9] Συναδηνός τις ἐξ ἀνατολῶν ὁρμώμενος, ἐκ γένους λαμπροῦ ... προσήκων αὐτῷ (sc. Βοτανειάτῃ) κατὰ γένος, *Alexias*, i, p. 155.

fourteenth centuries when they intermarried with other wealthy aristocrats including the Palaiologoi.[1]

It is not clear how the thirteenth-century Synadenoi acquired the name of Doukas. They may have been the descendants of Andronikos Synadenos[2] who was married to Zoe, a daughter of Konstantinos Angelos and a sister of Ioannes *40* and Andronikos *39*. It is also possible that they were related to a certain Synadenos, described as one τῶν ἐπιφανῶν,[3] who in c. 1224 was implicated in the conspiracy of Andronikos Nestongos against Batazes.

192. Konstantinos Doukas Synadenos: As an imperial official, Konstantinos Doukas Synadenos signed a document (τὸ ἐκδοτήριον τῆς μοναχῆς Μάρθας τῆς Θρᾳκησίνης) dated July 1274.[4] Nothing else is known of the man; he may have been a brother of Ioannes *193*.

193. Ioannes Komnenos Angelos Doukas Synadenos: The family of the *megas stratopedarches*[5] Ioannes is known from the *Typikon* of the convent of *Βεβαίας 'Ελπίδος* in Constantinople, founded by his wife. Pachymeres always calls him Synadenos,[6] but Ioannes himself also claimed ancestry with the Komnenoi.[7] He participated in several campaigns. In c. 1276, together with Michael Kaballarios, he led an army against Ioannes Doukas *52* of Thessaly but was defeated and captured.[8] In 1281 he took part in a campaign in Epirus to repulse the Angevin invaders.[9] Two years later he was ordered to join forces with the Byzantine fleet.[10] It should also be noted that Ioannes possessed a private library, two items of which have come down to us.[11]

Ioannes Synadenos married Theodora, a daughter of Konstantinos Palaiologos *149*.[12] They had four children: Ioannes *194*, Theodoros *196*, Euphrosyne *198*, and another daughter of unknown name. Presumably this last one was once spoken of as a candidate bride for the Bulgarian king Theodore Svetoslav.[13]

---

[1] For the members of the family during the later Byzantine period see H. Omont, 'Portraits de différents membres de la famille des Comnène peints dans le *Typicon* du monastère de Notre-Dame-de-Bonne-Espérance à Constantinople', *REG*, 17 (1904), 361–73; Delehaye, *Deux Typica*, pp. 143–51; P. Lemerle, *Actes de Kutlumus* (Paris, 1945), pp. 68–9; G. I. Theocharides, ''*Άγνωστα τοπογραφικὰ τῆς Θεσσαλονίκης ἐξ ἀνεκδότου ἐγγράφου τῆς ἐν 'Αγίῳ ''Ορει μονῆς Διονυσίου* ', *Μακεδονικά*, 5 (1961/3), 3.

[2] For the man see V. Laurent, 'Andronic Synadénos ou la carrière d'un haut fonctionnaire byzantin au XIIe siècle', *REB*, 20 (1962), 210–14.

[3] Akrop., p. 37.

[4] '*Ο δοῦλος τοῦ κραταιοῦ καὶ ἁγίου ἡμῶν αὐθέντου καὶ βασιλέως Κωνσταντῖνος ὁ Δούκας ὁ Συναδηνός, οἰκείᾳ χειρὶ προέταξα*, MM, IV, p. 106.

[5] Cf. R. Guilland, 'Etudes sur l'histoire administrative de l'empire byzantin: le stratopédarque et le grand stratopédarque , *BZ*, 46 (1953), 74–5.

[6] Pach., I, p. 411, 412, and 512; II, pp. 69 and 267.

[7] *Εἰς Κομνηνοὺς μὲν καὶ Συναδηνοὺς σαφῶς τὸ γένος ἀνέφερε τῷ τοῦ μεγάλου δὲ στρατοπεδάρχου καὶ πρό γε τῶν γάμων πρὸς τοῦ βασιλέως ὑψώθη λαμπρῶς ἀξιώματι*, Delehaye, *Deux Typica*, p. 24; cf. the compounds used: '*Ιωάννης Κομνηνὸς Δούκας Συναδηνὸς καὶ μέγας στρατοπεδάρχης καὶ κτήτωρ*, ibid., p. 13; *τοῦ μεγάλου στρατοπεδάρχου 'Αγγέλου Δούκα τοῦ Συναδηνοῦ κυροῦ Ιωάννου*, ibid., p. 81. He is also referred to in a poem of Philes (Miller), II, p. 164.

[8] Pach., I, pp. 411–12; cf. D. J. Geanakoplos, *Emperor Michael Palaeologus and the West* (Cambridge, Mass., 1958), p. 297.

[9] Pach., I, p. 512; cf. Geanakoplos, op. cit., pp. 331–3.   [10] Pach., II, p. 69.

[11] R. Devreesse, *Introduction à l'étude des manuscrits grecs* (Paris, 1954), p. 94.

[12] Papadopulos, *Genealogie der Palaiologen*, p. 9, no. 11.

[13] Cf. Pach., II, p. 267.

Ioannes died as the monk Ioakeim on 6 February[1] of an unknown year before 1345.[2]

194. Ioannes Komnenos Doukas Palaiologos Synadenos: He was a son, thought to be the elder,[3] of Ioannes *193* and Theodora and carried the rank of *megas kontostablos*.[4] The name 'Palaiologos' was obviously inherited from his mother. Ioannes married Thomais *195*,[5] but no children of his are mentioned. His mother speaks of a plot of land and some unspecified houses as belonging to him.[6]

195. Thomais Komnene Doukaina Laskarina Kantakouzene Palaiologina: Thomais was the wife of Ioannes *194* and she obviously inherited the names of Laskaris and Kantakouzenos from her parents and that of Palaiologos from her husband. She died on 11 February before the *Typikon* was written and had already embraced the monastic life with the name of Xene.[7]

196. Theodoros Komnenos Doukas Synadenos: Theodoros was a son of Ioannes *193* and Theodora and took an active part in the fourteenth-century civil strives. His name is given as Doukas,[8] Komnenos Doukas Synadenos,[9] or more frequently simply Synadenos.[10] He is also once called Palaiologos Synadenos.[11]

---

[1] Ὡσαύτως ποιήσετε μνημόσυνα καθ'ἑκάστην τοῦ χρόνου περίοδον τὴν ἔκτην τοῦ φεβρουαρίου μηνὸς καὶ ὑπὲρ τοῦ μακαρίου κτήτορος ὑμῶν τοῦ μεγάλου στρατοπεδάρχου Ἀγγέλου Δούκα τοῦ Συναδηνοῦ κυροῦ Ἰωάννου, τοῦ διὰ τοῦ θείου καὶ ἀγγελικοῦ σχήματος μετονομασθέντος Ἰωακεὶμ μοναχοῦ, Delehaye, *Deux Typica*, p. 81.

[2] *Terminus ante quem* of Theodora's *Typikon*; see R. Janin, *Les Eglises et les Monastères* (Paris. 1953), p. 166. The document was certainly written after 1310; cf. Delehaye, *Deux Typica*, p. 148.

[3] Delehaye, *Deux Typica*, p. 149.

[4] Ἰωάννης Κομνηνὸς Δούκας Συναδηνὸς ὁ μέγας κονόσταυλος, Delehaye, *Deux Typica*, p. 13; κυροῦ Ἰωάννου τοῦ Παλαιολόγου καὶ μεγάλου κονοσταύλου, ibid., pp. 82 and 91; cf. R. Guilland, 'Etudes sur l'histoire administrative de l'empire byzantin: le grand connétable', *B*, 19 (1949), 108; Papadopulos, *Genealogie der Palaiologen*, pp. 9–10, no. 12. Kant., I, p. 133, refers to him as τὸν μέγαν κονόσταυλον Ἰωάννην Παλαιολόγον, τὸν πρωτοστράτορος ἀδελφόν, but Papadopulos, *Genealogie der Palaiologen*, pp. 79–80, no. 128, wrongly distinguishes this man from Ioannes.

[5] The portraits of Ioannes and his wife are accompanied by the legends: Ἰωάννης Κομνηνὸς Δούκας Συναδηνὸς ὁ μέγας κονόσταυλος καὶ υἱὸς τῶν κτητόρων. Εἰρήνη Λασκαρίνα Κομνηνὴ Δούκαινα ἡ Παλαιολογίνα ἡ μεγάλη κονοσταύλισσα καὶ νύμφη τῆς κτητορίσσης, Delehaye, *Deux Typica*, p. 13. The name Eirene may be a mistake for Thomais; this seems more likely than a second marriage of Ioannes, cf. the editor's comments ibid., pp. 149–50.

[6] ... τῶν μεγάλων οἰκημάτων τῶν περιποθήτων μου υἱῶν ... τῶν δύο περιβολίων τοῦ τε περιποθήτου μου υἱοῦ κυροῦ Ἰωάννου τοῦ μεγάλου κονοσταύλου καὶ τῆς μονῆς, ibid., p. 95.

[7] Τῷ μηνὶ φεβρουαρίῳ ια' τελείσθωσαν τὰ μνημόσυνα τῆς περιποθήτου μου νύμφης, τῆς γυναικός φημι τοῦ φιλτάτου μου υἱοῦ κυροῦ Ἰωάννου τοῦ Παλαιολόγου τοῦ μεγάλου κονοσταύλου, κυρᾶς Θωμαΐδος Κομνηνῆς Δουκαίνης Λασκαρίνης τε Καντακουζηνῆς τῆς Παλαιολογίνης, τῆς διὰ τοῦ θείου καὶ ἀγγελικοῦ σχήματος μετονομασθείσης Ξένης μοναχῆς, Delehaye, *Deux Typica*, p. 91; her name is also given as Θωμαΐς Παλαιολογῖνα ἡ Καντακουζηνή, ibid., p. 84.

[8] κυροῦ Θεοδώρου τοῦ Δούκα τοῦ πρωτοστράτορος, Delehaye, *Deux Typica*, pp. 82 and 91.

[9] Θεόδωρος Κομνηνὸς Δούκας Συναδηνὸς ὁ πρωτοστράτωρ καὶ υἱὸς τῶν ἐκτητόρων, ibid., p. 13.

[10] Greg., I, pp. 301, 432, 441, 446; II, pp. 623 and 633; Kant., I, pp. 367, 459; II, pp. 77, 191, 298 etc. For Theodoros see Papadopulos, *Genealogie der Palaiologen*, p. 10, no. 13; R. Guilland, 'Etudes de titulature et de prosopographie byzantines: le protostrator', pp. 168–9; P. Lemerle, *Actes de Kutlumus* (Paris, 1945), pp. 68–9; F. Dölger, *Aus den Schatzkammern des Heiligen Berges* (Munich, 1948), p. 146.

[11] ... πρωτοστράτορος κυροῦ Θεοδώρου Παλαιολόγου τοῦ Συναδηνοῦ, L. Petit, *Actes de Xénophon* (St Petersburg, 1903), p. 80.

Theodoros Synadenos used to live at Bizye in Thrace where he possessed extensive estates and had great power.[1] He was described as being of the same age as Michael IX,[2] and, therefore, he must have been born in about 1277. Theodoros was among the first supporters of Andronikos III in 1321 and energetically assisted him until 1328. In 1330 he was sent as governor to Mesembria,[3] subsequently to Epirus (1336),[4] and in 1341 to Thessalonica[5] from which he was expelled by the Zealots in the summer of 1342[6] and returned to Constantinople where he now made peace with his enemy Alexios Apokaukos.[7] However, he was soon confined to his house and remained under guard until he died in c. 1346.[8]

In the course of his career Theodoros held the titles: *domestikos epi tēs trapezēs* (1321),[9] *protostrator*,[10] and *protovestiarios* (after 1342).[11]

Theodoros married Eudokia *197* and became the father of at least two daughters: Theodora *199* and Anna *200*.

197. Eudokia Doukaina Komnene Synadene Palaiologina: She was a daughter of Theodoros Doukas Mouzakios *128*[12] and became the wife of Theodoros *196*. The compound form of her name[13] is that of her husband's family. Eudokia died after 1345.

198. Euphrosyne Komnene Doukaina Palaiologina: Euphrosyne[14] was a daughter of Ioannes *193* but had been 'promised' to God since childhood and became a nun. She was the second founder of Βεβαίας 'Ελπίδος and added some chapters to the original *Typikon* in the second half of the fourteenth century.

199. Theodora Komnene Doukaina Raoulaina Palaiologina: She was a daughter of Theodoros *196* and Eudokia *197* who died before the *Typikon* was written on 23 July after having assumed the monastic name of Theodosia.[15] Her unmentioned husband may have been a Raoul.

---

[1] Πρωτοστράτωρ γὰρ ὁ τούτου (sc. Μανουὴλ τοῦ 'Ασάνη) πενθερὸς ἐκεῖ (sc. ἐν Βιζύῃ) τὴν οἰκίαν ἔχων ἐξαρχῆς κτήσεις τε πλείστας καὶ μεγάλας εἶχεν ἐν αὐτῇ, καὶ τῶν συγγενῶν καὶ τῶν οἰκείων ἐκεῖ πολλοὶ κατῴκουν, ὑφ᾽ ὧν ἤγετο σχεδὸν ἡ πόλις, Kant., II, p. 491.

[2] Greg., I, p. 301.   [3] Τὸν πρωτοστράτορα εἰς Μεσημβρίαν ἄρχοντα πέμπει, Kant., I, p. 459.

[4] 'Επὶ πᾶσιν ἀποδείξας στρατηγὸν καὶ τἆλλα πάντα ὡς ἂν αὐτῷ ἐδόκει διοικησάμενος, Kant., I, p. 504.

[5] Θεσσαλονίκης μὲν γάρ, καὶ τῶν πέριξ Στρυμόνος τοῦ ποταμοῦ πόλεων, ἣν ἐπίτροπος ὁ πρωτοστράτωρ, Θεόδωρος Συναδηνός, Greg., II, p. 623; ὅ τε πρωτοστράτωρ Συναδηνὸς Θεσσαλονίκης ἐπιτροπεύων, Kant., II, p. 77; cf. p. 191.

[6] Greg., II, pp. 633–5,

[7] Kant., II, p. 492.   [8] Ibid.   [9] Greg., I, p. 301.

[10] Cf. Guilland, 'Protostrator', pp. 168–9.

[11] Kant., II, p. 492; cf. R. Guilland, 'Fonctions et dignités des eunuques', *EB*, 2 (1944), 219.

[12] Delehaye, *Deux Typica*, p. 94.

[13] Εὐδοκία Δούκαινα Κομνηνὴ Συναδηνὴ ἡ Παλαιολογῖνα ἡ πρωτοστρατόρισσα καὶ νύμφη τῆς κτητορίσσης, ibid., p. 13. Eudokia is presumably the Συναδηνή, mentioned by Kant., II, p. 296, as being in prison in Thessalonica in 1342.

[14] Εὐφροσύνη μοναχὴ Κομνηνὴ Δούκαινα Παλαιολογῖνα καὶ θυγάτηρ τῶν ἐκτητόρων, Delehaye, *Deux Typica*, p. 14; κυρᾶς Εὐφροσύνης τῆς Παλαιολογίνης, ibid., p. 81; κυρὰ Εὐφροσύνη ἡ Παλαιολογῖνα, ibid., p. 96; cf. Papadopulos, *Genealogie der Palaiologen*, p. 11, no. 15.

[15] Τῇ κγ΄ τοῦ ἰουλίου μηνὸς ὀφείλουσι γίνεσθαι τὰ μνημόσυνα τῆς περιποθήτου ἐγγόνης μου, τῆς θυγατρὸς τοῦ περιποθήτου μου υἱοῦ κυροῦ Θεοδώρου Δούκα τοῦ πρωτοστράτορος, κυρᾶς Θεοδώρας Κομνηνῆς Δουκαίνης 'Ραουλαίνης τῆς Παλαιολογίνης, τῆς διὰ τοῦ θείου καὶ ἀγγελικοῦ σχήματος μετονομασθείσης Θεοδοσίας μοναχῆς, Delehaye, *Deux Typica*, p. 91; cf. Papadopulos, *Genealogie der Palaiologen*, p. 10, no. 14.

200. Anna Komnene Doukaina Palaiologina Asanina: Anna was a daughter of Theodoros *196* and Eudokia *197* and became the wife of the *megas primikērios* Manuel Asan, a brother-in-law of Ioannes VI Kantakouzenos.[1] She was the mother of the *sebastokrator* Andronikos Asan.[2]

201. Euphrosyne Doukaina Palaiologina: She was an unspecified grand-daughter of Ioannes *193* and Theodora and married the *prōtosebastos* Konstantinos Komnenos Raoul Palaiologos.[3] Other information on her is lacking.

202. Melane: Melane (evidently a nun's name) was a scion of the families of Synadenos, Skouterios, Strategopoulos, and Doukas (the Angelos branch) and became the wife of the *prōtoierakarios* Demetrios Palaiologos.[4] She had three children but apparently she outlived them all. At the end of her life Melane retired to a convent and Philes wrote her epitaph.[5]

SYRANERES

203. Doukas Syraneres: He appears as a witness at Serres in a document of November 1345.[6]

SYROPOULOS

Συρόπουλος originally meant some one who came from Syria.[7] Syropouloi appear in Byzantium quite frequently from the twelfth century onwards.

204. Syropoulos Doukas: The only Syropoulos who assumed the name of Doukas belongs to the post-Byzantine period. He was a priest in Thessalonica and also a scribe who wrote cod. Esphigmenou *87* (Athous 2100), a πατερικόν, on 10 May 1474. The colophon of the manuscript reads: Ἐτελειώθη ἡ θεία

---

[1] Kant., I, p. 125; II, p. 491. Their portraits are accompanied by the inscription: Μανουὴλ ʽΡαοὺλ ᾿Ασάνης καὶ μέγας πριμικήριος καὶ γαμβρὸς τῆς κτητορίσσης· ῎Αννα Κομνηνὴ Δούκαινα Παλαιολογῖνα ᾿Ασανῖνα ἡ μεγάλη πριμικήρισσα καὶ ἐγγόνη τῆς κτητορίσσης, Delehaye, *Deux Typica*, p. 13; cf. Papadopulos, *Genealogie der Palaiologen*, p. 12, no. 18.

[2] Papadopulos, *Genealogie der Palaiologen*, p. 12, no. 18.

[3] Κωνσταντῖνος Κομνηνὸς ʽΡαοὺλ ὁ Παλαιολόγος ὁ πρωτοσεβαστὸς καὶ γαμβρὸς τῆς κτητορίσσης· Εὐφροσύνη Δούκαινα Παλαιολογῖνα ἡ πρωτοσεβαστὴ καὶ ἐγγόνη τῆς κτητορίσσης, Delehaye, *Deux Typica*, p. 13; cf. Papadopulos, *Genealogie der Palaiologen*, pp. 12–13, no. 20.

[4]
Πατρίδα μὲν δὴ τὴν καλὴν ἔσχον πόλιν,
γεννήτορας δὲ τοὺς κατ᾽αὐτὴν ὀλβίους,
ἢ τί λέγειν χρὴ Συναδηνοὺς ἐνθάδε,
Σαμψὼν Γαβαλᾶν, ἀλλὰ καὶ Σκουτερίους,
Στρατηγοπούλους, Δούκας ᾿Αγγελωνύμους,
πρωθιερακάριον ὡς ὁμευνέτην
ἐκ Περσίδος φανέντα ʽΡωμαίοις μέγαν
ᾧ Βασιλικὸς ἦν τάχα τοὐπώνυμον

Philes (Miller), I, pp. 87–8; cf. Papadopulos, *Genealogie der Palaiologen*, pp. 73–4, no. 109.

[5] Philes (Miller), I, pp. 86–8; Philes (Martini), pp. 69–73.

[6] Petit, *Actes de Chilandar*, p. 281.

[7] Cf. similar ἐθνικὰ ending in -πουλος in K. Amantos, ʽ Τουρκόπωλοι ᾽, ʽΕλληνικά, 6 (1933), 325–6. Some bearers of the name in Laurent, *Médaillier Vatican*, pp. 206–7.

δέλτος διὰ χειρὸς ἐμοῦ τοῦ ἁμαρτωλοῦ Συροπούλου τοῦ Δούκα ἁγιοσοφίτου δομεστίκου καὶ λαμπαδαρίου Θεσσαλονίκης (...) μηνὶ μαΐου ι΄ ἰνδ. η΄ ἡμέρᾳ Τετράδῃ ἔτος ͵ϛλπβ΄.¹

I am inclined to identify this *domestikos* and *lampadarios* Syropoulos Doukas with a writer of ecclesiastical music of the same name who wrote χερουβικὰ and is considered of unknown date.²

TARCHANEIOTES

It is very probable that the family name Tarchaneiotes (Ταρχανειώτης) derived from Ταρχάνιον,³ a village in Thrace mentioned in 1298.⁴ The Tarchaneiotai were a noble and wealthy house, attested since the eleventh century, and during the period of the Palaiologoi they repeatedly intermarried with members of the ruling family. The name of Doukas must have been adopted by them in the thirteenth century. It may have been passed to them through the Angeloi.

205. Tarchaneiotes Angelos Doukas (Komnenos): Philes wrote two short poems for him⁵ but does not give his first name. He seems to have been an army man who died as a monk at a comparatively young age.⁶

206. Komnenos Tarchaneiotes Doukas Kantakouzenos: He is known from the poem Philes wrote for his death.⁷ He was killed quite young in military action, either in Serbia or in Bulgaria. Philes remarks that N descended from 'emperors' and that his father had been *megas domestikos tēs basilikēs trapezēs*.⁸

---

¹ Sp. P. Lampros, Κατάλογοι τῶν ἐν ταῖς μοναῖς τοῦ ʽΑγίου ʺΟρους ʽΕλληνικῶν κωδίκων, I (Cambridge, 1895), p. 180; Vogel–Gardthausen, *Schreiber*, p. 411. The 8th indiction does not correspond to the year 1475. 1θ May 1475, was indeed a Wednesday.

² Cf. Spyridon Lauriotes and S. Eustratiades, Κατάλογος τῶν κωδίκων τῆς Μεγίστης Λαύρας (Cambridge, Mass., 1925), p. 449.

³ K. I. Amantos, ʽ Σύμμεικτα: Πόθεν τὸ ὄνομα Ταρχανειώτης ʼ, ʽΕλληνικά, 2 (1929), 435–6. For the family see D. A. Zakythinos, ʽ Μιχαὴλ Μάρουλλος Ταρχανειώτης, ʺΕλλην ποιητὴς τῶν χρόνων τῆς ʼΑναγεννήσεως ʼ, ΕΕΒΣ, 5 (1929), 201, n. 3; P. Lemerle, *Actes de Kutlumus* (Paris, 1945), pp. 124–5.

⁴ In Metochites' Πρεσβευτικός, Sathas, *MB*, I, p. 161.   ⁵ Philes (Martini), pp. 135–7

⁶ The first poem entitled ʼΕπιτάφιοι ʼΑγγέλῳ τῷ Ταρχανειώτῃ describes him as

Ταρχανειώτης ʺΑγγελος θνητὸς Δούκας
Κομνηνοφυὴς τὴν τιμὴν ἄρχων μέγας,

Philes (Martini), p. 136.

⁷ ʼΕπιτάφιοι Κομνηνῷ Δούκᾳ τῷ Καντακουζηνῷ πεσόντι ἐν γῇ βαρβάρων, Philes (Martini), pp. 125–6, vv. 36.

⁸ The poem begins:

ʺΑωρε νεκρὲ καὶ πρὸ καιροῦ πρεσβῦτα,
Κομνηνέ (βαβαὶ τοῦ κενοῦ τοῦδε κτύπου)
Ταρχανειῶτα Δούκα (παπαὶ τῶν κρότων)
Καντακουζηνέ (ταῦτα γὰρ κλήσεις ἔχεις),
πῶς ἄρα, πῶς πέπτωκας ἐν γῇ βαρβάρων;
καὶ γὰρ ἀγαθῆς εὑρεθεὶς ῥίζης κλάδος
(ἐπεὶ βασιλεῖς εἰς τὸ πᾶν ἔσχες γένος,
ὁ δὲ σπορεὺς ἦν ὡς μέγας καὶ τὴν φύσιν
τῆς βασιλικῆς τραπέζης δομέστικος).

The identity of this official ἐπὶ τῆς τραπέζης remains unknown. R. Guilland, 'Fonctions et dignités des eunuques', *EB*, 3 (1945), 187, mentions only three holders of that office, none of whom can possibly be taken as the father of N.

Shortly before his death,[1] N became the son-in-law of a likewise unidentified nephew of the emperor[2] — perhaps of Andronikos II. The reference to the wife of the *megas domestikos*[3] (presumably Ioannes Kantakouzenos) points to the period 1328–41 as the time of N's death.

207. Manuel Doukas Tarchaneiotes: Manuel Doukas Tarchaneiotes is mentioned in three documents of the monastery of Koutloumousiou of the year 1375. Not much personal detail can be gathered from them. The first document is a private letter of Manuel, who signs as 'Manuel Tarchaneiotes', to his brother (see below), communicating a decision of their father who was then *megas chartophylax* at Thessalonica.[4] The second document bears Manuel's full signature,[5] and in the third one he is spoken of as *oikeios* to the emperor and *kephalē* of the town of Serres.[6]

208. Doukas Tarchaneiotes: He was a brother of Manuel *207* and likewise a son of the unknown *megas chartophylax* of Thessalonica.[7]

TORNIKES

Originally a branch of the Armenian princely house of Taron (the Taronitai), the family of Tornikios (*Τορνίκιος* later *Τορνίκης*) had been active since the middle of the tenth century but did not achieve distinction until the eleventh. Their prominent representative Leon Tornikes who revolted in 1048 had his residence and his support in Adrianople.[8] Later on the Tornikai married into the Byzantine aristocracy, and some of their members distinguished themselves in learning.[9] In 1258 the Tornikai are mentioned as having been related to

---

[1]   κάθευδε λοιπόν, ὦ πρὸ μικροῦ νυμφίε,
Philes (Martini), p. 126, v. 27.
[2]   γαμβρὸν δ'ἐπ'αὐτῇ δυστυχῶς τῇ φιλτάτῃ
                             ἀδελφιδοῦς ἄνακτος ἐκτήσατό σε,
Philes (Martini), p. 126, vv. 13–14.
[3]   ἡ τοῦ μεγάλου σύζυγος δομεστίκου,
Philes (Martini), p. 126, v. 18.
[4] Lemerle, op. cit., p. 125.
[5] Ὁ δοῦλος τοῦ κραταιοῦ καὶ ἁγίου ἡμῶν αὐθέντου καὶ βασιλέως Μανουὴλ Δούκας ὁ Ταρχανειώτης, ibid., p. 130.   [6] Ibid., p. 131.
[7] Τῷ γλυκυτάτῳ χρυσῷ καὶ ἁγίῳ μου αὐθέντῃ καὶ ἀδελφῷ, τῇ καρδίᾳ μου τὰ ὀμμάτιά μου, Δούκᾳ τῷ Ταρχανειώτῃ, ibid., p. 125. The editor (p. 124) considers that this Doukas Tarchaneiotes is actually Manuel, the signatory of the other two documents. The signatory of the first document Manuel Tarchaneiotes, is taken as his brother and Lemerle is inclined to explain the name Manuel, supposedly borne by the two brothers, as a copyist's error. It appears more likely that the name Manuel refers to one brother and Doukas Tarchaneiotes (mentioned in the passage cited above), to the second.   [8] Kedr., II, p. 561; Attal., p. 22; Psellos, II, p. 14.
[9] For the family and its members see N. Adontz, 'Les Taronites à Byzance', B, 11 (1936), 30–42; idem, 'Tornik le moine', B, 13 (1938), 143–64; idem, 'Observations sur la généalogie des Taronites', B, 14 (1959), 407–13. On the Armenian origins of the family see N. Akinean, 'Die Genealogie der Tornikier' in *Untersuchungen zur Geschichte der armenischen Literatur* (Vienna, 1938), pp. 49–88 (in Armenian with German summary and inaccessible to me), cf. *BZ*, 38 (1938), 520; P. Charanis, 'The Armenians in the Byzantine Empire', *BS*, 22 (1961), 229–30 and n. 173 for further bibliography; R. Browning, 'The Patriarchal School at Constantinople in the Twelfth century', B, 33 (1963), 34–8.

Ioannes III Batatzes,[1] and this may perhaps explain the name of Doukas which some of them bear in the fourteenth century. It is possible that an unknown Tornikes was married to a sister of Batatzes.

209. Isaakios Komnenos Doukas Tornikes: Isaakios is only mentioned as the husband of Maria Palaiologina *151*.[2] He died as the monk Ioasaph on 8 January of an unknown year before the *Typikon* of *Βεβαίας Ἐλπίδος* was written[3] (1310/45). Isaakios became the father of Andronikos *210*.

210. Andronikos Komnenos Doukas Palaiologos Tornikes: The *parakoimōmenos* Andronikos Tornikes is the only known son of Isaakios *209* and Maria *151*. The name Palaiologos was inherited from his mother. Like his father, Andronikos became a monk under the name of Antonios and died on 3 July of an unknown year before the *Typikon* was written.[4] He seems to have married a lady of the Tzamplakon family who died before 1356.[5]

TRICHAS

The epithet τριχᾶς is appropriate for a man with thick hair.[6] Several persons carrying the name of Trichas are known: Konstantinos Trichas in 1197;[7] Philes wrote an epitaph for Ioannes Trichas;[8] Manuel Trichas is mentioned in 1357;[9] Andronikos Trichas was υἱὸς Τριχᾶ τοῦ φύλακος ἐκείνου (*c*. 1400);[10] Theodora ἡ Τριχάδαινα lived in 1401 and was the mother of another Trichas.[11]

211. Ioannes Doukas Trichas: Ioannes was a *logothetes tōn oikeiakōn* in the Empire of Trebizond and was sent by his emperor to Jerusalem as a legate where he signed a will dated November 1344.[12]

[1] The Tornikai had τὸ πρὸς τὸ ἀμφιβαλλόμενον ἰσχυρὸν τὸ ἀπὸ πατρὸς οἰκεῖον καὶ ἀδελφικὸν ἐν γράμματι πρὸς τὸν τοῦ νέου (sc. Ioannes IV) πάππον καὶ βασιλέα Ἰωάννην τὸν Δούκαν, Pach., II, p. 64.

[2] Papadopulos, *Genealogie der Palaiologen*, p. 8, no. 8.

[3] Τῇ δὲ ὀγδόῃ τοῦ ἰανουαρίου μηνὸς τελείσθωσαν καὶ τὰ τοῦ ἀνδρὸς αὐτῆς (sc. *Μαρίας*) μνημόσυνα κυροῦ Ἰσαακίου Κομνηνοῦ Δούκα τοῦ Τορνίκη, τοῦ διὰ τοῦ θείου καὶ ἀγγελικοῦ σχήματος μετονομασθέντος Ἰωάσαφ μοναχοῦ, see Delehaye, *Deux Typika*, p. 92.

[4] Μηνὶ ἰουλίῳ γ′ τελείσθωσαν τὰ μνημόσυνα τοῦ περιποθήτου μου ἀνεψιοῦ, τοῦ υἱοῦ αὐτῶν (sc. Ἰσαακίου καὶ Μαρίας) κυροῦ Ἀνδρονίκου Κομνηνοῦ Δούκα Παλαιολόγου τοῦ Τορνίκη καὶ παρακοιμουμένου (sic), τοῦ διὰ τοῦ θείου καὶ ἀγγελικοῦ σχήματος μετονομασθέντος Ἀντωνίου μοναχοῦ, Delehaye, *Deux Typica*, p. 93; cf. Papadopulos, *Genealogie der Palaiologen*, p. 8, no. 9.

[5] See G. I. Theocharides, ' Οἱ Τζαμπλάκωνες. Συμβολὴ εἰς τὴν Βυζαντινὴν Μακεδονικὴν προσωπογραφίαν τοῦ ΙΔ′ αἰῶνος ', Μακεδονικά, 5 (1961/3), 173. This is based on a document of 1356 of Arsenios Tzamplakon who speaks of τὴν αὐταδέλφην μου ἐκείνην παρακοιμωμένην τὴν Τορνικῖναν, ibid., p. 156.

[6] For the name see K. Amantos in Ἑλληνικά, 7 (1934), 266.

[7] MM, VI, p. 140.

[8] See M. I. Gedeon, ' Μανουὴλ τοῦ Φιλῆ ἱστορικὰ ποιήματα ', Ἐκκλησιαστικὴ Ἀλήθεια, 3 (1883), 247. This is probably the same as the *sebastos* Ioannes Trichas of MM, I, p. 170.

[9] MM, I, p. 375.

[10] MM, II, p. 406.

[11] MM, II, p. 511.

[12] Ὁ δοῦλος τοῦ ἁγίου καὶ κραταιοῦ αὐθέντου καὶ βασιλέως, ὁ καὶ ἀποκρισιάριος, παρὼν ἐπὶ τῇ διαθήκῃ ταύτῃ καὶ στηρίξας καὶ βεβαιώσας αὐτὴν ὑπογράφω Ἰωάννης Δούκας Τριχᾶς ὁ λογοθέτης τῶν οἰκειακῶν, see Papadopoulos–Kerameus, Ἀνάλεκτα, II, p. 257; cf. Chrysanthos, Ἡ Ἐκκλησία Τραπεζοῦντος (Athens, 1933), p. 514.

TSAPHAS

212. Ioannes Tsaphas Doukas Oursinos: The name of Ioannes Tsaphas
Doukas Oursinos (i.e. Orsini) is found in a chrysobull of Symeon Urosh
Palaiologos dated in January 1361. The authenticity of this document is not
above suspicion.[1] He is mentioned as *megas kontostablos* and as σύντεκνος to
Symeon[2] which probably means that Ioannes was the god-father to one of
Symeon's children. Symeon recognises Ioannes as lord of Leucada and certain
towns in the mainland. Ioannes Tsaphas[3] was claimed as the ancestor of the
Doukatarioi.

TZYKANDELES

The surname Tzykandeles (Τζυκανδήλης) with its variants is attested since the
eleventh century. Leon Tzykandelos is probably the first mentioned.[4] Choniates
mentions a Goudelios Tzykandeles[5] who also participated in the synod of 1166[6]
and must have been one of the notables of the time. A well-known scribe
Manuel Tzykandeles flourished in 1358–70.[7] Contemporary, and possibly
identical, with him is a member of the family who figures in the epistolography
of the period.[8] Ὁ Τζυκανδάλης (sic) κῦρ Φίλιππος lived in 1400.[9] Another scribe
was Demetrios Kykandeles who was active in 1445.[10] In the fifteenth century
we meet another bearer of the name, Alexios Atzikanteles.[11]

213. Demetrios Tzykandeles Doukas: In an Ἐπίγραμμα εἰς ναὸν ἐν ᾧ
ἡ τῆς Θεομήτορος Κοίμησις, written by Manuel Philes, we read:

Κομνηνοφυὴς ταῦτά σοι Τζυκανδήλης
Δημήτριος καὶ Δούκας εὐνοίας χάριν[12]

Demetrios Tzykandeles Doukas who had commissioned the poet to compose the

---

[1] See the discussion in L. Vranoussis, Χρονικὰ Ἠπείρου (Ioannina, 1962), pp. 69–85.

[2] Ὁ περιπόθητος καὶ γλυκύτατος πατὴρ καὶ σύντεκνος τῆς βασιλείας μου, μέγας κοντόσταυλος κύριος
Ἰωάννης Τσάφας Οὐρσῖνος Δούκας,, MM, iii, p. 128.

[3] C. Hopf, *Chroniques gréco-romanes* (Berlin, 1873), p. 529, gives his name as 'Jean Ciaffa, comte
titulaire de Leucadia, 1361'.

[4] N. M. Panagiotakis, 'Λέων ὁ Διάκονος. Βιογραφικά. Χειρόγραφα καὶ ἐκδόσεις', reprinted from
ΕΕΒΣ, 34 (1965), 16, no. 2.

[5] Chon., p. 163; Skout., p. 253.

[6] *PG*, 140, cols. 236B and 253C. Two of his seals have been preserved, see Laurent, *Collection
Orghidan*, pp. 239–40, nos. 478–9.

[7] Vogel–Gardthausen, *Schreiber*, pp. 281–2; Sp. P. Lampros, ' Λακεδαιμόνιοι βιβλιογράφοι καὶ
κτήτορες κωδίκων κατὰ τοὺς μέσους αἰῶνας καὶ ἐπὶ Τουρκοκρατίας', *NE*, 4 (1907), 167–74. This may
be Tzykandeles ὁ Βυζάντιος who copied the Greek translation of the *Summa Theologica* at the
command of Kantakouzenos, cf. M. Rackl, 'Die griechische Übersetzung der Summa Theologica
des hl. Thomas von Aquin', *BZ*, 24 (1923/4), 52.

[8] P. Enepekides, 'Der Briefwechsel des Mystikers Nikolaos Kabasilas', *BZ*, 46 (1953), 34;
R.-J. Loenertz, *Démétrius Cydonès, Correspondance*, i (Rome, 1956), pp. 43, 74, and 89.

[9] MM, ii, p. 331.

[10] J. Bick, *Die Schreiber der Wiener Griechischen Handschriften* (Vienna, 1920), p. 46, no. 36.

[11] Lampros, op. cit., p. 176.

[12] Philes (Miller), ii, p. 135.

dedication must have been a wealthy man, but he is not otherwise known. The church seems to have been built by a grandfather of his.[1] He apparently descended from a branch of the Komnenoi (*Κομνηνοφυής*), and it is possible that he acquired the name of Doukas through them.

214. Georgios Doukas Tzykandeles: Georgios Doukas Tzykandeles signs a court decision in Thessalonica in June 1375.[2] He may have been a *katholikos krites* in that city.[3] This Georgios should be the same as the Georgios Doukas Tzykandelenos (sic) who issued an unpublished document dated February indiction I[4] (? 1363, 1378, 1393).

ZARIDES

215. Ioannes Doukas Zarides: The brothers Andronikos and Ioannes Zaridai are familiar names in the epistolography of the fourteenth century. Especially noteworthy is the exchange of letters between the two brothers and Georgios Lakapenos.[5] Andronikos is also the recipient of several letters written by well-known figures of the period.[6]

The name of Doukas, attributed to Ioannes Zarides, has been looked upon as suspect,[7] yet it must be accepted as authentic since it has been twice transmitted independently elsewhere.[8] Ioannes was a young man in *c.* 1295 and flourished during the first decades of the fourteenth century. In 1322 he was a member of a mission that went to Thessalonica to escort the widow of Michael IX to the capital.[9] Ioannes Zarides had landed property in Asia Minor where he stayed, at least temporarily, busy with his correspondence.[10] Planudes

---

[1]   καὶ τόνδε σοι τὸν οἶκον αὐχῶν παππόθεν.
Ibid.

[2] Ὁ δοῦλος τοῦ κραταιοῦ καὶ ἁγίου ἡμῶν αὐθέντου καὶ βασιλέως Γεώργιος Δούκας ὁ Τζυκανδήλης, see G. I. Theocharides, *Μία διαθήκη καὶ μία δίκη Βυζαντινή* (Thessalonica, 1962), p. 49.

[3] Ibid., pp. 78–9.

[4] Chr. Ktenas, ' Τὰ κειμηλιαρχεῖα τῆς ἐν Ἁγίῳ Ὄρει Ἄθω ἱερᾶς, βασιλικῆς, πατριαρχικῆς καὶ σταυροπηγιακῆς μονῆς τοῦ Δοχειαρίου ', *ΕΕΒΣ*, 7 (1930), 111.

[5] See S. Lindstam, *Georgii Lacapeni et Andronici Zaridae epistulae XXXII cum epimerismis Lacapeni* (Gothenburg, 1924). An incomplete earlier edition idem, *Georgii Lacapeni epistulae X priores cum epimerismis editae* (Uppsala, 1910).

[6] Cf. the notices on this Andronikos in M. Treu, *Maximi monachi Planudis epistulae* (Breslau, 1892), pp. 223–5; K. Krumbacher, *Geschichte der byzantinischen Literatur* (Munich, 1897²), pp. 559–60; R. Guilland, *Nicéphore Grégoras, Correspondance* (Paris, 1927), pp. 387–8.

[7] Krumbacher, op. cit., p. 560; A. H(eisenberg) in *BZ*, 20 (1911), 550–1.

[8] Cod. Xeropotamou 71 (Athous 2404) of the fourteenth century contains the inscription Γεωργίου Λακαπηνοῦ καὶ Ἰωάννου Δούκα τοῦ Ζαρίδου ἐπιστολαὶ ἀμοιβαῖαι, *Lacapeni epistulae X*, p. xxv; cf. p. xlvii; letter xxi of the collection bears the title καὶ αὕτη ἡ ἐπιστολὴ τοῦ Λακαπηνοῦ κυροῦ Γεωργίου. ἔγραψε δὲ οἶμαι πρὸς τὸν Ζαρίδην κυρὸν Ἰωάννην τὸν Δούκαν, see *Lacapeni epistulae XXXII*, p. 135.

[9] Kant., i, pp. 130 and 150.

[10] Lakapenos writes to him: ἦ που σὺ τρυφᾶς ἐν Ἀσίᾳ καθήμενος καὶ νῦν μὲν θήραις καὶ λειμῶσι καὶ δένδρεσι, νῦν δ᾽ ἃ τούτων ἀμείνω, ποιητῶν τε βίβλοις καὶ λογογράφων τόκοις καὶ σοφιστῶν τεχνήμασιν συχνὸν ἐγὼ χρόνον τῶν σῶν διάγων ἀνήκοος καὶ μήτε τὰ τῆς φίλης κεφαλῆς δεχόμενος γράμματα, *Lacapeni epistulae XXXII*, pp. 71–2.

wrote to him three letters in *c.* 1295,[1] and Georgios Lakapenos at least four.[2]

At the close of the thirteenth century Ioannes Zarides married an unknown lady and became the father of some children.[3]

[1] Treu, op. cit., nos xxx (pp. 49–50), xxxix (pp. 58–9), and xlii (pp. 61–2). The Zaridai brothers are also referred to in a letter to Alexios Doukas Philanthropenos *170* (οἱ δὲ σοὶ καὶ ἐμοὶ Ζαρίδαι, ibid., p. 147[70]).

[2] *Lacapeni epistulae XXXII*, nos. iii (pp. 15–16), vii (pp. 40–1), ix (pp. 71–4), and xxi (pp. 135–6); cf. p. vi.

[3] In the first letter of Planudes (see above n. 1) it is implied that Ioannes was about to be married. Lakapenos writes: ἥσθην δὲ καὶ υἱεῖ τῷ νέῳ καὶ χαριστήρια τῆς αὑτοῦ γενέσεως καὶ αὐτὸς ἀνῆψα τῷ Θεῷ καὶ ηὐξάμην γε αὐτῷ καὶ εὔχομαι ὁπόσα ἂν αὐτοὶ οἱ τεκόντες εἴξησθε, *Lacapeni epistulae XXXII*, p. 136.

PART IV

DOUKAI OF UNKNOWN FAMILY BACKGROUND

Apart from the descendants of the imperial family and those Doukai who belonged to other families but used the name, from the twelfth century onwards several other persons are found who are called Doukai although their exact family connections and background remain unknown. The male line of the imperial house in all likelihood did not outlive the twelfth century and some of the Doukai of that period, sketched in this section, may have been descendants of Ioannes *13*. The rest, except for a few who were obviously members of obscure and humble provincial stock, seem to have sprung from families other than the Doukai. In Part III there are indeed many instances of those who had abandoned their patronymic proper and assumed the name of Doukas to which they had a right through a female line. Most of those treated in this section must be regarded as having acted similarly. They belonged to other houses but had chosen, or were mentioned by, the name of Doukas. It must however be pointed out that some of those Doukai sketched here (like the Andronikoi and the Konstantinoi of the twelfth century) may be identical with persons included in the previous sections. But the names and the dating alone do not provide sufficient evidence to afford identification.

The court poetry of the twelfth century, so valuable in other respects for knowledge of contemporary prosopography, contains numerous references to persons who are only spoken of with the fashionable epithets of *Doukoblastos* and *Doukophyes*. These may never have been called Doukai. The few cases of this kind examined here (nos. 223 and 228–32) must therefore be seen as a sample of a considerable group whose claim to a place in the prosopography of this work has not been conclusively proved.

I have also appended to this section a list of those Doukai who are known from sigillography and who have not been identified in other sections. Again, some of these may be known only from their seals, while others may be identical with individuals of the same name already sketched.

TWELFTH CENTURY

216. Leon Doukas: Leon Doukas was a priest and lived in Calabria. His name occurs as a witness in a local document of the year 1115/16.[1]

217. Anna Doukaina: Kallikles wrote a short poem for the *sebaste* Anna Doukaina.[2] From it we also learn that she became the wife of Alexios *138*.[3]

218. Maria Doukaina: Maria Doukaina, who became the wife of Alexios Kontostephanos, a son of Stephanos Kontostephanos and Anna the daughter of Ioannes II Komnenos,[4] is mentioned in a couple of poems by Prodromos.[5] Her ancestry is totally unknown. Alexios died after 1170, and Maria bore to him a number of children,[6] none of whom appears to have employed the compound cognomen Doukas Kontostephanos which is not attested anywhere.

219. Na (Doukaina): In an epithalamium, probably written by Niketas Eugeneianos, reference is made to a certain lady of the Doukas family[7] who became the bride of an otherwise unknown Komnenos.

220. Andronikos Doukas: In the course of the Hungarian campaign of 1165 and during the siege of Semlin, Andronikos Doukas, then under the command of the future emperor Andronikos Komnenos, is reported to have performed deeds of bravery.[8] Nothing more is heard on him, but it is possible that he should be identified with Andronikos *39*.

---

[1] *Παπᾶς Λέων ὁ Δούκας μαρτυρῶν ὑπέγραψα*, see Sp. P. Lampros, ''Ὀκτὼ ἀνέκδοτα ἔγγραφα ὧν πέντε ἐκ τῆς Σικελίας καὶ τῆς Κάτω Ἰταλίας ', *NE*, 7 (1910), 37.

[2] *Εἰς τὴν εἰκόνα τοῦ Σωτῆρος τὴν κοσμηθεῖσαν παρὰ τῆς σεβαστῆς κυρᾶς Ἄννης τῆς Δουκαίνης,* see Kallikles, p. 337.

[3]
         Πλὴν ἀλλ'ἄναξ Ἄνναν με σὺν Ἀλεξίῳ
         τῷ συζυγοῦντι Παλαιολόγῳ σκέποις
         Κομνηνοδούκᾳ· κλάδον ἐκ Δουκῶν γένους.
Ibid.

[4] For this particular branch of the Kontostephanoi see H. Grégoire, 'Notes épigraphiques. XII. — La famille des Kontostéphanes et le monastère d'Elegmi', *Revue de l'Instruction Publique en Belgique*, 52 (1909), 152–61. For the career of Alexios see Laurent, *Médaillier Vatican*, pp. 192–4.

[5] In the first poem, dedicated to her husband, the author calls her
         τὴν ἀπὸ Δουκῶν ἱκέτιν σου Μαρίαν,
see L. Sternbach, 'Spicilegium Prodromeum', *Rozprawy Akademii Umiejętności. Wydział Filologiczny.* Serye II. 14 (1904), 348. The other poem is in fact an epitaph for Alexios, and reference to Maria is made in the verses:
         ἡ γὰρ καταστράπτουσα κάλλει χαρίτων
         πανευγενὴς Δούκαινα, σὴ κλεινὴ δάμαρ
         ξένον φιλοτίμημα γυναικῶν γένους,
ibid., p. 359. This is considered by Sternbach, ibid., p. 367, by Grégoire, op. cit., p. 155, and by Chalandon, *Les Comnène*, II, pp. 216–17, n. 7, as applying to the wife of Andronikos Kontostephanos, a brother of Alexios, but in fact the text is ambiguous and in all probability refers to our Maria.

[6] Cf. Laurent, *Médaillier Vatican*, p. 194, no. 2, in contrast to Sternbach, op. cit., p. 349.

[7]
         ἡ δὲ χαρίτων στεφάνῃ κοσμουμένη
         χρυσῆν ἐφέλκει σειρὰν ἐκ Δουκῶν γένους,
see C. Gallavotti, 'Novi Laurentianis codicis analecta', *SBN*, 4 (1935), 235, vv. 59–60.

[8] Kinn., pp. 246–7.

221. Konstantinos Doukas: After the Byzantine defeat at Myriokephalon (17 September 1176), the emperor dispatched a group of his officers to repel another attack by the Turks. The group included a young man called Konstantinos Doukas.[1] This Konstantinos must be clearly distinguished from Makrodoukas 226.[2]

222. Konstantinos Doukas: The *sebastos* Konstantinos Doukas is known from a badly preserved manuscript notice which speaks briefly of his career and records his death.[3] According to this notice, Konstantinos was sent by the emperor Manuel I Komnenos to defend Ancona and was there besieged for seven months by the combined forces of the German emperor Frederick Barbarossa and Venice.[4] Subsequently he was created a *dux* in Dalmatia, Dyrrachion, and Spalato.[5] Konstantinos fell ill with pleurisy at his home and died after seven days on 8 April 1179.

This man cannot be identified with any of the several homonymi who are known.

223. Maria (Doukaina): Maria, described as Δουκόβλαστος, is mentioned as being the wife of the much abused Alexios Komnenos,[6] a son of Andronikos the elder brother of Manuel I. Nothing is known about her.

224. Eudokia Doukaina: She is only known from a single reference to an anonymous epigram of the twelfth century.[7]

225. Konstantinos Doukas: A spurious document, relevant to the establishment of the famous twelve noble families in Crete, bearing the date of October 1183 and preserved in a later and probably distorted text, is allegedly issued by 'the *dux* and cousin of our mighty, glorious, and most holy lord and emperor of Constantinople, and head of the island of Crete, Konstantinos Doukas *megas hetaireiarches*'.[8] This Konstantinos is usually taken to be Mak-

---

[1] Chon., p. 251; Skout., p. 294.

[2] First, Choniates never calls Konstantinos 226 a Doukas but only Makrodoukas and secondly the latter, already married in 1166, could hardly have been described as a very young man ten years later. Choniates describes our Konstantinos as νεανίαν ἄρτι ὑπηνήτην καὶ κατὰ τῶν φυτῶν τὰ εὐγενῆ καρπογονεῖν πρὸ ὥρας ἐπαγγελλόμενον.

[3] See B. de Montfaucon, *Palaeographia Graeca* (Paris, 1708), p. 47. The notice is found in cod. Par. gr. 1564, fol. 18r, but some words at the end have been lost through being cut by the binder and little improvement on Montfaucon's text is possible. Indiction II should however be corrected to XII.

[4] The incident is also known from Kinn., pp. 288–9, and Chon., p. 262, and refers to the year 1173. Some western sources speak of an imperial envoy Konstantinos at Ancona during this period (cf. Chalandon, *Les Comnène*, II, p. 597) who must undoubtedly be Doukas.

[5] Chalandon, *Les Comnène*, II, p. 490, quoting western sources, mentions a *sebastos* Konstantinos who was in Spalato in 1171. It is quite probable that again this is Doukas in which case the dating for his assignments, implied by the manuscript notice, is wrong.

[6] See Lampros, ' Μαρκιανὸς 524 ', p. 36. Alexios became the fatal counsellor and perhaps lover of the dowager empress Maria of Antioch in 1180–83 and was finally blinded and thrown into prison by Andronikos I Komnenos (Chon., p. 472). On the man see the note in R. Guilland, 'Etudes de titulature et de prosopographie byzantines: Le protostrator', *REB*, 7 (1949), 162, and especially De Jongh, *Généalogie des Comnène*, p. 58.

[7] Lampros, ' Μαρκιανὸς, 524 ', p. 166.

[8] 'Ο δούκας καὶ ἐξάδελφος τοῦ κραταιοῦ καὶ ἐνδόξου καὶ ἁγιωτάτου ἡμῶν αὐθεντὸς καὶ βασιλέως Κωνσταντινουπόλεως καὶ κεφαλὴ τῆς νήσου Κρήτης Κωνσταντῖνος Δούκας καὶ μέγας ἑταιρειάρχης, see MM, III, p. 237. There is also a critical edition by E. Gerland, *Histoire de la Noblesse crétoise*

rodoukas *226*, who was in fact a cousin of the then emperor Alexios II Komnenos.[1] But this is only a guess since the evidence for the existence of the present Konstantinos Doukas is very doubtful.

226. Konstantinos Doukas: A number of references occurring between the years 1166 and 1185 mention the name of Konstantinos Doukas. It appears that all of them belong to one man, occasionally called Makrodoukas,[2] who figured prominently during the late Komnenian period. His own family connections cannot be established. Sometime before 1166 he married a daughter of the *sebastokrator* Isaakios, the elder brother of Manuel I Komnenos.[3] His signature can be seen in two official documents of 2 and 6 March 1166.[4] In 1170 he accompanied the emperor on an expedition in Asia Minor,[5] and he also participated in the unfortunate campaign which culminated in the disaster of Myriokephalon on 17 September 1176.[6]

During the reign of Andronikos I, Makrodoukas managed for a while to gain the confidence of the sovereign, but in the end the ill-judged support he gave to his nephew Isaakios Komnenos cost him his life. Isaakios had seized Cyprus, thus rousing the hostility of the emperor who revenged himself on

---

au Moyen Age (Paris, 1907), pp. 90–8, where the two existing Greek versions together with an old Italian translation are given. The formula βασιλεὺς Κωνσταντινουπόλεως is not Byzantine but western, see for instance another example in G. Schirò, 'Manuele II Paleologo incorona Carlo Tocco despota di Gianina', *B*, 29/30 (1959/60), p. 229; cf. D. A. Zakythinos, ''Ανέκδοτον βυζαντινὸν κτητορικὸν ἐκ Βορείου 'Ηπείρου', *ΕΕΒΣ*, 14 (1938), 293 (a Greek document presumably under strong western influence: τοῦ ἁγίου ἡμῶν βασιλέως κῦρ 'Ανδρονίκου Κωνσταντινουπόλεως καὶ πάσης 'Ρωμανίας). Gerland, op. cit., pp. 24–8, attempts to show that the date should be corrected to 1191, but this is rightly challenged by G. Ostrogorsky, *Pour l'Histoire de la féodalité byzantine* (Brussels, 1954), p. 44. The name of Konstantinos Doukas is also met in some later Cretan heraldic texts (cf. Gerland, op. cit., pp. 100 and 110) which, however, all derive from the document of 1183. For this document see also Dölger, *Regesten*, III, p. 90, no. 1561; N. B. Tomadakis, ' Τὸ χρυσόβουλλον τῶν Κομνηνῶν ', *Περιοδικὸν Δελτίον Βιβλιοθήκης Κρητικοῦ Φιλολογικοῦ Συλλόγου*, 1 (Chania, 1928), pp. 65 ff. (inaccessible to me); G. A. Sephakas, 'Τὸ χρυσόβουλλον 'Αλεξίου Β' Κομνηνοῦ καὶ τὰ δώδεκα ἀρχοντόπουλλα', *Κρητικὰ Χρονικά*, 2 (1948), 129–40; Ostrogorsky, op. cit., pp. 43–5; M. I. Manousakas, ' Συμβολὴ εἰς την ἱστορίαν τῆς Κρητικῆς οἰκογενείας Χορτάτση ', *ΕΕΒΣ*, 26 (1956), 272–3; F. Thiriet, *La Romanie vénitienne au Moyen Age* (Paris, 1959), pp. 113 and 130; S. Borsari, *Il dominio veneziano a Creta nel XIII secolo* (Naples, 1963), pp. 16–17, who regards the nucleus of the document as authentic.

---

[1] C. Hopf, *Geschichte Griechenlands vom Beginne des Mittelalters bis auf die neuere Zeit* (Leipzig, 1867), I, p. 179, and others following him.

[2] Choniates always calls him Μακροδούκας which at that time presumably did not yet specify a particular cognomen, but was perhaps only a distinctive nickname which eventually came to be used as a family name.

[3] In *PG*, 140, cols. 236B and 253B, he is called γαμβρός to the emperor which, in this case, means that Konstantinos had married one of Manuel I's nieces. This is actually what Kinn., p. 268, explicitly says. Chon., p. 379, is more specific and explains that his wife was the sister of Theodora, the notorious mistress of Andronikos I Komnenos, who was a daughter of the *sebastokrator* Isaakios Komnenos. Chon., p. 377, describes Makrodoukas as a maternal uncle of Isaakios Komnenos, the 'tyrant' of Cyprus, who was likewise a nephew of Theodora. We have an epithalamium of Prodromos, celebrating the wedding of an unspecified Doukas with a Komnene who was a granddaughter of Ioannes II *109*. This (*PG*, 133, col. 1353A) could refer to the marriage of Makrodoukas as S. Papademetriou, *Theodor Prodrom* (Odessa, 1905), p. 406, maintains.

[4] *PG*, 140, cols. 236B and 253B.

[5] Kinn., p. 268.

[6] Chon., pp. 233–4 and 245; Skout., p. 285.

those who had backed the rebel. Both Makrodoukas and Andronikos *104* were imprisoned and on Ascension Day, 30 May 1185, they were publicly accused of high treason and were condemned to be stoned to death. Makrodoukas' body, still alive, was carried to the district of the Mangana where it was dismembered.[1]

Konstantinos Makrodoukas is mentioned as holding two dignities: *pansebastos sebastos* in 1166[2] and *panypersebastos* in 1185.[3]

227. Doukas: The *notarios* Doukas is known from his signature[4] to a document of the monastery of the Saviour near Messina in Sicily, dated to 1188.[5]

228. Anna (Doukaina): The name of an Anna, certainly connected with the Doukas family, and her husband Ioannes Komnenos, joint-founders of the Pammakaristos monastery in Constantinople, exists in a twelfth-century inscription the original of which is now lost

'Ιωάννου φρόντισμα Κομνηνοῦ τόδε
῍Αννης τε ρίζης Δουκικῆς τῆς συζύγου
οἷς ἀντιδοῦσα πλουσίαν, ἁγνή, χάριν
τάξαις ἐν οἴκῳ τοῦ Θεοῦ μονοτρόπους[6]

It is not possible to identify the couple.

229. Maria (Doukaina): Maria, called *Doukoblastos*, lived in the twelfth century and was the wife of Ioannes Komnenos.[7] Both she and her husband are otherwise unknown.

230. Anna Komnene (Doukaina): Anna Komnene, *Doukoblastos* on her mother's side, was the wife of Alexios, a son of Manuel Anemas and Theodora the daughter of Ioannes II. From the epitaph for Alexios we learn that before his death he assumed the monastic habit taking the name of Athanasios. Anna became the mother of a child and died shortly afterwards.[8]

231. Eirene (Doukaina): The extant text of a lost seal speaks of a certain Eirene *Doukophyēs* as the wife of the *sebastos* Andronikos Komnenos, a son of

---

[1] Chon., pp. 377, 379–82, and 384; Skout., pp. 341–3; cf. F. Cognasso, 'Partiti politici e lotti dinastiche in Bisanzio alla morte di Manuele Comneno', *Memorie della Reale Accademia delle Scienze di Torino. Scienze morali, storiche e filologiche*, 62 (1912), 277. Chon., p. 381, speaks of Makrodoukas' γεραρὸν τῆς ἡλικίας καὶ τὴν τοῦ πλούτου βαθύτητα.

[2] *PG*, 140, col. 253B.   [3] Chon., p. 407.

[4] 'Ο εὐτελὴς δοῦνας νοτάριος ὑπέγραψα ἰδιοχείρως, see S. Cusa, *I Diplomi greci ed arabi di Sicilia* (Palermo, 1868), p. 529. I correct δοῦνας to the more likely Δούκας.

[5] The date seems to be uncertain.

[6] Last edited by C. Mango and E. J. W. Hawkins, 'Report on Field Work in Istanbul and Cyprus, 1962–1963', *DOP*, 18 (1964), 328, who discuss earlier views concerning the founders of the monastery.

[7]   'Ιωάννην με Κομνηνόν, Σῶτερ, σκέποις
     ἅμα συνεύνῳ Δουκοβλάστῳ Μαρία,
see Lampros, ' Μαρκιανὸς 524 ', p. 175. De Jongh, *Généalogie des Comnène*, p. 74, no. 11, is inclined to consider Ioannes as being Ioannes Komnenos Batatzes.

[8]   ᾧ (sc. 'Αλεξίῳ) συζυγεῖσα δεξιαῖς σὺν ἐλπίσιν
     ῍Αννα Κομνηνὴ Δουκόβλαστος μητρόθεν
     τῆς φύσεως ἄγαλμα χαρίτων γέμον
     μικρὸν συνανθεῖ καὶ συνεκφθίνει τάχος.
     ἐν σχοῦσα τέκος . . .
see Lampros, ' Μαρκιανὸς 524 ', pp. 163–4.

                                               P.T.D.

Ioannes Rogerios and Maria the eldest daughter of Ioannes II.[1] Her husband is occasionally encountered in the later part of the twelfth century.

232. Ioannes (Doukas): A poem of Nikephoros Chrysoberges, presumably dating from the last quarter of the twelfth century, is devoted to a certain πορφυρανθής (daughter of a porphyrogenitus?) Eirene who had lately become a nun. A passing reference is made to her husband Ioannes who is called *Doukophyēs*.[2] The editor identified him with Ioannes Kantakouzenos who is known to have married Eirene, a sister of Isaakios II Angelos.[3] If this is so, the word πορφυρανθής would then be inappropriate.

233. Andronikos Doukas: Andronikos Doukas is mentioned in around 1198 when as a very young man he successfully led a Byzantine army against the Turks.[4]

In a later document, dated in March 1300,[5] reference is made to a certain *logothetēs tōn sekretōn* Andronikos Doukas who had issued another document on the orders of an emperor Alexios Komnenos in favour of the Xenophon monastery on Mount Athos.[6] It has been suggested that the emperor in question is actually Alexios I,[7] but this appears extremely unlikely since the only Andronikos (*16*) to have lived under Alexios I could not have held this office. It is more appropriate to place Doukas either under Alexios II or, preferably, under Alexios III (who liked to style himself as Komnenos[8]) in which case an identification with the above Andronikos is possible.

234. Isaakios Doukas: The name of the *sebastos*, *oikeios*, and *vestiarites* Isaakios Doukas is included among the high dignitaries in an imperial *sēmeiōma* of 2 March 1166.[9]

---

1   Σφράγισμα γραφῶν Δουκοφυοῦς Εἰρήνης
Κομνηνὸς Ἀνδρόνικος ᾗ συνεζύγη
αὐτοκρατοῦντος Μανουὴλ ἀδελφόπαις
ἐκ πορφυρανθοῦς βασιλίσσης Μαρίας,

see Lampros, ' Μαρκιανὸς 524 ', pp. 49–50; Laurent, *Bulles métriques*, p. 166, no. 470. For Andronikos see L. Stiernon, 'Notes de titulature et de prosopographie byzantines: A propos de trois membres de la famille Rogerios', *REB*, 22 (1964), 191–7.

2   Τῆς πορφυρανθοῦς οὗτος Εἰρήνης τύπος,
ᾗ Δουκοφυεῖ συνεζύγη δεσπότῃ
τὴν κλῆσιν αὐχήσαντι τὴν Θεοῦ χάριν.
Καλλύνεται μὲν ἐκ στολῆς βασιλίδος
καὶ χρυσοτεύκτων ἀμφίων τῶν τοῦ κράτους,

see S. G. Mercati, 'Poesie giambiche di Niceforo Chrysoberges, metropolita di Sardi', *Miscellanea Giovanni Galbiati*, II (=*Fontes Ambrosiani* 26, Milan, 1951), pp. 265–6. It is not clear whether *despotes* here represents a dignity conferred upon Ioannes or not.

3 Ibid., p. 259.

4 Alexios III στέλλει τὸν Δούκαν Ἀνδρόνικον νεανίαν πρώτως ὑπηνέτην τῷ Πέρσῃ συμπλακησόμενον. Ὁ δὲ μεθ' ὧν ἡγεμόνευεν, ὀψὲ ποιεῖται τὴν κατὰ τῶν Τούρκων ἔφοδον, Chon., p. 657; cf. Skout., p. 421.

5 Cf. Dölger, *Regesten*, IV, p. 32, no. 2226.

6 L. Petit, *Actes de Xénophon* (St Petersburg, 1903), p. 30.

7 Ibid., p. 7; Dölger, *Regesten* III, p. 58, no. 1294. F. Dölger, *Beiträge zur byzantinischen Finanzverwaltung, besonders des 10. und 11. Jahrhunderts* (Leipzig, 1927), p. 18, no. 1, is uncommitted.

8 Chon., p. 605.

9 Τοῦ σεβαστοῦ καὶ οἰκείου βεστιαρίτου τοῦ κραταιοῦ καὶ ἁγίου ἡμῶν βασιλέως, κυροῦ Ἰσαακίου τοῦ Δούκα, see *PG*, 140, col. 237A.

THIRTEENTH CENTURY

235. Konstantinos Doukas: After the flight of Alexios V during the night of 12/13 April 1204, on the eve of Constantinople's fall to the Franks, there emerged two young candidates for the vacant throne of Byzantium. These were Konstantinos Laskaris and Konstantinos Doukas. As is well-known, the proclamation of the former was finally agreed upon.[1]

Konstantinos Doukas is not heard again. It is, however, possible that he should be identified with Konstantinos *44*.

236. Daniel Doukas: Daniel, called Doukas (Δανιὴλ λεγόμενος Δούκας) lived towards the beginning of the thirteenth century and was presumably a monk. He built the monastery τῶν Σποδῶν around an already existing church in the island of Cos.[2]

237. Ioannes Doukas: The existence of Ioannes Doukas is revealed only by the notice which his unknown father wrote on the occasion of his birth. According to this, Ioannes was born on 20 April 1276.[3]

238. Doukas: A gloss on the upper margin of cod. Laur. Conv. soppr. 206 (s. x), fol. 19v, reads: ἔχει ὁ Δούκας κόλας λβ′. It is possible that this notice comes from the age of Planudes (late thirteenth century) in which case it may refer to the scholar's intimate friend Alexios Doukas Philanthropenos *171*. But it could also come from a later period and speak of a (scribe?) Doukas who had in his possession 32 leaves of writing paper.[4]

239. Theodoros Doukas: An imperial document dated in February 1250 mentions a deceased Theodoros Doukas as having land in Asia Minor adjoining an estate of the monastery of Lembiotissa.[5]

FOURTEENTH CENTURY

240. Demetrios Doukas(?): A portrait in Kahriye Djami, the Byzantine Μονὴ τῆς Χώρας which was restored by Theodoros Metochites early in the fourteenth century, bears the inscription: Δημήτρι(ος Δ ?)ούκας.[6]

---

[1] Chon., p. 756; Skout., p. 448. On this question cf. B. Sinogowitz, 'Über das byzantinische Kaisertum nach dem vierten Kreuzzuge (1204–1205)', *BZ*, 45 (1952), 352.

[2] MM, VI, p. 185.

[3] See H. O. Coxe, *Catalogi codicum mss. Bibliothecae Bodleianae*, I (Oxford, 1853), p. 443, who, however, does not give the text found in cod. Cromwell 16, fol. 29v. The notice reads: Ἐγεννήθη ὁ ἠός μου ὁ Ἰω(άννης) ὁ Δούκας ἀπριλλίου εἰς τὰς εἴκοσι ἡμέρα σαββάτῳ πρωὶ ἐνδικτιώνος τετάρτης ἔτει ͵ϛψπδ′. It should be noted that 20 April 1276, was not Saturday but Monday. The manuscript is a gospel and at one time belonged to the library of the Pantokrator monastery at Constantinople, cf. the notice (by a different hand) on fol. 353v: Τετραευάγγελον μονῆς τοῦ Παντοκράτορος καὶ Σωτῆρος Χριστοῦ.

[4] See S. Kugéas, 'Analecta Planudea', *BZ*, 18 (1909), 111–13.

[5] See MM, IV, p. 216; cf. Dölger, *Regesten*, III, p. 22, no. 1802. The date of the document has been established by F. Dölger, 'Chronologisches und Prosopographisches zur byzantinischen Geschichte des 13. Jahrhunderts', *BZ*, 27 (1927), 314.

[6] P. A. Underwood, 'Notes on the Work of the Byzantine Institute in Istanbul 1955–56', *DOP*, 12 (1958), 277.

241. Michael Doukas: He was the paternal grandfather of Doukas *258* the historian, and it is claimed that he descended from the ever noble Doukai.[1] In the summer of 1346, following the fall of Alexios Apokaukos, Michael was saved from being killed during the persecution of the partisans of Kantakouzenos whom he supported in Constantinople. He had to escape to the Turks of Asia Minor. Eventually he settled in Ephesus and declined to return to Constantinople, seeing that sooner or later all Byzantine lands were destined to fall to the Turks. Michael's grandson praises him for his learning, especially in medicine.[2]

242. Doukas: A reference to an unknown Doukas who lived in about the middle of the fourteenth century is found in a manuscript notice. He was the possessor of a theological work.[3]

243. Doukaina: A piece of land belonging to an unspecified Doukaina in the island of Lemnos is spoken of in a document of October 1355.[4] It seems that the word $\Delta o \dot{v} \kappa a \iota v a$ is here a surname and not a rank.[5]

244. Doukas: Doukas was a physician from Imbros who lived in the fourteenth century or earlier.[6]

245. Ioannes Doukas: On cod. Xeropotamou *108* (s. xiv–xv) there is a notice, perhaps a fragment of a now lost short chronicle, to the effect that an otherwise unknown $\mathit{'I\omega \acute{a} v v \eta s\ \Delta o \acute{v} \kappa a s\ \acute{o}\ \Sigma a \kappa \epsilon \lambda \lambda \acute{a} \rho \iota o s}$ was born in January 1373.[7]

246. Doukas: In the will of the *megas primikērios* Ioannes,[8] dated on 1 August 1384, there is a postscript which speaks of his two children Palaiologopoulos and Doukas.[9] These were presumably their surnames.

---

[1] $\mathit{\Gamma \acute{\epsilon} v \epsilon \iota\ \tau \epsilon\ \kappa a \tau a \gamma \acute{o} \mu \epsilon v o s\ \tau \hat{\omega} v\ \dot{a} v \acute{\epsilon} \kappa a \theta \epsilon v\ \Delta o \upsilon \kappa \hat{\omega} v\ \kappa \grave{a} \kappa\ \tau \hat{\eta} s\ a \dot{v} \tau \hat{\eta} s\ \sigma \epsilon \iota \rho \hat{a} s\ \chi \rho \upsilon \sigma \acute{o} \kappa o \sigma \mu o s\ \kappa \rho \acute{\iota} \kappa o s}$, Doukas, p. 47.

[2] Doukas, pp. 46–7.

[3] $\mathit{'E \kappa\ \tau o \hat{v}\ a \dot{v} \tau o \hat{v}\ \beta \iota \beta \lambda \acute{\iota} o \upsilon\ \acute{o} \pi \epsilon \rho\ \kappa a \grave{\iota}\ \acute{o}\ \Delta o \acute{v} \kappa a s\ \acute{\epsilon} \chi \epsilon \iota}$. The phrase $\mathit{\acute{o} \pi \epsilon \rho\ \kappa a \grave{\iota}\ \acute{o}\ \Delta o \acute{v} \kappa a s\ \acute{\epsilon} \chi \epsilon \iota}$ has been crossed out. The notice is found in cod. Vat. gr. 604, fol. 35r. See R. Devreesse, *Codices Vaticani Graeci*. III *Codices 604–866* (Vatican, 1950), p. 4; cf. G. Mercati, *Notizie ed altri appunti* (Vatican, 1931), p. 260.

[4] $\mathit{\pi \lambda \eta \sigma \acute{\iota} o v\ \tau \hat{\eta} s\ \gamma \hat{\eta} s\ \tau \hat{\eta} s\ \Delta o \upsilon \kappa a \acute{\iota} v \eta s}$, F. Dölger, *Aus den Schatzkammern des Heiligen Berges* (Munich, 1948), p. 210.

[5] If the lady in question had been a $\mu \epsilon \gamma \acute{a} \lambda \eta\ \delta o \acute{v} \kappa a \iota v a$, that is the wife of a *megas dux*, the word $\mu \epsilon \gamma \acute{a} \lambda \eta$ would not have been omitted. Cf. $\mathit{\kappa a \tau \grave{a}\ \tau \grave{\eta} v\ \mu o v \grave{\eta} v\ \tau \hat{\eta} s\ \mu \epsilon \gamma \acute{a} \lambda \eta s\ \delta o \upsilon \kappa a \acute{\iota} v \eta s\ \mu \eta \tau \rho \grave{o} s\ \tau \hat{\eta} s\ \Sigma \upsilon \rho \gamma \iota a v v \acute{\iota} v \eta s}$, Devreesse, loc. cit.; Mercati, op. cit., p. 261. To this $\mu \epsilon \gamma \acute{a} \lambda \eta\ \delta o \acute{v} \kappa a \iota v a$ Philes wrote a poem, see Philes (Miller), I, p. 297.

[6] $\mathit{'E \pi \acute{\iota} \theta \epsilon \mu a\ \sigma \tau o \mu a \chi \acute{\iota} o \upsilon\ \Delta o \acute{v} \kappa a\ \iota a \tau \rho o \hat{v}\ 'I \mu \pi \rho \acute{\iota} o \upsilon\ \acute{o}\ \chi a \lambda a o \sigma \tau \acute{o} \mu a \chi o s}$, found in K. I. Amanos, ' $\mathit{'I a \tau \rho o \sigma o \phi \iota \kappa \grave{o} s\ \kappa \hat{\omega} \delta \iota \xi}$ ', $\mathit{'A \theta \eta v \hat{a}}$, 43 (1931), 155. The manuscript was written in 1599 (cf. ibid., p. 148, no. 2), but the work itself, in the view of Amantos, was composed in the fourteenth century (ibid., p. 150).

[7] A. Guillou and J. Bompaire, 'Recherches au Mont Athos', *BCH*, 82 (1958), 182; cf. Bompaire, *Actes de Xéropotamou*, p. 29.

[8] Ioannes' surname is unknown. He is called a $\gamma a \mu \beta \rho \acute{o} s$ of the emperor Ioannes V and had a brother the *megas stratopedarches* Alexios; for the two see P. Lemerle, *Philippes et la Macédonie orientale à l'époque chrétienne et byzantine* (Paris, 1945), pp. 206–13. The wife of Ioannes was Anna Asanina Kontostephanina. Can Ioannes be the *megas primikerios* Ioannes Palaiologos, son of Demetrios (Papadopulos, *Genealogie der Palaiologen*, p. 82, no. 136)?

[9] $\mathit{\dot{\epsilon} \grave{a} v\ \dot{\epsilon} \kappa\ \tau \hat{\omega} v\ \delta \acute{v} o\ \mu o \upsilon\ \pi a \iota \delta \acute{\iota} \omega v\ \tau o \hat{v}\ \Pi a \lambda a \iota o \lambda o \gamma o \pi o \acute{v} \lambda o \upsilon\ \kappa a \grave{\iota}\ \tau o \hat{v}\ \Delta o \acute{v} \kappa a}$, L. Petit, *Actes de Pantocrator* (St Petersburg, 1903), p. 15.

247. Doukas (?): There is a notice on cod. Panteleemonos 736 (Athous 6246), fol. 223r, referring to the children of a priest called Doukas(?). According to this, his second son Konstas was born on 22 November 1396, and his third son Theologos on 7 November 1402.[1] It is possible that the word Doukas here, if correct, denotes the first name of the priest.

248. Doukas Epikernes: Doukas Epikernes[2] was apparently an imperial official and in June 1397, when the Turks captured Argos, he was at Nauplion.[3]

249. Philippos Doux: Philippos was a priest who probably flourished in 1400.[4] In a signed promise to the patriarch he solemnly pledges that he will perform his sacerdotal duties properly.[5]

250. Ioannes Doukas: Ioannes Doukas was *megas dioikētēs* of Thessalonica, most probably at the end of the fourteenth century or the beginning of the fifteenth. According to an imperial *prostagma*, he issued a document, dated May indiction VIII, by which he gives certain estates to the monastery of Docheiariou of Mount Athos.[6]

FIFTEENTH CENTURY

251. Doukas: A letter of donation, dated on 1 June 1405 and signed by the hellenized Serb ʻΡαδοσθλάβος Σάμπιας, speaks of his two sons: Doukas and Laskaris.[7]

252. Georgios Doukas(?): The bibliographer Γεώργιος Δούκ(ας?) was active in 1421.[8] His name is uncertain.

---

[1] Ἡ γέννα Δούκα(;) ἱερέως. Ἔτους ͵ϛλε΄ μηνὶ νοεμβρίῳ κβ΄ ἐγεννήθη ὁ δεύτερος ὑμῶν υἱὸς ὁ Κώνστας. Ὁ δὲ Θεολόγος ὁ τρίτος ἡμῶν υἱὸς ἐγεννήθη τῷ ͵ϛλια΄ ἔτει μηνὶ νοεμβρίῳ ζ΄; see Sp. P. Lampros, Κατάλογοι τῶν ἐν ταῖς μοναῖς τοῦ Ἁγίου Ὄρους ἑλληνικῶν κωδίκων, II (Cambridge, 1900), p. 423.

[2] It is not clear whether Epikernes signifies a title or a family name here.

[3] Καὶ τὸν αὐτὸν χρόνον εὑρέθη εἰς τὸ Ἀνάπλι Δούκας ὁ Ἐπικέρνης; see Sp. P. Lampros and K. I. Amantos, Βραχέα Χρονικά (Athens, 1932), p. 47. W. Miller, The Latins in the Levant: A History of Frankish Greece (1204–1566) (London, 1908), p. 347, no. 1, seems to confuse this Doukas Epikernes with Stephanos, the brother of Ioannes 58, whom he calls Stephen Doukas Chlapen.

[4] The document bears the date September indiction IX; the year 1400 is the editors' assumption.

[5] The text in MM, II, pp. 426–7. There is a contemporary Philippos Doukas Aprenos 64 who seems to be a different person.

[6] Chr. Ktenas, ʻ Τὰ κειμηλιαρχεῖα τῆς ἐν Ἁγίῳ Ὄρει Ἄθω ἱερᾶς βασιλικῆς, πατριαρχικῆς καὶ σταυροπηγιακῆς μονῆς τοῦ Δοχειαρίου ʼ, ΕΕΒΣ, 7 (1930), 110; E. Kourilas, ʻʻΟ κατάλογος τῶν ἐπισήμων ʼἈθωνικῶν ἐγγράφων τοῦ Οὐσπένσκη ʼ, ΕΕΒΣ, 8 (1931), 72.
Among the signatures of a document of December 1376 there is one reading: Ὁ δοῦλος τοῦ κραταιοῦ καὶ ἁγίου ἡμῶν αὐθέντου καὶ βασιλέως Δούκας ὁ . . ., see M. Goudas, ʻʻΑφιερωτήριον Θεοδώρας Παλαιολογίνης τῆς Φιλανθρωπηνῆς ʼ, Δελτίον Χριστιανικῆς Ἀρχαιολογικῆς Ἑταιρείας, 2, ι-ιι (1925), p. 17. As his name is incomplete, it is not possible to identify him.

[7] St. Binon, Les origines légendaires et l'Histoire de Xéropotamou et de Saint-Paul de l'Athos (Louvain, 1942), p. 278; cf. p. 292. The text has been edited by Eulogios Hagiopaulites, ʻΤὰ κειμήλια τοῦ Ἁγίου Ὄρους: Αὐτοκρατορικὰ χρυσόβουλλα ʼ, Νέα Ἐποχή, 1 (1925), 705.

[8] A. Turyn, The Byzantine Manuscript Tradition of the Tragedies of Euripides (Urbana, Ill., 1957), p. 150.

253. Doukaina: On 6 June 1422, an otherwise unknown Doukaina gave, on behalf of an equally unknown Radene, five *nomismata* to an official of the metropolis of Thessalonica.[1]

254. Duca Lathra: Duca Lathra—the name is peculiar—is known from a Venetian document. In 1429 he lived in Kastoria in Macedonia, having previously been abducted by the Turks. Later on he came to Thessalonica. Doukas was a brave soldier and he sought to enter the Venetian service in the city guard. He was admitted to this with the monthly wage of 300 aspra. In Thessalonica he married the daughter of an Ioannes Radenos. Doukas could have been originally of Corfu as his mother and a brother of his were resident in that island.[2]

255. Doukas Milca: His name is included among the noble inhabitants of Thessalonica to whom the Venetian senate approved a monthly allowance of 120 aspra in 1425. The form Δούκας Μίλκα is the Greek version of an unknown Venetian form.[3]

256. Doukas: Doukas (Δούκας ταπεινὸς νοτάριος τῆς ἁγιωτάτης τοῦ Θεοῦ Μεγάλης Ἐκκλησίας) is a known scribe and presumably a divine. He flourished in 1435 in Constantinople as a notary to the church of St Sophia.[4]

257. Ioannes Doukas: The church melodist Δούκας ὁ λαοσυνάκτης[5] who seems to have flourished during the last years of the Byzantine empire, should be distinguished from the contemporary musician Doukas Syropoulos*204*.[6] His full name is given in a seventeenth-century manuscript as Ἰωάννης Δούκας καὶ λαοσυνάκτης ἁγιοσοφίτης.[7] The word ἁγιοσοφίτης implies that he was in the service of St Sophia either as a priest or as a deacon. Ioannes Doukas composed μαθήματα τοῦ μεγάλου ἑσπερινοῦ and μαθήματα καλοφωνικά.[8]

258. Doukas: Doukas, the historian of the last days of Byzantium, is only known as a person from what can be gathered from his own work.[9] His grand-

---

[1] Ἐλάβομεν διὰ τῆς Δούκαινας ἀπὸ τῆς Ῥαδηνῆς νομίσματα ε΄ καὶ ἐδόθη ἐνέχυρον σταυρὸς κτλ.; see S. Kugéas, 'Notizbuch eines Beamten der Metropolis in Thessalonike aus dem Anfang des XV. Jahrhunderts', *BZ*, 23 (1914/19), 144, no. 9.

[2] See K. A. Mertzios, Μνημεῖα Μακεδονικῆς Ἱστορίας (Thessalonica, 1947), pp. 85–6.

[3] Ibid., p. 50.

[4] Vogel–Gardthausen, *Schreiber*, p. 113; cf. Turyn, op. cit., p. 199, n. 194; F. Dölger, *Byzantinische Diplomatik* (Ettal, 1956), p. 260.

[5] Λαοσυνάκτης is a common church office; cf. Μοσχιανὸς ὁ λαοσυνάκτης, Συμεὼν ὁ λαοσυνάκτης in S. Eustratiades and Arcadios, *Catalogue of the Greek Manuscripts in the Library of the Monastery of Vatopedi on Mt Athos* (Cambridge, Mass., 1924), p. 276. For the word see D. B. Bagiakakos, ' Ἡ ἐκκλησιαστικὴ γλῶσσα καὶ ἡ μεσαιωνικὴ καὶ ἡ νεοελληνικὴ ὀνοματολογία ', Ἀθηνᾶ, 63(1959), 217.

[6] In some manuscripts of church music the distinction is not clearly made; see for instance Papadopoulos-Kerameus, Ἱεροσολυμιτικὴ Βιβλιοθήκη, I, p. 248.

[7] Cod. Lauras 1657, Spyridon Lauriotes and S. Eustratiades, *Catalogue of the Greek Manuscripts in the Library of the Laura on Mount Athos* (Cambridge, Mass., 1925), p. 292; cf. p. 451.

[8] Ibid., p. 449.

[9] V. Grecu, *Ducas Istoria Turco-Bizantină (1341–1462)* (Bucharest, 1958). Bibliographies on the man and his work in M. E. Colonna, *Gli storici bizantini dal IV al XV secolo. I. — Storici profani* (Naples, 1956), pp. 39–41; Gy. Moravcsik, *Byzantinoturcica* (Berlin, 1958), I, pp. 247–51. Recent additions: C. J. G. Turner, 'Pages from Late Byzantine Philosophy of History', *BZ*, 57 (1964), 356–8; M. Dinić, 'Dukin prevodilač o boyu na Kosovu', *Zbornik Radova Vizantoloshkog Instituta*, 8/2 (1964), 53–67.

father was Michael *241*, but his parents as well as his first name remain unknown. Doukas may have been born, most probably in Asia Minor, during the last decade of the fourteenth century and had been in the service of the Genoese rulers of the Aegaean from early manhood. In 1451 and 1452 he was in Adrianople on an official mission, and in 1455 he brought the taxes on behalf of the Gattilusi to the Turks. He was still alive in 1462 during the capture of Mitylene by the Turks and he may have died then.[1]

259. Michael Doukas: Michael Doukas was a priest and *sakellarios* of Philadelphia in Asia Minor. He was the possessor of a manuscript. His date is unknown.[2]

---

[1] Cf. the passages from his history cited and discussed by N. B. Tomadakis, Περὶ ἁλώσεως τῆς Κωνσταντινουπόλεως (*1453*). Συναγωγὴ κειμένων (Athens, 1953), pp. 20–24. The only reference to the historian I have been able to find outside his work is the concluding passage of list of emperors (short chronicle?) in cod. *Panagiou Taphou 102* which reads: 1455 . . . ὁ Δούκας φέρει ἕνα τέλος ἤτοι δόσιμον ἐκ μέρους τοῦ πρίγγιπος τῆς Λέσβου ἤτοι τῆς Μιτυλήνης; see Papadopoulos-Kerameus, Ἱεροσολυμιτικὴ Βιβλιοθήκη, IV, p. 100. There is no doubt that the Doukas here is the historian and the incident referred to is in fact described in detail in his history: Καὶ τῇ πρώτῃ τοῦ αὐγούστου (= 1455) ἐστάλθην ἐγὼ παρὰ τοῦ νέου ἡγεμόνος, τοῦ υἱοῦ αὐτοῦ, Δομνίκου τοῦ Γατελούζου, ἐν Ἀνδριανουπόλει τοῦ δοῦναι τοὺς κατ᾽ ἔτος διδομένους φόρους, Doukas, p. 411.

[2] Cod. 58 of Παναγίας (Chalke), fol. 1: Μιχαὴλ πρεσβυτέρου τοῦ Δούκα σακελλαρίου Φιλαδελφείας συναξάριον ἔχων ἐξ μῆνας μόνον; see Athenagoras, ʻ Κατάλογος τῶν χειρογράφων τῆς ἐν Χάλκῃ μονῆς τῆς Παναγίας ʼ, ΕΕΒΣ, 11 (1935), 157.

NAMES KNOWN ONLY FROM SEALS

The names that follow are those of persons known only from extant seals. These individuals cannot at present be further identified. There are of course several other seals belonging to known Doukai which have already been dealt with. It is however quite possible that some of the persons enumerated below are identical with other Doukai of the same name described in the main part of the work.

260. Andronikos Doukas: Undated seal:

Δούκαν σεβαστὸν ᾿Ανδρόνικόν με σκέποις[1]

261. Ioannes Doukas: Undated:

᾿Επισφραγίζεις ἡ ξυνωρὶς μαρτύρων
Δούκα σεβαστοῦ τὰς γραφὰς ᾿Ιωάννου.[2]

262 Ioannes Doukas: He was a descendant of emperors:

Σφραγὶς σεβαστοῦ ᾿Ιωάννου τοῦ Δούκα
ῥίζαν γένους ἔχοντος ἐκ βασιλέων.[3]

263. Ioannes (Doukas): End of twelfth century:

[Σφραγὶς πέφυκα] τῶν γραφῶν ᾿Ιωάννου
... δουκικῆς ῥίζης κλάδου.[4]

264. Konstantinos Doukas: A seal of the eleventh or the twelfth century:

Γραφὰς σφραγίζω Κωνσταντίνου τοῦ Δούκα.[5]

265. Maria Doukaina: Thirteenth century:

Σφραγὶς σεβαστῆς Μαρίας τῆς Δουκαίνης.[6]

266. Michael Doukas: Eleventh or twelfth century:

Σφραγὶς σεβαστοῦ Μιχαὴλ αὕτη Δούκα.[7]

267. Michael Doukas: A *prōtokouropalatēs*:

Κύριε, βοήθει Μιχαὴλ πρωτοκουροπαλάτῃ τῷ Δούκᾳ.[8]

268. Michael Komnenodoukas: Twelfth or thirteenth century:

Παρεμβολὴ καθάπερ ἀγγέλου κύκλῳ
εἰμὶ Μιχαὴλ ὧδε Κομνηνοδούκας.[9]

---

[1] Laurent, *Bulles métriques*, p. 40, no. 108.
[2] Laurent, *Bulles métriques*, p. 48, no. 134.
[3] Ibid., p. 153, no. 440. The editor thinks that he is the same as the previous one.
[4] Laurent, *Collection Orghidan*, p. 218, no. 428.
[5] Laurent, *Bulles métriques*, p. 30, no. 76.
[6] Ibid., p. 233, no. 698.
[7] Ibid., p. 155, no. 444.
[8] K. Konstantopoulos, Βυζαντιακὰ μολυβδόβουλλα (Athens, 1917), no. 292a.
[9] M. Froehner, 'Bulles métriques', *Annuaire de la Société Française de Numismatique et d'Archéologie*, 8 (1884), 330, no. 83.

269. Nikephoros Doukas: A descendant of emperors:

Σφραγὶς σεβαστοῦ Νικηφόρου τοῦ Δούκα
ῥίζαν γένους ἔχοντος ἐκ βασιλέων.[1]

270. Theodoros Doukas: A *sebastos* and *protostrator* Theodoros Doukas is known from a thirteenth-century seal:

Σφραγὶς σεβαστοῦ Θεοδώρου πρωτοστράτορος τοῦ Δούκα.[2]

This cannot be Theodoros Doukas Synadenos *196*.

---

[1] Laurent, *Bulles métriques*, p. 156, no. 447.
Another seal (ibid., p. 155, no. 446)

Σφραγὶς σεβαστοῦ Νικηφόρου τοῦ Δούκα

probably belongs to the same man.

[2] V. Laurent, 'Sceaux byzantins inédits', *BZ*, 33 (1933), 349; R. Guilland, 'Etudes de titulature et de prosopographie byzantines: Le protostrator', *REB*, 7 (1949), 162, places him under Isaakios II (1185–95).

THE DOUKAI AFTER 1453

The examination of the prosopography of the Doukai after 1453 falls outside the chronological limits of this survey. The short sketches that follow are only intended to illustrate the continuity of the name[1] at a time when Greek social conditions had undergone a profound change. They should be seen as examples of a large number of similar cases. But in spite of this continuity, it should be emphasised that there can be no genealogical connection between the Doukai of the Byzantine period and those found after 1453. Indeed the majority of the Doukai in the years after 1453 seem to have owed their designation to a first name Doukas which became progressively more common and which could easily be turned into a surname.

Demetrios Doukas: The Cretan Demetrios Doukas (c. 1480 — after 1527) became a pioneer of Greek studies in the West. Besides being a close collaborator of Aldus Manutius in Venice, he was also instrumental in initiating Greek learning in Spain where he prepared a famous edition of the Polyglot Bible (1521).[2]

Doukas: Doukas was a tailor of Mitylene and having turned down the overtures of a married woman he was falsely accused and consequently put to death by the Turks on 24 April 1564. The Church counts him among its martyrs.[3]

Ioannes Doukas: He lived during the second half of the seventeenth century and is the addressee of a letter by Eugenios Ioannoulios.[4]

Ioannes Doukas: Ioannes Doukas was *voivode* of Moldavia in the second half of the seventeenth century. The sources variously describe him as Vlach, Greek, or Albanian.[5]

Konstantinos Doukas: He was a son of the former and is sometimes called Δουκουτζέλης. He was also a ruler of Moldavia during the years 1693–6 and 1700–3. Some letters of Konstantinos Doukas have been preserved.

Doukas: A seal portraying St George and St Demetrios bears the inscription: Δούκας δοῦλος Χριστοῦ ἔτος 1692.[6]

---

[1] The continuity has been wrongly challenged by G. Stamnopoulos, Βόλτες ὀνοματολογικές. Σειρὰ πρώτη (Athens, 1929), p. 118, who explains the modern name as a shortened form of a non-existent surname.

[2] On this man see D. J. Geanakoplos, *Greek Scholars in Venice* (Cambridge, Mass., 1962), pp. 223–55.

[3] Nikodemos Hagioreites, Νέον Μαρτυρολόγιον (Athens, 1961³), pp. 59–60; K. Doukakis, Μέγας Συναξαριστής. Ἀπρίλιος (Athens, 1892), pp. 401–2; S. Eustratiades, Ἁγιολόγιον τῆς Ὀρθοδόξου Ἐκκλησίας (Athens, n.d.), p. 120.

[4] S. Eustratiades, "Ἐπιστολαὶ Εὐγενίου Ἰωαννουλίου τοῦ Αἰτωλοῦ", Ἑλληνικά, 8 (1935), 279–80, no. 73.

[5] Cf. E. Kourilas, 'Γρηγόριος ὁ Ἀργυροκαστρίτης', Θεολογία, 11 (1933), 217–19.

[6] *Collections sigillographiques de MM. Gustave Schlumberger et Adrien Blanchet* (Paris, 1914), p. 191, no. 650.

Triantaphyllos Douka: A Macedonian mentioned in a letter of 8 June 1702, as Τριαντάφυλλος Θοδωρῆ Δούκα.[1]

Ioannes Doukas: Shipper of a cargo of merchandise on 10 May 1710.[2]

Zacharias Doukas: Abbot of the monastery of Panachrantos (island of Andros) before 1732.[3]

Michael Doukas: An eighteenth-century philosopher and scholar from the town of Siatista in western Macedonia. He had remained for sometime in Vienna where his anti-Christian disposition brought him trouble with the Austrian authorities. He returned to his home town and was subsequently confined to the monasteries of Meteora and Mount Athos where he ended his days being generally regarded as insane.[4]

Stephanos Doukas: A Greek secretary to Ali Pasha of Jannina at the beginning of the nineteenth century.[5]

Triantaphyllos Doukas: He was a native of Castoria and in 1807 published at Budapest an Ἱστορία τῶν Σλαβενο-Σέρβων συντεθεῖσα διὰ στίχων πολιτικῶν.[6]

Konstantinos M. Doukas: Of Siatista, he published a Πρακτικὴ Ἀριθμητικὴ in Vienna in 1820.[7]

Neophytos Doukas: Neophytos Doukas, the learned divine (1760–1845) was one of the most respected educationalists and scholars after the creation of the modern Greek state. He came from Epirus.

---

[1] K. D. Mertzios, Μνημεῖα Μακεδονικῆς Ἱστορίας (Thessalonica, 1947), p. 267.

[2] Ibid., p. 270.

[3] E. I. Karpathios, Ἡ ἐν Ἄνδρῳ Ἱερὰ Μονὴ Παναχράντου (Athens, 1938), pp. 215–16.

[4] Cf. K. N. Sathas, Νεοελληνικὴ Φιλολογία (Athens, 1868), p. 554.

[5] Sp. P. Lampros, ' Ἡ ἑλληνικὴ ὡς ἐπίσημος γλῶσσα τῶν σουλτάνων ', NE, 5 (1908), 78.

[6] D. S. Gines and V. G. Mexas, Ἑλληνικὴ Βιβλιογραφία, 1800–1863, 1 (Athens, 1939), p. 79, no. 473; cf. A. Horváth, Οὐγγροελληνικὴ βιβλιογραφία (Budapest, 1940), p. 41, no. 24.

[7] Gines–Mexas, op. cit., p. 202, no. 1268.

THE DERIVATIVES

There are several surnames which obviously owe their existence to the name of Doukas although, with the probable exception of Doukitzes, it cannot be claimed that there is any genealogical link between them. Certain of these surnames are attested during the Byzantine period; others are not. Again, some of them (e.g. Doukaites) come presumably from the surname Doukas, while others (e.g. Doukides) were derived from a first name Doukas and were in all probability coined after 1453.

DOUKAINAS

Doukainas (Δούκαινας) is a matronymic form, directly deriving from the female surname Δούκαινα.[1] I have not been able to find an example in the Byzantine period, and the only case where it is cited as a surname dates from modern times.[2]

DOUKAITES

The family name Doukaites (Δουκαΐτης) can be plausibly explained from the existence of a Byzantine locality τὰ Δούκα or a monastery called τοῦ Δούκα. Nothing, however, of that sort is attested in the sources. The resident on an estate τὰ Δούκα — perhaps originally belonging to the Doukas family — or perhaps in a monastery of this name, could properly have been called ὁ Δουκαΐτης. There are several bearers of the name from the eleventh century onwards.

Ioannes Doukaites: The priest Ioannes Doukaites became a monk under the name of Alexios and composed a poem in nineteen verses to the Theotokos. The manuscript containing this poem was written in the eleventh century.[3]

Leon Doukaites: A seal, thought to be of the mid-twelfth century, reads [Λέ]οντος [ἐ]ἰμὶ [σφραγὶς τοῦ Δου]καΐτου.[4]

---

[1] On the ending -αινα see D. I. Georgakas, 'Συμβολὴ εἰς τὴν τοπωνυμικὴν ἔρευναν', 'Ἀθηνᾶ, 48 (1938), especially pp. 15–22.

[2] In the book of G. Stamnopoulos, Βόλτες ὀνοματολογικές. Σειρὰ πρώτη (Athens, 1929), p. 295.

[3] Εἰς τὴν δέσποιναν ἡμῶν Θεοτόκον στίχοι δι'ἐξομολογήσεως δεητικοὶ ἁμαρτωλοῦ 'Ἀλεξίου τάχα καὶ μοναχοῦ τοὔνομα παπᾶ 'Ἰωάννου τοῦ Δουκαΐτη, in cod. Batopediou 107, fol. 277v; see S. Eustratiades and Arcadios, Catalogue of Greek Manuscripts in the Library of the Monastery of Vatopedi on Mount Athos (Cambridge, Mass., 1925), p. 29.

[4] Laurent, Collection Orghidan, p. 227, no. 448.

Doukaites: A Doukaites, whose first name remains unknown, was a contemporary of the patriarch Georgios (Gregorios) Kyprios (1283–9). Letter no. 104 of Georgios is addressed to him.[1]

The name of another Doukaites is found in the fourteenth-century cod. Ambr. gr. 784; Τῷ πρωτοβεστιαρίῳ χαίρειν ὁ Δουκαΐτης.[2] Finally in a note on cod. Vat. gr. 1366 (s. XIII) εἰς τὴν γῆν τοῦ Λουκαΐτου[3] we should probably read τοῦ Δουκαΐτου.

Manuel Doukaites: The *pansebastos* Manuel Doukaites wrote a homily in honour of the prophet Elias which is preserved in a fourteenth-century manuscript, the cod. Barocci 197, fol. 623r–630r.[4] It is possible that Manuel should be identified with the correspondent of Georgios Kyprios.

Philaretos Doukaites: A reference to a monk Philaretos Doukaites is contained in the title of a work preserved in a sixteenth-century manuscript.[5]

DOUKAKES

Doukakes (Δουκάκης) is one of the diminutives of Doukas. No bearer of the name has been traced during the Byzantine period, but in the less distant past several of them are heard of.

Giannakis Doukakes: His name appears in the form 'Jannachi Ducachi' in a Venetian inventory of the inhabitants of Zarnata in Mane, made in 1690.[6]

Doukakes: He lived in the late eighteenth century and is the subject of a couple of epigrams by his contemporary Epiphanios Demetriades.[7]

Doukakes: A family of that name was very prominent in the region of Kalamata in the Peloponnesus early in the nineteenth century.[8] Some of its members played a part in the Greek Revolution.

---

[1] S. Eustratiades, ' Κυροῦ Γρηγορίου τοῦ Κυπρίου ἐπιστολαί ', 'Εκκλησιαστικὸς Φάρος, 1 (1908), 90; the text ibid., 3 (1909), 36.

[2] E. Martini and D. Bassi, *Catalogus codicum graecorum Bibliothecae Ambrosianae* (Milan, 1906), II, p. 785.

[3] G. Mercati and P. Franchi de'Cavalieri, *Codices Vaticani graeci*, 1 (Rome, 1923), p. 162.

[4] Λόγος εἰς τὸν μέγαν καὶ ἔνδοξον τοῦ Χριστοῦ προφήτην 'Ηλίαν συγγραφεὶς παρὰ τοῦ πανσεβάστου Μανουὴλ τοῦ Δουκαΐτου, H. O. Coxe, *Catalogi codicum manuscriptorum Bibliothecae Bodleianae*, 1 (Oxford, 1853), col. 350, no. 71.

[5] Πρὸς τὸν σοφώτατον Μανουηλίτην τοῦ Φιλαρέτου τοῦ γέροντος κυροῦ Δουκαΐτου; See E. Rostagno and N. Festa, 'Indice dei codici greci Laurenziani non compresi nel catalogo del Bandini', *Studi Italiani di Filologia Classica*, 1 (1883), 198.

[6] 'Li nomi della comunità di Zarnata' in S. B. Kougeas, "Αναφορὰ τῶν Βοιτυλιωτῶν πρὸς τὴν 'Ενετικὴν Δημοκρατίαν ', Πελοποννησιακά, 2 (1957), 429, no. 39.

[7] "Ετερον ἐπὶ τῇ ξενίσει ἑαυτοῦ ὑπὸ Δουκάκη and 'Ιαμβικὸν εἰς Δουκάκην, see Sp. P. Lampros, 'Κώδικες τῆς Βιβλιοθήκης Σπυρίδωνος Π. Λάμπρου ', ΝΕ, 17 (1923), 299.

[8] M. B. Sakellariou, 'Η Πελοπόννησος κατὰ τὴν δευτέραν Τουρκοκρατίαν (1715–1821) (Athens, 1939), p. 140.

DOUKATARIOS

Two adventurous persons under the name of Οὐρσῖνος Δουκατάριος appear towards the end of the sixteenth century, and they attempted to trace their supposed titles and descent from Ioannes Doukas Tsaphas Oursinos *212*, claims which were confirmed by the German emperor Rudolf II (1576–1612). Nikolaos Oursinos (Orsini) Doukatarios wrote a letter to Guglielmo Orsini, a high official in the German court, while his son Georgios applied directly to the emperor. They are also mentioned in a couple of other letters of the period.[1]

DOUKAKOS, DOUKATOS

Doukakos (Δουκάκος) and Doukatos (Δουκᾶτος) appear to be comparatively modern forms, having apparently originated in Mane and in Cephalonia[2] respectively.

DOUKIDES

The form Doukides (Δουκίδης) derives from a first name Δούκας rather than from the surname itself. It is only found during the more recent period.

Demetrios Doukides: He was a scribe who in 1809 copied the apocalyptic collection of Agathangelos.[3]

Azarias Doukides: Azarias Doukides was a monk who in 1834–8 was in charge of the Greek church of St George at Vienna.[4]

---

[1] Georgios writes to Rudolf: 'Ἐγὼ γάρ, ὦ Καῖσαρ, . . . τὰς καθολικάς σοι τῶν γραφῶν προσεκόμισα, χρυσαῖς ἐγκεχαραγμένας σφραγῖσιν, ἐν αἷς τοῖς ἐμοῖς δισπάπποις, ἄλλως τε Ἰωάννη Ζάφῳ τῷ Οὐρσίνῳ μεγάλῳ τῆς τῶν Σέρβων αὐλῆς κοντοσταύλῳ, παρὰ τῶν τῆς Ἑλλάδος τε καὶ Σερβίας ἀρχόντων καὶ δεσποτῶν ἐκείνων τῶν τόπων, ἡ ἀρχὴ μετὰ καὶ τοῦ τίτλου τοῦ Δούκα, δέδοται τε καὶ ἐπιβεβαιοῦται ὥσπερ ἐξ αὐτῶν τῶν γραφῶν καταφανὲς ἐστί; see K. N. Sathas, *Τουρκοκρατουμένη Ἑλλάς* (Athens, 1869), p. 180. For other references to the Doukatarioi see I. K. Romanos ' *Γρατιανὸς Ζώρζης*' in *Ἱστορικὰ Ἔργα* (Corfu, 1959), pp. 309–10; X. A. Siderides, ' *Γαβριὴλ Σεβήρου ἱστορικὴ ἐπιστολή*', *Ἐκκλησιαστικὸς Φάρος*, 11 (1913), 7, 9, 18, 19, and 25–6; L. Vranoussis, *Χρονικὰ Ἠπείρου* (Jannina, 1962), pp. 69–80. Could *Γεώργιος Δουκάτωρ*, mentioned by K. N. Sathas, *Νεοελληνικὴ Φιλολογία* (Athens, 1868), p. 294, be the present Georgios Doukatarios?

[2] For the ending -ᾶτος see K. I. Amantos, ' *Τοπωνυμικὰ σύμμεικτα*', '*Ἀθηνᾶ*, 22 (1910), 203.

[3] '*Ἐγράφθη ἡ παροῦσα ὅρασις παρ'ἐμοῦ Δημητρίου τοῦ Δουκίδου* . . . ,αωθ' ἰανουαρίου κς'; see Sp. P. Lampros, *Κατάλογοι τῶν ἐν ταῖς μοναῖς τοῦ Ἁγίου Ὄρους Ἑλληνικῶν κωδίκων*, II (Cambridge, 1900), p. 235.

[4] S. Eustratiades, '*Ὁ ἐν Βιέννῃ ναὸς τοῦ ἁγίου μεγαλομάρτυρος Γεωργίου*', *Ἐκκλησιαστικὸς Φάρος*, 10 (1912), 73.

DOUKISSAS

The surname Doukissas (Δούκισσας) is indirectly connected with Doukas since, being a matronymic, it derives from the word δούκισσα (duchess) which had in the meantime been turned into a baptismal name. At the same time it must be remembered that Δούκισσα is also found as the feminine form of Doukas in place of Doukaina.[1] Doukissas has been used as a surname in the island of Andros from at least the eighteenth century onwards.[2]

DOUKITZES

Doukitzes (Δουκίτζης) is a diminutive of Doukas.[3] The form appears as early as 1059 and may be applied to Ioannes *13*.[4] Bearers of the name are occasionally met.

Ioannes Doukitzes: The seal of the *patrikios* Ioannes Doukitzes has been preserved: Κύριε, βοήθει 'Ιωάννη πατρικίῳ τῷ Δουκίτζῃ.[5] It may belong to Ioannes *13*.

Ioannes Doukitzes: He is only mentioned in a document of 1357.[6]

DOUKOPOULOS

The name Δουκόπουλος (cf. Argyropoulos, Palaiologopoulos and the like) also derives from that of Doukas and is found several times during the later Byzantine period.[7] Some of the Doukopouloi belonged to the nobility.

Georgios Doukopoulos: Georgios Doukopoulos is known from a document of the year 1179/80. He was apparently an official in the service of the *dux* of Thessalonica Alexios Pegonites and was sent by him to investigate on the spot a dispute between certain inhabitants of Hierissos and the Athonite monastery of Batopedi.[8]

[1]   ὁ πατήρ μας κατάγεται ἀπὸ τῶν Κινναμάδων
       ἡ δὲ μήτηρ μας Δούκισσα, γένους τοῦ Κωνσταντίνου
see J. Mavrogordato, *Digenes Akrites* (Oxford, 1956), p. 18, vv. 265–66.

[2] Δημοτικὴ Βιβλιοθήκη, Andros, MS. 10, fol. 54r and 244r; D. P. Paschalis, 'Μητρωνυμικὰ τῆς νήσου "Ανδρου,' 'Επετηρὶς τῆς Λαογραφικῆς καὶ 'Ιστορικῆς 'Εταιρείας Κυκλαδικοῦ Πολιτισμοῦ καὶ Τέχνης, I (1935), 10.

[3] Cf. the explanation of Zon., III, p. 707, for the name of Nikephoritzes who was ὑποκοριζόμενος διὰ τὴν νεότητα Νικηφορίτζης ὠνόμαστο καὶ ὥσπερ ἐπωνυμίαν ἔσχηκε τοῦτο.

[4] See above on Ioannes *13*, n. 4.

[5] The seal was published by St. Maslev, 'Vizantiiski olovni pechati ot Pliska i Preslav', *Isvestiya na Arkheologicheskiya Institut*, 20 (1955), 456, who read Δουκιτζί(ω) instead of Δουκίτζι. Cf. the correction of V. L(aurent) in *BZ*, 49 (1956), 541, who attributed it to the *katepano* of Edessa Ioannes Doukitzes (=Ioannes *13*?).   [6] MM, I, p. 372.

[7] It is possible that the modern surname Λουκόπουλος originated from Δουκόπουλος rather than from Λουκᾶς; see K. I. Amantos, 'Ιστορία τοῦ Βυζαντινοῦ κράτους, II (Athens, 1957²), p. 385.

[8] M. Goudas, ' Βυζαντιακὰ ἔγγραφα τῆς ἐν "Αθω ἱερᾶς μονῆς τοῦ Βατοπεδίου ', ΕΕΒΣ, 4 (1927), 212.

Demetrios Doukopoulos: A *praktikon* dated to October 1300 makes reference to an estate in Macedonia, 'previously in the possession of Demetrios Doukopoulos'.[1]

Petros Doukopoulos: References to the *sebastos* Petros Doukopoulos occur between the years 1292 and 1339. He was a wealthy landowner and a document of his dated 1292, in which he dedicates a piece of land together with a mill to the monastery of Iberon, gives some indication about his family. The grandmother of Petros was called (as a nun) Makrina, and the monastic names of his parents were Ignatios and Euphemia while his father's brother was Gerasimos. Petros had a brother Manuel. By his marriage to Maria (a daughter of Nikolaos and Anastasia), Petros had a daughter Christodoule (also a nun).[2] An estate of Petros Doukopoulos at Lozikin is mentioned in a chrysobull of December 1324.[3] Other properties of his are known from documents of December 1324[4] and October 1327.[5] By May 1339 he is already dead.[6]

Demetrios Doukopoulos Manikaites: He flourished in about the middle of the fourteenth century[7] and was probably an imperial official. Manikaites is known as a correspondent of Nikolaos Kabasilas[8] and Demetrios Kydones.[9]

KALODOUKAS

Καλοδούκας, that is the 'good Doukas', has been used as a surname since the beginning of the thirteenth century. It is also employed in later times.[10]

Nikolaos Kalodoukas[11]: Nikolaos Kalodoukas was a physician and a correspondent of Michael Choniates during the latter's exile at Ceos. Choniates wrote him three letters,[12] the second of which deals with medical matters.

---

[1] L. Petit, *Actes de Xénophon* (St Petersburg, 1903), p. 33; cf. Dölger, *Regesten*, IV, p. 31, no. 2221.

[2] Ioakeim Iberites, ''Αφιερωτήριον Πέτρου σεβαστοῦ Δουκοπούλου', Γρηγόριος ὁ Παλαμᾶς, I (1917), 789–91. The document is signed by ὁ δοῦλος τοῦ κραταιοῦ καὶ ἁγίου ἡμῶν αὐθέντου καὶ βασιλέως Πέτρος σεβαστὸς ὁ Δουκόπουλος.

[3] Petit, *Actes de Chilandar*, p. 209; cf. Dölger, *Regesten*,IV, p. 101, no. 2519. The same is referred to in 1342, see Regel et al., *Actes Zographou*, p. 80.

[4] Petit, *Actes de Chilandar*, pp. 212–13.

[5] Ibid., pp. 239–41.   [6] Τοῦ Δουκοπούλου ἐκείνου κῦρ Πέτρου, ibid., p. 274.

[7] Τοῦ δούλου τοῦ κραταιοῦ καὶ ἁγίου ἡμῶν αὐθέντου καὶ βασιλέως Δημητρίου Δουκοπούλου τοῦ Μανικαΐτου, see V. Laurent in *EO*, 30 (1931), 348.

[8] P. Enepekides, 'Der Briefwechsel des Mystikers Nikolaos Kabasilas', *BZ*, 46 (1953), 42–3. The letter is dated by the editor probably before 1345.

[9] Kydones wrote four letters to him, of which the most notable is the first one (1372–3?). In this he complains that Doukopoulos considered Kydones as a heretic (R.-J. Loenertz, *Démétrius Cydonès, Correspondance*, II [Rome, 1956], pp. 153–5), this showing that the former belonged to the anti-unionist side.

An anonymous letter refers to Manikaites as a good but poor man (τὸν μὲν τρόπον χρηστὸς ὤν, τὴν δὲ τύχην πτωχός, ἐπιπλεῖον δυσπραγεῖ, ibid., p. 176.

[10] It is found in the island of Syme in 1712; see N. D. Chaviaras, ' Μητρωνυμικὰ ὀνόματα ἐν Σύμῃ ', *NE*, 3 (1906), 255.

[11] In the text he is repeatedly called Καλοδούκης which does not make sense.

[12] Sp. P. Lampros, Μιχαὴλ 'Ακομινάτου τοῦ Χωνιάτου τὰ Σωζόμενα, II (Athens, 1880), pp. 147–8, 234–7, and 263–67. In p. 263 he is called ἀρχίατρος.

Kalodoukas was unable to visit Choniates at Ceos and sent him a book with the works of Galenos.

Gregorios Kalodoukas: Together with Georgios Tzimiskes, Kalodoukas was sent as ambassador of Michael VIII in Venice in 1268.[1]

Ioannes Kalodoukas: He is mentioned in a document of December 1330.[2]

KONTODOUKAS

The surname Κοντοδούκας, that is 'short Doukas', is attested at least once during the Byzantine period. A patriarchal ἀπόφασις of June 1401 refers to a deacon Kontodoukas who had married the daughter of the nun Καλλονὴ ἡ Πουζουλοῦ and was now pressing his mother-in-law to hand over to him all the promised dowry. Kontodoukas and his wife lived at Selybria.[3]

MAKRODOUKAS

The earliest use of the form Μακροδούκας ('long Doukas') is found in Choniates who designates Konstantinos 226 in this manner. Then it is not until the fourteenth century that persons bearing this surname are found.

Makrodoukas: Makrodoukas was the commander (ἄρχων) of the town of Vodena in Macedonia when it was stormed by Dušan in 1349. He was allowed to go free by the Serbs.[4]

Nikolaos Makrodoukas: He is mentioned in several documents of the year 1399 and one of them refers to him as *oikeios* to the emperor.[5] Makrodoukas is called γαμβρός of a Leon Modas and in November 1399 the care of the church of St Theodoroi in Lemnos was given to him.[6] He had a daughter who became the wife of Manuel Palaiologos Raoul.[7]

Makrodoukas: Makrodoukas was *megas logariastes* to the court of Trebizond and representative of his ruler to the council of Florence where he signed the union.[8]

---

[1] TT, II, pp. 101–2; cf. D. J. Geanakoplos, *Michael Palaeologus and the West* (Cambridge, Mass., 1959), Dölger, *Regesten*, III, p. 54, no. 1261.

[2] Petit, *Actes de Chilandar*, pp. 252–3; cf. Dölger, *Regesten*, IV, p. 145, no. 2766.

[3] MM, II, pp. 502–5.

[4] Kant., III., p. 161. A document of 1253 speaks of an estate belonging to a Makrodoukas (Petit, *Actes de Chilandar*, p. 190), who may be the same as the present one.

[5] Ὁ οἰκεῖος τῷ κρατίστῳ καὶ ἁγίῳ μου αὐτοκράτορι κῦρ Νικόλαος ὁ Μακροδούκας, MM, II, p. 452.

[6] MM, II, pp. 322–3.

[7] MM, II, pp. 304–12; cf. Papadopulos, *Genealogie der Palaiologen*, p. 92, no. 175, who wrongly calls him Nikolaos Makrydux.

[8] Chrysanthos, Ἡ Ἐκκλησία Τραπεζοῦντος (Athens, 1933), p. 280; J. Gill, *The Council of Florence* (Cambridge, 1959), pp. 141 and 263.

Simon (or **Symeon**) **Makrodoukas:** He was a manuscript copyist who flourished in the fifteenth century and wrote cod. Vind. med. gr. 17, which contains medical works by Ioannes Aktouarios.[1]

MAKRYDOUKAS

Makrydoukas does not differ in meaning from Makrodoukas, though there is a slight variation in form ($\mu\alpha\kappa\rho\acute{o}s > \mu\alpha\kappa\rho\acute{v}s + \Delta o\acute{v}\kappa\alpha s$).

Makrydoukas: He is mentioned as being dead in a document of 17 June 1325. Makrydoukas had a brother called Ioannes Triakontaphyllos and a daughter who was betrothed to a Georgios Kaballarios but on account of consanguinity the marriage was not permitted. From the document in question[2] it is possible to trace this relationship.

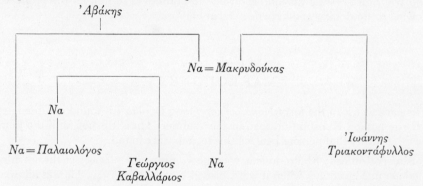

Maria Makrydoukaina: A manuscript notice preserves the date of her death which occurred on 24 June 1362. Maria was a nun with the name of Martha in religious life.[3]

MASTRODOUKAS

There is a reference to a certain Mastrodoukas who died on 11 September 1592.[4] In all probability this is a surname here.

[1] The colophon reading Ἐτελειώθη ἡ παροῦσα βίβλος διὰ χειρὸς Σίμωνος τοῦ Μακροδούκα τῇ κϛ' τοῦ παρόντος φεβρουαρίου τῆς παρούσης πρώτης ἰνδικτιῶνος used to be found on fol. 243 which is no longer extant. For references see J. Bick, *Die Schreiber der Wiener griechischen Handschriften* (Vienna, 1920), p. 114, no. 179.

[2] MM, 1, pp. 139–40. Papadopulos, *Genealogie der Palaiologen*, pp. 80–81, no. 132, is wrong in calling the man 'Palaiologos Makrydukas'.

[3] Μηνὶ ἰουνίῳ κδ' ἡμέρα Παρασκευῇ τὸ γενέσιον τοῦ ἁγίου καὶ ἐνδόξου Προδρόμου καὶ βαπτιστοῦ Ἰωάννου ὥρα θ' τῆς ἡμέρας ἐκοιμήθη ἡ δούλη τοῦ Θεοῦ Μαρία ἡ Μακρυδούκενα, ἡ διὰ τοῦ θείου καὶ ἀγγελικοῦ σχήματος μετονομασθεῖσα Μάρθα μοναχή, ἔτους ͵ϛωσ'. See Sp. P. Lampros, ' Ἐνθυμήσεων ἤτοι χρονικῶν σημειωμάτων συλλογὴ πρώτη ', *NE*, 7 (1911), 144, no. 69.

[4] ... ἐκοιμήθη ὁ μακαρίτης ὁ ἐξάδελφός μου Μαστροδούκας; see Dionysios, *Συμπληρωματικὸς κατάλογος τῶν χειρογράφων τῆς βιβλιοθήκης τῆς Ἱερᾶς Μονῆς Λειμῶνος ἐν Λέσβῳ*, (Athens, 1947), pp. 7–8.

MAURODOUKAS

Already by the middle of the twelfth century the names Mauros (the black one) and Maurodoukas had been applied to Ioannes Doukas Kamateros *99* by certain western sources,[1] but it may have been given as a nickname to this high official, whose full names are well known.

Theodora Maurodoukaina: Theodora is spoken of in a letter of Ioannes Apokaukos as εὐγενεστάτη, a word that points to an aristocratic background. She was pledged to make a pilgrimage to the Holy Sepulchre but by reason of various obstacles, mainly the presence of the Latins in the holy places, had to abandon this. Apokaukos promptly absolved Theodora from her oath.[2] The letter was probably written in *c.* 1216.

PAPADOUKAS

Παπαδούκας is a comparatively modern form, obviously deriving from a Christian name Doukas. The earliest reference which I have found, dates from 1617. In that year the *archon* Ioannes Papadoukas paid for the copying of cod. *Iberon* 464 (Athous 4585).[3]

[1] See above Ioannes *99*, p. 128, n. 12.

[2] See the text in Papadopoulos-Kerameus, Ἀνάλεκτα, II, pp. 361–2.
In the novel of Ph. Koukoules, Ὁ ἄρχων Καλόθετος (Athens, 1932), one of the characters is called Maurodoukas.

[3] Ἐτελειώθη ἡ παροῦσα διήγησις Βαρλαὰμ καὶ Ἰωάσαφ διὰ χειρὸς Μιχαὴλ Ἀριόλου τοῦ ἐξ Ἀθηνῶν καὶ ἐπαιδώθη διὰ συνδρομῆς καὶ ἐξόδου τοῦ ἐντημωτάτου ἐν ἄρχουσι κυροῦ Ἰωάννου Παπαδούκα ἐν ἔτει ͵αχιζ΄ ἰουλίῳ θ΄, Sp. P. Lampros, Κατάλογοι τῶν ἐν ταῖς Βιβλιοθήκαις τοῦ Ἁγίου Ὄρους Ἑλληνικῶν κωδίκων 1 (Cambridge, 1895), p. 149.

NAMES

(in the Doukas family)

Ninth-Century Doux
1. N

Tenth-Century Doukes
2. Andronikos
3. Konstantinos
4. Gregoras
5. Stephanos
6. Michael
7. Nikolaos

Lydoi
8. Andronikos
9. Christophoros
10. Bardas

Eleventh-Century Doukai
11. Andronikos
12. Konstantinos
13. Ioannes
14. Michael
15. N
16. Andronikos
17. Konstantios
18. Anna
19. Theodora
20. Zoe
21. Andronikos
22. Konstantinos
23. Konstantinos

Eleventh and Twelfth Centuries
24. Michael
25. Ioannes
26. Eirene
27. Anna
28. Theodora
29. N
30. Konstantinos
31. Theodora
31a. Na
32. Eirene
33. Zoe

NAMES

(in other families)

Adrianos
34. Petros

Agallon
35. Eudokia
36. Ioannes

Akropolites
37. Maria
38. Theodora

Angelos
39. Andronikos
40. Ioannes
41. Alexios
42. Theodoros
43. Manuel
44. Konstantinos
45. Michael
46. Demetrios
47. Anna
48. Michael
49. Nikephoros
50. Ioannes
51. Demetrios-Michael
52. Ioannes

53. Thomas
54. Konstantinos
55. Ioannes
56. Ioannes
57. Nikephoros
58. Ioannes
59. Maria

Apokaukos
60. Georgios

Aprenos
61. N
62. Manuel
63. Andronikos
64. Philippos
65. Demetrios

Arianites
66. Michael

Asan
67. Andronikos
68. Ioannes
69. Ioannes

Atrapes
70. Manuel

Balsamon
71. Theodora

Batatzes
72. Ioannes
73. Isaakios
74. Theodora
75. Theodoros
76. Ioannes

Boumbalis
77. Maria

Bryennios
78. Ioannes
79. Eirene
80. Alexios

Chandrenos
81. N

Choumnos
82. Michael

Chrysaphes
83. Manuel

Dalassenos
84. Konstantinos

Diasorenos
85. N
86. Pantoleon

Exazenos
87. Konstantinos

Gabras
88. Manuel

Glabas
89. Michael
90. Konstantinos
91. Theodote
92. Markos

Iagaris
93. Manuel

Kabasilas
94. Demetrios
95. N

Kalamanos
96. Konstantinos

Kalothetos
97. Ioannes

Kamateros
98. Andronikos
99. Ioannes
100. Basileios
101. Euphrosyne
102. Stephanos
103. N
104. Andronikos

Katrares
105. Ioannes

Kaukadenos
106. N

Komnenos
107. Anna

108. Ioannes
109. Ioannes
110. N
111. Alexios

Koresses
112. N

Kourtikes
112a. Na
113. Ioannes
114. Georgios

Laskaris
115. Eirene
116. Manuel

Limpidares
117. Konstantinos

Machoneos
118. N

Malakes
119. Ioannes
120. Nikephoros

Maliasenos
121. Konstantinos
122. Nikolaos

Mamalis
123. Andreas

Mandromenos
124. Demetrios

Melachrinos
125. Ioannes

Mourtzouphlos
126. Alexios
127. Isaakios

Mouzakios
128. Theodoros

Mouzalon
129. Ioannes

Neokaisareites
130. Ioannes

Nestongos
131. Alexios
132. Konstantinos
133. N
134. N

Palaiologos
135. Nikephoros
136. Andronikos
137. Michael
138. Alexios
139. Georgios
140. Konstantinos
141. Andronikos
142. Michael
143. Andronikos
144. Eirene
145. Michael
146. Theodoros
147. Demetrios
148. Konstantinos
149. Konstantinos
150. Andronikos
151. Maria
152. Ioannes
153. Maria
154. Anna
155. Euphrosyne
156. Manuel
157. N
158. Eudokia

Paraspondylos
159. Na

Petraliphas
160. Maria
161. Andronikos
162. Theodora
163. Anna

Petzikopoulos
164. Demetrios
165. Maria

Philanthropenos
166. Alexios
167. Michael
168. Theodora
169. Eirene
170. Eirene
171. Alexios

172. N
173. Georgios
174. Nikephoros
175. Na
176. Zoe

Prasomales
177. N

Prinkips
178. Ioannes

Radenos
179. Stephanos

Raoul
180. Konstantinos
181. Ioannes

Sarantenos
182. N
183. Alexandros
184. Nikolaos
185. Anna

Sebastopoulos
186. Helene

Sgouropoulos
187. N

Sgouros
188. Andronikos

Spartenos
189. Theodoros

Sphrantzes
190. Gabriel(?)

Strabomytes
191. N

Synadenos
192. Konstantinos
193. Ioannes
194. Ioannes
195. Thomais
196. Theodoros
197. Eudokia

198. Euphrosyne
199. Theodora
200. Anna
201. Euphrosyne
202. Melane

Syraneres
203. N

Syropoulos
204. N

Tarchaneiotes
205. N
206. N
207. Manuel
208. N

Tornikes
209. Isaakios
210. Andronikos

Trichas
211. Ioannes

Tsaphas
212. Ioannes

Tzykandeles
213. Demetrios
214. Georgios

Zarides
215. Ioannes

Unidentified

Twelfth Century
216. Leon
217. Anna
218. Maria
219. Na
220. Andronikos
221. Konstantinos
222. Konstantinos
223. Maria
224. Eudokia
225. Konstantinos
226. Konstantinos
227. N
228. Anna

229. Maria
230. Anna
231. Eirene
232. Ioannes
233. Andronikos
234. Isaakios

Thirteenth Century
235. Konstantinos
236. Daniel
237. Ioannes
238. N
239. Theodoros

Fourteenth Century
240. Demetrios
241. Michael
242. N
243. Na
244. N
245. Ioannes
246. N
247. N
248. N
249. Philippos
250. Ioannes

Fifteenth Century
251. N
252. Georgios
253. Na
254. N
255. N
256. N
257. Ioannes
258. N
259. Michael

Seals
260. Andronikos
261. Ioannes
262. Ioannes
263. Ioannes
264. Konstantinos
265. Maria
266. Michael
267. Michael
268. Michael
269. Nikephoros
270. Theodoros

TITLES

Apographeus: Ioannes *178*

basileopatōr: Michael *142*

co-emperors: Andronikos *16*, Konstantios *17*, Konstantinos *23*, Michael *145*

despotai: Theodoros *42*, Manuel *43*, Konstantinos *44*, Demetrios *46*, Michael *48*, Nikephoros *49*, Demetrios-Michael *51*, Thomas *53*, Ioannes *56*, Nikephoros *57*, Konstantinos *140*, Michael *142*, Demetrios *147*, Konstantinos *148*

domestikoi tōn scholōn: Andronikos *2*(?), Konstantinos *3*, Manuel *116*

domestikos (ecclesiastical): N *204*

emperors: Konstantinos *12*, Michael *14*, Theodoros *42*, Ioannes *72*, Theodoros *75*, Ioannes *76*, Ioannes *108*, Alexios *126*, Michael *142*, Andronikos *143*

empresses: Eirene *26*, Theodora *74*, Euphrosyne *101*, Eirene *115*, Eirene *144*

eparchoi: Andronikos *98*, Ioannes *99*

epi tēs trapezēs: Michael *167*, Theodoros *196*

epi tōn deēseōn: Andronikos *98*

epi tou stratou: Theodoros *128*, N *133*

kaisares: Ioannes *13*, Konstantinos *149*

katholikos kritēs: Georgios *214* (?)

kouropalatēs: Michael *89*

lampadarioi (ecclesiastical): Manuel *83*, N *204*

laosynaktēs: Ioannes *257*

logothetai tou dromou: Ioannes *99*, Basileios *100*

logothetēs tōn oikeiakōn: Ioannes *211*

logothetēs tōn sekretōn: Andronikos *233*

megas dioikētēs: Ioannes *250*

megaloi domestikoi: Andronikos *21*, Andronikos *141*

megaloi drungarioi tēs viglēs: Georgios *60*, Andronikos *98*, Ioannes *129*

megaloi duces: Ioannes *25*, Michael *142*, Alexios *166*(?)

megaloi hetaireiarchai: Ioannes *99*, N *133*, Georgios *139*, Georgios *173*, Konstantinos *225*

megaloi kontostabloi: Michael *89*, Michael *142*, Ioannes *194*, Ioannes *212*

megas notarios: Michael *6*(?)

megaloi papiai: Michael *89*, Demetrios *94*, N *134*

megas stratopedarches: Ioannes *193*

oikeioi: Petros *34*, Manuel *62*, Isaakios *73*, Ioannes *99*, Andreas *123*, Michael *167*, Ioannes *178*, Theodoros *189*, N *191*, Manuel *207*, Isaakios *234*

pansebastoi sebastoi: Ioannes *25*, Isaakios *73*, Andronikos *98*, Ioannes *99*, Basileios *100*, Georgios *139*, Manuel *156*, Konstantinos *226*

panypersebastoi: Nikephoros *57*, Konstantinos *226*

parakoimōmenos: Andronikos *210*

parakoimōmenos tēs megalēs sphendonēs: Konstantinos *132*

patrikīoi: Andronikos *2*, Andronikos *8*

pinkernai: Michael *89*, Alexios *131*, Alexios *171*

porphyrogennētoi: Konstantios *17*, Zoe *20*, Konstantinos *23*, Anna *107*, Ioannes *108*, Theodoros *146*, Demetrios *147*, Konstantinos *148*

primikērioi: Isaakios *127*, N *133*

prōtokouropalatēs: Michael *267*

prōtonotarios: Basileios *100*

prōtopansebastos: Andronikos *141*(?)

prōtoproedroi: Andronikos *21*, Konstantinos *22*

prōtospatharioi: Michael *6*(?), Andronikos *11*

prōtostratores: Konstantinos *22*, Michael *24*, Andronikos *63*, Michael *89*, Alexios *166*(?), Theodoros *196*, Theodoros *270*

protovestiarioi: Andronikos *21*, Alexios *126*, Ioannes *181*, Theodoros *196*

prōtovestiaritēs: Ioannes *72*

sakellarios (ecclesiastical): Michael *259*

sebastoi: Michael *24*, Ioannes *25*, Konstantinos *30*, Alexios *80*, Konstantinos *96*, Andronikos *98*, Ioannes *99*, Basileios *100*, Nikephoros *135*, Andronikos *136*, Michael *137*, Georgios *139*, Konstantinos *180*, Konstantinos *222*, Isaakios *234*, Andronikos *260*, Ioannes *261*, Michael *266*, Nikephoros *269*, Theodoros *270*

sebastokratores: Ioannes *40*, Ioannes *52*, Konstantinos *54*, Ioannes *55*, Isaakios *73*, Konstantinos *149*

vestarchēs: Konstantinos *12*

vestiaritēs: Isaakios *234*

INDEX